TODD KARR'S
BIBLIOGRAPHY OF MAGIC

Volume 1
Aalto to Denise

TODD KARR'S
BIBLIOGRAPHY OF MAGIC

Conjuring Books from 1584 to Today

Volume 1
Aalto to Denise

FOREWORD BY
DAVID COPPERFIELD

THE MIRACLE FACTORY
2025

I dedicate this bibliography with love to my mother, Joan M. Karr, PhD, who taught me about research during childhood trips to the University of Michigan. — *Todd Karr*

Todd Karr
Todd Karr's Bibliography of Magic

First edition 2025

The Miracle Factory
Los Angeles

Copyright 2025 Todd Karr
All rights reserved

The contents of this work may not be utilized in any form without the written permission of the publisher.

Back cover photo: Todd Karr in his Los Angeles library

Volume 1: Aalto to Denise
Volume 2: Dennerlein to Hummerston
Volume 3: Humphrey to Pomeroy
Volume 4: Ponsin to Zver

FOREWORD

David Copperfield

As a young boy starting to develop my magic, my focus was to create new presentations – new illusions and plot lines where the story and plot were as important as the magic itself.

All my focus was purely on that – and as my career expanded, I didn't find the time to do research into the amazing world of magic literature.

I was filming T.V. shows and creating new illusions and routines. I probably believed that not knowing what had been done in the past would help me not be influenced.

Then all of a sudden, in 1991, my friend Mike Caveney told me that one of the world's most important libraries of magic books, formerly owned by esteemed author John Mulholland, was going to be split up if it wasn't rescued by a singular individual.

So I instantly became the owner of an 80,000-piece renowned magic library and countless historical artifacts, literally from one day to the other. My Mulholland Library doubled in size when the Leslie Cole Collection became available, followed by many other acquisitions.

To be honest, at first I really didn't quite get it. I was still so focused on moving forward with my own creations. But then I realized that contained in those books and artifacts were stories, too.

The individuals who wrote these books, the individuals who performed their creations had amazing stories similar in many ways to what I was going through. That was a revelation. I finally got it.

I became immersed in what had come before me, immersed in the magic of the past. It was wondrous. It was a revelation to realize that a century ago the magicians of the past cared about the details in the way that I care about the details today.

Libraries are a great source of inspiration for all of us and remind us how people took the time to put their hard work into written form for future generations.

Entering this wonderful community of magicians who focus on books and literature has also rewarded me with friendships that I would have never had before. That has been a wonderful gift.

– David Copperfield
Las Vegas, 2025

ACKNOWLEDGMENTS

My sincere thanks to David Copperfield for his eloquent foreword and for sharing the treasures of his International Museum and Library of the Conjuring Arts during my research; to Byron E. Walker for his unparalleled knowledge of magic books and for answering my endless questions about bibliographical details; and to the following for patiently assisting me:

William Kalush of Conjuring Arts; the directors of the Robert Lund Collection at the American Museum of Magic; William Goodwin, librarian of the Academy of Magical Arts' William W. Larsen, Sr. Memorial Library; Bill Abbott; Allan Ackerman; James Alan; Ron and Tracy Aldrich; Alfonso; Stan Allen; Pablo Amira; Michael Ammar; Gene Anderson; Luka Andrews; Jon Armstrong; Doug Atkinson and his Magicref website; Steve Axtell; Sara Ballantine; Steve Banachek; Larry Barnowsky; Denis Behr and his Conjuring Archive site; Allen Berlinski; Jay Scott Berry; James Biss; David Britland; Christopher Broughton; Janet Budd; Don Bursell; John Cannon; Kathy Carini; John Carney; Mike Caveney; Levent Cimkentli for his valuable photography advice; Rudy Coby; Jordan Kotler; Kent Cummins; George L. Daily, Jr.; Sam Dalal; Jason Dean; Eric DeCamps; Chris "Doc" Dixon; Steve Drury; Gabe Fajuri; Erick Fearson; Tim Felix; John Ferrentino; Justin Flom; Steve Forte; Joe Fox; Louie Foxx; Gary Frank; David Gabbay; John Gaughan; Aaron Gillam; David Ginn; Andi Gladwin; Paul Gordon; Tim J. Goswick; Charles W. Greene III; Tony Griffith; John Guastaferro; James Hagy; Russell Hall; Keith Hart; Pit Hartling; Lawrence Hass; Richard Hatch; Murray Hatfield; Docc Hilford; John Hinchliffe; Scott Hitchcock; Jeff Hobson; Vanina Hodges; Mark and Sue Holstein; Will Houstoun; Mike Hutchinson; Kevin James; Joshua Jay; John and Julia Jefferson; Luke Jermay; Ross Johnson; Bruce Kalver; Joan and Ernest Karr; Sierra Karr; Ian Keable; Chris Kenner; Kostya Kimlat; Jim Kleefeld; Michal Kociolek; Danny Korem; David Kovac; Paul Kozak; Inés la Maga; Duane Laflin; Michael Lair; Mark Lemon; Roman LePree; Mark Leveridge; John Luka; Vito Lupo; Christopher Manos; Chuck Martinez; Jeff McBride; David Meyer; Stephen Minch; Steve Mitchell; Mondre; Dean Montalbano; Arthur Moses; Michael Murray; Lupe Nielsen; Pedro Nieves; François Normag; Kyle Norman; Andrew Normansell; Marc Oberon; Tom Ogden; Terry Perrett; Chris Pilsworth; Andrew Portala; Didier Puesch; Kyle Purnell; Marco Pusterla; Charlie Randall; Mike Rappa; Robert Rath; David Regal; Dennis Regling; Quentin Reynolds; Raymond Ricard; Jim Robertson; Paul Romhany; Danny Rudnick; Peter Samelson; Thomas Sawyer; Doug Scheer; George Schindler; Mark Setteducati; Artem Shchukin; David Schwaninger; Mark Setteducati; Phil Shaw; John Signa; Rocco Silano; Myles Sinclair; Marc Sky; Samuel Patrick Smith; Dan Stapleton; Jim Steinmeyer; Mark Strivings; Jamy Ian Swiss; George Tait; Mike Thornton; Brick Tilley; Mark Tripp; Tim Trono; John Tudor; Raven Tukwe; Philemon Vanderbeck; Steve Varro; Paul Vigil; Luca Volpe; Steve Wachner; Kaleb Wade; James A. Ward; Chris Wasshuber; Jeff Wawrzaszek; Ken Weber; Michael Weber; Richard Webster; Jeremy Weiss; Scott Wells; Adam Wilber; Mike Williams; R. Paul Wilson; Meir Yedid.

– *Todd Karr*

PREFACE

Todd Karr

Welcome to perhaps the most comprehensive bibliography of magic books ever published. In this set, you'll find details of over 23,000 conjuring works from around the globe from 1584 to 2025. Whether you're seeking a rare antiquarian pamphlet or a modern classic, whether you're researching the source of a card sleight or studying mentalism or manipulations, Houdini or Doug Henning, you'll likely find what you're looking for in these pages.

I've spent over six years preparing this bibliography and a lifetime of reading and collecting magic books. I started my first magic library when I was nine with a paperback edition of Henry Hay's *Amateur Magician's Handbook*. I now have over 15,000 volumes in my bookcases, including many finely produced with beautiful Victorian gilt-adorned covers and ornate engravings, though I also love any cheaply made booklet sold by some starry-eyed small-town performer before being lost to time and forgotten.

As a journalist and historian, I'm a stickler for facts, and I've done my best to check the details to make sure they're as accurate as possible. If you do find errors or omissions, I invite you to contact me.

It's not often that David Copperfield talks about his literary world and his role as owner of one of the world's finest magic libraries, and it's an honor to have his essay open this bibliography. Many of the rarest works that you'll find here have been carefully preserved in his Las Vegas collection.

I've often wished that an extensive research tool like this existed to assist my many quests for information over the years when I've developed effects as a performer or created my publishing company's historical works. I'll be using it in my own future research, and I hope that this epic study of conjuring literature will also soon become one of your favorite tools to improve your techniques, to rediscover wonderfully unexpected secrets, and to explore the vast, subtle, and long-lived art of the magician.

– *Todd Karr*
Los Angeles, 2025

A GUIDE TO THE BIBLIOGRAPHY

I've tried to make this bibliography as clearly structured as possible for easy use, so feel free to jump in and start your research or just flip through the pages to enjoy the parade of books. For further background, the following are a few guideposts.

Sources

The core of this set is my personal library of over 15,000 magic books, so you'll find scattered notes about an author's inscription in my copy of his work or the specific number of a limited edition that I own.

I've also added 8,000 more books from various other sources to make this bibliography as complete and useful as possible. You'll find a list of my major sources at the end of this guide.

Entries with the note "Information not verified by physical copy" means that it's not from my library and that I haven't personally examined it. In other cases, I've noted the collector's library where I looked over a work.

For antiquarian books, I sifted through the important English-language conjuring bibliographies of Stanyon, Clarke and Blind, Price, Hall, Heyl, Findlay, Toole Stott, and others, plus journal articles, university library catalogs, private collection databases, early publishing lists, reviews of works in print, copyright records, and auction descriptions.

I gathered many details about modern books from the authors themselves, who kindly answered my unexpected questions about their labors-of-love. I also contacted publishers, illustrators, editors, and translators; queried used magic-book dealers and collectors worldwide about elusive works; and searched through bibliographies, auction listings, magic-shop catalogs, used-book mailings, and magazine ads. Book reviews and articles in bygone magic magazines often supplied essential facts like size, binding, and page counts, as well as a wealth of easily overlooked minor titles.

A number of excellent online databases also saved the day many times with important information, including William Kalush's Ask Alexander; Denis Behr's Conjuring Archive; Doug Atkinson's Magicref; and the Academy of Magical Arts' library catalog.

Accuracy

Despite my care measuring each book in my library by hand and double-checking facts, some errors and omissions may have inevitably crept in. When necessary, I plan to produce a revised edition of this set to repair errors, fill in missing information, and document omitted works, so I hope readers will send me their corrections and notes in the hopes of creating a better record of these magic books. Please email me at my Miracle Factory website: www.miraclefactory.net.

I'll also of course welcome donations of books to my library for inclusion in any future revised edition of this set. Any readers who wish to send me a complimentary copy of a book can mail it to my company's address in Los Angeles, which can be found on The Miracle Factory's site. Thank you in advance.

Scope

Todd Karr's Bibliography of Magic lists over 23,000 conjuring works from 1584 to 2025, most in English, along with a wealth of antiquarian and modern French titles and important books in other languages.

I've focused closely on performance magic: the art of sleight-of-hand, the simulated magic of the stage magician. You'll therefore find very few books here on spirit mediums, con men, juggling, and other allied topics, although I've made exceptions for tangential works that I felt should be recorded as interesting parts of an author's writings or magic literature in general.

I have also exhaustively recorded variants and later editions that will allow you to follow the entire publishing history of many important writings that have never before been fully documented.

In addition, for each individual author, I've attempted to trace their entire published output, and for every magic publisher, I have tried to find every book the company released.

The entries are nearly all actual physical books: cloth-bound tomes, modern casebound volumes, aged pamphlets, stapled lecture notes, paperback books, and other printed forms, though you'll still find a few select ebooks and CDs that I felt were significant.

Note that I've limited catalogs mainly to historic reproductions and hybrid catalog-books, and the magazines included here are mostly collected sets issued by the original publisher or anthologized reprints.

Believing that there are no unimportant magic books, I've included numerous stapled instructions, dittoed manuscripts, advertising premium booklets, magic-set manuals, and early pulp publications. I also have a soft spot for obscure titles by small-time authors and publishers, so you'll find countless little-known works here, waiting for you to rediscover them.

As to the scope of subjects, I've not only detailed thousands of texts on significant topics like card techniques and mentalism but also paid attention to many genres often underrepresented in conjuring bibliographies, such as gospel magic, children's shows, and bizarre magick.

Author

Books without a credited author appear in the opening entries as "Anonymous," alphabetized by their titles. Uncredited works published by well-known magic dealers have mainly been listed under the name of the company or of the publisher himself.

Where a book by a prominent magician has been authored with the help of another writer or editor, I've generally listed the work under the name of the featured magician, where you might reasonably look first. You'll thus find *The Dai Vernon Book of Magic* listed under "Vernon, Dai," for instance, and not under the name of the actual writer, Lewis Ganson. In addition, Ganson's own list of entries begins with a suggestion of performers whose works he wrote, including Dai Vernon.

I have added other logical cross-references throughout the set, so if you search under Leon Nathanson's name for his 1966 classic *Slydini Encores,* a note will direct you to look under "Slydini."

Authors using stage names have generally been noted under their pseudonyms and not their real names, so you won't need to remember that Houdini's actual surname was Weiss, for example.

In cases where the real name and pen name are both well-known, I've opted for the more prolific name and added a cross-reference to guide you to the right place. For example, looking up books by Max Maven will send you to his more frequent credit, Phil Goldstein, and author Ned Williams' name will lead you to books listed under his better-known stage name of Robert Harbin.

Binding

I've tried to accurately describe the binding of every book, but because styles of binding can be easily confused, here are some brief definitions of the main types in these entries:

Boards: Sturdy printed cardboard covers, not cloth-covered. Often used in children's books.
Brads: Metal fasteners with long tabs that are spread flat.
Casebound: Hardbound with printing on smooth, sturdy covers and spine; distinct from cloth-bound works.
Coil: Spiral wire passing through holes. Often confused with comb binding.
Cloth: Cloth-covered boards. Often simply referred to as "hardbound." I have not obsessively distinguished between various types of cloth.
Comb: Plastic spine with pairs of curved tabs passing through slots. Often confused with coil binding.
Leather: Actual and not simulated leather binding. Please note that a leather cover in an entry may refer to a rebound copy in my collection and not to the book's original binding.
Perfect: Short for "perfect binding." Pages glued inside the flat spine of a folded paper cover, sometimes referred to as "paperback" or "softbound."

I have expanded the term "perfect bound" to include all books with signatures gathered inside a flat spine, as opposed to being stapled. I have also applied this description to antiquarian booklets with flat spines whose binding is often given the vague bibliographic term "wraps." I have here used the term "wraps" sparingly, reserving it for actual examples of books with their original brittle covers wrapped around groups of pages.

Saddle-stitch: The printing industry term for folded pages stapled through the center. The description originally referred to folded books sewn with actual thread instead of metal staples.
Stapled: Stapled in a corner or down the side.
Stapled with tape: Stapled down the side, then reinforced with a strip of cloth tape.
Strip binding: Thin plastic spine snapped onto the long edges of the pages.

Cover Color

Determining the shade of a cover has often proven surprisingly challenging to assess, so please be aware of my subjective attempts to distinguish nuances of pink from salmon, beige from tan, and other close calls.

Editions and Variants

I've extensively traced the publishing history of many of the books listed here through their subsequent editions and printings, in some cases dozens of versions over several decades.

These additional entries are far from mere variants. They help identify unusual copies, establish a publishing chronology, and offer insights into changing tastes in design. A book's longevity can also indicate prolonged sales, popular appeal, or enduring literary quality.

Date and Location

To provide a better sense of the origin of these books, I have spent many hours seeking dates and publishing locales, often by combing through magazine ads, magic-literature reviews, club reports, lecture announcements, and often by asking the writer himself.

Where I've failed to find a specific date, I've tried to at least provide an estimate to situate the work in a general era.

For readers unfamiliar with abbreviations for American states, please consult this complete list:

Alabama (AL), Alaska (AK), Arizona (AZ), Arkansas (AR), California (CA), Colorado (CO), Connecticut (CN), Delaware (DE), Florida (FL), Georgia (GA), Hawaii (HI), Idaho (ID), Illinois (IL), Indiana (IN), Iowa (IA), Kansas (KS), Kentucky (KY), Louisiana (LA), Maine (ME), Maryland (MD), Massachusetts (MS), Michigan (MI), Minnesota (MN), Mississippi (MS), Missouri (MO), Montana (MT), Nebraska (NE), Nevada (NV), New Hampshire (NH), New Jersey (NJ), New Mexico (NM), New York (NY), North Carolina (NC), North Dakota (ND), Ohio (OH), Oklahoma (OK), Oregon (OR), Pennsylvania (PA), Rhode Island (RI), South Carolina (SC), South Dakota (SD), Tennessee (TN), Texas (TX), Utah (UT), Vermont (VT), Virginia (VA), Washington (WA), West Virginia (WV), Wisconsin (WI), Wyoming (WY)

Topics

To convey a general sense of the contents of each book, I've added up to four subject descriptions, including both broad categories and more specific details, but please note that these topics do not necessarily cover every single aspect of a publication.

WORKS CONSULTED

The following sources provided helpful information in compiling this bibliography:

Alfredson, James B. and Daily, George L., Jr., *A Bibliography of Conjuring Periodicals in English 1791-1983* (1986), Magicana for Collectors, York

Blyth, Will, "A List of Books in the Magic Circle Library," *The Magic Circular* (August 1927), The Magic Circle, London

Braun, John, *Of Legierdemaine and Diverse Juggling Knacks: Columns from The Linking Ring, 1949-1966* (1999), Ken Klosterman, Loveland

Burlingame, H. J., "Bibliotheca Magica: A Classified List of Important Works on Natural and Occult Magic, Conjuring, and Amusements" in *Tricks in Magic vol. III* (1898), author, Chicago

Christopher, Maurine with Hansen, George, *The Milbourne Christopher Library 1589-1900* (1994) and *The Milbourne Christopher Library II 1901-1996* (1998), Mike Caveney's Magic Words, Pasadena

Clarke, Sidney W. and Blind, Adolphe, *A Bibliography of Conjuring and Kindred Deceptions* (1920), George Johnson, London

Donister, Colin (compiler), *The Magic Circle Catalogue of the Reference and Lending Library* (1952), The Magic Circle, London

Evans, Henry Ridgely, "Bibliography of Natural Magic and Prestidigitation," in Albert A. Hopkins, *Magic, Scientific Diversions, and Stage Illusions* (1897), Munn, New York

Fechner, Christian, *Bibliographie de la Prestidigitation Française et des Arts Annexes* (1994), author, Paris

Findlay, David W., *Ninth Collectors Annual* (1975), author, St. Albans

Findlay, James B., *How's Your Library?* (1958), Ireland Magic, Chicago

Findlay, James B., *Scottish Conjuring Bibliography* (1951), author, Shanklin

Forrester, Stephen, *A Bibliography of Classic Authors in Magic and Related Arts* (1993), author, Calgary

Hagy, James, *Magic for Free: 1887-1945*, vols. 1 and 2 (2006), author, Shaker Heights

Hall, Trevor H., *A Bibliography of Conjuring Books in English from 1580 to 1850* (1957), Carl W. Jones, Minneapolis

Hall, Trevor H., *Mathematicall Recreations: An Exercise in Seventeenth-Century Bibliography* (1969), Leeds Studies in Bibliography and Textual Criticism, Leeds

Hall, Trevor H., *Old Conjuring Books* (1972), Duckworth, London

Hall, Trevor H. and Muir, Percy, *Some Printers and Publishers of Conjuring Books and Other Ephemera 1800-1850* (1976), Elmete Press, Leeds

Heyl, Edgar G., *A Contribution to Conjuring Bibliography – English Language 1580 to 1850* (1963), author, Baltimore

Heyl, Edgar G., *Cues for Collectors* (1964), Ireland Magic, Chicago

Heyl, Edgar G., *A Survey of Conjuring Books, to Which is Added English and European Conjuring Books Prior to 1700* (1997), William Kalush, New York

Huber, Volker and Thies, Christian, *Bibliographie des Deutschsprachigen Schrifttums zur Zauberkunst* (2019), Volker Huber, Offenbach

Jiménez-Martínez, Enrique, "Minguet and His Deceptions in Plain Sight," *Gibecière*, vol. 4, no. 2 (Summer 2009), pp. 19-60

Kalush, William, "Antoine Castelli and His Physical Amusements," *Gibecière*, vol. 5, no. 1 (Winter 2010), pp. 141-178

Marshall, Frances Ireland with Lund, Robert, *Magic Bookman* (1974), Magic Inc., Chicago

McCullagh, Brian, *Under the Southern Cross: Australian Published Magic Books 1858-2000* (2001), author, Sydney

Meyer, David, *Howard Thurston's Card Tricks: An Illustrated and Descriptive Checklist of Various Editions Covering a 50-Year Period* (1991), author, Glenwood

Moses, Arthur, *The Houdini Pitchbooks* (2022), author, Fort Worth

Potter, Jack, *The Master Index to Magic in Print* (1964-75), Micky Hades, Calgary

Pratt, Bert, *Browsing Around in Magic* (1972), Magic Inc., Chicago

Price, Harry, *Short Title Catalogue of Works on Psychical Research, Spiritualism, Magic, etc.* (1929), National Laboratory of Psychical Research, London

Price, Harry, *Supplement to Short Title Catalogue of Works on Psychical Research, Spiritualism, Magic, etc.* (1935), University of London Council for Psychical Investigation, London

Ricard, Raymond, *A Short Title History and Checklist of Wee Books 1800-2005* (2005), author, Providence

Ruegg, Théodore, *Bibliographie de la Prestidigitation Française Ancienne et Moderne* (1931), author, Dijon

Smith, H. Adrian, *Catalogue of Conjuring Books in English Contained in the Library of H. Adrian Smith* (c. 1950), Brown University, Providence

Snader, Craige M., Jr., *The Annotated Bibliography Chronological (A.B.C.) of Weird and Bizarre* (1994), author, Mexico City

Sperber, Burton, *A Checklist of Conjuring Catalogs* (2007), author, Malibu

Stanyon, Ellis, *A Bibliography of Conjuring* (1899), author, London

Toole Stott, Raymond, *A Bibliography of English Conjuring 1569-1876* (1976), Harpur and Sons, Derby

Toole Stott, Raymond, *A Bibliography of English Conjuring 1569-1876 vol. 2* (1978), Harpur and Sons, Derby

Trost, Nick, *Jonathan H. Green: The Reformed Gambler* (2003), author, Columbus

Voignier, Jacques, *Catalogue d'une Bibliothèque de Prestidigitation: Éditions des XVIème, XVIIème, XVIIIème Siècle* (2004), author, Paris

Voignier, Jacques, "Who Was the Author of *Recréation Mathématique* (1624)?", *Perennial Mystics*, no. 9 (1991), pp. 5-48, James Hagy, Shaker Heights

Whaley, Bart, *Encyclopedic Dictionary of Magic 1584-1988* vols. 1 and 2 (1989), Jeff Busby Magic, Oakland

Whaley, Bart, *Who's Who in Magic* (1990), Jeff Busby Magic, Oakland

Young, Morris N., *Bibliography of Memory* (1961), Chilton Co., Philadelphia and New York

TODD KARR'S
BIBLIOGRAPHY
OF MAGIC

Conjuring Books from 1584 to Today

Volume 1
Aalto to Denise

BIBLIOGRAPHY OF MAGIC

Anonymous, *16 Tours de Cartes Pour les Amateurs de Magie.* (c. 1970) Altenburg-Stralsunder, Stuttgart, Germany. Folded. White. 4 pp. 4.75 x 3.5 in. Bound oblong. 17 individual folded card-trick booklets in set with cards, one with advice. Cards, Card set. French.

Anonymous, *24 Tricks from Your Vest Pocket.* (1943) Magic House of Charles, Hollywood, CA. Stapled. Tan. 24 pp. 3 x 5 in. Alan Wakeling illustration on cover. Beginner, Stunts.

Anonymous, *25 Amazing Card Tricks with a Miracle Pack of Magic Cards.* (n.d.) Watson Card Co., Sydney. Saddle-stitch. 20 pp. 3.5 x 4.75 in. (Information not verified by physical copy.) See McCullagh, "Under the Southern Cross." Cards, Gimmicked decks.

Anonymous, *25 Lessons in Hypnotism.* (c. 1955) Top Hat Magic Co., Evanston, IL. Perfect. White. 34 pp. 5.25 x 7.5 in. New cover on antique pages. Hypnotism.

Anonymous, *31 Tours de Magie Blanche.* (n.d.) France. Saddle-stitch. Beige. 32 pp. 4.75 x 7 in. (Measurements and other information have been recorded as accurately as possible.) Beginner. French.

Anonymous, *35 Magic Tricks.* (1987) AMAV Industries, New York. Saddle-stitch. White. 17 pp. 5.25 x 8.25 in. Beginner, Magic set manual.

Anonymous, *50 Tricks with Scotch and Soda.* (1995) That's Magic, Rancho Cordova, CA. Saddle-stitch. Color. 22 pp. 5.5 x 8.5 in. Coins, Gimmicks.

Anonymous, *84 New Card Tricks.* (1907) Wehman, New York. Perfect. White, orange, red, blue, yellow. 58 pp. 4.75 x 7.25 in. Cards. Pulp.

Anonymous, *84 New Card Tricks.* (1907) Wehman, New York. Perfect. White, orange, red, blue, yellow. 58 pp. 4.75 x 7.25 in. Different ads inside and on back cover. Cards. Pulp.

Anonymous, *84 New Card Tricks.* (1907) Wehman, New York. Perfect. White, red, blue, yellow. 58 pp. 4.75 x 7.25 in. Green ad on back. Cards. Pulp.

Anonymous, *84 New Card Tricks.* (1907) Wehman, New York. Perfect. White, red, blue, yellow. 58 pp. 4.75 x 7.25 in. Red ad on back. Cards. Pulp.

Anonymous, *101 Magic Tricks.* (n.d.) S. S. Adams, Asbury Park, NJ. Saddle-stitch. Black, purple, yellow. 32 pp. 4.25 x 5.75 in. Front stamped with 25-cent price. Beginner.

Anonymous, *102 E-Z Magic Tricks!* (1976) D. Robbins, Brooklyn, NY. Saddle-stitch. White, yellow, brown. 32 pp. 5.25 x 8.5 in. In Adams' "Abracadabra Magic Set." Magic set manual.

BIBLIOGRAPHY OF MAGIC

Anonymous, *110 Great Magic Tricks.* (1978) S. S. Adams, Neptune, NJ. Saddle-stitch. Tan. 28 pp. 5 x 7 in. (Measurements and other information have been recorded as accurately as possible.) Beginner.

Anonymous, *125 Card Tricks.* (c. 1910) Wehman, New York. Saddle-stitch. Yellow, red, black. 86 pp. 5 x 7 in. Bald goateed magician. Header says "Tricks and Diversions with Cards." Cards. Pulp.

Anonymous, *125 Card Tricks.* (c. 1910) Wehman, New York. Perfect. Yellow, red, black. 86 pp. 4.75 x 7.25 in. Bald goateed magician. No ad on back cover. Header says "Tricks and Diversions with Cards." Cards. Pulp.

Anonymous, *125 Card Tricks.* (c. 1910) Wehman, New York. Perfect. White, red, black. 86 pp. 5 x 7 in. Bald goateed magician. Header says "Tricks and Diversions with Cards." Cards. Pulp.

Anonymous, *125 Card Tricks.* (c. 1910) Wehman, New York. Perfect. Brown. Cover text: Black; 86 pp. 5 x 7.25 in. Text from "Thurston's Card Tricks." Smoking man with fan of Aces on cover. Header says "Tricks and Diversions with Cards." Cards. Pulp.

Anonymous, *125 Tricks with Cards or Sleight of Hand.* (n.d.) Johnson Smith and Co., Detroit. Perfect. Brown. 86 pp. 5.25 x 7.5 in. Smoking man with fan of Aces. Ad on back for Telegraph Set. No Thurston text. Cards. Pulp.

Anonymous, *125 Tricks with Cards or Sleight of Hand.* (n.d.) Detroit. Perfect. White. 86 pp. 4.75 x 7 in. Smoking man with fan of Aces. No publisher listed. No Thurston text. Cards. Pulp.

Anonymous, *125 Tricks with Cards or Sleight of Hand.* (n.d.) Johnson Smith and Co., Detroit. Perfect. Green. 64 pp. 5.25 x 7.5 in. Text from "Thurston's Card Tricks." Smoking man with fan of Aces on cover. Cards. Pulp.

Anonymous, *125 Tricks with Cards or Sleight of Hand.* (n.d.) Johnson Smith and Co., Detroit. Perfect. Light green. 64 pp. 5.25 x 7.5 in. Text from "Thurston's Card Tricks." Smoking man with fan of Aces on cover. Cards. Pulp.

Anonymous, *125 Tricks with Cards or Sleight of Hand.* (n.d.) Johnson Smith and Co., Detroit. Perfect. Olive. 64 pp. 5.25 x 7.5 in. Text from "Thurston's Card Tricks." Smoking man with fan of Aces on cover. Cards. Pulp.

Anonymous, *125 Tricks with Cards or Sleight of Hand.* (n.d.) Johnson Smith and Co., Racine, WI. Perfect. Orange. 64 pp. 5.25 x 7.5 in. Text from "Thurston's Card Tricks." Smoking man with fan of Aces on cover. Cards. Pulp.

Anonymous, *125 Tricks with Cards or Sleight of Hand.* (n.d.) Johnson Smith and Co., Detroit. Perfect. Purple. 64 pp. 5.25 x 7.5 in. Text from "Thurston's Card Tricks." Smoking man with fan of Aces on cover. Ad on back for Mocar model airplane. Cards. Pulp.

Anonymous, *125 Tricks with Cards or Sleight of Hand.* (n.d.) Johnson Smith and Co., Detroit. Perfect. Red. 64 pp. 5.25 x 7.5 in. Text from "Thurston's Card Tricks." Smoking man with fan of Aces on cover. Cards. Pulp.

Anonymous, *125 Tricks with Cards or Sleight of Hand.* (n.d.) Johnson Smith and Co., Detroit. Perfect. Tan. 64 pp. 5.25 x 7.5 in. Text from "Thurston's Card Tricks." Smoking man with fan of Aces on cover. Cards. Pulp.

Anonymous, *125 Tricks with Cards or Sleight of Hand.* (n.d.) Johnson Smith and Co., Detroit. Perfect. Brown. 64 pp. 5.25 x 7.5 in. Text from "Thurston's Card Tricks." Smoking man with fan of Aces on cover. Ad on back for Card Miracles. Cards. Pulp.

Anonymous, *125 Tricks with Cards or Sleight of Hand.* (n.d.) Johnson Smith and Co., Detroit. Perfect. Beige. 64 pp. 5.25 x 7.5 in. Text from "Thurston's Card Tricks." Smoking man with fan of Aces and no. 1174 on cover. Cards. Pulp.

Anonymous, *153 Tricks of Magic.* (n.d.) Western Printing Co., Racine, WI. Perfect. Red. 64 pp. 4 x 5.25 in. Beginner, Cards. Pulp.

Anonymous, *200 Easy Conjuring Tricks and Parlour Pastimes.* (c. 1910) R. March and Co., London. Saddle-stitch. Orange. 32 pp. 5.25 x 8.25 in. Revised version of "How to Perform One Hundred Conjuring Tricks."

Anonymous, *250 Parlor Tricks or Magic Made Easy.* (c. 1868) 28 pp. 5.75 x 8.75 in. Toole Stott no. 546. (Measurements and other information have been recorded as accurately as possible.) Beginner.

Anonymous, *250 Parlor Tricks or Magic Made Easy.* (n.d.) C. W. Bates and Co., Boston. Saddle-stitch. Dark blue. 28 pp. 5.75 x 8.5 in. Bates label on generic cover. Beginner. Pulp.

Anonymous, *250 Parlor Tricks or Magic Made Easy.* (n.d.) Dorn Book Co., Chicago. Saddle-stitch. Tan. 32 pp. 5.75 x 8.5 in. Beginner. Pulp.

Anonymous, *250 Parlor Tricks or Magic Made Easy.* (n.d.) Dorn Book Co., Chicago. Saddle-stitch. Light tan. 32 pp. 5.75 x 8.5 in. Beginner. Pulp.

Anonymous, *250 Parlor Tricks or Magic Made Easy.* (n.d.) Johnson Smith and Co., Racine, WI. Saddle-stitch. Tan. Cover text: Green; 28 pp. 6 x 8.5 in. Beginner. Pulp.

Anonymous, *250 Parlor Tricks or Magic Made Easy.* (n.d.) Johnson Smith and Co., Detroit. Saddle-stitch. Gray. 32 pp. 5 x 7.5 in. Beginner. Pulp.

Anonymous, *250 Parlor Tricks or Magic Made Easy.* (n.d.) Johnson Smith and Co., Detroit. Saddle-stitch. Red. 32 pp. 5 x 7.5 in. Beginner. Pulp.

Anonymous, *250 Parlor Tricks or Magic Made Easy.* (n.d.) Johnson Smith and Co., Detroit. Perfect. Tan. 32 pp. 5 x 7.5 in. Beginner. Pulp.

BIBLIOGRAPHY OF MAGIC

Anonymous, *1,200 Amusements et Recréations de Société, Les.* (n.d.) Le Bailly, Paris. Perfect. Beige. Multiple sections. 4 x 6 in. Bound with "L'Ancienne et la Nouvelle Collection de Tours de Cartes" and "L'Ancienne et la Nouvelle Collection de Tours de Physique." Beginner. Pulp. French.

Anonymous, *Adams' Entertain with Magic.* (n.d.) S. S. Adams, Asbury Park, NJ. Saddle-stitch. White. 12 pp. 4.5 x 5.75 in. In Adams' "Entertain with Magic" set. Magic set manual.

Anonymous, *Adventures of Ajeeb: The Wonderful Automaton, The.* (c. 1880) Deltje and Cutting, New York. Saddle-stitch. Olive. 24 pp. (Information not verified by physical copy.) Automata, History.

Anonymous, *Adventures of Ajeeb: The Wonderful Automaton, The.* (1996) Connolly Conjuring, New Milford, NJ. Saddle-stitch. Beige. 24 pp. 4.5 x 6.75 in. With reproduction ad card and pink booklet. #204 of 300. Automata, History.

Anonymous, *Adroit Escamoteur ou Recueil de Nouveaux Tours, L'.* (c. 1860) Author, Epinal, France. 23 pp. (Information not verified by physical copy.) Credited to "a student of M. Comte." French.

Anonymous, *Adroit Escamoteur ou Recueil de Nouveaux Tours, L'.* (1851) Author, Epinal, France. Perfect. Blue. 108 pp. (Information not verified by physical copy.) Early magic. French.

Anonymous, *After Dinner Tricks and Puzzles.* (1896) Chase and Sanborn, Boston. Saddle-stitch. Color. 12 pp. 3.75 x 5 in. Back cover says "For Sale by J. B. Holton, West Charleston, VT." Beginner, Stunts, Premium.

Anonymous, *Alpha-Power's Course in Magic.* (n.d.) Alpha Power Co., Australia. 13 pp. 8.25 x 13.25 in. (Information not verified by physical copy.) See McCullagh, "Under the Southern Cross." Beginner, Course.

Anonymous, *Amateur's Guide, including the Art of Legerdemain, The.* (1838) Thomas Richardson, Derby, UK. 24 pp. 4 x 7.25 in. (Information not verified by physical copy.) Toole Stott no. 916. Beginner.

Anonymous, *Amateur's Guide to Magic and Mystery, The.* (1874) Frank M. Reed, New York. Perfect. Beige. 58 pp. 4.5 x 5.75 in. Beginner.

Anonymous, *Amateur's Guide to Magic and Mystery and the Black Art Fully Exposed, The.* (1895) J. S. Ogilvie Publishing Co., New York. Perfect. Gray. Cover text: Black; 58 pp. 5.25 x 7.5 in. Beginner. Pulp.

Anonymous, *Amateur's Guide to Magic and Mystery and the Black Art Fully Exposed, The.* (n.d.) J. S. Ogilvie Publishing Co., New York. Perfect. Yellow, black. 58 pp. 4.75 x 7 in. Beginner. Pulp.

Anonymous, *Amateur's Guide to Magic and Mystery and the Black Art Fully Exposed, The.* (n.d.) J. S. Ogilvie Publishing Co., New York. Perfect. Yellow, red, black. 58 pp. 5.25 x 7.5 in. Beginner. Pulp.

BIBLIOGRAPHY OF MAGIC

Anonymous, *Amazing Magical Jell-o Desserts.* (1977) General Foods Corp., White Plains, NY. Casebound. White. 95 pp. 7.75 x 6.75 in. Bound oblong. Beginner, Stunts, Premium.

Anonymous, *Amazing Mumford Forgets the Words!, The.* (1979) Western Publishing Co., Racine, WI. Boards. Yellow. 24 pp. 6.5 x 8 in. Muppets character book. Fiction, Children's book.

Anonymous, *Ambassador Hood's Magic Book.* (1956) Hood Magic Flavored Drinks, Boston. Saddle-stitch. Beige. 32 pp. 6 x 9 in. Dated by offer expiration. Beginner, Premium.

Anonymous, *Amusement for Winter Evenings.* (c. 1800) M. C. Springsguth, London. 36 pp. 4.25 x 6.5 in. (Information not verified by physical copy.) Toole Stott no. 15. Early magic.

Anonymous, *Ancienne et la Nouvelle Collection des Tours de Cartes, L'.* (c. 1860) Le Bailly, Paris. Perfect. Gray. Cover text: Colors; 108 pp. 3.75 x 6 in. Cards. French.

Anonymous, *Ancienne et la Nouvelle Collection des Tours d'Escamotage, L'.* (c. 1860) S. Bornemann, Paris. Beige. 108 pp. 4 x 6 in. Beginner, Cards, Cups and Balls. French.

Anonymous, *Ancienne et la Nouvelle Collection des Tours d'Escamotage, L'.* (c. 1860) S. Bornemann, Paris. Beige. 108 pp. 4 x 6 in. Label of Le Record du Rire on Bd. St. Martin. Retitled edition of "Les 1,200 Amusements." Beginner, Cards, Cups and Balls. French.

Anonymous, *Ancienne et la Nouvelle Collection des Tours de Physique, L'.* (c. 1860) S. Bornemann, Paris. Beige. 108 pp. 4 x 6 in. Pages of plates in back; two sections of book. Beginner, Cards, Cups and Balls. French.

Anonymous, *Antidote ou le Contrepoison des Chevaliers d'Industrie ou Joueurs de Profession, L'.* (2018) Hachette, Paris. Perfect. Yellow. 115 pp. 6.25 x 9.25 in. Reprint of 1768 edition. Cards, Gambling. French.

Anonymous, *Art de S'Amuser en Société, L'.* (1868) Ferdinand Sortorius, Paris. Perfect. Olive. 137 pp. 4.5 x 6.75 in. Beginner, Cards. French.

Anonymous, *Art of Conjuring Made Easy, The.* (1822) S. King, New York. 24 pp. 4.5 x 7.75 in. (Information not verified by physical copy.) Toole Stott no. 62. Early magic, Beginner.

Anonymous, *Art of Conjuring Made Easy, The.* (1822) Dean and Munday, London. 34 pp. 4 x 7 in. (Information not verified by physical copy.) Toole Stott no. 64. Early magic, Beginner.

Anonymous, *Art of Conjuring Made Easy, The.* (1823) W. Boradaile, New York. 24 pp. 4.25 x 7 in. (Information not verified by physical copy.) Toole Stott no. 63. Early magic, Beginner.

Anonymous, *Art of Conjuring Made Easy, The.* (c. 1840) Samuel and John Keys, Devonport, UK. 12 pp. 4 x 7 in. (Information not verified by physical copy.) Toole Stott no. 65. Early magic, Beginner.

Anonymous, *Art of Conjuring Made Easy, The.* (1860) T. Richardson, Derby, UK. 12 pp. 3.5 x 5.5 in. (Information not verified by physical copy.) Toole Stott no. 66. Early magic, Beginner.

Anonymous, *Art of Conjuring or Legerdemain Made Easy, The.* (c. 1812) W. Mason, London. 28 pp. 4 x 6.75 in. (Information not verified by physical copy.) Toole Stott no. 61. Early magic, Beginner.

Anonymous, *Art of Conjuring or Legerdemain Made Easy, The.* Third edition. (c. 1815) W. Mason, London. 28 pp. 4 x 7.5 in. (Information not verified by physical copy.) Toole Stott no. 932. Early magic, Beginner.

Anonymous, *Art of Legerdemain.* (1832) J. Pitts, London. 1 pp. 14.25 x 19.75 in. (Information not verified by physical copy.) Toole Stott no. 67. Broadsheet. Early magic, Beginner.

Anonymous, *Art of Magic, The.* (c. 1900) Folded. Beige. 4 pp. 5 x 7 in. Cover from Wehman edition. Jay Marshall noted it as John Northern Hilliard's copy. Beginner. Pulp.

Anonymous, *Art of Magic, Ventriloquism with Punch and Judy.* (c. 1875) Dick's Publishing House, New York. 16 pp. (Information not verified by physical copy.) Toole Stott no. 1339. Beginner.

Anonymous, *Art of Mind Reading, The.* (c. 1870) Excelsior House, New York. 40 pp. (Information not verified by physical copy.) Toole Stott no. 1340. Mentalism.

Anonymous, *Art of Mind Reading, The.* (c. 1870) Jesse Haney and Co., New York. 40 pp. 4.5 x 7.5 in. (Information not verified by physical copy.) Toole Stott no. 68. Early magic, Beginner.

Anonymous, *Art of Stage Mind Reading, or Second Sight, The.* (1913) National Stage Instructing Co., New York. Perfect. Pink. 55 pp. 5.25 x 7.75 in. Title page says "Improved Manuscript of Second Sight or Mind Reading." Mentalism, Second Sight. Pulp.

Anonymous, *Art of Ventriloquism, The.* (c. 1870) F. M. Reed, New York. 80 pp. (Information not verified by physical copy.) Toole Stott no. 1341. Ventriloquism.

Anonymous, *Art Secret des Illusionnistes, L'.* (1973) Bibliothèque Forney, Paris. Perfect. White. 144 pp. 5 x 9.5 in. A.F.A.P. exhibit. Bibliography, Exhibit, History.

Anonymous, *B.G.L. Conjuring Booklet, The.* (c. 1920) B.G.L. Co., London. Saddle-stitch. White. 19 pp. 4 x 6.25 in. From "The All British Box" magic set. In Copperfield collection. Magic set manual, Beginner.

Anonymous, *Beezer Broadway Book of Mystery and Magic, The.* (c. 1924) D. C. Thomson and Co., London. Saddle-stitch. Color. 52 pp. 2.75 x 4.25 in. In Copperfield collection. Beginner, Premium.

Anonymous, *Big Book o'Tricks, The.* (c. 1910) Edward Smith and Co., London. Saddle-stitch. Orange. 16 pp. 7.25 x 9.75 in. In Copperfield collection. Beginner. Pulp.

Anonymous, *Bits of Patter.* (1915) Minneapolis. Saddle-stitch. Tan. 11 pp. 6.25 x 9 in. (Measurements and other information have been recorded as accurately as possible.) Patter.

Anonymous, *Black Art Fully Exposed and Laid Bare, The.* (c. 1875) F. M. Reed, New York. 58 pp. 4.75 x 6 in. (Information not verified by physical copy.) Toole Stott no. 938. Beginner.

Anonymous, *Black Art Fully Exposed and Laid Bare, The.* (c. 1876) J. S. Ogilvie Publishing Co., New York. 58 pp. 4.75 x 6 in. (Information not verified by physical copy.) Toole Stott no. 939. Beginner.

Anonymous, *Black Art of Magic Made Easy.* (c. 1874) New York Popular Publishing, New York. 64 pp. 4.25 x 6.75 in. (Information not verified by physical copy.) Toole Stott no. 95. Beginner.

Anonymous, *Black Art, or Magic Made Easy.* (1907) Wehman, New York. Perfect. Beige. 61 pp. 4.75 x 7 in. Beginner. Pulp.

Anonymous, *Black Art, or Magic Made Easy.* (1907) Wehman, New York. Perfect. Light blue. 61 pp. 4.75 x 7 in. Beginner. Pulp.

Anonymous, *Black Art, or Magic Made Easy, The.* (1869) Robert M. DeWitt, New York. Yellow. 64 pp. 4.5 x 6.75 in. (Information not verified by physical copy.) Toole Stott no. 94. Beginner.

Anonymous, *Black Magic: A Handbook of Cabalistic Phenomena, Prestidigitation, and Illusionary Science by Clarabell, Wizard Extraordinary.* (c. 1950) Luden's, Chicago. Folded. White. 2 pp. 17 x 11 in. In "Howdy Doody's Magic Kit." Magic set manual, Beginner.

Anonymous, *Bluff, The.* (2000) Author. Saddle-stitch. Red. 8 pp. 5.5 x 8.5 in. (Measurements and other information have been recorded as accurately as possible.) Cards, Torn and Restored Card.

Anonymous, *Book for All: Card Tricks and Conjuring.* (c. 1900) March, Cady, and Co., London. Saddle-stitch. White. 16 pp. 5.5 x 8.5 in. In Copperfield collection. Cards, Beginner. Pulp.

Anonymous, *Book o'Tricks.* (c. 1912) Edward Smith and Co., London. Saddle-stitch. Orange. 16 pp. 7.25 x 9.75 in. Title page has title "Smith's Book of Tricks." In Copperfield collection. Beginner. Pulp.

Anonymous, *Book o'Tricks.* (1937) A & P Bakers. Saddle-stitch. Red. 22 pp. 3.5 x 5.75 in. A & P Soft Twist Bread ad on back cover. Beginner, Stunts, Premium, Promotion.

Anonymous, *Book of Chemical Wonders, Secrets, and Mysteries of the World, The.* (n.d.) Johnson Smith and Co., Racine, WI. Saddle-stitch. Gray. 31 pp. 5 x 7.25 in. Beginner, Stunts, Chemical.

Anonymous, *Book of Experiments.* (1850) Boston. 64 pp. 4.25 x 6 in. (Information not verified by physical copy.) Toole Stott no. 102. Beginner.

Anonymous, *Book of Magic.* (c. 1940) D. R. Burnside, Glasgow. Saddle-stitch. Beige. 16 pp. 7.5 x 9.75 in. In Copperfield collection. Beginner. Pulp.

Anonymous, *Book of Magic.* (c. 1940) D. R. Burnside, Glasgow. Saddle-stitch. Blue. 16 pp. 7.5 x 9.75 in. In Copperfield collection. Beginner. Pulp.

Anonymous, *Book of Magic, The.* (1835) W. & R. Inglis, Glasgow. 24 pp. 3.75 x 6 in. (Information not verified by physical copy.) Toole Stott no. 104. Beginner.

Anonymous, *Book of Magic and Christmas Conjuring, The.* (c. 1920) Allied Newspapers, Manchester, UK. Saddle-stitch. Red. 26 pp. 4 x 5.75 in. Supplement inside "Boys' Magazine." In Copperfield collection. Beginner, Stunts, Premium.

Anonymous, *Book of Magic and the Art of Ventriloquism Made Easy.* (c. 1870) New York Popular Publishing, New York. 16 pp. 4.5 x 7.25 in. (Information not verified by physical copy.) Toole Stott no. 945. Beginner, Ventriloquism.

Anonymous, *Book of Magic or the Young Conjuror's Guide, The.* (c. 1840) Robert Inglis, Glasgow. 12 pp. 3.5 x 5 in. (Information not verified by physical copy.) Toole Stott no. 105. Beginner.

Anonymous, *Book of Magic or the Young Conjuror's Guide: How to Do Everything!, The.* (1840) Robert Inglis, Glasgow. 12 pp. 3.25 x 5.5 in. (Information not verified by physical copy.) Toole Stott no. 106. Beginner.

Anonymous, *Book of New Coin Tricks.* Text of Downs' "Modern Coin Manipulation." Miniature book. (1912) Royal Publishing, Philadelphia. Perfect. Red, yellow. 58 pp. 4 x 5 in. Devilish magician with interlocked fingers. Coins. Pulp.

Anonymous, *Book of New Coin Tricks.* Text of Downs' "Modern Coin Manipulation." Miniature book. (1913) Ottenheimer, Baltimore, MD. Perfect. Red, yellow. 64 pp. 4 x 5 in. Devilish magician with interlocked fingers. Coins. Pulp.

Anonymous, *Book of Parlor Tricks.* Miniature book. (1895) Multum in Parvo Library, Boston. Saddle-stitch. Tan. 16 pp. 2.75 x 4.25 in. Beginner. Pulp.

Anonymous, *Book of Secrets*. (n.d.) National Publishing Co., Sydney. Saddle-stitch. 33 pp. 6 x 9 in. (Information not verified by physical copy.) See McCullagh, "Under the Southern Cross." Beginner.

Anonymous, *Book of Tricks*. (c. 1914) Daisy Bank Publishing, Manchester. Saddle-stitch. Tan. 32 pp. 5.5 x 8.5 in. Presented by Goldston to The Magicians' Club in London, 1913. Signed by Will Goldston. Beginner.

Anonymous, *Book of Tricks*. (c. 1914) Daisy Bank Publishing, Manchester. Saddle-stitch. Orange. 32 pp. 5.5 x 8.5 in. In Copperfield collection. Beginner.

Anonymous, *Book of Tricks*. (c. 1914) Daisy Bank Publishing, Manchester. Saddle-stitch. Beige, blue. 32 pp. 5.5 x 8.5 in. In Copperfield collection. Beginner.

Anonymous, *Book of Tricks*. (c. 1914) Daisy Bank Publishing, Manchester. Saddle-stitch. Beige. 32 pp. 5.5 x 8.5 in. Price on cover: three pennies. In Copperfield collection. Beginner.

Anonymous, *Book of Tricks*. (c. 1914) Daisy Bank Publishing, Manchester. Saddle-stitch. Tan. 32 pp. 5.5 x 8.5 in. Price on cover: three pennies. In Copperfield collection. Beginner.

Anonymous, *Book of Tricks*. (c. 1914) Daisy Bank Publishing, Manchester. Saddle-stitch. Yellow. 32 pp. 5.5 x 8.5 in. Price on cover: three pennies. In Copperfield collection. Beginner.

Anonymous, *Book of Tricks*. Third printing. (c. 1914) Daisy Bank Publishing, Manchester. Saddle-stitch. Orange. 32 pp. 5.5 x 8.5 in. Cover states "Third issue." In Copperfield collection. Beginner.

Anonymous, *Boy Magician, The.* (2008) Hearst Books, New York. Perfect. Gray. 191 pp. 5.25 x 7.25 in. From vintage magazine articles. Beginner, History.

Anonymous, *Boy's Book of Magic, The.* (c. 1840) J. and W. Robertson, Glasgow. 16 pp. 2.75 x 4.25 in. (Information not verified by physical copy.) Toole Stott no. 108. Beginner.

Anonymous, *Boy's Book of Conjuring, The.* (c. 1928) Ward, Lock and Co., London. Cloth. Olive. Cover text: Black; 222 pp. 5.25 x 7.5 in. Retitled edition of "The Art of Modern Conjuring" (1910) with no author listed instead of "A Modern Magician." Green dust jacket. Beginner.

Anonymous, *Boy's Book of Conjuring, The.* (c. 1928) Ward, Lock and Co., London. Cloth. Tan. Cover text: Black; 222 pp. 5.25 x 7.5 in. Dust jacket. Retitled edition of "The Art of Modern Conjuring" by "A Modern Magician" (1910). Thinner pages. Beginner.

Anonymous, *Boy's Book of Conjuring, The.* (c. 1928) Ward, Lock and Co., London. Cloth. Tan. Cover text: Black; 222 pp. 5.25 x 7.5 in. Retitled edition of "The Art of Modern Conjuring" by "A Modern Magician" (1910). Beginner.

Anonymous (ed. by Eugene Stone), *Boy's Book of Conjuring, The.* (1952) Ward, Lock and Co., London. Cloth. Red. Cover text: Silver; 208 pp. 5 x 7.5 in. Dust jacket. Retitled edition of "The Art of Modern Conjuring" by "A Modern Magician" (1910). Beginner.

Anonymous (ed. by Eugene Stone), *Boy's Book of Conjuring, The.* (1953) Ward, Lock and Co., London. Cloth. Brown. Cover text: Silver; 208 pp. 5 x 7.5 in. Dust jacket. Retitled edition of "The Art of Modern Conjuring" by "A Modern Magician" (1910). Beginner.

Anonymous, *Boy's Book of Magic, The.* Eighth impression. (1957) Burke Publishing, London. Cloth. Blue. 192 pp. 5.5 x 8.75 in. Dust jacket. Beginner, Children's book.

Anonymous, *Boy's Conjurer, The.* (1866) Maddick and Pottage, London. 164 pp. 8 x 10 in. (Information not verified by physical copy.) Toole Stott no. 954. Beginner.

Anonymous, *Boy's Conjuror, The.* (1863) Hamilton, Adams, and Co., London. 16 pp. (Information not verified by physical copy.) Toole Stott no. 1345. Beginner.

Anonymous, *Boys of England Conjuring Book, The.* (1870) Boys of England, London. Saddle-stitch. Beige. 32 pp. 6 x 8.25 in. Published by British youth magazine. In Copperfield collection. Beginner.

Anonymous, *Boys of England Conjuring Book, The.* (c. 1870) Boys of England, London. Saddle-stitch. Beige. 16 pp. 5.25 x 8 in. Different layout. In Copperfield collection. Beginner.

Anonymous, *Boys' Own Book, The.* (1864) Lockwood, London. Cloth. Brown. 624 pp. 4.75 x 6.5 in. (Measurements and other information have been recorded as accurately as possible.) Beginner, Stunts.

Anonymous, *British Boy's Book of Magic and Mystery, The.* (c. 1890) P. W. Forbes, Birmingham, UK. Saddle-stitch. Light blue. 16 pp. 5 x 7.5 in. Author uncredited. Attribution from Findlay, "Price One Penny," 1967. In Copperfield collection. Beginner, Stunts.

Anonymous, *Broadway Book of Conjuring, The.* (c. 1921) D. C. Thomson and Co., London. Saddle-stitch. Blue. 52 pp. (Information not verified by physical copy.) See Hagy, "Magic for Free." Beginner, Premium.

Anonymous, *Broadway Book of Conjuring, The.* (c. 1921) D. C. Thomson and Co., London. Saddle-stitch. Color. 52 pp. (Information not verified by physical copy.) See Hagy, "Magic for Free." Beginner, Premium.

Anonymous, *By Far the Best Book of Conjuring Tricks.* (c. 1910) R. March and Co., London. Saddle-stitch. Light green. 26 pp. 6 x 8.25 in. Mind reader and spectator on cover. Same contents as "How to Perform One Hundred Conjuring Tricks." In Copperfield collection. Beginner, Mentalism. Pulp.

Anonymous, *By Far the Best Book of Conjuring Tricks.* (c. 1910) R. March and Co., London. Saddle-stitch. Orange. 26 pp. 6 x 8.25 in. Mind reader and spectator on cover. Same contents as "How to Perform One Hundred Conjuring Tricks." In Copperfield collection. Beginner, Mentalism. Pulp.

Anonymous, *Captain Midnight's Trick and Riddle Book.* (1939) Skelly Oil Co. Stapled. Red, blue. 64 pp. 2.5 x 3.5 in. Beginner, Premium.

Anonymous, *Card and Conjuring Tricks and Book of Riddles.* (c. 1919) W. Foulsham and Co., London. Saddle-stitch. Beige. 14 pp. 4.75 x 7.25 in. In Copperfield collection. Beginner, Cards, Riddles.

Anonymous, *Card Tricks.* (c. 1925) March, Cady, and Co., London. Saddle-stitch. Beige, blue, red. 16 pp. 5.5 x 8.5 in. In Copperfield collection. Beginner, Cards. Pulp.

Anonymous, *Card Tricks for the Amateur Magician.* (1921) U. S. Playing Card Co., Cincinnati, OH. Saddle-stitch. Beige. 14 pp. 4.5 x 7.25 in. Cards, Premium.

Anonymous, *Card Tricks for the Amateur Magician.* Second edition. (1923) U. S. Playing Card Co., Cincinnati, OH. Saddle-stitch. Beige. 28 pp. 4.5 x 7.25 in. Cards, Premium.

Anonymous, *Casanovia's Great Book of Magic.* (c. 1870) New York Popular Publishing, New York. 16 pp. 4 x 6.25 in. (Information not verified by physical copy.) Toole Stott no. 147. Beginner.

Anonymous, *Cassell's Book of Indoor Amusements, Card Games, and Fireside Fun.* (1881) Cassell and Co., London. Cloth. Green, red. 224 pp. 6 x 8.25 in. Beginner, Children's book, Stunts, Games.

Anonymous, *Cassell's Book of Indoor Amusements, Card Games, and Fireside Fun.* (1973) Cassell and Co., London. Cloth. Red. 224 pp. 6 x 8.25 in. Reprint of 1881 edition. Beginner, Children's book, Stunts, Games.

Anonymous, *Champion Card Tricks for Everybody.* (1920) Felix McGlennon Ltd., London. Folded. Beige. 8 pp. 7.25 x 9.75 in. Author credited from Newmann library catalog. Cards, Beginner. Pulp.

Anonymous, *Champion Parlour Tricks.* (1920) Felix McGlennon Ltd., London. Folded. Beige. 8 pp. 7.25 x 9.75 in. Author credited from Newmann library catalog. Beginner. Pulp.

Anonymous, *Chandu, White King of Magic Trick Set.* (n.d.) Folded. White. 12 pp. 3.25 x 6.75 in. From "Chandu White King of Magic Trick Set." Magic set manual, Beginner.

Anonymous, *Charles Dickens, Conjuror.* (1995) Saddle-stitch. White. 20 pp. 5 x 7 in. Reprint of 1912 "Magic Circular" article. Biography, History.

Anonymous, *Checkerboard Squarecrow Book of Magic.* (n.d.) Chex Cereal. Folded. Red, black, white. 16 pp. 3.5 x 5.5 in. Beginner, Premium.

Anonymous, *Chemical Magic.* (1952) Porter-Spear Co., Hagerstown, MD. Saddle-stitch. Yellow, red. 29 pp. 5 x 7.75 in. Chemical, Manual.

Anonymous, *Chemical Magic Manual.* (1952) Porter-Spear Co., Hagerstown, MD. Saddle-stitch. Yellow, red. 29 pp. 5 x 8 in. Chemical, Manual.

Anonymous, *Children's Game Book with Tricks and Puzzles.* (n.d.) Charles E. Graham and Co., New York. Boards. Red, green. 156 pp. 7.25 x 9.75 in. Beginner, Stunts, Puzzles, Children's book.

Anonymous, *Christian Conjurer vols. 1-5.* (1995) "Son" Shine Ministries, Holiday, FL. Comb. Light blue. Multiple sections. (Information not verified by physical copy.) Reprint of 1954 to 1961 issues. Magazine, Gospel magic.

Anonymous, *Clever Carroll's Combination Work of Ventriloquism, Magic, and Songs.* (c. 1869) New York Popular Publishing, New York. 16 pp. 3.5 x 6 in. (Information not verified by physical copy.) Toole Stott no. 1003. Beginner, Ventriloquism.

Anonymous, *Close-Up Floating Light Bulb.* (n.d.) Supreme Magic, Bideford, UK. Stapled. White. 5 pp. 8.5 x 11 in. Stage, Floating Light Bulb.

Anonymous, *Comedy Act for Magician in "One."* (n.d.) Stapled. White. 4 pp. 8.5 x 11 in. Mimeographed. White and tan pages. Comedy, Patter.

Anonymous, *Como's Book of Magic.* (c. 1870) George Whitehead and Sons, Huddersfield, UK. 19 pp. 5 x 6.5 in. (Information not verified by physical copy.) Toole Stott no. 1004. Beginner.

Anonymous, *Companion to the Endless Amusement, A.* (1831) James Gilbert, London. 215 pp. 3.5 x 5.75 in. (Information not verified by physical copy.) Toole Stott no. 172. Early magic, Beginner.

Anonymous, *Complete Art of Conjuring, The.* (c. 1820) J. Bailey, London. 32 pp. 4.25 x 7.25 in. (Information not verified by physical copy.) Toole Stott no. 173. Early magic, Beginner.

Anonymous, *Complete Conjuror, The.* (1812) Thomas Tegg, London. 36 pp. 4.5 x 6.5 in. (Information not verified by physical copy.) Toole Stott no. 1005. Early magic, Beginner, Cards, Dice.

Anonymous, *Complete Conjuror, The.* (c. 1840) J. Russell, Birmingham, UK. 12 pp. 3.5 x 5 in. (Information not verified by physical copy.) Toole Stott no. 175. Early magic, Beginner, Cards, Dice.

Anonymous, *Complete Manual for Adams' Real Magic Sets.* (n.d.) S. S. Adams, Asbury Park, NJ. Saddle-stitch. Olive. 15 pp. 5.25 x 8 in. In Adams' 1914 "Real Magic" set. Magic set manual.

Anonymous, *Confessions of a Medium.* (1882) Griffith and Farran, London. Cloth. Brown. 232 pp. 5.25 x 7.5 in. Spiritualism, Mediums, Exposés.

Anonymous, *Confidential Secrets of the Great Magicians.* (2017) Fun Inc., Chicago. Saddle-stitch. White. 32 pp. 5.5 x 8 in. In "Secrets of the Great Magicians" magic set. Magic set manual.

Anonymous, *Conjurer's Kit Book, The.* (n.d.) Waterlow and Sons Ltd., London. Stapled inside boards. Color. 18 pp. 15 x 10.5 in. Bound oblong. Foreword by Jasper Maskelyne. Oversize. Beginner, Punch-out effects.

Anonymous, *Conjuring and Card Tricks with Diagrams.* (n.d.) Daisy Bank Publishing, Manchester. Saddle-stitch. White. 16 pp. 10 x 14.75 in. Oversize. Beginner.

Anonymous, *Conjuring, or Magic Made Easy.* (c. 1870) New York Popular Pub. Co., New York. 16 pp. 4.75 x 6.75 in. (Information not verified by physical copy.) Toole Stott no. 176. Beginner.

Anonymous, *Conjuring, or Magic Made Easy.* (c. 1871) Benedict Popular Pub. Co., New York. 57 pp. 4.25 x 7 in. (Information not verified by physical copy.) Toole Stott no. 176. Beginner.

Anonymous, *Conjuring, or Magic Made Easy.* (c. 1873) Benedict Popular Pub. Co., New York. 57 pp. 4.75 x 6.75 in. (Information not verified by physical copy.) Toole Stott no. 177. Beginner.

Anonymous, *Conjuring Tricks and Catches.* (c. 1920) Allied Newspapers, Manchester. Saddle-stitch. White. 26 pp. 4 x 5.75 in. Supplement inside "Boys' Magazine." In Copperfield collection. Beginner, Stunts.

Anonymous, *Conjuring Tricks and Experiments.* (c. 1928) London. Saddle-stitch. Pink. 16 pp. 5 x 7.5 in. Findlay suggested this title may have been a magic-set manual. From "British Series." In Copperfield collection. Beginner. Pulp.

Anonymous, *Conjuring Tricks and Experiments.* (c. 1928) London. Saddle-stitch. Blue. 12 pp. 5 x 7.5 in. (Information not verified by physical copy.) Beginner. Pulp.

Anonymous, *Conjuring Tricks to Amuse All.* (c. 1912) R. March and Co., London. 32 pp. 5.75 x 8.75 in. In Copperfield collection. Beginner. Pulp.

Anonymous, *Conjuror Unmasked, or the Magical Mirror, The.* (1795) W. Lane, London. 144 pp. 4 x 6.75 in. (Information not verified by physical copy.) Toole Stott no. 182. Early magic.

Anonymous, *Conjuror Unmasked, or the Magical Mirror, The.* (c. 1811) J. Sadler, J. Eves, and M. Clements, London. 48 pp. 4.25 x 6.75 in. (Information not verified by physical copy.) Toole Stott no. 183. Early magic.

Anonymous, *Conjuror Unmasked, or the Whole Art and Mystery of Slight of Hand, The.* (1824) T. Hughes, London. 1824 pp. 4 x 6.75 in. (Information not verified by physical copy.) Toole Stott no. 184. Early magic.

Anonymous, *Conjuror's Guide, The.* (1808) Arliss and Huntsman, London. 36 pp. 5 x 7 in. (Information not verified by physical copy.) Toole Stott no. 1007. Early magic.

Anonymous, *Conjuror's Magazine, The.* (1792) W. Locke, London. Multiple sections. 5.25 x 8.25 in. (Information not verified by physical copy.) Toole Stott no. 179. Vol. 1, 494 pp.; vol. 2, 520 pp.; vol. 3, 250 pp. Magazine, Early magic, Beginner.

Anonymous, *Conjuror's Museum, or Hocus Pocus in Perfection, The.* (n.d.) M. C. Springsguth, London. 36 pp. 4.5 x 7 in. (Information not verified by physical copy.) Toole Stott no. 1008. Early magic.

Anonymous, *Conjuror's Repository, The.* (c. 1803) T. and R. Hughes, London. 146 pp. 2.75 x 7.5 in. (Information not verified by physical copy.) Toole Stott no. 180. Early magic.

Anonymous, *Conjuror's Repository, The.* Second edition. (c. 1805) W. Lewis, London. 146 pp. 4.25 x 7.5 in. (Information not verified by physical copy.) Toole Stott no. 181. Toole Stott notes that the title page lists Dewick as publisher. Early magic.

Anonymous, *Conjuror's Repository, The.* (1987) Walter B. Graham, Omaha. Leatherette. Brown. 146 pp. 4.5 x 7.5 in. Reprint of c. 1803 Hughes edition. #171 of 300. History, Early magic.

Anonymous, *Cute Tricks.* (1905) A. H. Kraus, Milwaukee, WI. Saddle-stitch. Beige. 24 pp. 5.25 x 7 in. Ad on back for printing company. Stunts, Impromptu, Close-Up.

Anonymous, *Daisy Bank Book for Amusing Electrical Tricks.* (c. 1914) Daisy Bank Publishing, Manchester and London. Saddle-stitch. Beige. 31 pp. 5.5 x 8.5 in. In Copperfield collection. Beginner, Electrical. Pulp.

Anonymous, *Daisy Bank Book for Amusing Electrical Tricks.* (c. 1914) Daisy Bank Publishing, Manchester and London. Saddle-stitch. Salmon. 31 pp. 5.5 x 8.5 in. In Copperfield collection. Beginner, Electrical. Pulp.

Anonymous, *Daisy Bank Book for Amusing Electrical Tricks.* (c. 1914) Daisy Bank Publishing, Manchester and London. Saddle-stitch. Yellow. 31 pp. 5.5 x 8.5 in. In Copperfield collection. Beginner, Electrical. Pulp.

Anonymous, *Daisy Bank Book for Winter Evenings.* (c. 1914) Daisy Bank Publishing, Manchester and London. Saddle-stitch. Yellow. 31 pp. 5.5 x 8.5 in. In Copperfield collection. Beginner, Stunts. Pulp.

Anonymous, *Daisy Bank Book of Electrical and Mechanical Tricks.* (c. 1914) Daisy Bank Publishing, Manchester and London. Saddle-stitch. Beige. 31 pp. 5.5 x 8.5 in. In Copperfield collection. Beginner, Electrical, Science magic. Pulp.

Anonymous, *Daisy Bank Book of Electrical and Mechanical Tricks.* (c. 1914) Daisy Bank Publishing, Manchester and London. Saddle-stitch. Light green. 31 pp. 5.5 x 8.5 in. In Copperfield collection. Beginner, Electrical, Science magic. Pulp.

Anonymous, *Daisy Bank Book of Electrical and Mechanical Tricks.* (c. 1914) Daisy Bank Publishing, Manchester and London. Saddle-stitch. Orange. 31 pp. 5.5 x 8.5 in. In Copperfield collection. Beginner, Electrical, Science magic. Pulp.

Anonymous, *Daisy Bank Book of Magic, The.* (c. 1914) Daisy Bank Publishing, Manchester and London. Saddle-stitch. Gray. 31 pp. 5.5 x 8.5 in. Beginner. Pulp.

Anonymous, *Daisy Bank Book of Magic, The.* (c. 1914) Daisy Bank Publishing, Manchester and London. Saddle-stitch. Green. 31 pp. 5.5 x 8.5 in. In Copperfield collection. Beginner. Pulp.

Anonymous, *Daisy Bank Book of Magic, The.* (c. 1914) Daisy Bank Publishing, Manchester and London. Saddle-stitch. Orange. 31 pp. 5.5 x 8.5 in. In Copperfield collection. Beginner. Pulp.

Anonymous, *Daisy Bank Book of Magic, The.* (c. 1914) Daisy Bank Publishing, Manchester and London. Saddle-stitch. Yellow. 31 pp. 5.5 x 8.5 in. In Copperfield collection. Beginner. Pulp.

Anonymous, *Daisy Bank Book of Magic, The.* (c. 1914) Daisy Bank Publishing, Manchester and London. Saddle-stitch. Orange. 31 pp. 5.5 x 8.5 in. Price on cover: two pennies. In Copperfield collection. Beginner. Pulp.

Anonymous, *Daisy Bank Book of Magic, The.* (c. 1914) Daisy Bank Publishing, Manchester and London. Saddle-stitch. Orange. 31 pp. 5.5 x 8.5 in. Price on cover: three pennies. In Copperfield collection. Beginner. Pulp.

Anonymous, *Dante's Secret Instructions.* (1964) Dante Productions, Rochester, NY. Saddle-stitch. White. 27 pp. 5.5 x 8.5 in. The set's "Dante" was Barrett Kirkendall, not illusionist Harry Jansen. From "Dante's Do-It-Yourself Magic Show" set. Magic set manual, Beginner.

Anonymous, *Dante's Secret Instructions.* (1965) Dante Productions, Rochester, NY. Folded. White. 15 pp. 4 x 6 in. From "Dante's Magic Show Junior Show" set. Magic set manual, Beginner.

Anonymous, *Dante's Secret Instructions.* (1965) Dante Productions, Rochester, NY. Saddle-stitch. Red, white. 24 pp. 4.75 x 6.75 in. From "Dante's Magic Show Party Show" set. Magic set manual, Beginner.

Anonymous, *David Copperfield's Tricks: Top Secret!* (2004) Books on Demand, Norderstedt, Germany. Perfect. Black. 186 pp. 6 x 8.75 in. "Copperfield's" misspelled in title as "Copperfields." Illusions, Television magic, Patents. German.

Anonymous, *Dean's New Book of Parlour Magic, or Tricks for the Drawing Room.* (1862) Dean and Son, London. 6 pp. 7.5 x 10.75 in. Movable pieces. (Information not verified by physical copy.) Toole Stott 1026. Beginner.

Anonymous, *Diary of a Prison Magician.* (2018) Vanishing Inc., Rancho Cordova, CA. Perfect. Black. 105 pp. 6 x 6 in. Astonishing Essays no. 3. Essays.

Anonymous, *Dick Tracy's Secret Detective Methods and Magic Tricks.* (1939) Quaker Oats Co., Chicago. Perfect. Green. 64 pp. 5 x 7.5 in. Beginner, Stunts, Premium, Cryptography.

Anonymous, *Directions for "Hokus Pokus Conjuring Tricks."* (n.d.) Spears Toys. Saddle-stitch. Brown. 16 pp. 6 x 9 in. Included in Spear's "Conjuring Tricks" magic set. Magic set manual, Beginner.

Anonymous, *Disneyland's Mystifying Magic Book: Magic from the Haunted Mansion in Disneyland.* (1970) Walt Disney Productions. Saddle-stitch. Black, purple, green. 59 pp. 6 x 9 in. Beginner.

Anonymous, *Do It Again Magic Tricks.* (1960) Whitman, Racine, WI. Saddle-stitch. Green. 8 pp. 10 x 14 in. Punch-out pieces. Beginner, Punch-out effects, Children's book.

Anonymous, *Drawing Room Magic.* (1868) Cassell, Petter, and Galpin, London. Cloth. Black. 90 pp. 4 x 6.5 in. Blind-embossed cover. Beginner.

Anonymous, *Easy Card Tricks.* (1912) Francis Griffiths, London. Perfect. Beige. 62 pp. 4.75 x 7.25 in. In Copperfield collection. Cards, Beginner.

Anonymous, *Easy Conjuring Tricks.* (1912) Francis Griffiths, London. Perfect. Beige. 62 pp. 4.75 x 7.25 in. (Measurements and other information have been recorded as accurately as possible.) Beginner.

Anonymous, *Easy-to-Do Card Tricks.* (n.d.) Levenson's Radio, Sydney. 32 pp. 5.5 x 7.5 in. (Information not verified by physical copy.) See McCullagh, "Under the Southern Cross." Cards, Beginner.

Anonymous, *Easy Tricks and Magic. Conjuring Without Sleight-of-Hand.* (n.d.) Saddle-stitch. Green. 48 pp. 4.75 x 7.25 in. Beginner, Stunts.

Anonymous, *Easy Tricks and Magic.* (c. 1920) Vawser and Wiles, London. Saddle-stitch. Color. 48 pp. 4.75 x 7.25 in. Beginner.

Anonymous, *Easy Tricks with Cards.* (c. 1916) Felix McGlennon Ltd., London. Saddle-stitch. Beige. 32 pp. 4 x 6.25 in. In Copperfield collection. Cards, Beginner.

Anonymous, *Easy Tricks with Cards.* (c. 1916) Felix McGlennon Ltd., London. Saddle-stitch. Light green. 32 pp. 4 x 6.25 in. In Copperfield collection. Cards, Beginner.

Anonymous, *Easy Tricks with Cards.* (c. 1916) Felix McGlennon Ltd., London. Saddle-stitch. Red. 32 pp. 4 x 6.25 in. In Copperfield collection. Cards, Beginner.

Anonymous, *Emperor of Conjurors Exploded, The.* (1815) J. Lee, London. 36 pp. 4.25 x 6.75 in. (Information not verified by physical copy.) Toole Stott no. 252. Early magic, Beginner.

Anonymous, *Endless Amusement.* (c. 1819) Gye and Balne, London. 216 pp. 4 x 6 in. (Information not verified by physical copy.) Toole Stott no. 255. Beginner, Cards.

Anonymous, *Endless Amusement.* Second edition. (c. 1820) Thorp and Burch, London. 216 pp. 3.75 x 6 in. (Information not verified by physical copy.) Toole Stott no. 256. Beginner, Cards.

Anonymous, *Endless Amusement.* Second edition. (1821) M. Carey and Sons, Philadelphia. 216 pp. 4 x 6 in. (Information not verified by physical copy.) Toole Stott no. 257. Beginner, Cards.

Anonymous, *Endless Amusement.* Third edition. (c. 1821) Thorp and Burch, London. 216 pp. 3.75 x 6 in. (Information not verified by physical copy.) Toole Stott no. 258. Beginner, Cards.

Anonymous, *Endless Amusement.* Third edition. (1822) M. Carey and Sons, Philadelphia. 216 pp. 4 x 6.25 in. (Information not verified by physical copy.) Toole Stott no. 259. Beginner, Cards.

Anonymous, *Endless Amusement.* Fourth edition. (1822) Thorp and Burch, London. 216 pp. 4 x 6.25 in. (Information not verified by physical copy.) Toole Stott no. 260. Beginner, Cards.

Anonymous, *Endless Amusement.* Fifth edition. (1830) James Gilbert, London. 216 pp. 4 x 6.25 in. (Information not verified by physical copy.) Toole Stott no. 261. Beginner, Cards.

Anonymous, *Endless Amusement.* (1831) W. C. Borradaile, New York. Boards. Tan. 216 pp. 3.5 x 6 in. Toole Stott no. 262. Beginner, Cards.

Anonymous, *Endless Amusement.* Sixth edition. (1834) Henry Washbourne, Thomas Tegg and Sons, London. 216 pp. 3.75 x 5 in. (Information not verified by physical copy.) Toole Stott no. 263. Beginner, Cards.

Anonymous, *Endless Amusement.* (1835) William Milner, Halifax. Cloth. Tan. 263 pp. 3.75 x 5.75 in. Toole Stott no. 264. Beginner, Cards, Science magic.

Anonymous, *Endless Amusement, The.* (1837) Thomas Tegg and Sons, London. 215 pp. 3.5 x 6 in. (Information not verified by physical copy.) Toole Stott no. 268. Beginner.

Anonymous, *Endless Amusement.* Seventh edition. (1839) Henry Washbourne and Thomas Tegg and Sons, London. Boards. Tan. 214 pp. 3.75 x 5.75 in. Toole Stott no. 265. Beginner, Cards.

Anonymous, *Endless Amusement.* Seventh edition. (1847) Lee and Blanchard, Philadelphia. Cloth. Red. 200 pp. 4.5 x 6.75 in. Toole Stott no. 266. Beginner, Cards.

Anonymous, *Endless Amusement.* (1853) Clark, Austin, and Smith, New York. 201 pp. 4.25 x 6.75 in. Toole Stott no. 267. Beginner, Cards.

Anonymous, *Endless Amusement for Youth.* (c. 1840) J. A. Wood, London. 36 pp. 3.5 x 5.5 in. (Information not verified by physical copy.) Toole Stott no. 269. Beginner, Early magic.

Anonymous, *Endless Amusements.* (1842) Theodore Abbot, Boston. 108 pp. 3.5 x 6 in. (Information not verified by physical copy.) Toole Stott no. 270. Beginner.

Anonymous, *Endless Amusements.* Second edition. (1842) Theodore Abbot, Boston. 108 pp. 3.5 x 5.75 in. (Information not verified by physical copy.) Toole Stott no. 271. Beginner.

Anonymous, *Endless Amusements.* Second edition. (1845) Theodore Abbot, Boston. 108 pp. 4 x 6.25 in. (Information not verified by physical copy.) Toole Stott no. 272. Beginner.

Anonymous, *Endless Amusements.* Twelfth edition. (1846) Theodore Abbot, Boston. 108 pp. 4 x 6.25 in. (Information not verified by physical copy.) Toole Stott no. 273. Beginner.

Anonymous, *England's Compleat Jester – to Which is Added Hocus Pocus.* (1721) Thomas Norris, London. 160 pp. 3.25 x 5.75 in. (Information not verified by physical copy.) Toole Stott no. 276. Beginner.

Anonymous, *Entertainer, The.* (n.d.) International Tailoring Co., New York. Saddle-stitch. Gold. 16 pp. 6.25 x 8.25 in. 2 pp. Parlor Magic section. "Downs Library" handwritten on cover. Beginner, Premium.

Anonymous, *Escamoteur de Bonne Société, L'.* (c. 1870) Bernardin-Bechet, Paris. Perfect. Beige. 108 pp. 3.75 x 6 in. Beginner, Stunts. French.

Anonymous, *Every Boy's Book of Conjuring Tricks and Magic.* (c. 1875) W. S. Fortey, London. Saddle-stitch. Pink. 8 pp. 5.25 x 8.5 in. Title page: "The Great Wizard's Handbook of Conjuring and Magic: Tricks with Cards." In Copperfield collection. Beginner. Pulp.

Anonymous, *Every Little Boy's Book.* (1864) George Routledge and Sons, London. Cloth. Green. 376 pp. 5 x 7.25 in. Conjuring section on p. 338. Beginner, Games, Stunts.

Anonymous, *Expert at Cards: Magic Card Tricks Anyone Can Do, The.* (c. 1930) Stein Publishing House, Chicago. Perfect. White, red. 128 pp. 5.25 x 7.75 in. From Kunard, Romanoff. Blank spine. Cards. Pulp.

Anonymous, *Expert at Cards: Magic Card Tricks Anyone Can Do, The.* (c. 1930) Stein Publishing House, Chicago. Perfect. Red, black. 128 pp. 5.25 x 7.75 in. Spine says "Magic Card Tricks Anyone Can Do." Cards. Pulp.

Anonymous, *Expert at Cards: Magic Card Tricks Anyone Can Do, The.* (c. 1930) Stein Publishing House, Chicago. Perfect. Red, black. 128 pp. 5.25 x 7.75 in. Spine says "Ordinary Card Tricks Anyone Can Do." Cards. Pulp.

Anonymous, *Expert at Cards: Magic Card Tricks Anyone Can Do, The.* (c. 1930) Stein Publishing House, Chicago. Perfect. Red, black. 128 pp. 5.25 x 7.75 in. Blank spine. Different cover with perpendicular Aces. Cards. Pulp.

Anonymous, *Extreme Magic.* (2000) Trickshop. Stapled. White. 25 pp. 8.5 x 11 in. (Measurements and other information have been recorded as accurately as possible.) Cards, Close-Up.

Anonymous, *Famous 6 Card Mysteries, The.* (n.d.) Folded. Beige. 3 pp. 3.75 x 5.5 in. (Measurements and other information have been recorded as accurately as possible.) Cards, Si Stebbins.

Anonymous, *Feats of Balancing.* (1945) Carstairs Bros. Distilling Co., Baltimore, MD. Saddle-stitch. Yellow, red, black. 32 pp. 3.75 x 5.5 in. In Copperfield collection. Beginner, Stunts, Premium.

Anonymous, *Feats of Genuine Mind Reading.* (n.d.) Chicago Magic Co., Chicago, IL. Stapled. White. 4 pp. 8.5 x 11 in. Mimeographed. (Information not verified by physical copy.) Mentalism.

Anonymous, *Five Card Sharpers and the Fortune Teller, The.* (n.d.) Union Gospel Printing, Cleveland, OH. Saddle-stitch. Beige. 6 pp. 3 x 4.5 in. Cards, Cheating, Religious tract.

Anonymous, *Fortune Telling with Cards.* (1978) La Croix Publishing Co., Belleville, MI. Saddle-stitch. Red. 3 pp. 6.25 x 7.5 in. Includes two-page perforated label sheet with cards. Fortune-telling.

Anonymous, *Forty Tricks with Cards.* (c. 1914) Daisy Bank Publishing, Manchester, UK. Saddle-stitch. Orange. 32 pp. 5.5 x 8.5 in. Text-only cover. In Copperfield collection. Cards, Beginner. Pulp.

Anonymous, *Forty Tricks with Cards.* (c. 1914) Daisy Bank Publishing, Manchester, UK. Saddle-stitch. Beige. 32 pp. 5.5 x 8.5 in. Hands with cards on cover. In Copperfield collection. Cards, Beginner. Pulp.

Anonymous, *Forty Tricks with Cards.* (c. 1914) Daisy Bank Publishing, Manchester, UK. Saddle-stitch. Light green. 32 pp. 5.5 x 8.5 in. Hands with cards on cover. Cards, Beginner. Pulp.

Anonymous, *Forty Tricks with Cards.* (c. 1914) Daisy Bank Publishing, Manchester, UK. Saddle-stitch. Olive. 32 pp. 5.5 x 8.5 in. Hands with cards on cover. Cards, Beginner. Pulp.

Anonymous, *Forty Tricks with Cards.* (c. 1914) Daisy Bank Publishing, Manchester, UK. Saddle-stitch. Orange. 32 pp. 5.5 x 8.5 in. Hands with cards on cover. In Copperfield collection. Cards, Beginner. Pulp.

Anonymous, *Forty Tricks with Cards.* (c. 1914) Daisy Bank Publishing, Manchester, UK. Saddle-stitch. Purple. 32 pp. 5.5 x 8.5 in. Hands with cards on cover. In Copperfield collection. Cards, Beginner. Pulp.

Anonymous, *Forty Tricks with Cards.* (c. 1914) Daisy Bank Publishing, Manchester, UK. Saddle-stitch. Salmon. 32 pp. 5.5 x 8.5 in. Hands with cards on cover. In Copperfield collection. Cards, Beginner. Pulp.

Anonymous, *Forty Tricks with Cards.* (c. 1914) Daisy Bank Publishing, Manchester, UK. Saddle-stitch. Beige. 32 pp. 5.5 x 8.5 in. Hand with fan of Ten to Ace of Diamonds. In Copperfield collection. Cards, Beginner. Pulp.

Anonymous, *Forty Tricks with Cards.* (c. 1914) Daisy Bank Publishing, Manchester, UK. Saddle-stitch. Light green. 32 pp. 5.5 x 8.5 in. Hand with fan of Ten to Ace of Diamonds. In Copperfield collection. Cards, Beginner. Pulp.

Anonymous, *Forty Tricks with Cards.* (c. 1914) Daisy Bank Publishing, Manchester, UK. Saddle-stitch. Orange. 32 pp. 5.5 x 8.5 in. Hand with fan of Ten to Ace of Diamonds. In Copperfield collection. Cards, Beginner. Pulp.

Anonymous, *Forty Tricks with Cards.* (c. 1914) Daisy Bank Publishing, Manchester, UK. Saddle-stitch. Yellow. 32 pp. 5.5 x 8.5 in. Hand with fan of Ten to Ace of Diamonds. In Copperfield collection. Cards, Beginner. Pulp.

Anonymous, *Fred Flintstone the Magician.* (1974) Peter Pan Industries, Newark, NJ. Saddle-stitch. Pink. 24 pp. 7 x 7.5 in. From book and record set. Label says "cassette" instead of "record." Beginner, Children's book.

Anonymous, *Fun Doctor, The.* (c. 1907) Tricks Publishing, New York. Cloth. Gray. 115 pp. 5.25 x 7.75 in. From Selbit publishing partnership. Humor.

Anonymous, *Fun with Magic.* (n.d.) Miller and Hollis Inc., Boston. Folded. Blue. 6 pp. 4 x 6 in. Folded. Promotion for candy company. Beginner, Premium.

Anonymous, *Fun, Magic, and Mystery.* (c. 1912) Ottenheimer, Baltimore, MD. Perfect. White, yellow, red, black. 58 pp. 4 x 5.25 in. Magician, witch, and ventriloquist on front cover. Beginner, Stunts. Pulp.

Anonymous, *Fun, Magic, and Mystery.* (c. 1916) Wehman Bros., New York. Saddle-stitch. Yellow, green. 62 pp. 3.75 x 5 in. Small edition of "New Book of Fun, Magic, and Mystery." Magician and Rising Cards on front cover. Beginner, Stunts. Pulp.

Anonymous, *Fun, Magic, and Mystery.* (c. 1916) Wehman Bros., New York. Perfect. White, pink, green. 62 pp. 3.75 x 5 in. Small edition of "New Book of Fun, Magic, and Mystery." Four square images on front cover. Beginner, Stunts. Pulp.

Anonymous, *Fun, Magic, and Mystery.* (c. 1916) Wehman Bros., New York. Perfect. White, pink, green. 62 pp. 3.75 x 5 in. Small edition of "New Book of Fun, Magic, and Mystery." Magician and Rising Cards on front cover. Beginner, Stunts. Pulp.

Anonymous, *Fun, Magic, and Mystery. 1.* (c. 1970) Johnson Smith and Co., Detroit. Saddle-stitch. White. 16 pp. 5.5 x 8.5 in. Different material. Reprints from Dunninger's "Popular Magic." Beginner. Pulp.

Anonymous, *Games of Skill and Conjuring.* (1860) Routledge, Warne, and Routledge, London. 128 pp. 4.5 x 6.75 in. (Information not verified by physical copy.) Toole Stott no. 312. Paginated as 376-502. Beginner, Stunts.

Anonymous, *Games of Skill and Conjuring.* (1861) Routledge, Warne, and Routledge, London and New York. 128 pp. 4.5 x 6.75 in. (Information not verified by physical copy.) Toole Stott no. 313. Paginated as 376-502. Beginner, Stunts.

Anonymous, *Games of Skill and Conjuring.* (1861) Routledge, Warne, and Routledge, London. Cloth. Blue. 128 pp. 4.25 x 6.75 in. Toole Stott no. 314. Paginated as 2-128. Beginner, Stunts.

Anonymous, *Games of Skill and Conjuring.* (1862) Routledge, Warne, and Routledge, London and New York. 128 pp. 4.25 x 6.75 in. (Information not verified by physical copy.) Toole Stott no. 315. Paginated as 2-128. Beginner, Stunts.

Anonymous, *Games of Skill and Conjuring.* (1865) George Routledge and Sons, London and New York. 128 pp. 4.25 x 6.75 in. (Information not verified by physical copy.) Toole Stott no. 316. Paginated as 2-128. Beginner, Stunts.

Anonymous, *Games of Skill and Conjuring.* (1870) George Routledge and Sons, London. Cloth. Orange. 128 pp. 4.75 x 7 in. Toole Stott no. 317. Paginated as 376-502. Beginner, Stunts.

Anonymous, *Georges Méliès: À la Conquête du Cinématographe.* (2011) Studio Canal, Paris. Casebound. Black. 128 pp. 9.75 x 11.25 in. Includes three DVDs. Biography, Cinema, History. French.

Anonymous, *Goofy Card Tricks.* (1977) Western Publishing Co., Racine, WI. Saddle-stitch. White. 64 pp. 5.5 x 3.5 in. In "Goofy Card Tricks" magic set. Cards, Magic set manual.

Anonymous, *Gran Curso de Magia y Prestidigitación.* (2000) Editorial de Vecchi, Barcelona. Cloth. Black. 478 pp. 7 x 9.75 in. Dust jacket. Beginner. Spanish.

Anonymous, *Great Chinese Wizard's Hand-Book of Magic, The.* (n.d.) Hurst and Co., New York. Saddle-stitch. Green. 64 pp. 5 x 6.75 in. Toole Stott no. 319. Beginner.

Anonymous, *Great Men's Revello, or Sealed Letter Reading, The.* (n.d.) Author. Stapled. Purple. 3 pp. 8.5 x 11 in. Mimeographed. (Information not verified by physical copy.) Mentalism, Impression pad.

Anonymous, *Great Wizard's Hand Book of Magic, The.* (1850) W. S. Fortey, London. 8 pp. 4 x 7.5 in. (Information not verified by physical copy.) Toole Stott no. 321. Beginner.

Anonymous, *Great Wizard's Handbook of Magic, The.* (1850) W. S. Fortey, London. 8 pp. 5 x 7.25 in. (Information not verified by physical copy.) Toole Stott no. 320. Beginner.

Anonymous, *Great Wizard's Handbook of Mystery and Magic, The.* (c. 1850) W. S. Fortey, London. 8 pp. 5 x 7.25 in. (Information not verified by physical copy.) Toole Stott no. 1365. Beginner.

Anonymous, *Hand-Book of Conjuring and Parlour Magic, The.* (c. 1910) F. H. Wakelin and Co., London. Saddle-stitch. 16 pp. Toole Stott nos. 328, 1071. Price: one penny. Magic set manual.

Anonymous, *Hand-Book of Conjuring and Parlour Magic, The.* (c. 1920) F. H. Wakelin and Co., London. Saddle-stitch. Beige, red, green. 16 pp. 4.75 x 7 in. Toole Stott nos. 328, 1071. Price: two pennies. In Copperfield collection. Magic set manual.

Anonymous, *Hand-Book of Magic, The.* (1839) Robert Tyas, London. 64 pp. 3.25 x 4.5 in. (Information not verified by physical copy.) Toole Stott nos. 328, 1071. Magic set manual.

Anonymous, *Handcuff Trick, The.* (n.d.) D. Robbins, Brooklyn, NY. Folded. White. 4 pp. 5.5 x 8.5 in. In envelope marked "How to Be a Handcuff King." Escapes, Handcuffs.

Anonymous, *Hanky Panky.* (n.d.) Hanky Panky Toys, Netherlands. Saddle-stitch. Black. 16 pp. 5.25 x 7.5 in. In "Hanky Panky" magic set. Magic set manual.

Anonymous, *Have You Seen This One?* (n.d.) Heath and Milligan Mfg. Co. Saddle-stitch. White, red, black. 15 pp. 3.75 x 5 in. Promotional booklet with recipes and card tricks. Cards, Premium, Recipes.

Anonymous, *Heller's Book of Magic.* (1898) Henry J. Wehman, New York. Perfect. Tan. 144 pp. 4.75 x 7 in. Material from Theobald, "Magic and Its Mysteries." Beginner. Pulp.

Anonymous, *Heller's Book of Magic.* (1898) Henry J. Wehman, New York. Perfect. Yellow. 100 pp. 4.75 x 7.5 in. Beginner. Pulp.

Anonymous, *Heller's Book of Magic.* (n.d.) Johnson Smith and Co., Detroit. Perfect. Brown. 102 pp. 5.25 x 7.25 in. Beginner. Pulp.

Anonymous, *Heller's Book of Magic.* (n.d.) Johnson Smith and Co., Detroit. Perfect. Tan. 102 pp. 5.25 x 7.25 in. Beginner. Pulp.

Anonymous, *Heller's Book of Magic.* (n.d.) Perfect. Tan, blue. 89 pp. 4.75 x 7 in. No publisher or date noted. Beginner. Pulp.

Anonymous, *Herman's Black Art: Magic Made Easy.* (n.d.) Royal Publishing Co., Philadelphia. Perfect. Light green. 94 pp. 5.25 x 7 in. Material from Dean, "Hocus Pocus." Beginner. Pulp.

Anonymous, *Hermann's Art of Magic.* (n.d.) Wehman, New York. Perfect. Light green. 91 pp. 4.75 x 7.25 in. Contents from "Herrmann's Book of Magic" (1902, Drake). Beginner. Pulp.

Anonymous, *Hermann's Art of Magic.* (n.d.) Wehman, New York. Perfect. Orange. 91 pp. 4.75 x 7.25 in. Contents from "Herrmann's Book of Magic" (1902, Drake). Beginner. Pulp.

Anonymous, *Hermann's Art of Magic.* (n.d.) Wehman, New York. Perfect. Tan. 91 pp. 4.75 x 7.25 in. Contents from "Herrmann's Book of Magic" (1902, Drake). Back cover shows "Wehman's Wizard Manual." Beginner. Pulp.

Anonymous, *Hermann's Art of Magic.* (n.d.) Wehman, New York. Perfect. White. 91 pp. 4.75 x 7 in. No ad on back. Beginner. Pulp.

Anonymous, *Hermann's Art of Magic.* (n.d.) Wehman, New York. Perfect. Beige, red. 91 pp. 4.75 x 7 in. Books ad on back. Beginner. Pulp.

Anonymous, *Herrman's Black Art.* (1908) Henry J. Wehman, New York. Perfect. Tan. 122 pp. 4.75 x 7 in. Contains occult magic only. Occult. Pulp.

Anonymous, *Herrman's Black Art: Magic Made Easy.* (n.d.) Royal Publishing, Philadelphia. Perfect. Yellow. 94 pp. 5.25 x 7.25 in. Material from Dean, "Hocus Pocus." Beginner, Cards. Pulp.

Anonymous, *Herrman's Tricks With Cards.* (1891) Street and Smith, New York. Perfect. White, olive, red, black. 145 pp. 5.25 x 7.5 in. Material from Hoffmann. In Copperfield library copy, Adelaide Herrmann inscription says her late husband did not write this work. Cards. Pulp.

Anonymous, *Herrman's Tricks With Cards.* (n.d.) Stein Publishing House, Chicago. Perfect. Yellow. 100 pp. 5.25 x 7.75 in. Contains 6 pp. on Canfield and material from Hoffmann, "Modern Magic." Cards. Pulp.

Anonymous, *Herrman's Tricks With Cards.* (n.d.) Stein Publishing House, Chicago. Perfect. Beige. 100 pp. 5.25 x 8 in. Contains 6 pp. on Canfield and material from Hoffmann, "Modern Magic." Cards. Pulp.

Anonymous, *Herrmann's Book of Magic.* (n.d.) Stein Publishing House, Chicago. Perfect. Red, beige. Multiple sections. 5.25 x 7.5 in. From "Tricks in Magic" and Hoffmann, "Modern Magic." Cards. Pulp.

Anonymous, *Herrmann's Book of Magic.* (n.d.) Stein Publishing House, Chicago. Perfect. Bright red, beige. Multiple sections. 5.25 x 7.5 in. From "Tricks in Magic" and Hoffmann, "Modern Magic." Cards. Pulp.

Anonymous, *Herrmann's Book of Magic.* (n.d.) Stein Publishing House, Chicago. Perfect. Dark blue, beige. Multiple sections. 5.25 x 7.5 in. From "Tricks in Magic" and Hoffmann, "Modern Magic." Cards. Pulp.

Anonymous, *Herrmann's Wizards' Manual.* (n.d.) Stein Publishing House, Chicago. Saddle-stitch. White, blue. Multiple sections. 5.25 x 7.5 in. From "Tricks in Magic" and Hoffmann, "Modern Magic." Cards. Pulp.

Anonymous, *Herrmann's Wizards' Manual.* (n.d.) Stein Publishing House, Chicago. Saddle-stitch. Yellow, red. Multiple sections. 5.25 x 7.5 in. From "Tricks in Magic" and Hoffmann, "Modern Magic." Cards. Pulp.

Anonymous, *Herrmann's Wizards' Manual.* (n.d.) Stein Publishing House, Chicago. Perfect. Yellow, blue. 66 pp. 5.25 x 7.5 in. From "Tricks in Magic" and Hoffmann, "Modern Magic." Cards. Pulp.

Anonymous, *Histoire des Grecs, ou de Ceux Qui Corrigent la Fortune au Jeu, Première Partie, L'.* (1758) L'Habile Joueur, La Haye. Leather. Brown. 215 pp. 3.75 x 6.25 in. Set of three volumes. Marbled endpapers. Gambling, Cards, Cheating, Early magic. French.

Anonymous, *Histoire des Grecs, ou de Ceux Qui Corrigent la Fortune au Jeu, Seconde Partie, L'.* (1758) L'Habile Joueur, La Haye. Leather. Brown. 237 pp. 3.75 x 6.25 in. Second book of set. Gambling, Cards, Cheating, Early magic. French.

Anonymous, *Histoire des Grecs, ou de Ceux Qui Corrigent la Fortune au Jeu, Troisième Partie, L'.* (1758) L'Habile Joueur, La Haye. Leather. Brown. 179 pp. 3.75 x 6.25 in. Third book of set. Gambling, Cards, Cheating, Early magic. French.

Anonymous, *History and Analysis of the Supposed Automaton Chess Player, The.* (1826) Hilliard, Gray, and Co., Boston. 24 pp. 4.75 x 8.25 in. (Information not verified by physical copy.) Toole Stott no. 421. History, Automata, Automaton chess player.

Anonymous, *Hocus Pocus.* (2008) City Museum at Old Treasury Melbourne, Melbourne. Saddle-stitch. Brown. 56 pp. 5.75 x 8.25 in. History, Museum guide.

Anonymous, *Hocus Pocus Junior: The Anatomy of Legerdemain or The Art of Jugling.* (1634) T. Harper, London. 56 pp. 5.75 x 7 in. (Information not verified by physical copy.) Toole Stott no. 356. Early magic, Beginner.

Anonymous, *Hocus Pocus Junior: The Anatomy of Legerdemain or The Art of Jugling.* Second edition. (1635) T. Harper, London. 64 pp. 5.25 x 7 in. (Information not verified by physical copy.) Toole Stott no. 357. Early magic, Beginner.

Anonymous, *Hocus Pocus Junior: The Anatomy of Legerdemain or The Art of Jugling.* Third edition. (1638) Francis Grove, London. 64 pp. 5.5 x 7.5 in. (Information not verified by physical copy.) Toole Stott no. 358. Early magic, Beginner.

Anonymous, *Hocus Pocus Junior: The Anatomy of Legerdemain or The Art of Jugling.* Fourth edition. (1654) G. Dawson, London. 64 pp. 5.25 x 7.25 in. (Information not verified by physical copy.) Toole Stott no. 359. Early magic, Beginner.

Anonymous, *Hocus Pocus Junior: The Anatomy of Legerdemain or The Art of Jugling.* Fifth edition. (1658) G. Dawson, London. 64 pp. 5.5 x 7.25 in. (Information not verified by physical copy.) Toole Stott no. 360. Early magic, Beginner.

Anonymous, *Hocus Pocus Junior: The Anatomy of Legerdemain or The Art of Jugling.* Sixth edition. (1663) G. Dawson, London. 64 pp. 5.25 x 7 in. (Information not verified by physical copy.) Toole Stott no. 361. Early magic, Beginner.

Anonymous, *Hocus Pocus Junior: The Anatomy of Legerdemain or The Art of Jugling.* Seventh edition. (1671) G. Purslow, London. 64 pp. 5.25 x 6.75 in. (Information not verified by physical copy.) Toole Stott no. 362. Early magic, Beginner.

Anonymous, *Hocus Pocus Junior: The Anatomy of Legerdemain or The Art of Jugling.* Eighth edition. (c. 1671) London. 57 pp. 5.25 x 7 in. (Information not verified by physical copy.) Toole Stott no. 363. Early magic, Beginner.

Anonymous, *Hocus Pocus Junior: The Anatomy of Legerdemain or The Art of Jugling.* Ninth edition. (1682) T. H., London. 57 pp. 5.75 x 7.5 in. (Information not verified by physical copy.) Toole Stott no. 364. Early magic, Beginner.

Anonymous, *Hocus Pocus Junior: The Anatomy of Legerdemain or The Art of Jugling.* Tenth edition. (1683) J. Deacon, London. 57 pp. 5.25 x 7.25 in. (Information not verified by physical copy.) Toole Stott no. 365. Early magic, Beginner.

Anonymous, *Hocus Pocus Junior: The Anatomy of Legerdemain or The Art of Jugling.* Eleventh edition. (1686) J. Deacon, London. 58 pp. 5.25 x 7 in. (Information not verified by physical copy.) Toole Stott no. 366. Early magic, Beginner.

Anonymous, *Hocus Pocus Junior: The Anatomy of Legerdemain or The Art of Jugling.* Twelfth edition. (1691) J. Deacon, London. 58 pp. 5.5 x 7.75 in. (Information not verified by physical copy.) Toole Stott no. 367. Early magic, Beginner.

Anonymous, *Hocus Pocus Junior: The Anatomy of Legerdemain or The Art of Jugling.* Thirteenth edition. (1697) J. Deacon, London. 58 pp. 5.5 x 7 in. (Information not verified by physical copy.) Toole Stott no. 368. Early magic, Beginner.

Anonymous, *Hocus Pocus Junior: The Anatomy of Legerdemain or The Art of Jugling.* Thirteenth edition with additions. (1706) J. Deacon, London. 58 pp. 4.5 x 7 in. (Information not verified by physical copy.) Toole Stott no. 369. See also "Old Hocus Pocus" for the retitled fourteenth and fifteenth editions. Early magic, Beginner.

Anonymous, *Hocus Pocus Junior: The Anatomy of Legerdemain or The Art of Jugling.* (1707) B. Deacon, London. 16 pp. 4.5 x 7 in. (Information not verified by physical copy.) Toole Stott no. 370. Early magic, Beginner.

For the fourteenth, fifteenth, seventeenth, and eighteenth editions of "Hocus Pocus Junior," see the 1708 and 1740 editions of "The Old Hocus Pocus" and the 1814 and 1817 editions of "Hocus Pocus, or The Whole Art of Legerdemain in Perfection."

Anonymous, *Hocus Pocus Junior.* (1950) John McArdle. Cloth. Green. 60 pp. 5.25 x 7.25 in. Limited to 50 copies. History, Early magic, Beginner.

Anonymous, *Hocus Pocus Junior.* (1997) Steve Burton Magic, Cypress, TX. Leatherette. Black. 60 pp. 5.25 x 7.25 in. Reprint of 1634 edition. #21 of 300. History, Early magic, Beginner.

Anonymous, *Hocus Pocus Magic.* (1953) Samuel Lowe Co., Kenosha, WI. Boards. Red. 23 pp. 6.25 x 7.75 in. A "Bonnie Spinwheel" book. Lenticular cover. Children's book, Beginner.

Anonymous, *Hocus Pocus, or A New Book of Legerdemain.* (c. 1765) Aldermary Church-Yard, London. 8 pp. 4.5 x 7 in. (Information not verified by physical copy.) Toole Stott no. 376. Early magic, Beginner.

Anonymous, *Hocus Pocus, or Legerdemain Curiosities.* (c. 1720) George Conyers, London. 12 pp. (Information not verified by physical copy.) Toole Stott no. 372. Information from copy in British Museum. Early magic, Beginner.

Anonymous, *Hocus Pocus, or Slight of Hand Explained.* (1826) T. Hughes, London. 38 pp. 5 x 7.5 in. (Information not verified by physical copy.) Toole Stott no. 380. Early magic, Beginner.

Anonymous, *Hocus Pocus, or The Art of Conjuration.* (1792) W. Lane, London. 144 pp. 3.25 x 5.75 in. (Information not verified by physical copy.) Toole Stott no. 378. Early magic, Beginner.

Anonymous, *Hocus Pocus, or The Art of Conjuration.* (1795) W. Lane, London. 140 pp. 3 x 6.25 in. (Information not verified by physical copy.) Toole Stott no. 1081. Early magic, Beginner.

Anonymous, *Hocus Pocus, or The Art of Conjuring Made Easy.* (1827) Freeman Scott, Philadelphia. 71 pp. 3 x 5.5 in. (Information not verified by physical copy.) Toole Stott no. 381. Early magic, Beginner.

Anonymous, *Hocus Pocus, or The Art of Legerdemain.* (c. 1790) Treen, Coventry, UK. 8 pp. 4 x 6.5 in. (Information not verified by physical copy.) Toole Stott no. 377. Early magic, Beginner.

Anonymous, *Hocus Pocus, or The New and Complete Art of Conjuring.* (c. 1820) J. Bailey, London. 32 pp. 4.25 x 7 in. (Information not verified by physical copy.) Toole Stott no. 379. Early magic, Beginner.

Anonymous, *Hocus Pocus, or The True Art of Legerdemain.* (c. 1860) Murphy, New York. 38 pp. 3.75 x 6 in. (Information not verified by physical copy.) Toole Stott no. 384. Early magic, Beginner.

Anonymous, *Hocus Pocus, or The True Art of Legerdemain.* (c. 1862) Murphy, New York. 72 pp. 3.75 x 5.75 in. (Information not verified by physical copy.) Toole Stott no. 385. Early magic, Beginner.

Anonymous, *Hocus Pocus, or The Whole Art of Legerdemain in Perfection.* Seventeenth edition. (1814) E. Duyckinck, New York. 107 pp. (Information not verified by physical copy.) See Heyl, "Cues for Collectors." Early magic, Beginner.

Anonymous, *Hocus Pocus, or The Whole Art of Legerdemain in Perfection.* Eighteenth edition. (1817) Munroe and Francis, Boston. 107 pp. (Information not verified by physical copy.) See Heyl, "Cues for Collectors." Early magic, Beginner.

Anonymous, *Hocus Pocus, or The Whole Art of Legerdemain in Perfection.* (c. 1846) William Walker, Otley, UK. 24 pp. 3.75 x 6.75 in. (Information not verified by physical copy.) Toole Stott no. 383. Early magic, Beginner.

Anonymous, *Hocus Pocus, or The Whole Art of Legerdemain, Laid Open.* (c. 1760) James Byrn and T. Wilkinson, Dublin. 143 pp. 3.5 x 6 in. (Information not verified by physical copy.) Toole Stott no. 374. Early magic, Beginner.

Anonymous, *Hocus Pocus, or The Whole Art of Legerdemain, Laid Open.* (c. 1774) Thomas WIlkinson, Dublin. 143 pp. 3.5 x 6 in. (Information not verified by physical copy.) Toole Stott no. 375. Early magic, Beginner.

Anonymous, *Hocus Pocus, or The Whole Art of Conjuring.* (c. 1846) Turner and Fisher, New York. 72 pp. 3.75 x 6 in. (Information not verified by physical copy.) Toole Stott no. 382. Early magic, Beginner.

Anonymous, *Holiday Frolics.* (1830) W. Strange and J. Clements, London. 36 pp. 3.75 x 6 in. (Information not verified by physical copy.) Toole Stott no. 387. Early magic, Beginner.

Anonymous, *Home Amusements.* (1910) Fleischmann Co. Saddle-stitch. Color. 12 pp. 3.5 x 5.5 in. (Measurements and other information have been recorded as accurately as possible.) Beginner, Premium.

Anonymous, *Houdin's Mysteries of Magic, from The Magician's Guide, and Conjuring Made Easy.* (c. 1875) G. Blackie and Co., New York. 55 pp. (Information not verified by physical copy.) Toole Stott no. 1168. Beginner.

Anonymous, *Houdini and Walt Disney.* (1979) Pendulum Press, West Haven, CT. Perfect. Green. 63 pp. 5.5 x 8 in. Houdini, Biography, Children's book.

Anonymous, *Houdini's Magic Secrets.* (1967) Platt and Munk, New York. Saddle-stitch. Blue. 46 pp. 7.75 x 8.75 in. Magic set manual, Houdini.

Anonymous, *How 'Tis Done, or The Secret Out.* (1864) Hunter and Co., Hinsdale, NH. 16 pp. 4.25 x 6.75 in. (Information not verified by physical copy.) Toole Stott no. 396. Gambling, Cheating, Cards, Dice.

Anonymous, *How 'Tis Done, or The Secret Out.* (n.d.) C. E. Curtiss, Lehigh, NY. Saddle-stitch. Orange. 16 pp. 6 x 8.75 in. Gambling, Cards, Cheating.

Anonymous, *How It's Done Between You and Me.* (n.d.) Redhill Products, Long Island, NY. Saddle-stitch. Red. 18 pp. 5.25 x 6.75 in. Magic set manual.

Anonymous, *How to Be a Clairvoyant.* (1905) Frederick J. Drake, Chicago. Cloth. Gray. 79 pp. 4.25 x 6.5 in. Clinton Burgess bookplate. Hypnotism.

Anonymous, *How to Be a Magician for School, Club, Church.* (n.d.) Saddle-stitch. Beige. 22 pp. 5.5 x 3 in. Bound oblong. Promotional ideas for business. Beginner, History, Business, Promotion.

Anonymous, *How to Become a Conjuror.* (n.d.) Willsons', Leicester, UK. Saddle-stitch. Yellow. 86 pp. 5 x 7.5 in. Beginner.

Anonymous, *How to Become a Lightning Calculator.* Miniature book. (1894) Multum in Parvo Library, Boston. Saddle-stitch. Tan. 12 pp. 2.75 x 4.25 in. Mathematical, Lightning calculation. Pulp.

Anonymous, *How to Control Fair Dice.* (c. 1949) H. C. Evans and Co., Chicago. Folded. White. 12 pp. 3.75 x 5.5 in. No publisher noted. (Measurements and other information have been recorded as accurately as possible.) Dice, Cheating.

Anonymous, *How to Control Fair Dice.* (1976) Busby Enterprises, Oakland, CA. Saddle-stitch. White. 16 pp. 5.25 x 8 in. Dice, Cheating.

Anonymous, *How to Do 100 "Moo"gic Tricks.* (n.d.) S. S. Adams, Asbury Park, NJ. Saddle-stitch. White. 32 pp. 4.25 x 6 in. Promotion for "Moo" restaurant. Beginner, Stunts, Promotion.

Anonymous, *How to Do Card Tricks Easily Manipulated.* (c. 1920) Daisy Bank Publishing, Manchester. Saddle-stitch. Red, green, white. 31 pp. 5.5 x 8.25 in. Cards.

Anonymous, *How to Do Electrical and Mechanical Tricks.* (c. 1914) Daisy Bank Publishing, Manchester and London. Saddle-stitch. Beige. 31 pp. 5.5 x 8.5 in. In Copperfield collection. Beginner, Electrical, Science magic. Pulp.

Anonymous, *How to Do Electrical and Mechanical Tricks.* (c. 1914) Daisy Bank Publishing, Manchester and London. Saddle-stitch. Orange. 31 pp. 5.5 x 8.5 in. In Copperfield collection. Beginner, Electrical, Science magic. Pulp.

Anonymous, *How to Do Snoopy the Magician Magic Tricks.* (n.d.) Helm Toy Co., New York. Saddle-stitch. White. 8 pp. 3.5 x 2.5 in. Bound oblong. In "Snoopy the Magician Magic Set." Magic set manual.

Anonymous, *How to Give Conjuring Entertainments at Home.* (n.d.) James Henderson and Sons, London. Saddle-stitch. Tan. 64 pp. 5.5 x 8.5 in. Beginner, Stunts.

Anonymous, *How to Learn the Art of Ventriloquism.* Miniature book. (1896) Multum in Parvo Library, Boston. Saddle-stitch. Tan. 16 pp. 2.75 x 4.25 in. Ventriloquism. Pulp.

Anonymous, *How to Perform One Hundred Conjuring Tricks.* (c. 1910) R. March and Co., London. Saddle-stitch. White. 10 pp. 5 x 7.5 in. In Copperfield collection. Beginner. Pulp.

Anonymous, *How to Perform One Hundred Conjuring Tricks.* (c. 1910) R. March and Co., London. Saddle-stitch. Blue. 26 pp. 5.25 x 8 in. In Copperfield collection. Beginner. Pulp.

Anonymous, *How to Perform the Magic Tricks of Voodini.* (1967) Transogram Inc., New York. Loose pages. White. 2 pp. 12 x 7.75 in. In "Mr. Magician" magic set. Magic set manual, Beginner, Puzzles.

Anonymous, *How to Win at Draw Poker.* (n.d.) Johnson Smith and Co., Detroit. Perfect. Brown. 22 pp. 5.25 x 7.5 in. Cards, Cheating, Card games, Poker.

Anonymous, *Illusions: L'Art de la Magie.* (2017) McCord Museum, Montreal. Cloth. Black. Cover text: Gold; 248 pp. 10 x 12 in. French edition. History, Posters, Exhibit catalog, Collecting. French.

Anonymous, *Illusions: The Art of Magic.* (2017) McCord Museum, Montreal. Cloth. Black. Cover text: Gold; 248 pp. 10 x 12 in. History, Posters, Exhibit catalog, Collecting.

Anonymous, *Illustrated Story of Magic, The.* (1960) Gilberton World-Wide Publications, Inc., New York. Perfect. Red. 64 pp. 6.5 x 10 in. "The World Around Us," no. 25, September 1960. Comic book, History, Biography.

Anonymous, *Incomparable Testot, The.* (2005) Projection Box, East Sussex, UK. Saddle-stitch. Red. 36 pp. 8.25 x 11.75 in. Introduction by Edwin A. Dawes. Biography, History.

Anonymous, *Indoor Tricks and Games.* (n.d.) Success Publishing Co., London. Saddle-stitch. Beige, red, blue. 64 pp. 4.75 x 7.25 in. Beginner, Cards.

Anonymous, *Instructions for Adams' Abracadabra Magic Set.* (n.d.) S. S. Adams, Asbury Park, NJ. Saddle-stitch. White. 18 pp. 4.5 x 6 in. In Adams' "Abracadabra Magic Set." Magic set manual.

Anonymous, *Instructions for Adams' Hocus-Pocus Magic Set.* (n.d.) S. S. Adams, Asbury Park, NJ. Saddle-stitch. White. 11 pp. 4 x 5.5 in. In Adams' "Hocus-Pocus Magic Set." Magic set manual.

Anonymous, *Instructions for Adams' Hokus-Pokus Magic Set.* (1962) S. S. Adams, Asbury Park, NJ. Saddle-stitch. White. 16 pp. 4.75 x 6 in. In Adams' "Hocus-Pocus Magic Set." Magic set manual.

Anonymous, *Instructions for Adams' Party Magic Set.* (n.d.) S. S. Adams, Neptune, NJ. Saddle-stitch. White. 17 pp. 4.5 x 6.5 in. In Adams' "Party Magic Set." Magic set manual.

Anonymous, *Instructions for no. 311 and 312 Magician's and Magic Comic Dress-Up Set.* (n.d.) H. Davis Toy Co., Newark, NJ. Folded. White. 8 pp. 4.25 x 5.75 in. In "Magic and Magicians Comic Dress-Up Set" magic set. Magic set manual.

Anonymous, *Instructions for the Ubiquitous and Multiplying Thimble.* (c. 1901) Ornum's, London. Stapled. White. 8.5 x 11 in. Mimeographed. (Information not verified by physical copy.) Thimbles, Manipulation.

Anonymous, *Instructions in Conjuring and Stage-Magic.* (1881) E. G. Rideout, Inc., New York. Saddle-stitch. Olive. 94 pp. 4.75 x 7.25 in. Beginner, Stage.

Anonymous, *Invisible Lady, The.* (1807) London. 4 pp. 4.75 x 8.25 in. (Information not verified by physical copy.) Toole Stott no. 412. Early magic, Illusions.

Anonymous, *It's All in Knowing How.* (n.d.) Calvert Distillers Corp., New York. Saddle-stitch. Brown. 14 pp. 3.5 x 5.25 in. Promotional booklet for Calvert whiskey. Beginner, Stunts, Premium.

Anonymous, *Jacques Vaucanson.* (1983) Musée National des Techniques, Paris. Perfect. Beige. 57 pp. 6 x 8.75 in. Biography, Automata, History. French.

Anonymous, *Jemima Carstairs' Book of Party Magic.* (1934) Schoolgirl, London. Folded. White. 16 pp. 3.75 x 5.5 in. Supplement to "The Schoolgirl" magazine. In Copperfield collection. Beginner.

Anonymous, *Juegos de Manos.* (1900) Saturnino Calleja, Madrid. Casebound. Beige. 302 pp. 3.25 x 4.75 in. Beginner. Spanish.

Anonymous, *Jumbo Hocus Pocus.* (1972) Uitgave Hausemann & Hötte, Amsterdam. Perfect. Red, green, black. 283 pp. 4 x 7 in. Beginner. Dutch.

Anonymous, *Karmos.* (c. 1920) Stapled. White. 16 pp. 8.5 x 11 in. Mimeographed. Based on Kellar's routine. Mentalism, Code acts.

Anonymous, *Kay Conjuring Booklet, The.* (n.d.) Kay Sports and Games, London. Folded. White. 4 pp. 5.25 x 8.25 in. In "Kay Conjuring Tricks" set. Magic set manual.

Anonymous, *Kellar's Wizards' Manual.* (c. 1910) Arthur Westbrook Co., Cleveland, OH. Perfect. White, blue. Multiple sections. 5 x 7 in. From "Hocus Pocus Junior," Hoffmann. Beginner, Cards, Hypnotism. Pulp.

Anonymous, *Kellar's Wizards' Manual.* (c. 1910) J. S. Ogilvie Publishing Co., New York. Perfect. White, blue. 69 pp. 4.75 x 7 in. From "Hocus Pocus Junior," Hoffmann. Beginner, Cards, Hypnotism. Pulp.

Anonymous, *Kellar's Wizards' Manual.* (c. 1910) Royal Publishing Co., Philadelphia. Perfect. Light blue. 69 pp. 5 x 7.25 in. From "Hocus Pocus Junior," Hoffmann. Beginner, Cards, Hypnotism. Pulp.

Anonymous, *Keller's Variety Entertainments.* (c. 1902) Drake Publishing, Chicago. Perfect. Black, red, gray. 188 pp. 4.25 x 6.5 in. From "Bunkum Entertainments." Stunts. Pulp.

Anonymous, *Keller's Variety Entertainments.* (c. 1902) Drake Publishing, Chicago. Perfect. Black, red, white. 188 pp. 4.25 x 6.5 in. From "Bunkum Entertainments." Has publisher's name on bottom of front cover. Stunts. Pulp.

Anonymous, *Learn How to Be a Handcuff King and Mystery Man.* (1941) Johnson Smith and Co., Detroit. Saddle-stitch. Olive. 22 pp. 5.25 x 7.5 in. Escapes, Handcuffs. Pulp.

Anonymous, *Learn How to Be a Handcuff King and Mystery Man.* (1941) Johnson Smith and Co., Detroit. Saddle-stitch. Tan. 22 pp. 5.25 x 7.5 in. Escapes, Handcuffs. Pulp.

Anonymous, *Learn the Tricks.* (1990) Mystical Ventures, Los Angeles. Folded. White. 12 pp. 3 x 5 in. Nestlé promotion. Magic with chocolate bar packaging. Beginner, Premium.

Anonymous, *Legerdemain, or the Mysteries of the Black Art Revealed.* (n.d.) Edwin Dipple, London. Saddle-stitch. White. 30 pp. 5 x 7.5 in. In Copperfield collection. Beginner. Pulp.

Anonymous, *Lessons in Magic.* (1970) Tenyo, Tokyo. Saddle-stitch. White, blue. 19 pp. 5.75 x 8.25 in. In "Can Be a Magician" set. Magic set manual, Beginner.

Anonymous, *Life Savers Book-o-Magic.* (1931) Life Savers Inc., Port Chester, NY. Saddle-stitch. Black. 34 pp. 4.75 x 6.25 in. Beginner, Premium.

Anonymous, *Little Book o' Tricks, The.* (c. 1908) Edward Smith and Co., London. Saddle-stitch. Beige. 24 pp. 4.25 x 7 in. In Copperfield collection. Beginner, Stunts. Pulp.

Anonymous, *London Conjuror, or Art of Legerdemain, The.* (1812) R. Harrild, London. 36 pp. 4.5 x 6 in. (Information not verified by physical copy.) Toole Stott nos. 435, 1104. Beginner.

Anonymous, *London Conjuror, or Art of Legerdemain, The.* (1813) R. Harrild, London. 36 pp. 4.5 x 7.5 in. (Information not verified by physical copy.) Toole Stott no. 436. Beginner.

Anonymous, *Look Alikes.* (1981) Philadelphia Magic Co., Philadelphia. Stapled. Beige. 2 pp. 5.75 x 8.5 in. Mimeographed inside printed cover. Pen and ink cover by Earle Oakes. Stapled text pages folded inside independent cover. Includes cards. Cards.

Anonymous, *Magic: A Treatise of Modern Magical Mysteries.* (n.d.) Stein Publishing House, Chicago. Saddle-stitch. Beige, blue. 16 pp. 5.25 x 7.75 in. Magician with cornucopia on cover. Beginner. Pulp.

Anonymous, *Magic and Mysteries.* (1924) Stein Publishing House, Chicago. Saddle-stitch. Red. 15 pp. 8.75 x 11.75 in. Various material on allied arts. Beginner.

Anonymous, *Magic and Mystery.* (n.d.) London. Saddle-stitch. Beige, red, blue. 18 pp. 4.75 x 7 in. (Measurements and other information have been recorded as accurately as possible.) Beginner.

Anonymous, *Magic and Mystery Unveiled.* (c. 1870) Hurst and Co., New York. Perfect. Light blue. 66 pp. 4.75 x 7 in. Toole Stott no. 463. In Copperfield collection. Beginner.

Anonymous, *Magic and Tack-a-Note.* (1993) Kee-West Productions, Mayo, MD. 31 pp. (Information not verified by physical copy.) Close-Up, Stage, Adhesives.

Anonymous, *Magic Book: How to Put On Your Own Magic Show.* (1977) Hallmark Cards, Inc. Saddle-stitch. Blue. 24 pp. 5.75 x 8.25 in. Formerly "Quick Tricks Magic Book." Beginner, Children's book.

Anonymous, *Magic Book of Mystifying Tricks.* (n.d.) Skinner Manufacturing Co., Omaha. Perfect. Red, black, white. 24 pp. 3.25 x 6 in. Beginner.

Anonymous, *Magic Book, or The Whole Art of Legerdemain, The.* (c. 1820) F. Cunningham, Glasgow. 24 pp. 3.5 x 6.5 in. (Information not verified by physical copy.) Toole Stott no. 465. Beginner.

Anonymous, *Magic, Cards, Coins, and Mystery Made Easy.* (c. 1909) Albert's Music Store, Sydney. 98 pp. 4 x 6.25 in. (Information not verified by physical copy.) See McCullagh, "Under the Southern Cross." Beginner.

Anonymous, *Magic for Everybody.* (1944) Popular Mechanics Press, Chicago. Saddle-stitch. 16 pp. (Information not verified by physical copy.) See Hagy, "Magic for Free." Beginner, Premium.

Anonymous, *Magic for Home and Stage.* (1929) Shrewsbury Publishing Co., Chicago. Cloth. Orange. 150 pp. 4.75 x 7 in. Material from Hoffmann, "Modern Magic." Beginner.

Anonymous, *Magic for Home and Stage.* (1929) Shrewsbury Publishing Co., Chicago. Perfect. Brown. 150 pp. 4.75 x 7 in. Material from Hoffmann, "Modern Magic." Beginner.

Anonymous, *Magic for Home and Stage.* (1941) Stein Publishing House, Chicago. Perfect. Yellow. 150 pp. 5.25 x 7.75 in. Magician holding top hat and 25-cent price on cover. Beginner. Pulp.

Anonymous, *Magic for Home and Stage.* (n.d.) Stein Publishing House, Chicago. Saddle-stitch. Red. 22 pp. 5.25 x 8 in. Magician holding top hat on cover. Beginner. Pulp.

Anonymous, *Magic for Home and Stage.* (1941) Stein Publishing House, Chicago. Perfect. Red. 150 pp. 5.25 x 7.75 in. Magician with cornucopia on cover. Cover says "Magic: A Treatise on Modern Magical Mysteries." Beginner. Pulp.

Anonymous, *Magic for Home and Stage.* (1941) Stein Publishing House, Chicago. Perfect. Yellow. 150 pp. 5.25 x 7.75 in. Magician with cornucopia on cover. Cover says "Magic: A Treatise on Modern Magical Mysteries." Beginner. Pulp.

Anonymous, *Magic for the Amateur Magician.* (1907) Wehman, New York. Perfect and staples. Yellow. 64 pp. 4.75 x 7.5 in. Contents from Wehman's "Black Art, or Magic Made Easy." Beginner, Cards, Coins. Pulp.

Anonymous, *Magic Fun for Everyone.* (1940) Frigidaire Corp., Dayton, OH. Saddle-stitch. Black, yellow. 23 pp. 3.5 x 5.5 in. Beginner, Stunts, Premium.

Anonymous, *Magic Handbook.* (1961) Science and Mechanics Magazine, New York. Perfect. Black. 160 pp. 6.5 x 9.25 in. Beginner.

Anonymous, *Magic Handbook.* (1968) Science and Mechanics Magazine, New York. Perfect. Red. 112 pp. 6.5 x 9.25 in. Beginner.

Anonymous, *Magic Instruction: Large Magic Set no. 1.* (1975) Chu's Magic, Hong Kong. Saddle-stitch. White. 18 pp. 5.75 x 8.25 in. In "Chu's Magic Set no. 1." Magic set manual.

Anonymous, *Magic: Instructions for 70 Tricks.* (n.d.) Merit, UK. Saddle-stitch. Pink. 21 pp. 5.5 x 8.5 in. Magic set manual, Beginner.

Anonymous, *Magic Made Easy.* (n.d.) Saddle-stitch. Red, black. 30 pp. 5.25 x 7.75 in. Cover subtitle: "279 Amazing Parlor Tricks." Illustrations in red and black. No publisher or locale noted. Beginner. Pulp.

Anonymous, *Magic Made Easy.* (1910) Wehman, New York. Perfect. Blue, red. 58 pp. 4 x 5 in. Magician and doves from hat in front of table on cover. Beginner. Pulp.

Anonymous, *Magic Made Easy.* (1910) Wehman, New York. Perfect. Blue, red. 58 pp. 4 x 5 in. Magician and doves from hat in front of table on cover. Different back cover. Beginner. Pulp.

Anonymous, *Magic Made Easy.* (1910) Wehman, New York. Perfect. Green, red. 58 pp. 4 x 5 in. Magician and doves from hat in front of table on cover. Beginner. Pulp.

Anonymous, *Magic Made Easy.* (n.d.) Ottenheimer, Baltimore, MD. Perfect. Yellow, red. 59 pp. 4 x 5 in. Two tables on cover. Beginner. Pulp.

Anonymous, *Magic Made Easy!* (1950) Vital Publications, New York. Saddle-stitch. White, black. 15 pp. 6 x 9 in. Beginner.

Anonymous, *Magic Mirror, or Conjuror's Companion, The.* (c. 1812) Knevett, Arliss, and Baker, London. 38 pp. 4.5 x 7.5 in. (Information not verified by physical copy.) Toole Stott no. 466. Beginner.

Anonymous, *Magic, Mirth, and Mystery.* (1874) Happy Hours Co., New York. 16 pp. (Information not verified by physical copy.) Toole Stott no. 1115. Beginner.

Anonymous, *Magic, Mirth, and Mystery, etc.* (c. 1886) Australian Magical Depot, Sydney. 56 pp. 5.25 x 8.5 in. (Information not verified by physical copy.) See McCullagh, "Under the Southern Cross." Beginner, Catalog.

Anonymous, *Magic Omnibook.* (1946) Saddle-stitch. Purple. Cover text: Brown; 48 pp. 8.25 x 10.75 in. Compilation of pages from "Conjurors' Magazine." Stage, Close-Up, Magazine.

Anonymous, *Magic, or An Easy Way to Do Tricks.* (c. 1872) G. F. Hanson, New York. 49 pp. 4 x 6.25 in. (Information not verified by physical copy.) Toole Stott no. 467. Beginner.

Anonymous, *Magic, or An Easy Way to Do Tricks.* (c. 1873) G. F. Hanson, New York. 49 pp. 4 x 6.25 in. (Information not verified by physical copy.) Toole Stott no. 468. Beginner.

Anonymous, *Magic Oracle, or Conjuror's Guide.* (c. 1850) Glasgow. 24 pp. 3.75 x 6.25 in. (Information not verified by physical copy.) Toole Stott no. 471. Beginner.

Anonymous, *Magic Oracle, or The Black Art Made Easy, The.* (c. 1867) J. Jones, Boston. 66 pp. 4.5 x 6 in. (Information not verified by physical copy.) Toole Stott no. 469. Beginner.

Anonymous, *Magic Oracle, or The Black Art Made Easy, The.* (1868) Yankee Blade Office, Boston. 95 pp. 3.75 x 5.5 in. (Information not verified by physical copy.) Toole Stott no. 470. Beginner.

Anonymous, *Magic Set.* (1969) Otto Maier, Ravensburg, Germany. Saddle-stitch. White. 12 pp. 11.75 x 8.25 in. Bound oblong. In Creative Playthings "Magic Set." Magic set manual.

Anonymous, *Magic Show Book, The.* (2016) Dorling Kindersley Books, Amsterdam. Casebound. Silver, black. 31 pp. 8.75 x 11.25 in. Children's book, Pop-up book.

Anonymous, *Magic Show Hocus Pocus.* (1985) Koninklijke, Amsterdam. Perfect. Blue. 159 pp. 4 x 7 in. Beginner. Dutch.

Anonymous, *Magic Simplified.* (c. 1900) Atlas Trick and Novelty Co., Chicago. Saddle-stitch. Tan. 12 pp. 5.75 x 8.75 in. Combination of book and catalog. Beginner, Catalog. Pulp.

Anonymous, *Magic to Amaze Your Friends.* (n.d.) Charles Hansen's Laboratory, Little Falls, NY. Saddle-stitch. Color. 20 pp. (Information not verified by physical copy.) See Hagy, "Magic for Free." Beginner, Premium.

Anonymous, *Magic Touch, The.* (1934) Arnold Tours, Boston. Folded. Yellow. 12 pp. 3.25 x 5.5 in. Travel brochure with images and descriptions of Indian magic. Indian magic.

Anonymous, *Magic Tricks from Nestlé Quik.* (1978) Nestlé. Saddle-stitch. Pink. 20 pp. 5.5 x 8.5 in. Promotion for Quik chocolate mix. Beginner, Stunts, Promotion.

Anonymous, *Magic Tricks Instruction Book.* (2000) Marks and Spencer, London. Saddle-stitch. White. 21 pp. 2.5 x 5.5 in. In Simpsons "Duff Beer Magic Set." Magic set manual, Beginner.

Anonymous, *Magic Tricks Made Easy.* (1989) Reader's Digest, Australia. Saddle-stitch. 40 pp. 3.75 x 5.5 in. (Information not verified by physical copy.) See McCullagh, "Under the Southern Cross." Beginner.

Anonymous, *Magic with a Stacked Deck.* (n.d.) Repro Magic, London. 55 pp. (Information not verified by physical copy.) Cards, Prearranged deck.

Anonymous, *Magic You Can Do!* (n.d.) Southern California Savings, Garden Grove, CA. Saddle-stitch. Red. 12 pp. 6 x 8 in. Beginner, Premium.

Anonymous, *Magical Mirror, or the Art of Legerdemain Laid Open.* (1810) T. and R. Hughes, London. 74 pp. 4 x 6 in. (Information not verified by physical copy.) Toole Stott no. 477. Beginner.

Anonymous, *Magician Exposed, The.* (1850) Turner and Fisher, Philadelphia. 44 pp. 3 x 5.5 in. (Information not verified by physical copy.) Toole Stott no. 479. Beginner.

Anonymous, *Magician, or the Magic of the Sciences, The.* (1834) W. Strange, London. 106 pp. 4 x 6 in. (Information not verified by physical copy.) Toole Stott no. 478. Beginner.

Anonymous, *Magician's Instructor, The.* (1870) Fisher and Denison, New York. 233 pp. 3.25 x 5 in. (Information not verified by physical copy.) Toole Stott no. 480. Beginner.

Anonymous, *Manual of Greatest Magic.* (c. 1927) Petrie-Lewis Mfg. Co., New Haven, CT. Saddle-stitch. White, red, blue. 24 pp. 6 x 3.25 in. Bound oblong. From "Aladdin Magic Outfit." Tarbell ad on back. Magic set manual, Beginner.

Anonymous, *Manuel de l'Amateur des Tours de Cartes.* (c. 1864) Delarue, Paris. Perfect. Beige. 84 pp. 3.75 x 6 in. Four fold-out plates and Pinetti-type image on back. Cards.

Anonymous, *Manual de Magia Matematica con los Cartas.* (1996) Editorial de Vecchi, Barcelona. Perfect. Red. 173 pp. 6.75 x 9.5 in. Cards, Mathematical magic.

Anonymous, *Manuel des Sorciers, Le.* Second edition. (1802) Metier, Paris. Perfect. Tan. 228 pp. 4 x 7 in. Original wraps, frontispiece. Woodcuts similar to Decremps. Beginner. French.

Anonymous, *March's Illustrated (200) Conjuring Tricks – and Easy, Too.* (c. 1910) R. March and Co., London. Saddle-stitch. Beige. 26 pp. 6 x 8.25 in. Hindu Mango Tree Trick on cover. Same contents as "How to Perform One Hundred Conjuring Tricks." In Copperfield collection. Beginner, Mentalism. Pulp.

Anonymous, *March's Illustrated (200) Conjuring Tricks – and Easy, Too.* (c. 1910) R. March and Co., London. Saddle-stitch. Light blue. 26 pp. 6 x 8.25 in. Hindu Mango Tree Trick on cover. Same contents as "How to Perform One Hundred Conjuring Tricks." In Copperfield collection. Beginner, Mentalism. Pulp.

Anonymous, *March's Illustrated (200) Conjuring Tricks – and Easy, Too.* (c. 1910) R. March and Co., London. Saddle-stitch. White. 26 pp. 6 x 8.25 in. Hindu Mango Tree Trick on cover. Same contents as "How to Perform One Hundred Conjuring Tricks." In Copperfield collection. Beginner, Mentalism. Pulp.

Anonymous, *March's Illustrated (200) Conjuring Tricks – and Easy, Too.* (c. 1910) R. March and Co., London. Saddle-stitch. Yellow. 26 pp. 6 x 8.25 in. Hindu Mango Tree Trick on cover. Same contents as "How to Perform One Hundred Conjuring Tricks." In Copperfield collection. Beginner, Mentalism. Pulp.

Anonymous, *Mars Mickey Mouse Club Magic Manual.* (n.d.) Mars Inc., Chicago. Envelope. White. 2 pp. 8 x 20 in. Folded. From "Mickey Mouse Club Magic Kit." Magic set manual.

Anonymous, *Master Key Systems.* (c. 1930) Hunt and Co., Chicago. Saddle-stitch. White. 20 pp. 3.5 x 6.25 in. Stacking, shuffles sections. Cards, Run-up systems.

Anonymous, *Master Key Systems.* (n.d.) S. F. Card Co., San Francisco. Saddle-stitch. White. 20 pp. 5.25 x 8.25 in. S.F. Card Co. stamp; Stacking, shuffles sections. Cards.

Anonymous, *Master Key Systems.* (n.d.) Saddle-stitch. White. 20 pp. 5.25 x 8.25 in. Stacking, shuffles sections. (Measurements and other information have been recorded as accurately as possible.) Cards.

Anonymous, *Master Key Systems.* (n.d.) Saddle-stitch. Yellow. 20 pp. 5.25 x 8.25 in. Reprint credited to Ernie Bryan and Duane Duvall. Cards.

Anonymous, *Masters of Illusion: Jewish Magicians of the Golden Age.* (2011) Los Angeles Conference on Magic History, Los Angeles. Saddle-stitch. Color. 60 pp. 6 x 9 in. History, Exhibit.

Anonymous, *Mattel's Magic Show Stoppers Showcase Super Secret Instructions and Showmanship Hints.* (1969) Mattel, El Segundo, CA. Saddle-stitch. Color. 23 pp. 7 x 5.5 in. Bound oblong. Includes four 2 pp. 11 x 14 in. instruction sheets. Magic set manual, Beginner, Showmanship.

Anonymous, *Mazda Mystic Ring Magic Book, The.* (1974) Mazda Mystic Ring, Chicago. Saddle-stitch. Silver. 36 pp. 5.5 x 8.5 in. Beginner, History, Magic clubs.

Anonymous, *Melbourne Parlour Magician, The.* (1875) John Pyrke and Co., Melbourne. 48 pp. 4.75 x 7.25 in. (Information not verified by physical copy.) See McCullagh, "Under the Southern Cross." Beginner.

Anonymous, *Mental Nuts to Crack.* (1928) Stein Publishing House, Chicago. Perfect. Beige, orange. 126 pp. 5.25 x 7.75 in. Drawing-room magic and coin magic sections. Beginner, Cards, Coins, Puzzles.

Anonymous, *Mephisto's Firecracker.* (1929) Petrie-Lewis Mfg. Co., New Haven, CT. Saddle-stitch. White. 3 pp. 8.5 x 11 in. (Information not verified by physical copy.) Stage, Apparatus.

Anonymous, *Merlin's Magic Show.* (2011) Hanky Panky Toys, Thailand. Saddle-stitch. Blue. 34 pp. 6.75 x 9.75 in. Magic set manual.

Anonymous, *Merveilleux Tours de Cartes, Les.* (n.d.) Le Bailly, Paris. Perfect. Beige. 93 pp. 3.5 x 5.75 in. Cards, Beginner. French.

Anonymous, *Mickey Mouse Magic Book, The.* (1974) Random House, New York. Casebound. Blue. 40 pp. 6.75 x 9.5 in. Beginner, Children's book.

Anonymous, *Mickey Mouse Magic Tricks.* (1977) Walt Disney Productions, Racine, WI. Saddle-stitch. White, red. 67 pp. 5.5 x 3.5 in. Bound oblong. Beginner, Children's book.

Anonymous, *Mickey Mouse the Magician.* (1981) Franklin Watts Inc., New York. Boards. Blue. 12 pp. 7 x 9.25 in. With puppet and hole through book. Fiction, Children's book.

Anonymous, *Mind-Blowing Magic.* (2003) Marvin's Magic, Herts, UK. Saddle-stitch. Blue. 26 pp. 5.75 x 8.25 in. Magic set manual.

Anonymous, *Modern Illusions.* (1974) O'Neal Magic, Rockbridge, OH. 36 pp. (Information not verified by physical copy.) Illusions.

Anonymous, *Modern Magic and Morgan's Sapolio.* (1887) Enoch Morgan's Sons, Philadelphia and New York. Saddle-stitch. White, blue, orange, black. 16 pp. 3.5 x 5.25 in. In Copperfield collection. Promotion for soap company. Beginner, Stunts, Premium.

Anonymous, *Modern Magic: The Newest, Simplest, and Best Tricks.* (c. 1850) Shenton, Cheltenham, UK. Saddle-stitch. Yellow. 12 pp. 4.25 x 7 in. (Information not verified by physical copy.) Toole Stott no. 493. Beginner.

Anonymous, *Modern Pastime, or Indoor Amusements.* (n.d.) Frederick Warne and Co., London. Cloth. Brown. 179 pp. 4.25 x 6 in. Period signature of owner. Beginner, Stunts, Cards.

Anonymous, *Monte Carlo Secret Service.* (1925) Perfect. Red, black. 96 pp. 5.75 x 8.75 in. (Measurements and other information have been recorded as accurately as possible.) Gambling, Cards, Cheating.

Anonymous, *Moody's Book of Magic.* (1870) New York Popular Publishing, New York. Saddle-stitch. 28 pp. 5 x 7.25 in. (Information not verified by physical copy.) Toole Stott no. 494. Beginner.

Anonymous, *More Than Sixty Tricks for the Amateur Conjurer.* (c. 1900) R. March and Co., London. Saddle-stitch. Blue. 16 pp. 6 x 8.25 in. Magician producing tree on cover. In Copperfield collection. Beginner.

Anonymous, *More Than Sixty Tricks for the Amateur Conjurer.* (c. 1900) R. March and Co., London. Saddle-stitch. Green. 16 pp. 6 x 8.25 in. Magician producing tree on cover. In Copperfield collection. Beginner.

Anonymous, *More Than Sixty Tricks for the Amateur Conjurer.* (c. 1900) R. March and Co., London. Saddle-stitch. Orange. 16 pp. 6 x 8.25 in. Magician producing tree on cover. In Copperfield collection. Beginner.

Anonymous, *More Than Sixty Tricks for the Amateur Conjurer.* (c. 1900) R. March and Co., London. Saddle-stitch. Pink. 16 pp. 6 x 8.25 in. Magician producing tree on cover. In Copperfield collection. Beginner.

Anonymous, *More Than Sixty Tricks for the Amateur Conjurer.* (c. 1900) R. March and Co., London. Saddle-stitch. Tan. 16 pp. 6 x 8.25 in. Magician producing tree on cover. In Copperfield collection. Beginner.

Anonymous, *Mr. Clown's Winter Nights Entertainment.* (1859) G. Abington, London. 48 pp. 4.75 x 7 in. (Information not verified by physical copy.) Toole Stott no. 497. Beginner, Cards.

Anonymous, *Mr. Tricko Magic Set.* (n.d.) Remco Industries Inc., Harrison, NJ. Accordion fold. White, black, red. 12 pp. 5.25 x 8 in. From "Mr. Tricko Magic Set." Magic set manual.

Anonymous, *Mr. Ree: From Blazing Comics nos. 1-5.* (n.d.) Classic Comics Library. Saddle-stitch. Brown. 29 pp. 8.5 x 11 in. Comics, History.

Anonymous, *Mueller Report Blow Book.* (n.d.) Stapled. Red, white, blue. Unpaginated. 8.5 x 11 in. Blow book in file folder marked "Top Secret" shows text, redacted, or blank. Blow book.

Anonymous, *Mysteries of Sleight of Hand: Book 1.* (n.d.) Semloh Publishing Co., Detroit. Saddle-stitch. Red. 12 pp. 3.25 x 6.25 in. In Copperfield collection. Cards, Close-Up.

Anonymous, *Mysteries of the Magic Wand, The.* (1928) Porter Chemical Co., Hagerstown, MD. Saddle-stitch. Red. 16 pp. 4.75 x 7.5 in. Chemical, Manual.

Anonymous, *Mysteries of the Mystic Seven, The.* (n.d.) Northampton, UK. Stapled with tape. Blue. 30 pp. 8 x 10 in. Mimeographed. Effects by Horace Goldin. Stage, Close-Up.

Anonymous, *New and Improved Hocus Pocus, or Art of Legerdemain, A.* (1808) Arliss and Huntsman, London. 36 pp. 4.25 x 6.75 in. (Information not verified by physical copy.) Toole Stott no. 502. Beginner, Early magic.

Anonymous, *New Art of Conjuring and Magic.* (c. 1875) William S. Fortey, London. 16 pp. 5.75 x 9 in. (Information not verified by physical copy.) Toole Stott no. 503. Beginner.

Anonymous, *New Art of Hocus Pocus Revived.* (1808) T. D. Dewick, London. 38 pp. 4.25 x 7.5 in. (Information not verified by physical copy.) Toole Stott no. 504. Beginner, Early magic.

Anonymous, *New Art of Hocus Pocus Revived.* (1808) T. and R. Hughes, London. 38 pp. 4.25 x 7.5 in. (Information not verified by physical copy.) Toole Stott no. 505. Beginner, Early magic.

Anonymous, *New Book of 150 Parlor Tricks and Games.* (1905) Wehman, New York. Perfect. Blue, red, black. 106 pp. 4.75 x 7 in. Magician with egg, hat, hank on cover. Green ad for books on back. Beginner. Pulp.

Anonymous, *New Book of 150 Parlor Tricks and Games.* (1905) Wehman, New York. Perfect. Green, red, black. 106 pp. 4.75 x 7.25 in. Magician with egg, hat, hank on cover. Green ad for books on back. Beginner. Pulp.

Anonymous, *New Book of 150 Parlor Tricks and Games.* (1905) Wehman, New York. Perfect. Green, red, black. 106 pp. 4.75 x 7.25 in. Magician with egg, hat, hank on cover. Red ad for books on back. Beginner. Pulp.

BIBLIOGRAPHY OF MAGIC

Anonymous, *New Book of 150 Parlor Tricks and Games.* (1939) Wehman, New York. Perfect. Yellow, green. 106 pp. 4.75 x 7.25 in. Magician with egg, hat, hank on cover. Beginner. Pulp.

Anonymous, *New Book of 150 Parlor Tricks and Games.* (1939) Wehman, New York. Perfect. Green, white. 106 pp. 4.75 x 7.25 in. Magician with egg, hat, hank on cover. Beginner. Pulp.

Anonymous, *New Book of 153 Tricks.* (1907) Wehman, New York. Perfect. White. 58 pp. 3.75 x 5 in. Magician with ribbons on cover. Red ads on back. Beginner. Pulp.

Anonymous, *New Book of 153 Tricks.* (1907) Wehman, New York. Perfect. White. 58 pp. 3.75 x 5 in. Magician with ribbons on cover. Blue ads on back. Beginner. Pulp.

Anonymous, *New Book of 153 Tricks.* (1907) Wehman, New York. Perfect. Yellow. 58 pp. 3.75 x 5 in. Magician with ribbons on cover. Beginner. Pulp.

Anonymous, *New Book of Card Tricks.* (n.d.) Ottenheimer, Baltimore, MD. Perfect. White, black, red. 58 pp. 4 x 5 in. Cover says "New Card Tricks" with Devil and rising cards, and "Printed in USA." Says Copyright 1913 Royal Pub. Spine upper and lower case. Cards. Pulp.

Anonymous, *New Book of Card Tricks.* (n.d.) Ottenheimer, Baltimore, MD. Perfect. White, black, red. 58 pp. 4 x 5 in. Cover says "New Card Tricks" with Devil and rising cards. Says Copyright 1913 Royal Pub. Spine all caps. Cards. Pulp.

Anonymous, *New Book of Card Tricks.* (n.d.) Ottenheimer, Baltimore, MD. Perfect. White, black, red. 58 pp. 4 x 5 in. Cover says "New Card Tricks" with Devil and rising cards. Says Copyright 1913 Royal Pub. Spine all caps. Different back cover. Cards. Pulp.

Anonymous, *New Book of Card Tricks: Tricks and Diversions with Cards.* (n.d.) Royal Publishing, Philadelphia. Perfect. White, green, red. 96 pp. 5 x 7 in. Headers say "Tricks with Cards" and "Hocus Pocus." Cards. Pulp.

Anonymous, *New Book of Coin Tricks.* Text of Downs' "Modern Coin Manipulation." (n.d.) Ottenheimer, Baltimore, MD. Perfect. Red, yellow. 64 pp. 4 x 5 in. Mustached magician rolling sleeve on yellow background with red around title. Coins.

Anonymous, *New Book of Fun, Magic, and Mystery.* (1905) Wehman Bros., Detroit. Saddle-stitch. Beige, orange, green. 16 pp. 8 x 10.75 in. In Copperfield collection. Beginner, Cards. Pulp.

Anonymous, *New Book of Fun, Magic, and Mystery.* (c. 1916) Johnson Smith and Co., Detroit. Saddle-stitch. Pink. 48 pp. 7.75 x 10.75 in. Beginner, Cards. Pulp.

Anonymous, *New Book of Fun, Magic, and Mystery.* (c. 1916) Johnson Smith and Co., Detroit. Saddle-stitch. Yellow. 48 pp. 7.75 x 10.75 in. Beginner, Cards. Pulp.

Anonymous, *New Book of Mysteries, A.* (c. 1910) Saddle-stitch. Gray. 14 pp. 8.5 x 11.5 in. Four vignettes on cover with rising smoke and large "Price 25 Cents." In Copperfield collection. Beginner. Pulp.

Anonymous, *New Book of Tricks.* (n.d.) Johnson Smith and Co., Detroit. Perfect. Red. 96 pp. 5.25 x 7.5 in. Cover says "Social-Entertainer Tricks." Spine says "Social Entertainer and Tricks." Beginner. Pulp.

Anonymous, *New Book of Tricks.* (n.d.) Johnson Smith and Co., Detroit. Perfect. Orange. 96 pp. 5.25 x 7.5 in. Cover says "Social-Entertainer Tricks." Spine says "Social Entertainer and Tricks." Beginner. Pulp.

Anonymous, *New Book of Tricks.* (n.d.) Perfect. Beige, blue. 94 pp. 4.75 x 7.25 in. No publisher noted. Cover says "Social-Entertainer Tricks." Title page says "Social Entertainer: Amusements and Tricks Simplified." Beginner. Pulp.

Anonymous, *New Complete and Extraordinary Method of Telling Fortunes by Cards – and Deceptions in Cards, A.* (1818) C. Sample, Madras, India. 115 pp. (Information not verified by physical copy.) Toole Stott no. 1385. Fortune-telling, Cards.

Anonymous, *New Conjuror's Museum and Magical Magazine.* (1803) Tegg and Castleman, London. Multiple sections. 4.25 x 7 in. (Information not verified by physical copy.) Toole Stott no. 506. Beginner, Magazine, Early magic.

Anonymous, *New Conjurors' Museum or Hocus Pocus in Perfection, The.* (c. 1805) M. C. Springsguth, London. 32 pp. 4.25 x 7 in. (Information not verified by physical copy.) Toole Stott no. 507. Beginner, Early magic.

Anonymous, *New Handbook of Magic, The.* (c. 1850) W. S. Fortey, London. 8 pp. 5 x 7.5 in. (Information not verified by physical copy.) Toole Stott no. 1134. Beginner, Early magic.

Anonymous, *New Hocus Pocus, The.* (c. 1850) Glasgow. 24 pp. 3.5 x 6.75 in. (Information not verified by physical copy.) Toole Stott no. 508. Beginner, Early magic.

Anonymous, *New Hocus Pocus, or the Art of Legerdemain Improved, The.* (1806) B. Mace, London. 40 pp. 4.25 x 6.75 in. (Information not verified by physical copy.) Toole Stott no. 509. Beginner, Early magic.

Anonymous, *New London Conjuror, or the Whole Art of Legerdemain Explained, The.* (c. 1855) T. Duggan, London. 64 pp. 4.75 x 7 in. (Information not verified by physical copy.) Toole Stott no. 510. Beginner, Early magic.

Anonymous, *New Universal Conjuror, The.* (c. 1850) C. Elliot, London. 16 pp. 5 x 7.5 in. (Information not verified by physical copy.) Toole Stott no. 513. Beginner, Early magic.

Anonymous, *New Universal Conjuror, The.* (c. 1864) T. Duggan, London. 32 pp. 4.25 x 6.75 in. (Information not verified by physical copy.) Toole Stott no. 514. Beginner, Early magic.

Anonymous, *NoneSuch Mindreader.* (1898) Merrell-Soule Co., Syracuse, NY. Saddle-stitch. Beige, red. 24 pp. 4 x 5 in. Promotion for food company. Pages with 10 to 15 images. Works by magic age cards principle. Mentalism, Premium.

Anonymous, *Nouveau Choix de Tours de Cartes.* (n.d.) Librairie de Théodore Lefèvre, Paris. Perfect. Beige. 104 pp. 3.75 x 6 in. Beginner, Cards. French.

Anonymous, *Nouveaux Tours de Cartes, Les.* (n.d.) Librairie du Mystère, Paris. Saddle-stitch. Beige. 16 pp. 4.5 x 5.5 in. Beginner, Cards. French.

Anonymous, *Oh!* (n.d.) Saddle-stitch. Purple. 20 pp. 7 x 5 in. Bound oblong. From cigarette cards by Austria Company. Beginner, Stunts, Trade cards.

Anonymous, *Old 3 Shell Game, The.* (c. 2004) School for Scoundrels, Los Angeles. Stapled. Yellow. 2 pp. 8.5 x 11 in. Cover and one page with reprint from 1952 "Racket Squad in Action" comic book. Three Shell Game.

Anonymous, *Old Army Game, The.* (2004) School for Scoundrels, Los Angeles. Stapled. Beige. 8 pp. 8.5 x 11 in. Reproduced in "The Old Maestro's Play Book," published by Whit Haydn, 2004. Three Shell Game.

Anonymous, *Old Hocus Pocus: Being the Anatomy of Legerdemain or The Whole Art of Jugling, The.* Fourteenth edition. (c. 1708) T. Norris, London. 144 pp. 3.25 x 5.5 in. (Information not verified by physical copy.) Toole Stott no. 371. Fourteenth edition of "Hocus Pocus Junior." Beginner, Early magic.

Anonymous, *Old Hocus Pocus: Being the Anatomy of Legerdemain or The Whole Art of Jugling, The.* Fifteenth edition. (c. 1740) R. Ware, C. Hitch, and J. Hodges, London. 135 pp. 3.25 x 5.75 in. (Information not verified by physical copy.) Toole Stott no. 373. Fifteenth edition of "Hocus Pocus Junior." Beginner, Early magic.

Anonymous, *Old Magician's Notebook.* (n.d.) Stapled. White. 12 pp. 8.75 x 13.75 in. (Measurements and other information have been recorded as accurately as possible.) Text in all caps. Illusions, Stage.

Anonymous, *Oriental Magic: Tricks You Can Do.* (1934) Jaffre Products, New York. Stapled with tape. Blue. Cover text: Pink; 48 pp. 5 x 7.25 in. John Northern Hilliard's personal copy with his bookplate. Signed by John Northern Hilliard. Beginner, Premium.

Anonymous, *Our Hand Has Never Lost Its Skill.* (c. 1947) Schaefer Brewing Co., Brooklyn, NY. Saddle-stitch. Red. 13 pp. 3.25 x 5 in. Beginner, Stunts, Premium.

Anonymous, *Out to Lunch.* (2022) Marchand de Trucs, Lorient, France. Perfect. Black. 124 pp. 4.75 x 7.5 in. Mentalism, Out to Lunch, Gimmicks. French.

Anonymous, *Over 50 Card Tricks.* (1906) Edward Smith and Co., London. Saddle-stitch. Green. 8 pp. 8.25 x 11 in. Cards, Beginner. Pulp.

Anonymous, *Over 50 Card Tricks.* (1927) March, Cady, and Co., London. Saddle-stitch. Beige, blue, red. 8 pp. 9 x 11.25 in. In Copperfield collection. Cards, Beginner. Pulp. French.

Anonymous, *Oxo Book of Magic, The.* (1934) Oxo Limited, London. Saddle-stitch. Black, red. 19 pp. (Information not verified by physical copy.) See Hagy, "Magic for Free." Beginner, Premium.

Anonymous, *Parfait Escamoteur, Le.* (1868) Le Bailly, Paris. Perfect. Salmon. 100 pp. 3.75 x 6 in. (Measurements and other information have been recorded as accurately as possible.) Beginner. French.

Anonymous, *Parlor Conjurer, or Magic Made Easy, The.* (c. 1930) Johnson Smith and Co., Detroit. Perfect. Olive. 32 pp. 5 x 7.5 in. Same as "Wehman's Parlor Conjurer." Beginner, Cards. Pulp.

Anonymous, *Parlor Conjurer, or Magic Made Easy, The.* (c. 1930) Johnson Smith and Co., Detroit. Saddle-stitch. Beige. Cover text: Blue; 32 pp. 4 x 6.25 in. Same as "Wehman's Parlor Conjurer." Beginner, Cards. Pulp.

Anonymous, *Parlor Conjurer, or Magic Made Easy, The.* (c. 1930) Johnson Smith and Co., Detroit. Saddle-stitch. Tan. Cover text: Blue; 32 pp. 4 x 6.25 in. Same as "Wehman's Parlor Conjurer." Beginner, Cards. Pulp.

Anonymous, *Parlor Conjurer, The.* (c. 1889) J. and R. Maxwell, London. Saddle-stitch. Red. 32 pp. 4.75 x 7.25 in. In Copperfield collection. Beginner.

Anonymous, *Parlor Magic.* (c. 1857) H. J. Wehman, New York. 31 pp. 4 x 6.75 in. (Information not verified by physical copy.) Toole Stott no. 683. Beginner.

Anonymous, *Parlor Magic.* (1889) Worthington Co., New York. Cloth. Red. 191 pp. 5.25 x 7.5 in. Franklin Edition. Beginner, Stunts, Science magic.

Anonymous, *Parlor Magic.* (1889) Worthington Co., New York. Cloth. Green. 191 pp. 5.25 x 7.5 in. Franklin Edition. Tissue over frontispiece of "Alice in Wonderland" with card fountain. Beginner, Stunts, Science magic.

Anonymous, *Parlor Magic.* (1889) John W. Lovell Co., New York. Cloth. Gray. 191 pp. 5.25 x 7.5 in. Beginner, Stunts, Science magic.

Anonymous, *Parlor Magic.* (1894) F. W. Lupton, New York. Saddle-stitch. Beige. 64 pp. 5.75 x 8.25 in. No. 36 in "People's Hand Book Series." Beginner.

Anonymous, *Parlor Magic.* (1894) Butler Brothers, New York and Chicago. Cloth. Brown. 191 pp. 5.25 x 7.5 in. Tissue over frontispiece of "Alice in Wonderland" image with card fountain. Beginner, Stunts, Science magic.

Anonymous, *Parlor Tricks with Cards.* (1907) Wehman, New York. Saddle-stitch. Beige. 58 pp. 3.75 x 5 in. Same as "84 New Card Tricks" as noted on cover. Cards. Pulp.

Anonymous, *Parlour Magic.* (1838) Whitehead and Co., London. Cloth. Brown. 183 pp. 4.75 x 6 in. Red frontispiece emblem. Toole Stott no. 532. Beginner.

Anonymous, *Parlour Magic.* Revised edition. (1838) H. Perkins, Philadelphia. Cloth. Brown. 175 pp. 5 x 6.25 in. Toole Stott no. 535. Beginner.

Anonymous, *Parlour Magic.* (c. 1838) Munroe and Francis, Boston. Boards. Beige. 191 pp. 4.75 x 5.75 in. Toole Stott no. 533. Beginner.

Anonymous, *Parlour Magic.* (c. 1840) Tilt and Bogue, London. Cloth. Brown. 183 pp. 4.75 x 6 in. Toole Stott no. 536. Blind-stamped front and back covers. Beginner.

Anonymous, *Parlour Magic.* (c. 1844) Munroe and Francis, Boston. 191 pp. 4.5 x 5.25 in. (Information not verified by physical copy.) Toole Stott no. 534. Beginner.

Anonymous, *Parlour Magic.* Third edition. (1853) David Bogue, London. Cloth. Red. 259 pp. 5 x 6.25 in. Toole Stott no. 537. Beginner.

Anonymous, *Parlour Magic.* Third edition. (1853) David Bogue, London. Cloth. Green. 259 pp. 5 x 6.25 in. Toole Stott no. 537. Beginner.

Anonymous, *Parlour Magic.* Fourth edition. (1858) W. Kent and Co., London. 259 pp. 4.75 x 5.75 in. (Information not verified by physical copy.) Toole Stott no. 538. Beginner.

Anonymous, *Parlour Magic.* Fifth edition. (1861) W. Kent and Co., London. Cloth. Blue. Cover text: Gold; 259 pp. 5.25 x 6.25 in. Toole Stott no. 539. Blind-stamped front and back covers. Beginner.

Anonymous, *Parlour Magic.* Fifth edition. (1861) Samuel French, London. 259 pp. 4.75 x 5.5 in. (Information not verified by physical copy.) Toole Stott no. 540. Beginner.

Anonymous, *Parlour Magic.* Fifth edition. (1861) Thomas Hailes Lacy, London. 259 pp. 4.25 x 6 in. (Information not verified by physical copy.) Toole Stott no. 541. Beginner.

Anonymous, *Parlour Magic.* Fifth edition. (1863) Bickers, London. 259 pp. 4.75 x 5.5 in. (Information not verified by physical copy.) Toole Stott no. 541. Beginner.

Anonymous, *Parlour Magic.* (n.d.) Philadelphia. Boards. Beige. 191 pp. 4.75 x 5.75 in. (Measurements and other information have been recorded as accurately as possible.) Beginner.

Anonymous, *Parlour Magic: A Handbook of Conjuring, Legerdemain, and Mystery.* (c. 1865) Cameron and Ferguson, Glasgow. 64 pp. 3.5 x 5.75 in. (Information not verified by physical copy.) Toole Stott no. 542. Beginner.

Anonymous, *Parlour Magic: Simple Tricks and Puzzles for Little Folks.* (c. 1906) Colman's Mustard, Norwich, UK. Saddle-stitch. 20 pp. (Information not verified by physical copy.) See Hagy, "Magic for Free." Beginner, Premium.

Anonymous, *Parlour Magician, The.* (1863) London. 55 pp. (Information not verified by physical copy.) Toole Stott no. 1144. Beginner.

Anonymous, *Parlour Magician, The.* (c. 1873) London. 52 pp. (Information not verified by physical copy.) Toole Stott no. 1145. Beginner.

Anonymous, *Parlour Magician, The.* (1876) Hamley's, London. 46 pp. (Information not verified by physical copy.) Toole Stott no. 1388. Beginner.

Anonymous, *Parlour Tricks.* (c. 1925) Felix McGlennon Ltd., London. Saddle-stitch. Orange. 16 pp. 3.5 x 4.75 in. Stanley Collins bookplate. Beginner.

Anonymous, *Parlour Tricks.* (c. 1925) Felix McGlennon Ltd., London. Saddle-stitch. Beige. 16 pp. 3.5 x 4.75 in. In Copperfield collection. Beginner.

Anonymous, *Peter Pan: no. 2 Magic Box instructions.* (c. 1966) Peter Pan Playthings, UK. Saddle-stitch. Yellow. 12 pp. 3.5 x 4.75 in. In "My Magic Box" set. Magic set manual.

Anonymous, *Peter Pan Peanut Butter Magic Kit instructions.* (n.d.) Fun Inc., Chicago. Folded. Beige. Cover text: Green; 8 pp. 2.75 x 4.25 in. From Peter Pan Peanut Butter magic kit by Derby Foods. Magic set manual.

Anonymous, *Peter Pan: The DeLuxe Magic Set Instructions.* (1968) Peter Pan Playthings, UK. Saddle-stitch. Yellow. 20 pp. 3.5 x 4.75 in. In "DeLuxe Magic" set. Magic set manual.

Anonymous, *Peter Pan: The Five Star Magic Box Instructions.* (1967) Peter Pan Playthings, UK. Saddle-stitch. Pink. 23 pp. 3.5 x 4.75 in. In "Five Star Magic" set. Magic set manual.

Anonymous, *Peter Pan: The Super Magic Set Instructions.* (c. 1967) Peter Pan Playthings, UK. Saddle-stitch. Olive. 12 pp. 3.75 x 5 in. In "Super Magic" set. Magic set manual.

Anonymous, *Petit Manuel de l'Escamoteur.* (n.d.) Delarue, Paris. Perfect. Green. 106 pp. 3.75 x 6 in. Beginner, Cards. French.

Anonymous, *Petit Sorcerer, or The Conjuror Unmasked, The.* (1808) T. and R. Hughes, London. 38 pp. 4 x 7 in. (Information not verified by physical copy.) Toole Stott no. 558. Beginner. French.

Anonymous, *Philosophical Recreations.* (1820) Thomas Hughes, London. Cloth. Blue. 200 pp. 3.75 x 6 in. Beginner, Early magic, Cards.

Anonymous, *Physique Amusante, La.* (1913) Éditions Foster, Paris. Saddle-stitch. Blue. 16 pp. 6.25 x 8.5 in. Cover illustration later used for back cover of Martin Gardner's 2015 "Impromptu." Beginner, Premium. French.

Anonymous, *Physique Amusante: Les Secrets de Quelques Tours Faciles et Impressionants.* (c. 1910) France. Folded. Beige. 7 pp. 4.5.x 5.5 in. Same format as "Tours de Cartes Inédits." Beginner. French.

Anonymous, *Play with Tricks.* (1955) Edwin A. Sirks Ltd., Heaton, UK. Saddle-stitch. Green. 12 pp. 9.5 x 9.5 in. Beginner, Children's book.

Anonymous, *Porky Pig and Bugs Bunny: Just Like Magic!* Fourth printing. (1978) Western Publishing Co., Racine, WI. Boards. Green. 22 pp. 6.5 x 8 in. Muppets character book. Fiction, Children's book.

Anonymous, *Practical Magician and Ventriloquist's Guide, The.* (1876) Hurst and Co., New York. 92 pp. 4.75 x 7.25 in. (Information not verified by physical copy.) Toole Stott no. 578. Beginner, Ventriloquism.

Anonymous, *Practical Magician and Ventriloquist's Guide, The.* (n.d.) Lipkind, New York. Perfect. White. Cover text: Blue; 92 pp. 5 x 7.25 in. Beginner, Ventriloquism. Pulp.

Anonymous, *Practical Magician and Ventriloquist's Guide, The.* (2018) Dover, New York. Perfect. Brown. 106 pp. 5.5 x 8.5 in. Beginner, Ventriloquism.

Anonymous, *Preciosa, or The Little Gypsy's Present.* (1799) W. Kemmish, London. 84 pp. 4 x 6.75 in. (Information not verified by physical copy.) Toole Stott no. 579. Fortune-telling, Beginner, Cards.

Anonymous, *Premier Amateur Conjuring Book.* (1926) CBP, Bristol, UK. Folded. Beige. Cover text: Red; 8 pp. 4.75 x 7.25 in. Beginner.

Anonymous, *Prestidigitateur? Mais Pourquoi Pas!* (n.d.) Montaubon, France. Accordion fold. Beige. 8 pp. 4.5 x 5.5 in. Beginner.

Anonymous, *Prestidigitation, or Magic Made Easy.* (1865) Hunter and Co., Hinsdale, NH. 64 pp. 4 x 5.75 in. (Information not verified by physical copy.) Toole Stott no. 580. Beginner.

Anonymous, *Prestidigitation, or Magic Made Easy.* Sixteenth edition. (c. 1870) Hunter and Co., Hinsdale, NH. Tan. 64 pp. (Information not verified by physical copy.) Toole Stott no. 1158. Beginner.

Anonymous, *Presto Change, or Magic Made Easy.* (1869) Fisher and Denison, New York. 134 pp. 3.25 x 5 in. (Information not verified by physical copy.) Toole Stott no. 581. Beginner.

Anonymous, *Presto Magic for Boys and Girls.* (1945) John Martin's House Inc., Racine, WI. Comb. Red, black. Unpaginated. 8.25 x 7.25 in. Bound oblong. Six metal bands as comb binding. Beginner, Children's book.

Anonymous, *Presto Magic Show 1 Instruction Manual.* (1975) Pressman Corp., New York. Saddle-stitch. Black. 29 pp. 5.25 x 8.25 in. In "Presto Magic Show 1" magic set. Magic set manual, Beginner.

Anonymous, *Presto Magic Show 2 Instruction Manual.* (1975) Pressman Corp., New York. Saddle-stitch. Black. 31 pp. 5.25 x 8.25 in. In "Presto Magic Show 2" magic set. Magic set manual, Beginner.

Anonymous, *Psychic Fakery.* (n.d.) Author. Stapled. Pink. 8 pp. 8.5 x 11 in. Mimeographed. (Measurements and other information have been recorded as accurately as possible.) Mentalism, Spirit effects.

Anonymous, *Quick Tricks Magic Book, The.* (1977) Hallmark Cards, Inc. Saddle-stitch. Orange. 24 pp. 5.75 x 8.25 in. Beginner, Children's book.

Anonymous, *Real Conjuror, The.* (1822) J. Smith, London. 36 pp. 4.25 x 7.25 in. (Information not verified by physical copy.) Toole Stott no. 594. Beginner, Early magic.

Anonymous, *Real New London Conjuror, The.* (c. 1816) J. Fairburn, London. 13 pp. 4.25 x 7 in. (Information not verified by physical copy.) Toole Stott no. 595. Beginner, Early magic.

Anonymous, *Real New London Conjuror, The.* (c. 1818) J. Fairburn, London. 36 pp. 4.5 x 7.5 in. (Information not verified by physical copy.) Toole Stott no. 596. Beginner, Early magic.

Anonymous, *Recueil de Tours de Physiques Amusantes.* (1877) Delarue, Paris. Perfect. Beige. 192 pp. 4.75 x 7.5 in. Bearded performer on cover. Beginner, Cards. French.

Anonymous, *Recueil de Tours de Physiques Amusantes.* (1877) Delarue, Paris. Perfect. Yellow. 192 pp. 4.75 x 7.25 in. Beginner, Cards. French.

BIBLIOGRAPHY OF MAGIC

Anonymous, *Recueil des Plus Jolis Tours de Cartes Contenant Tous les Tours Anciens et Modernes.* (c. 1870) Delarue, Paris. Boards. Blue, black. 106 pp. 3.75 x 5.5 in. Beginner, Cards. French.

Anonymous, *Ripley's Believe It or Not! Magic and Magicians.* (1982) Ripley Books, Toronto. Casebound. Green. 61 pp. 8 x 10.25 in. History, Children's book.

Anonymous, *Robert Heller's System of Second Sight Explained.* (1885) Eureka Trick and Novelty, New York. Saddle-stitch. Beige. 24 pp. 4 x 6.5 in. In Copperfield collection. Mentalism, Second Sight.

Anonymous, *Routledge's Handbook of Conjuring.* (1868) George Routledge and Sons, London. Boards. Green, red, black. 64 pp. 4.25 x 6.5 in. Toole Stott nos. 615, 1070. Beginner, Cards.

Anonymous, *Royal Balmoral Hand-Book of Magic.* (1850) Robert Inglis, Glasgow. 24 pp. 3 x 4.5 in. (Information not verified by physical copy.) Toole Stott no. 616. Beginner.

Anonymous, *Rules and Instructions for 25 Party Games for You to Play.* (1952) Whitman Publishing, Racine, WI. Saddle-stitch. Green. 12 pp. 6 x 8 in. Beginner, Stunts, Games, Party games.

Anonymous, *Saputello in Conversazione, Il.* (1859) Livorno, Italy. Perfect. Beige. 411 pp. 4 x 5.5 in. Beginner, Early magic. Italian.

Anonymous, *Scientific Mysteries.* (1891) Office of the Chemist and Druggist, London. Cloth. Brown. 100 pp. 5 x 7.25 in. Science magic, Chemical magic.

Anonymous, *Scooby-Doo's Box of Magic Tricks Instruction Book.* (1977) Rand McNally, New York. Saddle-stitch. Black. 8 pp. 6 x 8 in. From "Scooby Doo's Box of Magic Tricks" set. Magic set manual.

Anonymous, *Sealpackerchief Magic.* (1938) International Handkerchief. Accordion fold. White, blue, red. 8 pp. 2.75 x 5 in. Beginner, Stunts, Handkerchiefs, Premium.

Anonymous, *Second Sight.* (c. 1976) Ghastly Gallimaufry, Campbell, CA. (Information not verified by physical copy. Bibliographical details are as accurate as possible.) Mentalism.

Anonymous, *Second Sight Mystery Exposed, The.* (1867) Joseph Winterburn and Co., San Francisco. 16 pp. (Information not verified by physical copy.) Toole Stott no. 1179. Mentalism, Second Sight.

Anonymous, *Secret of an Eastern Professor in Magic and Conjuring Out Called the Wizard's Manual.* (1901) Y. Paul and Co., Calcutta. Perfect. Tan. 118 pp. 4.25 x 7 in. Beginner.

Anonymous, *Secret of the Great Handcuff Trick.* (1907) Mutual Book Co., Boston. Saddle-stitch. White. 31 pp. 3.75 x 6 in. Escapes, Handcuffs.

Anonymous, *Secrets du Maître Sorcier, Les.* (1968) Capiepa, Paris. Saddle-stitch. Black, red, white. 72 pp. 5 x 7 in. Magic set manual. French.

Anonymous, *Secrets of Ancient and Modern Magic, The.* (1875) Ideal Novelty Co., Palmyra, PA. Saddle-stitch. Tan. 12 pp. 5.25 x 7.5 in. Toole Stott no. 621. Full-cover Broom Suspension illustration. Large ad section. Beginner, Cards. Pulp.

Anonymous, *Secrets of Ancient and Modern Magic.* (1880) Gem Novelty Co., Palmyra, PA. Cloth. Orange. 64 pp. 4.75 x 7.25 in. Earliest version. Rebound in orange cloth. Beginner, Stunts.

Anonymous, *Secrets of Ancient and Modern Magic, The.* (n.d.) Johnson Smith and Co., Detroit. Perfect. Beige. 64 pp. 5 x 7.5 in. Broom Suspension vignette. New contents. Beginner, Stunts. Pulp.

Anonymous, *Secrets of Ancient and Modern Magic, The.* (n.d.) Johnson Smith and Co., Detroit. Perfect. Olive. 64 pp. 5.25 x 7.75 in. Broom Suspension vignette. New contents. Beginner, Stunts. Pulp.

Anonymous, *Secrets of Ancient and Modern Magic, The.* (n.d.) Johnson Smith and Co., Detroit. Perfect. Tan. 64 pp. 5 x 7.5 in. Broom Suspension vignette. New contents. Beginner, Stunts. Pulp.

Anonymous, *Secrets of Ancient and Modern Magic, The.* (n.d.) Johnson Smith and Co., Detroit. Perfect. Red. 64 pp. 5.25 x 7.75 in. Broom Suspension vignette. New contents. Cover has stock number. Small ad section. Beginner, Stunts. Pulp.

Anonymous, *Secrets of Ancient and Modern Magic, The.* (n.d.) Johnson Smith and Co., Detroit. Perfect and staples. Gray. 64 pp. 5.25 x 7.75 in. Broom Suspension vignette. New contents. Cover has stock number. Small ad section. Beginner, Stunts. Pulp.

Anonymous, *Secrets of Ancient and Modern Magic, The.* (n.d.) Johnson Smith and Co., Detroit. Perfect and staples. Brown. 64 pp. 5.25 x 7.75 in. Broom Suspension vignette. New contents. Cover has stock number. Small ad section. Beginner, Stunts. Pulp.

Anonymous, *Secrets of Ancient and Modern Magic.* (n.d.) Wehman Bros., New York. Saddle-stitch. Yellow. Cover text: Maroon; 94 pp. 4.75 x 7.25 in. Stage, Illusions. Pulp.

Anonymous, *Secrets of Ancient and Modern Magic, The.* (n.d.) Wehman Bros., New York. Perfect. Light green, brown. 94 pp. 4.75 x 7.25 in. Full-cover Broom Suspension illustration. Beginner, Stunts. Pulp.

Anonymous, *Secrets of Ancient and Modern Magic, The.* (n.d.) Wehman Bros., New York. Saddle-stitch. Light green, brown. 94 pp. 4.75 x 7.25 in. Full-cover Broom Suspension illustration. Beginner, Stunts. Pulp.

Anonymous, *Secrets of Ancient and Modern Magic, The.* (n.d.) Wehman Bros., New York. Perfect. White, brown. 94 pp. 4.75 x 7.25 in. Full-cover Broom Suspension illustration. Holden ad on back cover. Beginner, Stunts. Pulp.

Anonymous, *Secrets of Ancient and Modern Magic, The.* (n.d.) Wehman Bros., New York. Perfect. White, brown. 94 pp. 4.75 x 7 in. Full-cover Broom Suspension illustration. 10-cent books ad on back cover. Beginner, Stunts. Pulp.

Anonymous, *Secrets of Ancient and Modern Magic, The.* (n.d.) Wehman Bros., New York. Saddle-stitch. White, red. 94 pp. 4.75 x 7.25 in. Full-cover Broom Suspension illustration. Beginner, Stunts. Pulp.

Anonymous, *Secrets of Famous Magicians.* (c. 1930) Allied Newspapers, Manchester. Saddle-stitch. Red, blue, white. 27 pp. 4 x 5.75 in. Supplement to "Boys' Magazine." Beginner, History, Houdini.

Anonymous, *Secrets of the Great Magicians.* (n.d.) Saddle-stitch. Color. 14 pp. 4 x 3.5 in. Bound oblong. Promotion for Vick's. Beginner, History, Premium.

Anonymous, *Secrets of Ventriloquism.* Miniature book. (n.d.) Johnson Smith and Co., Racine, WI. Saddle-stitch. Beige. 12 pp. 3 x 4.25 in. Ventriloquism.

Anonymous, *Secrets of Ventriloquism and Vocal Illusions.* (n.d.) Johnson Smith and Co., Detroit. Perfect. Blue, white. 70 pp. 5.25 x 7.75 in. Ventriloquism.

Anonymous, *See?* (n.d.) Bausch and Lomb Optical Co., Rochester, NY. Saddle-stitch. Green. 16 pp. 3.5 x 6.25 in. Beginner, Stunts, Premium.

Anonymous, *Selection of Fifty Games, from Those Played by the Automaton Chess Player.* (1820) London. 76 pp. 4.25 x 6.75 in. (Information not verified by physical copy.) Toole Stott no. 419. History, Automata, Automaton chess player.

Anonymous, *Selection of the Most Entertaining and Surprising Recreations and Deceptions on Cards.* (n.d.) India. 113 pp. 3.75 x 6 in. (Information not verified by physical copy.) Toole Stott no. 622. Beginner.

Anonymous, *Senior Magic Set.* (1967) Creative Playthings, Princeton, NJ. Saddle-stitch. White. 28 pp. 6 x 5.5 in. Bound oblong. In Creative Playthings "Senior Magic Set." Magic set manual. Dutch.

Anonymous, *Sequel to the Endless Amusement.* (1825) Thomas Boys, London. 215 pp. 3.5 x 5.75 in. (Information not verified by physical copy.) Toole Stott no. 623. Beginner.

Anonymous, *Sesame Street Put and Play Magic Show.* (1981) Western Publishing Co., Racine, WI. Saddle-stitch. Green. 12 pp. 8.25 x 11 in. Colorforms-type book with pieces. Children's book.

Anonymous, *Shadowgraph.* (c. 1900) Richmond Range Co., Norwich, CT. Saddle-stitch. Color. 8 pp. 3.5 x 4.75 in. Another: Royal Tailor, Chicago and New York. Shadowgraphy, Premium.

Anonymous, *Shadowgraph.* (c. 1900) Royal Tailors, Chicago and New York. Saddle-stitch. Color. 8 pp. 3.5 x 4.75 in. Shadowgraphy, Premium.

Anonymous, *Simple and Clever Tricks by Cards.* (c. 1881) R. March and Co., London. Saddle-stitch. Green. 29 pp. 5 x 7 in. Title page says "Tricks with Playing Cards." Right header says "March's Book on Conjuring." Cards.

Anonymous, *Simple Magic Tricks.* (n.d.) S. S. Adams, Asbury Park, NJ. Saddle-stitch. Black, purple, yellow. 32 pp. 5 x 7 in. In Adams' "Hocus-Pocus Magic Set." Beginner.

Anonymous, *Simple Magic Tricks.* (n.d.) Benson Trading Co., Melbourne. Saddle-stitch. 28 pp. 5 x 7.25 in. (Information not verified by physical copy.) Licensed from D. Robbins. See McCullagh, "Under the Southern Cross." Beginner.

Anonymous, *Simple Tricks with Coins and Bills.* (n.d.) Stapled. Yellow, red. 8 pp. 8.5 x 11 in. Mimeographed. Coins, Bills, Stunts, Close-Up.

Anonymous, *Sleight of Hand: The Amusing Conjurer.* (c. 1845) Imprimerie de Wittersheim, Paris. Sewn covers. Green. 11 pp. 5 x 7 in. Explains apparatus effects. In Smith collection at Brown University. Single-sided pages. Beginner, Apparatus, Cups and Balls.

Anonymous, *Smith's Weekly Christmas Conjurer.* (1904) Smith's Weekly, UK. Saddle-stitch. Beige. 16 pp. 5.75 x 8.5 in. In Copperfield collection. Beginner.

Anonymous, *Smut Magic.* (1978) Busby-Corin, Oakland, CA. Comb. Blue. 14 pp. 8.5 x 11 in. (Measurements and other information have been recorded as accurately as possible.) Comedy, Risqué.

Anonymous, *Sneaky Pete's Magic Show.* (n.d.) Remco, Newark, NJ. Saddle-stitch. Blue. 10 pp. 5.25 x 8.25 in. Magic set manual.

Anonymous, *Sneaky Pete's Magic Show: How to Be a Magician.* (n.d.) Remco, Newark, NJ. Saddle-stitch. Red. 15 pp. 5.25 x 8.25 in. In set no. 701. Magic set manual.

Anonymous, *Snoopy the Great and His Amazing Magic Colorforms.* (1974) Colorforms Inc., Norwood, NJ. Folded. Color. 4 pp. 4.25 x 5 in. In "Snoopy the Great" Colorforms set. Magic set manual.

Anonymous, *Somnolency.* (1913) Chicago Magic Co., Chicago, IL. Stapled. White. 4 pp. 8.5 x 11 in. Carbon copy. (Information not verified by physical copy.) Mentalism.

BIBLIOGRAPHY OF MAGIC

Anonymous, *Soyer Prestidigitateur! 2ème Album.* (n.d.) France. Saddle-stitch. Pink. 16 pp. 7.5 x 5.75 in. Beginner. French.

Anonymous, *Speaking Figure and the Automaton Chess-Player Exposed and Detected, The.* (1784) J. Stockdale, London. 20 pp. 4.25 x 7 in. (Information not verified by physical copy.) Toole Stott no. 417. History, Automata, Automaton chess player.

Anonymous, *Spear's Conjuring Tricks.* (n.d.) Spear's Games, UK. Folded. Green. 6 pp. 6 x 8.5 in. (Measurements and other information have been recorded as accurately as possible.) Magic set manual.

Anonymous, *Special Effects with Fire and Smoke.* (1985) Theatre Effects Inc. Comb. Red. 124 pp. 5.5 x 8.5 in. Special effects, Fire, Smoke.

Anonymous, *Spiritualism Exposed.* Miniature book. (1896) Multum in Parvo Library, Boston. Saddle-stitch. Tan. 16 pp. 2.75 x 4.25 in. Spiritualism.

Anonymous, *Star-Magic.* (n.d.) Magic Star Conjuring Sets, UK. Saddle-stitch. Green. 17 pp. 4.75 x 7.25 in. In Magic Star "Conjuring Set." Magic set manual.

Anonymous, *Strathmore Magic Table Set: Instructions for Complete Magic Show.* (1947) Strathmore Company, Aurora, IL. Saddle-stitch. Red, blue, black. 12 pp. 7 x 4 in. In Strathmore "Magic Table Set." Magic set manual.

Anonymous, *System for Card Signals.* (n.d.) Stapled with paper cover. Orange. 6 pp. 5.5 x 9 in. Mimeographed. Cards, Cheating, Gambling.

Anonymous, *That Old Crow Magic: Magic Tricks and Mixing Tips.* (c. 1975) Old Crow Distillery, Frankfort, KY. Folded. Black. 10 pp. 3.5 x 7.5 in. Brochure with bar magic and recipes. Beginner, Premium, Bar magic, Recipes.

Anonymous, *Thought Reader, The.* (c. 1890) J. and R. Maxwell, London. Saddle-stitch. Red. 32 pp. 4.75 x 7.25 in. In Copperfield collection. Beginner, Mentalism, Stage.

Anonymous, *Three Crow Book of Games, Tricks, and Puzzles.* (n.d.) John Bird Co., Rockland, ME. Saddle-stitch. Yellow. 32 pp. 6 x 9.25 in. Beginner, Stunts.

Anonymous, *Tours d'Escamotage Faciles et Captivants.* (1932) Bernardin-Bechet, Paris. Perfect. Red. 61 pp. 5.75 x 7.5 in. Beginner. French.

Anonymous, *Tours de Cartes.* (n.d.) Bernardin-Bechet, Paris. Saddle-stitch. Beige. 23 pp. 3.75 x 5.75 in. Cards. French.

Anonymous, *Tours de Cartes: Incroyable Mais Vrai!* (n.d.) Saddle-stitch. Beige. 12 pp. 4 x 5.25 in. Ending has initials "H.R." Cards. French.

Anonymous, *Tours de Cartes Inédits.* (c. 1910) Folded. Beige. 7 pp. 4.5.x 5.5 in. Same format as "Physique Amusante: Les Secrets de Quelques Tours Faciles et Impressionants." Cards. French.

Anonymous, *Tricks and Delusions.* (c. 1855) Edward Duncombe, London. 20 pp. 4.25 x 7 in. (Information not verified by physical copy.) Toole Stott no. 669. Beginner.

Anonymous, *Tricks and Diversions with Cards.* (n.d.) Hurst and Co., New York. Perfect. Green. Cover text: Gold; 90 pp. 4.75 x 6.75 in. Blind-embossed cover. Cards.

Anonymous, *Tricks and Teasers.* (1965) Highlights for Children Inc., Columbus, OH. Saddle-stitch. Orange, blue, white. 32 pp. 8.5 x 11 in. Beginner, Stunts.

Anonymous, *Tricks and Traps of America.* (n.d.) Saddle-stitch. Beige. 16 pp. 6 x 9 in. (Measurements and other information have been recorded as accurately as possible.) Con games.

Anonymous, *Tricks Every Boy and Girl Can Do.* (1953) Hart Toy Corp., New York. Perfect. Red. 64 pp. 5.5 x 8.25 in. Beginner, Children's book.

Anonymous, *Tricks for Amateurs of Both Sexes.* (1904) Marshall, Brookes, and Chalkley, London. Perfect. White, blue. 126 pp. 5.75 x 8.5 in. In Copperfield collection. Beginner. Pulp.

Anonymous, *Tricks in Legerdemain.* (c. 1905) Eichler Publishing Co., New York. Perfect. White, red, black. 123 pp. 4.5 x 5.75 in. Scarce. Beginner.

Anonymous, *Tricks of Magic.* Miniature book. (1923) Western Printing Co., Racine, WI. Stapled with tape. Blue. 48 pp. 3 x 3.75 in. Beige back cover, black tape. Beginner.

Anonymous, *Tricks of Mystery.* (c. 1930) Single page. Yellow. 1 pp. 12 x 19 in. Uncredited excerpts from Johnson Smith's "Learn How to Be a Handcuff King and Mystery Man." Beginner, Illusions, Escapes.

Anonymous, *Tricks That Boys Can Do.* (1920) Cortley Junior Clothes, New York. Saddle-stitch. Beige. 32 pp. 3 x 3.5 in. Miniature book for shoe promotion. Beginner, Stunts, Premium.

Anonymous, *Tricks with Cards.* (n.d.) Arthur Westbrook Co., Cleveland, OH. Perfect. Red, green, black. 24 pp. 6 x 9.25 in. Cards, Beginner.

Anonymous, *True and Easy Guide to Conjuring, The.* (c. 1815) G. Stevens, London. 28 pp. 4.5 x 7 in. (Information not verified by physical copy.) Toole Stott no. 670. Beginner, Early magic.

Anonymous, *True and Easy Guide to Conjuring, The.* (c. 1816) G. Stevens, London. 32 pp. 4.5 x 7.25 in. (Information not verified by physical copy.) Toole Stott no. 671. Beginner, Early magic.

Anonymous, *Universal Conjuror, or The Whole Art of Legerdemain, The.* (1829) T. and J. Allman, London. 28 pp. 4.75 x 7 in. (Information not verified by physical copy.) Toole Stott no. 672. Beginner, Early magic.

Anonymous, *Universal Conjuror, or The Whole Art of Legerdemain, The.* (1830) Orlando Hodgson, London. 27 pp. 4.5 x 7.75 in. (Information not verified by physical copy.) Toole Stott no. 673. Toole Stott mentions a number of variants. Beginner, Early magic.

Anonymous, *Universal Conjuror, or The Whole Art of Legerdemain, The.* (1832) T. Allman, London. 20 pp. 4.25 x 7.5 in. (Information not verified by physical copy.) Toole Stott no. 674. Beginner, Early magic.

Anonymous, *Universal Conjuror, or The Whole Art of Legerdemain, The.* (c. 1832) M. Bassan, London. 36 pp. 4.25 x 6.5 in. (Information not verified by physical copy.) Toole Stott no. 675. Beginner, Early magic.

Anonymous, *Ventriloquism Explained and Jugglers' Tricks, or Legerdemain Exposed.* (1834) J. S. and C. Adams, Amherst, MA. Cloth. Beige. 156 pp. 4 x 6.25 in. Toole Stott no. 678. Ventriloquism, Beginner, Early magic.

Anonymous, *Verbeck's Trance Vision, or Silent Thought.* (n.d.) Chicago Magic Co., Chicago, IL. Stapled. White. 9 pp. 8.5 x 11 in. Mimeographed. Method of Yank Hoe and Omene. (Information not verified by physical copy.) Mentalism.

Anonymous, *Wehman's New Book of Parlor Games.* (1895) Henry J. Wehman, New York. Perfect. Tan, blue. 116 pp. 4.75 x 7 in. Ad on back for "New Book of Tricks." Games. Pulp.

Anonymous, *Wehman's New Book of Tricks and Ventriloquist's Guide.* (1889) Henry J. Wehman, Chicago. Perfect. White, black, red. 112 pp. 4.75 x 7 in. Goateed magician onstage with apparatus. Cover address is 125 W. Madison. Beginner. Pulp.

Anonymous, *Wehman's New Book of Tricks and Ventriloquist's Guide.* (1889) Henry J. Wehman, New York. Perfect. White, black, red. 112 pp. 4.75 x 7 in. Goateed magician onstage with apparatus. Cover address is 130 Park Row. Beginner. Pulp.

Anonymous, *Wehman's New Book of Tricks and Ventriloquist's Guide.* (1889) Henry J. Wehman, Chicago. Perfect. White, black, red. 112 pp. 4.75 x 7 in. Goateed magician onstage with apparatus. Cover address is 85 and 87 E. Madison. Beginner. Pulp.

Anonymous, *Wehman's New Book of Tricks and Ventriloquist's Guide.* (1889) Henry J. Wehman, New York. Perfect. Tan. 112 pp. 4.75 x 7 in. Goateed magician onstage with apparatus. Cover has no street address, just city. Beginner. Pulp.

Anonymous, *Wehman's New Book of Tricks and Ventriloquist's Guide.* (1889) Henry J. Wehman, New York. Perfect. White, green. 112 pp. 4.75 x 7 in. Goateed magician onstage with apparatus. Cover has no street address, just city. Beginner. Pulp.

Anonymous, *Wehman's New Book of Tricks and Ventriloquist's Guide.* (n.d.) Wehman Bros., New York. Perfect. Yellow. 89 pp. 5 x 7.5 in. New cover with magician in circle. Beginner. Pulp.

Anonymous, *Wehman's Parlor Conjurer.* (n.d.) Henry J. Wehman, New York. Perfect. Yellow. 32 pp. 4.75 x 7 in. Beginner, Cards. Pulp.

Anonymous, *Whole Art and Mystery of Modern Gaming Fully Expos'd and Detected.* (1726) J. Roberts and T. Cox, London. 111 pp. 7.75 x 10 in. (Information not verified by physical copy.) Toole Stott no. 703. Gambling, Cheating.

Anonymous, *Whole Art of Conjuring, or Hocus Pocus.* (1849) Fisher and Brother, Philadelphia, New York, Boston. 102 pp. 3.5 x 5.5 in. (Information not verified by physical copy.) Toole Stott no. 704. Beginner, Early magic.

Anonymous, *Whole Art of Conjuring, or Hocus Pocus.* (c. 1850) Fisher and Brother, Philadelphia, New York, Boston. Multiple sections. 3.5 x 6 in. (Information not verified by physical copy.) Toole Stott no. 705. Beginner, Early magic.

Anonymous, *Whole Art of Conjuring, or Hocus Pocus.* (c. 1850) Fisher and Brother, Philadelphia, New York, Boston. 72 pp. 3.75 x 6.25 in. (Information not verified by physical copy.) Toole Stott no. 706. Beginner, Early magic.

Anonymous, *Whole Art of Hocus Pocus, The.* (1812) Thomas Tegg, London. 22 pp. 4 x 6.75 in. (Information not verified by physical copy.) Toole Stott no. 707. Beginner, Early magic.

Anonymous, *Whole Art of Legerdemain in Perfection, The.* (1939) William Bradford Press, New York. Cloth. Green. 15 pp. 5 x 7.25 in. Limited to 400 copies. Beginner, Early magic.

Anonymous, *Whole Art of Legerdemain, or Hocus Pocus in Perfection, The.* (c. 1737) J. Smart, Wolverhampton, UK. 24 pp. 4 x 6.25 in. (Information not verified by physical copy.) Toole Stott no. 708. Beginner, Early magic.

Anonymous, *Whole Art of Legerdemain, or Hocus Pocus in Perfection, The.* (c. 1750) London. 24 pp. 3.5 x 6.25 in. (Information not verified by physical copy.) Toole Stott no. 709. Beginner, Early magic.

Anonymous, *Whole Art of Legerdemain, or Hocus Pocus in Perfection, The.* (c. 1755) London. 24 pp. 3.5 x 6.5 in. (Information not verified by physical copy.) Toole Stott no. 710. Beginner, Early magic.

Anonymous, *Whole Art of Legerdemain, or Hocus Pocus in Perfection, The.* (c. 1760) London. 24 pp. 3.5 x 6.25 in. (Information not verified by physical copy.) Toole Stott no. 711. Beginner, Early magic.

Anonymous, *Whole Art of Legerdemain, or Philosopher in Good Humor, The.* (1807) T. and R. Hughes, London. 38 pp. 4 x 6 in. (Information not verified by physical copy.) Toole Stott no. 712. Beginner, Early magic.

Anonymous, *Whole Art of Legerdemain, or Philosopher in Good Humor, The.* (c. 1810) J. Bailey, London. 28 pp. 4.5 x 7.75 in. (Information not verified by physical copy.) Toole Stott no. 714. Beginner, Early magic.

Anonymous, *Whole Art of Legerdemain, or Philosopher in Good Humor, The.* (1811) J. Kendrew, London. 38 pp. 4.5 x 7.5 in. (Information not verified by physical copy.) Toole Stott no. 715. Beginner, Early magic.

Anonymous, *Whole Art of Legerdemain, or Philosopher in Good Humor, The.* (c. 1812) J. D. Dewick, London. 38 pp. 4.25 x 7.5 in. (Information not verified by physical copy.) Toole Stott no. 713. Beginner, Early magic.

Anonymous, *Whole Art of Legerdemain, or Philosopher in Good Humor, The.* (1832) J. Kendrew, London. 36 pp. 4.5 x 7.5 in. (Information not verified by physical copy.) Toole Stott no. 716. Beginner, Early magic.

Anonymous, *Whole Art of Legerdemain, or The Black Art, The.* (c. 1820) T. Hughes, London. 38 pp. 4.25 x 7 in. (Information not verified by physical copy.) Toole Stott no. 717. Beginner, Early magic.

Anonymous, *Whole Art of Legerdemain, or The Conjurer Unmasked, The.* (c. 1830) Thomas Richardson, Derby, UK. 24 pp. 4.5 x 7.5 in. (Information not verified by physical copy.) Toole Stott no. 718. Beginner, Early magic.

Anonymous, *Whole Art of Legerdemain, or Hocus Pocus, The.* (1830) C. V. Nickerson, Baltimore. 72 pp. 3.75 x 6 in. (Information not verified by physical copy.) Toole Stott no. 719. Beginner, Early magic.

Anonymous, *Whole Art of Legerdemain, or Hocus Pocus, The.* (1830) C. V. Nickerson, Baltimore. 72 pp. 3.75 x 6 in. (Information not verified by physical copy.) Toole Stott no. 720. Different text and illustrations. Beginner, Early magic.

Anonymous, *Whole Art of Legerdemain, or Hocus Pocus, The.* (1831) C. V. Nickerson, Baltimore. 72 pp. 3.75 x 6 in. (Information not verified by physical copy.) Toole Stott no. 720. Beginner, Early magic.

Anonymous, *Whole Art of Legerdemain, or Hocus Pocus, The.* (1832) C. V. Nickerson, Baltimore. 72 pp. 3.75 x 6 in. (Information not verified by physical copy.) Toole Stott no. 721. Beginner, Early magic.

Anonymous, *Whole Art of Legerdemain, or Hocus Pocus, The.* (1833) C. V. Nickerson, Baltimore. 72 pp. 3.75 x 6 in. (Information not verified by physical copy.) Toole Stott no. 722. Beginner, Early magic.

Anonymous, *Whole Art of Legerdemain, or Hocus Pocus in Perfection, The.* (c. 1850) C. M. Warren, Dublin. 144 pp. 3.75 x 5.5 in. (Information not verified by physical copy.) Toole Stott no. 727. Beginner, Early magic.

Anonymous, *Whole Art of Legerdemain, or Hocus Pocus Laid Open and Explained, The.* (1831) R. Schoyer, New York. 71 pp. 3.5 x 5.5 in. (Information not verified by physical copy.) Toole Stott no. 723. Beginner, Early magic.

Anonymous, *Whole Art of Legerdemain, or Hocus Pocus Laid Open and Explained, The.* (1833) N. C. Nafis, Philadelphia. 71 pp. 3.5 x 5.75 in. (Information not verified by physical copy.) Toole Stott no. 724. Beginner, Early magic.

Anonymous, *Whole Art of Legerdemain, or Hocus Pocus Laid Open and Explained, The.* (c. 1840) Nafis and Cornish, New York. 71 pp. 3.5 x 5.75 in. (Information not verified by physical copy.) Toole Stott no. 725. Beginner, Early magic.

Anonymous, *Whole Art of Legerdemain, or Hocus Pocus Laid Open and Explained, The.* (1850) W. A. Leary and Co., Philadelphia. 71 pp. 4 x 5.75 in. (Information not verified by physical copy.) Toole Stott no. 726. Beginner, Early magic.

Anonymous, *Whole Art of Legerdemain, or Hocus Pocus Laid Open and Explained, The.* (c. 1852) J. and J. Gihon, Philadelphia. 71 pp. 3.5 x 5.75 in. (Information not verified by physical copy.) Toole Stott no. 728. Beginner, Early magic.

Anonymous, *Whole Art of Legerdemain, or Hocus Pocus Laid Open and Explained, The.* (1853) Leary and Getz, Philadelphia. 71 pp. 4 x 5.75 in. (Information not verified by physical copy.) Toole Stott no. 729. Beginner, Early magic.

Anonymous, *Whole Art of Legerdemain, or Hocus Pocus Laid Open and Explained, The.* (c. 1856) Fisher and Brother, Philadelphia. 72 pp. 4 x 7 in. (Information not verified by physical copy.) Toole Stott no. 730. See Heyl, "Cues for Collectors." Beginner, Early magic.

Anonymous, *Winnie-the-Pooh Magic Tricks.* Second printing. (1980) Golden Press, Racine, WI. Saddle-stitch. Color. 23 pp. 8 x 8 in. Book shaped like a pot of honey. Beginner, Fiction.

Anonymous, *Winter Evening's Amusement, A.* (1870) J. Harkness, Preston, UK. 8 pp. 3.25 x 4.75 in. (Information not verified by physical copy.) Toole Stott no. 735. Beginner.

Anonymous, *Wizard, The.* (1848) Ely and Allen, Chillcothe, OH. 96 pp. 4.25 x 6.5 in. (Information not verified by physical copy.) Toole Stott no. 738. Beginner.

Anonymous, *Wizard of the North: Life Story of John Henry Anderson.* (1984) Hocas Magazine, London. Clip. White. 65 pp. 6 x 8.25 in. Reprints from "People's Journal," Glasgow, June 1 to August 17, 1901. Biography, History.

Anonymous, *Wizard's Book of Magic, The.* (1865) J. and W. Robertson, Glasgow. 32 pp. 2.75 x 4.25 in. (Information not verified by physical copy.) Toole Stott no. 739. Beginner.

Anonymous, *Wizard's Fireside Book of Magic, The.* (1869) J. M. Miller, Edinburgh. Saddle-stitch. Beige. 32 pp. 3 x 4.75 in. Toole Stott no. 740. In Copperfield collection. Beginner.

Anonymous, *Wizard's Hand-Book of Magic, The.* (1839) George Love, Glasgow. 64 pp. 3 x 4.75 in. (Information not verified by physical copy.) Toole Stott no. 742. Beginner.

Anonymous, *Wizard's Mammoth Collection.* (c. 1910) London. Saddle-stitch. Orange. 16 pp. 8 x 10.25 in. Top of cover says "The 20th Century Wonder Book." In Copperfield collection. Beginner. Pulp.

Anonymous, *Wizard's Pocket Book, The.* (1863) Clarkson, Shallard, and Co., Melbourne and Sydney. 16 pp. (Information not verified by physical copy.) Toole Stott no. 1207. Beginner.

Anonymous, *Wonderful Book of Conjuring Tricks.* (c. 1915) Milner and Co., London. Saddle-stitch. Beige. 48 pp. 5.5 x 8.5 in. Cover says just "Conjuring Tricks." Magician producing fishbowl on cover. In Copperfield collection. Beginner. Pulp.

Anonymous, *Wonderful Book of Conjuring Tricks.* (c. 1915) Milner and Co., London. Saddle-stitch. Green. 48 pp. 5.5 x 8.5 in. Cover says just "Conjuring Tricks." Magician producing fishbowl on cover. In Copperfield collection. Beginner. Pulp.

Anonymous, *Wonderful Book of Conjuring Tricks.* (c. 1915) Milner and Co., London. Saddle-stitch. Pink. 48 pp. 5.5 x 8.5 in. Cover says just "Conjuring Tricks." Magician producing fishbowl on cover. In Copperfield collection. Beginner. Pulp.

Anonymous, *Wonderful Book of Conjuring Tricks.* (c. 1920) Daisy Bank Publishing, Manchester. Saddle-stitch. White, blue, red, black. 32 pp. 5.5 x 8.25 in. Cover says just "Conjuring Tricks." Hands cracking egg into top hat on cover. In Copperfield collection. Beginner. Pulp.

Anonymous, *Wonderful Conjuror, or Hocus Pocus in Perfection, The.* (c. 1800) T. Brandard, Birmingham, UK. 28 pp. 4.5 x 7.5 in. (Information not verified by physical copy.) Toole Stott no. 743. Beginner, Early magic.

Anonymous, *Wonderful Mysteries Fully Explained.* (1909) Leicester, UK. Saddle-stitch. Olive. 8 pp. 5.5 x 8.5 in. Beginner.

Anonymous, *Wray's Parlor Magic and Songs.* (1870) Times Steam Press, Cairo, Egypt. 16 pp. 4 x 5.75 in. (Information not verified by physical copy.) Toole Stott no. 745. Beginner.

Anonymous, *Young Man's Book of Amusement, The.* (1850) William Milner, Halifax. Cloth. Black. 384 pp. 3.25 x 5.25 in. Milton A. Bridges bookplate. Beginner, Cards.

Anonymous, *Zauber-Bilderbuch. Magic Picture Book.* (n.d.) Germany. Stapled with tape. Green, red. 15 pp. 3.75 x 5.5 in. Blow-book. Blow book. German.

Aalto, Simo, *Arctic Bells.* (1992) Author, Kempele, Finland. 15 pp. (Information not verified by physical copy.) Lecture notes. Close-Up, Bells.

Aalto, Simo, *Hot Arctic Magic.* (1999) Author, Kempele, Finland. Comb. Color. 22 pp. 8.25 x 11.75 in. Lecture notes. Close-Up, Ice, Matrix.

Aaronson, Sam, *26 Originals: Harry Roz-On Ring.* (1957) Roche Magic Studio, New York. Stapled. Pink. 23 pp. 8.5 x 11 in. Mimeographed. Cards, Close-Up, Stage.

Aaronson, Sam, *Lecture no. 1.* (1960) Author, W. Englewood, NJ. Stapled. Orange. 18 pp. 8.5 x 11 in. Mimeographed. Lecture notes. Cards, Coins.

Abbott Magic Co., *49 Easy-to-Do Card Tricks with Any Deck.* (1943) Abbott Magic Co., Colon, MI. Saddle-stitch. Silver. Cover text: Blue; 32 pp. 4.25 x 6.75 in. Cards.

Abbott Magic Co., *50 Crazy Card Stunts.* (1941) Abbott Magic Co., Colon, MI. Stapled. White. 7 pp. 5.5 x 8.5 in. Cards.

Abbott Magic Co., with Grant, U. F., *50 Ways to Produce a Silk.* (1941) Abbott Magic Co., Colon, MI. Stapled. Tan. 6 pp. 8.5 x 11 in. Silks, Stage.

Abbott Magic Co., with Grant, U. F., *50 Ways to Produce a Silk.* (c. 1980) Abbott Magic Co., Colon, MI. Folded. White. 5 pp. 8.5 x 11 in. Silks, Stage.

Abbott Magic Co., *2017 Abbott's Compendium, The.* (2017) Abbott Magic Co., Colon, MI. Perfect. Green. 557 pp. 8.5 x 11 in. History.

Abbott Magic Co., *Abbott Magic Collection vol. 1: The Percy Abbott Years.* (2018) Abbott Magic Co., Colon, MI. Perfect. Purple. 141 pp. 8.5 x 11 in. History.

Abbott Magic Co., *Abbott Magic Collection vol. 2: The Recil Bordner Years.* (2018) Abbott Magic Co., Colon, MI. Perfect. Orange. 139 pp. 8.5 x 11 in. History.

Abbott Magic Co., *Abbott Magic Collection vol. 3: The Greg Bordner Years.* (2018) Abbott Magic Co., Colon, MI. Perfect. Green. 140 pp. 8.5 x 11 in. History.

Abbott Magic Co., *Abbott Magic Collection vol. 4: Secrets and Routines.* (2018) Abbott Magic Co., Colon, MI. Perfect. Green. 140 pp. 8.5 x 11 in. Stage, Close-Up.

Abbott Magic Co., *Abbott Magic Collection vol. 5: Mentalism.* (2018) Abbott Magic Co., Colon, MI. Perfect. Yellow. 141 pp. 8.5 x 11 in. Mentalism.

Abbott Magic Co., *Abbott Magic Collection vol. 6: The Halloween Magic.* (2018) Abbott Magic Co., Colon, MI. Perfect. Green. 140 pp. 8.5 x 11 in. Stage, Séances, Illusions, Holiday magic.

Abbott Magic Co., *Abbott Magic Collection vol. 7: Stage Illusion Plans.* (2018) Abbott Magic Co., Colon, MI. Perfect. Green. 141 pp. 8.5 x 11 in. Illusions.

Abbott Magic Co., *Abbott Magic Collection vol. 8: Grand Illusion Plans.* (2018) Abbott Magic Co., Colon, MI. Perfect. Purple. 140 pp. 8.5 x 11 in. Illusions.

Abbott Magic Co., *Abbott Magic Collection vol. 9: Carnival Magic.* (2018) Abbott Magic Co., Colon, MI. Perfect. Pink. 140 pp. 8.5 x 11 in. Stage, Sideshow.

Abbott Magic Co., *Abbott Magic Collection vol. 10: Gospel Magic Routines.* (2018) Abbott Magic Co., Colon, MI. Perfect. Gray. 140 pp. 8.5 x 11 in. Gospel magic.

Abbott Magic Co., *Abbott Magic Collection vol. 11: Ventriloquism.* (2018) Abbott Magic Co., Colon, MI. Perfect. Purple. 140 pp. 8.5 x 11 in. Ventriloquism.

Abbott Magic Co., *Abbott Magic Collection vol. 12: Coin Magic and Routines.* (2018) Abbott Magic Co., Colon, MI. Perfect. Yellow. 140 pp. 8.5 x 11 in. Coins.

Abbott Magic Co., *Abbott Magic Collection vol. 13: Rope Magic and Routines.* (2018) Abbott Magic Co., Colon, MI. Perfect. Green. 142 pp. 8.5 x 11 in. Rope.

Abbott Magic Co., *Abbott Magic Collection vol. 14: Card Magic and Routines.* (2018) Abbott Magic Co., Colon, MI. Perfect. Purple. 140 pp. 8.5 x 11 in. Cards.

Abbott Magic Co., *Abbott Magic Collection vol. 15: Silk Magic and Routines.* (2018) Abbott Magic Co., Colon, MI. Perfect. Purple. 142 pp. 8.5 x 11 in. Silks.

Abbott Magic Co., *Abbott Magic Collection vol. 16: Paper Magic and Routines.* (2018) Abbott Magic Co., Colon, MI. Perfect. Purple. 140 pp. 8.5 x 11 in. Paper.

Abbott Magic Co., *Abbott Magic Collection vol. 17: Escape Routines.* (2018) Abbott Magic Co., Colon, MI. Perfect. Purple. 141 pp. 8.5 x 11 in. Escapes.

Abbott Magic Co., *Abbott Magic Collection vol. 18: Supplement and Potpourri.* (2018) Abbott Magic Co., Colon, MI. Perfect. Pink. 140 pp. 8.5 x 11 in. Stage, Close-Up.

Abbott Magic Co., *Abbott's Chinese Coins.* (1938) Abbott Magic Co., Colon, MI. Single page. Green. 11 x 8.5 in. Printed oblong. Illustrations by Tarbell. Coins, Chinese coins, Chinese 16-coin routine.

Abbott Magic Co., *Abbott's Chinese Coins.* (1938) Abbott Magic Co., Colon, MI. Loose pages. White. 4 pp. 8.5 x 11 in. Mimeographed. Coins, Chinese coins, Chinese 16-coin routine.

Abbott Magic Co., *Abbott's Cups and Balls Routine.* (c. 1939) Abbott Magic Co., Colon, MI. Folded. White. 4 pp. 6 x 9 in. (Information not verified by physical copy.) Cups and Balls, Manual.

Abbott Magic Co., *Abbott's Cups and Balls Routine.* (1957) Abbott Magic Co., Colon, MI. Stapled. White. 3 pp. 8.5 x 11 in. (Information not verified by physical copy.) Cups and Balls, Manual.

Abbott Magic Co., *Abbott's Illusions.* (2017) Abbott Magic Co., Colon, MI. Perfect. Dark blue. 461 pp. 8.5 x 11 in. Illusions.

Abbott Magic Co., *Abbott's Latest Acrobatic Cane.* (1946) Abbott Magic Co., Colon, MI. Stapled. Pink. 2 pp. 8.5 x 11 in. Mimeographed. Canes, Suspensions, Thread, Stage.

Abbott Magic Co., *Abbott's Magic and the American Side Show.* (2020) Abbott Magic Co., Colon, MI. Perfect. Orange. 520 pp. 8.5 x 11 in. Sideshows, Illusions, History.

Abbott Magic Co., with Karson, Joe, *Abbott's Neck Twister.* (c. 1950) Abbott Magic Co., Colon, MI. Stapled. White. 2 pp. 8.5 x 11 in. Mimeographed. Illusions.

Abbott Magic Co., *Abbott's Poster Book: The Art of the Get-Together.* (2022) Abbott Magic Co., Colon, MI. Casebound. Brown. 77 pp. 8.5 x 11.25 in. History, Conventions.

Abbott Magic Co., *Abbott's Rising-Floating Dancing Silk.* (1932) Abbott Magic Co., Colon, MI. Stapled. White. 3 pp. 8.5 x 11 in. Mimeographed. Silks, Floating effects.

Abbott Magic Co., *Abbott's Three Star Special.* (1942) Abbott Magic Co., Colon, MI. Stapled. Pink. 3 pp. 8.5 x 11 in. Mimeographed. (Information not verified by physical copy.) Stage, Silks, Bills, Apparatus.

Abbott Magic Co., *Abbott's Ten.* (c. 1973) Supreme Magic, Bideford, UK. Saddle-stitch. White. 8 pp. 8 x 10 in. (Information not verified by physical copy.) Cards.

Abbott Magic Co., with Koran, Al, *Abbott's Unique Cigarette Case.* (1948) Abbott Magic Co., Colon, MI. Stapled. White. 2 pp. 8.5 x 11 in. Mimeographed. (Information not verified by physical copy.) Cards, Cigarettes, Card Case.

BIBLIOGRAPHY OF MAGIC

Abbott Magic Co., *Abbott's Wrist Tie.* (1934) Abbott Magic Co., Colon, MI. Single page. Orange. 2 pp. 6 x 9 in. Includes "Coat Changing Routine." Illustrated by Sid Lorraine. Rope, Escapes.

Abbott Magic Co., *Aga Levitation.* (c. 1947) Abbott Magic Co., Colon, MI. Stapled. Tan. 7 pp. 8.5 x 11 in. Mimeographed. Levitations, Illusions, Plans.

Abbott Magic Co., *All Fair Rope Trick.* (1948) Abbott Magic Co., Colon, MI. Stapled. White. 3 pp. 8.5 x 11 in. Mimeographed. Rope, Cut and Restored Rope.

Abbott Magic Co., *And Some Left Over.* (1948) Abbott Magic Co., Colon, MI. Stapled. White. 2 pp. 8.5 x 11 in. Mimeographed. Bottles, Glasses, Liquids.

Abbott Magic Co., *Best-Yet Cigarette.* (1935) Abbott Magic Co., Colon, MI. Stapled. White. 2 pp. 8.5 x 11 in. Mimeographed. Invented by Percy Abbott. Folded in green printed envelope. Cigarettes, Gimmicks.

Abbott Magic Co., *Best-Yet Penetration.* (1943) Abbott Magic Co., Colon, MI. Stapled. White. 2 pp. 8.5 x 11 in. Mimeographed. Rope, Stage.

Abbott Magic Co., *Bottoms Up.* (1948) Abbott Magic Co., Colon, MI. Stapled. White. 2 pp. 8.5 x 11 in. Mimeographed. Bottles, Comedy.

Abbott Magic Co., *Bouquets and Blossoms: 25 Tricks with Spring Flowers.* (1957) Abbott Magic Co., Colon, MI. Stapled. White. 9 pp. 8.5 x 11 in. Flowers, Gimmicks.

Abbott Magic Co., *Bouquets and Blossoms: 25 Tricks with Spring Flowers.* (1960) Supreme Magic, Bideford, UK. Stapled. White. 9 pp. 8.5 x 11 in. (Information not verified by physical copy.) Flowers, Gimmicks.

Abbott Magic Co., *Box Escape.* (c. 1955) Abbott Magic Co., Colon, MI. Single page. White. 8.5 x 11 in. Mimeographed. Abbott's Secret Service release. Folded in pink envelope with rubber-stamped title. Escapes, Illusions.

Abbott Magic Co., *Boy to Rabbit Illusion.* (1944) Abbott Magic Co., Colon, MI. Stapled. White. 4 pp. 8.5 x 11 in. Illusions, Rabbits, Stage, Instructions.

Abbott Magic Co., *Chain Handcuffs.* (1953) Abbott Magic Co., Colon, MI. Stapled. White. 2 pp. 8.5 x 11 in. Mimeographed. Escapes, Handcuffs.

Abbott Magic Co., with Grant, U. F., *Chinese Magic and Illusions.* (1937) Abbott Magic Co., Colon, MI. Stapled. Blue, red. 12 pp. 8.5 x 11 in. Mimeographed. Asian magic, Stage.

Abbott Magic Co., with Grant, U. F., *Chinese Magic and Illusions.* (1937) Abbott Magic Co., Colon, MI. Stapled with tape. Orange, black. 12 pp. 8.5 x 11 in. Mimeographed. Asian magic, Stage.

Abbott Magic Co., *Comedy Tonight!* (1983) Abbott Magic Co., Colon, MI. Saddle-stitch. White. 60 pp. 8.5 x 11 in. Comedy.

Abbott Magic Co., *Confoundit Dollar.* (1934) Abbott Magic Co., Colon, MI. Stapled. White. 3 pp. 8.5 x 11 in. Mimeographed. Bills, Pulls, Gimmicks.

Abbott Magic Co., *Conjuring with Cards vol. 1: The Nick Trost Collection.* (2024) Abbott Magic Co., Colon, MI. Perfect. Black. 364 pp. 8.5 x 11 in. Cards.

Abbott Magic Co., *Conjuring with Cards vol. 2: The Maven/Marlo Collection.* (2024) Abbott Magic Co., Colon, MI. Perfect. Blue. 382 pp. 8.5 x 11 in. Cards.

Abbott Magic Co., *Conjuring with Cards vol. 3: The Marketed Effects Collection.* (2024) Abbott Magic Co., Colon, MI. Perfect. Blue. 383 pp. 8.5 x 11 in. Cards.

Abbott Magic Co., with Grant, U. F., *Counterfeit Card Miracles.* (c. 1934) Abbott Magic Co., Colon, MI. Loose pages. White. 3 pp. 8.5 x 11 in. Mimeographed. In printed envelope. Same as Grant version below, titled "Grant's Counterfeit Card Miracles." Cards.

Abbott Magic Co., with Grant, U. F., *Counterfeit Card Miracles no. 2.* (c. 1934) Abbott Magic Co., Colon, MI. Loose pages. White. 3 pp. 8.5 x 11 in. Mimeographed. In printed envelope. Same as Grant version below, titled "Grant's Counterfeit Card Miracles." Cards.

Abbott Magic Co., *Dark Energy Secrets.* (2020) Abbott Magic Co., Colon, MI. Perfect. Purple. 534 pp. 8.5 x 11 in. Bizarre magick, Halloween, Séances.

Abbott Magic Co., *Dark Matter Secrets.* (2014) Abbott Magic Co., Colon, MI. Perfect. Black. 412 pp. 8.5 x 11 in. Bizarre magick, Halloween, Séances.

Abbott Magic Co., *Decades.* (2014) Abbott Magic Co., Colon, MI. Perfect. Beige. 102 pp. 6 x 9 in. (Measurements and other information have been recorded as accurately as possible.) History.

Abbott Magic Co., *Dwarf Act, The.* (1957) Abbott Magic Co., Colon, MI. Stapled. Olive. 6 pp. 8.5 x 11 in. Mimeographed. Stage, Comedy.

Abbott Magic Co., *Dynamic Glasses.* (1935) Abbott Magic Co., Colon, MI. Folded. Tan. 3 pp. 5.5 x 8 in. (Information not verified by physical copy.) Glasses, Stage.

BIBLIOGRAPHY OF MAGIC

Abbott Magic Co., *Escapes.* (1955) Abbott Magic Co., Colon, MI. Stapled. White. 58 pp. 8.5 x 11 in. Mimeographed. Orange back cover. Escapes.

Abbott Magic Co., *Escapes.* (1955) Abbott Magic Co., Colon, MI. Saddle-stitch. Blue. 51 pp. 8.25 x 10.75 in. Later edition. Escapes.

Abbott Magic Co., *Escapes.* (1979) Supreme Magic, Bideford, UK. Saddle-stitch. Purple. 68 pp. 7.25 x 9.75 in. Escapes.

Abbott Magic Co., *Escapes.* (1995) Abbott Magic Co., Colon, MI. Saddle-stitch. Beige. 47 pp. 8.5 x 11 in. (Measurements and other information have been recorded as accurately as possible.) Escapes.

Abbott Magic Co., *Exclusive!* (c. 1935) Abbott Magic Co., Colon, MI. Loose pages. Tan. 6 pp. 7.75 x 11 in. Mimeographed. Signed by Percy Abbott. Stage.

Abbott Magic Co., *Feather Bouquets: Suggested Methods of Production.* (c. 1930) Abbott Magic Co., Colon, MI. Single page. Yellow. 5 x 8 in. (Information not verified by physical copy.) Stage, Feather flowers.

Abbott Magic Co., *Floating Handkerchief.* (c. 1940) Abbott Magic Co., Colon, MI. Stapled. White. 2 pp. 8.5 x 11 in. Mimeographed. (Information not verified by physical copy.) Handkerchiefs.

Abbott Magic Co., *Get-Together Reference Book: 2022 Edition.* (2022) Abbott Magic Co., Colon, MI. Perfect. White, black. 60 pp. 5 x 8 in. History, Reference, Conventions.

Abbott Magic Co. (ed. by Neil Foster), *Great Blackstone: World's Greatest Magician and His Show of 1001 Wonders, The.* (1970) Abbott Magic Co., Colon, MI. Saddle-stitch. White. 48 pp. 8.5 x 11 in. Biography, History.

Abbott Magic Co. (ed. by Neil Foster), *Great Blackstone: World's Greatest Magician and His Show of 1001 Wonders, The.* (2024) Abbott Magic Co., Colon, MI. Perfect. Brown, tan, white. 49 pp. 8.5 x 11 in. Biography, History.

Abbott Magic Co., *Handcuff Escape.* (c. 1955) Abbott Magic Co., Colon, MI. Single page. White. 8.5 x 11 in. Mimeographed. Abbott's Secret Service release. Escapes, Handcuffs.

Abbott Magic Co., *Haunted Hank.* (1941) Abbott Magic Co., Colon, MI. Stapled. White. 4 pp. 8.5 x 11 in. Mimeographed. Handkerchiefs, Animations.

Abbott Magic Co., *Hellstromism.* (1935) Abbott Magic Co., Colon, MI. Stapled. Green. 7 pp. 8.5 x 11 in. Mimeographed. Mentalism, Contact mind-reading.

Abbott Magic Co., *Hindoo Rope Trick.* (c. 1945) Abbott Magic Co., Colon, MI. Stapled. White. 2 pp. 8.5 x 11 in. Mimeographed. Rope, Illusions.

Abbott Magic Co., *Illusion Secrets.* (1934) Abbott Magic Co., Colon, MI. Stapled. Olive. 32 pp. 8.5 x 11 in. Mimeographed. See also similarly named 1934 U. F. Grant booklet. Illusions.

Abbott Magic Co., *Illusions!* (1989) Abbott Magic Co., Colon, MI. Coil. Pink. 177 pp. 8.5 x 11 in. (Measurements and other information have been recorded as accurately as possible.) Illusions.

Abbott Magic Co., *Illusions! Illusions!* (1989) Abbott Magic Co., Colon, MI. Comb. Pink. 177 pp. 8.5 x 11 in. Clear acetate covers. Illusions.

Abbott Magic Co., *Improved Girl in Fish Bowl.* (1951) Abbott Magic Co., Colon, MI. Loose pages. White. 6 pp. 8.5 x 11 in. Mimeographed. Illusions, Optics, Manual.

Abbott Magic Co., *Instanto Deck, The.* (1945) Abbott Magic Co., Colon, MI. Stapled. White. 2 pp. 8.5 x 11 in. Mimeographed. Cards, Gimmicked decks.

Abbott Magic Co., *Intimate Card and Cigarette Tricks.* (1935) Abbott Magic Co., Colon, MI. Stapled with tape. Green. 26 pp. 5.25 x 8.25 in. Cards, Cigarettes, Close-Up.

Abbott Magic Co., *Jumbo Card Tricks.* (1937) Abbott Magic Co., Colon, MI. Stapled with tape. Olive. 12 pp. 8.5 x 11 in. Mimeographed. Cards, Manipulation, Jumbo cards.

Abbott Magic Co., *Magic Card System.* (1943) Abbott Magic Co., Colon, MI. Saddle-stitch. Brown. 20 pp. 4.25 x 7 in. Cards, Prearranged deck.

Abbott Magic Co., *Magic Card System.* (1973) Supreme Magic, Bideford, UK. Stapled with tape. Gray. 13 pp. 8 x 10.25 in. Mimeographed. Cards, Prearranged deck.

Abbott Magic Co., with Martineau, Francis, *Magic Skipper, The.* (1945) Abbott Magic Co., Colon, MI. Single page. White. 8.5 x 11 in. Mimeographed. (Information not verified by physical copy.) Rope.

Abbott Magic Co., *Marvel Question Board.* (1957) Abbott Magic Co., Colon, MI. Stapled. White. 4 pp. 8.5 x 11 in. Mimeographed. (Information not verified by physical copy.) Mentalism, Question and answer.

Abbott Magic Co., *Neck and Wrist Cuffs.* (c. 1960) Abbott Magic Co., Colon, MI. Stapled. White. 4 pp. 8.5 x 11 in. Mimeographed. (Information not verified by physical copy.) Mentalism, Question and answer.

Abbott Magic Co., with Fox, Karrell, *Night Cap Tear.* (1950) Abbott Magic Co., Colon, MI. Single page. White. 8.5 x 11 in. Mimeographed. (Information not verified by physical copy.) Paper, Hats, Comedy.

Abbott Magic Co., *Nine Unearthed at Midnight.* (2016) Abbott Magic Co., Colon, MI. Perfect. Purple. 57 pp. 8.5 x 11 in. Mentalism, Séances.

Abbott Magic Co., *No-Knot Cut Rope.* (c. 1950) Abbott Magic Co., Colon, MI. Stapled. White. 2 pp. 8.5 x 11 in. Mimeographed. (Information not verified by physical copy.) Rope, Cut and Restored Rope.

Abbott Magic Co., *Nu-Coin in Lemon.* (1940) Abbott Magic Co., Colon, MI. Single page. White. 8.5 x 11 in. Mimeographed. Coins, Close-Up, Stage.

Abbott Magic Co., *Practical Patter.* (1935) Abbott Magic Co., Colon, MI. Stapled with tape. Orange. 24 pp. 5.25 x 8 in. Patter.

Abbott Magic Co., *Practical Patter.* (1935) Abbott Magic Co., Colon, MI. Stapled. Green. 18 pp. 8.5 x 11 in. Mimeographed. Patter.

Abbott Magic Co., with Francis, Douglas, *Rainbow Sponge Ball Routine.* (1950) Abbott Magic Co., Colon, MI. Stapled. White. 2 pp. 8.5 x 11 in. Mimeographed. Sponge balls, Close-Up.

Abbott Magic Co., *Séance Houdini 26:26: The 100 Year Houdini Séance.* (2023) Abbott Magic Co., Colon, MI. Perfect. Black. 97 pp. 8.5 x 11 in. Séance, Spirit effects, Houdini.

Abbott Magic Co., *Simplified Memory Act.* (1935) Abbott Magic Co., Colon, MI. Stapled with paper cover. Yellow. 4 pp. 5.5 x 8.25 in. Mimeographed. Memory.

Abbott Magic Co., *Source, The.* (1988) Abbott Magic Co., Colon, MI. Comb. White. 124 pp. 8.5 x 11 in. Anthology. Gospel magic.

Abbott Magic Co., *Spirit Spooks.* (1947) Abbott Magic Co., Colon, MI. Stapled. White. 2 pp. 8.5 x 11 in. Mimeographed. Spirit effects.

Abbott Magic Co., *Strange Secrets vol. 1.* (1984) Abbott Magic Co., Colon, MI. Saddle-stitch. White, black, blue. 90 pp. 8.5 x 11 in. Text in all caps. Bizarre magick, Mentalism, Psychic, Séance.

Abbott Magic Co., *Strange Secrets vol. 2.* (1984) Abbott Magic Co., Colon, MI. Saddle-stitch. White, black, blue. 104 pp. 8.5 x 11 in. Text in all caps. Bizarre magick, Mentalism, Psychic, Séance.

Abbott Magic Co., *Strange Secrets: The Addenda.* (1984) Abbott Magic Co., Colon, MI. Saddle-stitch. White, red. 54 pp. 8.5 x 11 in. Text in all caps. Bizarre magick, Mentalism, Psychic, Séance.

Abbott Magic Co., *Sympathetic Silk Tricks.* Second edition. (1947) Abbott Magic Co., Colon, MI. Stapled. Orange. 7 pp. 8.5 x 11 in. Mimeographed. Silks.

Abbott Magic Co., *Super-X Levitation.* (c. 1970) Abbott Magic Co., Colon, MI. Folded. White. 6 pp. 8.5 x 11 in. Illusions, Suspensions, Manual.

Abbott Magic Co., *Talk! A Panorama of Professional Prose Palaver and Polished Poetical Patter: A Pastiche.* (1984) Abbott Magic Co., Colon, MI. Saddle-stitch. White. 79 pp. 8.5 x 11 in. Patter, Comedy, Emcee.

Abbott Magic Co., *Target: Midnight.* (2022) Abbott Magic Co., Colon, MI. Perfect. Black. 572 pp. 8.5 x 11 in. Illusions.

Abbott Magic Co., *Ten: An Intimate Fooler.* (c. 1935) Abbott Magic Co., Colon, MI. Saddle-stitch. Beige. 5 pp. 3.5 x 5 in. With envelope. Cards.

Abbott Magic Co., *Tops 1963 Trick Annual.* (1963) Abbott Magic Co., Colon, MI. Saddle-stitch. White. 34 pp. 8.5 x 11 in. Supplement to "Tops." Cards, Close-Up, Stage.

Abbott Magic Co. (ed. by Neil Foster), *Tops Pictorial Album of Magicians.* (1966) Abbott Magic Co., Colon, MI. Saddle-stitch. White. 88 pp. 8.5 x 11 in. Signed by John Braun, Karrell Fox, Arnold Furst, Gene Gordon, Bob Lewis, Bruce Posgate. History, Photography.

Abbott Magic Co. (ed. by Gordon Miller), *Tops Treasury of Ball Manipulation.* (1999) Abbott Magic Co., Colon, MI. Coil. Light blue. 104 pp. 5.5 x 8.5 in. Balls, Manipulation.

Abbott Magic Co. (ed. by Neil Foster), *Tops Treasury of Cigarette Magic.* (1965) Abbott Magic Co., Colon, MI. Saddle-stitch. Yellow. 22 pp. 8.5 x 11 in. Cigarettes, Manipulation.

Abbott Magic Co. (ed. by Neil Foster), *Tops Treasury of Dove Magic.* (1965) Abbott Magic Co., Colon, MI. Saddle-stitch. White, green. 28 pp. 8.5 x 11 in. Doves, Stage.

Abbott Magic Co. (ed. by Neil Foster), *Tops Treasury of Illusions.* (1965) Abbott Magic Co., Colon, MI. Saddle-stitch. Blue. 100 pp. 8.5 x 11 in. Illusions.

Abbott Magic Co. (ed. by Neil Foster), *Tops Treasury of Illusions.* (1965) Abbott Magic Co., Colon, MI. Saddle-stitch. Tan. 100 pp. 8.5 x 11 in. Illusions.

Abbott Magic Co. (ed. by Gordon Miller), *Tops Treasury of Thimble Magic.* (1999) Abbott Magic Co., Colon, MI. Coil. Gray, red. 107 pp. 5.5 x 8.5 in. Thimbles, Manipulation.

Abbott Magic Co., *Whirling Dervish.* (1944) Abbott Magic Co., Colon, MI. Stapled. White. 2 pp. 8.5 x 11 in. Mimeographed. Rope, Escapes.

Abbott Magic Co., *Workshop Plans for Abbott's Electric Chair Illusion.* (n.d.) Abbott Magic Co., Colon, MI. Stapled. White. 4 pp. 8.5 x 11 in. Mimeographed. Illusions.

Abbott, Bill, *Cabaret Card Magic.* (2008) Author, St. Augustine, FL. Saddle-stitch. Black. 19 pp. 8.25 x 11 in. Cards, Close-Up.

Abbott, Bill, *Cocktail Card Magic.* (2009) Author, St. Augustine, FL. Saddle-stitch. Black. 26 pp. 8.5 x 11 in. Cards, Close-Up.

Abbott, Bill, *House Party Magic.* (2011) Author, St. Augustine, FL. Saddle-stitch. Blue. 21 pp. 8.5 x 11 in. (Information not verified by physical copy.) Cards, Close-Up.

Abbott, Bill, *People-Pleasing Magic.* (2006) Author, St. Augustine, FL. Stapled. White. 22 pp. 8.5 x 11 in. (Information not verified by physical copy.) Lecture notes. Cards, Close-Up.

Abbott, Bill, *Smart-Stuff.* (2009) Author, St. Augustine, FL. Wire binding. White. 49 pp. 5.5 x 8.5 in. Cards, Close-Up.

Abbott, Bill, *Table Magic.* (2010) Author, St. Augustine, FL. Saddle-stitch. Black. 27 pp. 8.5 x 11 in. Cards, Close-Up.

Abbott, David P., *Behind the Scenes with the Mediums.* First edition. (1907) Open Court, Chicago. Cloth. Beige. Cover text: Brown; 328 pp. 5.5 x 8 in. Mentalism, Spiritualism.

Abbott, David P., *Behind the Scenes with the Mediums.* Second edition. (1908) Open Court, Chicago. Cloth. Beige. Cover text: Maroon; 336 pp. 5.5 x 8 in. Mentalism, Spiritualism.

Abbott, David P., *Behind the Scenes with the Mediums.* Third revised edition. (1909) Open Court, Chicago. Cloth. Beige. Cover text: Brown; 340 pp. 5.5 x 8 in. Mentalism, Spiritualism.

Abbott, David P., *Behind the Scenes with the Mediums.* Fourth revised edition. (1912) Open Court, Chicago. Cloth. Beige. Cover text: Red, black; 340 pp. 5.5 x 8 in. Owl on cover. Mentalism, Spiritualism.

Abbott, David P., *Behind the Scenes with the Mediums*. Fifth revised edition. (1916) Open Court, Chicago. Perfect. Beige. Cover text: Red, black; 340 pp. 5.25 x 7.5 in. Mentalism, Spiritualism.

Abbott, David P., *Behind the Scenes with the Mediums*. Fifth revised edition. (1916) Open Court, Chicago. Cloth. Beige. Cover text: Brown; 340 pp. 5.5 x 8 in. Signed by David P. Abbott. Mentalism, Spiritualism.

Abbott, David P., *Behind the Scenes with the Mediums*. Fifth revised edition. (1916) Open Court, Chicago. Cloth. Beige. Cover text: Black; 340 pp. 5.5 x 8 in. Different color of cover text. Mentalism, Spiritualism.

Abbott, David P., *Behind the Scenes with the Mediums*. Sixth edition. (1926) Open Court, Chicago. Cloth. Beige. Cover text: Brown; 340 pp. 5.5 x 8 in. Incorrectly stated as "Fifth Revised Edition" like previous 1916 printing. Mentalism, Spiritualism.

Abbott, David P., with Graham, Walter, *David P. Abbott's Book of Mysteries*. (1977) Modern Litho, Inc., Omaha. Cloth. Light blue. 183 pp. 8.5 x 11 in. Signed by Walter Graham, Carl Ballantine. #316. Beginner, Stage.

Abbott, David P., with Graham, Walter, *David P. Abbott's Book of Mysteries*. (1977) Modern Litho, Inc., Omaha. Cloth. Dark blue. 183 pp. 8.5 x 11 in. #240. Beginner, Stage.

Abbott, David P., *History of a Strange Case, The*. (1908) Open Court, Chicago. Perfect. Blue. 50 pp. 6 x 9 in. Spiritualism.

Abbott, David P., with Teller; Karr, Todd, *House of Mystery: The Magic Science of David P. Abbott vols. 1-2*. Deluxe edition. (2005) The Miracle Factory, Los Angeles. Cloth. Black. 388 pp. 8 x 10 in. Dust jacket. In box with ribbon tie, DVD. Signed by Katlyn Breene, Todd Karr, Teller. #1 of 100. Biography, Spiritualism, Mentalism, Stage.

Abbott, David P., with Teller; Karr, Todd, *House of Mystery: The Magic Science of David P. Abbott vol. 1: Behind the Scenes*. (2005) The Miracle Factory, Los Angeles. Cloth. Black. 388 pp. 8 x 10 in. Dust jacket. Signed by Teller. Biography, Spiritualism, Mentalism, Stage.

Abbott, David P., with Teller; Karr, Todd, *House of Mystery: The Magic Science of David P. Abbott vol. 2: The Book of Mysteries*. (2005) The Miracle Factory, Los Angeles. Cloth. Black. 392 pp. 8 x 10 in. Dust jacket. Signed by Teller. Biography, Close-Up, Mentalism, Stage.

Abbott, David P., *Independent Voices, Movement of Objects Without Contact, and Spirit Portraits*. (1911) Open Court, Chicago. Stapled. Blue. 15 pp. 5.75 x 8.75 in. (Information not verified by physical copy.) Spiritualism, Exposés.

Abbott, David P., *Library of the World's Best Mystery and Detective Stories: Oriental: Modern Magic*. First edition. (1908) Review of Reviews Company, New York. Cloth. Beige. Cover text: Black; 304 pp. 5 x 7.5 in. Excerpts from "Behind the Scenes with the Mediums." Spiritualism, Exposés.

Abbott, David P., *Lock and Key Library: Real Life*. Second edition. (1915) Review of Reviews Company, New York. Cloth. Red. Cover text: Gold; 162 pp. 4.75 x 7 in. Excerpts from "Behind the Scenes with the Mediums." Spiritualism, Exposés.

Abbott, David P., *Marvelous Creations of Joseffy, The.* (1908) Open Court, Chicago. Saddle-stitch. Black. Cover text: Orange; 24 pp. 6.25 x 9.25 in. Biography, Illusions, Stage.

Abbott, David P., *Marvelous Creations of Joseffy, The.* (2001) Chuck Romano, South Elgin, IL. Saddle-stitch. Black. 32 pp. 5.75 x 8.75 in. #43 of 250. Biography, Exposés, Stage.

Abbott, David P., *Spirit Portrait Mystery: Its Final Solution, The.* (1913) Open Court, Chicago. Saddle-stitch. Tan. 33 pp. 6 x 9 in. Spiritualism, Exposés.

Abbott, David P., *Wonder Girl, The.* (1992) Walter B. Graham, Omaha. Saddle-stitch. White. 32 pp. 8.5 x 11 in. Mentalism, Biography, Psychic.

Abbott, Percy (See also Grant, U. F.), *Comedy Magic.* (1934) Abbott Magic Co., Colon, MI. Folded. White, green. 16 pp. 8.5 x 11 in. Comedy.

Abbott, Percy, *Comedy Magic.* (1934) Abbott Magic Co., Colon, MI. Saddle-stitch. Orange. 16 pp. 8.5 x 11 in. Later edition with new typesetting. Comedy.

Abbott, Percy, *Easy Ventriloquism.* (1937) Abbott Magic Co., Colon, MI. Saddle-stitch. White, purple. 8 pp. 5.25 x 8.25 in. Includes gimmick. Later edition. Ventriloquism.

Abbott, Percy, *Lifetime in Magic, A.* (1960) Abbott Magic Co., Colon, MI. Perfect. Gold. 132 pp. 6 x 8.75 in. Biography.

Abbott, Percy, *Lifetime in Magic, A.* (1960) Abbott Magic Co., Colon, MI. Perfect. Light blue. 132 pp. 6 x 8.75 in. Biography.

Abbott, Percy, *Magic for Magicians.* (1934) Abbott Magic Co., Colon, MI. Saddle-stitch. Blue. 64 pp. 6 x 9 in. Signed by Percy Abbott. Stage.

Abisch, Roz, with Kaplan, Boche, *Easy-to-Do Magic Tricks.* (1984) Weekly Reader Books, Middletown, CT. Saddle-stitch. Blue. 80 pp. 5.25 x 8 in. Beginner, Children's book.

Abisch, Roz, with Kaplan, Boche, *Mixed Bag of Magic Tricks.* (1973) Walker and Co., New York. Cloth. Red. 64 pp. 5.75 x 8.25 in. Dust jacket. Beginner, Children's book.

Abisch, Roz, with Kaplan, Boche, *Mixed Bag of Magic Tricks.* (1977) Grosset and Dunlap, New York. Perfect. Gray. 80 pp. 8.25 x 10.75 in. Beginner, Children's book.

Abraham, R. M., *Diversions and Pastimes.* (1933) Constable, London. Cloth. Green. 153 pp. 5.5 x 7.75 in. Dust jacket. Mathematical, Stunts, Puzzles, Cards.

Abraham, R. M., *Diversions and Pastimes.* (1964) Dover, New York. Perfect. Orange. 122 pp. 5.5 x 8.5 in. Mathematical, Stunts, Puzzles, Cards.

Abraham, R. M., *Winter Nights Entertainments.* (1932) Constable, London. Cloth. Blue. 186 pp. 5.5 x 7.75 in. Mathematical, Stunts, Puzzles, Cards.

Abram, David, *Becoming Animal.* (2010) Pantheon, New York. Cloth. Blue. 313 pp. 6.25 x 9.5 in. Dust jacket. Essays.

Abram, David, *Joker is Wild, The.* (1982) Author, Baldwin, NY. Stapled. Beige. 6 pp. 8.5 x 11 in. Theory, Essays, Close-Up, Cards.

Abram, David, *Spell of the Sensuous, The.* (1996) Pantheon, New York. Cloth. Green. 326 pp. 6.5 x 9.5 in. Dust jacket. Essays.

Abrams, Max, *Annemann: The Life and Times of a Legend.* Limited deluxe edition. (1992) L & L Publishing, Tahoma, CA. Leather. Black. 621 pp. 9 x 11.5 in. Slipcase. Signed by Max Abrams. #76 of 100. Biography, Mentalism, Cards.

Abrams, Max, *Annemann: The Life and Times of a Legend.* (1992) L & L Publishing, Tahoma, CA. Cloth. Black. 621 pp. 8.75 x 11.25 in. Dust jacket. Biography, Mentalism, Cards.

Abrams, Max, *Complete J. G. Thompson Jr. Bibliography and the Index to "The Miracle Makers."* (1976) Author, Los Angeles. Strip binding. Yellow. 21 pp. 8.5 x 11 in. #147 of 500. Bibliography, Reference, Index.

Absolon, *Street Magic.* (1988) Author, Prague. Stapled. Yellow. 21 pp. 8.5 x 11 in. (Measurements and other information have been recorded as accurately as possible.) Lecture notes. Street magic, Stage, Close-Up.

Accum, Frederick C., *Chemical Amusement.* (1817) Thomas Boys, London. 191 pp. 4.25 x 7 in. (Information not verified by physical copy.) Toole Stott no. 1. Early magic, Chemical magic.

Accum, Frederick C., *Chemical Amusement.* Second edition. (1818) Thomas Boys, London. 360 pp. 4 x 6.75 in. (Information not verified by physical copy.) Toole Stott no. 2. Early magic, Chemical magic.

Accum, Frederick C., *Chemical Amusement.* Third edition. (1818) Thomas Boys, London. 360 pp. 4.5 x 7.25 in. (Information not verified by physical copy.) Toole Stott no. 3. Early magic, Chemical magic.

Accum, Frederick C., *Chemical Amusement.* (1818) Mr. Carey and Son, Philadelphia. 217 pp. 4.5 x 7.75 in. (Information not verified by physical copy.) Toole Stott no. 5. Early magic, Chemical magic.

Accum, Frederick C., *Chemical Amusement.* Fourth edition. (1819) Thomas Boys, London. 430 pp. 4 x 6.75 in. (Information not verified by physical copy.) Toole Stott no. 4. Early magic, Chemical magic.

Accum, Frederick C., *Chemical Amusement.* Fourth edition. (1821) Thomas Boys, London. 430 pp. 4 x 6.75 in. (Information not verified by physical copy.) Toole Stott no. 913. Early magic, Chemical magic.

Acer, David (See also Bronson, Rick; Sankey, Jay), *7 by Michel Huot.* (2003) Author, Montreal. Saddle-stitch. White. 36 pp. 5.5 x 8.5 in. (Information not verified by physical copy.) Cards, Close-Up.

Acer, David, *7 by Patrik Kuffs.* (2004) Author, Montreal. Saddle-stitch. White. 32 pp. 5.5 x 8.5 in. (Information not verified by physical copy.) Cards, Close-Up.

Acer, David, *7 by Rick Bronson.* (2005) Author, Montreal. Saddle-stitch. White. 38 pp. 5.5 x 8.5 in. (Information not verified by physical copy.) Cards, Close-Up.

Acer, David, *Bread and Butter.* (1991) Author, Montreal. Stapled. Beige. 23 pp. 8.5 x 11 in. (Information not verified by physical copy.) Cards, Close-Up.

Acer, David, with Sankey, Jay, *Cross Roads.* (2000) Authors, Montreal. Saddle-stitch. Beige. 17 pp. 8.5 x 11 in. Lecture notes. Cards, Close-Up.

Acer, David, *Keys to the Kingdom.* (1992) Camirand Academy of Magic, Quebec. Saddle-stitch. White, blue. 12 pp. 5.5 x 8.5 in. (Information not verified by physical copy.) Close-Up, Paddles.

Acer, David, *More Power to You.* (2011) Hermetic Press, Seattle. Cloth. Yellow, blue. 182 pp. 7.25 x 10 in. Dust jacket. Close-Up, Stage.

Acer, David, *Natural Selections.* (1995) Camirand Academy of Magic, Quebec. Cloth. Black. 148 pp. 6.75 x 10 in. Dust jacket. Cards, Close-Up.

Acer, David, *Natural Selections vol. 2.* (1998) Camirand Academy of Magic, Quebec. Cloth. Black. 201 pp. 6.75 x 10.25 in. Dust jacket. Cards, Close-Up.

Acer, David, *Not Actual Size.* (1995) Author, Montreal. Comb. White. 28 pp. 8.5 x 11 in. Lecture notes. Cards, Close-Up.

Acer, David, *Plot Thickens, The.* (c. 1990) Author, Montreal. Stapled. Gray. 24 pp. 8.5 x 11 in. (Information not verified by physical copy.) Cards, Close-Up.

Acer, David, *Random Acts of Magic.* (2004) Camirand Academy of Magic, Quebec. Cloth. Black. 350 pp. 6.5 x 10 in. Dust jacket. Cards, Close-Up.

Acer, David, *Richard Sanders: Close-Up Assassin.* (1998) Camirand Academy of Magic, Quebec. Saddle-stitch. Color. 88 pp. 5.5 x 8.5 in. Cards, Close-Up.

Acer, David, *Selections from The Magic Menu: Tricks, Tips, and Interviews.* (1999) Author, Montreal. Stapled. Beige. 26 pp. 8.5 x 11 in. (Information not verified by physical copy.) Cards, Close-Up, Strolling magic.

Acer, David, *Sudden Impact.* (1998) Author, Montreal. Stapled. Beige. 16 pp. 8.5 x 11 in. Lecture notes. Close-Up, Stage.

Acer, David, *This is a Circle.* (2001) Author, Montreal. Stapled. Blue. 16 pp. 8.5 x 11 in. Lecture notes. Close-Up, Cards.

Acer, David, *Toast and Jam.* (1993) Author, Montreal. Stapled. White. 19 pp. 8.5 x 11 in. (Information not verified by physical copy. Bibliographical details are as accurate as possible.) Cards, Close-Up.

Acer, David, *Views: Insight into the World of Professional Magic, The.* (2003) Author, Montreal. Stapled. Blue. 38 pp. 8.5 x 11 in. (Information not verified by physical copy.) Showmanship, Interviews, Theory.

Acer, David, *You Are Here.* (1999) Author, Montreal. Stapled. White. 22 pp. 8.5 x 11 in. (Information not verified by physical copy.) Lecture notes. Cards, Close-Up, Stage.

Ackerman, Allan, *52 Minutes of Cards.* (1980) Author, Las Vegas. (Information not verified by physical copy.) Lecture notes. Cards.

Ackerman, Allan, *Ackerman 2004.* (2004) Author, Las Vegas. Comb. White. 54 pp. 8.5 x 11 in. Includes DVD. Signed by Allan Ackerman.

Ackerman, Allan, *Al Cardpone.* (1996) Author, Las Vegas. Stapled. Blue. 43 pp. 8.5 x 11 in. Signed by Allan Ackerman. Lecture notes. Cards.

Ackerman, Allan, with Lovick, John, *All-In vol. 1.* (2024) Vanishing Inc., Rancho Cordova, CA. Cloth. Green. 218 pp. 8.75 x 11.25 in. Two-volume set in slipcase. Cards.

Ackerman, Allan, with Lovick, John, *All-In vol. 2.* (2024) Vanishing Inc., Rancho Cordova, CA. Cloth. Red. 211 pp. 8.75 x 11.25 in. Two-volume set in slipcase. Cards.

Ackerman, Allan, with Lovick, John, *All-In vols. 1-2.* Deluxe edition. (2024) Vanishing Inc., Rancho Cordova, CA. Cloth. Black. 218 pp. 8.75 x 11.25 in. Two-volume set in slipcase (Information not verified by physical copy.) Cards.

Ackerman, Allan, *Baker's Dozen.* (2014) Author, Las Vegas. (Information not verified by physical copy.) Lecture notes. Cards.

Ackerman, Allan, *Card Theater.* (2019) Author, Las Vegas. Comb. White. 107 pp. 8.5 x 11 in. (Information not verified by physical copy.) Lecture notes. Cards.

Ackerman, Allan, *Cardjurer, The.* (2012) Author, Las Vegas. Comb. Yellow. 110 pp. 8.5 x 11 in. (Information not verified by physical copy.) Lecture notes. Cards.

Ackerman, Allan, *Classic Handlings.* (1999) Author, Las Vegas. Stapled. Salmon. 37 pp. 8.5 x 11 in. Signed by Allan Ackerman. Cards.

Ackerman, Allan, *Day of Magic Lecture Notes.* (1992) Author, Las Vegas. Comb. Gray. 25 pp. 8.5 x 11 in. Lecture notes. Cards.

Ackerman, Allan, *Esoterist, The.* (1971) Paul Diamond Magic, Ft. Lauderdale, FL. Saddle-stitch. Blue. 45 pp. 8.5 x 11 in. Gems of Magic Book no. 2. Signed by Allan Ackerman. Cards.

Ackerman, Allan, *Esoterist, The.* (1971) Paul Diamond Magic, Ft. Lauderdale, FL. Saddle-stitch. Dark blue. 45 pp. 5.5 x 8.5 in. Gems of Magic Book no. 2. Signed by Allan Ackerman. Cards.

Ackerman, Allan, *Esoterist, The.* (1971) Paul Diamond Magic, Ft. Lauderdale, FL. Cloth. Black. 45 pp. 8.5 x 11 in. Gems of Magic Book no. 2. Signed by Allan Ackerman. Cards.

Ackerman, Allan, *Esoterist, The.* (n.d.) Paul Diamond Magic, Ft. Lauderdale, FL. Saddle-stitch. Green. 45 pp. 5.5 x 8.5 in. Later reprint. Gems of Magic Book no. 2. Signed by Allan Ackerman. Cards.

Ackerman, Allan, *Every Move a Move.* (1992) Author, Las Vegas. Comb. Tan. 24 pp. 8.5 x 11 in. (Measurements and other information have been recorded as accurately as possible.) Lecture notes. Cards.

Ackerman, Allan, *Here's My Card.* (1978) Gamblers Book Club, Las Vegas. Perfect. White. 109 pp. 5.25 x 8.25 in. Signed by Allan Ackerman. Cards.

Ackerman, Allan, *How to Tame a Moose.* (1995) Author, Las Vegas. Stapled. Green. 61 pp. 8.5 x 11 in. Signed by Allan Ackerman. Lecture notes. Cards.

Ackerman, Allan, *I Can't Believe It's Not All Cards Lecture Tour.* (1997) Author, Las Vegas. Stapled. Yellow. 33 pp. 8.5 x 11 in. Lecture notes. Cards.

Ackerman, Allan, *Las Vegas Kardma.* Deluxe edition. (1994) A-1 MultiMedia, El Dorado Hills, CA. Leather. Red. Cover text: Gold; 176 pp. 8.5 x 11 in. Slipcase. Signed by Allan Ackerman. #21 of 125. Cards.

Ackerman, Allan, *Magic Castle Lecture Notes.* (1991) Author, Las Vegas. Comb. Beige. 30 pp. 8.5 x 11 in. (Information not verified by physical copy.) Lecture notes. Cards.

Ackerman, Allan, *Magic Mafia Effects.* (1970) Author, Las Vegas. Comb. Yellow. 39 pp. 8.5 x 11 in. Foreword by Ed Marlo. Signed by Allan Ackerman. Cards.

Ackerman, Allan, *Wednesday Nights.* (1994) Author, Las Vegas. Stapled. Green. 32 pp. 8.5 x 11 in. Signed by Allan Ackerman. Cards.

Adair, Ian (See also De Courcy, Ken; Hooper, Edwin), *6 Stunning Card Tricks.* (2020) Author, Barnstable, UK. Saddle-stitch. Yellow. Only 10 copies privately published. Series of six booklets mailed to friends from 2020 to 2021. Beginner.

Adair, Ian, *100 Magic Tricks.* (1991) Chartwell Books, London. Cloth. Black. 128 pp. 8.75 x 11.25 in. (Measurements and other information have been recorded as accurately as possible.) Beginner.

Adair, Ian, *À la Zombie.* (1965) Supreme Magic, Bideford, UK. Stapled with tape. Blue, white. 32 pp. 8 x 9.75 in. Mimeographed. Stage, Zombie.

Adair, Ian, *À la Zombie Plus.* (1970) Supreme Magic, Bideford, UK. Comb. Blue, white. 53 pp. 8 x 10 in. Stiff boards. Blue comb binding. Stage, Zombie.

Adair, Ian, *A1 Magic by Al.* (1987) Supreme Magic, Bideford, UK. Saddle-stitch. Red, white, black. 43 pp. 5.75 x 8.25 in. (Information not verified by physical copy.) Stage.

Adair, Ian, *Adair Devils.* (1985) Supreme Magic, Bideford, UK. 12 pp. (Information not verified by physical copy.) Lecture notes. Stage.

Adair, Ian, *Adair's Ideas.* (1959) Supreme Magic, Bideford, UK. Stapled with tape. Light green, purple. 24 pp. 7.75 x 9.75 in. Doves, Stage.

Adair, Ian, *Adair's Ideas on Kids' Magic.* (2011) Pages 2 Stages Publishing, UK. Perfect. Colors. 182 pp. 5.75 x 8.25 in. (Information not verified by physical copy.) Children's magic.

Adair, Ian, *Adair's Magical Menu: Course 1: Entertaining Children.* (1961) Supreme Magic, Bideford, UK. Saddle-stitch. 18 pp. 5.75 x 8.75 in. Course, Children's magic.

Adair, Ian, *Adair's Magical Menu: Course 2: Mental Magic.* (1961) Supreme Magic, Bideford, UK. Saddle-stitch. White, green. 20 pp. 5.75 x 8.75 in. Course, Mentalism.

Adair, Ian, *Adair's Magical Menu: Course 3: Illusions.* (1962) Supreme Magic, Bideford, UK. Saddle-stitch. White, blue. 30 pp. 5.75 x 8.75 in. Color Sorcar section. Course, Illusions.

Adair, Ian, *Balloon Business.* (1988) Supreme Magic, Bideford, UK. Saddle-stitch. Pink. 24 pp. 8 x 10 in. (Information not verified by physical copy.) Balloons.

Adair, Ian, *Balloon-o-Dove.* (1963) Supreme Magic, Bideford, UK. Stapled with tape. Light purple. 7 pp. 7.75 x 9.75 in. Doves, Balloons.

Adair, Ian, *Birthday Magic for Kid's Shows.* (2013) Pages 2 Stages Publishing, UK. Perfect. Orange, white. 122 pp. 5.75 x 8.25 in. (Information not verified by physical copy.) Children's magic.

Adair, Ian, *Blindfold Bafflers.* (1999) Supreme Magic, Bideford, UK. 14 pp. (Information not verified by physical copy.) Blindfolds, Mentalism.

Adair, Ian, *Cabaret Dove Act.* (1962) Supreme Magic, Bideford, UK. Stapled with tape. Green. 19 pp. 7.75 x 9.75 in. Doves, Stage.

Adair, Ian, *Cabaret Dove Act.* (1962) Supreme Magic, Bideford, UK. Stapled with tape. Red. 19 pp. 7.75 x 9.75 in. Doves, Stage.

Adair, Ian, *Cedric RIchardson's Paint Book.* (2000) Mystic House Publications, Devon, UK. Stapled. Green. 21 pp. 5.75 x 8.25 in. (Information not verified by physical copy.) Doves, Stage.

Adair, Ian, *Cedric's Commercial Routines nos. 1-20.* (n.d.) Magician Adair Publications, UK. Stapled. Orange. 5.75 x 8.25 in. Series of twenty booklets. (Information not verified by physical copy.) Children's magic.

Adair, Ian, *Cedric's Tried and Tested Routines for Kids' Shows.* (c. 2012) Pages 2 Stages Publishing, UK. Perfect. Red. 5.75 x 8.25 in. (Information not verified by physical copy.) Children's magic.

Adair, Ian, *Classical Dove Secrets.* (1964) Supreme Magic, Bideford, UK. Stapled with tape. Red, white. 21 pp. 8 x 10 in. Silk-screened cover. (Information not verified by physical copy.) Doves, Apparatus, Stage.

Adair, Ian, with Geddes, John, *Comedy Magic of John Geddes, The.* (2016) Silver Sceptre Publishing, UK. Perfect. Red. 182 pp. 5.75 x 8.25 in. (Information not verified by physical copy.) Children's magic.

Adair, Ian, *Complete Guide to Card Conjuring, The.* (1980) A. S. Barnes and Co., London. Cloth. Red. 108 pp. 6.5 x 9.5 in. Dust jacket. Cards.

Adair, Ian, *Complete Guide to Conjuring, The.* (1979) A. S. Barnes and Co., New York. Cloth. Red. 160 pp. 6.5 x 9.5 in. Dust jacket. Beginner.

Adair, Ian, *Conjuring as a Craft.* (1972) A. S. Barnes and Co., South Brunswick, NJ. Cloth. Red. 160 pp. 5.5 x 8.75 in. Dust jacket. Beginner.

Adair, Ian, *"Dealing" with Magic: The Rise and Fall of the Supreme Magic Company.* (2010) Pages 2 Stages Publishing, UK. Perfect. Colors. 180 pp. 5.75 x 8.25 in. Signed by Ian Adair. History, Dealers.

Adair, Ian, *Diary of a Dove-Worker.* (1964) Supreme Magic, Bideford, UK. Stapled with tape. Red, white. 24 pp. 8 x 10 in. Silk-screened cover. (Information not verified by physical copy.) Doves, Stage.

Adair, Ian, *Dove Classics.* (1961) Supreme Magic. Stapled with tape. Red. 20 pp. 7.75 x 9.75 in. (Measurements and other information have been recorded as accurately as possible.) Doves, Stage.

Adair, Ian, *Dove Dexterity.* (1963) Supreme Magic, Bideford, UK. Saddle-stitch. White, black. 24 pp. 5 x 8 in. Doves, Stage.

Adair, Ian, *Dove Magic Encore.* (1960) Supreme Magic, Bideford, UK. Stapled with tape. Orange. 19 pp. 7.75 x 9.75 in. Doves, Stage.

Adair, Ian, *Dove Magic Finale.* (1960) Author, Kilmarnock, UK. Saddle-stitch. White. 19 pp. 5.5 x 8.75 in. (Measurements and other information have been recorded as accurately as possible.) Doves, Stage.

Adair, Ian, *Dove Magic part 1.* (1961) Supreme Magic, Bideford, UK. Stapled with tape. Pink. 21 pp. 7.75 x 9.75 in. Youthful portrait of author on cover. Doves, Stage.

Adair, Ian, *Dove Magic part 1.* (1961) Supreme Magic, Bideford, UK. Stapled with tape. Light green. 21 pp. 7.75 x 9.75 in. Doves, Stage.

Adair, Ian, *Dove Magic part 2.* (1960) Supreme Magic, Bideford, UK. Stapled with tape. Blue. 19 pp. 7.75 x 9.75 in. Doves, Stage.

Adair, Ian, *Doves from Silks.* (1961) Supreme Magic, Bideford, UK. Stapled with tape. Brown. 10 pp. 7.75 x 9.75 in. Doves, Silks, Stage.

Adair, Ian, *Doves from Silks.* (1961) Supreme Magic, Bideford, UK. Stapled with tape. Orange. 10 pp. 7.75 x 9.75 in. Doves, Silks, Stage.

Adair, Ian, *Doves in Magic.* (1961) Supreme Magic, Bideford, UK. Stapled with tape. Orange. 12 pp. 7.75 x 9.75 in. Doves, Stage.

Adair, Ian, *Edwin: Supreme Magician.* (1995) Martin Breese, London. Saddle-stitch. White. 5.75 x 8.25 in. Included in Sound of Magic's audio cassette set. Biography.

Adair, Ian, *Encyclopedia of Children's Magic, The.* (1991) Supreme Magic, Bideford, UK. Cloth. Red. 414 pp. 8.25 x 10.25 in. Dust jacket. Children's magic.

Adair, Ian, *Encyclopedia of Dove Magic vol. 1.* (1968) Supreme Magic, Bideford, UK. Cloth. Blue. 316 pp. 7.25 x 10 in. Dust jacket. Doves, Stage.

Adair, Ian, *Encyclopedia of Dove Magic vol. 2.* (1972) Supreme Magic, Bideford, UK. Cloth. Blue. 407 pp. 7.25 x 10 in. Dust jacket. Doves, Stage.

Adair, Ian, *Encyclopedia of Dove Magic vol. 3.* (1973) Supreme Magic, Bideford, UK. Cloth. Blue. 317 pp. 7.25 x 10 in. Dust jacket. Doves, Stage.

Adair, Ian, *Encyclopedia of Dove Magic vol. 4.* (1975) Supreme Magic, Bideford, UK. Cloth. Blue. 438 pp. 7.25 x 10 in. Dust jacket. Doves, Stage.

Adair, Ian, *Encyclopedia of Dove Magic vol. 5.* (1987) Supreme Magic, Bideford, UK. Cloth. Blue. 372 pp. 7.25 x 10 in. Dust jacket. Doves, Stage.

Adair, Ian, *Fertile Mind of Ian Adair: A Celebration, The.* (2000) Author, Barnstable, UK. Saddle-stitch. Yellow. 36 pp. 5.75 x 8.25 in. (Information not verified by physical copy.) Close-Up, Stage.

Adair, Ian, *Football Club Final Prediction.* (2014) Silver Sceptre Publishing, UK. Comb. White. 5.75 x 8.25 in. (Information not verified by physical copy.) Mentalism, Publicity stunts.

Adair, Ian, *Further Dove Classics.* (1962) Supreme Magic, Bideford, UK. Stapled with tape. Blue. 21 pp. 7.75 x 9.75 in. Doves, Stage.

Adair, Ian, *Further Dove Classics.* (1962) Supreme Magic, Bideford, UK. Stapled with tape. White. 21 pp. 7.75 x 9.75 in. Doves, Stage.

Adair, Ian, *Hand Puppet Magic.* (2011) Pages 2 Stages Publishing, UK. Perfect. Colors. 166 pp. 5.75 x 8.25 in. (Information not verified by physical copy.) Children's magic, Puppetry.

Adair, Ian, *Heads Off.* (1965) Supreme Magic, Bideford, UK. 7 pp. (Information not verified by physical copy. Bibliographical details are as accurate as possible.) Doves, Stage.

Adair, Ian, *Hitting the Headlines: The Perfect Headline Prediction.* (2014) Author, Barnstable, UK. Comb. Beige. (Information not verified by physical copy.) Mentalism, Newspaper, Publicity stunts.

Adair, Ian, *How to Become a Supreme Magician.* (1997) Supreme Magic, Bideford, UK. Saddle-stitch. Yellow. 88 pp. 5.75 x 8.25 in. Showmanship, Theory, Promotion, Business.

Adair, Ian, *Ian Adair Lecture-Demonstration, The.* (1968) Supreme Magic, Bideford, UK. Saddle-stitch. White, blue. 14 pp. 6.5 x 7.75 in. Actual ribbon on cover. Signed by Ian Adair. Lecture notes. Close-Up, Stage.

Adair, Ian, *Ian Adair's 21.* (1962) Supreme Magic, Bideford, UK. Stapled with tape. Yellow. 26 pp. 7.75 x 9.75 in. Doves, Stage.

Adair, Ian, *Ian Adair's Mind Blowing Mentalism.* (2023) MagicSeen, Norton, UK. Perfect. Yellow, black. 144 pp. 6 x 9 in. Mentalism.

Adair, Ian, *Kids' Effects and Routines Using Standard Props.* (2012) Pages 2 Stages Publishing, UK. Perfect. Blue. 108 pp. 5.75 x 8.25 in. (Information not verified by physical copy.) Children's magic.

Adair, Ian, *Kids' Show Routines Using Changing Bags.* (2012) Pages 2 Stages Publishing, UK. Perfect. 5.75 x 8.25 in. (Information not verified by physical copy.) Children's magic, Change bag, Apparatus.

Adair, Ian, *Kids' Show Selection.* (2012) Pages 2 Stages Publishing, UK. Perfect. Yellow, black. 152 pp. 6 x 9 in. Mentalism.

Adair, Ian, *KnowHow Book of Jokes and Tricks, The.* (1977) Supreme Magic, Bideford, UK. Stapled with tape. Blue. 21 pp. 7.75 x 9.75 in. Doves, Stage.

Adair, Ian, *Magic.* (c. 1975) Usborne Publishing, London. Saddle-stitch. Red. 4 x 6 in. (Information not verified by physical copy.) Beginner.

Adair, Ian, *Magic on the Wing.* (c. 1965) Supreme Magic, Bideford, UK. Stapled with tape. Orange. 8 x 10 in. (Information not verified by physical copy.) Doves.

Adair, Ian, with Amery, Heather, *Magic on the Wing.* (1989) Usborne Publishing, London. Saddle-stitch. Color. 32 pp. 8.5 x 11 in. Beginner.

Adair, Ian, *Magic Step-by-Step.* (1972) Arco Publications, New York. Perfect. Yellow. 155 pp. 4.25 x 7 in. (Measurements and other information have been recorded as accurately as possible.) Beginner.

Adair, Ian, *Magic Tricks: Secrets of the Master Magician.* (1995) Chartwell Books, Edison, NJ. Casebound. Color. 48 pp. 8.75 x 11.25 in. Dust jacket. Beginner.

Adair, Ian, *Magic Wand Book, The.* (2012) Pages 2 Stages Publishing, UK. Perfect. Blue. 206 pp. 5.75 x 8.25 in. (Information not verified by physical copy.) Wands, Comedy, Children's magic.

Adair, Ian, *Magic with Doves.* (c. 1958) Diamond Magic Co., Kilmarnock, UK. Stapled with tape. Beige. 8 x 10 in. (Information not verified by physical copy.) Doves, Stage.

Adair, Ian, *Magic with Doves.* (1962) Supreme Magic, Bideford, UK. Stapled with tape. White. 19 pp. 7.75 x 9.75 in. (Information not verified by physical copy.) Doves, Stage.

Adair, Ian, *Magic with Latex Budgies.* (1950) Supreme Magic, Bideford, UK. Stapled with tape. White, purple. 13 pp. 8 x 9.75 in. Silkscreened cover. Gimmicks, Birds, Canaries.

Adair, Ian, *Microphone Techniques.* (1993) Supreme Magic, Bideford, UK. Saddle-stitch. White. 5.75 x 8.25 in. (Information not verified by physical copy.) Stagecraft, Showmanship.

Adair, Ian, *More Modern Dove Classics.* (1962) Supreme Magic, Bideford, UK. Stapled with tape. Blue. 19 pp. 7.75 x 10 in. (Information not verified by physical copy.) Doves, Stage.

Adair, Ian, *More Terrific-Trix for Kid's Shows.* (2011) Pages 2 Stages Publishing, UK. Perfect. Colors. 192 pp. 5.75 x 8.25 in. (Information not verified by physical copy.) Children's magic.

Adair, Ian, *Mouse Animation: The Tom Harris Way.* (2003) Mystic House Publications, Devon, UK. Saddle-stitch. Yellow, blue. 24 pp. 5.5 x 8 in. Close-Up, Silks.

Adair, Ian, *New Doves from Silks Methods.* (1963) Supreme Magic, Bideford, UK. Stapled with tape. Light green. 12 pp. 7.75 x 9.75 in. Doves, Silks, Stage.

Adair, Ian, *Novel Notions.* (1981) Supreme Magic, Bideford, UK. Saddle-stitch. Red. 48 pp. 5.75 x 8.75 in. (Measurements and other information have been recorded as accurately as possible.) Stage.

Adair, Ian, *More Novel Notions for Kids' Shows.* (2013) Pages 2 Stages Publishing, UK. Perfect. Black. 124 pp. 5.75 x 8.25 in. (Information not verified by physical copy.) Children's magic.

Adair, Ian, *Oceans of Notions.* (1973) Supreme Magic, Bideford, UK. Cloth. Blue. 88 pp. 7.75 x 10 in. Dust jacket. Stage.

Adair, Ian, *Paddle Antics.* (1971) Supreme Magic, Bideford, UK. Comb. Red, black, white. 45 pp. 8 x 9.75 in. Paddle effects, Close-Up.

Adair, Ian, *Papercrafts.* (1975) David and Charles, London. Cloth. Black. 80 pp. 7.5 x 9.75 in. Dust jacket. Paper, Origami.

Adair, Ian, *Pot-Pourri: The Collected Magic of Ian Adair.* (1963) Supreme Magic, Bideford, UK. Stapled with tape. Green. 19 pp. 8 x 10 in. (Information not verified by physical copy.) Close-Up, Stage.

Adair, Ian, *Rainbow Dove Routines.* (1961) Supreme Magic, Bideford, UK. Stapled with tape. Green. 17 pp. 7.75 x 9.75 in. Silk-screened cover. (Information not verified by physical copy.) Doves, Stage.

Adair, Ian, *Rainbow Dove Routines.* (1961) Supreme Magic, Bideford, UK. Stapled with tape. Red. 17 pp. 7.75 x 9.75 in. Doves, Stage.

Adair, Ian, *Spotlite on Doves.* (1966) Supreme Magic, Bideford, UK. Stapled with tape. Red, white. 23 pp. 8 x 9.75 in. Doves, Stage.

Adair, Ian, *"Supreme" Lifetime in Magic, A.* (2013) Silver Sceptre Publishing, UK. Perfect. Green. 200 pp. 5.75 x 8.25 in. (Information not verified by physical copy.) Business, Dealers, Magic shops, History.

Adair, Ian, *Television Card Manipulations.* (1967) Supreme Magic, Bideford, UK. Saddle-stitch. Orange, red. 55 pp. 4.75 x 7.75 in. Cards, Television magic, Manipulation.

Adair, Ian, *Television Card Manipulations.* (1967) Supreme Magic, Bideford, UK. Cloth. Maroon. Cover text: Gold; 55 pp. 4.75 x 7.75 in. (Information not verified by physical copy.) Cards, Television magic, Manipulation.

Adair, Ian, *Television Dove Magic.* (1963) Supreme Magic, Bideford, UK. Saddle-stitch. Red. 87 pp. 5.5 x 8.5 in. Doves, Television magic, Stage.

Adair, Ian, *Television Dove Steals.* (1968) Supreme Magic, Bideford, UK. Saddle-stitch. White. 23 pp. 6 x 8.5 in. Doves, Television magic, Stage.

Adair, Ian, *Television Puppet Magic.* (1969) Supreme Magic, Bideford, UK. Cloth. Blue. 176 pp. 5.25 x 8.25 in. Dust jacket. Puppetry, Television magic.

Adair, Ian, *Terrific-Trix for Kids' Shows.* (2010) Pages 2 Stages Publishing, UK. Perfect. Colors. 204 pp. 5.75 x 8.25 in. (Information not verified by physical copy.) Children's magic.

Adair, Ian, *There's Children's Magic in the Air.* (1997) Ideas Associated, Barnstable, UK. Saddle-stitch. Orange. 28 pp. 5.75 x 8.25 in. (Information not verified by physical copy.) Children's magic.

Adair, Ian, *Thinking Tricks.* (2014) Silver Sceptre Publishing, UK. Perfect. Blue, black, white. 110 pp. 5.75 x 8.25 in. (Information not verified by physical copy.) Close-Up, Stage.

Adair, Ian, *Tricks and Stunts with the Rubber Dove.* (1964) Supreme Magic, Bideford, UK. Stapled with tape. Light green, red. 11 pp. 7.75 x 9.75 in. Doves, Stage, Comedy.

Adair, Ian, with De Courcy, Ken, *Tricks, Gags, and Notions Using Magic Slush Powder.* (1991) Supreme Magic, Bideford, UK. Saddle-stitch. White. 28 pp. 5.75 x 8.25 in. Liquids, Close-Up, Stage.

Adair, Ian, *Twin Dove Production.* (1971) Supreme Magic, Bideford, UK. Saddle-stitch. White. 11 pp. 5.75 x 8.25 in. (Information not verified by physical copy.) Doves, Stage.

Adair, Ian, *Valuable Tips for Children's Entertainers.* (2007) Mystic House Publications, UK. Stapled with tape. Blue. 76 pp. 8 x 10 in. (Information not verified by physical copy.) Children's magic, Tips.

Adair, Ian, *Watch the Birdie.* (1963) Supreme Magic, Bideford, UK. Stapled with tape. Purple. 28 pp. 8.25 x 10 in. Mimeographed inside printed cover. Doves, Stage.

Adair, Ian, *Whiteboard Bat, The.* (2014) Funtime Innovations, Calcutta. Saddle-stitch. Tan. 38 pp. 5.75 x 8.25 in. Paddle effects, Close-Up.

Adair, Ian, *You Don't Have to Be Crazy to Be a Magic Dealer – But It Helps.* (2014) Silver Sceptre Publishing, UK. Perfect. Red. 76 pp. 5.75 x 8.25 in. (Information not verified by physical copy.) Business, Dealers, Magic shops, History.

Adams, Bertram, *Adamathica.* (1921) Author, Boston, MA. Black. 15 pp. 4.25 x 2.75 in. (Information not verified by physical copy.) Cards.

Adams, Graham, *Graham Adams Cut and Restored Rope, The.* (1928) Author, UK. Stapled. White. 5 pp. 8.5 x 11 in. (Information not verified by physical copy.) Rope, Cut and Restored Rope.

Adams, Graham, *Mr. S. W. Erdnase: His Book.* (1931) Author, UK. Stapled. White. 103 pp. 8.25 x 11.75 in. Only six copies published. (Information not verified by physical copy.) Cards, Erdnase, History.

Adams, Howard (See also Wagner, Bob), *666 Mentalism.* (2007) Leaping Lizards Magic, Orlando, FL. Perfect. Black, red. 132 pp. 8.5 x 11 in. (Information not verified by physical copy.) Mentalism.

Adams, Howard, *Matchalot Mentalism.* (2009) Leaping Lizards Magic, Orlando, FL. Casebound. Black, purple. 378 pp. 8.5 x 11 in. (Information not verified by physical copy.) Mentalism.

Adams, Howard, *Mathcasts Aspelonu.* (2003) H & R Magic Books, Humble, TX. Casebound. White, black, red. 167 pp. 8.5 x 11 in. Mathematical, Mentalism.

Adams, Howard, *Mindespa.* (2008) Leaping Lizards Magic, Orlando, FL. Perfect. Gray. 160 pp. 8.5 x 11 in. (Information not verified by physical copy.) Reprint of series of twelve booklets. Mentalism.

Adams, Howard, *Mindespa chap. 1: Dungeon of Deception.* (1984) Author, Torrance, CA. Stapled. 10 pp. 8.5 x 11 in. (Information not verified by physical copy.) Mentalism.

Adams, Howard, *Mindespa chap. 2: Cavern of Cremation.* (1984) Author, Torrance, CA. Stapled. Orange. 9 pp. 8.5 x 11 in. With handwritten correction note by Adams attached inside back cover. Signed by Howard Adams. #65 of 103. Mentalism.

Adams, Howard, *Mindespa chap. 3: Computer of Catastrophe.* (n.d.) Author, Torrance, CA. Stapled. 8.5 x 11 in. (Information not verified by physical copy. Bibliographical details are as accurate as possible.) Mentalism.

Adams, Howard, *Mindespa chap. 4: Tunnel of Terror.* (n.d.) Author, Torrance, CA. Stapled. 8.5 x 11 in. (Information not verified by physical copy. Bibliographical details are as accurate as possible.) Mentalism.

Adams, Howard, *Mindespa chap. 5: Doorway to Doomsday.* (n.d.) Author, Torrance, CA. Stapled. 8.5 x 11 in. (Information not verified by physical copy. Bibliographical details are as accurate as possible.) Mentalism.

Adams, Howard, *Mindespa chap. 6: Portal of Peril.* (1992) Author, Torrance, CA. Stapled. 8.5 x 11 in. (Information not verified by physical copy. Bibliographical details are as accurate as possible.) Mentalism.

Adams, Howard, *Mindespa chap. 7: Hallway of Horror.* (n.d.) Author, Torrance, CA. Stapled. 8.5 x 11 in. (Information not verified by physical copy. Bibliographical details are as accurate as possible.) Mentalism.

Adams, Howard, *Mindespa chap. 8: Entrance to Eternity.* (1994) Author, Torrance, CA. Stapled. 8.5 x 11 in. (Information not verified by physical copy. Bibliographical details are as accurate as possible.) Mentalism.

Adams, Howard, *Mindespa chap. 9: Exit to Evil.* (n.d.) Author, Torrance, CA. Stapled. 8.5 x 11 in. (Information not verified by physical copy. Bibliographical details are as accurate as possible.) Mentalism.

Adams, Howard, *Mindespa chap. 10: Down Under Downpour.* (1999) Author, Laguna Niguel, CA. Stapled. 16 pp. 8.5 x 11 in. (Information not verified by physical copy.) Mentalism.

Adams, Howard, *Mindespa chap. 11: Down Under Deluge.* (1999) Author, Laguna Niguel, CA. Stapled. Blue. 14 pp. 8.5 x 11 in. Signed by Howard Adams. #38 of 115. Mentalism.

Adams, Howard, *Mindespa chap. 12: Down Under Dealights.* (1999) Author, Laguna Niguel, CA. Stapled. 12 pp. 8.5 x 11 in. (Information not verified by physical copy.) Mentalism.

Adams, Howard, *O.I.C.U.F.E.S.P.* (2008) Leaping Lizards Magic, Orlando, FL. Perfect. Black. 200 pp. 8.5 x 11 in. (Information not verified by physical copy.) Reprint of series of ten booklets. Cards, Mentalism, E.S.P. cards.

Adams, Howard, *O.I.C.U.F.E.S.P. vol. 1: Ten Brand New E.S.P. Card Miracles.* (1979) Author, Torrance, CA. Stapled. Yellow. 20 pp. 8.5 x 11 in. Cards, Mentalism, E.S.P. cards.

Adams, Howard, *O.I.C.U.F.E.S.P. vol. 2: Ten More Brand New E.S.P. Card Miracles.* (1979) Author, Torrance, CA. Stapled. Green. 18 pp. 8.5 x 11 in. Cards, Mentalism, E.S.P. cards.

Adams, Howard, *O.I.C.U.F.E.S.P. vol. 3: Further Brand New E.S.P. Card Miracles.* (1980) Author, Torrance, CA. Stapled. Orange. 18 pp. 8.5 x 11 in. Cards, Mentalism, E.S.P. cards.

Adams, Howard, *O.I.C.U.F.E.S.P. vol. 4: E.S.P. Card and Mental Miracles Return.* (1980) Author, Torrance, CA. Stapled. Pink. 18 pp. 8.5 x 11 in. Cards, Mentalism, E.S.P. cards.

Adams, Howard, *O.I.C.U.F.E.S.P. vol. 5: Son of E.S.P. Card and Mental Miracles, The.* (1980) Author, Torrance, CA. Stapled. Blue. 18 pp. 8.5 x 11 in. Cards, Mentalism, E.S.P. cards.

Adams, Howard, *O.I.C.U.F.E.S.P. vol. 6: Ghost of E.S.P. Card and Mental Miracles, The.* (1980) Author, Torrance, CA. Stapled. Beige. 18 pp. 8.5 x 11 in. Cards, Mentalism, E.S.P. cards.

Adams, Howard, *O.I.C.U.F.E.S.P. vol. 7: Matheight Miracles.* (1981) Author, Torrance, CA. Stapled. Tan. 18 pp. 8.5 x 11 in. Cards, Mentalism, Mathematical.

Adams, Howard, *O.I.C.U.F.E.S.P. vol. 8: 21 Cidentaquin Variations.* (1980) Author, Torrance, CA. Stapled. Orange. 18 pp. 8.5 x 11 in. Cards, Mentalism, E.S.P. cards.

Adams, Howard, *O.I.C.U.F.E.S.P. vol. 9: With Packets and Rows.* (1982) Author, Torrance, CA. Stapled. Green. 18 pp. 8.5 x 11 in. Cards, Mentalism, E.S.P. cards.

Adams, Howard, *O.I.C.U.F.E.S.P. vol. 10: Tulefta: The Ramasee Prophesy.* (1982) Author, Torrance, CA. Stapled. Orange. 13 pp. 8.5 x 11 in. Cards, Mentalism.

Adams, M. P., *Rich Uncle from Fiji, The.* (1911) Author, Melbourne. Stapled. Brown. 110 pp. (Information not verified by physical copy.) Gambling, Cheating, Three-Card Monte.

Adams, M. P., *Rich Uncle from Fiji, The.* (c. 1978) Gamblers Book Club, Las Vegas. Saddle-stitch. Brown. 64 pp. 5.25 x 8.25 in. Gambling, Cheating, Three-Card Monte.

Adams, Martin, *Gate vol. 1, The.* (2011) Author. Saddle-stitch. Black. 36 pp. 5.75 x 8.25 in. (Information not verified by physical copy. Bibliographical details are as accurate as possible.) Mentalism.

Adams, Martin, *Gate vol. 2, The.* (2011) Author. Saddle-stitch. Black. 20 pp. 5.75 x 8.25 in. (Information not verified by physical copy. Bibliographical details are as accurate as possible.) Mentalism.

Adams, Martin, *Nexus.* (2009) Author. Saddle-stitch. Black. 28 pp. (Information not verified by physical copy. Bibliographical details are as accurate as possible.) Mentalism.

Adams, Morley, *Boy's Own Book of Indoor Games and Recreations, The.* (1912) Religious Tract Society, London. Cloth. Red. 439 pp. 6.25 x 9.25 in. Beginner, Stunts, Games.

Adams, Morley, *Boy's Own Book of Indoor Games and Recreations, The.* (n.d.) Boys' Own Paper, London. Cloth. Red. 439 pp. 6.25 x 9 in. Beginner, Stunts, Games.

Adams, Morley, *Tricks That Anyone Can Do.* (1911) L. Upcott Gill, London. Sewn covers. Orange. 96 pp. 5 x 7.25 in. Cards, Stunts, Beginner.

Adams, Peter, *Wizard's Magic Book, The.* (1930) Whitman, Racine, WI. Perfect. Orange. 158 pp. 6 x 7.75 in. (Measurements and other information have been recorded as accurately as possible.) Beginner.

Adams, Ralph, *Original Illusions of Ralph Adams, The.* (1994) Author, Santa Maria, CA. Perfect. Gold. 93 pp. 8.5 x 11 in. Illusions, Biography.

Adams, Rory, *Only Ideas.* (2018) Author, UK. Perfect. Blue. 162 pp. (Information not verified by physical copy.) Creativity, Routining.

Adams, Si, *Snappy Rope Patter.* (c. 1972) Author, Milwaukee, WI. Saddle-stitch. 25 pp. 5.5 x 8.5 in. (Measurements and other information have been recorded as accurately as possible.) Patter, Rope.

Adept, An, *Grand Exposé of the Science of Gambling, A.* (1860) Frederic A. Brady, New York. Cloth. Green. 194 pp. 4.5 x 5.5 in. In Byron Walker collection. Gambling, History, Cards, Cheating.

Adept, An, *Grand Exposé of the Science of Gambling, A.* (2010) Magicana, Toronto. Cloth. Brown. 167 pp. 5 x 5.5 in. New edition of 1860 original. Gambling, History, Cards, Cheating.

Adolphus, *Coincidentalism.* (1993) Author, Bel Air, MD. Saddle-stitch. Light green. 17 pp. 5.5 x 8.5 in. Mentalism.

Adrion, Alexander (See also Berlinski, Allen), *Kunst zu Zaubern, Die.* (1978) DuMont, Köln, Germany. Cloth. Black. 284 pp. 6.75 x 9.25 in. History. German.

Adrion, Alexander, *Zauberkabinett.* (1980) DuMont, Köln, Germany. Cloth. Blue. 157 pp. 6.75 x 9.25 in. History. German.

Ady, Thomas, *Candle in the Dark, A.* (1655) Robert Ibbitson, Smithfield, UK. 172 pp. 5 x 7.25 in. (Information not verified by physical copy.) Toole Stott no. 6. Early magic.

Ady, Thomas, *Candle in the Dark, A.* (1656) Robert Ibbitson, Smithfield, UK. 172 pp. 5.5 x 7.25 in. (Information not verified by physical copy.) Toole Stott no. 7. Early magic.

Ady, Thomas, *Candle in the Dark, A.* (1994) Stevens Magic, Wichita, KS. Cloth and leather. Black. 172 pp. 5.5 x 7.75 in. Reprint. #64 of 300. History, Early magic.

Agnew the Magician, *17 Simple But Mystifying Tricks.* (1937) Signal Oil Co., New York. Saddle-stitch. Blue. 16 pp. 3.5 x 5.5 in. Sequel to Carl E. Zamloch's Signal Oil booklet. Beginner, Premium, Stunts.

Agosta-Meynier (Auguste Meynier), *Prestidigitateur, Le.* (1919) Author, Paris. Leather. Brown. 588 pp. 6.5 x 9.75 in. Collected issues nos 1-72. Signed by Agosta-Meynier. Magazine. French.

Ainsley, Arthur, *Water Wizardry.* (1922) C. Arthur Pearson Ltd., London. Boards. Yellow. 124 pp. 5 x 7.25 in. Ad for Houdini's "Magical Rope Ties and Escapes." Liquids, Stage.

Åkerlind-Casino, Jonnie, *Svensk Bibliografi för Trollkarlar.* (1963) Svensk Magisk Cirkels, Stockholm. Perfect. Yellow, pink. 233 pp. 6.75 x 9.25 in. Signed by Jonnie Akerlind-Casino. #233. Bibliography. Swedish.

Akimoto, Tadashi, *Visible Phenomena.* (n.d.) Topit Company, Tokyo. Saddle-stitch. Pink. 26 pp. 5.75 x 8.25 in. Cards, Coins, Matrix.

Akonak, Amark, *ABC of Magic Tricks, The.* (2001) Russia. Casebound. Black. 110 pp. 5.25 x 8.25 in. Title is an approximated translation. (Measurements and other information have been recorded as accurately as possible.) Beginner. Russian.

Al the Only (Alfred Ulman, Jr.), with Karr, Todd (ed.), *Business of Restaurant Magic, The.* First edition. (September 1984) Author, Hamtramck, MI. Stapled. Beige, red. 58 pp. 8.5 x 11 in. With Al the Only label on text page. Inscribed to editor Todd Karr. Signed by Al the Only. Business, Restaurant magic.

Al the Only, with Karr, Todd (ed.), *Business of Restaurant Magic, The.* Revised edition. (July 1985) Author, Hamtramck, MI. Comb. Beige, red. 58 pp. 8.5 x 11 in. With Al the Only label on text page and table tent in back cover. Business, Restaurant magic.

Al the Only, with Karr, Todd (ed.), *Business of Restaurant Magic, The.* Third edition. (July 1987) Author, Hamtramck, MI. Comb. White, black. 58 pp. 8.5 x 11 in. Signed by Al the Only. Business, Restaurant magic.

Al the Only, *It's Not Always Wine and Roses, But Sometimes You Get a Free Lunch: Life on a School Show Tour.* (1983) Author, Hamtramck, MI. Stapled. Gray, red. 30 pp. 8.5 x 11 in. Lecture notes. Business.

Al the Only, *Magic Graveyard, The.* (2014) Magical Presentations, Inc., Lahaina, HI. Perfect. Gray. 229 pp. 6 x 9 in. Signed by Al the Only. History, Biography.

Al the Only, *Magic Graveyard, The.* (2014) Magical Presentations, Inc., Lahaina, HI. Perfect. Blue. 229 pp. 6 x 9 in. Signed by Al the Only. History, Biography.

Al the Only, *Magic Graveyard, The.* (2015) Magical Presentations, Inc., Lahaina, HI. Perfect. Blue. 251 pp. 6 x 9 in. Signed by Al the Only. History, Biography.

Al the Only, *Magic Graveyard, The.* (2017) Magical Presentations, Inc., Lahaina, HI. Perfect. Blue, gold. 292 pp. 6 x 9 in. Signed by Al the Only. History, Biography.

Al the Only, *Magic Graveyard, The.* (2019) Magical Presentations, Inc., Lahaina, HI. Perfect. Blue, gold. 399 pp. 6 x 9 in. Proof copy. Signed by Al the Only. History.

Aladdin, *Aladdin's Mental Miracle.* (1957) Author, Newton Centre, MA. Stapled. White. 5 pp. 8.5 x 11 in. Mimeographed. (Information not verified by physical copy.) Mentalism, Book tests.

Aladdin the Magician, *World's Greatest Magic Tricks.* (1976) Paragon Products, Inc., Pompano Beach, FL. Saddle-stitch. White, red. orange. 15 pp. 8.5 x 5.5 in. Bound oblong. Beginner.

Alan, David, *Hiding Your Bullets.* (2021) David Alan Productions. Saddle-stitch. White. 10 pp. 5.5 x 8.5 in. Fold-out photo page. Rope, Magnets, Building.

Alan, Don, *Close-Up Time.* First printing. (1951) Ireland Magic Co., Chicago. Saddle-stitch. Yellow. 20 pp. 5.5 x 8.5 in. Close-Up.

Alan, Don, *Close-Up Time.* Third printing. (1970) Magic Inc., Chicago. Saddle-stitch. Yellow. 20 pp. 5.5 x 8.5 in. Close-Up.

Alan, Don, *Close-Up Time.* Sixth printing. (1980) Magic Inc., Chicago. Saddle-stitch. Yellow. 20 pp. 5.5 x 8.5 in. Signed by Don Alan. Close-Up.

Alan, Don, *Don Alan Lecture.* (c. 1960) Top Twenty School of Magic, Chicago. Stapled. White. 2 pp. 8.5 x 11 in. (Information not verified by physical copy.) Lecture notes.

Alan, Don, *Don Alan's Bowl Routine.* (1953) Martin's Magic Shop, Peoria, IL. Single page. White. 2 pp. 8.5 x 13 in. Benson Bowl, Close-Up, Sponge balls.

Alan, Don, *Don Alan's Professional Presentation of the Chop Cup.* (c. 1970) Magic Inc., Chicago. Saddle-stitch. White, blue. 7 pp. 5.5 x 8.25 in. All text printed in blue. Chop Cup, Close-Up.

Alan, Don, *Great Put-On, The.* (c. 1975) Logan Pritchett, Little Rock, AR. Saddle-stitch. Black. 5.5 x 8.5 in. With jumbo cards. Version of McCombical Prediction.(Information not verified by physical copy.) Cards, Jumbo cards.

Alan, Don, with Racherbaumer, Jon, *In a Class by Himself: The Legacy of Don Alan.* (2000) L & L Publishing, Tahoma, CA. Cloth. Maroon. 269 pp. 8.5 x 11 in. Dust jacket. Close-Up, Biography.

Alan, Don, with Fields, Eddie, *Invisible Deck, The.* (n.d.) Haines House of Cards, Norwood, OH. Single page. White. 5.5 x 8.5 in. Cards, Invisible Deck, Gimmicked decks.

Alan, Don, *Just Good Fun.* (c. 2000) Author, Chicago. Saddle-stitch. Blue. 16 pp. 8.5 x 11 in. (Measurements and other information have been recorded as accurately as possible.) Lecture notes. Close-Up.

Alan, Don, *Pretty Sneaky.* First edition. (1956) Ireland Magic Co., Chicago. Saddle-stitch. Yellow, green. 48 pp. 5.25 x 8.25 in. Close-Up.

Alan, Don, *Pretty Sneaky.* Second edition. (1960) Ireland Magic Co., Chicago. Saddle-stitch. Yellow, red, pink. 48 pp. 5.5 x 8.5 in. Close-Up.

Alan, Don, *Pretty Sneaky.* Sixth printing. (1977) Magic Inc., Chicago. Saddle-stitch. Yellow. 48 pp. 5.5 x 8.5 in. Close-Up.

Alan, Don, *Professional Presentation of the Don Alan Chop Cup: Don Alan's Original Chop Cup Routine, The.* (c. 1974) Rings 'n' Things, Jennings, MO. Saddle-stitch. White. 12 pp. 5.5 x 8.5 in. Chop Cup, Close-Up, Balls.

Alan, Don, *Rubber Circus, The.* (1958) Ireland Magic Co., Chicago. Saddle-stitch. Green. 16 pp. 5.5 x 8.5 in. Jay Marshall essay "Bits of Balloons" with history. Balloons, History.

Alan, James, *Seventeen Secrets from the Sid Lorraine Hat and Rabbit Club.* (2012) Sid Lorraine Hat and Rabbit Club, Toronto. Perfect. Green. 56 pp. (Information not verified by physical copy.) Close-Up, Stage.

Alan, James, *Seventeen Secrets from the Sid Lorraine Hat and Rabbit Club vol. 2.* (2013) Sid Lorraine Hat and Rabbit Club, Toronto. Perfect. 56 pp. (Information not verified by physical copy.) Close-Up, Stage.

Alan, Wayne, *Patented Illusions: The World's Best-Kept Secrets vol. 1.* (1980) Author, Mt. Rainier, MD. Comb. 105 pp. (Information not verified by physical copy.) History, Patents, Illusions.

Albenice, *Reel Magic.* (1941) Nat Louis, New York. Cloth. Blue. 56 pp. 5.25 x 8.25 in. (Measurements and other information have been recorded as accurately as possible.) Reels, Gimmicks, Silks.

Albenice, *Reel Magic.* (1941) Nat Louis, New York. Cloth. Red. Cover text: Gold; 56 pp. 5.25 x 8.25 in. Reels, Gimmicks, Silks.

Albenice, *Reel Magic.* (1950) Louis Tannen, New York. Perfect. White, blue. 88 pp. 5.5 x 8.5 in. Later edition. Reels, Gimmicks, Silks.

Alber (Jean-Jacques Edouard Graves), *De l'Illusion: Son Mécanisme Psycho-Social.* (1909) Librairie Bloud, Paris. Perfect. Tan. 118 pp. 4.75 x 7.5 in. Theory, Psychological, Sociology. French.

Alber, *Grands Trucs de la Prestidigitation Décrits et Expliqués, Les.* (1904) E. Mazo, Paris. 288 pp. (Information not verified by physical copy.) Beginner. French.

Alber, *Manuel du Prestidigitateur.* (1927) Albin Michel, Paris. Perfect. Light green. 179 pp. 4.75 x 7.5 in. Beginner. French.

Alber, *Narrations du Prestidigitateur, Les.* (1895) E. Mazo, Paris. 296 pp. (Information not verified by physical copy.) Humor, Shadowgraphy. French.

Alber, *Petits Secrets Amusants, Les.* (1921) Hachette, Paris. Cloth. Maroon. Cover text: Gold; 183 pp. 5.75 x 9 in. Beginner. French.

Alber, *Prestidigitation à la Portée de Tout le Monde, La.* (1899) E. Mazo, Paris. 32 pp. (Information not verified by physical copy.) Beginner. French.

Alber, *Prestidigitation Moderne, La.* (1927) Albin Michel, Paris. Perfect. Gray. 263 pp. 4.75 x 7.25 in. Beginner, Mentalism. French.

Alber, *Questions Amusantes.* (1932) Alexis Redier, Paris. 110 pp. (Information not verified by physical copy.) Humor. French.

Alber, *Théâtres d'Ombres Chinoises, Les.* (1896) E. Mazo, Paris. 139 pp. (Information not verified by physical copy.) Shadowgraphy. French.

Alber, *Trente Ans d'un Art Mystérieux.* (1924) A. Clerc, St. Amand, France. Perfect. Tan. 208 pp. 4.5 x 7.25 in. Biography. French.

Alber, *Une–Deux–Disparaissez.* (1930) Alexis Redier, Paris. 188 pp. (Information not verified by physical copy.) Beginner. French.

Albers, Alfred, *Complete Guide to Teaching Magic, The.* Second edition. (2002) Author, Virginia Beach, VA. Clip. White. 44 pp. 8.5 x 11 in. First edition was published 1997. Educational.

Alberstat, Paul, *Can You Keep a Secret?* (2002) AB Stage Craft, Canada. Comb. White. 87 pp. 8.5 x 11 in. Mentalism, Cards, Close-Up.

Alberti, Giuseppe Antonio, *Giuochi Numerici Fatti Arcani Palesati, I.* (1745) Venice, Italy. 154 pp. (Information not verified by physical copy.) Early magic, Mathematical magic, Cups and Balls. Italian.

Alberti, Giuseppe Antonio, *Giuochi Numerici Fatti Arcani Palesati, I.* (1747) Borghi, Bologna, Italy. 313 pp. 5 x 7.25 in. In Copperfield collection. Early magic, Mathematical magic, Cups and Balls. Italian.

Alberti, Giuseppe Antonio, *Giuochi Numerici Fatti Arcani Palesati, I.* (1749) Volpe, Bologna, Italy. 72 pp. 5 x 7.25 in. In Copperfield collection. Early magic, Mathematical magic, Cups and Balls. Italian.

Alberti, Giuseppe Antonio, *Giuochi Numerici Fatti Arcani Palesati, I.* (1788) Venice, Italy. (Information not verified by physical copy.) Early magic, Mathematical magic, Cups and Balls. Italian.

Alberti, Giuseppe Antonio, *Giuochi Numerici Fatti Arcani Palesati, I.* (1795) Giuseppe Orlandelli, Venice, Italy. Cloth. Brown. 154 pp. 5.25 x 8 in. Early magic, Mathematical magic, Cups and Balls. Italian.

Alberti, Giuseppe Antonio, *Giuochi Numerici Fatti Arcani Palesati, I.* (1814) Presso Michele Morelli, Naples, Italy. (Information not verified by physical copy.) Early magic, Mathematical magic, Cups and Balls. Italian.

Alberti, Giuseppe Antonio, *Giuochi Numerici Fatti Arcani Palesati, I.* (1815) Molinari, Venice, Italy. (Information not verified by physical copy.) Early magic, Mathematical magic, Cups and Balls. Italian.

Albertus, *Entertaining: Conjuring, Hypnotism, Muscle Reading, Mind Reading.* (1922) Gardner, Vernon Publishing Co., Pentre. Perfect. Red. 118 pp. 4.75 x 7 in. Stage, Cards, Muscle reading, Hypnotism.

Albo, Robert J., with Lewis, Eric C., *Classic Magic with Apparatus vol. 1: The Oriental Magic of the Bambergs.* (1973) San Francisco Book Co., Piedmont, CA. Cloth. Red. 228 pp. 9.25 x 12.25 in. With correction sheet. Numbered edition. Unnumbered copy. Stage, History.

Albo, Robert J., with Burger, Marvin; Page, Patrick, *Classic Magic with Apparatus vol. 2.* (1976) Author, Piedmont, CA. Cloth. Red. 208 pp. 9.25 x 12.25 in. With correction sheet. Numbered edition. Unnumbered copy. Stage, History.

Albo, Robert J., *Classic Magic with Apparatus vol. 3: More Classic Magic with Apparatus.* (1977) Author, Piedmont, CA. Cloth. Red. 265 pp. 9.25 x 12.25 in. Numbered edition. Unnumbered copy. Stage, History, Posters.

Albo, Robert J., *Classic Magic with Apparatus vol. 4: Further Classic Magic with Apparatus.* (1979) Author, Piedmont, CA. Cloth. Red. 229 pp. 9.25 x 12.25 in. Stage, History, Posters.

Albo, Robert J., *Classic Magic with Apparatus vol. 5: Still Further Classic Magic with Apparatus.* (1985) Author, Piedmont, CA. Cloth. Red. 423 pp. 9.25 x 12.25 in. Stage, History, Apparatus.

Albo, Robert J., *Classic Magic with Apparatus vol. 6: Final Classic Magic with Apparatus.* (1986) Author, Piedmont, CA. Cloth. Red. 416 pp. 9.25 x 12.25 in. Stage, History, Apparatus.

Albo, Robert J., *Classic Magic with Apparatus vol. 7: Classic Magic Index.* (1986) Author, Piedmont, CA. Cloth. Red. 267 pp. 9.25 x 12.25 in. Index, History, Apparatus.

Albo, Robert J., *Classic Magic with Apparatus vol. 8: Classic Magic Supplement.* (1986) Author, Piedmont, CA. Binder. Red. Multiple sections. 9.25 x 12.25 in. History, Apparatus.

Albo, Robert J., *Classic Magic with Apparatus vol. 8: Classic Magic Supplement: Floyd G. Thayer.* (1986) Author, Piedmont, CA. Loose pages. White. 12 pp. 8.5 x 11 in. Supplement to "Classic Magic vol. 8." Collecting, History, Apparatus.

Albo, Robert J., *Classic Magic with Apparatus vol. 8: Classic Magic Supplement: "Forcing" Books and Book Tests.* (1986) Author, Piedmont, CA. Loose pages. Green. 16 pp. 8.5 x 11 in. Collecting, History, Forcing, Book tests.

Albo, Robert J., *Classic Magic with Apparatus vol. 8: Classic Magic Supplement: The Okito Timeline.* (1986) Author, Piedmont, CA. Loose pages. White. 16 pp. 8.5 x 11 in. Supplement to book. Collecting, History, Apparatus.

Albo, Robert J., *Classic Magic with Apparatus vol. 8: Classic Magic Supplement no. 2.* (1986) Author, Piedmont, CA. 167 pp. (Measurements and other information have been recorded as accurately as possible.) History, Apparatus.

Albo, Robert J., *Classic Magic with Apparatus vol. 8: Magic.* (1986) Author, Piedmont, CA. 20 pp. (Measurements and other information have been recorded as accurately as possible.) Museum guide, Apparatus, History.

Albo, Robert J., *Classic Magic with Apparatus vol. 8: Magic Collecting.* (1986) Author, Piedmont, CA. Saddle-stitch. Blue. 16 pp. 8.5 x 11 in. With exhibit brochure, article, and mirror. Collecting, History.

Albo, Robert J., *Classic Magic with Apparatus vol. 8: Magic Supplement.* (1986) Author, Piedmont, CA. 108 pp. (Measurements and other information have been recorded as accurately as possible.) History, Apparatus.

Albo, Robert J., *Classic Magic with Apparatus vol. 8: The Magic Apparatus Collection of Robert J. Albo, M.D.* (1986) Author, Piedmont, CA. 10 pp. Museum guide, Apparatus, History.

Albo, Robert J., *Classic Magic with Apparatus vol. 8: The Magic of Okito.* (1986) Author, Piedmont, CA. Saddle-stitch. Green. 8 pp. 8.5 x 11 in. Collecting, History, Biography.

Albo, Robert J., *Classic Magic with Apparatus vol. 8: Zauber Klingl.* (1986) Author, Piedmont, CA. Saddle-stitch. Purple. 12 pp. 8.5 x 11 in. With flyer. Collecting, Apparatus, History.

Albo, Robert J., *Classic Magic with Apparatus vol. 9: Additional Classic Magic with Apparatus.* (1998) Author, Piedmont, CA. Cloth. Red. 260 pp. 9.25 x 12.25 in. With errata sheet and supplement. Limited to 1000 copies. Unnumbered copy. Stage, History, Posters.

Albo, Robert J., *Classic Magic with Apparatus vol. 10: History and Mystery of Magic.* (2001) Author, Piedmont, CA. Cloth. Red. 444 pp. History, Apparatus.

Albo, Robert J., *Classic Magic with Apparatus vol. 11: Laboratories of Legerdermain.* (2005) Author, Piedmont, CA. Cloth. Red. 486 pp. History, Apparatus.

Albo, Robert J., *Magic of Germany, The.* (n.d.) Author, Piedmont, CA. Saddle-stitch. Blue. 16 pp. 8.5 x 11 in. Collecting, History.

Albo, Robert J., *Thoughts and Reminiscences on the History and Mystery of Magic.* (2004) Author, Piedmont, CA. Perfect. Red. 70 pp. 8.5 x 11 in. Signed by Robert J. Albo. History, Collecting, Apparatus.

Albo, Robert J., *Ultimate Okito, The.* (2007) Author, Piedmont, CA. Cloth. Green. 162 pp. 9.25 x 12.25 in. Slipcase. Includes folder with eight DVDs. Limited to 400 sets. Stage, History.

Albo, Robert J., *Ultimate Okito Addendum, The.* (2008) Author, Piedmont, CA. Cloth. Green. 118 pp. 9.25 x 12.25 in. Limited to 400 copies. Stage, History.

Albo, Robert J., *Ultimate Okito Encore, The.* (2012) Marge Albo, Piedmont, CA. Cloth. Green. 54 pp. 9.25 x 12.25 in. Slipcase. With printed extras. Limited to 320 copies. Stage, History.

Albo, Robert J., with Schwartz, Philip M., *Ultimate Thayer, The.* (2010) Authors, Orlando, FL. Cloth. Black. Multiple sections. 9.25 x 12.25 in. Slipcase. Vol. 1, 242 pp.; vol. 2, 226 pp. Includes ten DVDs. Limited to 400 sets. Stage, History, Manufacturers.

Alborough, John, *Mainly Manipulative Magic.* (1978) Supreme Magic, Bideford, UK. Cloth. Red. 92 pp. 7.5 x 10 in. Dust jacket. Balls, Silks, Manipulation.

Albrecht, Don, *Magic Cartoons of Albrecht, The.* (1988) Jeff Busby Magic, Oakland, CA. Comb. White, yellow, blue. 50 pp. 11 x 8.5 in. Bound oblong. Art, Cartoons.

Albright, Howard P., *Advanced Card Magic.* (1948) Abbott Magic Co., Colon, MI. Stapled with tape. White. 19 pp. 8.5 x 11 in. Mimeographed. Signed by Leo Behnke. Cards.

Albright, Howard P., *Advanced Card Magic.* (1948) Abbott Magic Co., Colon, MI. Stapled. Yellow. 19 pp. 5.5 x 8.5 in. Mimeographed. 8.5 x 11 in. pages folded inside cover. Cards.

Albright, Howard P., *Advanced Card Magic.* (1948) Gen Publications, London. Saddle-stitch. Blue. 24 pp. 5.5 x 8.5 in. Cards.

Albright, Howard P., *Advanced Card Magic.* (1980) Supreme Magic, Bideford, UK. Saddle-stitch. White. Cover text: Purple; 24 pp. 5.25 x 8.25 in. Cards.

Albright, Howard P., *Blankety-Blank Routine, The.* (1936) Author, Albany, NY. Stapled with paper cover. Orange. 5 pp. 6 x 9 in. Mimeographed. Includes envelope with blank-back card. Cards.

Albright, Howard P., *Blankety-Blank Routine with a Borrowed Deck.* (1936) Abbott Magic Co., Colon, MI. Stapled with paper cover. Yellow. 4 pp. 5.5 x 8.25 in. Mimeographed. Cards.

Albright, Howard P., *Cards-o-Destiny.* (1936) Unique Magic Studios, Albany, NY. Stapled with paper cover. 3 pp. Mimeographed. (Information not verified by physical copy. Bibliographical details are as accurate as possible.) Cards, Fortune-telling.

Albright, Howard P., *Comic Combination for Children's Shows.* (c. 1936) Unique Magic Studios, Albany, NY. Stapled with paper cover. Orange. 3 pp. 8.5 x 11 in. Mimeographed. Cards, Paper, Comedy, Children's magic.

Albright, Howard P., *Duo-Mentality.* (1935) Unique Magic Studios, Albany, NY. Stapled with paper cover. 6 pp. 6 x 9 in. Mimeographed. (Information not verified by physical copy. Bibliographical details are as accurate as possible.) Cards.

Albright, Howard P., *Eagle Eyes.* (1938) Unique Magic Studios, Albany, NY. 8.5 x 11 in. Mimeographed. (Information not verified by physical copy.) Bills, Mentalism.

Albright, Howard P., *Educated Cards, The.* Advanced Card Magic no. 8. (1937) Unique Magic Studios, Albany, NY. Stapled. White. 2 pp. 8.5 x 11 in. Mimeographed. With one-page "Instantaneous Method for Determining the Number of Letters Required to Spell Any Card." (Information not verified by physical copy.) Cards, Spelling effects.

Albright, Howard P., *Five-Star Packet.* (1948) Albright, Howard P., Albany, NY. Stapled. White. 7 pp. 8.5 x 11 in. Mimeographed. Folded inside printed cover. Stage, Needle Swallowing.

Albright, Howard P., *Forbidden Wisdom.* (1948) Abbott Magic Co., Colon, MI. Stapled with paper cover. Olive. 20 pp. 8.5 x 11 in. Mimeographed. Folded inside printed cover. Cards, Fortune-telling.

Albright, Howard P., *Forbidden Wisdom.* (n.d.) Supreme Magic, Bideford, UK. 24 pp. (Information not verified by physical copy.) Cards, Fortune-telling.

Albright, Howard P., *Forbidden Wisdom.* (c. 1960) Unique Magic Studios, Elsmere, NY. Stapled with paper cover. Beige. 13 pp. 5.75 x 8.5 in. Mimeographed. Cards, Fortune-telling.

Albright, Howard P., *Gileegaloo Bird, The.* (1935) Unique Magic Studios, Albany, NY. Stapled with paper cover. 6 pp. Mimeographed. (Information not verified by physical copy. Bibliographical details are as accurate as possible.) Cards.

Albright, Howard P., *Goofy Card, The.* Advanced Card Magic no. 1. (1937) Unique Magic Studios, Albany, NY. Stapled. White. 2 pp. 8.5 x 11 in. Mimeographed. With one-page "Useful Card Sleights." (Information not verified by physical copy.) Cards.

Albright, Howard P., *Humdinger, The.* (1938) Unique Magic Studios, Albany, NY. Stapled. White. 3 pp. 8.5 x 11 in. Mimeographed. (Information not verified by physical copy. Bibliographical details are as accurate as possible.) Cards.

Albright, Howard P., *Intuition, or What?* Advanced Card Magic no. 4. (1937) Unique Magic Studios, Albany, NY. Stapled with paper cover. Yellow. 1 pp. 4.25 x 9.25 in. Mimeographed. Cards.

Albright, Howard P., *Kard Kapers.* (1934) Unique Magic Studios, Albany, NY. Saddle-stitch. Orange. 15 pp. 4.25 x 9.25 in. Inscribed to Dariel Fitzkee. Signed by Howard P. Albright. Cards.

Albright, Howard P., *Klever Kard Kodes.* (1934) Unique Magic Studios, Albany, NY. Saddle-stitch. Yellow. 35 pp. 4.25 x 9.25 in. Cards.

Albright, Howard P., *Klever Kard Kodes.* (1950) Abbott Magic Co., Colon, MI. Stapled with paper cover. Tan. 21 pp. 8.5 x 11 in. Mimeographed. Cards.

Albright, Howard P., *Lady Luck Card Effects.* (1933) Unique Magic Studios, Albany, NY. Saddle-stitch. Yellow. 21 pp. 4.25 x 9.25 in. Inscribed to Dariel Fitzkee. Signed by Howard P. Albright. Cards.

Albright, Howard P., *Lucky Number.* Advanced Card Magic no. 10. (1937) Unique Magic Studios, Albany, NY. White. 1 pp. 8.5 x 11 in. Mimeographed. (Information not verified by physical copy.) Cards.

Albright, Howard P., *Mental Power, or Cards That Answer Their Names.* (1934) Unique Magic Studios, Albany, NY. Stapled. Yellow. 7 pp. 4.25 x 9.25 in. Mimeographed. Cards.

Albright, Howard P., *Message from the Sky, A.* (1934) Unique Magic Studios, Albany, NY. Stapled. Blue. 29 pp. 4.25 x 9.25 in. Mimeographed. Cards.

Albright, Howard P., *Mind of Mephistopheles, The.* Advanced Card Magic no. 3. (1937) Unique Magic Studios, Albany, NY. White. 1 pp. 8.5 x 11 in. Mimeographed. (Information not verified by physical copy.) Cards.

Albright, Howard P., *Novelty Card Magic.* (1935) Unique Magic Studios, Albany, NY. Saddle-stitch. Green. 20 pp. 4.25 x 9.25 in. Includes printed card gimmicks. Cards.

Albright, Howard P., *Oracle Act, The.* (1937) Abbott Magic Co., Colon, MI. Loose pages. White. 6 pp. 8.5 x 11 in. Mimeographed. Cards, Fortune-telling, Mentalism.

Albright, Howard P., *Party Pak no. 1.* (1936) Abbott Magic Co., Colon, MI. Mimeographed. (Information not verified by physical copy. Bibliographical details are as accurate as possible.) Close-Up, Stage.

Albright, Howard P., *Party Trix à la Carte.* (1948) Abbott Magic Co., Colon, MI. Stapled with paper cover. Olive. 11 pp. 5.25 x 8.5 in. Mimeographed. Cards.

Albright, Howard P., *Party Trix à la Carte.* (c. 1957) Supreme Magic, Bideford, UK. Stapled with tape. Red. 10 pp. 8 x 9.75 in. Mimeographed inside printed cover. Cards.

Albright, Howard P., *Peculiarities of the Pasteboards, The.* (1934) Unique Magic Studios, Albany, NY. Saddle-stitch. Yellow. 6 pp. 4.25 x 9.25 in. Mimeographed. Cards.

Albright, Howard P., *Persistent Card, The.* Advanced Card Magic no. 2. (1937) Unique Magic Studios, Albany, NY. Stapled. White. 3 pp. 8.5 x 11 in. Mimeographed. (Information not verified by physical copy.) Cards.

Albright, Howard P., *Psychic Dealer.* (n.d.) Unique Magic Studios, Albany, NY. Stapled with paper cover. Yellow. 1 pp. 4.25 x 9.25 in. Mimeographed. Cards, Mentalism.

Albright, Howard P., *Simplified Interpretation of the Cards.* (c. 1931) Unique Magic Studios, Albany, NY. Stapled with paper cover. 5 pp. 4.25 x 9.25 in. (Information not verified by physical copy.) Cards, Fortune-telling.

Albright, Howard P., *Slate Stunts.* (1938) Author, Albany, NY. Stapled with paper cover. 6 pp. Mimeographed. (Information not verified by physical copy. Bibliographical details are as accurate as possible.) Slates.

Albright, Howard P., *Super-Psychic Mental Effects.* (1933) Unique Magic Studios, Albany, NY. Saddle-stitch. Yellow. 35 pp. 4.25 x 9.25 in. Stamps of Bert Allerton and Hornmann. Mentalism.

Albright, Howard P., *Super-Psychic Mental Effects.* (1933) Unique Magic Studios, Albany, NY. Saddle-stitch. Yellow. 35 pp. 4.25 x 9.25 in. Sid Lorraine bookplate. Mentalism.

Albright, Howard P., *Super-Psychic Mental Effects.* (1948) Abbott Magic Co., Colon, MI. Saddle-stitch. White. 52 pp. 4.75 x 7.25 in. Mentalism.

Albright, Howard P., *Super-Psychic Mental Effects.* (1948) Abbott Magic Co., Colon, MI. Saddle-stitch. Tan. Cover text: Green; 52 pp. 4.75 x 7.25 in. Mentalism.

Albright, Howard P., *Super-Sensitive Fingertips.* (1933) Unique Magic Studios, Albany, NY. Saddle-stitch. Orange. 30 pp. 4.25 x 9.25 in. Individually numbered. #2330. Mentalism.

Albright, Howard P., *Super-Sensitive Fingertips.* Third edition. (n.d.) Unique Magic Studios, Albany, NY. Saddle-stitch. Orange. 30 pp. 4.25 x 9.25 in. Inscribed to Dariel Fitzkee. Signed by Howard P. Albright. Mentalism.

Albright, Howard P., *Super-Sensitive Fingertips.* (1948) Abbott Magic Co., Colon, MI. Saddle-stitch. Olive. 42 pp. 4.75 x 7.25 in. Mentalism.

Albright, Howard P., *Super-Sensitive Fingertips.* (1973) Supreme Magic, Bideford, UK. Stapled with tape. Olive. 18 pp. 8 x 10 in. Mimeographed. Mentalism.

Albright, Howard P., *Surprise Speller.* Advanced Card Magic no. 7. (1937) Author, Albany, NY. White. 1 pp. 8.5 x 11 in. Mimeographed. (Information not verified by physical copy.) Cards.

Albright, Howard P., *Triple Stop Disclosure.* Advanced Card Magic no. 9. (1937) Unique Magic Studios, Albany, NY. Stapled with paper cover. Yellow. 1 pp. 4.25 x 9.25 in. Mimeographed. Cards.

Albright, Howard P., *Uni-Mentality.* (1935) Unique Magic Studios, Albany, NY. Stapled. Beige. 5 pp. 5.5 x 8.5 in. Cards.

Albright, Howard P., *Variety Magic Pak.* (1948) Abbott Magic Co., Colon, MI. Mimeographed. (Information not verified by physical copy. Bibliographical details are as accurate as possible.) Close-Up, Stage.

Albright, Howard P., *With Two Decks.* (1942) Unique Magic Studios, Delmar, NY. Stapled with paper cover. 5 pp. Mimeographed. (Information not verified by physical copy. Bibliographical details are as accurate as possible.) Cards.

Albright, Howard P., *With Two Decks.* (1948) Abbott Magic Co., Colon, MI. Stapled with paper cover. Red. 4 pp. 5.5 x 8.5 in. Mimeographed. Cards.

Alburger, James, *Get Your Act Together.* Second printing. (1981) Author, San Diego. Perfect. White. 149 pp. 5.5 x 8.5 in. Showmanship.

Aldine Publishing Co., *Aldine Boys' Own Magic and Trick Handbooks no. 1: The Magic of Numbers.* (1894) Aldine Publishing Co., London. Saddle-stitch. Color. 32 pp. 5.5 x 8.5 in. All titles are as listed on the front cover, which may vary from the back-cover title. (Information not verified by physical copy.) Beginner, Mathematical.

Aldine Publishing Co., *Aldine Boys' Own Magic and Trick Handbooks no. 2: Tricks and Deceptions with Cards for Home Performance.* (1894) Aldine Publishing Co., London. Saddle-stitch. Color. 32 pp. 5.5 x 8.5 in. Back cover title: "Capital Tricks and Deceptions with Cards." Beginner, Cards.

Aldine Publishing Co., *Aldine Boys' Own Magic and Trick Handbooks no. 3: Magic Toys – How to Make Them.* (1894) Aldine Publishing Co., London. Saddle-stitch. Color. 32 pp. 5.5 x 8.5 in. Back cover title: "Magic Toys and How to Make Them." (Information not verified by physical copy.) Toys.

Aldine Publishing Co., *Aldine Boys' Own Magic and Trick Handbooks no. 4: Tricks in Mechanics for Home Construction and Amusement.* (1894) Aldine Publishing Co., London. Saddle-stitch. Color. 32 pp. 5.5 x 8.5 in. Back cover title: "Tricks in Mechanics." (Information not verified by physical copy.) Science magic.

Aldine Publishing Co., *Aldine Boys' Own Magic and Trick Handbooks no. 5: Amusing Sleight of Hand.* (1894) Aldine Publishing Co., London. Saddle-stitch. Color. 32 pp. 5.5 x 8.5 in. Back cover title: "Sleight of Hand." (Information not verified by physical copy.) Beginner, Second Sight.

Aldine Publishing Co., *Aldine Boys' Own Magic and Trick Handbooks no. 6: Chemical Tricks for Home Amusement and Instruction.* (1894) Aldine Publishing Co., London. Saddle-stitch. Color. 32 pp. 5.5 x 8.5 in. Back cover title: "Magical Tricks with Chemicals." (Information not verified by physical copy.) Chemical, Beginner.

Aldine Publishing Co., *Aldine Boys' Own Magic and Trick Handbooks no. 7: Curious and Amusing Puzzles.* (1894) Aldine Publishing Co., London. Saddle-stitch. Color. 32 pp. 5.5 x 8.5 in. Back cover title: "Curious and Amusing Puzzles." (Information not verified by physical copy.) Puzzles.

Aldine Publishing Co., *Aldine Boys' Own Magic and Trick Handbooks no. 8: Mechanical and Electrical Tricks.* (1894) Aldine Publishing Co., London. Saddle-stitch. Color. 32 pp. 5.5 x 8.5 in. Cover title: "Amusements in Electricity, Magnetism, and Galvanism." Beginner, Electrical, Science magic.

Aldini (See also Berg, Joe), *Aldini's Lecture Notes.* (1970) Magic Limited, Oakland, CA. Stapled. White. 11 pp. 8.5 x 11 in. Lecture notes. Cards, Close-Up, Stage.

Aldini, *Magic Sermonettes.* (1962) Abbott Magic Co., Colon, MI. Stapled. Light green. 31 pp. 8.5 x 11 in. Mimeographed. Gospel magic.

Aldini, *Novel Concepts in Magic.* (1970) Micky Hades, Calgary, Canada. Stapled with tape. Beige. 37 pp. 8.5 x 11 in. Cards.

Aldini, *New Concepts in Magic.* (1970) Micky Hades, Calgary, Canada. Stapled with tape. Tan. 37 pp. 8.5 x 11 in. Cards, Rope.

Aldini, *Novel Concepts with Cards.* (1970) Micky Hades, Calgary, Canada. Stapled with tape. Beige. 46 pp. 8.5 x 11 in. Cards.

Aldini, *Roughingly Yours.* (1969) Micky Hades, Calgary, Canada. Stapled with tape. Blue. 48 pp. 8.5 x 11 in. Cards, Rough and smooth.

Aldrich, Charles T., *Magic.* (c. 1905) Author, New York. Saddle-stitch. Green. 32 pp. 6 x 9 in. Cut-out cover. Beginner, Stunts, Souvenir book.

Aldrich, Steve, *Stacked Pack, The.* (1991) Zauberman Press, Lakewood, CO. Saddle-stitch. Pink. 47 pp. 5.25 x 8.5 in. #320. Cards, Prearranged deck, Prearranged deck.

Aleko, *What You Are and What You Are Not.* (c. 1925) Author, Philippines. Saddle-stitch. Pink. 24 pp. 4.5 x 8.25 in. Promotion for Greek mentalism duo. Fortune-telling, Pitch book.

Alemán, Camilo Vázquez, *Magic Castle Lecture Notes.* (2003) Author, Madrid. Stapled. Gray. 24 pp. 8.5 x 11 in. (Information not verified by physical copy.) Lecture notes. Close-Up, Stage.

Alex, Father, *Lecture Notes: Hand Mucking.* (2014) Author, Paris. Stapled. Olive. 16 pp. 8.25 x 11.75 in. (Information not verified by physical copy.) Lecture notes. Cards.

Alex, Lee, *Time for a Change?* (2009) Author, UK. Cloth. Black. 187 pp. 6.25 x 9.25 in. (Measurements and other information have been recorded as accurately as possible.) Quick change, Stage.

Alexander the Magician, *Magic Show Book, The.* (1950) Macmillan, New York. Cloth. Red. 145 pp. 5.25 x 8.25 in. Dust jacket. Beginner, Children's book.

Alexander, Alison, with Bower, Susie, *Science Magic.* (1986) Simon and Schuster, New York. Perfect. Blue. 45 pp. 7.25 x 10 in. Science magic, Children's book.

Alexander, C., *Crystal Gazing.* (1919) Author, Los Angeles. Saddle-stitch. Black. 32 pp. 5.25 x 7.5 in. Fortune-telling, Crystal gazing.

Alexander, C., *Crystal Gazing.* (c. 1920) Alexander Publishing Co., Los Angeles. Saddle-stitch. Yellow. 38 pp. 6.25 x 9.25 in. Fortune-telling, Crystal gazing.

Alexander, C., *Crystal Gazing and Mind Reading Act.* (n.d.) Author, Los Angeles. Stapled. White. 7 pp. 8.5 x 11 in. Mimeographed. (Information not verified by physical copy.) Mentalism, Crystal gazing.

Alexander, C., *Inner Secrets of Psychology vol. 1: Creative Thought Power, The.* (1924) C. Alexander Publishing Co., Los Angeles. Cloth. Black. 188 pp. 5.25 x 7.5 in. Self-help.

Alexander, C., *Inner Secrets of Psychology vol. 2: Personal Magnetism, The.* (1924) C. Alexander Publishing Co., Los Angeles. Cloth. Black. 195 pp. 5.25 x 7.5 in. (Information not verified by physical copy.) Self-help.

Alexander, C., *Inner Secrets of Psychology vol. 3: Psychology of Sex, The.* (1924) C. Alexander Publishing Co., Los Angeles. Cloth. Black. 219 pp. 5.25 x 7.5 in. (Information not verified by physical copy.) Self-help, Psychology.

Alexander, C., *Inner Secrets of Psychology vol. 4: Psychology of Health, The.* (1924) C. Alexander Publishing Co., Los Angeles. Cloth. Black. 229 pp. 5.25 x 7.5 in. Self-help, Psychology.

Alexander, C., *Inner Secrets of Psychology vol. 5: Astral-Plane Phenomena, The.* (1924) C. Alexander Publishing Co., Los Angeles. Cloth. Black. 191 pp. 5.25 x 7.5 in. (Information not verified by physical copy.) Self-help, Psychic.

Alexander, C., *Life and Mysteries of the Celebrated Dr. "Q," The.* First edition. (1921) Alexander Publishing Co., Los Angeles. Cloth. Orange. 124 pp. 6 x 9 in. Signed by C. Alexander. Mentalism, Second Sight.

Alexander, C., *Life and Mysteries of the Celebrated Dr. "Q," The.* Third printing. (1946) Nelson Enterprises, Columbus, OH. Cloth. Black. 166 pp. 6 x 9 in. T. A. Waters' copy from high school with pencil sketches inside cover. Signed by T. A. Waters. Mentalism, Second Sight.

Alexander, C., *Oriental Wisdom: Its Principles and Practices.* (1924) Alexander Publishing Co., Los Angeles. Cloth. Black. 557 pp. 6 x 9 in. (Information not verified by physical copy.) Signed by C. Alexander. Mentalism, Second Sight.

Alexander, C., *Slick Stuff for Slickers.* (1922) Thayer Magical Mfg. Co., Los Angeles. 12 pp. (Information not verified by physical copy.) Mentalism, Cards, Nail writer.

Alexander, C., *Thot Projection.* (1928) B. L. Gilbert, Chicago. Stapled. White. 2 pp. 8.5 x 11 in. Mimeographed. (Information not verified by physical copy.) Mentalism, Question and answer.

Alexander, David, *Complete Professional Pickpocket, The.* Revised edition. (2015) AMS Books, Nanaimo, Canada. Cloth. Blue. 100 pp. 6.5 x 9.5 in. Dust jacket. Pickpocket.

Alexander, Jack, *Thou Shalt Not Steal Except Magic Ideas.* (1983) Author, Warsaw, IN. Folded. White. 5.5 x 8.5 in. (Information not verified by physical copy. Bibliographical details are as accurate as possible.) Lecture notes. Gospel magic.

Alexander, Jörg, *F.F.F.F. 2000 Lecture Notes.* (2000) Author, Munich. Wire binding. White. 41 pp. 11 x 8.5 in. Bound oblong. (Information not verified by physical copy.) Lecture notes. Cards, Close-Up, Three Shell Game.

Alexander, Jörg, *S.A.M. Lecture Notes, The.* (2002) Author, Munich. Comb. White. 34 pp. 8.5 x 11 in. Lecture notes. Cards, Close-Up, Stage.

Alexander, Jörg, *Zauber Kunst Stücke.* (2000) Author, Munich. Cloth. Black. 64 pp. 8.5 x 8.5 in. Signed by Jörg Alexander. Cards.

Alexander, Jörg, *Zauber Kunst Stücke Band 2.* (2019) Author, Munich. Casebound. Black. 91 pp. 8.5 x 8.5 in. Signed by Jörg Alexander. Cards, Close-Up.

Alexander, Jörg, *Zauber Kunst Stücke Band 3.* (2011) Author, Munich. Casebound. Black. 79 pp. 8.5 x 8.5 in. Signed by Jörg Alexander. Cards, Close-Up.

Alexander, Prof. Max, *Parlour Magician: A Handy Book for the Amateur Conjuror, The.* (1876) H. G. Clarke and Co., London. 48 pp. (Information not verified by physical copy.) Toole Stott no. 1327. Beginner.

Alexander, Scott, *52.* (2022) Author, Lancaster, PA. Cloth. Black. 324 pp. 8.5 x 11 in. Dust jacket. Signed by Scott Alexander. #151 of 500. Cards, Stage, Close-Up.

Alexander, Scott, *Fakir Miracle, A.* (2012) Alexander Illusions, Lancaster, PA. Coil. White. 20 pp. 8.5 x 11 in. (Information not verified by physical copy.) Chop Cup, Close-Up.

Alexander, Scott, *MC's Guidebook, The.* (2022) Alexander Illusions, Lancaster, PA. Perfect. White. 90 pp. 8 x 10 in. With note from author. Emcee.

Alexander, Scott, *Stand Up Guy.* (2016) Alexander Illusions, Lancaster, PA. Perfect. White. 85 pp. 5.5 x 8.5 in. Cards, Stage, Close-Up.

Alexander, Scott, *Standing Up On Stage: Creating a Commercial and Effective Working Stand-Up Act.* (2012) Alexander Illusions, Lancaster, PA. Coil. White. 26 pp. 8.5 x 11 in. (Information not verified by physical copy.) Stage, Showmanship, Routining.

Alexander, Scott, *Standing Up On Stage with the Flying Ring.* (2012) Alexander Illusions, Lancaster, PA. Comb. White. 21 pp. 8.5 x 11 in. (Information not verified by physical copy.) Stage, Rings.

Alexander, Scott, *Super Fly.* (2013) Alexander Illusions, Lancaster, PA. Comb. White. 9 pp. 8.5 x 11 in. (Information not verified by physical copy.) Cards, Cards Across, Stage.

Alfonso (Alfonso Aceituno), *Alfonso 2001.* (2001) Author, Los Angeles. Stapled. Green. 8 pp. 8.5 x 11 in. (Information not verified by physical copy.) Lecture notes. Cards, Close-Up.

Alfonso, *Alfonso in the Capital.* (1994) Author, Los Angeles. Stapled. Tan. 11 pp. 8.5 x 11 in. (Information not verified by physical copy.) Lecture notes. Cards, Close-Up.

Alford, Jason, *Cyber Sessions: Underground Notes from Cyberia.* (1999) Author, Hammond, LA. Comb. Beige, black. 160 pp. 8.5 x 11 in. (Information not verified by physical copy.) Cards.

Alford, Jason, *Deal or No Deal.* (2008) The Second Deal, Hammond, LA. Saddle-stitch. White. 36 pp. 8.5 x 11 in. (Information not verified by physical copy.) Cards.

Alford, Jason, *Freebie.* (1999) Author, Hammond, LA. Saddle-stitch. Red. 34 pp. 5.5 x 8.5 in. (Information not verified by physical copy.) Lecture notes. Cards.

Alford, Jason, *Freebie 2.* (2000) Author, Hammond, LA. Saddle-stitch. Red. 24 pp. 5.5 x 8.5 in. (Information not verified by physical copy.) Lecture notes. Cards.

Alford, Jason, *Freebie 3.* (2002) Author, Hammond, LA. Saddle-stitch. Red. 34 pp. 5.5 x 8.5 in. (Information not verified by physical copy.) Lecture notes. Cards.

Alford, Jason, *Freebie 4.* (2003) Author, Hammond, LA. Saddle-stitch. Red. 32 pp. 5.5 x 8.5 in. (Information not verified by physical copy.) Lecture notes. Cards.

Alford, Jason, *Freebie 5.* (2004) Author, Hammond, LA. Saddle-stitch. Red. 32 pp. 5.5 x 8.5 in. (Information not verified by physical copy.) Lecture notes. Cards.

Alford, Jason, *Freebie 6.* (2005) Author, Hammond, LA. Saddle-stitch. Red. 49 pp. 5.5 x 8.6 in. (Information not verified by physical copy.) Lecture notes. Cards.

Alford, Jason, *Freebie 7.* (2006) Author, Hammond, LA. Saddle-stitch. Red. 29 pp. 5.5 x 8.7 in. (Information not verified by physical copy.) Lecture notes. Cards.

Alford, Jason, with Tams, Mark, *Freebie 8.* (2007) Author, Hammond, LA. Saddle-stitch. Red. 32 pp. 5.5 x 8.8 in. (Information not verified by physical copy.) Lecture notes. Cards.

Alford, Jason, *Thinking and Wondering.* (1998) Author, Hammond, LA. Comb. Blue. 34 pp. 8.5 x 11 in. (Information not verified by physical copy.) Cards.

Alfredson, James B., with Daily, George L., Jr., *Bibliography of Conjuring Periodicals in English 1791-1983, A.* (1986) Magicana for Collectors, York, PA. Cloth. Blue. 395 pp. 8.5 x 11 in. Bibliography, Magazines, History.

Alfredson, James B., *Jean Hugard.* (1997) Meyerbooks, Glenwood, IL. Cloth. Maroon. Cover text: Gold; 72 pp. 6 x 9.25 in. #401 of 750. Biography, History.

Alfredson, James B., with Schmitz, Bernhard, *Magic Bookplates.* (2022) Author, Remscheid, Germany. Cloth. Blue. Cover text: Silver; 485 pp. 8.5 x 11.75 in. Signed by Bernhard Schmitz. #203 of 300. Collecting, History, Bookplates.

Alfredson, James B., *Magical Ex Libris: A Checklist.* (1991) Author, Lansing, MI. Saddle-stitch. Beige. 60 pp. 4.75 x 8.25 in. Signed by James B. Alfredson. #107 of 110. Collecting, History, Bookplates.

Alfredson, James B., *Newmann the Pioneer Mentalist.* Second edition. (1990) Meyerbooks, Glenwood, IL. Cloth. Black. Cover text: Gold; 49 pp. 6 x 9.25 in. Limited to 250 copies. Biography, History.

Alfredson, James B., with Daily, George L., Jr., *Short Title Check List of Conjuring Periodicals in English, A.* (1976) Author, Lansing, MI. Comb. Red, black, white. 60 pp. 5.5 x 8.5 in. Signed by James B. Alfredson, George L. Daily. #177 of 200. Bibliography, Magazines, History.

Allan, Jamie, *Everything.* (2023) Author, UK. Casebound. Black. 436 pp. 12 x 12 in. Illusions, Stage, Showmanship, Routining.

Allen, Alexander, *Closer Than Before!* (1997) Author, Lincoln, UK. 25 pp. (Information not verified by physical copy.) Cards, Close-Up.

Allen, Alexander, *Natural and Close-Up.* (2009) Author, Lincoln, UK. 54 pp. (Information not verified by physical copy.) Cards, Close-Up, Stage.

Allen, Alexander, *Shared Secrets of Card Magic.* (1997) Author, Lincoln, UK. 135 pp. (Information not verified by physical copy.) Cards.

Allen, C. C., *Legend of Mac McDonald, The.* (1986) Author, Mesa, AZ. Comb. Beige. 34 pp. 8.5 x 11 in. Biography, Cards, Stage.

Allen, C. C., *Little Black Bag: A Complete Magic Act, The.* (1986) Author, Mesa, AZ. Comb. 40 pp. (Information not verified by physical copy.) Bags, Children's magic, Stage.

Allen, C. C., *Professor Presto's Paper Hat Book.* (1993) Dan Tong, Port Charlotte, FL. Saddle-stitch. Yellow. 26 pp. 5.5 x 8.5 in. Paper, Hats, Stage, Apparatus.

Allen, George, *History of the Automaton Chess-Player in America, The.* (1859) Rudd and Carleton, New York. Cloth. 563 pp. Article in Daniel Willard Fiske, "The Book of the First American Chess Congress," pp. 420-84. History, Automaton chess player, Automata.

Allen, George, *History of the Automaton Chess-Player in America, The.* (1998) Cauldron Press, Glen Burnie, MD. Coil. White. 64 pp. 5.5 x 8.5 in. Reprint of 1859 article. #27 of 300. History, Automaton chess player, Automata.

Allen, Harry, with Cook, Irv, *Lecture Notes of Impromptu Magic.* (1985) Magic Shop, Daytona Beach, FL. 12 pp. (Information not verified by physical copy.) Lecture notes. Close-Up, Stage.

Allen, Harry, *Sleight of Foot in Mouth.* (1985) Author, Daytona Beach, FL. Saddle-stitch. Orange. 23 pp. 5.5 x 8.5 in. Comedy, Jokes.

Allen, Harry, *Sleight of Lips: Book Four.* (1986) Author, Daytona Beach, FL. Saddle-stitch. Green. 24 pp. 5.5 x 8.5 in. Comedy, Jokes.

Allen, Harry, *Sleight of Mouth.* (1995) L & L Publishing, Tahoma, CA. Casebound. White. 177 pp. 6.25 x 9.25 in. Comedy, Jokes.

Allen, Harry, *Sleight of One Liners (For Lack of a Better Title): Book Five.* (1991) Author, Daytona Beach, FL. Comb. Beige, black. 49 pp. 5.5 x 8.5 in. Comedy, Jokes.

Allen, Harry, *Sleight of Tongue.* (1982) Author, Daytona Beach, FL. Saddle-stitch. Blue. 19 pp. 5.5 x 8.5 in. Comedy, Jokes.

Allen, Harry, *Sleight of Tongue in Cheek.* (1984) Author, Daytona Beach, FL. Saddle-stitch. Yellow. 24 pp. 5.5 x 8.5 in. Comedy, Jokes.

Allen, Jon, *1 Trick, 2 Names.* (1995) Author, UK. Saddle-stitch. 19 pp. 8.5 x 5.75 in. (Information not verified by physical copy. Bibliographical details are as accurate as possible.) Cards, Close-Up.

Allen, Jon, *"B" Movies, The.* (1995) Incorporate Magic, UK. Stapled. Green. 12 pp. 8.5 x 11 in. (Information not verified by physical copy. Bibliographical details are as accurate as possible.) Rubber bands.

Allen, Jon, *Director's Cut, The.* (1995) Author, UK. Stapled. Blue. 19 pp. 8.5 x 11 in. (Information not verified by physical copy. Bibliographical details are as accurate as possible.) Close-Up.

Allen, Jon, *Director's Cut: The Sequel, The.* (2003) Author, UK. Stapled. Red. 23 pp. 8.5 x 11 in. (Information not verified by physical copy. Bibliographical details are as accurate as possible.) Close-Up.

Allen, Jon, with Lovick, John, *Experience: The Magic of Jon Allen.* (2009) Vanishing Inc., Rancho Cordova, CA. Cloth. Blue. 198 pp. 8.75 x 11.25 in. Dust jacket. Cards, Close-Up.

Allen, Jon, with Lovick, John, *Experience: The Magic of Jon Allen.* Second edition. (2012) Vanishing Inc., Rancho Cordova, CA. Perfect. Gray. 206 pp. 8.5 x 11 in. (Information not verified by physical copy.) Cards, Close-Up.

Allen, Jon, *Experience: The Notes of Jon Allen.* (2009) Author, UK. Stapled. White. 24 pp. 8.5 x 11 in. Dust jacket. (Information not verified by physical copy.) Lecture notes. Cards, Close-Up.

Allen, Jon, *Interrobang Lecture, The.* (2017) Author, UK. Saddle-stitch. White. 22 pp. 5.5 x 8.5 in. (Information not verified by physical copy.) Lecture notes. Close-Up, Coins.

Allen, Jon, *Simple Magic Tricks.* (2004) Octopus, London. Perfect. Color. 128 pp. 9.25 x 7.5 in. (Measurements and other information have been recorded as accurately as possible.) Beginner.

Allen, Ken, *Do-It-Yourself Lecture.* (1952) Ken Allen Products, Union City, NJ. Stapled. Light green, red. 29 pp. 8.5 x 5.5 in. Bound oblong. Mimeographed. Lecture notes. Beginner.

Allen, Ken, *Mighty Micros.* (1959) Ken Allen Products, Union City, NJ. Stapled. Pink. 5 pp. 5.5 x 8.5 in. Mimeographed. Close-Up, Gimmicks.

Allen, Ken, *Pilfered Patter no. 1.* (1958) Ken Allen Products, Union City, NJ. Stapled. Beige. 23 pp. 8.5 x 5.5 in. Bound oblong. Mimeographed. Patter.

Allen, Ken, *T.I.P.S. (Tips, Ideas, Patter, and Suggestions).* (1959) Ken Allen Products, Union City, NJ. Saddle-stitch. White, black. 56 pp. 5.5 x 8.5 in. Signed by Ken Allen. Tips, Close-Up.

Allen, Ken, *What's New with Ken Allen.* Second printing. (1981) Author, Palisade Park, NJ. Stapled. Orange. 32 pp. 8.5 x 11 in. David Hoy library embossed seal and Klosterman rubber stamp. Close-Up, Stage.

Allen, Lee, *Lee Allen Lecture, The.* (c. 1978) Author, Lexington, KY. Stapled. White. 24 pp. 8.5 x 11 in. (Information not verified by physical copy.) Lecture notes. Children's magic, Close-Up, Stage.

Allen, Lieut. W., *Book on Ventriloquism.* (n.d.) Morrell Brothers Show Printing, Philadelphia. Saddle-stitch. White, red. 16 pp. 5 x 6.5 in. 2 pp. on dissolving knot, etc. "Art of Magic" full-page on back cover. Toole Stott no. 914. Ventriloquism, Beginner.

Allen, Lieut. W., *Book on Ventriloquism.* (c. 1871) Dick's Popular Publishing House, New York. Saddle-stitch. Tan. 16 pp. 5 x 6.75 in. 2 pp. on dissolving knot, etc. "Art of Magic" full-page on back cover. Toole Stott no. 915. Ventriloquism, Beginner.

Allen, Sam, *Sam Allen Lecture Notes: The First Five (Years, Not Tricks).* (1996) Author, Queensland, Australia. Stapled. 8 pp. 8.25 x 11.75 in. (Information not verified by physical copy.) Lecture notes. Close-Up, Stage.

Allen, Stan, with James, Kevin, *Broom Suspension: An Owner's Manual, The.* (1983) Stan Allen's IllusionSales, Los Alamitos, CA. Comb. Tan. 50 pp. 6.75 x 8.5 in. Illusions, Broom Suspension.

Allen, Stan, *Cruise Ship Magic.* (1984) Author, Los Alamitos, CA. Saddle-stitch. White. 20 pp. 5.5 x 8.5 in. Lecture notes. Business, Cruise ships.

Allen, Stan, *Inside Allen Lecture Notes.* (1989) Author, Lakewood, CA. Saddle-stitch. White, purple, black. 32 pp. 5.5 x 8.5 in. Signed by Stan Allen. Lecture notes. Showmanship, Close-Up, Stage.

Allen, Stan, *Magic Live 2016: 25 Years of "Magic."* (2016) Magic Live, Las Vegas. Saddle-stitch. Multiple sections. 8.5 x 11 in. Three 32 pp. and one 40 pp. booklets with writings by convention's performers and lecturers. Close-Up, Stage, Business, Conventions.

Allen, Stan, *Magic Live 2017: The Road Less Traveled.* (2017) Magic Live, Las Vegas. Saddle-stitch. Multiple sections. 8.5 x 11 in. Four 24 pp. booklets with writings by convention's performers and lecturers. Close-Up, Stage, Business, Conventions.

Allen, Stan, *Magic Live 2018: Questions.* (2018) Magic Live, Las Vegas. Saddle-stitch. Multiple sections. 8.5 x 11 in. Five booklets, three with 24 pp., two with 28 pp. Close-Up, Stage, Business, Conventions.

Allen, Stan, *Magic Live 2023: Beginnings.* (2023) Magic Live, Las Vegas. Perfect. Multiple sections. 8.5 x 11 in. 88 pp. "Magic" magazine. Also "Inside Magic Newsletter" with eight loose pages. Close-Up, Stage, Business, Conventions.

Allen, Stan, *Magic Live Lecture Notes.* (2001-2013) Magic Live, Las Vegas. Looseleaf binder. Black. Multiple sections. 8.5 x 11 in. With three-hole-punched pages printed for Magic Live convention in 2001, 2004, 2007, 2009, 2011, and 2013. Lecture notes. Close-Up, Stage, Business, Conventions.

Allen, Tom, *Garden Path.* (1999) Author, Sacramento, CA. Stapled. Green. 39 pp. 8.5 x 11 in. (Information not verified by physical copy. Bibliographical details are as accurate as possible.) Cards, Coins, Close-Up.

Allerton, Bert, *Bamboozle.* Stars of Magic series 3, no. 2. (1947) Stars of Magic, Inc., New York. Folded. White. 4 pp. 8.5 x 11 in. Bills, Short change.

Allerton, Bert, with Parrish, Robert, *Close-Up Magician, The.* First edition. (1958) Ireland Magic Co., Chicago. Cloth. Black. 72 pp. 6.25 x 9.5 in. Close-Up.

Allerton, Bert, with Parrish, Robert, *Close-Up Magician, The.* First edition. (1958) Ireland Magic Co., Chicago. Stapled with tape. Beige, red, black. 72 pp. 6.25 x 9.5 in. Close-Up.

Allerton, Bert, with Parrish, Robert, *Close-Up Magician, The.* Second printing. (1958) Ireland Magic Co., Chicago. Stapled with tape. Beige, red, black. 72 pp. 6.25 x 9.5 in. Close-Up.

Allerton, Bert, with Parrish, Robert, *Close-Up Magician, The.* Third printing. (1964) Ireland Magic Co., Chicago. Coil. White, red, black. 72 pp. 6 x 9 in. Close-Up.

Allerton, Bert, with Parrish, Robert, *Close-Up Magician, The.* Second printing of Magic Inc. reprint. (1974) Magic Inc., Chicago. Saddle-stitch. White, green. 72 pp. 5.5 x 8.5 in. Close-Up.

Allerton, Bert, with Parrish, Robert, *Close-Up Magician, The.* Third printing of Magic Inc. reprint. (1977) Magic Inc., Chicago. Saddle-stitch. White, purple. 72 pp. 5.5 x 8.5 in. Close-Up.

Allerton, Bert, *Pump Room Phantasy.* Stars of Magic series 3, no. 1. (1947) Stars of Magic, Inc., New York. Folded. White. 4 pp. 8.5 x 11 in. Cards.

Allesi, Ron, *Magic Collector's Portfolio.* (1987) Author, Dunkirk, NY. Loose pages. White. 16 pp. 8.5 x 11 in. Individual pages inside printed cover. Signed by Ron Allesi. #73. Collecting, Apparatus, History.

Allesi, Ron, *Magic of Ronal, The.* (1977) Micky Hades, Calgary, Canada. Comb. Blue. 47 pp. 8.5 x 11 in. (Measurements and other information have been recorded as accurately as possible.) Stage.

Allingham, Herbert, with Notaro, Joe, *Houdini's Schooldays.* (2023) Authors, Los Angeles. Casebound. Red. 291 pp. 6.25 x 9.25 in. Houdini, Fiction.

Alma (Maurice Mejean), *Jeu de Gobelets, Le.* (1945) Mayette, Paris. Perfect. Beige. 138 pp. 6.25 x 9.5 in. #241 of 650. Cups and Balls. French.

Alma (Maurice Mejean), *Nouveautés Cartomagiques.* (1945) Mayette, Paris. Perfect. Beige. 165 pp. 6.5 x 10 in. Signed by George Armstrong. #165 of 650. Cards. French.

Alma, Will, *Magical Patter.* (n.d.) Alma Magical Co., Melbourne. Stapled. 3 pp. 7.75 x 13 in. Folded. (Information not verified by physical copy.) See McCullagh, "Under the Southern Cross." Patter.

Alma, Will, *Methods of Forcing.* (n.d.) Alma Magical Co., Melbourne. Stapled. 4 pp. 7.75 x 13 in. Folded. (Information not verified by physical copy.) See McCullagh, "Under the Southern Cross." Forcing.

Alma, Will, *Money from Magic.* (n.d.) Alma Magical Co., Melbourne. Stapled. 4 pp. 7.75 x 13 in. Folded. (Information not verified by physical copy.) See McCullagh, "Under the Southern Cross." Business.

Alma, Will, *More Magical Patter.* (n.d.) Alma Magical Co., Melbourne. Stapled. 3 pp. 7.75 x 13 in. Folded. (Information not verified by physical copy.) See McCullagh, "Under the Southern Cross." Patter.

Almond, Philip C., *England's First Demonologist: Reginald Scot and "The Discoverie of Witchcraft."* (2014) I. B. Tauris, London. Perfect. Black. 246 pp. 5.5 x 8.5 in. Biography, History.

Almoznino, Albert, *Art of Hand Shadows, The.* (1970) Stravon Educational Press, New York. Perfect. Brown. 64 pp. 6 x 9 in. From Doug Henning collection; Henning stamp. Shadowgraphy.

Almoznino, Albert, *Art of Hand Shadows, The.* (1970) Stravon Educational Press, New York. Cloth. Yellow. 64 pp. 6 x 9 in. Shadowgraphy.

Alpha (Alain Falippou), *Lecture Notes - Notes de Conférence.* (1994) Académie de Magie Georges Proust, Paris. Stapled. Beige. 21 pp. 8.25 x 11.75 in. Lecture notes. Stage, Fire.

Altgelt, Frederick, *Mind Magic.* (1978) Magic Inc., Chicago. Saddle-stitch. Yellow. 24 pp. 5.5 x 8.5 in. (Measurements and other information have been recorded as accurately as possible.) Mentalism.

Alward, Gus and Nellie, *Alwards: America's Greatest Mind Readers, The.* (c. 1880) Authors. 12 pp. 4.25 x 6.75 in. Mentalism, Second Sight. Pulp.

Amac, *Third Man Walks Out, The.* (1951) William Kalman, Montreal. Stapled. (Information not verified by physical copy.) Cards, Three-Card Monte.

Amalfi, *Santa's Workshop and Other Christmas Magic.* (1957) Goodliffe Publications, Birmingham, UK. Saddle-stitch. Red, green, white. 51 pp. 5.5 x 8.5 in. Holiday magic, Christmas magic.

Amateur, Un, *Nouvelle Magie Blanche Dévoilée, La.* (1862) B. Renault et Cie., Paris. Perfect. Beige. 324 pp. 4.5 x 7.25 in. Fold-out frontispiece, plates. Beginner, Cards. French.

Amato, Bruce, *Feed 'Em and Fool 'Em.* (1988) Author, Hendersonville, TN. Saddle-stitch. Blue. 34 pp. 6.75 x 8.25 in. Signed by Bruce Amato. Close-Up, Restaurants.

Amato, Bruce, *This, That, and the Other.* (1991) Author, Hendersonville, TN. Saddle-stitch. Green. 23 pp. 5.5 x 8.5 in. Signed by Bruce Amato. Close-Up, Stage.

Amazia, *Book of Magic for the Amateur.* (n.d.) Author, Castleford, UK. Saddle-stitch. Yellow. 20 pp. 4 x 6.5 in. Beginner.

Ames, Eric, *Carl Hagenbeck's Empire of Entertainments.* (2008) University of Washington Press, Seattle. Perfect. Yellow. 336 pp. 8.5 x 10 in. History, Indian magic.

American Society for Psychical Research, *Proceedings A.S.P.R. 1926-1927 Vol. 3: The Margery Mediumship.* (1927) A.S.P.R., New York. Cloth. Black. 228 pp. 6.25 x 9.25 in. Scarce Margery signature. Signed by Margery (Mina Crandon). Spiritualism.

Amira, Pablo, *5 Miracles with 5 E.S.P. Cards.* (2011) Titanus Magic Productions, UK. Saddle-stitch. 37 pp. 5.5 x 8 in. (Information not verified by physical copy.) Mentalism, E.S.P. cards.

Amira, Pablo, *52.* (2016) Mentalism Center, Temuco, Chile. Perfect. 97 pp. 5.75 x 8.25 in. (Information not verified by physical copy.) Mentalism.

Amira, Pablo, *B'Cards.* (2016) Mentalism Center, Temuco, Chile. Perfect. 84 pp. 5.75 x 8.25 in. (Information not verified by physical copy.) Mentalism.

Amira, Pablo, *Birreal.* (2019) Mentalism Center, Temuco, Chile. Perfect. 83 pp. 4.25 x 6.75 in. (Information not verified by physical copy.) Mentalism.

Amira, Pablo, *Borrowed Time.* (2019) Mentalism Center, Temuco, Chile. Perfect. 103 pp. 4.25 x 6.75 in. (Information not verified by physical copy.) Mentalism.

Amira, Pablo, *Cartomantic Artifacts.* (2018) Mentalism Center, Temuco, Chile. Perfect. 100 pp. 5.75 x 8.25 in. (Information not verified by physical copy.) Mentalism.

Amira, Pablo, *E5P.* (2015) Mentalism Center, Temuco, Chile. Perfect. 150 pp. 5.75 x 8.25 in. (Information not verified by physical copy.) Mentalism.

Amira, Pablo, *Ideas About Pendulums.* (2011) Mentalism Center, Temuco, Chile. Casebound. 192 pp. 6 x 9 in. (Information not verified by physical copy.) Mentalism, Pendulums.

Amira, Pablo, *Impromptu and Colorful Prediction.* (2011) Titanus Magic Productions, UK. Saddle-stitch. 49 pp. 8 x 10.5 in. (Information not verified by physical copy.) Mentalism.

Amira, Pablo, *MentalRubik.* (2018) Mentalism Center, Temuco, Chile. Perfect. 58 pp. 5.75 x 8.25 in. (Information not verified by physical copy.) Mentalism, Rubik's Cube.

Amira, Pablo, *Minimal Mentalism II.* (2017) Mentalism Center, Temuco, Chile. Perfect. 74 pp. 5.75 x 8.25 in. (Information not verified by physical copy.) Mentalism.

Amira, Pablo, *Minimal Mentalism III.* (2019) Mentalism Center, Temuco, Chile. Perfect. 112 pp. 5.75 x 8.25 in. (Information not verified by physical copy.) Mentalism.

Amira, Pablo, *Minimal Mentalism IV.* (2020) Mentalism Center, Temuco, Chile. Perfect. 61 pp. 5.75 x 8.25 in. (Information not verified by physical copy.) Mentalism.

Amira, Pablo, *Minimal One-Man Act.* (2023) Mentalism Center, Temuco, Chile. Casebound. 85 pp. 5.75 x 8.25 in. (Information not verified by physical copy.) Mentalism.

Amira, Pablo, *Motivational Mentalism Virtual Act.* (2021) Mentalism Center, Temuco, Chile. Perfect. 85 pp. 5.75 x 8.25 in. (Information not verified by physical copy.) Mentalism.

Amira, Pablo, *Mysteries Anywhere.* (2011) Titanus Magic Productions, UK. Saddle-stitch. 56 pp. 5.5 x 8 in. (Information not verified by physical copy. Bibliographical details are as accurate as possible.) Mentalism.

Amira, Pablo, *Path of Mystery, The.* (2023) Mentalism Center, Temuco, Chile. Casebound. 206 pp. 5.75 x 8.25 in. (Information not verified by physical copy.) Mentalism.

Amira, Pablo, *Romantic Mentalism.* (2019) Mentalism Center, Temuco, Chile. Perfect. 65 pp. 5.75 x 8.25 in. (Information not verified by physical copy.) Mentalism.

Amira, Pablo, *Simply Mental.* (2017) Mentalism Center, Temuco, Chile. Casebound. 526 pp. 6 x 9 in. (Information not verified by physical copy.) Mentalism.

Amira, Pablo, *Simply Mental II.* (2020) Mentalism Center, Temuco, Chile. Casebound. 715 pp. 6 x 9 in. (Information not verified by physical copy.) Mentalism.

Amira, Pablo, *Symbolic Artifacts.* (2021) Mentalism Center, Temuco, Chile. Perfect. 118 pp. 5.75 x 8.25 in. (Information not verified by physical copy.) Mentalism.

Amira, Pablo, *Telepathic Artifacts.* (2019) Mentalism Center, Temuco, Chile. Perfect. 339 pp. 5.75 x 8.25 in. (Information not verified by physical copy.) Mentalism.

Ammar, Michael (See also Bennett, Doug; Fleischer, Adam J.; Harris, Paul; Roth, David), *Ammar.* (2010) Author, Windermere, FL. Saddle-stitch. Red. 20 pp. 8.5 x 11 in. Signed by Michael Ammar. Lecture notes. Close-Up, Stage.

Ammar, Michael, *Ammar Lecture Supplement 1998.* (1998) Author, Las Vegas. Saddle-stitch. 9 pp. 8.5 x 11 in. (Information not verified by physical copy.) Lecture notes. Cards, Coins, Close-Up, Theory.

Ammar, Michael, *Ammar Topit Pattern.* (2011) Author, Windermere, FL. Folded single page. Color. 18 x 24 in. Topit pattern for tailor. Topit, Gimmicks, Close-Up, Stage.

Ammar, Michael, *Bill to Lemon Closer.* (2006) Author, Austin, TX. Saddle-stitch. Blue. 12 pp. 5.75 x 8.25 in. (Information not verified by physical copy.) Stage, Bill in Lemon.

Ammar, Michael, *Coins Through Silk.* (1995) Author, Austin, TX. Stapled. Gray. 3 pp. 8.5 x 11 in. (Information not verified by physical copy. Bibliographical details are as accurate as possible.) Coins, Silks, Close-Up.

Ammar, Michael, *Command Performance Encore I, The.* (1980) Secret Service, Morgantown, WV. Saddle-stitch. Yellow. 28 pp. 8.5 x 11 in. Signed by Michael Ammar. Cards, Close-Up.

Ammar, Michael, *Command Performance Encore II, The.* (1981) Secret Service, Morgantown, WV. Saddle-stitch. Yellow. 44 pp. 8.5 x 11 in. Cards, Close-Up.

Ammar, Michael, *Command Performance Premier Issue, The.* (1980) Secret Service, Morgantown, WV. Saddle-stitch. Blue. 32 pp. 8.5 x 11 in. Signed by Michael Ammar. Cards, Close-Up.

Ammar, Michael, *Complete Cups and Balls, The.* (1998) L & L Publishing, Tahoma, CA. Cloth. Black. 172 pp. 8.5 x 11 in. Dust jacket. Close-Up, Cups and Balls.

Ammar, Michael, *Crazy Man's Handcuffs, The.* (1989) Magic City, Paramount, CA. Stapled. Pink. 8 pp. 8.5 x 11 in. Close-Up, Rubber bands.

Ammar, Michael, *Cups and Lemon, The.* (2008) Ammar Magic, Windermere, FL. Saddle-stitch. Blue. 10 pp. 8.5 x 11 in. Cups and Balls, Bill in Lemon, Close-Up.

Ammar, Michael, *Easy to Master Lecture.* (1995) Ammar Magic, Austin, TX. Saddle-stitch. Color. 16 pp. 8.25 x 11 in. Lecture notes. Close-Up, Cards, Topit.

Ammar, Michael, *Encore III.* (1983) Secret Service, Bluefield, WV. Cloth. Maroon. Cover text: Gold; 95 pp. 8.5 x 11 in. Dust jacket. Close-Up.

Ammar, Michael, with Losander, Dirk, *Exquisite Floating Wine Glass.* (2016) Authors, Las Vegas. Folded. Color. 4 pp. 8.5 x 11 in. Levitations, Close-Up, Stage, Zombie.

Ammar, Michael, *Floating Bill, The.* (1986) Author, Van Nuys. CA. Stapled. Yellow. 13 pp. 8.5 x 11 in. Lecture notes. Close-Up, Thread, Bills, Levitations.

Ammar, Michael, *Fourth World Lecture Tour.* (1993) Author, Austin, TX. Saddle-stitch. Green. 20 pp. 8.5 x 11 in. Lecture notes. Close-Up, Cards, Stage.

Ammar, Michael, *How to Negotiate Higher Performance Fees.* (1988) Author, Van Nuys. CA. Stapled. Blue. 12 pp. 8.5 x 11 in. Signed by Michael Ammar. Business.

Ammar, Michael, *I've Been Everywhere.* (c. 2014) Author, Windermere, FL. Saddle-stitch. Red. 20 pp. 8.5 x 11 in. Lecture notes. Close-Up, Cards, Coins.

Ammar, Michael, *Lecture Notes.* (1981) Author, Bluefield, WV. 10 pp. (Information not verified by physical copy.) Lecture notes. Close-Up, Cards, Coins.

Ammar, Michael, *Lecture Notes: April-May Lectures 1981.* (1981) Author, Bluefield, WV. 10 pp. As "Michael A. Ammar." (Information not verified by physical copy.) Lecture notes. Cards, Coins, Close-Up, Stage.

Ammar, Michael, *Lucid Astonishment.* (1993) Author, Austin, TX. Clip. White. 18 pp. 8.5 x 11 in. (Measurements and other information have been recorded as accurately as possible.) Lecture notes. Theory, Business.

Ammar, Michael, *Magic lecture notes.* (2000) Author, Westlake Village, CA. Saddle-stitch. White. 20 pp. 8.5 x 11 in. Lecture notes. Close-Up, Coins, Topit.

Ammar, Michael, *Magic of Michael Ammar, The.* Collector's Edition. (1999) L & L Publishing, Tahoma, CA. Cloth. Blue. 306 pp. Slipcase. Dust jacket. Signed and numbered. (Information not verified by physical copy.) Close-Up, Stage, Theory.

Ammar, Michael, *Magic of Michael Ammar, The.* First printing. (1999) L & L Publishing, Tahoma, CA. Cloth. Blue. 306 pp. 8.5 x 11 in. Dust jacket. Warmly inscribed to Jay Marshall. Signed by Michael Ammar, Hannah Ammar. Close-Up, Stage, Theory.

Ammar, Michael, *Magic of Michael Ammar, The.* Ninth printing. (1999) L & L Publishing, Tahoma, CA. Cloth. Blue. 306 pp. 8.5 x 11 in. Dust jacket. Close-Up, Stage, Theory.

Ammar, Michael, *Magic of Michael Ammar, The.* (2024) Murphy's Magic Supplies, Rancho Cordova, CA. Cloth. Black. 260 pp. 8.5 x 11 in. Dust jacket. Close-Up, Stage, Theory.

Ammar, Michael, with Fleischer, Adam J., *Magical Arts Journal.* Deluxe edition. (2010) Ammar Magic, Windermere, FL. Leather. Blue. 554 pp. 8.5 x 11 in. Signed by Michael Ammar, Adam J. Fleischer. Close-Up, Showmanship, Magazine.

Ammar, Michael, with Fleischer, Adam J., *Magical Arts Journal.* (2010) Ammar Magic, Windermere, FL. Casebound. White, brown. 554 pp. 8.5 x 11 in. Close-Up, Showmanship, Magazine.

Ammar, Michael, *Manual of Magic Psychology, A.* (1980) Author, Bluefield, WV. Stapled. Orange. 30 pp. 8.5 x 11 in. Inscribed "I hope you enter the Magician's Hut!" Signed by Michael Ammar. Theory, Psychology.

Ammar, Michael, *Michael Ammar Coin Clip, The.* (1983) Palmer Magic, Redwood City, CA. Saddle-stitch. White, blue. 12 pp. 5.5 x 8.5 in. Coins, Gimmicks.

Ammar, Michael, *Michael Ammar Lecture.* (2007) Author, Windermere, FL. 21 pp. (Information not verified by physical copy.) Lecture notes. Close-Up, Cards. Spanish.

Ammar, Michael, *Michael Ammar Notes.* (2016) Author, Windermere, FL. Saddle-stitch. Color. 19 pp. 8.5 x 11 in. Lecture notes. Close-Up, Cards.

Ammar, Michael, *Notes de Conférence.* (2004) Author, Windermere, FL. 16 pp. (Information not verified by physical copy.) Lecture notes. Close-Up, Stage. French.

Ammar, Michael, *Success and Magic.* (1984) Secret Service, Bluefield, WV. Saddle-stitch. Color. 36 pp. 8.5 x 11 in. Signed by Michael Ammar. Theory, Business.

Ammar, Michael, *Third National Tour Notes.* (1989) Author, Austin, TX. Saddle-stitch. Yellow. 16 pp. 8.5 x 11 in. Inscribed "I hope you'll use this." Signed by Michael Ammar. Lecture notes. Close-Up.

Ammar, Michael, *Topit Book, The.* (1983) Secret Service, Bluefield, WV. Cloth. Black. 119 pp. 8.5 x 11 in. Signed by Michael Ammar. Close-Up, Topit.

Ammar, Michael, *Topit Book 2.0, The.* Second edition. (2014) Author, Windermere, FL. Casebound. Tan. 200 pp. 8.5 x 11 in. Close-Up, Topit.

Ammar, Michael, *Visually Yours.* (1981) Author, Bluefield, WV. Saddle-stitch. Yellow. 6 pp. 5.5 x 8.5 in. Includes gimmicked card. Signed by Michael Ammar. Cards, Gimmicked cards, Gimmicks.

Amodei, Ivan, *Magic's Most Amazing Stories.* (2010) Eclipse P & D Inc., Los Angeles. Perfect. 256 pp. 6 x 9 in. (Information not verified by physical copy.) History, Essays.

Ancona, Daniele, *Bizarre Magic vol. 1.* Limited edition. (2018) Author, Italy. Casebound. Black. 526 pp. 8.25 x 11.5 in. Signed by Daniele Ancona. 50 copies. Bizarre magick. Italian.

And, Dr. Metin, *Magic in Istanbul.* (1978) Micky Hades, Calgary, Canada. Saddle-stitch. White. 67 pp. 6 x 9 in. History.

Anders, Franz, *Junge Tausenkünstler, Der.* (1877) Belhagen, Leipzig. Cloth. Brown. 320 pp. 5.25 x 7.75 in. Beginner, Stunts. German.

Anders, Franz, *Junge Tausenkünstler, Der.* (1989) Edition Olms, Zurich. Cloth. Black. 330 pp. 5.25 x 7.75 in. Reprint of 1890 edition. Beginner. German.

Anderson, A., *How to Become a Magician.* (1898) Frank Tousey, New York. Perfect. Pink, brown, yellow. 61 pp. 3.5 x 6 in. Beginner, Cards.

Anderson, A., *How to Become a Magician.* (1902) Frank Tousey, New York. Perfect. Color. 62 pp. 3.5 x 6 in. Beginner, Cards.

Anderson, A., *How to Do Chemical Tricks.* (1894) Frank Tousey, New York. Perfect. Tan, black. 64 pp. 3.5 x 6 in. Chemical.

Anderson, A., *How to Do Chemical Tricks.* (1898) Frank Tousey, New York. Perfect. White, blue. 64 pp. 4.25 x 6.5 in. Chemical.

Anderson, A., *How to Do Electrical Tricks.* (1902) Frank Tousey, New York. Perfect. White, blue. 64 pp. 4 x 6.25 in. Stunts, Electrical.

Anderson, A., *How to Do Forty Tricks with Cards.* (1902) Frank Tousey, New York. Perfect. Tan, blue. 62 pp. 4.25 x 6.5 in. Cards, Beginner.

Anderson, A., *How to Do Mechanical Tricks.* (1898) Frank Tousey, New York. Perfect. White, blue. 62 pp. 4 x 6.5 in. Stunts, Beginner.

Anderson, A., *How to Do Second Sight.* (1902) Frank Tousey, New York. Perfect. White, blue, red, brown. 60 pp. 3.5 x 6 in. In Copperfield collection. Mentalism, Second Sight.

Anderson, A., *How to Do Sixty Tricks with Cards.* (1898) Frank Tousey, New York. Perfect. Color. 62 pp. 4.25 x 6.5 in. Cards, Beginner.

Anderson, A., *How to Do Sixty Tricks with Cards.* (1900) Frank Tousey, New York. Perfect. White, green. 62 pp. 3.5 x 6 in. Cards, Beginner.

Anderson, A., *How to Do Sixty Tricks with Cards.* (1902) Frank Tousey, New York. Perfect. White, blue. 62 pp. 4.25 x 6.25 in. Different cover design. Cards, Beginner.

Anderson, A., *How to Do Sleight of Hand.* (1894) Frank Tousey, New York. Perfect. 64 pp. 3.5 x 6 in. Beginner, General.

Anderson, A., *How to Do Sleight of Hand.* (1898) Frank Tousey, New York. Perfect. Color. 64 pp. 3.5 x 6 in. Beginner, General.

Anderson, A., *How to Do Sleight of Hand.* (1902) Harry E. Wolff, New York. Perfect. White, blue. 64 pp. 3.5 x 6 in. Beginner, General.

Anderson, A., *How to Do the Black Art.* (1898) Frank Tousey, New York. Perfect. Tan. 62 pp. 4 x 6 in. (Measurements and other information have been recorded as accurately as possible.) Beginner.

Anderson, A., *How to Do Tricks.* (1890) Frank Tousey, New York. Perfect. Tan. 60 pp. 4.25 x 6.25 in. Fire-breathing card magician on cover. Second printing of 1881 edition. Beginner.

Anderson, A., *How to Do Tricks.* (1894) Frank Tousey, New York. Perfect. White. 60 pp. 3.5 x 6 in. (Measurements and other information have been recorded as accurately as possible.) Beginner.

Anderson, A., *How to Do Tricks.* (1898) Frank Tousey, New York. Perfect. White, blue, brown, yellow. 60 pp. 3.5 x 6 in. In Copperfield collection. Beginner.

Anderson, A., *How to Do Tricks.* (1902) Frank Tousey, New York. Perfect. White, blue. 60 pp. 3.5 x 6 in. (Measurements and other information have been recorded as accurately as possible.) Beginner.

Anderson, A., *How to Do Tricks with Numbers.* (1902) Frank Tousey, New York. Perfect. Tan, blue. 60 pp. 3.5 x 6 in. In Copperfield collection. Beginner.

Anderson, Brooks, *So – You Want to Make a Buck: The Magic Manner of R. Claude Enslow.* Second edition. (1977) Author, Kansas City, MO. Saddle-stitch. Green. 32 pp. 5.5 x 8.5 in. Business.

Anderson, Doug, *Drive 'Em Nuts!* (1984) Author, Sunnyvale, CA. Stapled. Blue. 21 pp. 8.5 x 11 in. Lecture notes. Close-Up, Stage.

Anderson, Doug, *Straight Talk About Theme Park Magic.* (1984) Author, Sunnyvale, CA. Cloth. Black. 151 pp. 8.5 x 11 in. Signed by Doug Anderson. #351. Lecture notes. Business, Theme parks.

Anderson, Eric, *$15,000 Newspaper Test, The.* (c. 2016) Author, San Diego. Stapled. White. 8.5 x 11 in. (Information not verified by physical copy.) Mentalism, Newspaper.

Anderson, Eric, *From the Streets to the Corporate Suites.* (2016) Author, San Diego. Stapled. White. 40 pp. 8.5 x 11 in. (Information not verified by physical copy.) Cards, Close-Up, Corporate shows.

Anderson, Eric, *Just Cards.* (c. 2016) Author, San Diego. Stapled. White. 8.5 x 11 in. (Information not verified by physical copy.) Lecture notes. Cards.

Anderson, Gene (See also Martyn, Topper), *Book, The.* Deluxe edition. (2016) Author, Midland, MI. Leather. Black. 256 pp. 8.5 x 11 in. Dust jacket. Slipcase. Signed by Gene Anderson. #45 of 50. Stage, Theory, Business, Close-Up.

Anderson, Gene, *Book, The.* First edition. (2016) Author, Midland, MI. Cloth. Black. 256 pp. 8.5 x 11 in. Dust jacket. Stage, Theory, Business, Close-Up.

Anderson, Gene, *Claude Crowe's Peace o' Paper.* (1970) Magic Inc., Chicago. Comb. Blue. 3 pp. 8.5 x 11 in. Signed by Gene Anderson. Torn and Restored Newspaper, Stage.

Anderson, Gene, *Gene Anderson's Newspaper Trick.* (1976) Magic Inc., Chicago. Saddle-stitch. Olive. 13 pp. 8.5 x 11 in. Torn and Restored Newspaper, Stage.

Anderson, Gene, with Marshall, Frances Ireland, *Newspaper Magic.* First edition. (1968) Magic Inc., Chicago. Saddle-stitch. Yellow. 144 pp. 8.5 x 11 in. Jay Marshall note: "First copy, July 1, 1968." Torn and Restored Newspaper, Stage, Newspaper.

Anderson, Gene, with Marshall, Frances Ireland, *Newspaper Magic.* First edition. (1968) Magic Inc., Chicago. Saddle-stitch. Yellow. 144 pp. 8.5 x 11 in. Torn and Restored Newspaper, Stage, Newspaper.

Anderson, Gene, with Marshall, Frances Ireland, *Newspaper Magic.* Fourth printing. (1976) Magic Inc., Chicago. Comb. White, blue. 144 pp. 8.5 x 11 in. Signed by Gene Anderson, Frances Marshall. Torn and Restored Newspaper, Stage, Newspaper.

Anderson, Gene, with Marshall, Frances Ireland, *Newspaper Magic.* Sixth printing. (1980) Magic Inc., Chicago. Comb. Green. 144 pp. 8.5 x 11 in. Signed by Gene Anderson. Torn and Restored Newspaper, Stage, Newspaper.

Anderson, Gene, with Marshall, Frances Ireland, *Newspaper Magic.* Seventh printing. (1983) Magic Inc., Chicago. Perfect. Blue. 144 pp. 8.75 x 11.25 in. Signed by Gene Anderson. Torn and Restored Newspaper, Stage, Newspaper.

Anderson, Gene, with Marshall, Frances Ireland, *Newspaper Magic.* (n.d.) Magic Inc., Chicago. Comb. White, black. 144 pp. 8.5 x 11 in. Torn and Restored Newspaper, Stage, Newspaper.

Anderson, Gene, *Part-Time Pro, The.* (1975) Author, Midland, MI. Saddle-stitch. Bright red. 30 pp. 5.5 x 8.5 in. Signed by Gene Anderson. Lecture notes. Business, Theory, Close-Up, Stage.

Anderson, Gene, *Part-Time Pro, The.* (1976) Author, Midland, MI. Saddle-stitch. Dark red. 30 pp. 5.5 x 8.5 in. Signed by Gene Anderson. Lecture notes. Business, Theory, Close-Up, Stage.

Anderson, Gene, *Part-Time Pro, The.* (1989) Author, Midland, MI. Saddle-stitch. Red. 20 pp. 5.5 x 8.5 in. Signed by Gene Anderson. Lecture notes. Business, Theory, Close-Up, Stage.

Anderson, Gene, *Part-Time Pro: Return Engagement, The.* (1983) Author, Midland, MI. Saddle-stitch. Blue. 20 pp. 5.5 x 8.5 in. Signed by Gene Anderson. Lecture notes. Business, Theory, Close-Up, Stage.

Anderson, Gene, *Perceptions and Deceptions.* (2010) Author, Midland, MI. Stapled. Green. 16 pp. 8.5 x 11 in. (Measurements and other information have been recorded as accurately as possible.) Stage, Close-Up.

Anderson, Gene, *Si Stebbins Card Routine.* (2005) Author, Midland, MI. Stapled. Blue. 6 pp. 8.5 x 11 in. Signed by Gene Anderson. Cards, Prearranged deck.

Anderson, Gene, *Squircle.* (1976) Author, Midland, MI. Folded. White. 2 pp. 8.5 x 11 in. Sold at lectures. With outer title sheet. Paper, Newspaper.

Anderson, Gene, *Squircle.* (n.d.) Author, Midland, MI. Stapled. White. 2 pp. 8.5 x 11 in. Includes Ken Brooke routine. Paper, Newspaper.

Anderson, Gene, *Star of David.* (1976) Author, Midland, MI. Folded. White. 2 pp. 8.5 x 11 in. Sold at lectures. With outer title sheet. Paper, Newspaper.

Anderson, George B., *Anthology.* (1980) Magic Inc., Chicago. Comb. White. Multiple sections. 5.5 x 8.5 in. Original booklets bound together with cover. Mentalism, Showmanship.

Anderson, George B., *Dynamite Mentalism.* (1979) Magic Inc., Chicago. Saddle-stitch. Blue. 28 pp. 5.5 x 8.5 in. Mentalism.

Anderson, George B., *George Anderson's Lecture Notebook.* (1980) Magic Inc., Chicago. Saddle-stitch. White. 35 pp. 5.5 x 8.5 in. Lecture notes. Mentalism.

Anderson, George B., *How to Be a Junior Magician.* (1959) Haywood Publishing Co., Chicago. Saddle-stitch. Light green. 63 pp. 5.5 x 8.25 in. Children's book, Beginner.

Anderson, George B., *It Must Be Mindreading.* First edition. (1949) Ireland Magic Co., Chicago. Saddle-stitch. Beige. 57 pp. 6 x 9 in. Mentalism.

Anderson, George B., *It Must Be Mindreading.* Second edition. (1949) Ireland Magic Co., Chicago. Saddle-stitch. Gray. 57 pp. 5.25 x 8.25 in. Mentalism.

Anderson, George B., *It Must Be Mindreading.* Third printing. (1963) Ireland Magic Co., Chicago. Saddle-stitch. Pink. 62 pp. 5.5 x 8.5 in. Mentalism.

Anderson, George B., *Let the Audience Do the Show.* (1980) Magic Inc., Chicago. Saddle-stitch. Green. 17 pp. 5.5 x 8.5 in. Showmanship, Stage, Close-Up.

Anderson, George B., *Magic Digest.* (1972) Digest Books, Northfield, IL. Perfect. Black. 288 pp. 8.5 x 11 in. (Measurements and other information have been recorded as accurately as possible.) Beginner.

Anderson, George B., *Magic Pendulum, The.* (1980) Magic Inc., Chicago. Saddle-stitch. Beige. 27 pp. 5.5 x 8.5 in. Mentalism, Pendulums.

Anderson, George B., *My Favorite Easy Mental Card Magic.* (1980) Magic Inc., Chicago. Saddle-stitch. Yellow. 24 pp. 5.5 x 8.5 in. Mentalism, Cards.

Anderson, George B., *My Favorite Sucker Card Tricks.* (1980) Magic Inc., Chicago. Saddle-stitch. Blue. 16 pp. 5.5 x 8.5 in. Mentalism, Cards.

Anderson, George B., *Overcoming Magic Hazards.* (1980) Magic Inc., Chicago. Saddle-stitch. Blue. 24 pp. 5.5 x 8.5 in. Discussion of Vernon Mental Force. Showmanship, Cards, Mentalism.

Anderson, George B., *You, Too, Can Read Minds.* (1968) Magic Inc., Chicago. Saddle-stitch. Blue. 63 pp. 5.5 x 8.5 in. Mentalism.

Anderson, H. E. P., *Biography of John Henry Anderson, The Great Wizard of the North.* (1858) John Tonks, Birmingham, UK. 24 pp. 5.75 x 9.75 in. (Information not verified by physical copy.) Toole Stott no. 59. History, Biography.

Anderson, Harry, *Anderson Illusion Lecture Notes.* (1979) Author, Los Angeles. Clip. Yellow. 15 pp. 8.5 x 11 in. Lecture notes. Mentalism, Stage, Memory, Cards.

Anderson, Harry, *Anderson Illusion Lecture Notes.* (c. 1980) Author, Los Angeles. Saddle-stitch. Yellow. 16 pp. 5.5 x 8.5 in. Lecture notes. Mentalism, Stage.

Anderson, Harry, *Games You Can't Lose.* (1989) Pocket Books, New York. Perfect. Red. 189 pp. 5.25 x 8.25 in. Bets, Cheating.

Anderson, Harry, *Games You Can't Lose.* (2001) Burford Books, Short Hills, NJ. Perfect. Yellow. 160 pp. 5.5 x 8.25 in. Signed by Harry Anderson. Bets, Cheating.

Anderson, Harry, *Last Monte, The.* (1992) Meir Yedid Magic, Rego Park, NY. 4 pp. (Information not verified by physical copy.) Cards, Monte.

Anderson, Harry, with Caveney, Mike, *Harry Anderson: Wise Guy.* (1993) Mike Caveney's Magic Words, Pasadena, CA. Cloth. Green. 187 pp. 8.75 x 9.5 in. Dust jacket. Signed by Harry Anderson. Biography, Stage, Cards.

Anderson, Harry, with Racherbaumer, Jon, *Magic 2 (Squared).* Special limited edition. (2008) Spade and Archer, Asheville, NC. Comb. White. 49 pp. 8.5 x 11 in. Bound backward. Signed by Harry Anderson. #70 of 200. Cards.

Anderson, Harry, with Racherbaumer, Jon, *Magic 2 (Squared).* Special limited edition. (2009) Spade and Archer, Asheville, NC. Comb. Blue. 49 pp. 8.5 x 11 in. Bound backward. Signed by Harry Anderson. #22. Cards.

Anderson, Harry, *Practical Magic.* (2011) Spade and Archer, Asheville, NC. Perfect. Green. 4.25 x 7 in. (Measurements and other information have been recorded as accurately as possible.) Book test, Mentalism.

Anderson, Harry, *Shadow and Other Card Mysteries, The.* (1982) Left-Handed League, Los Feliz, CA. Saddle-stitch. Orange. 24 pp. 5.5 x 8.5 in. Cards.

Anderson, Harry, *Tipping the Hat.* (2011) Spade and Archer, Asheville, NC. Perfect. Tan. 131 pp. 8.5 x 11 in. (Information not verified by physical copy.) Stage, Comedy.

Anderson, Harry, *Tipping the Hat.* Second printing. (2013) Spade and Archer, Asheville, NC. Perfect. Tan. 131 pp. 8.5 x 11 in. (Information not verified by physical copy.) Stage, Comedy.

Anderson, John Henry, *Anderson's Hand Book of Magic and Mystery.* (c. 1848) Author, Glasgow. Perfect. Yellow. 16 pp. 3 x 5 in. (Information not verified by physical copy.) Toole Stott no. 38. Early magic.

Anderson, John Henry, *Brains of Boston, The.* (1861) Author, Boston. 40 pp. 6 x 9 in. (Information not verified by physical copy.) Toole Stott no. 926. Humor, Puzzles.

Anderson, John Henry, *Complete Conjuror, with the Whole Art of Making Fireworks, The.* (c. 1833) J. Catnach, London. 12 pp. 4.25 x 6.75 in. (Information not verified by physical copy.) Toole Stott no. 174. Credited to "Wizard of the North." Toole Stott listed this title as "anonymous" because author was age 19. Beginner.

Anderson, John Henry, *Fashionable Science of Parlour Magic, The.* (1843) Author, London. Perfect. Blue. 72 pp. 4.25 x 7 in. (Information not verified by physical copy.) Toole Stott no. 17. Beginner.

Anderson, John Henry, *Fashionable Science of Parlour Magic, The.* Sixth edition. (c. 1845) Author, London. Perfect. Blue. 71 pp. 4.25 x 7 in. Toole Stott no. 917. In Copperfield collection. Beginner.

Anderson, John Henry, *Fashionable Science of Parlour Magic, The.* Seventh edition. (c. 1845) Author, London. 71 pp. 4.5 x 7 in. (Information not verified by physical copy.) Toole Stott no. 918. Beginner.

Anderson, John Henry, *Fashionable Science of Parlour Magic, The.* Eighth edition. (c. 1845) Author, London. 71 pp. 4.5 x 7 in. (Information not verified by physical copy.) Toole Stott no. 919. Beginner.

Anderson, John Henry, *Fashionable Science of Parlour Magic, The.* Tenth edition. (c. 1845) Author, London. 70 pp. 4.25 x 6.75 in. (Information not verified by physical copy.) Toole Stott no. 18. Beginner.

Anderson, John Henry, *Fashionable Science of Parlour Magic, The.* Eleventh edition. (c. 1845) Author, London. 72 pp. 4 x 7 in. (Information not verified by physical copy.) Toole Stott no. 19. Beginner.

Anderson, John Henry, *Fashionable Science of Parlour Magic, The.* Fourteenth edition. (c. 1845) Author, London. 72 pp. 3 x 6.75 in. (Information not verified by physical copy.) Toole Stott no. 20. Beginner.

Anderson, John Henry, *Fashionable Science of Parlour Magic, The.* Fifteenth edition. (c. 1846) Author, London. 71 pp. 3 x 6.75 in. (Information not verified by physical copy.) Toole Stott no. 1330. Beginner.

Anderson, John Henry, *Fashionable Science of Parlour Magic, The.* Sixteenth edition. (c. 1846) Author, London. 71 pp. 3 x 6.75 in. (Information not verified by physical copy.) Toole Stott no. 21. Beginner.

Anderson, John Henry, *Fashionable Science of Parlour Magic, The.* Seventeenth edition. (c. 1846) Author, London. 71 pp. 4.25 x 6 in. (Information not verified by physical copy.) Toole Stott no. 22. Beginner.

Anderson, John Henry, *Fashionable Science of Parlour Magic, The.* Twentieth edition. (c. 1846) Author, London. 78 pp. 4.25 x 6.75 in. (Information not verified by physical copy.) Toole Stott no. 23. Beginner.

Anderson, John Henry, *Fashionable Science of Parlour Magic, to which is added for the first time The Magic of Spirit Rapping, Writing Mediums, and Table Turning, The.* 21st edition. (c. 1847) Author, London. 160 pp. 4.5 x 6.75 in. (Information not verified by physical copy.) Toole Stott no. 24. Beginner.

Anderson, John Henry, *Fashionable Science of Parlour Magic, The.* 28th edition. (c. 1848) Author, London. 96 pp. 4.75 x 7 in. (Information not verified by physical copy.) Toole Stott no. 25. Beginner.

Anderson, John Henry, *Fashionable Science of Parlour Magic, The.* 29th edition. (c. 1848) Author, London. 95 pp. 4.75 x 7 in. (Information not verified by physical copy.) Toole Stott no. 1331. Beginner.

Anderson, John Henry, *Fashionable Science of Parlour Magic, The.* 29th edition. (c. 1848) Author, London. 95 pp. 4.75 x 7 in. (Information not verified by physical copy.) Ray Ricard library. Beginner.

Anderson, John Henry, *Fashionable Science of Parlour Magic, The.* 71st edition. (c. 1850) Godwin and Co., New York. 71 pp. 4.5 x 7 in. (Information not verified by physical copy.) Toole Stott no. 920. Estimated date has been changed to c. 1850. Beginner.

Anderson, John Henry, *Fashionable Science of Parlour Magic, The.* 84th edition. (c. 1851) Author, London. Perfect. Yellow. 62 pp. 4.5 x 7 in. (Information not verified by physical copy.) Toole Stott no. 26. Beginner.

Anderson, John Henry, *Fashionable Science of Parlour Magic, The.* 84th edition. (c. 1851) Author, London. 71 pp. 4 x 6.25 in. (Information not verified by physical copy.) Toole Stott no. 27. Beginner.

Anderson, John Henry, *Fashionable Science of Parlour Magic, The.* 84th edition. (1852) Brown, Philadelphia. 71 pp. 4.5 x 7 in. (Information not verified by physical copy.) Toole Stott no. 921. Beginner.

Anderson, John Henry, *Fashionable Science of Parlour Magic, The.* 85th edition. (1852) Stearns and Co., New York. 66 pp. 4.75 x 7.25 in. (Information not verified by physical copy.) Toole Stott no. 922. Beginner.

Anderson, John Henry, *Fashionable Science of Parlour Magic, The.* 85th edition. (1861) Dick and Fitzgerald, New York. Perfect. Red, yellow. 90 pp. 4.25 x 7.75 in. (Information not verified by physical copy.) Toole Stott no. 28. Beginner.

Anderson, John Henry, *Fashionable Science of Parlour Magic, The.* 85th edition. (c. 1861) Stearns and Co., New York. Perfect. Green. 71 pp. 4.5 x 7.5 in. (Information not verified by physical copy.) Toole Stott no. 29. Beginner.

Anderson, John Henry, *Fashionable Science of Parlour Magic, The.* 100th edition. (c. 1852) Author, London. 71 pp. 4.5 x 7 in. (Information not verified by physical copy.) Toole Stott no. 1332. Beginner.

Anderson, John Henry, *Fashionable Science of Parlour Magic, The.* 102nd edition. (c. 1852) Author, London. 71 pp. 4.5 x 7 in. (Information not verified by physical copy.) Toole Stott no. 1333. Beginner.

Anderson, John Henry, *Fashionable Science of Parlour Magic, The.* 104th edition. (c. 1852) Author, London. 95 pp. 4.25 x 7.25 in. (Information not verified by physical copy.) Toole Stott no. 923. Beginner.

Anderson, John Henry, *Fashionable Science of Parlour Magic, The.* 106th edition. (n.d.) Author, London. 95 pp. 4.75 x 7.25 in. (Information not verified by physical copy.) Toole Stott no. 30. Beginner.

Anderson, John Henry, *Fashionable Science of Parlour Magic, The.* 106th edition. (n.d.) Author, London. 95 pp. 4.75 x 7.25 in. (Information not verified by physical copy.) Toole Stott no. 30. Beginner.

Anderson, John Henry, *Fashionable Science of Parlour Magic, The.* 108th edition. (n.d.) Author, London. 95 pp. 4.5 x 6.75 in. (Information not verified by physical copy.) Toole Stott no. 31. Beginner.

Anderson, John Henry, *Fashionable Science of Parlour Magic, The.* 128th edition. (c. 1859) Author, London. 95 pp. 4.75 x 7 in. (Information not verified by physical copy.) Toole Stott no. 1334. Beginner.

Anderson, John Henry, *Fashionable Science of Parlour Magic, The.* 139th edition. (c. 1859) Author, London. 95 pp. 4.75 x 7 in. (Information not verified by physical copy.) Toole Stott no. 924. Beginner.

Anderson, John Henry, *Fashionable Science of Parlour Magic, The.* 140th edition. (c. 1860) Author, London. 128 pp. 4.75 x 7.25 in. (Information not verified by physical copy.) Toole Stott no. 33. Beginner.

Anderson, John Henry, *Fashionable Science of Parlour Magic, The.* 150th edition. (c. 1860) Author, London. 128 pp. 4.75 x 7.25 in. (Information not verified by physical copy.) Toole Stott no. 1335. Beginner.

Anderson, John Henry, *Fashionable Science of Parlour Magic, The.* 151st edition. (1860) Author, United States. Perfect. Red. 72 pp. 4.75 x 6.75 in. (Information not verified by physical copy.) Toole Stott no. 34. Beginner.

Anderson, John Henry, *Fashionable Science of Parlour Magic, The.* 250th edition. (c. 1864) Author, London. 128 pp. 4.5 x 7.25 in. (Information not verified by physical copy.) Toole Stott no. 35, 1336. Beginner.

Anderson, John Henry, *Fashionable Science of Parlour Magic, The.* (n.d.) Brian McCullagh, Queensland, Australia. Saddle-stitch. Brown. 48 pp. 4.25 x 7 in. Reprint of c. 1858 Australian edition. Beginner, Pitch book.

Anderson, John Henry, *Fashionable Science of Parlour Magic, The.* (n.d.) Author, London. Perfect. Black, red, beige. 95 pp. 4.75 x 7 in. Beginner, Pitch book.

Anderson, John Henry, *Great Wizard's Hand-Book of Magic, or Parlour Entertainment, The.* (n.d.) W. S. Fortey, London. White. 7 pp. 5 x 7.5 in. Cover and one sheet only. Beginner.

Anderson, John Henry, *Great Wizard's Hand-Book of Magic, or Parlour Entertainment, The.* (n.d.) Ryle and Paul, London. Yellow. 12 pp. 4.5 x 7 in. (Information not verified by physical copy.) Toole Stott no. 39. Beginner.

Anderson, John Henry, *Great Wizard's Hand-Book of Magic, or Parlour Entertainment, The.* (n.d.) W. J. Bailey, London. 12 pp. 4.25 x 7.25 in. (Information not verified by physical copy.) Toole Stott no. 40. Beginner.

Anderson, John Henry, *Great Wizard's Hand-Book of Magic, or Parlour Entertainment and Fortune Telling by Cards, The.* (n.d.) Author, London. 8 pp. 5 x 7.5 in. (Information not verified by physical copy.) Toole Stott no. 41. Beginner, Fortune-telling, Cards.

Anderson, John Henry, *Great Wizard's Hand-Book of Magic, or Parlour Entertainment and Fortune Telling with Cards.* (c. 1860) T. Whitton, London. 8 pp. 4.75 x 7 in. (Information not verified by physical copy.) Toole Stott no. 928. Beginner, Fortune-telling, Cards.

Anderson, John Henry, *Great Wizard's Hand-Book of Magic, or Parlour Entertainment, Containing also Fortune-Telling by Cards and the Rope Trick, The.* (n.d.) Author, London. 8 pp. 5 x 7.5 in. (Information not verified by physical copy.) Toole Stott no. 42. Beginner, Fortune-telling, Cards, Rope.

Anderson, John Henry, *Ladies' Budget of Wit, The.* (1852) Baker, Godwin, and Co., New York. 60 pp. 5.5 x 9 in. (Information not verified by physical copy.) Toole Stott no. 927. Humor, Puzzles.

Anderson, John Henry, *Magic of Spirit Rapping, Writing Mediums, and Table Turning, The.* (c. 1850) Author, London. 95 pp. (Information not verified by physical copy.) Toole Stott no. 1337. Spiritualism, Mediums, Exposés.

Anderson, John Henry, *Magical Grammar, or The Fashionable Science of Parlour Magic.* 129th edition. (n.d.) Author, London. 48 pp. 4.25 x 7 in. (Information not verified by physical copy.) Toole Stott no. 32. Beginner.

Anderson, John Henry, *Magical Grammar, or The Fashionable Science of Parlour Magic.* (c. 1858) Author, Melbourne. 48 pp. 4.25 x 7 in. (Information not verified by physical copy.) Toole Stott no. 925. Beginner.

Anderson, John Henry, *Opinions of the London and Provincial Press on the Unparalleled and Truly Scientific Performances of the Great Wizard of the North.* (1840) Mitchell, Heaton, and Mitchell, Liverpool, UK. 22 pp. 4.25 x 7 in. (Information not verified by physical copy.) Toole Stott no. 37. Biography, History, Souvenir book.

Anderson, John Henry, *Parlour Magic.* (c. 1845) Knight and Co., London. 12 pp. 4.25 x 7 in. (Information not verified by physical copy.) Toole Stott no. 36. Beginner.

Anderson, John Henry, *Professor Anderson at Brechin Castle, from the Note-Book of the Wizard of the North.* (n.d.) Author, London. 15 pp. 2.75 x 4 in. (Information not verified by physical copy.) Toole Stott no. 48. Biography, History.

Anderson, John Henry, *Professor Anderson's Expose of Spirit Rappings.* (1853) S. Booth, New York. 32 pp. 4.25 x 6.75 in. (Information not verified by physical copy.) Toole Stott no. 49. Spiritualism, Exposés.

Anderson, John Henry, *Professor Anderson's Grand Conundrum Competition Night.* (1850) W. GIlchrist, Glasgow. 34 pp. 4.5 x 7 in. (Information not verified by physical copy.) Toole Stott no. 43. Riddles, Souvenir book.

Anderson, John Henry, *Professor Anderson's Grand Conundrum Contest in the Music Hall, Birmingham.* (1857) John Tonks, Birmingham, UK. Perfect. Purple. 32 pp. 4.75 x 7 in. (Information not verified by physical copy.) Toole Stott no. 45. Riddles, Souvenir book.

Anderson, John Henry, *Professor Anderson's Magic Picture Gallery.* (1864) A. Nimmo, London. 5 x 7.25 in. (Information not verified by physical copy.) Toole Stott no. 53. Souvenir book.

Anderson, John Henry, *Professor Anderson's Notebook, or Recollections of His Continental Tour.* (n.d.) Author, London. 16 pp. 3 x 4 in. (Information not verified by physical copy.) Toole Stott no. 46. Biography.

Anderson, John Henry, *Professor Anderson's Notebook, or Recollections of His Continental Tour.* (n.d.) Author, London. 16 pp. 2.75 x 4.25 in. (Information not verified by physical copy.) Toole Stott no. 47. Biography.

Anderson, John Henry, *Wit of Aberdeen, The.* (1863) Author, Aberdeen, Scotland. 16 pp. 4 x 7.25 in. (Information not verified by physical copy.) Toole Stott no. 52. Humor.

Anderson, John Henry, *Wizard's Book of Conundrums, The.* (1852) T. W. Strong, New York. Perfect. Beige. 108 pp. 3.75 x 6 in. (Information not verified by physical copy.) Toole Stott no. 44. Riddles.

Anderson, John Henry, *Wizard of the North's Book of Magic, Cards, Handkerchiefs, Rugs, etc.* (c. 1850) Paul, London. 8 pp. (Information not verified by physical copy.) Toole Stott no. 741. Credited to Anderson's title of "Wizard of the North," but Toole Stott suggests it may have been an imitator. Beginner.

Anderson, Leslie, *Eight Brass Monkeys: Mental Magic of Leslie Anderson vol. 1.* (1982) Left-Handed League, Los Feliz, CA. Saddle-stitch. Yellow. 15 pp. 5.5 x 8.5 in. Mentalism.

Anderson, Melvin, *Repeat T & R (Torn and Restored) Card, The.* (1980) Author, Portland, OR. Saddle-stitch. Yellow. 36 pp. 5.5 x 8.5 in. (Information not verified by physical copy.) Cards, Torn and Restored Card.

Anderson, Oscar, *Illustrated and Alphabetical Enumeration of the Experiments in the Magic Programme of his Father's Professor Anderson's Entertainment.* (c. 1875) Wizard's Psycomantheum. 16 pp. 4 x 5.5 in. (Information not verified by physical copy.) Toole Stott no. 58. History, Biography.

Anderson, Scott K., *40 Tricks with a Hot Rod and Other Color-Change Rods.* (1986) D. Robbins, Brooklyn, NY. Saddle-stitch. White, red, black. 32 pp. 5.25 x 8.25 in. Hot Rod, Paddle effects, Close-Up, Apparatus.

Anderson, William H., *Short Bible Routines vol. 1.* (1992) Maher Studios, Racine, WI. Saddle-stitch. Yellow. 43 pp. 5.5 x 8.5 in. Gospel magic, Ventriloquism.

Andrade, Will, *50 Simple Card Tricks.* (n.d.) Author, Melbourne. 56 pp. (Information not verified by physical copy.) Cards, Beginner.

Andrade, Will, *70 Simple Card Tricks.* (n.d.) Author, Melbourne. 46 pp. (Information not verified by physical copy.) Cards, Beginner.

Andrade, Will, *Comedy Magic.* (n.d.) Author, Sydney. Stapled. 12 pp. 8 x 10.25 in. (Information not verified by physical copy.) See McCullagh, "Under the Southern Cross." Comedy.

Andrade, Will, *Easy Conjuring Tricks: Parlor Magic.* (c. 1911) Author, Melbourne. Saddle-stitch. 64 pp. 5.75 x 6.75 in. (Information not verified by physical copy.) See McCullagh, "Under the Southern Cross." Beginner.

Andrade, Will, *Magic Kettle Routine.* (n.d.) Author, Melbourne. Stapled. 3 pp. 8 x 10.25 in. (Information not verified by physical copy.) See McCullagh, "Under the Southern Cross." Stage, Kettle.

Andrade, Will, *Magic Up to Date.* (c. 1903) Author, Melbourne. Saddle-stitch. 89 pp. (Information not verified by physical copy.) See McCullagh, "Under the Southern Cross." Beginner.

Andrade, Will, *Magical Patter.* (n.d.) Author, Sydney. Stapled. 3 pp. 8 x 10.25 in. (Information not verified by physical copy.) See McCullagh, "Under the Southern Cross." Patter.

Andrade, Will, *Magical Patter.* (n.d.) Author, Sydney. Saddle-stitch. 8 pp. 8 x 10.25 in. (Information not verified by physical copy.) See McCullagh, "Under the Southern Cross." Patter.

Andrade, Will, *Simplified Card Fanning.* (n.d.) Author, Melbourne. Stapled. 6 pp. 8 x 10.25 in. (Information not verified by physical copy.) See McCullagh, "Under the Southern Cross." Cards, Fanning, Manipulation.

Andrade, Will, *Sleight of Hand.* (1945) Author, Melbourne. Cloth. Gray. 119 pp. 5.75 x 8.75 in. Dust jacket. Manipulation, Close-Up.

Andrade, Will, *Super Mentality.* (n.d.) Author, Sydney. Folded. 4 pp. 9 x 13 in. (Information not verified by physical copy.) See McCullagh, "Under the Southern Cross." Mentalism.

Andrade, Will, *Trip to Spookville, A.* (n.d.) Author, Sydney. Stapled. 8 pp. 5.25 x 8.75 in. (Information not verified by physical copy.) See McCullagh, "Under the Southern Cross." Spirit effects.

Andrade, Will, *X-Ray Eye, The.* (n.d.) Author, Sydney. Stapled. 9 pp. 5.25 x 8.25 in. (Information not verified by physical copy.) See McCullagh, "Under the Southern Cross." Mentalism.

Andreu, *Geheimnisse.* (2020) Author. Casebound. Blue. 144 pp. (Information not verified by physical copy. Bibliographical details are as accurate as possible.) Mentalism.

Andreu, *Mindsight.* (2015) Author. Casebound. Black. 74 pp. (Information not verified by physical copy. Bibliographical details are as accurate as possible.) Mentalism.

Andrews, Arthur J., *Incomparable.* (1955) Ed Konstant, East Meadow, NY. Stapled. White. 3 pp. 8.5 x 11 in. (Information not verified by physical copy.) Cards.

Andrews, Carl, Jr., *Magic from Maui.* (2003) Author, Maui, HI. 96 pp. (Information not verified by physical copy.) Close-Up, Coins, Cards.

Andrews, Carl, Jr., *Making a Living in Magic: Performing at Restaurants and Hotels.* (1999) Author, Maui, HI. 38 pp. (Information not verified by physical copy.) Business, Strolling magic, Promotion.

Andrews, John H., *Magic, Mirth, and Mystery: Magic Made Easy.* (c. 1900) Author, Philadelphia. Saddle-stitch. Light green. 12 pp. 5.25 x 7 in. In Copperfield collection. Beginner. Pulp.

Andrews, Luka, *Behind the Pine: A Magician's Guide to Bar Magic.* (2024) Author, Oak Creek, WI. Perfect. Black. 146 pp. 6 x 9 in. (Information not verified by physical copy.) Bar magic, Close-Up.

Andrews, Mark, *How to Pull a Super Model.* (1996) Dynamic FX Inc., London. 13 pp. (Information not verified by physical copy.) Close-Up, Stage.

Andrews, Max, *Sixteen Card Index Gems.* (1943) Max Andrews, London. Saddle-stitch. Red. 36 pp. 4.75 x 7.25 in. Cards, Card index.

Andrews, Max, *Sixteen Card Index Gems.* (1981) Supreme Magic, Bideford, UK. Saddle-stitch. Green. 36 pp. 4.75 x 7 in. Cards, Card index.

Andrews, Max, *Sixteen Thumb Tie Gems.* (1944) Max Andrews, London. Stapled with tape. Green, pink. 16 pp. 8 x 9.75 in. Mimeographed. Stage, Thumb Tie.

Andrews, Max, *Sixteen Thumb Tie Gems.* (1944) Max Andrews, London. Saddle-stitch. Beige. 50 pp. 4.75 x 7.25 in. Stage, Thumb Tie.

Andrews, Max, *Sixteen Thumb Tie Gems.* (1947) Max Holden, New York. Saddle-stitch. Beige. 50 pp. 4.75 x 7.25 in. With separate typed notes on Rosini version. Stage, Thumb Tie.

Andrews, Max, *Sixteen Thumb Tie Gems.* (1981) Supreme Magic, Bideford, UK. Saddle-stitch. White. 50 pp. 4.75 x 7.25 in. Stage, Thumb Tie.

Andrews, Val (See also Merry, Richard; Roy, Fergus), *Aqua-Whirl.* (1983) Supreme Magic, Bideford, UK. Saddle-stitch. Yellow. 8 pp. 7.75 x 9.75 in. Spinning glass on hoop. Juggling.

Andrews, Val, *Balloon Modeler's Companion.* (1982) Magico, New York. Saddle-stitch. Yellow. 35 pp. 5.25 x 8.5 in. Vol. 2 of "Manual of Balloon Modeling." Balloons.

Andrews, Val, *Big Show, The.* (1960) Supreme Magic, Bideford, UK. Stapled with tape. Blue. 21 pp. 8.25 x 10.25 in. Mimeographed. Stage, Patter.

Andrews, Val, *Bit of a Dog, A.* (1973) Supreme Magic, Bideford, UK. Stapled. White. 8 pp. 7.75 x 10 in. Ventriloquism, Puppetry.

Andrews, Val, *Cash in for Comedy.* (c. 1973) Supreme Magic, Bideford, UK. Stapled. White. 9 pp. 8 x 10 in. Signed by Val Andrews. Comedy.

Andrews, Val, *Chi-canery.* (1958) Supreme Magic, Bideford, UK. Stapled with tape. Yellow. 18 pp. 8.25 x 10.25 in. Mimeographed. Comedy, Stage, Circus.

Andrews, Val, *Circus Magic.* (c. 1959) Supreme Magic, Bideford, UK. Stapled with tape. Yellow. 18 pp. 8.25 x 10.25 in. Mimeographed. Comedy, Stage, Circus.

Andrews, Val, *Close-Up Comedy.* (1960) Supreme Magic, Bideford, UK. Stapled with tape. Tan. 16 pp. 8 x 10 in. Mimeographed. Comedy.

Andrews, Val, *Club Comedy.* (1964) Supreme Magic, Bideford, UK. Saddle-stitch. White, green. 14 pp. 8 x 9.75 in. Comedy.

Andrews, Val, *Coin and Card Magic of Bobby Bernard, The.* (1982) Magico, New York. Cloth. Black. 123 pp. 6 x 9.25 in. Coins, Cards.

Andrews, Val, *Comedy Book: From Here to Obscurity: The Comedy Magic of Val Andrews.* (1960) Abbott Magic Co., Colon, MI. Stapled. Blue. 16 pp. 8.5 x 11 in. Mimeographed. Comedy, Stage.

Andrews, Val, *Comedy for Comperes.* (1960) Supreme Magic, Bideford, UK. Stapled. Gray. 20 pp. 7.75 x 9.75 in. Mimeographed. Signed by Val Andrews. Emcee, Comedy.

Andrews, Val, *Comedy for Mentalists.* (1958) Corinda's Magic Studio, London. Stapled with tape. Green. 12 pp. 8 x 10 in. Mimeographed. Signed by Val Andrews. Comedy, Mentalism.

Andrews, Val, *Crazy Mindreading.* (c. 1973) Supreme Magic, Bideford, UK. Stapled with tape. Light blue. 4 pp. 8 x 10 in. Mimeographed. Mentalism, Comedy.

Andrews, Val, *Dante Scrapbook, The.* (1990) Author, London. Clip. Yellow. 52 pp. 8.25 x 11.75 in. (Measurements and other information have been recorded as accurately as possible.) Biography, History.

Andrews, Val, *David Devant: The Junior Partner.* (1988) Author, London. Saddle-stitch. Orange. 42 pp. 5.75 x 8.25 in. Signed by Val Andrews. #15. Biography, History.

Andrews, Val, *Dedicated Magic.* (1971) Unique Magic Studios, London. Cloth. Black. 154 pp. 6.5 x 9 in. Dust jacket. Stage.

Andrews, Val, *Dialogues for Use with "Supreme Vent-Skull": A Midsummer Night's Scream.* (c. 1973) Supreme Magic, Bideford, UK. Stapled with tape. Gray. 11 pp. 8 x 10.25 in. Mimeographed. Ventriloquism, Talking skull.

Andrews, Val, *Egg Bags and Egg Gags.* (1972) Supreme Magic, Bideford, UK. Stapled. Beige. 18 pp. 7.75 x 9.75 in. Mimeographed. Signed by Val Andrews. Egg Bag, Comedy.

Andrews, Val, *Explosive Comedy!* (c. 1977) Supreme Magic, Bideford, UK. Stapled. Tan. 14 pp. 8 x 10 in. Mimeographed. Comedy.

Andrews, Val, *Floorshow, Fun, and Phantasy.* (c. 1973) Supreme Magic, Bideford, UK. Stapled. Orange. 19 pp. 7.75 x 9.75 in. Mimeographed. Signed by Val Andrews. Comedy, Stage.

Andrews, Val, *Four Seasons in the Life of Val Andrews.* (1984) Micky Hades, Calgary, Canada. Comb. Beige. 73 pp. 8.5 x 11 in. Biography, Comedy, Stage.

Andrews, Val, *Fred Culpitt: A Brief Biography.* (2001) Abraxas Publications, Calgary, Canada. Comb. Blue. 42 pp. 8.5 x 11 in. Biography, History.

Andrews, Val, *Gift from the Gods, A.* (1981) Goodliffe Publications, Alcester, UK. Cloth. Green. 187 pp. 7.5 x 10 in. Dust jacket. Biography, History.

Andrews, Val, *Goodnight, Mr. Dante.* (1978) Goodliffe Publications, Alcester, UK. Cloth. Black. 111 pp. 5.5 x 8.75 in. Dust jacket. Biography, History.

Andrews, Val, *Great Carmo, The.* (2008) Arcady Press, London. Perfect. White. 99 pp. 5.5 x 8 in. (Measurements and other information have been recorded as accurately as possible.) Biography, History.

Andrews, Val, *Great Houdini Broadcasts, The.* (1981) Micky Hades, Calgary, Canada. Stapled with tape. Orange. 11 pp. 8.5 x 11 in. Houdini, Script, Radio.

Andrews, Val, *Great Lyle and His Cavalcade of Mystery, The.* (1989) Magical Treasury Productions, London. Saddle-stitch. Light blue. 29 pp. 5.75 x 8.25 in. Biography, History.

Andrews, Val, *Greatest Little Show on Earth, The.* (1971) Supreme Magic, Bideford, UK. Stapled with paper cover. Light green. 17 pp. 7.75 x 9.75 in. Mimeographed. Stage, Inventions.

Andrews, Val, *How Do You Doodle?* (1964) Supreme Magic, Bideford, UK. Stapled. Purple. 21 pp. 7.75 x 9.75 in. Mimeographed. Signed by Val Andrews. Chalk talk, Comedy.

Andrews, Val, *How to Give a Magic Lecture.* (1979) Micky Hades, Calgary, Canada. Stapled with tape. Yellow. 27 pp. 8.5 x 11 in. Business, Showmanship, Lecturing.

Andrews, Val, *How to Write a Magical Best Seller.* (1982) Magic Inc., Chicago. Stapled. Orange. 17 pp. 8.5 x 11 in. Business, Writing.

Andrews, Val, *Idiot at the Card Table, The.* (c. 1982) Supreme Magic, Bideford, UK. Stapled. White, green. 14 pp. 7.75 x 9.75 in. Mimeographed. Cards.

Andrews, Val, *Just for Starters: Thirty Ways to Open an Act.* (1980) Magico, New York. Saddle-stitch. Blue. 40 pp. 5.5 x 8.5 in. Comedy, Stage, Showmanship.

Andrews, Val, *Just Polly and Me.* (1983) Supreme Magic, Bideford, UK. Stapled with tape. Orange. 8 pp. 7.5 x 10 in. Ventriloquism, Comedy.

Andrews, Val, *Komedy for Kid Shows.* (1960) Corinda's Magic Studio, London. 25 pp. (Information not verified by physical copy.) Children's magic, Comedy.

Andrews, Val, *Kwickfire Klassics of Komedy.* (c. 1973) Supreme Magic, Bideford, UK. Stapled. Purple. 20 pp. 7.75 x 9.75 in. Mimeographed. Signed by Val Andrews. Comedy.

Andrews, Val, *Life: Dull It Ain't: Horace Goldin: The Tragedies and Triumphs of Horace Goldin.* (1983) Magical Treasury Productions, London. Comb. Yellow. 92 pp. 6 x 8.25 in. Biography, History.

Andrews, Val, *Life: Dull It Ain't: Horace Goldin: The Tragedies and Triumphs of Horace Goldin.* (2010) Arcady Press, London. Perfect and tape. White. 96 pp. 7 x 8.5 in. Biography, History.

Andrews, Val, *Lyle's Cavalcade of Magic.* (1983) Author, London. 26 pp. (Information not verified by physical copy.) Biography, History.

Andrews, Val, *Magic in Store: The Magic Pitchman's Handbook.* (1976) Micky Hades, Calgary, Canada. Stapled with tape. Blue. 45 pp. 8.5 x 11 in. Signed by Val Andrews. Pitchman act.

Andrews, Val, *Magic of Christmas, The.* (1989) Author, London. Saddle-stitch. Yellow. 12 pp. 5.75 x 8.25 in. Produced as a holiday gift for friends. Signed by Val Andrews. Essays, History.

Andrews, Val, *Magical Clown, The.* (1983) Supreme Magic, Bideford, UK. 24 pp. (Information not verified by physical copy.) Clowning, Comedy.

Andrews, Val, *Manual of Balloon Modeling vol. 1.* (1981) Magico, New York. Perfect. Yellow. 57 pp. 6 x 9 in. Gift from the publisher. Balloons.

Andrews, Val, *More Doodles.* (c. 1973) Supreme Magic, Bideford, UK. Stapled with tape. Light blue. 20 pp. 7.75 x 9.75 in. Mimeographed. Signed by Val Andrews. Chalk talk, Comedy.

Andrews, Val, *More Ventriloquial Vitality.* (1963) Supreme Magic, Bideford, UK. Stapled with tape. Green. 15 pp. 8 x 10 in. Mimeographed. Ventriloquism.

Andrews, Val, *Most Popular Trick in Magic!, The.* (1980) Magico, New York. Saddle-stitch. White. 32 pp. 5.25 x 8.25 in. Cards, Rising Cards.

Andrews, Val, *Murray.* (1974) Goodliffe Publications, Alcester, UK. Cloth. Black. 88 pp. 5.5 x 8.75 in. Dust jacket. Signed by Murray. Biography, History.

Andrews, Val, *Murray: The Encore.* (1988) Author, London. 72 pp. (Information not verified by physical copy.) Biography, History.

Andrews, Val, *Once Hung a Gilded Lamp: The Life and Times of Will Goldston.* (1986) Author, London. Clip. Yellow. 76 pp. 8.5 x 11.75 in. Signed by Val Andrews. #159 of 200. Biography, History.

Andrews, Val, *Original Comedy Magic.* (c. 1973) Supreme Magic, Bideford, UK. Stapled with tape. Green. 23 pp. 8 x 10.25 in. Mimeographed. Signed by Val Andrews. Comedy, Stage.

Andrews, Val, *Patter Supreme.* (1960) Supreme Magic, Bideford, UK. 16 pp. (Information not verified by physical copy.) Patter.

Andrews, Val, *Practical Guide to Ventriloquism, A.* (1977) Micky Hades, Calgary, Canada. Comb. Yellow. 33 pp. 8.5 x 11 in. Ventriloquism.

Andrews, Val, *Ropey Comedy.* (1963) Marzinni House of Magic, Reading, UK. Stapled with tape. Yellow, green. 14 pp. 7.75 x 9.75 in. Mimeographed. Comedy, Rope.

Andrews, Val, *Seven Keys of Kalanag.* (2009) Arcady Press, London. Perfect. White. 110 pp. 5.5 x 8 in. (Measurements and other information have been recorded as accurately as possible.) Biography, History.

Andrews, Val, *Shortcut to Showmanship.* (1981) Author, London. Stapled. White. 8 pp. 5.5 x 8.5 in. (Measurements and other information have been recorded as accurately as possible.) Showmanship.

Andrews, Val, *Showman-Ventriloquist, The.* (1963) Supreme Magic, Devon, UK. Stapled with tape. Orange. 17 pp. 8 x 10 in. Ventriloquism.

Andrews, Val, *Simplicity, Audacity, and Bluff.* (1979) Magico, New York. Saddle-stitch. White. 32 pp. 8.5 x 11 in. Theory, Misdirection, Stage, Comedy.

Andrews, Val, *Six Cabaret Vent Acts.* (1961) Supreme Magic, Bideford, UK. Stapled with tape. Orange. 14 pp. 8 x 10.25 in. Mimeographed. Ventriloquism, Snake Basket.

Andrews, Val, *Spook-Show-Stoppers.* (1963) Supreme Magic, Bideford, UK. Stapled with tape. Orange. 17 pp. 8.25 x 10.25 in. Mimeographed. Spirit effects, Spook shows.

Andrews, Val, *Stand and Deliver (the Gags!).* (1964) Supreme Magic, Bideford, UK. 21 pp. (Information not verified by physical copy.) Comedy.

Andrews, Val, *Taint all Magic But –.* (1962) Supreme Magic, Bideford, UK. Stapled. Orange, red. 11 pp. 7.75 x 9.75 in. Mimeographed. Later edition. Different cover design. Comedy.

Andrews, Val, *Taint all Magic But –.* (1962) Supreme Magic, Bideford, UK. Stapled with tape. Orange. 11 pp. 7.75 x 9.75 in. Mimeographed. Signed by Val Andrews. Comedy.

Andrews, Val, *Talking to a Snake.* (1961) Supreme Magic, Bideford, UK. Stapled with tape. Orange. 7 pp. 8 x 10 in. Mimeographed. Ventriloquism, Snake Basket.

Andrews, Val, *Tumbling Tumblers, The.* (1960) Unique Magic Studios, London. Stapled. Beige. 11 pp. 8 x 10 in. Mimeographed. Glasses, Stage.

Andrews, Val, *Unfaked Book Test.* (2007) L. Davenport and Co., London. Saddle-stitch. Tan. 8 pp. 5.75 x 8.25 in. Book tests, Mentalism.

Andrews, Val, *Val Andrews First American Tour Lecture Notes.* (1980) Author, London. Saddle-stitch. Yellow. 8 pp. 5.75 x 8.5 in. Signed by Val Andrews. Lecture notes. Stage, Close-Up.

Andrews, Val, *Val's Varieties.* (1962) Supreme Magic, Bideford, UK. 12 pp. (Information not verified by physical copy.) Stage.

Andrews, Val, *Ventertaining Dialogues.* (1964) Supreme Magic, Bideford, UK. (Information not verified by physical copy.) Ventriloquism.

Andrews, Val, *Ventriloquial Vitality.* (1963) Supreme Magic, Bideford, UK. (Information not verified by physical copy.) Ventriloquism.

Andrews, Val, *Vis-ability.* (1955) Author, London. Saddle-stitch. Pink. 20 pp. 6.5 x 8 in. Single-sided pages. Comedy, Gags.

Andrews, Val, *Wonderful Magic of Chefalo, The.* Second printing. (1983) Author, London. Saddle-stitch. Pink. 24 pp. 5.5 x 8.25 in. Features explanations of Chefalo's effects. Signed by Val Andrews. Biography, History, Stage.

Andrews, Val, *You're On Your Own.* (1972) Supreme Magic, Bideford, UK. Stapled. White. 14 pp. 8 x 10 in. Signed by Val Andrews. Emcee, Comedy.

Andrews, W. S., *Magic Squares and Cubes.* (1960) Dover, New York. Perfect. Blue. 419 pp. 5.25 x 8 in. Mathematical, Magic squares.

Andrieu, Pierre, *Souvenirs des Frères Isola.* (1943) Flammarion, Paris. Perfect. Beige. 236 pp. 4.75 x 7.25 in. Biography, Magicians in cinema, History. French.

Andrus, Jerry, *Andrus Card Control vol. 1.* (1976) J. A. Enterprises, Albany, OR. Comb. Yellow. 63 pp. 8.5 x 11 in. Signed by Jerry Andrus. Cards.

Andrus, Jerry, *Andrus Card Control vol. 2.* (1976) J. A. Enterprises, Albany, OR. Comb. Brown. 59 pp. 8.5 x 11 in. Signed by Jerry Andrus. #270. Cards.

Andrus, Jerry, *Andrus Deals You In.* Library Edition. (1956) Star Magic, Portland, OR. Cloth. Brown. 191 pp. 5.5 x 8.5 in. Dust jacket. Signed by Jerry Andrus. Cards.

Andrus, Jerry, *Andrus Deals You In.* Autograph Edition. (1956) Star Magic, Portland, OR. Perfect. Green. Cover text: Gold; 191 pp. 5.5 x 8.25 in. Signed by Jerry Andrus. Cards.

Andrus, Jerry, *Andrus Deals You In.* (1956) Star Magic, Portland, OR. Perfect. Teal, black. 191 pp. 5.5 x 8.25 in. Signed by Jerry Andrus. Cards.

Andrus, Jerry, *Andrus Deals Again.* (1957) Star Magic, Portland, OR. Saddle-stitch. White. 8 pp. 5.5 x 8.5 in. Signed by Jerry Andrus. Cards.

Andrus, Jerry, *Andrus Deals You In.* (1978) J. A. Enterprises, Albany, OR. Comb. Olive, black. 191 pp. 5.25 x 8 in. Signed by Jerry Andrus. Cards.

Andrus, Jerry, *Andrus Deals You In.* (2006) Chazpro, Joyce, WA. Coil. Black. 147 pp. 8.5 x 11 in. (Measurements and other information have been recorded as accurately as possible.) Cards.

Andrus, Jerry, *Andrus Notes.* (2004) Chazpro, Joyce, WA. Perfect. White. 100 pp. 8.5 x 11 in. Signed by Jerry Andrus. Lecture notes. Cards, Stage, Inventions.

Andrus, Jerry, *Five Dollar Trix.* (1973) J. A. Enterprises, Albany, OR. Comb. Yellow. 52 pp. 5.25 x 8 in. (Measurements and other information have been recorded as accurately as possible.) Coins, Bills.

Andrus, Jerry, *Kurious Kards.* (1973) J. A. Enterprises, Albany, OR. Comb. Red. 53 pp. 5.5 x 8.5 in. Signed by Jerry Andrus. Cards.

Andrus, Jerry, *Kurious Kards – Five Dollar Trix.* (2001) Chazpro, Joyce, WA. Saddle-stitch. Gray. 55 pp. 8.5 x 11 in. Combined second edition. Cards, Coins, Bills.

Andrus, Jerry, *Linking Pins.* (1955) Star Magic, Portland, OR. Folded. White. 8 pp. 7 x 9.75 in. (Measurements and other information have been recorded as accurately as possible.) Linking safety pins, Close-Up.

Andrus, Jerry, *Magia con Imperdibles.* (2010) Ediciones Marré, Barcelona. Perfect. Black, yellow. 120 pp. 6.75 x 9.75 in. Linking safety pins, Close-Up. Spanish.

Andrus, Jerry, *Miser's Miracle, The.* Second printing. (1961) J. A. Enterprises, Albany, OR. Saddle-stitch. Tan. 19 pp. 5.5 x 8.5 in. Signed by Jerry Andrus. Cards, Coins, Close-Up.

Andrus, Jerry, *Miser's Miracle, The.* (2000) Chazpro, Eugene, OR. Saddle-stitch. White. 18 pp. 5.5 x 8.5 in. Cards, Coins, Close-Up.

Andrus, Jerry, *More Sleightly Slanted.* (1974) Author, Albany, OR. Stapled. Yellow. 28 pp. 8.5 x 11 in. Lecture notes. Close-Up, Stage, Balls.

Andrus, Jerry, *More Sleightly Slanted.* Second edition. (1977) Author, Albany, OR. Saddle-stitch. Beige. 28 pp. 8.5 x 11 in. Signed by Jerry Andrus. Lecture notes. Close-Up, Stage, Balls.

Andrus, Jerry, *More Sleightly Slanted.* Second edition. (1977) Author, Albany, OR. Stapled. Yellow. 28 pp. 8.5 x 11 in. Lecture notes. Close-Up, Stage, Balls.

Andrus, Jerry, *Nameless Notes.* (1964) Author, Albany, OR. Saddle-stitch. Yellow. 4 pp. 8.5 x 11 in. With separate illustration sheets. Signed by Jerry Andrus. Lecture notes. Close-Up, Cards, Stage.

Andrus, Jerry, *Nameless Notes no. 2 (on Close-Up Magic).* (1970) Author, Albany, OR. Saddle-stitch. Beige. 14 pp. 5.25 x 8 in. Signed by Jerry Andrus. Lecture notes. Close-Up.

Andrus, Jerry, *Paradox Box.* (1997) Author, Albany, OR. Single page. Beige. 8.5 x 11 in. Template for illusionary box. Optical illusions.

Andrus, Jerry, *Safety Pin-Trix.* (1955) Star Magic, Portland, OR. Saddle-stitch. Beige. 70 pp. 5.75 x 8.75 in. Linking safety pins, Close-Up.

Andrus, Jerry, *Safety Pin-Trix.* (1972) Star Magic, Portland, OR. Saddle-stitch. Orange. 79 pp. 5.75 x 8.75 in. Signed by Jerry Andrus. Linking safety pins, Close-Up.

Andrus, Jerry, *Safety Pin-Trix.* (1972) Author, Albany, OR. Comb. Orange. 79 pp. 5 x 8 in. Signed by Jerry Andrus. Linking safety pins, Close-Up.

Andrus, Jerry, *Safety Pin-Trix.* (2006) Chazpro, Joyce, WA. Coil. White. 60 pp. 8.5 x 11 in. (Measurements and other information have been recorded as accurately as possible.) Linking safety pins, Close-Up.

Andrus, Jerry, *Sleeving from the Deck.* (1961) J. A. Enterprises, Albany, OR. Saddle-stitch. Gray. 18 pp. 6 x 8.5 in. Signed by Jerry Andrus. Cards, Sleeving.

Andrus, Jerry, *Sleightly Miraculous.* (1961) Author, Albany, OR. Saddle-stitch. Green. 15 pp. 6 x 8.5 in. Signed by Jerry Andrus. Cards.

Andrus, Jerry, *Sleightly Slanted.* (1974) Author, Albany, OR. Saddle-stitch. Blue. 16 pp. 8.5 x 11 in. Signed by Jerry Andrus. Lecture notes. Cards.

Andrus, Jerry, *Special Magic.* (1974) Author, Albany, OR. Stapled. Blue. 16 pp. 8.25 x 10.5 in. Lecture notes. Close-Up, Stage, Balls.

Andrus, Jerry, *Steals and Palms.* (1961) Author, Albany, OR. Saddle-stitch. Tan. 34 pp. 6 x 8.5 in. Signed by Jerry Andrus. Cards.

Andrus, Jerry, *Up Close with Andrus.* (1957) Author, Albany, OR. Saddle-stitch. Gray. 9 pp. 8.5 x 11 in. Illustration sheets. Signed by Jerry Andrus. Lecture notes. Close-Up, Cards.

Andrus, Jerry, *Up Close with Andrus.* (1957) Author, Albany, OR. Stapled. Yellow. 9 pp. 8.5 x 11 in. Illustration sheets. Signed by Jerry Andrus. Lecture notes. Close-Up, Cards.

Andrus, Jerry, *Wink Magic.* (1994) Japan. Casebound. Red. 45 pp. 8.75 x 12 in. Dust jacket. Optical illusions, Punch-out effects.

Andruzzi, Tony (as Maskelyn ye Mage. See also Raven, Anthony), *Daemon's Diary.* (1980) Author, Chicago. Saddle-stitch. White. 81 pp. 5.5 x 8.5 in. Bizarre magick.

Andruzzi, Tony (as Maskelyn ye Mage), *Grimoire of the Mages, The.* (1978) Author, Chicago. Suede. Brown. Cover text: Red; pp. (Information not verified by physical copy.) Limited to 250 copies. Bizarre magick.

Andruzzi, Tony (as Maskelyn ye Mage), *Legendary Scroll of Maskelyn ye Mage, The.* (1975) Author, Chicago. Scroll. Beige. 8.5 in. width. Bizarre magick.

Andruzzi, Tony, *Magazine Memory Act.* (1990) Flora and Company, Albuquerque, NM. Comb. Beige. 12 pp. 5.5 x 8.5 in. Memory, Mentalism.

Andruzzi, Tony (as Maskelyn ye Mage), *Negromicon of Maskelyn ye Mage, The.* (1977) Author, Chicago. Leather. Black. 89 pp. 8.5 x 11 in. Locked book. Limited to 350 copies. Bizarre magick.

Andy (as S. W. Erdnase III), *Expert at the Kitchen Table, The.* (2016) Author, Liverpool, NY. Saddle-stitch. Green. 46 pp. 5.5 x 8.5 in. All of the author's books were bonus items for subscribers to "The Jerx" website. Theory, Essays.

Andy (as S. W. Erdnase III), *Expert at the Kitchen Table, The.* (2024) Author, Liverpool, NY. Casebound. Green. 41 pp. 6 x 9 in. (Information not verified by physical copy.) Theory, Essays.

Andy, *Here Be Bunnies: Presentational Techniques.* (2020) Author, Liverpool, NY. Cloth. Gray. 293 pp. 6 x 9 in. (Information not verified by physical copy.) Theory, Essays, Showmanship.

Andy, *Jerx vol. 1, The.* (2016) Author, Liverpool, NY. Cloth. Black. 348 pp. 6 x 9 in. Inscribed to Todd Karr. Signed by "Andy Jerxmann." Close-Up, Cards, Mentalism.

Andy, *Magic for Young Lovers: Adding Emotional Elements to Magic.* (2018) Author, Liverpool, NY. Cloth. Black, red. 334 pp. 6 x 9 in. (Information not verified by physical copy.) Theory, Essays.

Andy, *Thinking of You: Mentalism.* (2019) Author, Liverpool, NY. Cloth. Black. 232 pp. 6 x 9 in. (Information not verified by physical copy.) Mentalism.

Andy, *White Wand Chronicles vol. 1: The Entertainer.* (2022) Author, Liverpool, NY. Casebound. Brown. 196 pp. 6 x 9 in. (Information not verified by physical copy.) Theory, Essays.

Andy, *White Wand Chronicles vol. 2: Young Girls are Coming to the Canyon.* (2023) Author, Liverpool, NY. Casebound. Red, yellow, blue. 223 pp. 6 x 9 in. (Information not verified by physical copy.) Theory, Essays.

Angel, Criss, with Kaufman, Richard, *Mindfreak: Secret Revelations.* (2008) Harper Entertainment, New York. Perfect. Color. 295 pp. 6 x 9 in. Biography, Beginner.

Angel, Criss, *Platinum Magic Kit Instruction Manual.* (2009) MPOA, Las Vegas. Perfect. Black. 99 pp. 5.5 x 8.25 in. From "Platinum Magic Kit." Magic set manual, Beginner.

Angel, Criss, *Professional Magic Kit Instruction Book.* (2015) MPOA, Las Vegas. Perfect. Black. 109 pp. 5.5 x 8.25 in. From "Professional Magic Kit." Magic set manual, Beginner.

Annemann, Theodore, *101 Methods of Forcing.* (1932) Author, New York. Stapled. Light green. 17 pp. 8.5 x 11 in. John Northern Hilliard's copy with his annotations. Cards, Mentalism, Forcing.

Annemann, Theodore, *202 Methods of Forcing.* (1933) Max Holden, New York. Saddle-stitch. Tan. 36 pp. 6 x 9 in. All caps on title page. Cards, Mentalism, Forcing.

Annemann, Theodore, *202 Methods of Forcing.* (1933) Max Holden, New York. Saddle-stitch. Dark tan. 36 pp. 6 x 9 in. Italics on title page. Cards, Mentalism, Forcing.

Annemann, Theodore, *202 Methods of Forcing.* Fourth printing. (1951) Max Holden, New York. Saddle-stitch. Tan. 36 pp. 6 x 9 in. Cards, Mentalism, Forcing.

Annemann, Theodore, *202 Methods of Forcing.* (1964) Magic Inc., Chicago. Saddle-stitch. Blue. 34 pp. 5.5 x 8.5 in. Cards, Mentalism, Forcing.

Annemann, Theodore, *202 Methods of Forcing.* Third Magic Inc. printing. (1973) Magic Inc., Chicago. Saddle-stitch. Red. 35 pp. 5.5 x 8.5 in. Cards, Mentalism, Forcing.

Annemann, Theodore, *202 Methods of Forcing.* Fourth Magic Inc. printing. (1974) Magic Inc., Chicago. Saddle-stitch. Light green. 35 pp. 5.5 x 8.5 in. Cards, Mentalism, Forcing.

Annemann, Theodore, *202 Methods of Forcing.* Third later Magic Inc. printing. (1976) Magic Inc., Chicago. Saddle-stitch. Dark green. 35 pp. 5.5 x 8.5 in. Cards, Mentalism, Forcing.

Annemann, Theodore, *202 Methods of Forcing.* Fourth later Magic Inc. printing. (1978) Magic Inc., Chicago. Saddle-stitch. Orange. 35 pp. 5.5 x 8.5 in. Cards, Mentalism, Forcing.

Annemann, Theodore, *202 Methods of Forcing.* Fifth later Magic Inc. printing. (1980) Magic Inc., Chicago. Saddle-stitch. Orange. 35 pp. 5.5 x 8.5 in. Cards, Mentalism, Forcing.

Annemann, Theodore, *202 Procédés de Forçage.* (1954) E. Sauty, Geneva, Switzerland. Perfect. Red. 85 pp. 5.75 x 8.5 in. Cards, Mentalism, Forcing. French.

Annemann, Theodore, *Annemann's $50.00 Manuscript.* (1976) Max Abrams, Los Angeles. Cloth. Blue. 22 pp. 8.5 x 11 in. New edition of original. #40 of 100. Cards, Mentalism.

Annemann, Theodore, *Annemann's Buried Treasures.* (1952) Sphinx Publishing Co., New York. Saddle-stitch. Red. 15 pp. 5.5 x 8.5 in. Cards, Mentalism.

Annemann, Theodore, *Annemann's Card Miracles and Annemann's Mental Mysteries.* (c. 1935) L. Davenport and Co., London. Cloth. Black. 40 pp. 5.75 x 8.5 in. Mentalism, Cards.

Annemann, Theodore, *Annemann's Card Miracles and Annemann's Mental Mysteries.* (1944) Stage Magic, Woodside, NY. Cloth. Orange. 40 pp. 6 x 9 in. Mentalism, Cards.

Annemann, Theodore, *Annemann's Card Miracles and Annemann's Mental Mysteries.* (1944) Stage Magic, Woodside, NY. Cloth. Red. 40 pp. 6 x 9 in. Mentalism, Cards.

Annemann, Theodore, *Annemann's Complete One-Man Mental and Psychic Routine.* (1935) Max Holden, New York. Saddle-stitch. Light tan. 24 pp. 6 x 9 in. Cover font different; probably later printing. Mentalism.

Annemann, Theodore, *Annemann's Complete One-Man Mental and Psychic Routine.* (1935) Max Holden, New York. Saddle-stitch. Light tan. 24 pp. 6 x 9 in. Cover font different; probably later printing. Mentalism.

Annemann, Theodore, *Annemann's Complete One-Man Mental and Psychic Routine.* (1935) Max Holden, New York. Saddle-stitch. Tan. 24 pp. 6 x 9 in. Mentalism.

Annemann, Theodore, *Annemann's Enigma.* Limited deluxe edition. (2019) The Miracle Factory, Los Angeles. Cloth. Black. 720 pp. 8.25 x 10.25 in. Dust jacket. Anthology. Blank cover, as published. With simulated "Jinx" and CD. Signed by Todd Karr, Max Maven. #1 of 100. Biography, Mentalism, Cards, Close-Up.

Annemann, Theodore, *Annemann's Enigma.* (2019) The Miracle Factory, Los Angeles. Cloth. Black. 720 pp. 8.25 x 10.25 in. Dust jacket. Anthology. With simulated "Jinx," CD, and "Master Subtleties" reprint. Biography, Mentalism, Cards, Close-Up.

Annemann, Theodore, *Annemann's Exclusive Manuscript.* (n.d.) Micky Hades, Calgary, Canada. Comb. White. 26 pp. 8.5 x 11 in. Hades' typeset version of the "Fifty Dollar Manuscript." Mentalism, Cards.

Annemann, Theodore, *Annemann's Exclusive Tricks with Borrowed Decks.* (n.d.) Folder. Blue. 19 pp. 8.5 x 11 in. Mimeographed. Pirated version. Mentalism, Cards.

Annemann, Theodore, *Annemann's Master Subtleties with Cards.* (2019) The Miracle Factory, Los Angeles. Stapled. White. 12 pp. 8.5 x 11 in. Reprint of c. 1928 Annemann booklet. Included in deluxe edition of "Annemann's Enigma" (2019). Signed by Todd Karr. #1 of 100. Cards.

Annemann, Theodore, *Annemann's Mental Bargain Effects.* (1935) Author, New York. Saddle-stitch. Beige. 12 pp. 6 x 9 in. Mentalism.

Annemann, Theodore, *Annemann's Mental Bargain Effects.* (1935) Author, New York. Saddle-stitch. Light pink. 16 pp. 6 x 9 in. Smooth cover. Mentalism.

Annemann, Theodore, *Annemann's Mental Bargain Effects.* (n.d.) Louis Tannen, New York. Saddle-stitch. Beige. 16 pp. 6 x 9 in. Uncoated cover. Mentalism.

Annemann, Theodore, *Annemann's Mental Mysteries.* (1929) Burling Hull, New York. Stapled inside boards. Silver. 12 pp. 6.25 x 9 in. Mimeographed. Red and black label on cover. Cards, Mentalism.

Annemann, Theodore (ed. by John J. Crimmins, Jr.), *Annemann's Miracles of Card Magic.* (1948) Max Holden, New York. Saddle-stitch. Beige, green. 109 pp. 6 x 9 in. Posthumous, compiled from "The Jinx." Cards.

Annemann, Theodore (ed. by John J. Crimmins, Jr.), *Annemann's Miracles of Card Magic.* (1964) Faber, London. Cloth. Blue. 158 pp. 5.25 x 8.25 in. Dust jacket. In Copperfield collection. Cards.

Annemann, Theodore (ed. by John J. Crimmins, Jr.), *Annemann's Miracles of Card Magic.* (1964) Faber, London. Cloth. Light red. 158 pp. 5.5 x 8 in. Dust jacket. Cards.

Annemann, Theodore (ed. by John J. Crimmins, Jr.), *Annemann's Miracles of Card Magic.* (1977) Dover, New York. Perfect. Color. 188 pp. 5.5 x 8.5 in. Dust jacket. Cards.

Annemann, Theodore, *Book Without a Name, The.* (1931) Max Holden, New York. Cloth. Maroon. Cover text: Black; 62 pp. 5.25 x 8.25 in. Rounded ornament on front cover. Inscribed to Stuart Robson. Signed by Theodore Annemann. Cards, Mentalism.

Annemann, Theodore, *Book Without a Name, The.* (1931) Max Holden, New York. Cloth. Red. Cover text: Black; 62 pp. 5.25 x 8.25 in. Pointed ornament and different font size on front cover. Cards, Mentalism.

Annemann, Theodore, *Book Without a Name, The.* (1931) Max Holden, New York. Cloth. Blue. 62 pp. 5.25 x 8 in. White label with blue text on cover. Cards, Mentalism.

Annemann, Theodore, *Book Without a Name, The.* (1931) Max Holden, New York. Cloth. Light blue. 62 pp. 5.25 x 8 in. Light blue label with blue text on cover. Cards, Mentalism.

Annemann, Theodore, *Book Without a Name, The.* (1931) Max Holden, New York. Cloth. Light blue. 62 pp. 5.25 x 7.75 in. White label with black text on cover. Cards, Mentalism.

Annemann, Theodore, *Book Without a Name, The.* (1931) Max Holden, New York. Cloth. Dark blue. Cover text: Gold; 62 pp. 5.25 x 8 in. Beige translucent dust jacket. Cards, Mentalism.

Annemann, Theodore, *Card Miracles.* (1929) Burling Hull, New York. Stapled inside boards. Silver. 12 pp. 6.25 x 9 in. Mimeographed. Posthumous. Compiled from "Sphinx" articles. Silver and black label on cover. Cards, Mentalism.

Annemann, Theodore, *Card Miracles.* (1929) Burling Hull, New York. Stapled inside boards. Green. 12 pp. 6.25 x 9 in. Mimeographed. Posthumous. Compiled from "Sphinx" articles. Silver and black label on cover. Cards, Mentalism.

Annemann, Theodore, *Card Miracles.* (1944) Stage Magic, Woodside, NY. Saddle-stitch. Yellow. 16 pp. 5.75 x 8.75 in. No label on title page. Incorrect "Mental Mysteries" title visible. Cards, Mentalism.

Annemann, Theodore, *Card Miracles.* (1944) Stage Magic, Woodside, NY. Saddle-stitch. Yellow. 16 pp. 5.75 x 8.75 in. Off-white label on title page. Cards, Mentalism.

Annemann, Theodore, *Card Miracles.* (1944) Stage Magic, Woodside, NY. Saddle-stitch. Yellow. 16 pp. 5.75 x 8.75 in. Silver foil label from earlier edition on title page. Cards, Mentalism.

Annemann, Theodore, *Dead Name Duplication, A.* Trick of the Month Club series 1, no. 1. (August 1931) Thayer Magical Mfg. Co., Los Angeles. Folded. Beige. 3 pp. 3.75 x 8.5 in. Mentalism.

Annemann, Theodore, *En Rapport.* (1937) Author, Waverly, NY. Stapled. Green. 15 pp. 6.5 x 10 in. Stapled inside larger folded cover. Mentalism, Second Sight.

Annemann, Theodore, *En Rapport.* (1937) Author, Waverly, NY. Stapled. Green. 15 pp. 6.5 x 9 in. Stapled inside larger folded cover. Mentalism, Second Sight.

Annemann, Theodore, *En Rapport.* (1937) Max Holden, New York. Saddle-stitch. Tan. 24 pp. 6 x 9 in. (Measurements and other information have been recorded as accurately as possible.) Mentalism.

Annemann, Theodore, *En Rapport / Patter in Rhyme by Bert Douglas.* (n.d.) D. Robbins, New York. Saddle-stitch. White, blue. 52 pp. 5.5 x 8.5 in. Double-sided book pairing these unrelated titles. Mentalism, Patter.

Annemann, Theodore, *Full Deck of Impromptu Card Tricks.* (1943) Max Holden, New York. Saddle-stitch. Beige, brown. 80 pp. 6 x 9 in. Cards, Impromptu, Mentalism.

Annemann, Theodore, *Full Deck of Impromptu Card Tricks.* (n.d.) Louis Tannen, New York. Saddle-stitch. Beige, brown. 80 pp. 6 x 9 in. Cards, Impromptu, Mentalism.

Annemann, Theodore, *Full Deck of Impromptu Card Tricks.* (n.d.) D. Robbins, Brooklyn, NY. Saddle-stitch. White, blue. 78 pp. 5.5 x 8.5 in. Cards, Impromptu, Mentalism.

Annemann, Theodore, *Incorporated Strange Secrets, The.* (1939) Max Holden, New York. Saddle-stitch. Beige. 20 pp. 6 x 9 in. Mentalism, Cards.

Annemann, Theodore, *Incorporated Strange Secrets, The.* (1983) D. Robbins, New York. Saddle-stitch. Blue. 19 pp. 5.5 x 8.5 in. Mentalism, Cards.

Annemann, Theodore, *Jinx 1-40 reprints.* Typeset reprints. (1941) L. Davenport and Co., London. Folded. White. Multiple sections. 8.5 x 11 in. Typeset reissues of the first forty issues. Magazine, Cards, Mentalism.

Annemann, Theodore, *Jinx 1-50, The.* First bound version. (1938) Author, New York. Cloth. Black. Cover text: Gold; 352 pp. 8.5 x 11 in. One of the early bound collections with the narrow-margin original printing of issue no. 1. No spine title. Magazine, Cards, Mentalism.

Annemann, Theodore, *Jinx 1-50, The.* First bound version. (1938) Author, New York. Cloth. Black. Cover text: Gold; 352 pp. 8.5 x 11 in. Early copy indicated by font on spine. Edges of pages tinted red. Lengthy inscription to William McCaffrey. Signed by Theodore Annemann. Magazine, Cards, Mentalism.

Annemann, Theodore, *Jinx 51-100, The.* First bound version. (1940) Author, New York. Cloth. Black. Cover text: Gold; 270 pp. 8.5 x 11 in. Early copy indicated by font on spine. Magazine, Cards, Mentalism.

Annemann, Theodore, *Jinx 100-151, The.* First bound version. (1942) Author, New York. Cloth. Black. Cover text: Gold; 270 pp. 8.5 x 11 in. Magazine, Cards, Mentalism.

Annemann, Theodore, *Jinx 1-50, The.* Second bound version. (1938) Author, New York. Cloth. Black. Cover text: Gold; 352 pp. 8.5 x 11 in. Set of three volumes with matching gold spine text. Magazine, Cards, Mentalism.

Annemann, Theodore, *Jinx 51-100, The.* Second bound version. (1940) Author, New York. Cloth. Black. Cover text: Gold; 270 pp. 8.5 x 11 in. Set of three volumes with matching gold spine text. Magazine, Cards, Mentalism.

Annemann, Theodore, *Jinx 100-151, The.* Second bound version. (1942) Author, New York. Cloth. Black. Cover text: Gold; 270 pp. 8.5 x 11 in. Set of three volumes with matching gold spine text. Magazine, Cards, Mentalism.

Annemann, Theodore, *Jinx 1-50, The.* Third bound version. (1963) Louis Tannen, New York. Cloth. Black. Cover text: Gold; 352 pp. 8.5 x 11 in. Reprints bound with original issues. Magazine, Cards, Mentalism.

Annemann, Theodore, *Jinx 51-100, The.* Third bound version. (1963) Louis Tannen, New York. Cloth. Black. Cover text: Gold; 270 pp. 8.5 x 11 in. Reprints bound with original issues. Magazine, Cards, Mentalism.

Annemann, Theodore, *Jinx 100-151, The.* Third bound version. (1963) Louis Tannen, New York. Cloth. Black. Cover text: Gold; 270 pp. 8.5 x 11 in. Reprints bound with original issues. Magazine, Cards, Mentalism.

Annemann, Theodore, *Jinx 1-50, The.* Fourth bound version. (n.d.) D. Robbins, Brooklyn, NY. Cloth. Black. Cover text: Gold; 352 pp. 8.5 x 11 in. Magazine, Cards, Mentalism.

Annemann, Theodore, *Jinx 51-100, The.* Fourth bound version. (n.d.) D. Robbins, Brooklyn, NY. Cloth. Black. Cover text: Gold; 270 pp. 8.5 x 11 in. Magazine, Cards, Mentalism.

Annemann, Theodore, *Jinx 100-151, The.* Fourth bound version. (n.d.) D. Robbins, Brooklyn, NY. Cloth. Black. Cover text: Gold; 270 pp. 8.5 x 11 in. Magazine, Cards, Mentalism.

Annemann, Theodore, *Jinx Program no. 1: A Club Act of Magic.* (1938) Max Holden, New York. Saddle-stitch. Yellow. 12 pp. 5.5 x 8.25 in. Mentalism, Cards.

Annemann, Theodore, *Jinx Program no. 1: A Club Act of Magic.* (1938) Max Holden, New York. Saddle-stitch. Bright yellow. 12 pp. 5.25 x 8.25 in. Mentalism, Cards.

Annemann, Theodore, *Jinx Program no. 2: A Mental Club Act.* (1938) Max Holden, New York. Saddle-stitch. Light blue. 16 pp. 5.5 x 8.25 in. Mentalism, Cards.

Annemann, Theodore, *Jinx Program no. 2: A Mental Club Act.* (n.d.) Louis Tannen, New York. Saddle-stitch. Light blue. 16 pp. 5.5 x 8.25 in. Mentalism, Cards.

Annemann, Theodore, *Jinx Program no. 2: Annemann's Mental Club Act.* (1956) George Armstrong, London. Saddle-stitch. Orange. 18 pp. 5.5 x 8.25 in. Mentalism, Cards.

Annemann, Theodore, *Jinx Program no. 3: A Magical Club Program.* (1938) Max Holden, New York. Saddle-stitch. Green. 20 pp. 5.5 x 8.25 in. Mentalism, Cards.

Annemann, Theodore, *Jinx Program no. 3: A Magical Club Program.* (1938) Max Holden, New York. Saddle-stitch. Blue. 20 pp. 5.5 x 8.25 in. Mentalism, Cards.

Annemann, Theodore, *Jinx Program no. 4: A "No Card" Mystery Act.* (1938) Max Holden, New York. Saddle-stitch. Yellow. 16 pp. 5.5 x 8.25 in. Mentalism, Cards.

Annemann, Theodore, *Jinx Program no. 5: "No Code" Telepathy.* (1938) Max Holden, New York. Saddle-stitch. Beige. 11 pp. 5.5 x 8.5 in. Mentalism, Cards, Second Sight.

Annemann, Theodore, *Jinx Program no. 5: "No Code" Telepathy.* (1938) Max Holden, New York. Saddle-stitch. Light beige. 11 pp. 5.25 x 8.25 in. Textured paper. Mentalism, Cards, Second Sight.

Annemann, Theodore, *Mental Mysteries.* (1944) Stage Magic, Woodside, NY. Saddle-stitch. Yellow-orange. 24 pp. 5.75 x 8.75 in. No label on title page. Incorrect title of dual edition visible. Cards, Mentalism.

Annemann, Theodore, *Mental Mysteries.* (1944) Stage Magic, Woodside, NY. Saddle-stitch. Yellow. 24 pp. 5.75 x 8.75 in. Silver foil label from earlier edition on title page. Cards, Mentalism.

Annemann, Theodore (trans. by Christian Chelman), *Mentalisme Pratique.* (2013) Fantaisium, Paris. Perfect. Black, white, yellow. 498 pp. 6.25 x 9.5 in. Translation of "Practical Mental Effects." Cards, Mentalism. French.

Annemann, Theodore (trans. by Philippe Billot), *Miracles Cartomagiques.* (2014) Fantaisium, Paris. Perfect. Black, white, yellow, sepia. 175 pp. 6.5 x 9.75 in. Translation of "Miracles of Card Magic." Cards, Mentalism. French.

Annemann, Theodore, *Ne Plus Ultra Reading Method.* Trick of the Month Club series 2, no. 2. (August 1932) Thayer Magical Mfg. Co., Los Angeles. Folded. Pink. 6 pp. 3.75 x 6.75 in. Mentalism.

Annemann, Theodore (John J. Crimmins, Jr.), *Practical Mental Effects.* (1944) Max Holden, New York. Cloth. Red. Cover text: Gold; 310 pp. 6.25 x 9.25 in. Posthumous, compiled from "The Jinx." Mentalism, Cards.

Annemann, Theodore (John J. Crimmins, Jr.), *Practical Mental Effects.* (1963) Louis Tannen, New York. Cloth. Red. Cover text: Gold; 310 pp. 6.25 x 9.25 in. Brown dust jacket. Posthumous, compiled from "The Jinx." Mentalism, Cards.

Annemann, Theodore (John J. Crimmins, Jr.), *Practical Mental Effects.* (1963) Louis Tannen, New York. Cloth. Red. Cover text: Gold; 310 pp. 6.25 x 9.25 in. Red dust jacket; later Tannen edition. Posthumous, compiled from "The Jinx." Mentalism, Cards.

Annemann, Theodore (John J. Crimmins, Jr.), *Practical Mental Effects.* (1983) Dover, New York. Perfect. Black. 310 pp. 5.5 x 8.5 in. Posthumous, compiled from "The Jinx." Mentalism, Cards.

Annemann, Theodore (John J. Crimmins, Jr.), *Practical Mental Effects.* (2000) D. Robbins, Brooklyn, NY. Cloth. Red. Cover text: Gold; 310 pp. 6.25 x 9.25 in. Red dust jacket. Posthumous, compiled from "The Jinx." Mentalism, Cards.

Annemann, Theodore (John J. Crimmins, Jr.), *Practical Mental Effects.* (2009) D. Robbins, Brooklyn, NY. Perfect. Color. 317 pp. 5.5 x 8.5 in. Posthumous, compiled from "The Jinx." Mentalism, Cards.

Annemann, Theodore, *Sh-h-h-h-! It's a Secret!* (1934) Author, New York. Stapled. Blue. 50 pp. 6 x 9 in. Inscribed "First copy off the press!" Signed by Theodore Annemann. Mentalism, Cards.

Annemann, Theodore, *Sh-h-h-h-! It's a Secret!* (1934) Max Holden, New York. Saddle-stitch. Blue. 50 pp. 6 x 9 in. Mentalism, Cards.

Annemann, Theodore, *Sh-h-h-h-! It's a Secret!* (1935) L. Davenport and Co., London. Cloth. Black. 50 pp. 5.75 x 8.5 in. Mentalism, Cards.

Annemann, Theodore, *Sh-h-h-h-! It's a Secret!* (c. 1944) L. Davenport and Co., London. Saddle-stitch. Pink. 50 pp. 5.5 x 8.5 in. Mentalism, Cards.

Annemann, Theodore, *Sh-h-h-h-! It's a Secret!* (n.d.) Louis Tannen, New York. Saddle-stitch. Blue. 50 pp. 6 x 9 in. Light blue image and text on cover. Mentalism, Cards.

Annemann, Theodore, *Sh-h-h-h-! It's a Secret!* (n.d.) Louis Tannen, New York. Saddle-stitch. Blue. 50 pp. 6 x 9 in. Light blue image with white text on cover. Mentalism, Cards.

Annemann, Theodore, *Strani Segreti.* (2013) George Marchese, Italy. Perfect. Black, red. 32 pp. 6 x 9 in. Translation of "Strange Secrets." Mentalism. Italian.

Anonymous "Psychic" Metal Bender, The, *Secret Tricks of Bending Metal Objects with Just Your Mind or How Those Big-Time "Psychics" on TV Fool You Every Time!, The.* (1976) Trade Winds Press, San Francisco. Saddle-stitch. White, red. 7 pp. 8.25 x 11 in. Metal bending, Psychic.

Ansbach, *Mysteries of Magic.* (1905) Ansbach Company, Hilldale, NJ. Saddle-stitch. Red, black, white. 41 pp. 5.75 x 8.25 in. Also mentions magic course. Beginner, Coins, Course.

Anthony, Sir (A. Vitez Keresztfalvy), *High Art of Gambling, The.* (1937) Monte Carlo Pub. Co., New York. Perfect. White, red, black. 94 pp. 4.74 x 6.25 in. Gambling, Cards, Cheating.

Anthony, Gene, *Penetra-Bill.* (1983) Emerson and West, Washington D.C. Comb. Yellow. 8 pp. 8.5 x 11 in. Bills, Cards, Close-Up.

Anthony, Walt, *Tales of Enchantment.* (2010) Spellbinding Entertainment, San Francisco. Perfect. Color. 252 pp. 7 x 10 in. Signed by Walt Anthony. Bizarre magick, Showmanship.

Antoine, Éric, *Abracadabra: La Baguette Volée.* (2022) Livres du Dragon d'Or, Paris. Perfect. Blue. 173 pp. 5.5 x 8.25 in. Fiction, Children's book. French.

Antoine, Éric, *Magic Optimystic.* (2018) Éditions Robert Lafont, Paris. Perfect. Pink. 205 pp. 6.5 x 8.75 in. Essays. French.

Antoine, Éric, *Petit Traité d'Éternelle Joie de Vivre.* (2020) Marabout, Vanves, France. Perfect. Pink. 247 pp. 5 x 7 in. Essays. French.

Anverdi, *50 Years of Magical Creations.* (1992) Mephisto Edition, Kortrijk, Belgium. Cloth. Brown. 190 pp. 8.5 x 12 in. Dust jacket. Stage, Inventions.

Anverdi, *Anverdi's Lecture Notes.* (n.d.) Author, Leiden, Netherlands. Saddle-stitch. Blue. 12 pp. 6.5 x 8.5 in. Signed by Anverdi. Lecture notes. Stage.

Anverdi, *Anverdi's Lecture Notes.* (1963) Author, Leiden, Netherlands. Saddle-stitch. Yellow. 24 pp. 6.25 x 9.25 in. (Information not verified by physical copy.) Lecture notes. Stage. Dutch.

Anverdi, *Anverdi's Lecture Notes.* (1964) Author, Leiden, Netherlands. Saddle-stitch. Green. 32 pp. 6.25 x 9.25 in. Lecture notes. Stage. Dutch.

Anverdi, *Anverdi's Miracles with Liquids.* (1965) Author, Leiden, Netherlands. Comb. Color. 44 pp. 6.5 x 9.25 in. Stage, Liquids.

Anverdi, *Geeft College.* Second edition. (1963) Author, Leiden, Netherlands. Saddle-stitch. Yellow, red, black. 32 pp. 6.5 x 8 in. Mimeographed. First edition was published in 1962. Lecture notes. Manipulation, Stage, Balls, Silks. Dutch.

Apel, Fred, *Fred's Ultimate Arrangement of the Si Stebbins Stack.* (2010) Author, West Bloomfield, MI. Perfect. 20 pp. (Information not verified by physical copy.) Cards, Si Stebbins, Prearranged deck.

Apel, Fred, *Imaginary Magic.* (1991) Author, West Bloomfield, MI. 20 pp. (Information not verified by physical copy.) Cards, Close-Up, Stage, Mentalism.

Apel, Fred, *Impromptu Magic.* (2016) Author, West Bloomfield, MI. Comb. 19 pp. 5.5 x 8.5 in. (Information not verified by physical copy.) Impromptu, Close-Up.

Apel, Fred, *Key Card Menu.* (2009) Author, West Bloomfield, MI. Perfect. 36 pp. 5.5 x 8.5 in. (Information not verified by physical copy.) Cards.

Apel, Fred, *Magic for Grandparents.* (2010) Author, West Bloomfield, MI. Perfect. (Information not verified by physical copy. Bibliographical details are as accurate as possible.) Cards.

Aragón, Woody, *Book in English, A.* (2011) Author, Madrid. Cloth. Black. 376 pp. 6.25 x 9.25 in. Dust jacket. Cards, Prearranged deck.

Aragón, Woody, *Memorandum.* (2017) Author, Madrid. Cloth. White. 383 pp. 7.25 x 10.25 in. Dust jacket. Cards, Prearranged deck.

Arai, Shin-Ichi, with Goldstein, Phil, *Shin-Ichi Arai's Affections.* (n.d.) Author, Japan. Saddle-stitch. Red. 15 pp. 8.25 x 12 in. Signed by Shin-Ichi Arai. Cards, Close-Up, Rope.

Arai, Shin-Ichi, with Saikawa, T., *On the Table.* (1983) Author, Japan. Saddle-stitch. White. 16 pp. 7 x 10 in. Cards, Close-Up. Japanese.

Arathorn, Mazarian, *Olde Magick for the New Age.* (2023) Author, UK. Casebound. Black. 153 pp. 6 x 9 in. (Information not verified by physical copy.) Mentalism, Bizarre magick.

Arcana, Homer, *E.S.P. Arcana.* (2013) Shop of Secrets. Saddle-stitch. Black, white. 40 pp. 8.5 x 11 in. Mentalism, E.S.P. cards.

Arcane, Peter (Trevor McCombie), *Elucidator, The.* (2005) Author, Edinburgh. (Information not verified by physical copy. Bibliographical details are as accurate as possible.) Mentalism, Cold reading.

Arce, Greg, *Deep Thought.* (2004) Author, Hialeah, FL. Saddle-stitch. Blue. 52 pp. 5.5 x 8.5 in. (Information not verified by physical copy.) Mentalism.

Arch, Dave, *Tricks for Trainers.* (1999) Human Resource Development, Omaha, NE. Perfect. Black. 153 pp. 8.5 x 11 in. Beginner, Psychology.

Archer, Danny (See also Martin, Marty), *Alone Again.* (2012) Author, Denver, CO. 20 pp. (Information not verified by physical copy.) Cards, Coins, Close-Up.

Archer, Danny, *Alone Again: Europe 2014.* (2014) Author, Denver, CO. Saddle-stitch. Blue. 20 pp. 6.75 x 8.25 in. (Information not verified by physical copy.) Lecture notes. Cards, Close-Up.

Archer, Danny, *Danny Archer's 3 Ball Routine.* (1998) Author, Denver, CO. Saddle-stitch. Yellow. 7 pp. 5.5 x 8.5 in. (Information not verified by physical copy.) Balls, Close-Up.

Archer, Danny, *On Target.* (2003) Author, Denver, CO. Saddle-stitch. Green. 23 pp. 6.75 x 8.5 in. (Measurements and other information have been recorded as accurately as possible.) Close-Up, Cards.

Archer, Danny, with Martin, Marty, *One to One-Hundred.* (c. 1990) Author, Denver, CO. Stapled. White. 6 pp. 8.5 x 11 in. (Information not verified by physical copy.) Bills, Close-Up.

Archer, Danny, *Still Working Alone.* (1997) Author, Denver, CO. Comb. Red. 13 pp. 8.5 x 11 in. Lecture notes. Close-Up, Cards, Mentalism, Stage.

Archer, Danny, *Working Alone.* (1994) Author, Denver, CO. Saddle-stitch. Yellow. 20 pp. 7 x 8.5 in. Lecture notes. Cards, Coins, Close-Up, Mentalism.

Archer, Danny, *Working Alone.* (1994) Author, Denver, CO. Comb. Yellow. 20 pp. 8.5 x 11 in. Another edition. Lecture notes. Cards, Coins, Close-Up, Mentalism.

Arcturus, *Psychic Magic.* (1986) Arcturus Productions. (Information not verified by physical copy. Bibliographical details are as accurate as possible.) Mentalism.

Arcuri, Larry (ed.), *Houdini Birth Research Committee's Report, The.* (1980) Magico Magazine, New York. Stapled. Yellow. 25 pp. 8.5 x 11 in. Houdini, History, Research.

Areny de Plandolit, Dr., *Bibliografia Española de la Prestidigitacion.* (1950) Casa Magicus, Madrid. Saddle-stitch. Gray. 50 pp. 6 x 8.25 in. Bibliography. Spanish.

Areny de Plandolit, Dr., *Maravillas de la Magia Moderna, Las.* (1931) Casa Editorial Maucci, Barcelona. Cloth. Red. 415 pp. 6.5 x 9.75 in. From Christopher library. Signed by Milbourne Christopher. Stage, Illusions, Beginner. Spanish.

Arioch, *Mouth to Mouth: A Collection of Thoughts and Uses for the Mouth Squeaker.* (c. 1980) Author, Ridgefield Park, NJ. Stapled. White. 14 pp. 5.5 x 8.5 in. Comedy, Gimmicks, Close-Up.

Arkane, Nikola, *In Plain Sight.* (2021) Author, Ireland. Perfect. Color. 70 pp. 5.5 x 8.5 in. (Information not verified by physical copy.) Close-Up, Comic book.

Arkane, Nikola, *Pop.* (2022) Author, Ireland. Perfect. Color. 130 pp. 6 x 8.25 in. (Information not verified by physical copy.) Close-Up, Showmanship.

Arkin, Charles, *Arkin's Favorite Mental Effects vol. 1.* (c. 2018) Author, Elm Grove, WI. Stapled. White. 6 pp. 8.5 x 11 in. Mentalism.

Arkin, Charles, *Artistry and Magic of 50 Illusions and Props Built by Jim Sommers.* (2018) Author, Elm Grove, WI. Coil. White. 118 pp. 8.5 x 11 in. #38 of 120. Illusions, Biography.

Arkin, Charles, *Magic in Wisconsin: The History of the Houdini Club of Wisconsin Conventions.* (2013) Author, Elm Grove, WI. Coil. White. 290 pp. 8.5 x 11 in. (Information not verified by physical copy. Bibliographical details are as accurate as possible.) History, Conventions, Houdini, Magic clubs.

Arkomanis, Perseus, *Mosaic.* (2021) Author, Greece. Perfect. Purple. 526 pp. 8.5 x 11 in. (Measurements and other information have been recorded as accurately as possible.) Mentalism.

Arkomanis, Perseus, *Tiles.* (2024) Author, Greece. Perfect. Blue. 350 pp. 8.5 x 11 in. (Information not verified by physical copy.) Mentalism.

Armes, Craig S., *Professional Séance, The.* (1990) Dark Artz Publishing, Los Gatos, CA. Saddle-stitch. White. 44 pp. 8.5 x 11 in. (Information not verified by physical copy.) Séances, Bizarre magick.

Armour. Richard, *Magic of the Scottish Conjurers Association.* (1947) Lloyd Jones, Oakland, CA. Saddle-stitch. Beige. 31 pp. 6 x 9 in. Close-Up, Stage, Magic clubs.

Armstrong, A. V., *Parlor Magic.* (n.d.) Acme Trick and Novelty, Pawtucket, RI. Saddle-stitch. Red. 24 pp. 3.5 x 4.75 in. (Information not verified by physical copy.) See Ricard, "Wee Books." Beginner.

Armstrong, Bruce (See also Hades, Micky), *Lecture Notes: A Presentation of Chimeric Ideas.* (c. 1976) Magic Inc., Chicago. Saddle-stitch. White. 32 pp. 5.5 x 8.5 in. Lecture notes. Stage, Close-Up.

Armstrong, George, *Challenge Instant Hypnotism and Mass Hypnotism.* (1950) George Armstrong, London. Saddle-stitch. Beige. 16 pp. 5.5 x 8.5 in. Mentalism, Hypnosis.

Armstrong, George, *Chandu's Psychoanalysis.* (1950) George Armstrong, London. Saddle-stitch. White, green. 12 pp. 5.5 x 8.25 in. Mentalism.

Armstrong, George, *Magic Wand Year Book 1946-7 Edition.* (1946) George Armstrong, London. Saddle-stitch. Tan. 80 pp. 5.25 x 8.25 in. Close-Up, Stage, History, Magazines.

Armstrong, George, *Magic Wand Year Book 1947-1948 Edition.* (1947) George Armstrong, London. Perfect. Orange. 96 pp. 5.5 x 8.5 in. Close-Up, Stage, History, Magazines.

Armstrong, George, *Magic Wand Year Book 1948-1949.* (1948) George Armstrong, London. Perfect. Orange. 92 pp. 5.5 x 8.5 in. Close-Up, Stage, History, Magazines.

Armstrong, George, *Premonition.* (1949) George Armstrong, London. Saddle-stitch. Beige. 12 pp. 5.5 x 8.5 in. Mentalism, Cards.

Armstrong, George, *Tricks of the Trade.* (1946) George Armstrong, London. Saddle-stitch. Tan. 23 pp. 5.25 x 7.75 in. Close-Up, Stage, Tips.

Armstrong, Jon, *How to Win: Essays and Routines for the Stand-Up Magician.* (2023) Author, Los Angeles. Perfect. Black. 103 pp. 6 x 9 in. Signed by Jon Armstrong. Theory, Showmanship, Stage.

Armstrong, Jon, *Magical Adventures of Jon Armstrong, The.* (2008) Author, Los Angeles. Stapled. 67 pp. 5.5 x 8.5 in. (Information not verified by physical copy.) Cards, Close-Up.

Armstrong, Jon, *Thoughts from a Former Boy Wonder.* (2006) Author, Los Angeles. Stapled. 30 pp. 5.5 x 8.5 in. (Information not verified by physical copy.) Cards, Close-Up.

Armstrong, Jon, *Year of the Starving Artist.* (c. 2005) Author, Los Angeles. Stapled. 24 pp. 5.5 x 8.5 in. (Information not verified by physical copy.) Cards, Close-Up.

Armstrong, Jon, *You Don't Know Union Jack!* (2007) Author, Los Angeles. Stapled. 21 pp. 5.5 x 8.5 in. (Information not verified by physical copy.) Cards, Close-Up.

Army, Dan, *Black: A Book of Deception and Psychology.* (2007) Author, Los Angeles. Perfect. Black. 81 pp. 5.75 x 8 in. (Measurements and other information have been recorded as accurately as possible.) Cards.

Arneson, D. J., *Doctor Graves Magic Book.* (1977) Charlton Press, Derby, CT. Perfect. White, green, purple. 62 pp. 5.25 x 8 in. Beginner, Children's book.

Arnold, Daniel, *Magic Square 2.0, The.* (2022) Spellcaster, New York. Saddle-stitch. Yellow. 32 pp. 8 x 8 in. Magic squares, Mathematical.

Arnold, Dean, *Dr. Lynn's Wonderful Telescope.* (2020) WhoDean Productions, Chapel Hill, NC. Coil. White, red. 34 pp. 9 x 7 in. Signed by Dean Arnold. #38 of 100. Biography, History, Optics, Patents.

Arnold, Dean, *Fairground Too, The.* (2015) Magic Words, Pasadena, CA. Leather. Black. 120 pp. 6.25 x 9.25 in. Bookmark with charm. Signed by Dean Arnold. #21 of 30. Biography, History, Collecting.

Arnold, Jeff, *1980 F.C.M. Lecture on Wells, Servantes, Body Loads.* (1980) Author, Gainesville, FL. Stapled. White. 8.5 x 11 in. (Information not verified by physical copy.) Lecture notes. Gimmicks, Body loads.

Arnold, Jeff, *Canes and Candles Lecture.* (1978) Author, Gainesville, FL. Stapled. White. 8.5 x 11 in. (Information not verified by physical copy.) Lecture notes. Canes, Candles.

Arnold, Jeff, *Silks.* (1976) Author, Gainesville, FL. Stapled. Yellow. 8.5 x 11 in. (Information not verified by physical copy.) Lecture notes. Silks, Gospel magic.

Arnold, Ned and Lois, *Great Science Magic Show, The.* (1979) Franklin Watts Inc., New York. Casebound. Blue, red, black. 99 pp. 7.75 x 10.25 in. Science magic, Beginner, Stunts, Children's book.

Arons, Harry, *How to Develop an Alarm Clock Mind.* (1948) Power Publishers, Newark, NJ. Stapled. Beige. 11 pp. 5.5 x 8.5 in. Mimeographed inside printed cover. Hypnotism, Self-help.

Aronson, Simon, *Aronson Approach, The.* (2012) Author, Chicago. Cloth. Black. 173 pp. 8.5 x 11 in. Dust jacket. Cards, Prearranged deck.

Aronson, Simon, *Art Decko.* (2014) Author, Chicago. Cloth. Black. 323 pp. 8.5 x 11 in. Dust jacket. Cards, Prearranged deck.

Aronson, Simon, *Bound to Please.* (1994) Author, Chicago. Cloth. Black. 179 pp. 8.5 x 11 in. Dust jacket. Cards, Prearranged deck.

Aronson, Simon, *Card Ideas of Simon Aronson, The.* (1978) Author, Chicago. Comb. White. 127 pp. 8.5 x 11 in. Foreword by Ed Marlo. Cards, Prearranged deck.

Aronson, Simon, *Lecture Notes.* (2003) Author, Chicago. 32 pp. (Information not verified by physical copy.) Lecture notes. Cards.

Aronson, Simon, *Memories Are Made of This.* (1999) Author, Chicago. Saddle-stitch. Pink. 29 pp. 8.5 x 11 in. Cards, Prearranged deck.

Aronson, Simon, with Solomon, David, *Sessions.* (1982) Savaco Ltd., Chicago. 138 pp. Dust jacket. (Information not verified by physical copy.) Cards, Prearranged deck.

Aronson, Simon, *Shuffle-Bored.* (1980) Author, Chicago. Saddle-stitch. Purple. 28 pp. 8.5 x 11 in. Cards, Prearranged deck.

Aronson, Simon, *Side-Swiped.* (2002) Murphy's Magic Supplies, Rancho Cordova, CA. 29 pp. (Information not verified by physical copy.) Cards, Close-Up.

Aronson, Simon, *Simply Simon.* (1995) Author, Chicago. Cloth. Black. 308 pp. 8.5 x 11 in. Dust jacket. Cards, Prearranged deck.

Aronson, Simon, *Stack to Remember, A.* (1979) Author, Chicago. Saddle-stitch. Yellow. 35 pp. 5.5 x 8.5 in. Cards, Prearranged deck.

Aronson, Simon, *Try the Impossible.* (2001) Author, Chicago. Cloth. Black. 288 pp. 8.5 x 11 in. Dust jacket. Cards, Prearranged deck.

Arrowsmith, G. E., *Arrowsmith's Assorted Mysteries.* (1967) Supreme Magic, Bideford, UK. Stapled with tape. White, blue. 43 pp. 8 x 9.75 in. Mentalism, Stage.

Arrowsmith, G. E., *Arrowsmith's Mystery Box.* (c. 1965) Supreme Magic, Bideford, UK. Stapled with tape. White, blue. 90 pp. (Information not verified by physical copy.) Mentalism, Stage.

Arrowsmith, G. E., *Exceptional Concepts.* (1980) Supreme Magic, Bideford, UK. Saddle-stitch. Orange, black, white. 84 pp. 7.25 x 9.75 in. Stage.

Arrowsmith, G. E., *Magical Mentalia.* (1942) Max Andrews, London. Perfect. Green. 66 pp. 5 x 7.25 in. (Measurements and other information have been recorded as accurately as possible.) Mentalism.

Arrowsmith, G. E., *Magical Mentalia.* (n.d.) Louis Tannen, New York. Saddle-stitch. Green. 66 pp. 5 x 6.75 in. Signed by Long Tack Sam. Mentalism.

Arrowsmith, G. E., *Magical Mentalia.* (1984) D. Robbins, Brooklyn, NY. Perfect. White. 67 pp. 5.5 x 8.5 in. Mentalism.

Arrowsmith, G. E., *Magical Originalia.* (1943) Max Andrews, London. Perfect. Tan. 67 pp. 4.75 x 7.25 in. Mentalism, Cards, Stage.

Art the Magician, *250 Magic Tricks Anyone Can Do!* Second edition. (1967) Padell Book Co., New York. Saddle-stitch. Red. 32 pp. 6 x 9 in. Psychedelic design. Beginner.

Artanis (Joe Sinatra), *Story of the Bottom Deal, The.* (1958) Author, New York. Loose pages. Tan. 3 pp. 8.5 x 11 in. With twenty 4.5 x 6.75 in. photo illustrations and 78-rpm record album in box. Cards, Bottom deal.

Arthur, Don, *Illusions in the Round.* (1993) Author, Jackson, MS. Casebound. Yellow. 123 pp. 8.75 x 11.5 in. (Measurements and other information have been recorded as accurately as possible.) Illusions.

Arthur, Gilles, *Magie.* (1982) Hachette, Paris. Casebound. Blue. 39 pp. 9 x 11.75 in. Comic book-style introductions. Beginner. French.

Arthur, Gilles, *Secrets des Mega-Illusions, Les.* (2006) Académie de Magie Georges Proust, Paris. Perfect. Color. 188 pp. 7.5 x 10.5 in. (Information not verified by physical copy.) Illusions, Television magic. French.

Arthur, R. E., *New Look for the Magic Show, The.* (1950) Ireland Magic Co., Chicago. Stapled. Orange. 22 pp. 8.5 x 11 in. Mimeographed. Business, Stagecraft, Backdrops.

Arthur, Thomas, *Life of Billy Purvis, The.* (c. 1875) T. Arthur, Newcastle-Upon-Tyne, UK. 144 pp. (Information not verified by physical copy.) Toole Stott no. 1302. Biography.

Arthur, Thomas, *Life of Billy Purvis, The.* (1875) Daniel Bowman, Newcastle-Upon-Tyne, UK. 200 pp. (Information not verified by physical copy.) Toole Stott no. 1304. Biography.

Arthur, Thomas, *Life of Billy Purvis, The.* Second edition. (1876) T. Arthur, Newcastle-Upon-Tyne, UK. 153 pp. (Information not verified by physical copy.) Toole Stott no. 1303. Biography.

Arthur, Thomas, *Life of Billy Purvis, The.* (1981) Frank Graham, Newcastle-Upon-Tyne, UK. Perfect. White. 149 pp. 4.75 x 7.25 in. Biography, History.

Artix, The, *Art of Thought Transference, The.* (c. 1950) Albert Wood and Son, Northwich, UK. Stapled with tape. Light blue. 10 pp. 4.25 x 7.25 in. Mentalism, Second Sight.

Asbury, Herbert, *Some Sharpers and Blacklegs at Mid-Century.* (1956) Public Library of Fort Wayne and Allen County, Fort Wayne, IN. Saddle-stitch. Beige. 54 pp. 5.5 x 8.25 in. Excerpt from "Sucker's Progress." Gambling.

Ascanio, Arturo de (trans. by Roberto Giobbi), *About the Handling of Double Cards.* (1981) Author, Madrid. Saddle-stitch. Green. 20 pp. 6 x 8.5 in. Lecture notes. Cards, Double lift.

Ascanio, Arturo de (trans. by Roberto Giobbi), *About the Handling of Double Cards.* (1981) Author, Madrid. Saddle-stitch. Blue. 20 pp. 6 x 8.5 in. Lecture notes. Cards, Double lift.

Ascanio, Arturo de, *Ascanio's All Backs.* (1984) Author, Madrid. Comb. White. 27 pp. 8.25 x 11.75 in. Inscribed to Dai Vernon by Ascanio. Signed by Arturo de Ascanio. Cards, All-backs routine.

Ascanio, Arturo de (trans. by Rafael Benatar), *Ascanio's All Backs.* (1989) Author, Madrid. Saddle-stitch. White. 29 pp. 6.25 x 8.5 in. Cards, All-backs routine.

Ascanio, Arturo de (trans. by Rafael Benatar), *Ascanio's Favorites 1: Aunt Henriette's Aces, The Trick I Would Show Dai Vernon.* (1989) Author, Madrid. Saddle-stitch. Yellow. 12 pp. 6 x 8.5 in. Cards.

Ascanio, Arturo de (trans. by Rafael Benatar), *Ascanio's Favorites 2: Sleightless Oil and Water, Aces with Love.* (1989) Author, Madrid. Saddle-stitch. Orange. 6 x 8.5 in. Cards, Oil and Water.

Ascanio, Arturo de (trans. by Rafael Benatar), *Ascanio's Favorites 3: Mentalism by Elimination.* (1989) Author, Madrid. Saddle-stitch. Tan. 16 pp. 6 x 8.5 in. Cards, Mentalism.

Ascanio, Arturo de (trans. by Rafael Benatar), *Ascanio's Favorites 4: About the Handling of Double Cards.* (1989) Author, Madrid. Saddle-stitch. Green. 20 pp. 6 x 8.5 in. Cards, Double lift.

Ascanio, Arturo de (trans. by José De La Torre), *Ascanio's World of Knives.* First edition. (1975) José's Studio, Belleville, NJ. Saddle-stitch. Blue. 95 pp. 5.25 x 8.25 in. Knives.

Ascanio, Arturo de (trans. by José De La Torre), *Ascanio's World of Knives.* Second edition. (1975) José's Studio, Belleville, NJ. Comb. Blue. 95 pp. 5.5 x 8.5 in. Knives.

Ascanio, Arturo de (trans. by José De La Torre), *Ascanio's World of Knives.* Revised edition. (2011) Meir Yedid Magic, Rego Park, NY. Perfect. Color. 142 pp. 6 x 9 in. Knives.

Ascanio, Arturo de, *Jours Noirs, Les.* (1997) Joker Deluxe, Paris. Perfect. Black. 96 pp. 5.75 x 8.25 in. (Measurements and other information have been recorded as accurately as possible.) Cards. French.

Ascanio, Arturo de (trans. by Jesus Etcheverry), *Magic of Ascanio vol. 1: The Structural Conception of Magic, The.* (2005) Páginas Libros de Magia, Madrid. Casebound. Gray. 296 pp. 6.75 x 9.25 in. Dust jacket. Cards, Theory.

Ascanio, Arturo de (trans. by Jesus Etcheverry), *Magic of Ascanio vol. 2: Studies of Card Magic, The.* (2006) Páginas Libros de Magia, Madrid. Casebound. Gray. 296 pp. 6.75 x 9.26 in. Dust jacket. Cards, Theory.

Ascanio, Arturo de (trans. by Jesus Etcheverry), *Magic of Ascanio vol. 3: More Studies of Card Magic, The.* (2008) Páginas Libros de Magia, Madrid. Casebound. Gray. 394 pp. 6.75 x 9.26 in. Dust jacket. Cards, Theory.

Ascanio, Arturo de (trans. by Jesus Etcheverry), *Magic of Ascanio vol. 4: Knives and Color Blindness, The.* (2008) Páginas Libros de Magia, Madrid. Casebound. Gray. 132 pp. 6.75 x 9.26 in. Dust jacket. Knives, Theory.

Ascanio, Arturo de (as Marcus), *Manejo de la Carte Doble, El.* (1980) Author, Spain. Stapled. Gray. 21 pp. 8.25 x 11.75 in. (Information not verified by physical copy.) Cards, Double lift. Spanish.

Ascanio, Arturo de (as Marcus), *Navajas y Daltonismo: Magia de las Navajas.* (1958) Sociedad Española de Ilusionismo, Barcelona. Perfect. Green. 250 pp. 4.75 x 6.75 in. Knives, Theory. Spanish.

Ascanio, Arturo de, *Psychology of Palming, The.* (1982) Author, Spain. Saddle-stitch. Green. 24 pp. 6 x 8.5 in. Cards, Theory, Palming.

Asher, Lee, *Card Magic and Playing Card Games Timeline.* (2022) Author, Toronto. Perfect. White. 104 pp. 5.25 x 8.25 in. Cards, History, Card games.

Asher, Lee, *Catch 33.* (2013) Author, Toronto. eBook. 27 pp. Printed from PDF. (Information not verified by physical copy.) Cards, Three-Card Monte.

Asher, Lee, *Close Cover Before Striking.* (2001) Author, Paris. Saddle-stitch. White. 28 pp. 5.5 x 8.5 in. Signed by Lee Asher. Cards.

Asher, Lee, *Hand Jobs.* (2001) Author, Paris. Saddle-stitch. White. 16 pp. 5.5 x 8.5 in. (Measurements and other information have been recorded as accurately as possible.) Signed by Lee Asher. Cards.

Asher, Lee, *Lecture Notes '99 – French Tour.* (1999) Author, Las Vegas. Saddle-stitch. White. 16 pp. 5.5 x 8.5 in. Signed by Lee Asher. Lecture notes. Cards.

Asher, Lee, *Pulp Friction.* (1998) Author, Las Vegas. Saddle-stitch. White. 16 pp. 5.5 x 8.5 in. (Measurements and other information have been recorded as accurately as possible.) Signed by Lee Asher. Cards.

Asher, Lee, *Sex Sells.* (1998) Author, Las Vegas. Saddle-stitch. White. 16 pp. 5.5 x 8.5 in. (Measurements and other information have been recorded as accurately as possible.) Signed by Lee Asher. Cards.

Asher, Lee, *Sleightly Difficult: The Magic of Lee Asher.* (1994) Author, Parkland, FL. Strip binding. Green. 18 pp. 8.5 x 11 in. (Measurements and other information have been recorded as accurately as possible.) Cards.

Asher, Lee, *Thinking Out Loud.* (1998) Author, Las Vegas. Saddle-stitch. White. 16 pp. 5.5 x 8.5 in. (Measurements and other information have been recorded as accurately as possible.) Signed by Lee Asher. Cards.

Asher, Lee, *Three Stylin'.* (2004) Author, Eugene, OR. Saddle-stitch. Green. 12 pp. 7 x 8.5 in. Includes poker chips. Coins, Poker chips.

Ashford, *Natural Born Cardshark.* (2001) Author, Paris. (Information not verified by physical copy. Bibliographical details are as accurate as possible.) Cards.

Astley, Philip, *Astley's System of Equestrian Education.* (1971) Volker Huber, Offenbach, Germany. Cloth. Orange. 206 pp. 5 x 8.25 in. Reprint of 1801 work by the circus pioneer and early magic showman. #247 of 250. Animal training.

Astley, Philip, *Natural Magic, or Physical Amusements Revealed.* (1785) Author, London. 45 pp. 4.25 x 6.75 in. (Information not verified by physical copy.) Toole Stott no. 69. Early magic, Beginner.

Astor, *Astor's Sealed Miracle no. 1: Antigravitron.* (2006) Author, Kakucs, Hungary. Saddle-stitch. Black. 16 pp. 5.75 x 8.25 in. (Measurements and other information have been recorded as accurately as possible.) Mentalism.

Astor, *Astor's Sealed Miracle no. 2: Supra Vision.* (2006) Author, Kakucs, Hungary. Saddle-stitch. Black. 8 pp. 5.75 x 8.25 in. Mentalism, Blindfolds.

Astor, *Astor's Sealed Miracle no. 3: Miracle Paper Tear.* (2007) Author, Kakucs, Hungary. Saddle-stitch. Black. 16 pp. 5.75 x 8.25 in. Newspaper.

Astor, *Astor's Twin Lights.* (2000) Author, Kakucs, Hungary. Saddle-stitch. Green. 5 pp. 5.75 x 8.25 in. (Information not verified by physical copy.) Candles, Stage.

Astor, *Production Tray.* (1995) Author, Kakucs, Hungary. Saddle-stitch. Green. 11 pp. 5.75 x 8.25 in. (Information not verified by physical copy.) Stage, Productions, Apparatus.

Astor, *Telepathie 1: Clip Boards.* (2000) Author, Kakucs, Hungary. Saddle-stitch. Green. 20 pp. 5.75 x 8.25 in. (Information not verified by physical copy.) Mentalism, Clip board.

Astor (ed.), *Top Secrets.* (2007) Trick Production, Kakucs, Hungary. Saddle-stitch. Black. 39 pp. 5.75 x 8.25 in. Effects by various magicians. Close-Up, Stage.

Atkins, Jeffery, *Atkins in Australia.* (1987) Author, UK. Gray. 12 pp. 8 x 10 in. (Information not verified by physical copy.) Lecture notes. Close-Up, Stage.

Atkins, Jeffery, *Atkins Touch, The.* (1975) Supreme Magic, Bideford, UK. Saddle-stitch. White, red, black. 20 pp. 6.75 x 8.75 in. Lecture notes. Stage.

Atkins, Jeffery, *Jeffery Atkins Lecture-Demonstration, The.* (1971) Supreme Magic, Bideford, UK. Saddle-stitch. White, red, blue. 8 pp. 6.5 x 8 in. Lecture notes. Stage.

Atkins, Jeffery, *Magic Kettle, The.* (1972) Supreme Magic, Bideford, UK. Saddle-stitch. Tan. 31 pp. 7.75 x 9.75 in. Stage, Any Drink Called For, Kettle.

Atkins, Jeffery, *Magic Medley.* (1971) Supreme Magic, Bideford, UK. Saddle-stitch. White. 16 pp. 8 x 10 in. (Information not verified by physical copy.) Stage.

Atmore, Joseph, *Dunninger Knows.* (2012) Author, San Jose, CA. Casebound. Black. 398 pp. 8.5 x 11 in. Signed by Joseph Atmore. Mentalism, History, Television magic.

Atmore, Joseph, *Dunninger's Brain Busters.* (2001) H & R Magic Books, Humble, TX. Cloth. Black. 111 pp. 6 x 9 in. Dust jacket. Mentalism.

Attwood, David J., *House of Magic, The.* (2020) Author, Victoria, Canada. Cloth. Black. 148 pp. 6.25 x 9.25 in. Dust jacket. Cards, Close-Up.

Auer, James, *N. E. Book Test, The.* (1947) Author, Kenosha, WI. Stapled. White. 2 pp. 8.5 x 11 in. (Information not verified by physical copy.) Mentalism, Book tests.

Auer, James, *Spirit is Willing, The.* (1961) Ireland Magic Co., Chicago. Saddle-stitch. Orange. 55 pp. 5.5 x 8.5 in. Mentalism.

Augier, Sieur, *Nouveau Dévelopement de Plusieurs Tours de Mains.* (1768) Author, Paris. 12 pp. (Information not verified by physical copy.) Includes a one-way deck effect, card stabbing, and the cross-cut force. Beginner, Cards, Coins, Cups and Balls. French.

Aurich, Rolf, *Kalanag: Die Kontrollierten Illusionen des Helmut Schreiber.* (2016) Verbrecher, Berlin, Germany. Perfect. Green. 179 pp. 4.75 x 6.75 in. Biography, History. German.

Austin, Guy K., *Practical Magic with Popular Patter.* (1919) Will Goldston Ltd., London. Saddle-stitch. Gray. 32 pp. 5.5 x 8.5 in. Patter, Stage.

Austin, Guy K., *Practical Magic with Popular Patter.* Second edition. (1924) Will Goldston Ltd., London. Boards. Green. 92 pp. 4.75 x 7.25 in. Patter, Stage.

Avadon, David (See also Berg, Joe), *Cutting Up Touches.* (2007) Squash Publishing, Chicago. Casebound. Black. 148 pp. 5.25 x 7.25 in. Pickpocket, History.

Aviles, Rich, *Above the Fold.* (2010) Vanishing Inc., Rancho Cordova, CA. Saddle-stitch. Brown. 76 pp. 6 x 9 in. (Information not verified by physical copy.) Cards.

Avis, Jack, with Jones, Lewis, *Ahead of the Pack.* (2002) Authors, London. Cloth. Black. 288 pp. 6.25 x 9.25 in. Dust jacket. Cards, Close-Up, Mentalism.

Avis, Jack, with Derris, John, *Vis à Vis.* (1998) Kaufman and Co., Washington D.C. Cloth. Black. 155 pp. 8.5 x 11 in. Dust jacket. Cards, Close-Up.

Axtell, Steve, *Ideas for Axtell Expressions Products.* (1987) Axtel Expressions, Ventura, CA. Saddle-stitch. 48 pp. 5.5 x 8.5 in. (Information not verified by physical copy.) Patter, Ventriloquism, Apparatus.

Ayala, Joaquin, *What I Think.* (2016) Author, Las Vegas. Saddle-stitch. White. 19 pp. 8.5 x 11 in. (Measurements and other information have been recorded as accurately as possible.) Showmanship, Theory.

Ayling, Will, *Art of Illusion, The.* (1968) Harry Stanley, London. Cloth. Red. 233 pp. 6.5 x 9.5 in. Dust jacket. Thick version. Stage, Illusions.

Ayling, Will, *Art of Illusion, The.* (1968) Harry Stanley, London. Cloth. Red. 233 pp. 6.5 x 9.5 in. Dust jacket. Thin version. Stage, Illusions.

Ayling, Will, *Art of Illusion, The.* Fourth impression. (1990) Supreme Magic, Bideford, UK. Cloth. Red. 196 pp. 6 x 8.75 in. Dust jacket. Stage, Illusions.

Ayling, Will, *Genie Presentations.* (1972) Supreme Magic, Bideford, UK. Cloth. Red. 163 pp. 7.75 x 10 in. Dust jacket. Stage, Illusions.

Ayling, Will, *Knowing the Chop Cup (and Other One Cup-One Ball Routines).* (1989) Supreme Magic, Bideford, UK. Saddle-stitch. Purple. 40 pp. 7.75 x 10 in. Chop Cup, Cups and Balls, Balls.

Ayling, Will, *Knowing the Egg Bag.* (1988) Supreme Magic, Bideford, UK. Saddle-stitch. Blue. 35 pp. 8 x 10 in. Egg Bag, Stage.

Ayling, Will, *Knowing the Rising Cards.* (1991) Supreme Magic, Bideford, UK. Saddle-stitch. Red, white. 27 pp. 8 x 10.5 in. Cards, Rising Cards.

Ayling, Will, *Knowing the Ropes.* (1987) Supreme Magic, Bideford, UK. Saddle-stitch. Red, white. 36 pp. 8 x 10 in. Rope, Stage.

Ayling, Will, *Liliputians, The.* (1987) Supreme Magic, Bideford, UK. Saddle-stitch. Orange. 67 pp. 7.75 x 10.25 in. Puppetry.

Ayling, Will, with Sharpe, S. H., *Oriental Conjuring and Magic.* (1981) Supreme Magic, Bideford, UK. Cloth. Black. 384 pp. 7.5 x 9.75 in. Dust jacket. Signed by S. H. Sharpe. Asian magic, Stage, Close-Up, History.

Ayling, Will, *Simply Magic.* (1976) Supreme Magic, Bideford, UK. Saddle-stitch. Blue. 16 pp. 6 x 8.5 in. Lecture notes. Stage, Close-Up.

Ayres, Micky, with Moreland, Robert, *Holy City Session, The.* (2004) Authors, Hilton Head, SC. 25 pp. Bound oblong. (Information not verified by physical copy.) Lecture notes. Cards.

B., J. T., *Drawing Room Magic.* (1867) Cassell, Petter, and Galpin, London and New York. 90 pp. 4 x 6.5 in. (Information not verified by physical copy.) Toole Stott no. 933. Beginner, Early magic.

B., J. T., *Drawing Room Magic.* (1868) Cassell, Petter, and Galpin, London and New York. 90 pp. 4 x 6.25 in. (Information not verified by physical copy.) Toole Stott no. 70. Beginner, Early magic.

B., J. T., *Drawing Room Magic.* (c. 1874) Happy Hours Co., New York. 88 pp. (Information not verified by physical copy.) Toole Stott no. 1342. Beginner, Early magic.

Bachet, Claude-Gaspar, *Problèmes Plaisans et Délectables, Qui Se Font Par des Nombres.* (1612) Pierre Rigaud, Lyons, France. Perfect. Gray. 172 pp. (Information not verified by physical copy.) Early magic, Mathematical magic, Cards. French.

Bachet, Claude-Gaspar, *Problèmes Plaisans et Délectables, Qui Se Font Par des Nombres.* Second edition. (1624) Pierre Rigaud, Lyons, France. Perfect. Gray. 247 pp. (Information not verified by physical copy.) Early magic, Mathematical magic, Cards. French.

Bachet, Claude-Gaspar, with Labosne, A. (ed.), *Problèmes Plaisans et Délectables, Qui Se Font Par des Nombres.* Third edition. (1874) Gauthier-Villars, Paris. Perfect. Gray. 247 pp. (Information not verified by physical copy.) Early magic, Mathematical magic, Cards. French.

Bachet, Claude-Gaspar, *Problèmes Plaisans et Délectables, Qui Se Font Par des Nombres.* Fourth edition. (1879) Paris. Perfect. Gray. 247 pp. (Information not verified by physical copy.) Early magic, Mathematical magic, Cards. French.

Bachet, Claude-Gaspar, *Problèmes Plaisans et Délectables, Qui Se Font Par des Nombres.* (1884) Gauthier-Villars, Paris. (Information not verified by physical copy.) Early magic, Mathematical magic, Cards. French.

Bachet, Claude-Gaspar, *Problèmes Plaisans et Délectables Qui Se Font Par des Nombres.* (1905) Gauthier-Villars, Paris. Perfect. Blue. 161 pp. (Information not verified by physical copy.) Early magic, Mathematical magic, Cards. French.

Backenstoss, Drew, *Architect of the Mind.* (2019) Haresign Press, Salt Lake City, UT. Casebound. Black. 326 pp. (Information not verified by physical copy.) Mentalism.

Bacon, Francis, *Sylva Sylvarum, or a Naturall Historie.* (1626) William Lee, London. 266 pp. 7.25 x 11.25 in. (Information not verified by physical copy.) Toole Stott no. 71.

Badcock, John, *Domestic Amusements, or Philosophical Recreations.* (c. 1823) T. Hughes, London. 210 pp. 3.75 x 6.25 in. (Information not verified by physical copy.) Toole Stott no. 78. Beginner, Early magic, Cards, Stunts.

Badcock, John, *Domestic Amusements, or Philosophical Recreations.* (1825) T. Hughes, London. 200 pp. 3.5 x 6 in. (Information not verified by physical copy.) Toole Stott no. 79. Beginner, Early magic, Cards, Stunts.

Badcock, John, *Domestic Amusements, or Philosophical Recreations.* (c. 1828) T. Hughes, London. 210 pp. 3.5 x 5.5 in. (Information not verified by physical copy.) Toole Stott no. 80. Beginner, Early magic, Cards, Stunts.

Badcock, John, *Philosophical Recreations, or Winter Amusements.* (1820) T. Hughes, London. Boards. Tan. 200 pp. 3.5 x 6.25 in. Toole Stott no. 75. Beginner, Early magic, Cards, Stunts.

Badcock, John, *Philosophical Recreations, or Winter Amusements.* (1822) T. Hughes, London. 200 pp. 3.5 x 6.25 in. (Information not verified by physical copy.) Toole Stott no. 76. Beginner, Early magic, Cards, Stunts.

Badcock, John, *Philosophical Recreations, or Winter Amusements.* (c. 1828) Knight and Bagshot, London. 200 pp. 3.5 x 6.25 in. (Information not verified by physical copy.) Toole Stott no. 77. Beginner, Early magic, Cards, Stunts.

Badman, Jamie, with Miller, Colin, *Underground Change, The.* (2002) Underground Collective, London. Comb. White, blue. 29 pp. 8.25 x 11.75 in. Cards.

Baffel, Will, *Easy Conjuring Without Apparatus.* (1922) George Routledge and Sons, London. Boards. Yellow. 143 pp. 5 x 7.25 in. Beginner, Cards.

Baffel, Will, *Easy Conjuring Without Apparatus.* Fourth impression. (1922) George Routledge and Sons, London. Boards. Color. 143 pp. 5 x 7.25 in. Beginner, Cards.

Bagshawe, Edward, *E. D. Proudlock's Routine with Thimbles.* First edition. (1936) Edward Bagshawe, London. Saddle-stitch. Beige. 32 pp. 6 x 9.5 in. Thimbles, Manipulation.

Bagshawe, Edward, *E. D. Proudlock's Routine with Thimbles.* Second edition. (1936) Edward Bagshawe, London. Saddle-stitch. Beige. 32 pp. 6 x 9.5 in. Thimbles, Manipulation.

Bagshawe, Edward, *E. D. Proudlock's Routine with Thimbles.* (c. 1946) L. Davenport and Co., London. Saddle-stitch. Black, white. 32 pp. 5.5 x 8.5 in. Thimbles, Manipulation.

Bagshawe, Edward, *Edward Proudlock's Version of the Sympathetic Silks.* (1936) Edward Bagshawe, London. Saddle-stitch. Beige. 26 pp. 6 x 9.5 in. Silks, Stage.

Bagshawe, Edward, *Exclusive Problems in Magic.* (1924) Edward Bagshawe, London. Perfect. Tan. 90 pp. 5.5 x 8.25 in. Stage.

Bagshawe, Edward, *Le Walke Mysteries, The.* (1936) Edward Bagshawe, London. Perfect. Gray. 60 pp. 5.5 x 8.5 in. Stage.

Bagshawe, Edward, *More Magical Mysteries.* (1925) Edward Bagshawe, London. Perfect. Beige. 83 pp. 5.5 x 8.5 in. Signed by Edward Bagshawe. Cards, Stage.

Bagshawe, Edward, *Novel Mysteries.* (1932) Edward Bagshawe, London. Cloth. Green. 232 pp. 4.75 x 7 in. Bound collection with each booklet signed by the publisher. Signed by Edward Bagshawe. Stage.

Bagshawe, Edward, *Novel Mysteries Part 1: Original Silk Effects.* (1932) Edward Bagshawe, London. Saddle-stitch. Beige. 44 pp. 5 x 7.25 in. Silks.

Bagshawe, Edward, *Novel Mysteries Part 2: Original Card Effects.* (1932) Edward Bagshawe, London. Saddle-stitch. Beige. 36 pp. 5 x 7.25 in. Cards.

Bagshawe, Edward, *Novel Mysteries Part 3: Original Pocket Effects.* (1932) Edward Bagshawe, London. Saddle-stitch. Beige. 36 pp. 5 x 7.25 in. Close-Up.

Bagshawe, Edward, *Novel Mysteries Part 4: Original Spiritualistic Effects.* (1932) Edward Bagshawe, London. Saddle-stitch. Beige. 36 pp. 5 x 7.25 in. Spiritualism, Mentalism.

Bagshawe, Edward, *Novel Mysteries Part 5: Miscellaneous Magic.* (1932) Edward Bagshawe, London. Saddle-stitch. Beige. 32 pp. 5 x 7.25 in. Stage.

Bagshawe, Edward, *Novel Mysteries Part 6: More Miscellaneous Magic.* (1932) Edward Bagshawe, London. Saddle-stitch. Beige. 32 pp. 5 x 7.25 in. Stage.

Bagshawe, Edward, *Novel Mysteries Part 1: Original Silk Effects.* Second edition. (1940) L. Davenport and Co., London. Saddle-stitch. Yellow, green. 44 pp. 5 x 7.25 in. Silks.

Bagshawe, Edward, *Novel Mysteries Part 2: Original Card Effects.* Second edition. (1942) L. Davenport and Co., London. Saddle-stitch. Yellow, red. 36 pp. 5 x 7.25 in. Cards.

Bagshawe, Edward, *Novel Mysteries Part 3: Original Pocket Effects.* Second edition. (1942) L. Davenport and Co., London. Saddle-stitch. Yellow, brown. 36 pp. 5 x 7.25 in. Close-Up.

Bagshawe, Edward, *Novel Mysteries Part 4: Original Spiritualistic Effects.* Second edition. (1940) Edward Bagshawe, London. Saddle-stitch. Yellow, green. 36 pp. 5 x 7.25 in. Spiritualism, Mentalism.

Bagshawe, Edward, *Novel Mysteries Part 5: Miscellaneous Magic.* Second edition. (1942) Edward Bagshawe, London. Saddle-stitch. Yellow, black. 32 pp. 5 x 7.25 in. Stage.

Bagshawe, Edward, *Novel Mysteries Part 6: More Miscellaneous Magic.* Second edition. (1942) L. Davenport and Co., London. Saddle-stitch. Yellow, blue. 32 pp. 5 x 7.25 in. Stage.

Bagshawe, Edward, *Proudlock's Egg Bag and Four-Ace Presentations.* (1938) Edward Bagshawe, London. Saddle-stitch. Beige. 28 pp. 6 x 9.5 in. Egg Bag, Cards, Stage.

Bagshawe, Edward, *Twenty Magical Novelties.* (1930) Edward Bagshawe, London. Boards. Green. 80 pp. 6 x 9.5 in. Stage.

Bai, Kurt, *MentalSport.* (2010) Author, Norway. Perfect. Black. 365 pp. 7 x 9.75 in. Stunts, Puzzles, Optical illusions. Norwegian.

Bailey, George, *Selling Your Show.* (1965) Author, Freeport, PA. 4 pp. (Information not verified by physical copy.) Lecture notes. Business, Promotion.

Bailey, Michael (See also Dawes, Edwin A.), *Bailey Formula, The.* (1972) Author, London. Saddle-stitch. White. 28 pp. 5.5 x 8.5 in. Signed by Michael Bailey. Stage, Showmanship.

Bailey, Michael, *How to Succeed in Corporate Magic.* (1998) Author, London. Stapled. White. 33 pp. 8.5 x 11 in. (Information not verified by physical copy.) Lecture notes. Business, Trade shows, Corporate shows.

Bailey, Michael, *Magic Business, The.* (1998) Author, London. Perfect. Blue. 391 pp. 8.25 x 11.5 in. Business, Promotion, Showmanship.

Bailey, Michael, *Magic Circle: Performing Magic Through the Ages, The.* (2007) Tempus, Stroud, UK. Cloth. Black. 288 pp. 6.25 x 9.5 in. Dust jacket. History, Clubs.

Bailey, S. Wilson, with Osborne, Harold, *Wrinkles.* (1911) Bailey-Tripp Co., Cambridgeport, MA. Perfect. Brown. 62 pp. 6 x 9 in. Cards, Stage.

Baillie, Ron, *Extra Sensory Perfection.* (1954) George Armstrong, London. Saddle-stitch. White, blue. 17 pp. 5.5 x 8.5 in. Mentalism, Billets.

Baillie, Ron, *Prepossessed.* (1951) Unique Magic Studios, London. Saddle-stitch. Beige, red. 10 pp. 5 x 7.75 in. Includes illustration sheet and sample window envelope. Mentalism.

Baillie, Ron, *Universal Mind, The.* (1952) George Armstrong, London. Saddle-stitch. White, red. 24 pp. 5.5 x 8.25 in. Mentalism.

Baird, Scott, *Hermit vol. 1, nos. 1-6, The.* (2022) Hermit Magazine, Calgary, Canada. Casebound. Black. 292 pp. 8.5 x 11 in. Magazine, Close-Up, Cards.

Baird, Scott, *Hermit vol. 1, nos. 7-12, The.* (2022) Hermit Magazine, Calgary, Canada. Casebound. Black. 287 pp. 8.5 x 11 in. Magazine, Close-Up, Cards.

Baird, Scott, *Hermit vol. 2, nos. 1-6, The.* (2023) Hermit Magazine, Calgary, Canada. Casebound. Black. 292 pp. 8.5 x 11 in. Magazine, Close-Up, Cards.

Baird, Scott, *Hermit vol. 2, nos. 7-12, The.* (2023) Hermit Magazine, Calgary, Canada. Casebound. Black. 292 pp. 8.5 x 11 in. Magazine, Close-Up, Cards.

Baker, Al (See also Carney, John), *Albaka.* (1933) Julien Proskauer, New York. Stapled with paper cover. Blue. 3 pp. 8.5 x 11 in. Mimeographed. Cover and one page. Folded. Cards, Mentalism.

Baker, Al, *Al Baker's Book.* (1933) Author, Brooklyn, NY. Stapled with paper cover. Orange. 25 pp. 6.25 x 9 in. Signed by Al Baker. Close-Up, Stage.

Baker, Al, *Al Baker's Book.* (1933) Author, Brooklyn, NY. Stapled with paper cover. Yellow. 25 pp. 6.25 x 9 in. Signed by Al Baker to Arthur Lloyd. Close-Up, Stage.

Baker, Al, *Al Baker's Book One.* (1933) L. Davenport and Co., London. Saddle-stitch. Green. 40 pp. 5.5 x 8.5 in. Close-Up, Stage.

Baker, Al, *Al Baker's Book One.* (1938) L. Davenport and Co., London. Saddle-stitch. Green. 38 pp. 5.5 x 8.5 in. Close-Up, Stage.

Baker, Al, *Al Baker's Book One.* (2006) Houdini Magic, Las Vegas. Saddle-stitch. Green. 39 pp. 5.5 x 8.5 in. Close-Up, Stage.

Baker, Al, *Al Baker's Book Two.* (1938) L. Davenport and Co., London. Perfect. Gray. 38 pp. 5.5 x 8.5 in. Close-Up, Stage.

Baker, Al, *Al Baker's Diminishing Cards.* (n.d.) Author, Brooklyn, NY. Folded. White. 2 pp. 5.5 x 8.5 in. Illustrations by Clayton Rawson. Cards, Diminishing Cards, Manual.

Baker, Al, *Al Baker's Dyeing Tube Method.* (1938) Author, Brooklyn, NY. Folded. White. 3 pp. 5.5 x 8.5 in. Silks, Gimmicks, Stage, Instructions.

Baker, Al, *Al Baker's Exclusive "Twenty-Five Dollar" Manuscript.* (n.d.) Anonymous. Stapled. Yellow. 15 pp. 8.5 x 11 in. Mimeographed. Unauthorized manuscript. Cover features the phrase "This Will Open Your Eyes." Cards, Mentalism, Stage.

Baker, Al, *Al Baker's Lock Spirit Slate.* (1934) Author, Brooklyn, NY. Folded. White. 4 pp. 5.5 x 8.5 in. Slates, Spirit effects, Stage, Manual.

Baker, Al, *Al Baker's Mental Magic.* First edition. (1949) Carl W. Jones, Minneapolis. Cloth. Red. 116 pp. 5.25 x 8 in. Dust jacket. Inscribed by Baker to Cardini: "He has millions of admirers and thousands of imitators." Signed by Al Baker. Mentalism.

Baker, Al, *Al Baker's Mental Magic.* Second impression. (1949) Carl W. Jones, Minneapolis. Cloth. Brown. 116 pp. 5.25 x 8 in. Dust jacket. Mentalism.

Baker, Al, *Al Baker's Mental Magic.* Third impression. (1949) Carl W. Jones, Minneapolis. Cloth. Blue. 116 pp. 5.25 x 8 in. Mentalism.

Baker, Al, *Al Baker's Pack.* (1932) Broadway Magic Shop, New York. Stapled with paper cover. Blue. 7 pp. 9 x 11.25 in. Mimeographed. Routines using one-way deck, short and wide cards. Cards.

Baker, Al, *Al Baker's Second Book.* (1935) Author, Brooklyn, NY. Saddle-stitch. Blue. 32 pp. 5.5 x 8.5 in. Close-Up, Stage.

Baker, Al, with Vernon, Dai, *Al-n-Dai.* (1941) Author, Brooklyn, NY. Stapled with paper cover. Blue. 3 pp. 8.5 x 11 in. Mimeographed. Cover and one page. Folded. Cards, Instructions.

Baker, Al, *"Al" Producto.* (1934) Author, Brooklyn, NY. Stapled with paper cover. Green. 2 pp. 8.5 x 11 in. Mimeographed. Cover and one page. Folded. Silks, Gimmicks.

Baker, Al, *Bakerscope, The.* (1936) Author, Brooklyn, NY. Folded. White. 4 pp. 5.5 x 8.5 in. Cards, Princess Card Trick, Manual.

Baker, Al, *Borrowed Cigarette Remade, A.* Trick of the Month Club series 1, no. 3. (October 1931) Thayer Magical Mfg. Co., Los Angeles. Folded. Blue. 2 pp. 3.75 x 8.5 in. Cigarettes.

Baker, Al, *Cardially Yours.* (1933) Author, Brooklyn, NY. Stapled. Orange. 11 pp. 8.5 x 11 in. Mimeographed. Signed by Al Baker. Cards.

Baker, Al, *Cardially Yours.* (1933) Author, Brooklyn, NY. Stapled. Orange. 11 pp. 9 x 11.25 in. Mimeographed. Signed by Al Baker. Cards.

Baker, Al, *Cards and Coins, The.* (1935) Author, Brooklyn, NY. Folded. White. 4 pp. 5.5 x 8.5 in. Cards, Coins, Matrix.

Baker, Al, with Wagner, William, *Checking the Dead Name, New Method Dead Name Duplication, and The Improved Floating Match.* Trick of the Month Club series 2, no. 12. (June 1933) Thayer's Studio of Magic, Los Angeles. Loose pages. Beige. 5 pp. 3.75 x 6.75 in. Mentalism, Matches.

Baker, Al, *Effects 1, 2, and 3: As Presented by Al Baker.* (1939) Author, Brooklyn, NY. Folded. White. 3 pp. 5.5 x 8.5 in. Cards, Gimmicked cards.

Baker, Al, with Bulson, Eugene, *Eugene Bulson's Notebooks About the Secrets of Al Baker vol. 1.* (1989) Jeff Busby Magic, Wallace, ID. 195 pp. (Information not verified by physical copy.) Close-Up, Stage, Notebook.

Baker, Al, with Bulson, Eugene, *Eugene Bulson's Notebooks About the Secrets of Al Baker vol. 2.* (1989) Jeff Busby Magic, Wallace, ID. 175 pp. (Information not verified by physical copy.) Close-Up, Stage, Notebook.

Baker, Al, *Just a Sweet Cake: Al Baker Speaks, June 1941.* (2009) Squash Publishing, Chicago. Saddle-stitch. Black. 31 pp. 8.5 x 5.5 in. Bound oblong. Biography, History.

Baker, Al, *Magical Ways and Means.* First edition. (1941) Carl W. Jones, Minneapolis. Cloth. Light blue. 135 pp. 7 x 10.25 in. Signed by Al Baker. Close-Up, Stage, Mentalism.

Baker, Al, *Magical Ways and Means.* Second edition. (1946) Carl W. Jones, Minneapolis. Cloth. Blue. 135 pp. 6.25 x 9.25 in. Signed by Al Baker. Close-Up, Stage, Mentalism.

Baker, Al, *Magical Ways and Means.* (2014) Houdini Publishing, Las Vegas. Perfect. Blue. 135 pp. 7 x 10.25 in. Reprint of 1941 edition. Close-Up, Stage, Mentalism.

Baker, Al, *Number Please.* (1935) Author, Brooklyn, NY. Folded. White. 4 pp. 5.5 x 8.5 in. Cards, Telephone effects, Mentalism.

Baker, Al, *Pet Secrets.* Limited deluxe edition. (1951) George Starke, New York. Cloth. Black. 111 pp. 6.25 x 9.25 in. Inscribed to Bill Clarke and signed a second time on the numbering page. Signed by Al Baker. #421 of 500. Close-Up, Stage, Mentalism.

Baker, Al, *Pet Secrets.* Second edition. (1951) Carl W. Jones, Minneapolis. Cloth. Red. 111 pp. 6.25 x 9.25 in. Close-Up, Stage, Mentalism.

Baker, Al, *Secret Ways of Al Baker, The.* Limited deluxe edition. (2003) The Miracle Factory, Seattle. Cloth. Black. 912 pp. 8.25 x 10.25 in. Dust jacket. In box with ribbon tie, with DVD. Signed by Katlyn Breene, Eugene Burger, John Carney, Todd Karr, Jay Marshall, Max Maven. #1 of 100. Close-Up, Stage, Biography.

Baker, Al, *Secret Ways of Al Baker, The.* (2003) The Miracle Factory, Seattle. Cloth. Black. 912 pp. 8.25 x 10.25 in. Dust jacket. Close-Up, Stage, Biography.

Baker, Al, *Thought Transcription.* (1937) Author, Brooklyn, NY. Stapled with paper cover. Blue. 2 pp. 8.5 x 11 in. Mimeographed. Cover and one page. Folded. Silks, Gimmicks.

Baker, Bob, *Shared Thoughts.* (1985) Bowl of Cherries Press, Jericho, NY. Comb. Blue. 91 pp. 8.5 x 11 in. Mentalism, Stage, Close-Up.

Baker, Harrison "Red," with Larsen, Milt, *Gags Galore.* (1949) Baker and Larsen, Hollywood, CA. Saddle-stitch. White. 14 pp. 5.5 x 8.5 in. Mimeographed. Comedy, Jokes, Patter.

Baker, Harrison "Red," *In the Aisles.* (1947) Author, Hollywood, CA. Stapled with paper cover. Yellow, red. 8 pp. 5.5 x 8.5 in. Comedy, Jokes, Patter.

Baker, Harrison "Red," with Larsen, Milt, *Jokers' Jackpot.* (1952) Baker and Larsen, Hollywood, CA. Stapled with paper cover. White. 11 pp. 5.5 x 8.5 in. (Information not verified by physical copy.) Comedy, Jokes, Patter.

Baker, Harrison "Red," with Larsen, Milt, *Wit Kit, The.* (1953) Yogi Magic Mart, Baltimore. Stapled with paper cover. Red, black. 13 pp. 5.5 x 8.25 in. Comedy, Jokes, Patter.

Baker, Harrison "Red," with Larsen, Milt, *Wit Parade, The.* (1955) Baker and Larsen, Hollywood, CA. Stapled with paper cover. White. 10 pp. 5.5 x 8.5 in. (Information not verified by physical copy.) Comedy, Jokes, Patter.

Baker, Harrison "Red," with Larsen, Milt, *You Asked for "Wit."* (1952) Baker and Larsen, Hollywood, CA. Stapled with paper cover. White. 9 pp. 5.5 x 8.5 in. Folded. Comedy, Jokes, Patter.

Baker, James W., *April Fool's Day Magic.* (1988) Lerner Publications, Minneapolis. Casebound. 48 pp. 6.25 x 6 in. (Information not verified by physical copy.) Holiday magic, Beginner.

Baker, James W., *Arbor Day Magic.* (1990) Lerner Publications, Minneapolis. Casebound. 48 pp. 6.25 x 6 in. (Information not verified by physical copy.) Holiday magic, Beginner.

Baker, James W., *Christmas Magic.* (1988) Lerner Publications, Minneapolis. Casebound. 48 pp. 6.25 x 6 in. (Information not verified by physical copy.) Holiday magic, Beginner.

Baker, James W., *Columbus Day Magic.* (1990) Lerner Publications, Minneapolis. Casebound. 48 pp. 6.25 x 6 in. (Information not verified by physical copy.) Holiday magic, Beginner.

Baker, James W., *Halloween Magic.* (1988) Lerner Publications, Minneapolis. Casebound. 48 pp. 6.25 x 6 in. (Information not verified by physical copy.) Holiday magic, Beginner.

Baker, James W., *Illusions Illustrated.* (1984) Lerner Publications, Minneapolis. Perfect. Brown. 120 pp. 8.5 x 8 in. Beginner.

Baker, James W., *Independence Day Magic.* (1990) Lerner Publications, Minneapolis. Casebound. 48 pp. 6.25 x 6 in. (Information not verified by physical copy.) Holiday magic, Beginner.

Baker, James W., *New Year's Magic.* (1989) Lerner Publications, Minneapolis. Casebound. 48 pp. 6.25 x 6 in. (Information not verified by physical copy.) Holiday magic, Beginner.

Baker, James W., *President's Day Magic.* (1989) Lerner Publications, Minneapolis. Casebound. 48 pp. 6.25 x 6 in. (Information not verified by physical copy.) Holiday magic, Beginner.

Baker, James W., *St. Patrick's Day Magic.* (1990) Lerner Publications, Minneapolis. Casebound. 48 pp. 6.25 x 6 in. (Information not verified by physical copy.) Holiday magic, Beginner.

Baker, James W., *Thanksgiving Magic.* (1989) Lerner Publications, Minneapolis. Casebound. 48 pp. 6.25 x 6 in. (Information not verified by physical copy.) Holiday magic, Beginner.

Baker, James W., *Valentine Magic.* (1988) Lerner Publications, Minneapolis. Casebound. White. 48 pp. 6.25 x 6 in. Holiday magic, Beginner.

Baker, Ken, *21 Himber Wallet Routines.* (1985) Author, Chicago. Saddle-stitch. Yellow. 16 pp. 5.5 x 8.5 in. Wallets, Bills, Close-Up, Cards.

Baker, Ken, *21 Himber Wallet Routines.* (1992) Magic Methods, Greenville, SC. Saddle-stitch. Beige. 14 pp. 5.25 x 8.5 in. Wallets, Bills, Close-Up, Cards.

Baker, Ken, *Comic Book, The.* (1985) Ken Baker's Magicland, Chicago. Saddle-stitch. 32 pp. (Information not verified by physical copy.) Comedy, Jokes, Gags.

Baker, Ken, *Hoo's Koin Box Routines.* (1975) Paul Diamond Magic, Ft. Lauderdale, FL. Saddle-stitch. Light green. 10 pp. 5.5 x 8.5 in. (Information not verified by physical copy.) Coins, Okito Coin Box, Close-Up.

Baker, Ken, *Lecture no. 68.* (c. 1978) Paul Diamond Magic, Ft. Lauderdale, FL. 38 pp. (Information not verified by physical copy.) Lecture notes. Close-Up, Stage.

Baker, Matt, *Buena Vista Shuffle Club, The.* (2019) Author, Atlanta. Cloth. Black. 264 pp. 6.25 x 9.25 in. Dust jacket. (Measurements and other information have been recorded as accurately as possible.) Cards.

Baker, Rev. William F., Jr., *Baker's Dozen, A.* (1983) Collector's World, Holiday, FL. Comb. Yellow. 44 pp. 8.5 x 11 in. Coins, Stage.

Baker, Rev. William F., Jr., *Basic Library for Magicians, A.* (1982) Collector's World, Holiday, FL. Stapled with paper cover. Blue. 18 pp. 8.5 x 11 in. Collecting, Bibliography, Reference.

Baker, Rev. William F., Jr., *Close-Up Gospel Magic.* (1989) Collector's World, Holiday, FL. 40 pp. (Information not verified by physical copy.) Close-Up, Gospel magic.

Baker, Rev. William F., Jr., *It's in the Coins.* (c. 1982) Collector's World, Holiday, FL. Comb. Green. 26 pp. 8.5 x 11 in. Single-sided pages. Coins, Close-Up.

Baker, Rev. William F., Jr., *Magic and Storytelling: Wonderful Partners!* (c. 1982) Collector's World, Holiday, FL. Stapled. Red. 8.5 x 11 in. (Information not verified by physical copy.) Lecture notes. Gospel magic, Storytelling magic.

Baker, Rev. William F., Jr., *Presentation Bits and Tips.* (c. 1982) Collector's World, Holiday, FL. Comb. Beige. 14 pp. 8.5 x 11 in. (Information not verified by physical copy.) Showmanship, Tips.

Baker, Roy, with Miller, Hugh, *Baker's Bonanza.* Second impression. (1978) Supreme Magic, Bideford, UK. Cloth. Black. 127 pp. 6 x 8.75 in. Dust jacket. Close-Up, Cards, Stage.

Baker, Roy, *Baker's Brainwaves.* (1981) Supreme Magic, Bideford, UK. Cloth. Dark blue. 159 pp. 6.25 x 9 in. Dust jacket. Children's magic, Stage.

Baker, Roy, *Baker's Capers.* (1983) Supreme Magic, Bideford, UK. Saddle-stitch. Gray. 32 pp. 8 x 9.75 in. Stage, Close-Up.

Baker, Roy, *Cards to Pocket.* (1976) Author, London. Stapled. White. 7 pp. 8 x 10 in. With illustration sheet. (Measurements and other information have been recorded as accurately as possible.) Cards.

Baker, Roy, *Miracle Shell-Coin Routines.* (1979) Supreme Magic, Bideford, UK. Stapled. White, red. 7 pp. 8 x 9.75 in. (Information not verified by physical copy.) Coins, Gimmicks.

Baker, Roy, *Time Flies.* (1983) Supreme Magic, Bideford, UK. Saddle-stitch. White, blue. 7 pp. 5.75 x 8.25 in. (Measurements and other information have been recorded as accurately as possible.) Stage.

Baker, Roy, *Yell-Up for Kids.* (1977) Supreme Magic, Bideford, UK. Stapled. White. 6 pp. 8 x 10 in. (Information not verified by physical copy.) Children's magic, Balls.

Bakner, Gérard, *Magie Enfantine.* (1986) Académie de Magie Georges Proust, Paris. Comb. Beige. 35 pp. 8.25 x 11.75 in. Children's magic.

Baldwin, Samri S., *Spirit Mediums Exposed.* (1879) Author, Melbourne. Saddle-stitch. Blue. 64 pp. 4.25 x 5.25 in. (Information not verified by physical copy.) See McCullagh, "Under the Southern Cross." Spiritualism, Mediums, Exposés.

Baldwin, Samri S., *Secrets of Mahatma Land Explained.* Second edition. (1895) Author, Hartford, CN. Boards. Blue. 120 pp. 7.25 x 9.5 in. This is the first edition of this title but designated as the second to reflect the earlier "Spirit Mediums Exposed" (1879), according to McCullagh, "Under the Southern Cross." Indian magic, History.

Baldwin, Samri S., *Secrets of Mahatma Land Explained.* Second edition. (1895) Author, Hartford, CN. Boards. Brown. 120 pp. 7.25 x 9.5 in. Indian magic, History.

Baldwin, Samri S., *Secrets of Mahatma Land Explained.* Second edition. (1895) Author, Hartford, CN. Boards. Yellow. 120 pp. 7.25 x 9.5 in. Indian magic, History.

Bamberg, David, *Fu Manchu: Una Vida Para la Magia.* (2024) Bazar de Magia, Buenos Aires. Casebound. Dark blue. 407 pp. 9.25 x 11.75 in. Biography, Illusions. Spanish.

Bamberg, David, *Illusion Show.* (1988) Meyerbooks, Glenwood, IL. Cloth. Blue. 331 pp. 7.25 x 10.25 in. Dust jacket. Biography, Illusions.

Banachek (Steve Shaw), *Banachek Lecture Notes.* (2009) Magic Inspirations, Houston, TX. Saddle-stitch. Black, white. 48 pp. 5.5 x 8.5 in. Lecture notes. Mentalism.

Banachek, *Banachek Lecture Notes no. 2.* (2016) Magic Inspirations, Houston, TX. Saddle-stitch. 19 pp. 8.5 x 11 in. (Information not verified by physical copy.) Lecture notes. Mentalism.

Banachek, *Banachek's 2005 Lecture.* (2005) Magic Inspirations, Houston, TX. Saddle-stitch. 48 pp. 5.5 x 8.5 in. (Information not verified by physical copy.) Lecture notes. Mentalism.

Banachek, *Key-Erect.* (1999) Magic Inspirations, Houston, TX. Comb. White. 9 pp. 8.5 x 11 in. (Information not verified by physical copy.) Mentalism, Keys, Risqué.

Banachek, *Pre-Thoughts.* (1990) Author, Houston, TX. Comb. Blue. 22 pp. 8.5 x 11 in. (Measurements and other information have been recorded as accurately as possible.) Mentalism.

Banachek, *Pre-Thoughts.* Fifth printing. (1999) Author, Houston, TX. Comb. Blue. 22 pp. 8.5 x 11 in. (Measurements and other information have been recorded as accurately as possible.) Mentalism.

Banachek, *Psychokinetic Time.* Second edition. (1999) Magic Inspirations, Houston, TX. Saddle-stitch. Beige. 24 pp. 5.5 x 8.5 in. Mentalism.

Banachek, *Psychokinetic Touches.* Eleventh printing. (2015) Magic Inspirations, Houston, TX. Coil. Beige. 10 pp. 8.5 x 11 in. Mentalism, PK Touch routines.

Banachek, *Psychological Subtleties.* Second edition, second printing. (2002) Magic Inspirations, Houston, TX. Casebound. Dark blue. 112 pp. 5.5 x 8.5 in. Mentalism, Psychological.

Banachek, *Psychological Subtleties 2.* Second edition, second printing. (2017) Magic Inspirations, Houston, TX. Cloth. White. 206 pp. 6.25 x 9.25 in. Dust jacket. Mentalism, Psychological.

Banachek, *Psychological Subtleties 3.* Second edition. (2017) Magic Inspirations, Houston, TX. Cloth. Red. 228 pp. 6.25 x 9.25 in. Dust jacket. Mentalism, Psychological.

Banachek, with Burlingame, H. J., *Psychophysiological Thought Reading.* (2002) Magic Inspirations, Houston, TX. Casebound. Gray. 91 pp. 5.5 x 8.75 in. Includes Burlingame's 1904 "How to Read People's Minds." Stage, Cards, Close-Up.

Banachek, *Radio: The Forgotten Showcase.* (n.d.) Author, Houston, TX. Strip binding. Blue. 5 pp. 8.5 x 11 in. Mentalism, Radio, Promotion.

Banachek, *Thick Thighs.* (2003) Banachek Inc., Houston, TX. Stapled. White. 9 pp. 8.5 x 11 in. (Measurements and other information have been recorded as accurately as possible.) Mentalism, Magazine tests.

Bandy, Father Albert R., *All About Linking Rings.* (1976) John D. Standridge, Mesquite, TX. Saddle-stitch. Green. 72 pp. 5.5 x 8.5 in. Linking Rings.

Bandy, Father Albert R., *Go Ahead, I'll Wait! More Magic of Johnny Brown.* (1975) John D. Standridge, Mesquite, TX. Vinyl cover. Brown. 100 pp. 5.5 x 8 in. Close-Up, Cards.

Bandy, Father Albert R., *Isn't That Good!?! The Magic of Johnny Brown.* (1974) John D. Standridge, Mesquite, TX. Vinyl cover. Brown. 101 pp. 5.5 x 8 in. Close-Up, Cards.

Bandy, Father Albert R., *Keep Magic Simple, Magicians.* (1980) Universal Magic Studio, Carrolltown, TX. 15 pp. (Information not verified by physical copy.) Cards, Close-Up, Stage.

Bandy, Father Albert R., *Magic Dove Gimmick: A Must for All Dove Workers, The.* (1980) Universal Magic Studio, Carrolltown, TX. 15 pp. (Information not verified by physical copy.) Doves, Gimmicks.

Banerjee, Ananta Deb, *Designed to Deceive.* (1998) Electro Fun, Calcutta. Saddle-stitch. 24 pp. 5.5 x 8.5 in. (Measurements and other information have been recorded as accurately as possible.) Mentalism.

Bannon, John (See also Gallo, Michael), *Avant Carde 1.* (1989) Author, Chicago. Saddle-stitch. Beige. 16 pp. 8.5 x 11 in. Cards.

Bannon, John, *Barrage.* (2023) 3 Monkeys Publishing, Lempdes, France. Perfect. Orange. 132 pp. 6.25 x 9.5 in. (Measurements and other information have been recorded as accurately as possible.) Cards.

Bannon, John, *Bullet Party.* (2011) Author, Chicago. Perfect. Red. 125 pp. 6 x 9 in. (Measurements and other information have been recorded as accurately as possible.) Cards.

Bannon, John, *Dear Mr. Fantasy.* (2004) Author, Chicago. Cloth. White. 197 pp. 6.25 x 9.25 in. Dust jacket. (Measurements and other information have been recorded as accurately as possible.) Cards.

Bannon, John, *Destination Zero.* (2015) Squash Publishing, Chicago. Cloth. Black. 209 pp. 7.5 x 10.25 in. Dust jacket. Cards.

Bannon, John, *Detour de Force.* (1991) A-1 MultiMedia, El Dorado Hills, CA. Saddle-stitch. Yellow, black. 8 pp. 5.5 x 8.5 in. Cards.

Bannon, John, *Djinn and Tonic.* (2017) Author, Chicago. Perfect. Black. 78 pp. 6 x 9 in. (Measurements and other information have been recorded as accurately as possible.) Cards.

Bannon, John, *Heart of the City.* (1990) Author, Chicago. Stapled. Yellow. 6 pp. 8.5 x 11 in. (Measurements and other information have been recorded as accurately as possible.) Cards.

Bannon, John, *High Caliber.* (2013) Squash Publishing, Chicago. Cloth. Gray. 305 pp. 7.25 x 10.25 in. Dust jacket. Signed by John Bannon. Cards.

Bannon, John, *High Caliber.* (2018) Tokyo Do Shuppan, Tokyo. Cloth. Gray. 334 pp. 7.5 x 10.25 in. Dust jacket. Cards. Japanese.

Bannon, John, *Impossibilia.* (1990) L & L Publishing, Tahoma, CA. Cloth. Blue. 142 pp. 8.5 x 11 in. Dust jacket. Cards.

Bannon, John, *Lucky.* (2016) Author, Chicago. Perfect. Black, white. 104 pp. 6 x 9 in. (Measurements and other information have been recorded as accurately as possible.) Cards.

Bannon, John, *Mega 'Wave and Other Fractal Adventures.* (2010) Fractal Productions, Chicago. Perfect. Orange. 73 pp. 6 x 9 in. Cards.

Bannon, John, *Mentalissimo.* (2016) Squash Publishing, Chicago. Cloth. Red. 216 pp. 7.5 x 10.25 in. Dust jacket. Cards, Mentalism.

Bannon, John, *Mirage.* (1986) Kee-West Productions, Edgewater, MD. Saddle-stitch. Beige. 58 pp. 5.5 x 8.25 in. Cards.

Bannon, John, *Open and Notorious.* (2009) Author, Chicago. 31 pp. (Information not verified by physical copy.) Cards.

Bannon, John, *Outnumbered.* (2024) 3 Monkeys Publishing, Lempdes, France. Perfect. Green. 112 pp. 6.25 x 9.5 in. (Measurements and other information have been recorded as accurately as possible.) Cards.

Bannon, John, *Queen Spirit.* (2021) Author, Chicago. Casebound. Red. 74 pp. 7.25 x 10.25 in. Title page says "(Smells Like) Queen Spirit." Cards.

Bannon, John, *Return of the Magnificent Seven, The.* (1989) Author, Chicago. Saddle-stitch. Gray. 8 pp. 5.5 x 8.5 in. Cards.

Bannon, John, *Secret Weapons.* (1990) Author, Chicago. Saddle-stitch. Yellow. 24 pp. 8.5 x 11 in. (Measurements and other information have been recorded as accurately as possible.) Cards.

Bannon, John, *Six. Impossible. Things.* (2009) Author, Chicago. Perfect. Black. 63 pp. 6 x 9 in. (Measurements and other information have been recorded as accurately as possible.) Cards.

Bannon, John, *Smoke and Mirrors.* (1991) Kaufman and Greenberg, New York. Casebound. Blue. 164 pp. 8.5 x 11 in. Cards.

Bannon, John, with Montier, Liam, *Triabolical.* (2011) Author, Chicago. Perfect. White. 52 pp. 6 x 6 in. Includes cards. Cards.

Bannon, John, *Very Hush-Hush.* (2023) Squash Publishing, Chicago. Cloth. Black. 254 pp. 7.25 x 10.25 in. Dust jacket. Cards.

Bannon, John, *Without.* (1989) Author, Chicago. Saddle-stitch. Beige. 16 pp. 8.5 x 11 in. (Measurements and other information have been recorded as accurately as possible.) Coins.

Barbaud, Roger, *Prestidigitation et Magie Blanche vol. 1: Tours de Cartes Sans Appareils.* (1933) Société Française d'Éditions Littéraires et Techniques, Paris. Perfect. Beige. 298 pp. 4.75 x 7.25 in. Cards, Beginner.

Barbaud, Roger, *Prestidigitation et Magie Blanche vol. 1: Tours de Cartes Sans Appareils.* (1947) Société Française d'Éditions Littéraires et Techniques, Paris. Perfect. Dark red. 198 pp. 4.25 x 7.25 in. Cards, Beginner.

Barbaud, Roger, *Prestidigitation et Magie Blanche vol. 2: Tours de Cartes Avec Appareils.* (1933) Société Française d'Éditions Littéraires et Techniques, Paris. Perfect. Beige. 316 pp. 4.75 x 7.25 in. Cards, Beginner.

Barbaud, Roger, *Prestidigitation et Magie Blanche vol. 3: Foulards et Drapeaux.* (1933) Société Française d'Éditions Littéraires et Techniques, Paris. Perfect. Beige. 336 pp. 4.75 x 7.25 in. Silks, Handkerchiefs, Flags.

Barbaud, Roger, *Prestidigitation et Magie Blanche vol. 4: Hydromagie.* (1933) Société Française d'Éditions Littéraires et Techniques, Paris. Perfect. Beige. 209 pp. 4.75 x 7.25 in. Liquids, Stage.

Barbaud, Roger, *Traité Complèt des Tours de Cartes.* (1910) Roret, Paris. Perfect. Tan. 302 pp. 3.75 x 5.75 in. Cards. French.

Barbaud, Roger, *Traité Complèt des Tours de Cartes: Deuxième Série.* (1912) Roret, Paris. Perfect. Tan. 320 pp. 3.75 x 6 in. Cards. French.

Barends, H. P., *International Magic Course.* (1934) International Magic Course, Jackson Heights, NY. Folder. Tan. 36 pp. 8.75 x 11.5 in. Course.

Bargatze, Stephen, *Four Tricks from All Four of Us.* (n.d.) Author, Nashville, TN. 21 pp. (Information not verified by physical copy.) Lecture notes. Comedy, Stage.

Bargatze, Stephen, *Magic of Stephen, The.* (1998) Author, Nashville, TN. Comb. White, black. 17 pp. 8.5 x 11 in. Lecture notes. Comedy, Stage, Showmanship.

Barkann, Roger, *Patent Pending.* (1944) Louis Tannen, New York. Saddle-stitch. Beige. 16 pp. 6 x 9 in. Stage, Political magic.

Barnello, E. (Edward A. Barnwell), *Red Demons, or Mysteries of Fire, The.* (1893) Author, Chicago. 16 pp. 4.5 x 5.75 in. (Information not verified by physical copy.) Fire-eating.

Barnes, H. Lee, *Dummy Up and Deal.* (2002) University of Nevada Press, Las Vegas. Perfect. Black. 140 pp. 6 x 9 in. Gambling, Cheating, Cards.

Barnett, Paul, with Tiner, Ron, *Conjuring Tricks.* (1992) Charles Letts and Co., London. Casebound. Green. 95 pp. 4.25 x 5.75 in. Dust jacket. Beginner, History.

Barnett, Paul, with Tiner, Ron, *Conjuring Tricks.* (1992) Bulfinch Press, Boston. Casebound. Blue. 96 pp. 4.25 x 5.75 in. Dust jacket. Beginner, History.

Barnett, Paul, with Tiner, Ron, *Conjuring Tricks.* (1998) Lorenz Books, New York. Casebound. Green. 95 pp. 4.5 x 5.75 in. Dust jacket. Beginner, History.

Barnhart, Norm, *Amazing Magic Tricks: Apprentice Level.* (2008) Capstone Press, Mankato, MN. 32 pp. (Information not verified by physical copy.) Beginner, Children's book.

Barnhart, Norm, *Amazing Magic Tricks: Beginner Level.* (2008) Capstone Press, Mankato, MN. 32 pp. (Information not verified by physical copy.) Beginner, Children's book.

Barnhart, Norm, *Amazing Magic Tricks: Expert Level.* (2008) Capstone Press, Mankato, MN. 32 pp. (Information not verified by physical copy.) Beginner, Children's book.

Barnhart, Norm, *Amazing Magic Tricks: Master Level.* (2008) Capstone Press, Mankato, MN. 32 pp. (Information not verified by physical copy.) Beginner, Children's book.

Barnhart, Norm, *Comedy Balloon Hats.* (1997) Author, St. Paul, MN. 20 pp. (Information not verified by physical copy.) Balloons, Comedy, Children's magic.

Barnhart, Norm, *Comedy Magic with Balloons.* (1992) Author, St. Paul, MN. 32 pp. (Information not verified by physical copy.) Balloons, Comedy, Children's magic.

Barnhart, Norm, *Good News for Children, The.* (1995) Author, St. Paul, MN. Saddle-stitch. Yellow. 24 pp. 5.25 x 8.5 in. Gospel magic, Children's magic.

Barnhart, Russell (See also Villiod, Eugène), *Beating the Wheel.* (1994) Lyle Stuart, New York. Perfect. Green. 216 pp. 5.75 x 8.75 in. Gambling, Roulette.

Barnhart, Russell, *Casino Gambling: Why You Win, Why You Lose.* (1979) Souvenir Press, London. Cloth. Yellow. 221 pp. 6.25 x 9.5 in. Dust jacket. Gambling.

Barnhart, Russell, *Gamblers of Yesteryear.* (1983) Gamblers Book Club, Las Vegas. Perfect. Yellow. 239 pp. 6 x 9 in. Gambling, History.

Barnhart, Russell, *Master Palm, The.* (1975) Magic Inc., Chicago. Comb. Yellow. 78 pp. 5.25 x 8.5 in. (Measurements and other information have been recorded as accurately as possible.) Cards, Palming.

Barnhart, Russell, *Master Palm, The.* Second printing. (1981) Magic Inc., Chicago. Saddle-stitch. Yellow. 78 pp. 5.25 x 8.5 in. Cards, Palming.

Barnhart, Russell, *Two Second Deals.* (1974) Magic Inc., Chicago. Comb. Red. 14 pp. 5.5 x 8.5 in. With actual photos attached. Cards, Second deal.

Barnhart, Russell, *Two Second Deals.* Reprint. (1982) Magic Inc., Chicago. Saddle-stitch. Pink. 16 pp. 5.5 x 8.5 in. Cards, Second deal.

Barnouw, Erik, *Magician and the Cinema, The.* (1981) Oxford University Press, New York. Cloth. Black. 128 pp. 6 x 9 in. Dust jacket. Signed by Erik Barnouw. Magicians in cinema, History.

Barnowsky, Larry, *21st Century Coin Mechanics.* (2005) Gyromagnetic Press, Cooperstown, NY. Casebound. Black, red. 160 pp. 8.5 x 11 in. Dust jacket. (Information not verified by physical copy.) Coins.

Barnowsky, Larry, *Book of Destiny, The.* (2011) Gyromagnetic Press, Cooperstown, NY. Casebound. Black. 368 pp. 8.5 x 11 in. Dust jacket. (Information not verified by physical copy.) Cards.

Barnowsky, Larry, *Counting on Deception.* (2013) Gyromagnetic Press, Cooperstown, NY. Casebound. Red. 256 pp. 8.5 x 11 in. Dust jacket. (Information not verified by physical copy.) Cards.

Barnowsky, Larry, *Kingdom of the Red.* (2007) Gyromagnetic Press, Cooperstown, NY. Casebound. Blue, red. 240 pp. 8.5 x 11 in. Dust jacket. (Information not verified by physical copy.) Cards, Close-Up.

Barnowsky, Larry, *Magica Analytica.* (2014) Gyromagnetic Press, Cooperstown, NY. Coil. Red. 104 pp. 8.5 x 11 in. (Information not verified by physical copy.) Cards, Coins, Close-Up.

Barnowsky, Larry, *Magica Analytica II.* (2015) Gyromagnetic Press, Cooperstown, NY. Coil. Red. 104 pp. 8.5 x 11 in. (Information not verified by physical copy.) Cards, Coins, Close-Up.

Barnowsky, Larry, *Magica III.* (2017) Gyromagnetic Press, Cooperstown, NY. Coil. Colors. 132 pp. 8.5 x 11 in. Also offered in deluxe hardbound leather edition. (Information not verified by physical copy.) Cards, Coins, Close-Up.

Barnowsky, Larry, *Magica IV: Secrets from the Vault.* (2018) Gyromagnetic Press, Cooperstown, NY. Coil. Purple. 150 pp. 8.5 x 11 in. Also offered in deluxe hardbound leather edition. (Information not verified by physical copy.) Cards, Coins, Close-Up.

Barnowsky, Larry, *Magica V.* (2019) Gyromagnetic Press, Cooperstown, NY. Coil. Black. 148 pp. 8.5 x 11 in. Also offered in deluxe hardbound leather edition. (Information not verified by physical copy.) Cards, Coins, Close-Up.

Barnowsky, Larry, *Magica VI.* (2024) Gyromagnetic Press, Cooperstown, NY. Coil. Black. 150 pp. 8.5 x 11 in. Also offered in deluxe hardbound leather edition. (Information not verified by physical copy.) Cards, Coins, Close-Up.

Barnum, Bill, *Fun with Stunts, Tricks, and Skits.* (1956) Padell Book Co., New York. Saddle-stitch. Blue. 32 pp. 5 x 7.25 in. Beginner, Stunts.

Barnum, Vance, with Dunn, Bruce, *Joe Strong: A Brief Biography of the Boy Wizard.* Miniature book. (1996) Bruce Dunn, Kalamazoo, MI. Saddle-stitch. Blue. 12 pp. 3 x 4.25 in. Wee Books by Dunn series 01-96. From "Joe Strong, the Boy Fire-Eater," 1916. History, Fiction.

Barnum, Vance, *Joe Strong and His Box of Mystery.* (1919) George Sully and Co., New York. Cloth. Olive. 214 pp. 4.75 x 7.25 in. Fiction.

Barnum, Vance, *Joe Strong the Boy Wizard.* (1916) George Sully and Co., New York. Cloth. Olive. 218 pp. 4.75 x 7.25 in. Fiction.

Barnum, Vance, *Joe Strong the Boy Wizard.* (1916) Whitman, Racine, WI. Cloth. Blue. 215 pp. 4.25 x 6.5 in. Fiction.

Barnum, Vance, *Joe Strong the Boy Wizard.* (1916) Whitman, Racine, WI. Cloth. Gray. 215 pp. 4.25 x 6.5 in. (Measurements and other information have been recorded as accurately as possible.) Fiction.

Barnum, Vance, *Joe Strong the Boy Wizard.* (1916) Whitman, Racine, WI. Cloth. Green. 215 pp. 4.25 x 6.5 in. (Measurements and other information have been recorded as accurately as possible.) Fiction.

Barnum, Vance, *Joe Strong the Boy Wizard.* (1916) Whitman, Racine, WI. Cloth. Orange. 215 pp. 4.25 x 6.5 in. (Measurements and other information have been recorded as accurately as possible.) Fiction.

Barnum, Vance, *Joe Strong the Boy Wizard.* (1921) Harrap, London. Cloth. Blue. 189 pp. 5 x 7.5 in. (Measurements and other information have been recorded as accurately as possible.) Fiction.

Barnum, Vance, *Joe Strong the Boy Wizard.* (1940) Whitman, Racine, WI. Cloth. Orange. 252 pp. 5.25 x 7.75 in. Dust jacket. Fiction.

Barnum, Vance, *Joe Strong the Boy Wizard.* (1940) Whitman, Racine, WI. Cloth. Yellow. 215 pp. 4 x 6.5 in. Dust jacket. Fiction.

Barnum, Vance, with Dunn, Bruce, *Vanishing Lady, The.* Miniature book. (1996) Bruce Dunn, Kalamazoo, MI. Saddle-stitch. Blue. 15 pp. 3 x 4.25 in. Wee Books by Dunn series 02-96. From "Joe Strong, the Boy Fire-Eater," 1916. History, Fiction.

Baron, Harry, *Better Magic: The Key to Improved Performances.* (1978) Kaye and Ward, London. Perfect. Pink. 94 pp. 4.25 x 7 in. (Information not verified by physical copy.) Beginner.

Baron, Harry, *Card Tricks.* (1977) Sphere Books, London. Perfect. Red. 128 pp. 4.25 x 7 in. Same text as "How to Do Card Tricks and Entertain People." Cards, Beginner.

Baron, Harry, *Card Tricks for Beginners.* Second printing. (1970) Emerson Books Inc., New York. Cloth. Blue. 136 pp. 5.75 x 8.75 in. Dust jacket. Cards, Beginner.

Baron, Harry, *Close-Up Magic for Beginners.* (1972) Kaye and Ward, London. Cloth. Blue. 160 pp. 5.5 x 8.75 in. Dust jacket. Beginner, Close-Up.

Baron, Harry, *Close-Up Magic for Beginners with Magic for Beginners.* (1978) Bell Publishing, New York. Cloth. Black. 156 pp. 6.25 x 9.25 in. Dust jacket. Beginner, Close-Up.

Baron, Harry, *How to Do Card Tricks and Entertain People.* (1960) Nicholas Kaye, London. Cloth. Black. 126 pp. 5.75 x 8.75 in. Dust jacket. Cards, Beginner.

Baron, Harry, *Instant Magic: The 65th Lecture.* (1980) British Magical Society, UK. 26 pp. (Information not verified by physical copy.) Lecture notes. Cards, Coins, Close-Up, Stage.

Baron, Harry, *Magic for Beginners.* (1967) Funk and Wagnalls, New York. Cloth. Black, red. 160 pp. 5.5 x 8.5 in. Dust jacket. Beginner.

Baron, Harry, *Magic for Beginners.* (1967) Kaye and Ward, London. Cloth. Blue. 159 pp. 5.5 x 8.5 in. Dust jacket. (Measurements and other information have been recorded as accurately as possible.) Beginner.

Baron, Harry, *Magic for Beginners.* (1995) Prima Publishing, Rocklin, CA. Perfect. Purple. 160 pp. 5.5 x 8.5 in. Beginner.

Baron, Harry, *Magic Simplified.* (1954) Nicholas Kaye, London. Cloth. Yellow. 112 pp. 5 x 7.5 in. Dust jacket. Beginner.

Baron, Harry, *My Best Card Trick.* (1953) Ridgmont Books, London. Saddle-stitch. Red. 31 pp. 5.5 x 8.5 in. Material by Avis, Haxton, Koran, Victor, Warlock. Cards.

Baron, Harry, *My Best Close-Up Trick.* (1954) Lyndon Books, Presteigne, UK. Saddle-stitch. Blue. 36 pp. 5.5 x 8.5 in. Material by Alex Elmsley, Edward Victor, Bobby Bernard. Close-Up.

Baron, Harry, *Peter Pan's Book of Tricks.* (n.d.) Peter Pan Playthings, UK. Saddle-stitch. Pink. 16 pp. 3.5 x 4.75 in. In "My Magic Box" set. Magic set manual.

Baron, Harry, *Peter Pan's Book of Tricks.* (n.d.) Peter Pan Playthings, UK. Saddle-stitch. White. 16 pp. 3.5 x 4.75 in. In "Five Star Magic" set. Magic set manual.

Baron, Harry, *Pick a Card, Any Card.* (1994) Prima Publishing, Rocklin, CA. Perfect. Blue. 126 pp. 5.5 x 8.5 in. Cards, Beginner.

Baronio, Tony, Jr., *On Location with Tony Baronio.* (1981) Author, Hazleton, PA. Comb. Green. 11 pp. 8.5 x 11 in. Cards, Close-Up.

Baronio, Tony, Jr., *Tony Baronio's Magic Lecture no. 1.* (n.d.) Author, Hazleton, PA. Comb. Yellow. 37 pp. 8.5 x 11 in. (Information not verified by physical copy.) Lecture notes. Cards, Close-Up.

Barr, George, *Entertaining with Number Tricks.* (1971) McGraw-Hill, New York. Casebound. Red. 143 pp. 5.5 x 8.25 in. Mathematical, Mentalism, Magic squares.

Barrows, Jack, *Introduction to Magic, An.* (1976) Elizabeth Ltd., East Lansing, MI. Comb. Blue. 95 pp. 5.5 x 8.5 in. #145. Showmanship, Marketing.

Barrows, Jack, *Introduction to Magic, An.* (1979) Micky Hades, Calgary, Canada. Saddle-stitch. Blue. 93 pp. 5.25 x 8.25 in. Showmanship, Marketing.

Barrows, Jack, *Magic Won.* (1978) Micky Hades, Calgary, Canada. Saddle-stitch. Yellow. 89 pp. 5.5 x 8.5 in. Showmanship, Stage.

Barry, Dick, *Champagne Goldfish Miracle.* (1979) Author, Newbury Park, CA. Saddle-stitch. Black. 12 pp. 7 x 8.5 in. Close-Up, Goldfish.

Barry, Dick, *Magic with Class.* Revised edition. (1998) Author, San Clemente, CA. Comb. Gold. 131 pp. 5.5 x 8.5 in. Props in envelope. Close-Up, Stage, Mentalism, Inventions.

Barry, Joseph, *Blackpool 2015 Inscrutable Notes.* (2015) Modus, UK. Saddle-stitch. Purple. 6 pp. 5.75 x 8.25 in. (Information not verified by physical copy.) Lecture notes. Cards.

Barry, Joseph, *Charlotte's Notes.* (2016) Modus, UK. Saddle-stitch. Black. 13 pp. 5.75 x 8.25 in. (Information not verified by physical copy. Bibliographical details are as accurate as possible.) Lecture notes. Cards.

Barry, Joseph, *Fifty.* (2014) Modus, UK. Saddle-stitch. Red. 14 pp. 5.75 x 8.25 in. (Information not verified by physical copy. Bibliographical details are as accurate as possible.) Cards.

Barry, Joseph, *Reverie.* (2014) Modus, UK. Saddle-stitch. Blue. 26 pp. 5.75 x 8.25 in. (Information not verified by physical copy. Bibliographical details are as accurate as possible.) Cards.

Barry, Sheila Anne, *Tricks and Stunts to Fool Your Friends.* (1978) Sterling Publishing, New York. Perfect. Red. 128 pp. 5.25 x 8.25 in. Beginner, Children's book.

Barto, El, *My Torn and Restored Paper Trick.* Trick of the Month Club series 1, no. 2. (September 1931) Thayer Magical Mfg. Co., Los Angeles. Folded. Green. 4 pp. 4 x 9 in. Beige text pages. Paper.

Barto, El, *Novel Handkerchief Production, A.* Trick of the Month Club series 2, no. 3. (September 1932) Thayer Magical Mfg. Co., Los Angeles. Folded. Pink. 2 pp. 3.75 x 6.75 in. Handkerchiefs.

Barton, Fred, *Land of Make Believe, The.* (1972) Goodliffe Publications, Alcester, UK. Cloth. Red. 67 pp. 5.5 x 8.75 in. Dust jacket. Children's magic.

Bartram, Richard, Jr., *Close-Up of the Damned.* (1985) Magic Methods, Greenville, SC. Saddle-stitch. Green. 45 pp. 8.5 x 11 in. Comic book-style illustrations. Cards, Close-Up.

Bartram, Richard, Jr., *Mystification.* (1993) Magic Methods, Greenville, SC. Perfect. White, black. 110 pp. 8.5 x 11 in. Cards.

Bartram, Richard, Jr., *Trephine: A Collection of Magic.* (1997) Magic Methods, Greenville, SC. Casebound. White, red. 182 pp. 8.75 x 11.25 in. Cards, Close-Up.

Basch, Ernst, *Cagliostro, Illustreiter Preis-Courant, Le.* (1979) Volker Huber, Offenbach, Germany. Boards. Yellow. 40 pp. 9.5 x 12.25 in. No. 2 of Huber reprint series. Slipcase. #43 of 250. Catalog reprint. German.

Batchelor, Tom, *Canadian Card Control.* (1971) Magic Inc., Chicago. Saddle-stitch. Yellow. 52 pp. 5.5 x 8.5 in. Cards.

Bates, Jimmy, *Baking a Cake.* (1959) Supreme Magic, Bideford, UK. Stapled. White. 11 pp. 7.75 x 9.75 in. Comedy, Children's magic.

Bauer, Jack, *One Hundred and One Card Tricks.* (n.d.) Magic Inc., Chicago. Saddle-stitch. White. 39 pp. 5.5 x 8.5 in. Cards.

Bauer, Joel, with Levy, Mark, *How to Persuade People Who Don't Want to Be Persuaded.* (2004) John Wiley and Sons, West Sussex, UK. Cloth. 242 pp. 6 x 9 in. Dust jacket. Business, Trade shows, Promotion, Marketing.

Bauer, Joel, *Hustle, Hustle.* (1983) Author, Los Angeles. Perfect. Gray. 138 pp. 8.5 x 11 in. (Measurements and other information have been recorded as accurately as possible.) Business.

Bauer, Joel, *Hustle, Hustle.* Fourth revised printing. (1992) Magic City, Paramount, CA. Comb. Gold. 164 pp. 8.5 x 11 in. Business.

Bauer, Joel, *Passion Into Profits Guide.* (1993) Author, North Hills, CA. Comb. Yellow. 138 pp. 8.5 x 11 in. Business, Promotion, Publicity.

Bauer, Ron (See also Hamman, Bro. John; Kort, Milton), *Basic Cups and Balls Technique.* (2004) Rings 'n' Things, Stamps, AR. Saddle-stitch. White. 14 pp. 5.5 x 8.5 in. Close-Up, Cups and Balls.

Bauer, Ron, *Chick Trick.* (2002) Author, Rochester, MI. Saddle-stitch. White. 20 pp. 5.5 x 8.5 in. (Measurements and other information have been recorded as accurately as possible.) Close-Up.

Bauer, Ron, *Complete Don Alan's Chop Cup, The.* (2005) Author, Rochester, MI. Saddle-stitch. White. 26 pp. 5.5 x 8.5 in. Close-Up, Chop Cup.

Bauer, Ron, *How to Perform Magic on Local TV.* (1980) Author, Rochester, MI. Stapled. White. 20 pp. 8.5 x 11 in. Lecture notes. Television magic, Stagecraft.

Bauer, Ron, *Private Studies: Don Alan's Devano Card Rise.* (1999) Author, Rochester, MI. Saddle-stitch. White. 16 pp. 5.5 x 8.5 in. Cards.

Bauer, Ron, *Private Studies no. 1: Ron Bauer's Gaddabout Coins Revisited.* (2000) Author, Rochester, MI. Saddle-stitch. White. 16 pp. 5.5 x 8.5 in. Close-Up, Coins.

Bauer, Ron, *Private Studies no. 2: Ron Bauer's Sudden Death Gypsy Curse.* (2000) Author, Rochester, MI. Saddle-stitch. White. 16 pp. 5.5 x 8.5 in. Cards, Close-Up, Three-Card Monte.

Bauer, Ron, *Private Studies no. 3: Tony Chaudhuri's Feminine Side.* (2000) Author, Rochester, MI. Saddle-stitch. White. 20 pp. 5.5 x 8.5 in. Close-Up, Cards.

Bauer, Ron, *Private Studies no. 4: Ron Bauer's Butch, Ringo, and Sheep.* (2002) Author, Rochester, MI. Saddle-stitch. White. 32 pp. 5.5 x 8.5 in. Close-Up.

Bauer, Ron, *Private Studies no. 5: Ron Bauer's Hornswoggled Again.* (2001) Author, Rochester, MI. Saddle-stitch. White. 20 pp. 5.5 x 8.5 in. Close-Up, Bills, Short change.

Bauer, Ron, *Private Studies no. 6: Ron Bauer's Owed to Poker Dan.* (2001) Author, Rochester, MI. Saddle-stitch. White. 16 pp. 5.5 x 8.5 in. Includes cards and folder. Cards, Close-Up.

Bauer, Ron, *Private Studies no. 7: Ron Bauer's Dixie!* (2002) Author, Rochester, MI. Saddle-stitch. White. 24 pp. 5.5 x 8.5 in. Close-Up, Bills.

Bauer, Ron, *Private Studies no. 8: Ron Bauer's The Cursed Ring.* (2000) Author, Rochester, MI. Saddle-stitch. White. 16 pp. 5.5 x 8.5 in. Close-Up, Rings.

Bauer, Ron, *Private Studies no. 9: Ron Bauer's Fair and Sloppy.* (2002) Author, Rochester, MI. Saddle-stitch. White. 32 pp. 5.5 x 8.5 in. Cards.

Bauer, Ron, *Private Studies no. 10: Charlie Miller's Left-Handed Hank.* Second edition. (2001) Author, Rochester, MI. Saddle-stitch. White. 28 pp. 5.5 x 8.5 in. Includes "Seven Corners" effect. Close-Up, Handkerchiefs, Silks.

Bauer, Ron, *Private Studies no. 11: Ron Bauer's Mechanical Deck.* (2001) Author, Rochester, MI. Saddle-stitch. White. 32 pp. 5.5 x 8.5 in. Cards.

Bauer, Ron, *Private Studies no. 12: Paul Chosse's Bar Bill Stunt.* Second edition. (2001) Author, Rochester, MI. Saddle-stitch. White. 32 pp. 5.5 x 8.5 in. Includes color labels; plus Powers' "Payoff" and Bauer's "Befuddler." Close-Up, Bills.

Bauer, Ron, *Private Studies no. 13: Senator Crandall's Cut-Up Card Trick.* (2003) Author, Rochester, MI. Saddle-stitch. White. 16 pp. 5.5 x 8.5 in. Uncorrected proof. Cards.

Bauer, Ron, *Private Studies no. 13: Senator Crandall's Cut-Up Card Trick.* (2003) Author, Rochester, MI. Saddle-stitch. White. 16 pp. 5.5 x 8.5 in. Cards.

Bauer, Ron, *Private Studies no. 14: Ron Bauer's Four Squares and a Knot.* (2003) Author, Rochester, MI. Saddle-stitch. White. 16 pp. 5.5 x 8.5 in. Uncorrected proof. Close-Up, Silks.

Bauer, Ron, *Private Studies no. 14: Ron Bauer's Four Squares and a Knot.* (2003) Author, Rochester, MI. Saddle-stitch. White. 16 pp. 5.5 x 8.5 in. Close-Up, Silks.

Bauer, Ron, *Private Studies no. 15: Ron Bauer's Siamese Goose Egg Bag.* (2003) Author, Rochester, MI. Saddle-stitch. White. 36 pp. 5.5 x 8.5 in. Stage, Egg Bag.

Bauer, Ron, *Private Studies no. 16: Ed Marlo's Time Machine.* (2003) Author, Rochester, MI. Saddle-stitch. White. 24 pp. 5.5 x 8.5 in. Includes business card. Cards.

Bauer, Ron, *Private Studies no. 17: Ron Bauer's Second Finger Top Deal.* (2004) Author, Rochester, MI. Saddle-stitch. White. 32 pp. 5.5 x 8.5 in. Cards.

Bauer, Ron, *Private Studies no. 18: Ron Bauer's Xerox Money.* (2000) Author, Rochester, MI. Saddle-stitch. White. 24 pp. 5.5 x 8.5 in. Includes stage bills. Close-Up, Bills, Wallets.

Bauer, Ron, *Private Studies no. 19: Milt Kort's All-Out Think-of-a-Card.* (2005) Author, Rochester, MI. Saddle-stitch. White. 24 pp. 5.5 x 8.5 in. Cards.

Bauer, Ron, *Private Studies no. 21: Brother Hamman's Final(ly) Aces.* (2006) Author, Rochester, MI. Saddle-stitch. White. 40 pp. 5.5 x 8.5 in. (Number 20 skipped in series.) Cards.

Bauer, Ron, *Private Studies no. 22: Jim Bergstrom's Hat Trick.* (2007) Author, Rochester, MI. Saddle-stitch. White. 32 pp. 5.5 x 8.5 in. Children's magic, Stage, Paper.

Bauer, Ron, *Private Studies no. 23: Ron Bauer's Gaddabout Coins Revisited.* (2000) Author, Rochester, MI. Saddle-stitch. White. 16 pp. 5.5 x 8.5 in. Coins, Close-Up.

Bauer, Ron, *Ron Bauer 2008 Lecture, The.* Revised edition. (2009) Author, Rochester, MI. Saddle-stitch. White. 32 pp. 5.5 x 8.5 in. Lecture notes. Stagecraft, Business, Stage, Cards.

Baukin, Larry, *Bizarre Magick: The Collector's Edition.* (2015) Author, Minneapolis. Cloth. Black. 268 pp. 8.5 x 11 in. Dust jacket. (Information not verified by physical copy.) Bizarre magick.

Baukin, Larry, *Book of Aleister Crowley, The.* (1997) Thaumysta Publishing Co., Minneapolis. Stapled. 48 pp. 5.5 x 8.5 in. (Information not verified by physical copy.) Bizarre magick.

Baukin, Larry, *Dr. Fathom's Amusements.* (1991) Invocational, Chicago. Stapled. 38 pp. 8.5 x 11 in. (Information not verified by physical copy.) Bizarre magick.

Baukin, Larry, *Laughing Souls and Other Bizarre Visitations.* (1995) Thaumysta Magic Co., Minneapolis. Coil. 49 pp. 8.5 x 11 in. (Information not verified by physical copy.) Bizarre magick.

Baukin, Larry, *Unholy Grail, The.* (2023) Author, Minneapolis. Casebound. Black. 84 pp. 8.5 x 11 in. (Information not verified by physical copy.) Bizarre magick.

Baumann, Fred C., *Card Splitting Technique.* (c. 1983) Author, Brooklyn, NY. Stapled. White. 4 pp. 8.5 x 11 in. (Measurements and other information have been recorded as accurately as possible.) Cards, Splitting cards.

Baumann, Fred C., *Magical Duet, A.* (1995) Author, Brooklyn, NY. 12 pp. (Information not verified by physical copy. Bibliographical details are as accurate as possible.) Coins.

Baumann, Fred C., *Metalogic.* New Stars of Magic vol. 1, no. 10. (1978) Louis Tannen, New York. Saddle-stitch. White. 6 pp. 8.5 x 11 in. Coins.

Baumann, Fred C., *Milestone in Coin Magic.* (1982) Louis Tannen, New York. Perfect. Blue. 94 pp. 6 x 9 in. (Measurements and other information have been recorded as accurately as possible.) Coins.

Baumann, Fred C., *Odyssey of Classic Coin Sleights.* (1983) Author, Brooklyn, NY. Comb. Yellow. 154 pp. 8.5 x 11 in. Signed by Fred C. Baumann. Coins.

Bavli, Guy, *Art of Metal Bending, The.* (1996) Author, Savion, Israel. Saddle-stitch. Black. 16 pp. 8.5 x 10.75 in. Metal bending, Spoon bending.

Bavli, Guy, *Bending Card, The.* (1995) Author, Savion, Israel. 8 pp. (Information not verified by physical copy.) Cards, Psychic.

Bavli, Guy, *Key Bending.* (1994) Author, Savion, Israel. Saddle-stitch. Purple. 14 pp. 5.75 x 8 in. Metal bending, Key bending.

Baxt, Robert, *Iraqi Most Wanted Deck: Tricks and Gags.* (2003) Magic City, Paramount, CA. Comb. Green. 18 pp. 8.5 x 11 in. Cards, Comedy, Wartime.

Baxt, Robert, *Laughter is the Best Misdirection!* (2004) Author, Los Angeles. Stapled. Orange. 18 pp. 8.5 x 11 in. Signed by Robert Baxt. Lecture notes. Cards, Comedy.

Baxt, Robert, *Stabbed in the Baxt.* (1989) Author, Los Angeles. Saddle-stitch. White. 26 pp. 8.5 x 11 in. Signed by Robert Baxt. Lecture notes. Cards, Comedy, Stage.

Baxter, Ian (See also Govan, Barry), *Burnt Offering.* (1984) Dexterity Promotions, Victoria, Australia. Stapled. 11 pp. (Information not verified by physical copy.) Lecture notes. Cards.

Baxter, Ian, *Ten on Deck.* (1970) Aladdin's Magic Shop, Melbourne. Saddle-stitch. White, black. 40 pp. 5.5 x 8.5 in. Cards.

Baxter, Ian, *Turnstile Pass, The.* (2002) Author, Wantirna South, Australia. Saddle-stitch. Gray. 23 pp. 5.75 x 8.25 in. (Measurements and other information have been recorded as accurately as possible.) Cards.

Baxter, Thomas, *20 Tips for Séance Workers.* (2011) Author, Vancouver, Canada. Perfect. Black. 52 pp. 6 x 9 in. Séances, Spirit effects, Mentalism.

Baxter, Thomas, *Action Cop, The.* Second edition. (2002) Author, Vancouver, Canada. Cloth. Gray. 103 pp. 5.75 x 8.75 in. (Measurements and other information have been recorded as accurately as possible.) Cards.

Baxter, Thomas, *Card Merely Thought Of, A.* Second edition. (2010) Author, Vancouver, Canada. Cloth. Blue. 108 pp. 6.25 x 9.25 in. Cards, Mentalism.

Baxter, Thomas, *Nail Writer Anthology, The.* (2015) H & R Magic Books, Humble, TX. Cloth. Black. 267 pp. 6.5 x 9.5 in. Dust jacket. Mentalism, Nail writer.

Baxter, Thomas, *Not a Dianoetic Rage.* (2014) Author, Vancouver, Canada. Cloth. Blue. 209 pp. 6.5 x 9.5 in. Dust jacket. (Measurements and other information have been recorded as accurately as possible.) Cards.

Baxter, Thomas, *Open Prediction Project, The.* Second edition. (2010) Author, Vancouver, Canada. Cloth. Blue. 293 pp. 6.25 x 9.25 in. Dust jacket. Cards.

Bayer, Constance Pole, *Great Wizard of the North, The.* (1990) Magic Art Book Co., Watertown, MA. Cloth. Black. 180 pp. 8.25 x 10.25 in. Dust jacket. Signed by Ray Goulet, Constance Pole Bayer. Biography, History.

Bayle, St. John, *Amateur Conjuring.* (1907) Abel Heywood and Sons, Manchester and London. Perfect. Yellow. 86 pp. 4.75 x 7.25 in. Beginner. Pulp.

B. C., Professor (Brian Corrigan), *Phasmology: The Bizarre Art of Paratheatrical Performance.* (2015) Author, Kansas City, KS. Casebound. 197 pp. (Information not verified by physical copy.) Bizarre magick.

Beam, Steve (See also Mogar, Joe; Robinson, Scott), *52: The Buffalo Gathering Notes.* (2017) Trapdoor Productions, Cayce, SC. Saddle-stitch. Brown. 46 pp. 8.5 x 11 in. (Information not verified by physical copy.) Cards.

Beam, Steve, *2011 F.F.F.F. Teach-A-Trick.* (2011) Trapdoor Productions, Cayce, SC. Saddle-stitch. 16 pp. 8.5 x 11 in. (Information not verified by physical copy.) Cards, Close-Up.

Beam, Steve, *Card Book, The.* (1979) Columbia Magic Shop, Cayce, SC. Comb. Red. 12 pp. 8.5 x 11 in. Effects with a comb-bound deck. Cards.

Beam, Steve, *Card Magic to Go.* (2016) Trapdoor Productions, Cayce, SC. Saddle-stitch. Yellow. 20 pp. 8.5 x 11 in. (Information not verified by physical copy. Bibliographical details are as accurate as possible.) Cards.

Beam, Steve, *Card Tricks After Hours.* (2022) Trapdoor Productions, Cayce, SC. Perfect. Blue. 43 pp. 8.5 x 11 in. (Information not verified by physical copy.) Cards.

Beam, Steve, *Card Tricks from Mount Olympus.* (1980) Trapdoor Productions, Cayce, SC. Comb. Blue. 73 pp. 5.5 x 8.5 in. Cards.

Beam, Steve, *Card Tricks That Kilt.* (2019) Trapdoor Productions, Cayce, SC. Saddle-stitch. Green. 24 pp. 8.5 x 11 in. (Information not verified by physical copy.) Cards.

Beam, Steve, *Cardquistador: El Yanqui y Sus Cartas, El.* (2014) Trapdoor Productions, Cayce, SC. Saddle-stitch. Blue. 20 pp. 8.5 x 11 in. (Information not verified by physical copy.) Cards. Spanish.

Beam, Steve, *Cartas y Cajones.* (2003) Trapdoor Productions, Cayce, SC. Saddle-stitch. White. 8 pp. 8.5 x 11 in. (Information not verified by physical copy.) Lecture notes. Cards.

Beam, Steve, *Changing of the Cards, The.* (1982) Author, Cayce, SC. Saddle-stitch. White, red, black. 39 pp. 5.5 x 8.5 in. (Measurements and other information have been recorded as accurately as possible.) Cards.

Beam, Steve, *Counter Attack.* (2008) Trapdoor Productions, Cayce, SC. Saddle-stitch. Red. 72 pp. 6.75 x 8.5 in. (Measurements and other information have been recorded as accurately as possible.) Cards.

Beam, Steve, *Diary of a Deranged Deck.* (1980) Author, Williston, SC. Saddle-stitch. White. 22 pp. 5.5 x 8.5 in. Signed by Steve Beam. Cards.

Beam, Steve, *F.F.F.F.-ing Great Card Moves.* (2011) Trapdoor Productions, Cayce, SC. Saddle-stitch. Black. 32 pp. 8.5 x 11 in. (Information not verified by physical copy.) Cards.

Beam, Steve, *Gift, The.* (2009) Trapdoor Productions, Cayce, SC. Saddle-stitch. White. 12 pp. 5.5 x 8.5 in. (Measurements and other information have been recorded as accurately as possible.) Cards.

Beam, Steve, *Gourmet Card Magic.* Second edition. (2012) Trapdoor Productions, Cayce, SC. Saddle-stitch. Black. 16 pp. 8.5 x 11 in. Cards, Coins, Close-Up.

Beam, Steve, *Hand-Picked Card Tricks.* (2001) Trapdoor Productions, Raleigh, NC. Coil. White, blue. 52 pp. 7 x 8.5 in. With 2 pp. insert. Cards.

Beam, Steve, with Morris, Don, *Inside Outs, or For My Next Trick I'll Try One That Works.* (1979) Author, Cayce, SC. Saddle-stitch. Gray. 28 pp. 5.5 x 8.5 in. (Information not verified by physical copy.) Cards, Outs, Showmanship.

Beam, Steve, *Magic for the British Aisles.* (1996) Author, Cayce, SC. Saddle-stitch. White. 20 pp. 8.5 x 11 in. (Measurements and other information have been recorded as accurately as possible.) Lecture notes. Cards.

Beam, Steve, *Magic: The Vanishing Art, or How to Turn a Trick for Fun and Profit.* (1979) Author, Cayce, SC. Comb. Yellow. 100 pp. 6.25 x 9.25 in. Cards, Coins, Close-Up.

Beam, Steve, *Magic with No Entertainment Value.* (1989) Trapdoor Productions, Cayce, SC. Saddle-stitch. Beige. 20 pp. 8.5 x 11 in. Signed by Steve Beam. Lecture notes. Cards, Close-Up.

Beam, Steve, *Magic with No Entertainment Value II.* (1993) Trapdoor Productions, Cayce, SC. Stapled. Gray. 20 pp. 8.5 x 11 in. Signed by Steve Beam. Lecture notes. Cards, Close-Up, Stage.

Beam, Steve, *Multiple Impact.* (1993) Trapdoor Productions, Knightdale, NC. Saddle-stitch. White. 16 pp. 5.5 x 8.25 in. Cards.

Beam, Steve, *Noteworthy.* (2008) Trapdoor Productions, Cayce, SC. Perfect. Yellow. 52 pp. 5.25 x 8.5 in. Bound at top. Designed to resemble a legal pad. Cards.

Beam, Steve, *Semi-Automatic Card Tricks vol. 1.* (1993) Trapdoor Productions, Cary, NC. Cloth. Black. 170 pp. 8.5 x 11 in. Dust jacket. Cards.

Beam, Steve, *Semi-Automatic Card Tricks vol. 2.* (1995) Trapdoor Productions, Cary, NC. Cloth. Black. 229 pp. 8.5 x 11 in. Dust jacket. Cards.

Beam, Steve, *Semi-Automatic Card Tricks vol. 3.* Second edition. (2003) Trapdoor Productions, Cary, NC. Cloth. Black. 239 pp. 8.5 x 11 in. Dust jacket. Cards.

Beam, Steve, *Semi-Automatic Card Tricks vol. 4.* (2002) Trapdoor Productions, Cary, NC. Cloth. Black. 264 pp. 8.5 x 11 in. Dust jacket. Cards.

Beam, Steve, *Semi-Automatic Card Tricks vol. 5.* (2004) Trapdoor Productions, Cary, NC. Cloth. Black. 256 pp. 8.5 x 11 in. Dust jacket. Cards.

Beam, Steve, *Semi-Automatic Card Tricks vol. 6.* (2006) Trapdoor Productions, Cary, NC. Cloth. Black. 247 pp. 8.5 x 11 in. Dust jacket. Cards.

Beam, Steve, *Semi-Automatic Card Tricks vol. 7.* (2006) Trapdoor Productions, Cary, NC. Cloth. Black. 246 pp. 8.5 x 11 in. Dust jacket. Cards.

Beam, Steve, *Semi-Automatic Card Tricks vol. 8.* (2010) Trapdoor Productions, Cary, NC. Cloth. Black. 319 pp. 8.5 x 11 in. Dust jacket. Cards.

Beam, Steve, *Semi-Automatic Card Tricks vol. 9.* (2015) Trapdoor Productions, Cary, NC. Cloth. Black. 255 pp. 8.5 x 11 in. Dust jacket. Cards.

Beam, Steve, *Semi-Automatic Card Tricks vol. 10.* (2015) Trapdoor Productions, Cary, NC. Cloth. Black. 255 pp. 8.5 x 11 in. Dust jacket. Cards.

Beam, Steve, *Semi-Automatic Card Tricks vol. 11.* (2018) Trapdoor Productions, Cary, NC. Cloth. Black. 320 pp. 8.5 x 11 in. Dust jacket. Cards.

Beam, Steve, *Semi-Automatic Card Tricks vol. 12.* (2020) Trapdoor Productions, Cary, NC. Cloth. Black. 344 pp. 8.5 x 11 in. Dust jacket. Cards.

Beam, Steve, *Semi-Automatic Card Tricks Cumulative Index vols. 1-12.* (2020) Trapdoor Productions, Cary, NC. Perfect. Yellow. 61 pp. 8.5 x 11 in. Index, Cards, Reference.

Beam, Steve, *Smokers.* (2021) Trapdoor Productions, Cary, NC. Casebound. Brown. 184 pp. 8.75 x 11.25 in. Dust jacket. With 14 of Hearts gag prediction. Cards.

Beam, Steve, *Sound Effects.* (1997) Trapdoor Productions, Cary, NC. Saddle-stitch. Gray. 24 pp. 8.5 x 11 in. Lecture notes. Cards.

Beam, Steve, *Spiral-Sliced Color Change, The.* (2006) Trapdoor Productions, Cayce, SC. Folded. White. 4 pp. 5.5 x 8.5 in. (Information not verified by physical copy.) Cards.

Beam, Steve, *Super Stack.* (1983) Trapdoor Productions, Cayce, SC. Saddle-stitch. Beige. 11 pp. 5.5 x 8.5 in. Cards, Prearranged deck.

Beam, Steve, *Tea Time with the Pasteboards.* (2016) Trapdoor Productions, Cayce, SC. Saddle-stitch. Blue. 20 pp. 5.25 x 8.5 in. (Information not verified by physical copy.) Cards.

Beam, Steve, *They Don't Make Trapdoors Like They Used To, or You Too Can Walk on Water.* (1978) Trapdoor Productions, Cayce, SC. Saddle-stitch. Beige. 42 pp. 6 x 9 in. Cards, Close-Up.

Beam, Steve, *Trapdoor vol. 1 1984-1988, The.* (2011) Trapdoor Productions, Cayce, SC. Cloth. Black. 510 pp. 8.75 x 11.25 in. Magazine, Cards, Close-Up.

Beam, Steve, *Trapdoor vol. 2 1989-1993, The.* (2011) Trapdoor Productions, Cayce, SC. Cloth. Black. 553 pp. 8.75 x 11.25 in. Magazine, Cards, Close-Up.

Beam, Steve, *Trapdoor vol. 3 1994-1998, The.* (2011) Trapdoor Productions, Cayce, SC. Cloth. Black. 630 pp. 8.75 x 11.25 in. Magazine, Cards, Close-Up.

Beam, Steve, *Underhand Shuffle, The.* (2001) Trapdoor Productions, Raleigh, NC. Saddle-stitch. White. 24 pp. 5.25 x 8.5 in. Cards.

Beam, Steve, *Vienna Notes.* (1995) Trapdoor Productions, Cayce, SC. Saddle-stitch. White. 16 pp. 8.5 x 11 in. Signed by Steve Beam. Lecture notes. Cards, Close-Up.

Bean, Gordon, *Color Blind Deck.* (1998) Author, Los Angeles. Saddle-stitch. Yellow. 5 pp. 5.5 x 8.5 in. With "The Well-Balanced Deck" 2 pp. insert.

Beasley, Thomas, *Stealing Doves: Lecture One – The Basics.* (n.d.) Author, Mooresville, IN. Saddle-stitch. Yellow. 9 pp. 8.5 x 11 in. Doves.

Beason, Chris, *State of the Act.* (2016) Author, Atlanta. Saddle-stitch. Blue, yellow. 20 pp. 5.5 x 8.5 in. (Information not verified by physical copy. Bibliographical details are as accurate as possible.) Close-Up, Coins.

Beau, Philippe, with Corty, Axelle, *Robert-Houdin: Le Roi des Magiciens.* (2016) Éditions à Dos d'Âne, Paris. Perfect. Purple. 45 pp. 4.25 x 6 in. Biography, Robert-Houdin. French.

Beaufort d'Auberval, Alphonse-Aimé, *Voyages et Séances Anecdotiques de M. Comte de Genève, Physico-Magiventriloque.* (n.d.) Hachette, Paris. Perfect. Yellow. 252 pp. 6.25 x 9.25 in. Reprint of 1816 edition. Biography.

Beaufort, Douglas, *Nothing Up My Sleeve!* (1938) Stanley Paul, London. Cloth. Beige. 287 pp. 6 x 9 in. (Measurements and other information have been recorded as accurately as possible.) Biography.

Beaumont, Dr. Henry (Doug Bush), *Famous 3 Shell Game, The.* (1975) Author, Atlanta. Stapled. Yellow. 13 pp. 8.5 x 11 in. Three Shell Game.

Beaumont, Dr. Henry, *Famous 3 Shell Game, The.* (c. 2004) School for Scoundrels, Los Angeles. Stapled. White, yellow. 15 pp. 8.5 x 11 in. Reprint with additional credit page. Three Shell Game.

Bebel, with Frame, Tom, *In Case of Emergency.* (2000) Author, Paris. Saddle-stitch. White. 14 pp. 7 x 8.5 in. (Measurements and other information have been recorded as accurately as possible.) Cards.

Bebel, *Nôtes de Conférence 1.* (2014) Author, Paris. Saddle-stitch. White. 24 pp. 8.5 x 11 in. (Information not verified by physical copy.) Lecture notes. Cards. French.

Bebel, *Nôtes de Conférence 2.* (2014) Author, Paris. Saddle-stitch. White. 29 pp. 5.5 x 8.5 in. (Information not verified by physical copy.) Lecture notes. Cards. French.

Bebel, *Transposition Asymétrique: Conférence 3.* (2014) Author, Paris. Saddle-stitch. White. 29 pp. 5.5 x 8.5 in. (Information not verified by physical copy.) Lecture notes. Cards. French.

Beck, Joycee, *Power Performance Skills.* (1996) Author, Riverside, CA. Stapled. Pink. 25 pp. 5.5 x 8.5 in. (Information not verified by physical copy.) Lecture notes. Showmanship, Theory.

Beck, Norman, with Kopf, Jared, *Beck is Back: Reflections of a Vagabond.* (2009) Author, Dallas, TX. Coil. White. 15 pp. 8.5 x 11 in. (Information not verified by physical copy.) Close-Up, Cards, Bets, Con games.

Beck, Norman, with Kopf, Jared, *Beckreations.* (2014) Author, Dallas, TX. Clip. White. 43 pp. 8.5 x 11 in. (Information not verified by physical copy.) Close-Up, Cards, Bets, Con games.

Beck, Norman, with Kopf, Jared, *Ear Full of Cider: The Magic and Short-Cons of Norman Beck, An.* (2006) Author, Dallas, TX. Coil. White. 60 pp. 8.5 x 11 in. Clear acetate cover. Signed by Norman Beck. Close-Up, Cards, Bets, Con games.

Beck, Norman, *It's Not the Miles You Have Traveled, It's the Stops You Have Made.* (2008) Author, Dallas, TX. Comb. White. 38 pp. 8.5 x 11 in. Clear acetate cover. Signed by Norman Beck. Lecture notes. Close-Up, Cards.

Beck, Norman, with Kopf, Jared, *Two Paper Cuts.* (2008) Author, Dallas, TX. Clip. White. 18 pp. 8.5 x 11 in. (Information not verified by physical copy.) Cards, Bottom deal.

Becker, Fred, *Animated Magic.* (2001) Author, Orlando, FL. Comb. White. 34 pp. 8.5 x 11 in. (Measurements and other information have been recorded as accurately as possible.) Stage.

Becker, Fred, *Cruise Magician's Handbook, The.* (1997) Magic Touch Shows, Orlando, FL. Comb. White. 240 pp. 8.5 x 11 in. Cruise ships, Business, Promotion.

Becker, Fred, *Video Promotions for Magicians.* (2001) Author, Phoenix, AZ. Perfect. White. 83 pp. 5.25 x 8.25 in. Business, Promotion, Video production.

Becker, Larry, *Entertaining Professional Mentalism.* (n.d.) Author, Carefree, AZ. Comb. White, black. 43 pp. 8.5 x 11 in. (Information not verified by physical copy.) Mentalism.

Becker, Larry, *Finishing Touches, The.* (1997) Author, Carefree, AZ. Coil. White. 43 pp. 8.5 x 11 in. (Information not verified by physical copy.) Mentalism.

Becker, Larry, *Larry Becker's Magic Castle Lecture.* (1984) Author, Carefree, AZ. Stapled. Tan. 11 pp. 8.5 x 11 in. (Information not verified by physical copy.) Lecture notes. Mentalism.

Becker, Larry, *Lecture Notes.* (1979) Author, Carefree, AZ. Stapled. Yellow. 14 pp. 8.5 x 11 in. (Information not verified by physical copy.) Lecture notes. Mentalism.

Becker, Larry, *Mentalism for Magicians.* (1981) Busby-Corin, Oakland, CA. Comb. White, black, red. 66 pp. 5.5 x 8.5 in. Mentalism.

Becker, Larry, *Mentalism for the Millennium.* (1998) Author, Phoenix, AZ. Comb. Beige. 8.5 x 11 in. (Information not verified by physical copy.) Mentalism.

Becker, Larry, with Earle, Lee, *Mentalism Super Symposium II.* (2004) Author, Phoenix, AZ. Comb. White. 50 pp. 8.5 x 11 in. (Information not verified by physical copy.) Mentalism.

Becker, Larry, *Mind Openers.* (c. 1985) Author, Carefree, AZ. Stapled. Beige. 18 pp. 8.5 x 11 in. (Measurements and other information have been recorded as accurately as possible.) Lecture notes. Mentalism.

Becker, Larry, *More Mentalism for Magicians.* (1990) Author, Carefree, AZ. Saddle-stitch. White, black. 30 pp. 5.5 x 8.5 in. (Information not verified by physical copy.) Mentalism.

Becker, Larry, *Mostly Card-Mental.* (1990) Author, Carefree, AZ. Stapled. Yellow. 16 pp. 8.5 x 11 in. (Information not verified by physical copy.) Lecture notes. Mentalism, Cards.

Becker, Larry, *Myth Mash! Larry Becker's Mental Card Lecture for Magicians Who Hate Card Tricks.* (1990) Author, Carefree, AZ. Saddle-stitch. Yellow. 15 pp. 5.25 x 8.5 in. Signed by Larry Becker. Lecture notes. Mentalism, Close-Up, Cards.

Becker, Larry, *Stunners!* (1996) Author, Carefree, AZ. Cloth. Black. Cover text: Silver; 464 pp. 8.5 x 11 in. Dust jacket. (Information not verified by physical copy. Bibliographical details are as accurate as possible.) Mentalism.

Becker, Larry, *Stunners! Plus!* (2002) Author, Phoenix, AZ. Perfect. Black. 674 pp. 8.5 x 11 in. (Measurements and other information have been recorded as accurately as possible.) Mentalism.

Becker, Larry, *Stunners! The Lecture.* (1997) Author, Phoenix, AZ. Saddle-stitch. Black. 28 pp. 8.5 x 11 in. (Information not verified by physical copy.) Lecture notes. Mentalism.

Becker, Larry, with Earle, Lee, *Symposium Secrets.* (1993) Author, Carefree, AZ. Comb. Red. 36 pp. 8.5 x 11 in. (Information not verified by physical copy.) Mentalism.

Becker, Larry, *Virtuosity.* (1999) Author, Carefree, AZ. Comb. Yellow. 27 pp. 8.5 x 11 in. (Measurements and other information have been recorded as accurately as possible.) Mentalism.

Becker, Larry, *World of Super Mentalism.* (1978) Louis Tannen, New York. Comb. Red. 154 pp. 8.5 x 11 in. (Measurements and other information have been recorded as accurately as possible.) Mentalism.

Becker, Larry, *World of Super Mentalism Book Two.* (1989) Magico Magazine, New York. Comb. White. 216 pp. 5.5 x 8.5 in. Mentalism.

Beckley, Timothy Green, *Dark Séance: The Fabulous Davenport Brothers.* (2015) Global Communications, New Brunswick, NJ. Perfect. Red. 194 pp. 8.5 x 11 in. Additional material by Arthur Conan Doyle. Spiritualism.

Beckley, Timothy Green, *Revealing the Bizarre Powers of Harry Houdini Updated.* (2014) Global Communications, New Brunswick, NJ. Perfect. Orange. 240 pp. 8.5 x 11 in. Additional material by Arthur Conan Doyle. Spiritualism, Houdini.

Beckmann, Darryl, *Life and Times of Alexander, The.* (1994) Rolling Bay Press, Rolling Bay, WA. Cloth. Blue. 207 pp. 8.5 x 11 in. Includes "Life and Mysteries of the Celebrated Dr. 'Q'" reprint. Signed by Darryl Beckmann, Sheila Lyons. #639 of 1000. Biography, Mentalism.

Beckmann, John, *History of Inventions and Discoveries, A.* (1797) J. Bell, London. 492 pp. 5 x 8.5 in. (Information not verified by physical copy.) Toole Stott no. 84. History, Automata.

Beckwith, Tobias, *Beyond Applause.* (2018) Triple Muse Publications, Richmond, CA. Perfect. White. 318 pp. 8 x 10 in. Business, Promotion.

Beckwith, Tobias, *Beyond Deception.* (2007) Triple Muse Publications, Richmond, CA. Cloth. Black. 123 pp. 6.25 x 9.25 in. Dust jacket. Showmanship, Theory.

Beckwith, Tobias, *Beyond Deception vol. 2.* (2014) Triple Muse Publications, Richmond, CA. Perfect. Black. 286 pp. 6 x 9 in. Showmanship, Theory.

Beckwith, Tobias, *Wizard's Way, The.* (2014) Triple Muse Publications, Richmond, CA. Perfect. Gray. 347 pp. 6 x 9 in. Showmanship, Scripting.

Beckwith, Tobias, *Wizard's Way to Powerful Presentations, The.* (2015) Triple Muse Publications, Richmond, CA. Perfect. Red. 112 pp. 6 x 9 in. Showmanship, Scripting.

Bedford, Charles M., *101 Magic Tricks.* (1945) S. S. Adams, Asbury Park, NJ. Saddle-stitch. Green. 16 pp. 6 x 9 in. Beginner, Stunts, Close-Up.

Bedford, Charles M., *Professional Card Secrets.* (1944) Author, Asbury Park, NJ. Stapled with paper cover. Green. 2 pp. 3.5 x 6 in. Mimeographed inside printed cover. Complete series of 12 booklets. Cards.

Bedwell, Ray, *Hidden Treasures of Magic.* (1971) Author, Brookfield, WI. Saddle-stitch. Light blue. 20 pp. 5.5 x 8.5 in. With "Vernon's Forgotten Trick." Close-Up, Cards, Stage.

Bedwell, Ray, *L'il Bit of Magic (for Young and Old Alike), A.* (1971) Author, Brookfield, WI. Stapled. 12 pp. 8.5 x 11 in. (Information not verified by physical copy.) Lecture notes. Close-Up, Stage.

Bedwell, Ray, *Magic to Do with the Stuff You've Got.* (1970) Author, Brookfield, WI. Brads. 30 pp. 8.5 x 11 in. Ditto. (Information not verified by physical copy.) Lecture notes. Close-Up, Stage.

Bedwell, Steve, *Flexing and Twisting.* (c. 1998) Author, London. Clip. White. 15 pp. 8.5 x 11 in. (Measurements and other information have been recorded as accurately as possible.) Signed by Steve Bedwell. Cards.

Bedwell, Steve, *Gold Reunion Notes, The.* (c. 2000) Author, London. Stapled. White. 15 pp. 8.5 x 11 in. Lecture notes. Cards, Close-Up, Stage.

Bedwell, Steve, *In Over Your Head!* (2000) Author, London. Folded. White. 16 pp. 5.5 x 8.5 in. (Measurements and other information have been recorded as accurately as possible.) Rope, Paper Balls Over Head.

Bedwell, Steve, *Parked Card and Other Manoeuvres.* (c. 1998) Author, London. Stapled. White. 14 pp. 8.5 x 11 in. (Measurements and other information have been recorded as accurately as possible.) Cards.

Bedwell, Steve, *Siamese Signatures and Other Oddities.* (1995) Author, London. Clip. White. 24 pp. 8.5 x 11 in. (Measurements and other information have been recorded as accurately as possible.) Cards.

Bedwell, Steve, *Thick Schtick!* (2000) Author, London. Saddle-stitch. Blue. 30 pp. 5.5 x 8.5 in. (Information not verified by physical copy. Bibliographical details are as accurate as possible.) Cards, Thick card.

Beecham, Mark, with Stirton, Neil, *Nine of Diamonds, The.* (2012) Authors, London. Cloth. Black. 139 pp. 6.25 x 9.25 in. Dust jacket. Cards.

Beedham, Ann, *Randini: The Man Who Helped Houdini.* (2009) Youbooks, Sheffield, UK. Perfect. Tan. 240 pp. Biography, Houdini, Escapes, History.

Beedie, Professor, *Conjuring Up-to-Date and How to Do It.* (c. 1914) Daisy Bank Publishing, Manchester, UK. Saddle-stitch. Beige. 32 pp. 5 x 7.5 in. Same contents as similarly titled booklets by Goldin and Prof. Yates. In Copperfield collection. Beginner. Pulp.

Begley, Adam, *Houdini: The Elusive American.* (2020) Yale University Press, New Haven, CT. Cloth. Red. 216 pp. 6 x 8.5 in. Dust jacket. Houdini, Biography.

Behnke, Leo (See also Blackstone, Harry, Jr.), *100 of the Greatest Magic Tricks of the Past 50 Years.* (1974) Pacific Games, N. Hollywood, CA. Saddle-stitch. White. 39 pp. 8.5 x 11 in. In "100 Greatest Magic Tricks" set. Magic set manual, Beginner.

Behnke, Leo, *Bag of Tricks Magic Show pts. 1 and 2.* (1975) Pacific Games, N. Hollywood, CA. Folded. White. 7 pp. 5.5 x 8.5 in. In "Bag of Tricks Magic Show" set in two parts. Magic set manual, Beginner.

Behnke, Leo, *Conservation of Magic, The.* (2000) Book Group, Las Vegas. Cloth. Black, beige. 260 pp. 6.25 x 9.25 in. Dust jacket. Collecting, History.

Behnke, Leo, *Corporate Presentations.* (1992) Book Group, Pasadena, CA. Cloth. Beige. 123 pp. 8.75 x 11.5 in. Bound inverted. Inscribed to Todd Karr. Signed by Leo Behnke. Trade shows, Business, Corporate shows.

Behnke, Leo, *Cues: Variations of the Second Sight Act.* (2005) Book Group, Las Vegas. Cloth. Beige. 137 pp. 8.5 x 11 in. Mentalism, Second Sight.

Behnke, Leo, *Entertaining Close-Up.* (1962) Owen Magic Supreme, Pasadena, CA. Stapled with tape. Black, white. 15 pp. 8.5 x 11 in. Text in all caps. Close-Up.

Behnke, Leo, *Entertaining on T.V.* (1977) Owen Magic Supreme, Alhambra, CA. Saddle-stitch. Black, white. 27 pp. 8 x 10.25 in. Close-Up, Television magic.

Behnke, Leo, *Entertaining with Cards.* (1962) Owen Magic Supreme, Pasadena, CA. Stapled with tape. Black, white. 25 pp. 8.5 x 11 in. Cards.

Behnke, Leo, *Fake Card Tricks.* (2002) Book Group, Las Vegas. Saddle-stitch. Red. 63 pp. 5.5 x 8.5 in. (Measurements and other information have been recorded as accurately as possible.) Cards.

Behnke, Leo, *Find the Ace.* (1993) Magic City, Paramount, CA. Saddle-stitch. Pink. 56 pp. 5.5 x 8.5 in. Cards, Three-Card Monte.

Behnke, Leo, *Houdini's School of Magic vol. 1.* (2009) Houdini Magic, Las Vegas. Perfect. Red. 185 pp. 5.5 x 8.5 in. Beginner.

Behnke, Leo, *How to Write a Magic Book.* Second edition. (2019) Book Group, Las Vegas. Perfect. Yellow. 60 pp. 6 x 9 in. Theory, Business.

Behnke, Leo, *Impromptu Magic from the Magic Castle.* (1980) J. B. Tarcher, Los Angeles. Cloth. Blue. 235 pp. 6.25 x 9.25 in. Dust jacket. Second-place prize for I.B.M. convention junior close-up contest. Signed by Steve Martin, Dai Vernon, Mark Wilson, and others. Beginner, Close-Up.

Behnke, Leo, *Incredible Dr. Jaks, The.* (2014) Salon de Magie, Loveland, OH. Cloth. Red. 248 pp. 7.25 x 10.25 in. Dust jacket. Includes prospectus. Signed by Leo Behnke. Biography, History, Close-Up, Mentalism.

Behnke, Leo, *Magic City Library vols. 1-20.* (1991) Magic City, Paramount, CA. Saddle-stitch. Multiple sections. 5.5 x 8.5 in. Twenty booklets in maroon slipcase. Close-Up, Stage, Cards.

Behnke, Leo, *Magic City Library of Magic vol. 1: Rope Magic.* (1990) Magic City, Paramount, CA. Saddle-stitch. Yellow. 36 pp. 5.5 x 8.5 in. Rope, Stage.

Behnke, Leo, *Magic City Library of Magic vol. 2: Linking Rings.* (1990) Magic City, Paramount, CA. Saddle-stitch. Blue. 32 pp. 5.5 x 8.5 in. Linking Rings, Stage.

Behnke, Leo, *Magic City Library of Magic vol. 3: Cups and Balls.* (1990) Magic City, Paramount, CA. Saddle-stitch. Purple. 32 pp. 5.5 x 8.5 in. Cups and Balls, Close-Up.

Behnke, Leo, *Magic City Library of Magic vol. 4: Magic with Canes.* (1990) Magic City, Paramount, CA. Saddle-stitch. Purple. 31 pp. 5.5 x 8.5 in. Canes, Apparatus, Stage.

Behnke, Leo, *Magic City Library of Magic vol. 5: Milk Pitcher.* (1990) Magic City, Paramount, CA. Saddle-stitch. White. 32 pp. 5.5 x 8.5 in. Milk pitcher, Apparatus, Stage.

Behnke, Leo, *Magic City Library of Magic vol. 6: Folding Coin.* (1990) Magic City, Paramount, CA. Saddle-stitch. Purple. 32 pp. 5.5 x 8.5 in. Folding coins, Coin in Bottle, Gimmicks.

Behnke, Leo, *Magic City Library of Magic vol. 7: Force Decks.* (1991) Magic City, Paramount, CA. Saddle-stitch. Yellow. 35 pp. 5.5 x 8.5 in. Cards, Gimmicked decks, Forcing.

Behnke, Leo, *Magic City Library of Magic vol. 8: Bill Tube.* (1991) Magic City, Paramount, CA. Saddle-stitch. Yellow. 35 pp. 5.5 x 8.5 in. Bill Tube, Apparatus, Close-Up, Bills.

Behnke, Leo, *Magic City Library of Magic vol. 9: Sponge Balls.* (1991) Magic City, Paramount, CA. Saddle-stitch. Pink. 29 pp. 5.5 x 8.5 in. Sponge balls, Close-Up.

Behnke, Leo, *Magic City Library of Magic vol. 10: Dime and Penny.* (1991) Magic City, Paramount, CA. Saddle-stitch. White. 31 pp. 5.5 x 8.5 in. Dime and Penny, Coins, Gimmicked coins.

Behnke, Leo, *Magic City Library of Magic vol. 11: Spring Flowers.* (1991) Magic City, Paramount, CA. Saddle-stitch. Purple. 31 pp. 5.5 x 8.5 in. Spring flowers, Stage, Gimmicks.

Behnke, Leo, *Magic City Library of Magic vol. 12: Card Boxes.* (1991) Magic City, Paramount, CA. Saddle-stitch. Purple. 28 pp. 5.5 x 8.5 in. Cards, Card Case, Apparatus, Close-Up.

Behnke, Leo, *Magic City Library of Magic vol. 13: Egg Bag.* (1991) Magic City, Paramount, CA. Saddle-stitch. Yellow. 28 pp. 5.5 x 8.5 in. Egg Bag, Stage, Apparatus.

Behnke, Leo, *Magic City Library of Magic vol. 14: Trick Decks.* (1991) Magic City, Paramount, CA. Saddle-stitch. White. 38 pp. 5.5 x 8.5 in. Cards, Gimmicked decks.

Behnke, Leo, *Magic City Library of Magic vol. 15: Reels.* (1991) Magic City, Paramount, CA. Saddle-stitch. Blue. 32 pp. 5.5 x 8.5 in. Reels, Gimmicks, Close-Up, Stage.

Behnke, Leo, *Magic City Library of Magic vol. 16: Wands.* (1991) Magic City, Paramount, CA. Saddle-stitch. Blue. 28 pp. 5.5 x 8.5 in. Wands.

Behnke, Leo, *Magic City Library of Magic vol. 17: Dove Pan.* (1991) Magic City, Paramount, CA. Saddle-stitch. Yellow. 23 pp. 5.5 x 8.5 in. Dove Pan, Apparatus, Stage, Doves.

Behnke, Leo, *Magic City Library of Magic vol. 18: Change Bags.* (1991) Magic City, Paramount, CA. Saddle-stitch. Pink. 28 pp. 5.5 x 8.5 in. Change bag, Apparatus, Stage.

Behnke, Leo, *Magic City Library of Magic vol. 19: Flash Paper.* (1991) Magic City, Paramount, CA. Saddle-stitch. Yellow. 25 pp. 5.5 x 8.5 in. Flash paper, Fire.

Behnke, Leo, *Magic City Library of Magic vol. 20: Zombie.* (1991) Magic City, Paramount, CA. Saddle-stitch. Gray, blue. 22 pp. 5.5 x 8.5 in. Zombie, Apparatus, Stage, Levitations.

Behnke, Leo, *Magic for Bartenders – Encore!* (1992) Magic City, Paramount, CA. Comb. Yellow. 80 pp. 8.5 x 11 in. Bar magic, Stunts, Bets, Close-Up.

Behnke, Leo, *Magic for Bartenders no. 3 Encore.* (2014) Magic City, Paramount, CA. Perfect. Orange. 72 pp. 8.5 x 11 in. Bar magic, Stunts, Bets, Close-Up.

Behnke, Leo, *Magic in Books, The.* (2009) H & R Magic Books, Humble, TX. Cloth. Gray. 120 pp. 6 x 9 in. Collecting, History.

Behnke, Leo, *Magic on Magicians.* (2023) Book Group, Las Vegas. Saddle-stitch. White, blue. 18 pp. 5.5 x 8.5 in. Comedy, Gags, Stage, Close-Up.

Behnke, Leo, *Magic Show Tonite!* Miniature book. (1999) Author, Las Vegas. Cloth. Brown. 73 pp. 2.75 x 2.75 in. Signed by Leo Behnke. #107 of 300. History, Miniature book.

Behnke, Leo, *Making of Playing Cards, The.* (2005) Book Group, Las Vegas. 14 pp. (Information not verified by physical copy.) Cards, History.

Behnke, Leo, *Other Stories, The.* (2015) Kirk D. Kaplan, Las Vegas. Cloth. Gray. 129 pp. 6 x 9 in. (Measurements and other information have been recorded as accurately as possible.) Biography, History.

Behnke, Leo, *Party Magic from the Magic Castle.* (1980) J. B. Tarcher, Los Angeles. Cloth. Orange. 239 pp. 6.25 x 9.25 in. Dust jacket. Second-place prize for I.B.M. convention junior close-up contest. Signed by Shari Lewis, Marvyn Roy, Mark Wilson, and others. Beginner, Close-Up.

Behnke, Leo, *Professional Close-Up.* (1995) Book Group, Las Vegas. Perfect. Black. 112 pp. 5.5 x 8.5 in. Signed by Leo Behnke. Close-Up.

Behnke, Leo, *Simple, Baffling Card Tricks.* (1992) Magic City, Las Vegas. Saddle-stitch. White. 63 pp. 5.5 x 8.5 in. Cards.

Behnke, Leo, *Taylor Made Magic: The Life of Merv Taylor.* (2022) Book Group, Las Vegas. Cloth. Black. 273 pp. 8.5 x 11.25 in. History of Merv Taylor magic company. Inscribed to Todd Karr with bookmark. Signed by Leo Behnke. History, Biography, Dealers, Manufacturers.

Behnke, Leo, *Thread Reference.* (1992) Magic City, Paramount, CA. Saddle-stitch. Black. 45 pp. 5.5 x 8.5 in. (Measurements and other information have been recorded as accurately as possible.) Thread.

Behnke, Leo, *Will Rock Presents.* (2007) Prentice Taylor, Laguna Beach, CA. Casebound. Yellow. 120 pp. 8.5 x 11 in. Biography, History.

Behr, Denis, *Handcrafted Card Magic.* Second printing. (2012) Author, Munich. Cloth. Blue. 94 pp. 6 x 8.5 in. Dust jacket. Cards.

Behr, Denis, *Handcrafted Card Magic vol. 2.* Second printing. (2013) Author, Munich. Cloth. Red. 93 pp. 6 x 8.5 in. Dust jacket. Cards.

Behr, Denis, *Handcrafted Card Magic vol. 3.* Second printing. (2018) Author, Munich. Cloth. Green. 93 pp. 6 x 8.5 in. Dust jacket. Cards.

Behr, Denis, *Lecture Notes 2011.* (2011) Author, Munich. 19 pp. (Information not verified by physical copy.) Lecture notes. Cards.

Belamy, Zakary, *Double Faces.* (2004) CC Editions, Chasseneuil, France. Casebound. White. 143 pp. 9.75 x 10.75 in. Dust jacket. With note and photo from author. Photography.

Belcher, Len, *Best of Belcher.* (1980) Supreme Magic, Bideford, UK. Cloth. Red. 152 pp. 8.25 x 10.25 in. Dust jacket. Children's magic, Stage.

Beldig, Marcus, *Double-Decker, The.* (2019) Author, Germany. 5 pp. (Information not verified by physical copy.) Mentalism, Envelopes.

Beldig, Marcus, *Florida Notes 2019, The.* (2019) Author, Germany. 25 pp. (Information not verified by physical copy.) Lecture notes. Mentalism.

Bell, Bob, *Inside Magic.* (1979) Micky Hades, Calgary, Canada. Comb. Blue. 52 pp. 8.5 x 11 in. (Measurements and other information have been recorded as accurately as possible.) Stage, Mentalism.

Bell, Don, *Man Who Killed Houdini, The.* (2004) Véhicule Press, Georgetown, Canada. Perfect. Orange. 260 pp. 5.5 x 8.5 in. History, Houdini.

Bell, Prof. M., *Conjuring Tricks Simple Magic.* (c. 1912) Gaskill, Jones, and Co., London. Saddle-stitch. Tan. 32 pp. 4 x 6.25 in. Cards, Beginner.

Bell, Prof. M., *Tricks with Cards.* (c. 1912) Gaskill, Jones, and Co., London. Saddle-stitch. Tan. 32 pp. 4 x 6.25 in. Cards, Beginner.

Bell, Ron, *If This Be Magic, Let It Be an Art.* (2005) Author, Victoria, Canada. Stapled. 32 pp. 8.5 x 11 in. (Information not verified by physical copy.) Cards, Close-Up.

Bellet, Caniel, *Promenades Amusantes.* (1913) Hachette, Paris. Cloth. Red. 192 pp. 5.75 x 9 in. Gilt floral. Handwritten 1913 student prize label on cover. Stunts, Science magic. French.

Bellew, Frank, *Art of Amusing, The.* (1866) Carleton, S. Low and Co., New York, London. Cloth. Green. 302 pp. 5 x 7.5 in. Toole Stott no. 89. Beginner, Stunts, Games.

Bellew, Frank, *Art of Amusing, The.* (1866) Carleton, S. Low and Co., New York, London. Cloth. Maroon. 302 pp. 5 x 7.5 in. Toole Stott no. 935. Same edition with an extra engraved title page. Beginner, Stunts, Games.

Bellew, Frank, *Art of Amusing, The.* (1867) Carleton, New York. Cloth. 302 pp. 5 x 7.5 in. (Information not verified by physical copy.) Toole Stott no. 936. Beginner, Stunts, Games.

Bellew, Frank, *Art of Amusing, The.* (1869) Carleton, S. Low and Co., New York, London. 302 pp. 5 x 7.5 in. (Information not verified by physical copy.) Toole Stott no. 937. Beginner, Stunts, Games.

Bellew, Frank, *Art of Amusing, The.* (1870) John Camden Hotten, London. Cloth. Red. 300 pp. 4 x 7.25 in. Toole Stott no. 90. Beginner, Stunts, Games.

Bellew, Frank, *Art of Amusing, The.* (1890) John Grant, London. Cloth. Tan. 299 pp. 4 x 7.25 in. Toole Stott no. 934. Beginner, Stunts, Games.

Bellman, Dan (See also Lewis, Eric C.), *Cheerful Conjuring.* (1938) Eric C. Lewis, Northampton, UK. Saddle-stitch. Red, white. 49 pp. 5.5 x 8.5 in. Stage, Close-Up, Cards.

Bellman, Dan, *Patter, Tricks, and Quips.* (1933) Edward Bagshawe, London. Brads. Gray. 14 pp. 8 x 6.75 in. Mimeographed. Folded. Introduction by Laurance Glen. Patter, Comedy, Close-Up, Stage.

Bellon, Alain, *Obsidian Oblique: The Bellon Billet Techniques.* (2003) Author, UK. Cloth. Brown. 85 pp. 8.5 x 11 in. Limited to 100 copies. (Information not verified by physical copy.) Mentalism, Billets.

Bellon, Alain, *Obsidian Oblique: The Bellon Billet Techniques.* (2003) Author, UK. Comb. Beige. 85 pp. 8.5 x 11 in. (Information not verified by physical copy.) Mentalism, Billets.

Beme, Sixten, *Complete Card Linking, The.* Second edition. (1981) El Duco, Mälmo, Sweden. Saddle-stitch. Black. 13 pp. 8.25 x 11.75 in. Cards, Linking cards.

Beme, Sixten, *Outsider.* (c. 1980) Author, Stockholm. Saddle-stitch. Yellow. 3 pp. 5.75 x 8.25 in. (Information not verified by physical copy.) Cards, Card Warp, Bills.

Bemrose, Paul, *Astley: Circus Genius.* (1992) Newcastle-Under-Lyme Borough Council, Newcastle-Under-Lyme, UK. Perfect. Beige, red. 58 pp. 5.75 x 8.25 in. Biography, History, Circus.

Ben, David, *Advantage Play: The Manager's Guide to Creative Problem Solving.* (2001) Key Porter Books, Toronto. Cloth. Red. 240 pp. 6.25 x 9.25 in. Dust jacket. Business, Erdnase.

Ben, David, *Alchemy.* (2022) Vanishing Inc., Rancho Cordova, CA. Perfect. White. 61 pp. 6 x 6 in. From publisher's "Western Adventure Retreat Gift Pack." (Information not verified by physical copy.) Cards, Close-Up.

Ben, David, *Ambitious Card, The.* (2003) Squash Publishing, Chicago. Saddle-stitch. White. 25 pp. 7 x 5.5 in. Bound oblong. Bonus to Ben's book "Tricks." Letter O of 26. Cards, Ambitious Card.

Ben, David, *Dai Vernon: A Biography.* (2006) Squash Publishing, Chicago. Cloth. Blue. 366 pp. 6.25 x 9.25 in. Dust jacket. Biography.

Ben, David, *Dai Vernon: The Spirit of Magic.* (2022) Magicana, Toronto. Perfect. Tan. 119 pp. 6.25 x 9.25 in. Dust jacket. Biography.

Ben, David, *Erdnase Unmasked.* (2012) Magicana, Canada. Perfect. Beige. 80 pp. 5.5 x 8.5 in. (Measurements and other information have been recorded as accurately as possible.) History, Cards, Erdnase.

Ben, David, *Experts at the Card Table, The.* (2015) Magicana, Canada. Cloth. Blue. 231 pp. 10.25 x 10.25 in. Dust jacket. Cards, Erdnase.

Ben, David, *Extension of Credit.* (1992) Author, Toronto. Stapled. White. 11 pp. 8.5 x 11 in. (Information not verified by physical copy.) Credit cards, Close-Up.

Ben, David, *Fringe, The.* (1985) Author, Toronto. Saddle-stitch. White. 24 pp. 5.5 x 8.5 in. (Information not verified by physical copy.) Cards, Close-Up.

Ben, David, *Habits.* (1992) Author, Toronto. Stapled. White, black. 11 pp. 8.5 x 11 in. (Information not verified by physical copy. Bibliographical details are as accurate as possible.) Close-Up.

Ben, David, *New York Notes.* (2003) Author, Toronto. Stapled. White. 29 pp. 8.5 x 11 in. (Information not verified by physical copy.) Lecture notes. Cards, Close-Up.

Ben, David, *Notes, The.* (1992) Author, Toronto. Stapled. White, black. 17 pp. 8.5 x 11 in. (Information not verified by physical copy. Bibliographical details are as accurate as possible.) Close-Up, Bills.

Ben, David, *Platform of Miracles, A.* (2002) Author, Toronto. Stapled. White. 54 pp. 8.5 x 11 in. (Information not verified by physical copy.) Lecture notes. Cards, Close-Up.

Ben, David, *Tricks.* (2003) Squash Publishing, Chicago. Leather. Black. 173 pp. 7.25 x 10.25 in. Dust jacket. With note from Ben. Letter O of 26. Close-Up, Cards, Stage.

Ben, David, *Untitled lecture notes.* (n.d.) Author, Toronto. Stapled. White, black. 17 pp. 8.5 x 11 in. Signed by David Ben. Lecture notes. Close-Up, Cards.

Ben, David, *Zarrow: A Lifetime of Magic.* (2008) Meir Yedid Magic, Fair Lawn, NJ. Cloth. Black. 463 pp. 9.25 x 12.25 in. Dust jacket. Cards, False shuffles, Zarrow shuffle.

Ben Ali, Ali (McClernon, Brian), *Ali Ben Ali's Impromptu Card Magic.* (1990) Magick Enterprises, Sheffield, UK. Saddle-stitch. Light blue. 17 pp. 5.75 x 8.25 in. (Information not verified by physical copy.) Cards, Impromptu.

Ben Ali, Ali (McClernon, Brian), *Ali Ben Ali's Utility Pack.* (1987) Magick Enterprises, Sheffield, UK. Saddle-stitch. Yellow. 16 pp. 5.75 x 8.25 in. Cards, Thick card, Gimmicks.

Ben Ali, Ali (McClernon, Brian), *Down Your Alley.* (1987) Magick Enterprises, Sheffield, UK. Wire binding. White, green. 61 pp. 8.25 x 11.75 in. (Information not verified by physical copy.) Cards, Close-Up, Theory.

Benatar, Rafael, *Antologia del Doble Lift.* (1991) Author, Madrid. Saddle-stitch. Blue. 16 pp. 5.75 x 8.25 in. (Information not verified by physical copy.) Cards, Double lift. Spanish.

Benatar, Rafael, *Benatar's Best.* (c. 2008) Author, Madrid. Coil. Yellow. 32 pp. 8.25 x 11.75 in. (Information not verified by physical copy. Bibliographical details are as accurate as possible.) Cards.

Benatar, Rafael, *Cartas Certificadas.* (1989) Author, Madrid. Perfect. Black. 135 pp. 6 x 9 in. (Information not verified by physical copy.) Cards. Spanish.

Benatar, Rafael, *Castle Notes.* (2004) Author, Madrid. Stapled. Gray. 15 pp. 8.5 x 11 in. Signed by Rafael Benatar. Lecture notes. Cards.

Benatar, Rafael, *Double-Card Technique.* (1993) Author, Madrid. Comb. Beige. 31 pp. 8.5 x 11 in. Lecture notes. Cards, Double lift.

Benatar, Rafael, *E-Cups: A Cups and Balls Routine.* (2012) Author, Madrid. Saddle-stitch. White. 26 pp. 5.75 x 8.25 in. Signed by Rafael Benatar. Cups and Balls.

Benatar, Rafael, *Parlour.* (2012) Author, Madrid. Saddle-stitch. White. 23 pp. 5.5 x 8.5 in. Signed by Rafael Benatar. Cards, Stage, Silks.

Benatar, Rafael, *Right Between the Eyes.* (2009) Author, Madrid. Saddle-stitch. White. 18 pp. 5.75 x 8.25 in. Signed by Rafael Benatar. Cards, Stage, Silks.

Benatar, Rafael, *Sleight of Phone: Lecture Notes F.F.F.F. 1999.* (1999) Author, Madrid. Stapled. Beige. 14 pp. 8.5 x 11 in. Lecture notes. Cards, Close-Up.

Benatar, Rafael, *Three Professional Card Routines.* (1993) Author, Madrid. Comb. Tan. 26 pp. 8.25 x 11.75 in. Signed by Rafael Benatar. Lecture notes. Cards.

Benatar, Rafael, *Three Professional Card Routines.* (1993) Author, Madrid. Stapled. Tan. 26 pp. 8.5 x 11 in. Signed by Rafael Benatar. Lecture notes. Cards.

Benatar, Rafael, *Transit Cups and Balls.* (1989) Author, Madrid. Saddle-stitch. Yellow. 20 pp. 6 x 8.5 in. Signed by Rafael Benatar. Cups and Balls.

Benatar, Rafael, *Tricks I Do All the Time.* (2010) Author, Madrid. Saddle-stitch. White. 47 pp. 5.5 x 8.5 in. Signed by Rafael Benatar. Cards.

Benatar, Rafael, *Twins with Rhythm.* (1996) Author, Madrid. Saddle-stitch. Beige. 16 pp. 5.75 x 8.25 in. Cards, Counts.

Bender, Carol, *Choose One from Column A.* (1992) Ickle Pickle Products, St. Louis, MO. Saddle-stitch. Green. 36 pp. 5.5 x 8.5 in. (Information not verified by physical copy.) Showmanship, Theory.

Bender, Steve, *20 of My Best.* (2005) Author, St. Louis, MO. Saddle-stitch. Green. 35 pp. 5.5 x 8.5 in. Close-Up, Stage, Comedy.

Bender, Steve, *After 10,000 Shows.* (1984) Author, St. Louis, MO. Saddle-stitch. Green. 22 pp. 5.5 x 8.5 in. Comedy, Stage.

Bender, Steve, *Bits and Pieces.* (1983) Author, St. Louis, MO. Saddle-stitch. Light blue. 25 pp. 5.5 x 8.5 in. Comedy, Stage.

Bender, Steve, *Do's, the Don'ts, the Pluses, the Minus: So You Want to Be a Dealer at a Convention, The.* (n.d.) Author, St. Louis, MO. Saddle-stitch. White. 5.5 x 8.5 in. Title spelled as printed on cover. (Information not verified by physical copy.) Business, Conventions, Dealers.

Bender, Steve, *Images.* (1985) Author, St. Louis, MO. Saddle-stitch. Beige. 28 pp. 5.5 x 8.5 in. Self-help, Showmanship.

Bender, Steve, *It's Fun to See Them Laugh.* Second printing. (1985) Author, St. Louis, MO. Saddle-stitch. Red. 27 pp. 5.5 x 8.5 in. Comedy, Stage.

Bender, Steve, *Laugh.* (1985) Author, St. Louis, MO. Saddle-stitch. Yellow. 16 pp. 5.5 x 8.5 in. Comedy, Clowning, Stage.

Bender, Steve, *Laughter is Contagious: Start an Epidemic.* (1982) Author, St. Louis, MO. Saddle-stitch. Beige. 24 pp. 5.5 x 8.5 in. (Information not verified by physical copy.) Comedy.

Bender, Steve, *Little Bit of This, A Little Bit of That, Some Brand New, Some Not, A.* (2006) Author, St. Louis, MO. Saddle-stitch. Purple. 26 pp. 5.5 x 8.5 in. Close-Up, Stage, Comedy.

Bender, Steve, *Magic's Greatest Illusion.* (1982) Author, St. Louis, MO. Saddle-stitch. Gray. 16 pp. 4.25 x 5.5 in. Business, Promotion.

Bender, Steve, *More Comedy and Magic.* (n.d.) Author, St. Louis, MO. Saddle-stitch. Red. 5.5 x 8.5 in. (Information not verified by physical copy.) Comedy, Stage.

Bender, Steve, *Mr. Pickle's Magic and Comedy.* (n.d.) Author, St. Louis, MO. Saddle-stitch. Green. 5.5 x 8.5 in. (Information not verified by physical copy.) Comedy, Stage.

Bender, Steve, *Sixteen of My Current Favorites.* (2002) Author, St. Louis, MO. Saddle-stitch. Beige. 18 pp. 5.5 x 8.5 in. (Information not verified by physical copy.) Close-Up, Stage, Comedy.

Bender, Steve, *Tableside Magic.* (n.d.) Author, St. Louis, MO. Saddle-stitch. Blue. 5.5 x 8.5 in. (Information not verified by physical copy.) Close-Up, Stage, Comedy.

Bender, Steve, *This, That, and Then Some.* (n.d.) Author, St. Louis, MO. Saddle-stitch. Yellow. 5.5 x 8.5 in. (Information not verified by physical copy.) Close-Up, Stage, Comedy.

Bender, Steve, *Unusual Beginning, An Entertaining End(s), and Some Good Stuff in the Middle, An.* (1993) Author, St. Louis, MO. Saddle-stitch. Yellow. 30 pp. 5.5 x 8.5 in. Close-Up, Stage, Comedy.

Bender, Steve, *What's New 2007.* (2007) Author, St. Louis, MO. Saddle-stitch. Pink. 14 pp. 5.5 x 8.5 in. Close-Up, Stage, Comedy.

Bender, Steve, *What's New 2011.* (2011) Author, St. Louis, MO. Saddle-stitch. Green. 19 pp. 5.5 x 8.5 in. Close-Up, Stage, Comedy.

Benge, Ken, *3 Ball Juggling.* Seventh printing. (1982) Magic Inc., Chicago. Saddle-stitch. Blue. 84 pp. 5.5 x 8.5 in. Juggling.

Bengel, Robert W., *Back-to-Basics II.* (1995) Author, Valrico, FL. Stapled with tape. Yellow. 56 pp. 8.5 x 11 in. Signed by Robert W. Bengel. Cards.

Bengel, Robert W., *Bengel's Best of Spades.* (1984) Author, Valrico, FL. Saddle-stitch. White. 34 pp. 8.5 x 11 in. (Measurements and other information have been recorded as accurately as possible.) Cards, Close-Up.

Bengel, Robert W., *Bengel's Best of Spades.* Second edition. (1995) Author, Valrico, FL. Saddle-stitch. White. 40 pp. 8.5 x 11 in. (Measurements and other information have been recorded as accurately as possible.) Cards, Close-Up.

Bengel, Robert W., *Bill Matrix.* (c. 2007) Author, Valrico, FL. Stapled. White. 4 pp. 8.5 x 11 in. (Information not verified by physical copy.) Bills, Coins, Matrix, Close-Up.

Bengel, Robert W., *Chock Full of Sleeves and Twist 'n' Shout.* (1996) Author, Valrico, FL. Saddle-stitch. Green. 20 pp. 8.5 x 11 in. (Information not verified by physical copy.) Cards, Close-Up.

Bengel, Robert W., *Close-Up Lecture no. 3.* (1995) Author, Valrico, FL. (Information not verified by physical copy.) Lecture notes. Cards.

Bengel, Robert W., *Corporate Ways and Means.* (1996) Author, Valrico, FL. Stapled. Light blue. 30 pp. 8.5 x 11 in. (Information not verified by physical copy.) Business, Cards, Coins, Close-Up.

Bengel, Robert W., *Fechter's Close-Up Convention Close-Up Lecture.* (1986) Author, Valrico, FL. 26 pp. 8.5 x 11 in. (Information not verified by physical copy.) Lecture notes. Cards, Coins.

Bengel, Robert W., *Getting Back to Basics.* (1992) Author, Tampa, FL. Stapled. Light blue. 84 pp. 8.5 x 11 in. Signed by Robert W. Bengel. Lecture notes. Cards, Coins, Theory.

Bengel, Robert W., *Information Super-Highway, The.* (1994) Author, Valrico, FL. 25 pp. 8.5 x 11 in. (Information not verified by physical copy.) Lecture notes. Coins, Close-Up.

Bengel, Robert W., *Matrix Times 6.* (1995) Author, Valrico, FL. Light blue. 24 pp. 8.5 x 11 in. (Information not verified by physical copy.) Coins, Matrix.

Bengel, Robert W., *Tannen's 23rd Jubilee Lecture.* (1985) Author, Valrico, FL. Stapled. Light green. 23 pp. 8.5 x 11 in. (Information not verified by physical copy.) Lecture notes. Cards, Coins, Close-Up.

Bengtson, Nicholas, *Abyss: The Revolutionary Coin in Bottle.* (2007) Atlas Enterprises, Denver, CO. Saddle-stitch. Black, purple. 20 pp. 5.5 x 8.5 in. (Information not verified by physical copy.) Coins, Coin in Bottle.

Bengtson, Nicholas, *Aquarius: The Definitive Cap in Bottle.* (2007) Atlas Enterprises, Denver, CO. Saddle-stitch. Black, blue. 24 pp. 5.5 x 8.5 in. (Information not verified by physical copy.) Close-Up, Bottles.

Bengtson, Nicholas, *Dreamweaver.* (2003) Atlas Enterprises, Denver, CO. Saddle-stitch. Blue. 18 pp. 5.5 x 8.5 in. (Information not verified by physical copy.) Safety pins, Close-Up.

Bengtson, Nicholas, *Skywalker.* (2007) Atlas Enterprises, Denver, CO. Saddle-stitch. Black. 24 pp. 5.5 x 8.5 in. (Measurements and other information have been recorded as accurately as possible.) Levitations.

Benham, W. Gurney, *Playing Cards: History of the Pack and Explanations of Its Many Secrets.* (1931) Ward, Lock and Co., London. Cloth. Green. 195 pp. 7.5 x 10 in. Card games, Cards, History.

Benham, W. Gurney, *Playing Cards: History of the Pack and Explanations of Its Many Secrets.* (1957) Spring Books, London. Cloth. Tan. 196 pp. 7.5 x 10 in. Dust jacket. Card games, Cards, History.

Benjamin, Arthur, *Magic of Maths, The.* (2015) Basic Books, New York. Perfect. Black. 321 pp. 5.5 x 8.25 in. Mathematical.

Benjamin, Arthur, with Shermer, Michael, *Mathemagics.* (1993) Lowell House, Los Angeles. Cloth. Red. 218 pp. 6.25 x 9.25 in. Dust jacket. Mathematical. German.

Benjamin, Arthur, with Shermer, Michael, *Mathe Magie.* (2010) Heyne, Munich. Perfect. Blue. 278 pp. 5.25 x 8 in. Mathematical. German.

Benjamin, Arthur, *Mathematics of Games and Puzzles, The.* (2013) Teaching Company, Chantilly, VA. Perfect. Blue. 302 pp. 5.25 x 7.5 in. Mathematical, Games, Puzzles.

Benjamin, Arthur, *Secrets of Benjamin.* (1981) Author, Cleveland, OH. Clip. White. 25 pp. 8.5 x 11 in. Signed by Arthur Benjamin. Lecture notes. Mathematical, Lightning calculation, Magic squares.

Benjamin, Arthur, with Shermer, Michael, *Secrets of Mental Math.* (2006) Three Rivers Press, New York. Perfect. Blue. 278 pp. 5.25 x 8 in. Signed by Arthur Benjamin. Mathematical.

Benjamin, Arthur, *Secrets of Mental Math, The.* (2011) The Great Courses, Chantilly, VA. Perfect. Blue. 161 pp. 5.25 x 7.5 in. Signed by Arthur Benjamin. Mathematical.

Benjilini, *Benjilini on Houdini.* (1994) Author, Brooklyn, NY. Saddle-stitch. White. 84 pp. 8.25 x 11 in. (Information not verified by physical copy.) Biography, Houdini, History.

Bennett, Doug, *Bewildering.* New Stars of Magic vol. 2, no. 2. (1984) Louis Tannen, New York. Saddle-stitch. White. 6 pp. 8.5 x 11 in. (Information not verified by physical copy.) Ring and rope.

Bennett, Doug, with Ammar, Michael, *Business Merger Book, The.* (1984) Author, Newport Beach, CA. Saddle-stitch. White, black. 17 pp. 5.5 x 8.5 in. Material by Michael Weber and Mark Green. Includes wallet and gimmick. Business cards, Close-Up.

Bennett, Doug, *Criss-Cross Cards.* (1982) Author, Newport Beach, CA. Saddle-stitch. White. 8 pp. 5.5 x 8.5 in. Cards.

Bennett, Doug, *Extra Sensory Deceptions.* (1982) Author, Vista, CA. Saddle-stitch. Black, red, white. 27 pp. 5.5 x 8.5 in. Close-Up, Cards, Stage.

Bennett, Horace, *All-Purpose "Show-Off" Rope Routine.* (1974) Magic Methods, Greenville, SC. Stapled. Red. 10 pp. 8.5 x 11 in. Folded. Rope.

Bennett, Horace, *Alternative Handlings.* (1983) Magic Methods, Greenville, SC. Comb. Black. 96 pp. 5.5 x 8.5 in. Close-Up, Cards, Coins.

Bennett, Horace, *Bennett's Best.* (1975) Magic Methods, Greenville, SC. Comb. Black. 115 pp. 5.5 x 8.5 in. (Measurements and other information have been recorded as accurately as possible.) Close-Up.

Bennett, Horace, *Bennett's Fourth Book.* (1981) Magic Methods, Greenville, SC. Comb. Black, white. 70 pp. 5.5 x 8.5 in. Coins, Cards.

Bennett, Horace, *Close-Up Lecture Notes.* (c. 1977) Author, Richmond, VA. Metal band. White. 15 pp. 8.5 x 11 in. Lecture notes. Close-Up, Cards.

Bennett, Horace, *Downs Palm Technique.* (1981) Author, Richmond, VA. Saddle-stitch. Yellow. 16 pp. 5.5 x 8.5 in. Coins.

Bennett, Horace, *Familiar Themes.* (1984) Magic Methods, Greenville, SC. Comb. Black, white. 111 pp. 5.25 x 8.5 in. Cards, Coins, Close-Up.

Bennett, Horace, *Horace Bennett's Prize Winning Magic.* (1983) Supreme Magic, Bideford, UK. Cloth. Red. 80 pp. 6.25 x 9 in. Dust jacket. Stage, Linking Rings, Silks.

Bennett, Horace, *Magic Afoot.* (1989) Magic Methods, Greenville, SC. Perfect. Red, white. 121 pp. 5.25 x 8.25 in. Stage.

Bennett, Horace, *On Your Feet.* (1978) Magic Methods, Greenville, SC. Comb. Black. 84 pp. 5.5 x 8.5 in. (Measurements and other information have been recorded as accurately as possible.) Close-Up.

Bennett, Horace, *With a Grain of Salt: Horace Bennett's Cups and Balls Routine.* (1978) Magic Methods, Greenville, SC. Saddle-stitch. Blue. 12 pp. 5.5 x 8.5 in. Excerpt from Bennett's "On Your Feet." Cups and Balls.

Bennett, Nils, *Creating New Magic.* (2004) Author, Stuttgart, Germany. Wire binding. Gray. 59 pp. 11.75 x 8.25 in. Bound oblong. Theory, Close-Up, Mentalism.

Benson, Roy (See also Levent with Karr, Todd), *Benson on Magic.* (1972) Author, New York. Brads. Yellow. 23 pp. 8.5 x 11 in. (Measurements and other information have been recorded as accurately as possible.) Lecture notes. Stage, Close-Up, Theory.

Bent, Mike, *Zero Gravity.* (1997) Author, Belmont, MA. Comb. White. 8 pp. 8.5 x 11 in. Silver seal on side. Levitations.

Bentine, Michael, *Michael Bentine's Magic Book.* (1972) Wolfe Publishing, London. Perfect. Red. 142 pp. 4.25 x 7.25 in. Magic advisor: Patrick Page. In Copperfield collection. Beginner.

Benzais, Johnny, *Best of Benzais, The.* (1967) Haines House of Cards, Norwood, OH. Saddle-stitch. Red. 62 pp. 5.5 x 8.5 in. Cards, Close-Up.

Bercelini, *Juwelen der Kartenkunst.* (1946) Luctor, Rotterdam, Netherlands. Cloth. Beige. 119 pp. 6.5 x 9.5 in. Dust jacket. Cards, Beginner. Dutch.

Berg, Harvey A., *Deceiva Las Vegas.* (2005) Author, Washingtonville, NY. Stapled. Black. 25 pp. 8.5 x 11 in. (Information not verified by physical copy.) Cards, Close-Up.

Berg, Harvey A., *Fermi Chronicles, The.* (2009) Author, Washingtonville, NY. Stapled. Black. 13 pp. 8.5 x 11 in. (Information not verified by physical copy. Bibliographical details are as accurate as possible.) Cards.

Berg, Harvey A., *Gospell.* Second revision. (2000) Author, Washingtonville, NY. Stapled. Blue. 20 pp. 8.5 x 11 in. Cards, Gospel magic.

Berg, Harvey A., *Intercept.* Fourth edition. (2001) Author, Washingtonville, NY. Stapled. White, black. 25 pp. 8.5 x 11 in. (Information not verified by physical copy.) Cards, Mentalism.

Berg, Harvey A., *Sleight of Mind.* (1997) Author, Washingtonville, NY. Comb. Beige. 40 pp. 8.5 x 11 in. (Information not verified by physical copy. Bibliographical details are as accurate as possible.) Cards, Mentalism.

Berg, Harvey A., *Three Degrees.* (2012) Meir Yedid Magic, Fair Lawn, NJ. Perfect. Brown. 57 pp. 6 x 9 in. Cards, Mentalism.

Berg, Harvey A., *Wanderings.* (1997) Author, Washingtonville, NY. Comb. Beige. 56 pp. 8.5 x 11 in. (Information not verified by physical copy. Bibliographical details are as accurate as possible.) Cards, Mentalism.

Berg, Joe (See also Hahne, Nelson C.), with Avadon, David; Lewis, Eric C., *Berg Book, The.* (1983) Joe Stevens, Wichita, KS. Cloth. Red. 315 pp. 8.5 x 11 in. Cards, Close-Up, Stage.

Berg, Joe, *Chinese Cups and Balls, The.* (1928) Joe Berg, Chicago. Folded. White. 3 pp. 5.5 x 8 in. Illustrated by Tarbell. Cups and Balls, Instructions.

Berg, Joe, *Here's New Magic.* (1937) Joe Berg, Chicago. Cloth. Black. Cover text: Gold; 63 pp. 5.5 x 8.5 in. Limited edition of 300 signed by authors. Signed by Joe Berg, Nelson C. Hahne. #201 of 300. Cards, Stage, Close-Up.

Berg, Joe, *Here's New Magic.* (1937) Joe Berg, Chicago. Saddle-stitch. Gray. 63 pp. 5.5 x 8.5 in. Cards, Stage, Close-Up.

Berg, Joe, with Aldini, Al, *Rough Stuff.* (1956) Berg's Magic Studio, Hollywood, CA. Saddle-stitch. Beige. 24 pp. 5.5 x 8.5 in. Cards, Rough and smooth.

Berg, Joe, with Aldini, Al, *Rough Stuff.* Second printing. (1967) Ireland Magic Co., Chicago. Saddle-stitch. Gray. 24 pp. 5.5 x 8.5 in. Cards, Rough and smooth.

Bergen, Edgar, *How to Become a Ventriloquist.* (1938) Grosset and Dunlap, New York. Cloth. Orange. 125 pp. 5 x 7.5 in. Ventriloquism.

Bergeron, Bev, *7-11.* (2006) Author, Orlando, FL. Saddle-stitch. White. 23 pp. 5.5 x 8.5 in. (Information not verified by physical copy.) Lecture notes. Stage, Close-Up.

Bergeron, Bev, *Bev Bergeron in Print.* (1975) Author, Orlando, FL. Saddle-stitch. White. 16 pp. 5.5 x 8.5 in. Signed by Bev Bergeron. Stage, Close-Up.

Bergeron, Bev, *Clown Magic.* (1988) Author, Orlando, FL. Saddle-stitch. White. 11 pp. 5.5 x 8.5 in. (Information not verified by physical copy.) Clowning, Balloons, Comedy.

Bergeron, Bev, *Comedy Magic.* (1981) Author, Orlando, FL. Saddle-stitch. White. 12 pp. 5.5 x 8.5 in. (Information not verified by physical copy.) Comedy.

Bergeron, Bev, *Damnant Quod Non Intelligent.* (1984) Author, Orlando, FL. Saddle-stitch. White. 12 pp. 5.5 x 8.5 in. Signed by Bev Bergeron. Lecture notes. Close-Up, Stage.

Bergeron, Bev, *Damnant Quod Non Intelligent.* (1984) Author, Orlando, FL. Saddle-stitch. Yellow. 12 pp. 5.5 x 8.5 in. Signed by Bev Bergeron. Lecture notes. Close-Up, Stage.

Bergeron, Bev, *Lecture 5.* (1994) Author, Orlando, FL. Saddle-stitch. Beige. 12 pp. 5.5 x 8.5 in. Signed by Bev Bergeron. Lecture notes. Close-Up, Stage.

Bergeron, Bev, *Magic Connection, The.* (2009) Author, Orlando, FL. Perfect. 208 pp. 5.5 x 8.5 in. (Information not verified by physical copy.) Fiction.

Bergeron, Bev, *Predicting Time.* (1989) Exclusive Magical Publications, Mexico City. Saddle-stitch. White, blue. 19 pp. 5.5 x 8.25 in. Mentalism.

Bergeron, Bev, *Willard the Wizard.* (1978) Lake Cane Publications, Orlando, FL. Cloth. Black. 154 pp. 8.5 x 11 in. Dust jacket. Biography.

Berglas, David, *Berglas Effects, The.* (2011) Kaufman and Co., Washington D.C. Cloth. Black. 394 pp. 8.5 x 11 in. Dust jacket. Includes 3D glasses, three DVDs. Secret fold-out at back of book. Mentalism.

Berglas, David, *David Berglas File no. 1, The.* (1976) Author, London. Saddle-stitch. Orange. 48 pp. 8.25 x 11.75 in. Stage, Cards, Close-Up.

Berglas, David, *David Berglas Lecture: 1976 Brighton Convention.* (1976) Author, London. Stapled. Beige. 24 pp. 8.25 x 11.75 in. (Information not verified by physical copy.) Lecture notes. Close-Up, Stage.

Berglas, David, *Lecture Notes.* (1991) Author, London. Comb. Orange. 19 pp. 8.25 x 11.75 in. Lecture notes. Stage, Close-Up, Mentalism.

Berglas, David, *Lecture Notes: ESPacology – The Ultimate Mental Routine.* (1996) Author, London. Coil. Blue. 29 pp. 8.25 x 11.75 in. (Information not verified by physical copy.) Lecture notes. Mentalism.

Berglas, David, *Lecture Notes: Matchmaker – The Ultimate Card in Balloon.* (1996) Author, London. Coil. Yellow. 23 pp. 8.25 x 11.75 in. (Information not verified by physical copy.) Lecture notes. Stage, Cards, Balloons.

Berglas, David, *Lecture Notes: The Ultimate Newspaper Prediction.* (1996) Author, London. Coil. Beige. 22 pp. 8.25 x 11.75 in. (Information not verified by physical copy.) Lecture notes. Mentalism.

Berglas, David, *Magic Made Easy.* (1960) Author, London. Saddle-stitch. Orange. 24 pp. 5.5 x 8.5 in. In David Berglas "Conjuring Tricks" set. Magic set manual.

Berglas, David, with Britland, David, *Mind and Magic of David Berglas, The.* (2002) Hahne, Burbank, CA. Cloth. Maroon. 566 pp. 8.75 x 10.25 in. Signed by David Britland. Mentalism.

Berglas, David, with Playfair, Guy Lyon, *Question of Memory, A.* (1988) Jonathan Cape, UK. Cloth. Black. 128 pp. 5.75 x 8.75 in. Dust jacket. Memory, Mnemonics.

Berglas, Marvin, *110 Amazing Magic Tricks with Everyday Objects.* (1998) Marvin's Magic, London. Saddle-stitch. Red. 40 pp. 5.5 x 8.5 in. (Information not verified by physical copy.) Beginner.

Berglas, Marvin, *Mind Reading Magic.* (2003) Alligator Books, UK. Casebound. Dark blue. 20 pp. 5.5 x 8.5 in. (Information not verified by physical copy.) Mentalism, Children's book.

Bergor, Ben, *Highlight Magic.* (1941) John Snyder, Norwood, OH. Cloth. Green. 31 pp. 5.75 x 8.25 in. Stage, Close-Up.

Bergor, Ben, *Lecture Notes of Ben Bergor.* (1941) Author, Madison, WI. Stapled. Tan. 22 pp. 8.5 x 11 in. Lecture notes. Business, Promotion.

Berkeley, with Rowland, T. B., *Card Tricks and Puzzles.* (1892) Frederick A. Stokes Co., New York. Cloth. Red, white. 120 pp. 4.5 x 7 in. Cards, Prearranged deck, Eight Kings.

Berkeley, with Rowland, T. B., *Card Tricks and Puzzles.* (1892) George Bell and Sons, London. Cloth. Red. 120 pp. 4.5 x 6.5 in. Cards, Prearranged deck, Eight Kings.

Berkeley, with Rowland, T. B., *Card Tricks and Puzzles.* (1894) George Bell and Sons, London. Cloth. Red. 120 pp. 4.5 x 6.5 in. Cards, Prearranged deck, Eight Kings.

Berkeley, with Rowland, T. B., *Card Tricks and Puzzles.* (1897) George Bell and Sons, London. Cloth. Red. 120 pp. 4.5 x 6.5 in. Cards, Prearranged deck, Eight Kings.

Berkeley, with Rowland, T. B., *Card Tricks and Puzzles.* (1899) George Bell and Sons, London. Cloth. Red. 120 pp. 4.5 x 6.5 in. Cards, Prearranged deck, Eight Kings.

Berkeley, with Rowland, T. B., *Card Tricks and Puzzles.* (1902) George Bell and Sons, London. Cloth. Red. 120 pp. 4.5 x 6.5 in. Cards, Prearranged deck, Eight Kings.

Berland, Samuel, *Amazing Tricks with Paper Cups.* (1962) Author, Chicago. Saddle-stitch. Green. 24 pp. 6 x 9 in. Stage, Cups.

Berland, Samuel, *Amazing Tricks with Paper Cups.* (n.d.) Author, Chicago. Saddle-stitch. Beige. 24 pp. 5.25 x 8.25 in. Later reprint. Stage, Cups.

Berland, Samuel, *Berland's Amazing Substitution.* (1940) Author, Chicago. Folder. Beige. Cover text: Blue; pp. 6 x 9 in. Three folded 8.5 x 11 mimeographed pages inside outer folder with props. Stage.

Berland, Samuel, *Berland's Delayed Action Cigarette Vanish.* (1934) Author, Chicago. Single page. White. 8.5 x 11 in. Oriented lengthwise. Cigarettes, Manipulation, Gimmicks.

Berland, Samuel, *Berland's Kit of Jumbo Card Tricks.* (1944) Author, Chicago. Saddle-stitch. Beige. 7 pp. 5.75 x 9 in. In printed envelope with giant cards and half-card gimmick. Cards, Jumbo cards.

Berland, Samuel, *Berland's New and Original Tricks.* (1933) Author, Chicago. Stapled. Black. 42 pp. 8.25 x 6.25 in. Bound oblong. Photographic illustration sheet. Stage, Close-Up.

Berland, Samuel, *Berland's Portfolio of More Exclusive Tricks.* (1970) Author, Chicago. Folder. Yellow. 28 pp. 8.5 x 11 in. Cover says: "Magic is Alive! Magic is Wonderful! YOU can make it come alive! YOU can make it wonderful!" Stage, Close-Up.

Berland, Samuel, *Berland's Soap Swindle.* (1943) Author, Chicago, IL. Saddle-stitch. Blue. 4 pp. 5.5 x 8.5 in. (Information not verified by physical copy.) Con games, Bills.

Berland, Samuel, *Berland's Tricks and Routines: Mark III.* (1964) Author, Chicago. Saddle-stitch. Beige. 20 pp. 8.5 x 11 in. Stage.

Berland, Samuel, *Berland's Triple Water Maze.* (1930) Author, Chicago, IL. Stapled. White. 3 pp. 8.5 x 11 in. Mimeographed. Harness and cord to produce glass of liquid. Glasses, Liquids.

Berland, Samuel, *Biltrix.* (1940) Author, Chicago. Saddle-stitch. Silver. 8 pp. 5.5 x 8.5 in. (Measurements and other information have been recorded as accurately as possible.) Close-Up, Bills.

Berland, Samuel, *Biltrix.* (1940) Author, Chicago. Saddle-stitch. Silver. 8 pp. 5.5 x 8.5 in. (Measurements and other information have been recorded as accurately as possible.) Close-Up, Bills.

Berland, Samuel, *Blue Ribbon Card Tricks.* (1942) Author, Chicago. Saddle-stitch. Beige. 29 pp. 6 x 9 in. (Measurements and other information have been recorded as accurately as possible.) Cards.

Berland, Samuel, *Book of Routines, vol. no. 1.* (1950) Ireland Magic Co., Chicago. Saddle-stitch. Beige. 32 pp. 6 x 9 in. Close-Up, Stage.

Berland, Samuel, *Carnival Cigarette, The.* (1929) Central Magic Co., Chicago. Single page. White. 5.5 x 8.5 in. Mimeographed. (Information not verified by physical copy.) Cigarettes, Torn and Restored Cigarette.

Berland, Samuel, *Close-Up Magic of Sam Berland, The.* (1986) Author, Chicago. Perfect. Black. 80 pp. 8.5 x 11 in. Cover says "The Magic of Sam Berland." Close-Up, Cards, Bills.

Berland, Samuel, *Devil Dollar.* (1938) Author, Chicago. Folder. Red. 4 pp. 5.5 x 8.5 in. Cover with envelope of props and 4 pp. manual. Bills, Close-Up.

Berland, Samuel, with Faber, Harry T., *Immortal Cigarette.* (1929) Central Magic Co., Chicago. Single page. White. 5.5 x 8.5 in. (Information not verified by physical copy.) Half-page. Cigarettes, Torn and Restored Cigarette.

Berland, Samuel, *Lecture for Close-Up.* (n.d.) Author, Chicago. Clip. Green. 44 pp. 8.5 x 11 in. Some single-sided pages. Signed by Sam Berland. Lecture notes. Close-Up.

Berland, Samuel, *Lecture Notes.* (n.d.) Author, Chicago. Stapled. White. 9 pp. 8.5 x 11 in. Lecture notes. Close-Up, Stage.

Berland, Samuel, *Magic of Sam Berland, The.* (1986) Author, Chicago. Perfect. Black. 80 pp. 8.5 x 11 in. Close-Up, Stage, x.

Berland, Samuel, *Match-Effex.* (1939) Author, Chicago. Saddle-stitch. Orange. 8 pp. 6 x 9 in. (Measurements and other information have been recorded as accurately as possible.) Close-Up, Matches.

Berland, Samuel, *More of Berland's Exclusive Tricks.* (1961) Author, Chicago. Stapled. Pink. 13 pp. 8.5 x 11 in. (Measurements and other information have been recorded as accurately as possible.) Stage.

Berland, Samuel, *More of Berland's Exclusive Tricks.* (1961) Author, Chicago. Comb. Pink. 13 pp. 8.5 x 11 in. (Measurements and other information have been recorded as accurately as possible.) Stage.

Berland, Samuel, *New Applause Winning Tricks.* (1961) Author, Chicago. Stapled. Gold. 14 pp. 8.5 x 11 in. (Measurements and other information have been recorded as accurately as possible.) Stage.

Berland, Samuel, *Novel Cigarette Tricks.* (1934) Author, Chicago. Perfect. Dark red. 48 pp. 5.25 x 7.75 in. (Measurements and other information have been recorded as accurately as possible.) Cigarettes.

Berland, Samuel, with Faber, Harry T., *Paper of Satan Finale.* (1930) Central Magic Co., Chicago. Stapled. White. 3 pp. 8.5 x 11 in. Bound at top. Mimeographed. (Information not verified by physical copy.) Original version released 1929. Paper, Stage.

Berland, Samuel, *Pirate Pack, The.* (1926) Author, Chicago. Single page. White. 8.5 x 11 in. Mimeographed. (Information not verified by physical copy.) Cards, Card stab.

Berland, Samuel, *Radio Match Trick, The.* (1926) Author, Chicago. Single page. White. 8.5 x 11 in. Mimeographed. (Information not verified by physical copy.) Matches.

Berland, Samuel, *Reminder Notes for Berland's Lecture.* (c. 1955) Author, Chicago. Stapled. White. 5 pp. 8.5 x 11 in. (Information not verified by physical copy.) Lecture notes. Close-Up, Stage.

Berland, Samuel, *Reminder Notes for Berland's Lecture no. 2.* (c. 1960) Author, Chicago. Stapled. White. 4 pp. 8.5 x 11 in. (Information not verified by physical copy.) Lecture notes. Close-Up, Stage.

Berland, Samuel, *Reminder Notes for Berland's Lecture no. 3.* (1968) Author, Chicago. Stapled. White. 8 pp. 8.5 x 11 in. (Information not verified by physical copy.) Lecture notes. Close-Up, Stage.

Berland, Samuel, *Reminder Notes for Berland's Lecture no. 4.* (c. 1970) Author, Chicago. Stapled. White. 6 pp. 8.5 x 11 in. (Information not verified by physical copy.) Lecture notes. Close-Up, Stage.

Berland, Samuel, *Sam Berland's Lecture: Tricks and Routines.* (1980) Author, Chicago. Clip. White. 29 pp. 8.5 x 11 in. Signed by Sam Berland. Lecture notes. Close-Up, Stage.

Berland, Samuel, *Silks from Nowhere.* (1938) Author, Chicago. Stapled. White. 4 pp. 8.5 x 11 in. Mimeographed. Silks, Stage.

Berland, Samuel, *Spirit Sealed Envelopes.* (1938) Author, Chicago. Folder. Red. Cover text: Silver; pp. 6 x 9 in. With one-page 8.5 x 11 in. mimeographed instruction sheet, gimmicks, and envelopes inside outer printed folder. Close-Up, Bills.

Berland, Samuel, *Supreme Thimble Act.* (1939) Author, Chicago. Saddle-stitch. Tan. 8 pp. 6 x 9 in. Pearl-finish cover. Advertised as "Thimble Act Supreme." Thimbles, Manipulation, Stage.

Berland, Samuel, *Tear-A-Bill.* (1938) Author, Chicago. Folded. Green. 2 pp. 6 x 9 in. Envelope with bills and printed instructions in folder. Bills.

Berland, Samuel, *Tricks for Today and Tomorrow 1970.* (1970) Author, Chicago. Saddle-stitch. Beige. 32 pp. 8.5 x 11 in. Stage.

Berland, Samuel, *Tricks with Watches.* (1942) Author, Chicago. Perfect. Orange. 64 pp. 6 x 9 in. Signed by Sam Berland. Stage, Watches.

Berland, Samuel, *Twenty Tricks with Wiztax.* Second edition. (1941) Berland Magical Creations, Chicago. Saddle-stitch. Yellow. 12 pp. 6 x 9 in. Envelope in back for gimmick material. Photo illustrations. Close-Up, Gimmicks, Adhesives.

Berland, Samuel, *Twenty Tricks with Wiztax.* (1962) D. Robbins, Brooklyn, NY. Saddle-stitch. Beige. 16 pp. 5.5 x 8.5 in. Close-Up, Gimmicks, Adhesives.

Berland, Samuel, *Xclusive Trix.* (1935) Author, Chicago. Stapled. Green. 25 pp. 8.5 x 7 in. Bound oblong. Mimeographed inside printed cover. Silver label on cover. Close-Up, Stage.

Berland, Samuel, *Xclusive Trix.* (1935) Author, Chicago. Saddle-stitch inside die-cut cover. Blue. 25 pp. 9 x 7 in. Mimeographed inside printed cover. Signed by Sam Berland. Close-Up, Stage.

Berlinski, Allen, *Purvis: The Newcastle Conjuror.* (1981) Steam Power, Northville, MI. Saddle-stitch. Beige. 38 pp. 8.5 x 11 in. Signed by Allen Berlinski. #28 of 150. Biography, History.

Berlinski, Allen, with Lund, Robert, *Wee Books series no. 1: Wisdoms of the Learned Pig.* Miniature book. (1993) Sun Dog Press, Northville, MI. Folded. Beige. 8 pp. 2.75 x 4.25 in. History.

Berlinski, Allen, with Lund, Robert, *Wee Books series no. 2: Pig Tale.* Miniature book. (1994) Sun Dog Press, Northville, MI. Folded. Gray. 8 pp. 2.75 x 4.25 in. History, Collecting.

Berlinski, Allen, with Meyer, David, *Wee Books series no. 3: A Collector's Tale.* Miniature book. (1995) Sun Dog Press, Northville, MI. Folded. Beige. 8 pp. 2.75 x 4.25 in. Signed by Allen Berlinski, David Meyer. History, Biography.

Berlinski, Allen, with Waldron, Dan, *Wee Books series no. 4: Magic's Greatest Gimmick.* Miniature book. (1996) Sun Dog Press, Northville, MI. Folded. Beige, red, black. 8 pp. 2.75 x 4.25 in. History, Essays.

Berlinski, Allen, with Hagy, James, *Wee Books series no. 5: A Fable for Collectors.* Miniature book. (1997) Sun Dog Press, Northville, MI. Folded. Beige, red, black. 8 pp. 2.75 x 4.25 in. History, Collecting.

Berlinski, Allen, with Adrion, Alexander, *Wee Books series no. 6: Antwerp at a Late Hour.* Miniature book. (2001) Sun Dog Press, Northville, MI. Folded. Green. 8 pp. 2.75 x 4.25 in. History.

Berlinski, Allen, with Dawes, Edwin A., *Wee Books series no. 7: The Conversion of a Magical Loner.* Miniature book. (2003) Sun Dog Press, Northville, MI. Folded. Beige, brown. 8 pp. 2.75 x 4.25 in. History, Collecting.

Berlinski, Allen, with Ricard, Ray, *Wee Books series no. 8: A Visit with H. Adrian Smith.* Miniature book. (2003) Sun Dog Press, Northville, MI. Folded. Beige, brown. 8 pp. 2.75 x 4.25 in. History, Biography, Collecting.

Berlinski, Allen, with Bamberg, Theo, *Wee Books series no. 9: On Hand Shadows.* Miniature book. (2005) Sun Dog Press, Northville, MI. Folded. Blue, white. 8 pp. 2.75 x 4.25 in. History, Shadowgraphy.

Berlinski, Allen, with Hatch, Richard, *Wee Books series no. 10: A Lesson in Timing.* Miniature book. (2005) Sun Dog Press, Northville, MI. Folded. Red, beige, yellow, black, blue. 8 pp. 2.75 x 4.25 in. Jay Marshall story. Signed by Richard Hatch. History, Essays.

Berlinski, Allen, *Wee Books series no. 11: Letters of Robert-Houdin.* Miniature book. (2009) Sun Dog Press, Northville, MI. Folded. Beige, red, brown. 8 pp. 2.75 x 4.25 in. History, Biography, Robert-Houdin.

Berlinski, Allen, *Wee Books series no. 12, checklist: Collection Plates.* Miniature book. (2009) Sun Dog Press, Northville, MI. Folded. Blue, red, black. 8 pp. 2.75 x 4.25 in. History, Collecting, Bookplates.

Berlinski, Allen, *Wee Books series no. 12, vol. 1: Collection Plates.* Miniature book. (2009) Sun Dog Press, Northville, MI. Folded. Blue, red, black. 8 pp. 2.75 x 4.25 in. History, Collecting, Bookplates.

Berlinski, Allen, *Wee Books series no. 12, vol. 2: Collection Plates.* Miniature book. (2009) Sun Dog Press, Northville, MI. Folded. Blue, red, black. 8 pp. 2.75 x 4.25 in. History, Collecting, Bookplates.

Berman, Sam, *How to Present Magic.* (1951) Author, Chicago. Stapled. 3 pp. 8.5 x 11 in. (Information not verified by physical copy.) Lecture notes. Showmanship.

Berman, Sam, *Principles and Sleights in Coin Manipulation.* (c. 1960) Author, Chicago. Stapled. 5 pp. 8.5 x 11 in. (Information not verified by physical copy.) Lecture notes. Coins, Manipulation.

Berman, Sam, *Sam Berman's Lecture Notes.* (1951) Author, Chicago. Stapled. Yellow. 11 pp. 8.5 x 11 in. (Information not verified by physical copy.) Lecture notes. Close-Up, Stage.

Bernard, *64 Tricks You Can Do.* (n.d.) Author, Melbourne. 48 pp. 6.75 x 8.25 in. (Information not verified by physical copy.) See McCullagh, "Under the Southern Cross." Beginner.

Bernard, Bobby, *Magic in Miniature.* (1958) Corinda's Magic Studio, London. Stapled. Orange. 12 pp. 8.5 x 11 in. Theory, Coins, Sleeving, Dice.

Bernhard, Robert E., *Psychology of Conjuring, The.* (1936) Author, Stanford, CA. Saddle-stitch. Blue. 15 pp. 5 x 7.75 in. Blackledge library. Signed by J. Elder Blackledge. Theory.

Bernhard, Robert E., *Publicity for Magicians.* (1940) Abbott Magic Co., Colon, MI. Saddle-stitch. Beige. 48 pp. 6 x 9 in. Business, Publicity.

Bernstein, Bruce, *1982 Lecture Notes.* (1982) Author, Chicago. Saddle-stitch. White. 19 pp. 5.5 x 8.5 in. (Information not verified by physical copy.) Lecture notes. Mentalism, Cards.

Bernstein, Bruce, *Bernstein Center Tear Technique.* (1980) Author, Chicago. Comb. Green. 18 pp. 8.5 x 11 in. Mentalism, Center Tear.

Bernstein, Bruce, *Bernstein on Number Predictions.* (1985) Author, Chicago. Saddle-stitch. Green. 16 pp. 5.5 x 8.5 in. Mentalism.

Bernstein, Bruce, *Classics.* (1998) Author, Chicago. Comb. Gray. 41 pp. 8.5 x 11 in. (Measurements and other information have been recorded as accurately as possible.) Mentalism, Center Tear.

Bernstein, Bruce, *Couples.* (1977) Paul Curry, Phoenicia, NY. Loose pages. Yellow. 4 pp. 8.5 x 11 in. (Measurements and other information have been recorded as accurately as possible.) Mentalism, Cards.

Bernstein, Bruce, *Going South with His Secrets.* (1994) Author, Chicago. Saddle-stitch. Gray. 24 pp. 8.5 x 11 in. Memorable inscription to Jay Marshall. Signed by Bruce Bernstein. Lecture notes. Mentalism.

Bernstein, Bruce, *Lecture Compendium, The.* (2006) Author, Chicago. Comb. Gray. 63 pp. 8.5 x 11 in. (Information not verified by physical copy.) Lecture notes. Mentalism, Cards.

Bernstein, Bruce, *Many Minds.* (2017) Author, Chicago. Comb. White, black, red. 16 pp. 8.5 x 11 in. Lecture notes. Mentalism, Cards.

Bernstein, Bruce, *Matter of Time, A.* (1987) Author, Chicago. Saddle-stitch. Gray. 47 pp. 8.5 x 11 in. (Information not verified by physical copy.) Mentalism, Cards.

Bernstein, Bruce, *Perception is Everything.* (1999) Author, Chicago. Comb. White. 34 pp. 8.5 x 11 in. (Measurements and other information have been recorded as accurately as possible.) Mentalism.

Bernstein, Bruce, *Psi-Kicks.* (1997) Author, Chicago. Comb. White. 56 pp. 8.5 x 11 in. (Measurements and other information have been recorded as accurately as possible.) Mentalism.

Bernstein, Bruce, *Psi-Tech.* (1985) Author, Chicago. Comb. Beige. 62 pp. 8.5 x 11 in. (Information not verified by physical copy. Bibliographical details are as accurate as possible.) Mentalism.

Bernstein, Bruce, *Psych-Out.* (1985) Magic Inc., Chicago. Saddle-stitch. Yellow. 12 pp. 5.5 x 8.25 in. Mentalism, Cards, Ten-card poker deal.

Bernstein, Bruce, *Psych-Out.* Fourth printing. (1998) Author, Chicago. Comb. Gray. 20 pp. 5.5 x 8.5 in. Mentalism, Cards, Ten-card poker deal.

Bernstein, Bruce, *Psych-Out Update.* (1986) Author, Chicago. Saddle-stitch. Yellow. 7 pp. 5.5 x 8.5 in. Mentalism, Cards, Ten-card poker deal.

Bernstein, Bruce, *Three.* (2004) Author, Chicago. Saddle-stitch. White. 25 pp. 8.5 x 11 in. (Measurements and other information have been recorded as accurately as possible.) Mentalism.

Bernstein, Bruce, *Twenty Effects for Psychic Entertainers.* (1981) Author, Chicago. Comb. Beige. 60 pp. 5.5 x 8.5 in. Mentalism.

Bernstein, Bruce, *Unreal.* (2013) Squash Publishing, Chicago. Cloth. Black, red. 242 pp. 7.25 x 10.25 in. (Measurements and other information have been recorded as accurately as possible.) Mentalism.

Berol, Felix, *Mnemotechnical Dictionary.* (1913) Funk and Wagnalls, New York. Cloth. Brown. 41 pp. 2.5 x 5 in. Memory.

Berol, William, *Card Memory.* (1920) Players Publishing Co., New York. Saddle-stitch. Beige. 32 pp. 4.5 x 6 in. Memory, Cards.

Berry, Jay Scott, *Éclair Miracle.* (c. 1986) Author, Simi Valley, CA. Single page. White. 2 pp. 8.5 x 11 in. Illustrated by James Hodges. Thumb tip, Light effects, Gimmicks.

Berry, Jay Scott, *Eclipse Effects.* (1990) CSI, Buckingham, VA. Saddle-stitch. Black. 20 pp. 5.5 x 8.5 in. Stage, Thumb tip, Gimmicks.

Berry, Jay Scott, *Genesis Scrolls.* (1989) CSI, Buckingham, VA. Saddle-stitch. White. 21 pp. 5.5 x 8.5 in. Stage, Zombie, Gimmicks.

Berry, Jay Scott, *Illusioneering 2001.* (2001) Author, Germany. Comb. White. 16 pp. 8.5 x 11 in. Lecture notes. Stage, Close-Up, Gimmicks, Inventions.

Berry, Jay Scott, *Magic for the New World.* (1986) Académie de Magie Georges Proust, Paris. Saddle-stitch. Black. 44 pp. 8.25 x 11.75 in. Stage, Smoke, Reels, Ring and rope.

Berry, Jay Scott, *Realizations.* (1983) Author, Barcelona. Loose pages. White. 15 pp. 8.5 x 11 in. Signed by Jay Scott Berry. Lecture notes. Theory, Stage.

Berry, Jay Scott, *Sunburst.* (1988) Author, Studio City, CA. Folded. White. 2 pp. 5.5 x 8.5 in. Thumb tip, Light effects, Gimmicks.

Berry, Jay Scott, *Symphony on the Ring and String.* (c. 1986) Author, Studio City, CA. Clip. White. 10 pp. 8.5 x 11 in. (Information not verified by physical copy.) Rings, String, Close-Up.

Berry, Jay Scott, *Totally Eclipse.* (1995) CSI, Buckingham, VA. Saddle-stitch. White. 24 pp. 5.5 x 8.5 in. Stage, Thumb tip, Gimmicks.

Berry, Jay Scott, *Triple Flash.* (1988) Author, Studio City, CA. Single page. White. 8.5 x 11 in. Illustrated by James Hodges. Thumb tip, Light effects, Gimmicks.

Bert, Guy, *Anneaux "Innovation," Les.* (1947) Guy Bert, Paris. Perfect. Beige. 92 pp. 5.5 x 8.75 in. Includes Hilliard ring moves. Linking Rings. French.

Bert, Guy, *Méthode Complète Pour le Jeu de Cartes dit "Radio."* (c. 1947) Guy Bert, Paris. Saddle-stitch. Beige. 8 pp. 4.75 x 6.25 in. Routines with forcing deck, half all-alike. Cards, Forcing.

Bert, Guy, *Optima, ou Leurs Meilleurs Expériences.* (c. 1947) Guy Bert, Paris. Saddle-stitch. Beige. 15 pp. 8.5 x 10.75 in. Material by Jules Dhotel and others. Stage, Close-Up, Biography. French.

Bert, Guy, with Lauret, E. and Hippolito, V., *Vade Mecum de la Magie part 1.* (1937) Author, Paris. Saddle-stitch. Maroon. 32 pp. 6.25 x 10 in. Beginner. French.

Bert, Guy, with Lauret, E. and Hippolito, V., *Vade Mecum de la Magie part 2.* (1937) Author, Paris. Saddle-stitch. Maroon. 16 pp. 6.25 x 10 in. Beginner. French.

Bert, Guy, with Lauret, E. and Hippolito, V., *Vade Mecum de la Magie part 3.* (1937) Author, Paris. Saddle-stitch. Maroon. 14 pp. 6.25 x 10 in. Beginner. French.

Bert, Guy, with Lauret, E. and Hippolito, V., *Vade Mecum de la Magie part 4.* (1937) Author, Paris. Saddle-stitch. Maroon. 15 pp. 6.25 x 10 in. Beginner. French.

Bert, Guy, with Lauret, E. and Hippolito, V., *Vade Mecum de la Magie part 5.* (1937) Author, Paris. Saddle-stitch. Maroon. 16 pp. 6.25 x 10 in. Beginner. French.

Bert, Guy, with Lauret, E. and Hippolito, V., *Vade Mecum de la Magie II: Annuaire Général de l'Illusion.* (1937) Author, Paris. Saddle-stitch. Orange. 16 pp. 6.25 x 10 in. Beginner. French.

Bertino, Prof., *Mystical Novelties Up-to-Date.* (1895) Author, Manchester, UK. Saddle-stitch. Beige. 15 pp. 4.75 x 7 in. In Copperfield collection. Close-Up, Stage.

Bertol, Louis, *Kid Stuff of Louis Bertol, The.* (1977) Magic Inc., Chicago. Comb. White. 96 pp. 5.5 x 8.5 in. Photos of Jay Marshall. Children's magic.

Bertram, Charles, with Dunn, Bruce, *Charles Bertram: Card Tricks.* Miniature book. (2001) Bruce Dunn, Kalamazoo, MI. Folder. Beige. Multiple sections. 2.75 x 4 in. Wee Books by Dunn. Set with two 16 pp. "Card Tricks" booklets in folder. From "London Magazine," 1903. History, Cards.

Bertram, Charles, *Isn't It Wonderful?* Limited deluxe edition. (1896) Swan Sonnenschein, London. Cloth. White. Cover text: Gold; 301 pp. 7.25 x 9.75 in. Biography, Cards.

Bertram, Charles, *Isn't It Wonderful?* (1896) Swan Sonnenschein, London. Cloth. Maroon. Cover text: Gold; 301 pp. 5.75 x 8.75 in. Biography, Cards.

Bertram, Charles, *Isn't It Wonderful?* (1899) Swan Sonnenschein, London. Perfect. Blue. 301 pp. 5.25 x 8.25 in. Biography, Cards.

Bertram, Charles, *Magician in Many Lands, A.* (1911) George Routledge and Sons, London. Cloth. Blue. Cover text: Gold; 315 pp. 5.25 x 8 in. Biography, History.

Bertram, Charles, *Magician in Many Lands, A.* (1911) George Routledge and Sons, London. Cloth. Maroon. Cover text: Gold; 315 pp. 5.25 x 8 in. Biography, History.

Bertram, Charles, *Magician in Many Lands, A.* (1911) George Routledge and Sons, London. Cloth. Red. Cover text: Gold; 315 pp. 5.25 x 8 in. Biography, History.

Bertram, Ross, *Bertram on Sleight of Hand.* (1996) Lee Jacobs Productions, Pomeroy, OH. Cloth. Green. 255 pp. 8.75 x 11.25 in. Dust jacket. Close-Up, Stage.

Bertram, Ross, *Blendo.* (1941) Abbott Magic Co., Colon, MI. Stapled. White. 3 pp. 8.5 x 11 in. (Measurements and other information have been recorded as accurately as possible.) Silks, Instructions.

Bertram, Ross, *Magic and Methods of Ross Bertram.* (1978) Magic Limited, Oakland, CA. Cloth. Tan. 163 pp. 8.5 x 11 in. Close-Up, Stage.

Bertram, Ross, *Ross Bertram on Coins.* Stars of Magic series 9, no. 1. (1951) Stars of Magic, Inc., New York. Saddle-stitch. White. 12 pp. 8.5 x 11 in. Coins, Close-Up.

Bessy, Maurice, with Duca, Lo, *Georges Méliès: Mage.* (1945) Prisma, Paris. Cloth. Black. 205 pp. 8 x 10.75 in. Includes 32-page facsimile manuscript of Méliès' autobiography, two reproduction business cards. #473 of 500. Magicians in cinema, Biography.

Bessy, Maurice, with Duca, Lo, *Georges Méliès: Mage.* (1945) Prisma, Paris. Cloth. Maroon. 205 pp. 8 x 10.75 in. Includes reproduction Méliès business card; orange promotional paper band. #1056 of 2000. Magicians in cinema, Biography.

Bey, Rayman, *Oriental Mysteries Revealed.* (c. 1930) Author, Sydney. 8 pp. (Information not verified by physical copy.) Beginner, Asian magic.

Bibik, Jeff, *Bibik Of Course! The 1991 Lecture World Tour.* (1991) Author, Chicago. Stapled. White. 10 pp. 8.5 x 11 in. Lecture notes. Close-Up.

Bich, Mathieu, *Discovery of a New World.* (2003) Author, Paris. Saddle-stitch. White. 18 pp. 5.5 x 8.5 in. (Information not verified by physical copy.) Cards, Close-Up.

Bich, Mathieu, *Lecture Notes 2002.* (2002) Author, Paris. Stapled. White. 16 pp. 5.5 x 8.5 in. (Information not verified by physical copy.) Lecture notes. Cards, Close-Up.

Bich, Mathieu, *Newsletter Tricks, The.* (2012) Author, Paris. Perfect. Purple. 62 pp. 7 x 10 in. With DVD. (Information not verified by physical copy.) Cards, Close-Up.

Bicknell, Frank M., *Blitzen the Conjurer.* (1906) Henry Altemus, Philadelphia. Cloth. Beige, orange. 130 pp. 4.75 x 7 in. Fiction.

Bieri, John C., *Poetic Patter for the Prestidigitator.* (1933) Author, Philadelphia. String. Red. 10 pp. 4 x 8.5 in. Early gospel magic book. Patter, Gospel magic.

Bigbee, North, *40 New Mental Effects.* (1962) The Elders, Dallas, TX. Cloth. Red. Cover text: Gold; 76 pp. 5.5 x 8.75 in. (Measurements and other information have been recorded as accurately as possible.) Mentalism.

Bigbee, North, *Stage Mentalism.* Second printing. (1969) Magic Inc., Chicago. Comb. Green. 72 pp. 8.5 x 11 in. Large format. Mentalism.

Bigbee, North, *Stage Mentalism.* Second printing. (1969) Magic Inc., Chicago. Saddle-stitch. Yellow. 72 pp. 5.5 x 8.75 in. Small version. Mentalism.

Bigelow, Norman, *Beyond Treason: The Houdini Code.* The Cord, vol. 6. (1985) Author, Fitchburg, MA. Stapled. White. 6 pp. 8.5 x 11 in. (Information not verified by physical copy.) Houdini, History.

Bigelow, Norman, *Bigelow Writings.* (1996) Author, Fitchburg, MA. Stapled. White. 15 pp. 8.5 x 11 in. (Information not verified by physical copy.) Escapes, History.

Bigelow, Norman, *Death Blow! Was Houdini Murdered?* (1983) October Creations, Fitchburg, MA. Stapled. White. 68 pp. 8.5 x 11 in. Houdini, History.

Bigelow, Norman, *Man from Beyond, The.* (c. 1990) Author, Fitchburg, MA. Stapled. White. 9 pp. 8.5 x 11 in. (Information not verified by physical copy.) Houdini, History.

Bigelow, Norman, *Margery's Medium.* (1985) Author, Fitchburg, MA. Stapled. White. 10 pp. 8.5 x 11 in. (Information not verified by physical copy.) Houdini, Mediums, History.

Bigelow, Norman, *Norman Bigelow Course in Escape Artistry: Lesson 1: Expert Manipulation in Handcuffs.* (1976) Mickey O Enterprises, Brooklyn, NY. Loose pages. White. 18 pp. 8.5 x 11 in. With 3 pp. supplement. (Information not verified by physical copy.) Escapes, Handcuffs, Course.

Bigelow, Norman, *Norman Bigelow Course in Escape Artistry: Lesson 2: Straitjackets.* (1976) Mickey O Enterprises, Brooklyn, NY. Loose pages. White. 25 pp. 8.5 x 11 in. With 3 pp. supplement. (Information not verified by physical copy.) Escapes, Straitjackets, Course.

Bilek, Phedon, *Hermes.* (2023) Haresign Press, UK. Perfect. Black. 295 pp. 6 x 9 in. (Information not verified by physical copy. Bibliographical details are as accurate as possible.) Mentalism, Code acts.

Bilek, Phedon, *Orion: The Hunter.* (2020) Haresign Press, UK. Cloth. Black. 295 pp. 7 x 10 in. (Information not verified by physical copy. Bibliographical details are as accurate as possible.) Mentalism.

Bilek, Phedon, *Orion: The Pleiades.* (2020) Haresign Press, UK. Cloth. Black. 303 pp. 7 x 10 in. (Information not verified by physical copy. Bibliographical details are as accurate as possible.) Mentalism.

Bilek, Phedon, *Orpheus.* (2024) Haresign Press, UK. Cloth. White. 328 pp. 7 x 10 in. (Information not verified by physical copy. Bibliographical details are as accurate as possible.) Mentalism.

Bilek, Phedon, *Proteus.* (2017) Haresign Press, UK. Perfect. Black. 133 pp. 5.5 x 8.5 in. (Information not verified by physical copy. Bibliographical details are as accurate as possible.) Mentalism.

Billings, Roy, *By-Play My Way.* (1949) Magic Circle, London. 9 pp. (Information not verified by physical copy.) Lecture notes.

Bilis, Bernard, *Close Up, French Style.* (1976) Magic Inc., Chicago. Saddle-stitch. Beige. 52 pp. 5.5 x 8.5 in. (Measurements and other information have been recorded as accurately as possible.) Cards.

Bilis, Bernard, *Close Up, French Style.* (1976) Magic Inc., Chicago. Saddle-stitch. Orange. 52 pp. 5.5 x 8.5 in. (Measurements and other information have been recorded as accurately as possible.) Cards.

Bilis, Bernard, *French Pasteboards.* (1980) Magical Publications, Sierra Madre, CA. Comb. Orange. 63 pp. 5.5 x 8.5 in. Cards.

Bilis, Bernard, *Notes de Conférence.* (1975) Author, Paris. Saddle-stitch. Red. 26 pp. 8.25 x 11.75 in. Lecture notes. Cards.

Billy, H., *Recueil de Tours de Cartes d'Après les Meilleurs Prestidigitateurs de Paris.* (n.d.) H. Billy, Paris. Folded. Beige. 8 pp. 5 x 6 in. Cards. French.

Binarelli, Tony, *Manual Tutor de Ilusionismo.* Second edition. (2001) Tutor, Madrid. Perfect. Green. 172 pp. 6 x 9.25 in. Beginner. Spanish.

Binarelli, Tony, *My Way to Mentalism.* (2000) Camirand Academy of Magic, Quebec. Cloth. Black. 222 pp. 6.75 x 9.75 in. Dust jacket. Mentalism.

Binarelli, Tony, *Playmagic.* (1976) Author, Rome. Saddle-stitch. Green. 18 pp. 8.25 x 11.75 in. (Information not verified by physical copy. Bibliographical details are as accurate as possible.) Lecture notes. Cards.

Binarelli, Tony, *Playmagic 2.* (1979) Author, Rome. Saddle-stitch. Red. 16 pp. 8.25 x 11.75 in. (Measurements and other information have been recorded as accurately as possible.) Cards.

Bingham, Euan, *20 Things Marlo Didn't Publish.* (c. 2003) Author, UK. Coil. Black. 5.75 x 8.25 in. (Information not verified by physical copy.) Cards.

Bingham, Euan, *Free from Filler.* (2003) Author, UK. Coil. Black. 26 pp. 5.75 x 8.25 in. (Information not verified by physical copy.) Cards.

Bingham, Euan, *MDP.* (c. 2003) Author, UK. Coil. Black. 5.75 x 8.25 in. (Information not verified by physical copy.) Cards.

Bingham, Euan, *Quirky Card Magic.* (c. 2003) Author, UK. Coil. Black. 5.75 x 8.25 in. (Information not verified by physical copy.) Cards.

Biow, Dick, *Sponge Ball King's Cups and Balls.* (1994) Robinson Wizard, New York. Saddle-stitch. Gray. 12 pp. 6 x 9 in. Cups and Balls.

Bird, Malcolm, with Dart, Alan, *Magic Handbook, The.* (1992) Chrysalis Books, San Francisco. Casebound. Blue. 87 pp. 9.25 x 10.25 in. Children's book, Beginner.

Bird, Malcolm, with Dart, Alan, *Magic Handbook, The.* (1992) Chrysalis Books, San Francisco. Perfect. Blue. 87 pp. 9 x 10 in. Children's book, Beginner.

Biro, Pete (See also Kaps, Fred; Koran, Al), *Biro's Dozen.* (c. 1971) Author, Los Angeles. Stapled. White. 4 pp. 8.5 x 11 in. (Information not verified by physical copy.) Lecture notes. Close-Up, Stage.

Biro, Pete, *Book Entitled Son of Greater Magic vol. 1, A.* (c. 1974) Author, Los Angeles. Saddle-stitch. Light blue. 8 pp. 7 x 8.5 in. Lecture notes. Close-Up, Stage.

Biro, Pete, *Book Entitled Son of Greater Magic vol. 1-1/2, A.* (1980) Author, Los Angeles. Saddle-stitch. Gray. 8 pp. 7 x 8.75 in. Signed by Pete Biro. Lecture notes. Close-Up, Stage.

Biro, Pete, *From Soup to Nuts!* (2011) Author, Los Angeles. Saddle-stitch. Black. 12 pp. 5.5 x 8.5 in. Close-Up, Glasses, Walnuts.

Biro, Pete, *Hindu Cups and Balls, The.* (2000) Author, Los Angeles. Saddle-stitch. White. 19 pp. 5.5 x 8.5 in. (Information not verified by physical copy.) Cups and Balls, Indian magic.

Biro, Pete, *Indian Cups and Balls, The.* (2000) Author, Los Angeles. Saddle-stitch. White. 19 pp. 5.5 x 8.5 in. Same as Biro's "Hindu Cups and Balls." (Information not verified by physical copy.) Cups and Balls, Indian magic.

Biro, Pete, *Magnet Magic Mini-Lecture.* (1968) Author, Los Angeles. Single page. White. 8.5 x 11 in. (Information not verified by physical copy.) Lecture notes. Magnets.

Biro, Pete, *Nutty Surprise.* Second edition. (2011) Author, Los Angeles. Saddle-stitch. Black. 16 pp. 5.5 x 8.5 in. Close-Up, Glasses, Walnuts.

Biro, Pete, *P. Biro Comedy Magic Lecture no. 3.* (1971) Los Angeles. Stapled. White. 5 pp. 8.5 x 11 in. (Information not verified by physical copy.) Lecture notes. Close-Up, Stage.

Biro, Pete, *Pete Biro Lecture Number One.* (1969) Author, Los Angeles. Clip. White. 5 pp. 8.5 x 11 in. (Measurements and other information have been recorded as accurately as possible.) Lecture notes. Close-Up, Stage.

Biro, Pete, *Pete Biro Tries Again! No. 2.* (1969) Author, Los Angeles. Stapled. White. 8 pp. 8.5 x 11 in. (Information not verified by physical copy.) Lecture notes. Close-Up, Stage.

Biro, Pete, *Pete Biro's Magic no. 1: Eggs, Bags, and Gags.* (2009) Author, Los Angeles. Saddle-stitch. Black. 24 pp. 5.5 x 8.5 in. Signed by Pete Biro. Egg Bag, Stage.

Biro, Pete, *Pete Biro's Magic no. 2: Give a Magician Enough Rope.* (2009) Author, Los Angeles. Saddle-stitch. Purple. 24 pp. 5.5 x 8.5 in. Signed by Pete Biro. Rope, Stage.

Biro, Pete, *Pete Biro's Magic no. 3: BOWLing with the Stars.* (2009) Author, Los Angeles. Saddle-stitch. Blue. 24 pp. 5.5 x 8.5 in. Signed by Pete Biro. Close-Up, Benson Bowl, Sponge balls.

Biro, Pete, *Pete Biro's Magic no. 4: The Magic of Emile Clifton.* (2009) Author, Los Angeles. Saddle-stitch. Red. 24 pp. 5.5 x 8.5 in. Signed by Pete Biro. Stage, Biography, History, Black magicians.

Biro, Pete, *Pete Biro's Magic no. 5: Indian Cups and Balls.* (2009) Author, Los Angeles. Saddle-stitch. Blue. 24 pp. 5.5 x 8.5 in. Signed by Pete Biro. Cups and Balls, Indian magic.

Biro, Pete, *Pete Biro's Magic no. 6: Comedy Linking Rings.* (2009) Author, Los Angeles. Saddle-stitch. Orange. 24 pp. 5.5 x 8.5 in. Signed by Pete Biro. Linking Rings, Comedy.

Biro, Pete, *Pete Biro's Magic no. 7: Fred Kaps' Cups and Balls and More.* (2009) Author, Los Angeles. Saddle-stitch. Green. 24 pp. 5.5 x 8.5 in. Signed by Pete Biro. Cups and Balls.

Biro, Pete, *Pete Biro's Magic no. 8: John Ramsay's Cups and Balls.* (2011) Author, Los Angeles. Saddle-stitch. Purple, orange. 28 pp. 5.5 x 8.5 in. Two booklets of the series are numbered 8. Cups and Balls.

Biro, Pete, *Pete Biro's Magic no. 8: Miscellaneous Miracles.* (2011) Author, Los Angeles. Saddle-stitch. Yellow. 24 pp. 5.5 x 8.5 in. Cards, Bills, Close-Up.

Biro, Pete, *Pete Biro's Magic no. 10: There Are No Rules: The Lost Lecture.* (2013) Author, Los Angeles. Saddle-stitch. 28 pp. 5.5 x 8.5 in. (Information not verified by physical copy.) History, Spook shows, Spirit effects.

Biro, Pete, *Pete Biro's Magic no. 13: Memoirs of a Spook Show Ghost.* (2013) Author, Los Angeles. Saddle-stitch. Green. 28 pp. 5.5 x 8.5 in. (Information not verified by physical copy.) Lecture notes. Close-Up, Stage, Showmanship.

Biro, Pete, *Pete Biro's Magical Mystery Tour.* (1972) Author, Los Angeles. Folded. White. 4 pp. 7 x 8.5 in. (Information not verified by physical copy.) Lecture notes. Close-Up, Stage, Showmanship.

Biro, Pete, *Real Secrets of the Chinese Linking Rings, The.* (2012) Stevens Magic, Wichita, KS. Casebound. Red. 242 pp. 8 x 10 in. Linking Rings, History.

Biro, Pete, *Ropes I Have Known.* (c. 1970) Author, Los Angeles. Single page. White. 8.5 x 11 in. (Information not verified by physical copy. Bibliographical details are as accurate as possible.) Lecture notes. Rope.

Biro, Pete, *Tomato Trick, The.* (c. 2000) Author, Los Angeles. Saddle-stitch. White. 20 pp. 8.5 x 11 in. (Information not verified by physical copy.) Bowl routines, Benson Bowl, Close-Up.

Bischof, Christian, *Diamonds of Performance vols. 1-2.* Deluxe edition. (2022) Author, Aarburg, Switzerland. Casebound. Gray. 230 pp. 7.5 x 10.75 in. Slipcase. (Information not verified by physical copy.) Two-volume set. Signed by Christian Bischof. #83 of 300. Mentalism.

Bischof, Christian, *Diamonds of Performance vol. 1.* (2022) Author, Aarburg, Switzerland. Casebound. Gray. 230 pp. 7.5 x 10.75 in. (Information not verified by physical copy.) Two-volume set. Mentalism.

Bischof, Christian, *Diamonds of Performance vol. 2.* (2022) Author, Aarburg, Switzerland. Casebound. Gray. 222 pp. 7.5 x 10.75 in. (Information not verified by physical copy.) Mentalism.

Bishop, Billy, *Life and Magic of Billy Bishop, "Bish the Magish," The.* (2000) David Charvet Studios, Tigard, OR. Perfect. Brown. 105 pp. 8 x 10 in. Biography, Stage.

Bishop, Billy, *Magic for Special Events and Self-Promotion.* (c. 2000) Author, Oak Park, IL. Stapled. White. 8.5 x 11 in. (Information not verified by physical copy.) Lecture notes. Business, Promotion, Showmanship.

Bishop, Glenn, *Tested Tricks for Table-Side Tricksters.* (2001) Author, St. Charles, MO. Comb. Yellow. 25 pp. 8.5 x 11 in. (Information not verified by physical copy.) Lecture notes. Cards, Close-Up, Strolling magic.

Bishop, Percy, *Tricks with Cards.* (c. 1920) Hearth and Home Library, UK. Saddle-stitch. Red. 31 pp. 5 x 7.25 in. In Copperfield collection. Cards, Beginner.

Bishop, Ron, *Laughter All the Way.* (1968) Goodliffe Publications, Birmingham, UK. Cloth. Orange. 130 pp. 5.75 x 9 in. Children's magic, Comedy.

Bishop, Ron, *On Ways and Means.* (c. 1975) Author, UK. Stapled. Blue. (Information not verified by physical copy. Bibliographical details are as accurate as possible.) Lecture notes. Close-Up, Stage.

Bishop, Washington Irving, *Houdin and Heller's Second Sight Explained.* (1880) John Menzies and Co., Edinburgh. Perfect. Beige, black. 78 pp. 5 x 7.25 in. Mentalism, Second Sight.

Biss, James, *Messing with Minds.* (2004) Wyllie Publishing, Hamilton, Canada. Perfect. Purple. 296 pp. 6 x 9 in. (Information not verified by physical copy.) Mentalism.

Biss, James, *Mind Blowing: Second Thoughts on Messing with Minds.* Extremely Mental Edition. (2008) Wyllie Publishing, Hamilton, Canada. Cloth. Black. 380 pp. 6 x 9 in. (Information not verified by physical copy.) Mentalism.

Biss, James, *Mind Blowing: Second Thoughts on Messing with Minds.* Second edition. (2009) Wyllie Publishing, Hamilton, Canada. Perfect. Black. 352 pp. 6 x 9 in. (Information not verified by physical copy.) Mentalism.

Bjorklund, Harry C., *Comic Trick Cartoons.* Second printing. (1937) Author, Minneapolis. Saddle-stitch. Yellow. 25 pp. 5.5 x 8.25 in. Chalk talk, Cartoons, Art.

Bjorklund, Harry C., *Comic Trick Cartoons.* (c. 1973) Magic Inc., Chicago. Saddle-stitch. Orange. 31 pp. 5.5 x 8.5 in. Bound reprints of five booklets. Chalk talk, Cartoons, Art.

Bjorklund, Harry C., *Comic Trick Cartoons collection.* (c. 1973) Magic Inc., Chicago. Comb. Orange. Multiple sections. 5.25 x 8.5 in. Bound reprints of five booklets. Chalk talk, Cartoons, Art.

Bjorklund, Harry C., *Chalk "Talkies."* (1929) Author, Minneapolis. Saddle-stitch. Orange. 31 pp. 5.5 x 8.25 in. Chalk talk, Cartoons, Art.

Bjorklund, Harry C., *Chalk "Talkies."* (c. 1973) Magic Inc., Chicago. Saddle-stitch. Blue. 31 pp. 5.5 x 8.5 in. Reprint. Chalk talk, Cartoons, Art.

Bjorklund, Harry C., *Comic Trick Cartoons: Book 2.* (1942) Author, Minneapolis. Saddle-stitch. Tan, black. 32 pp. 5.5 x 8.5 in. Chalk talk, Cartoons, Art.

Bjorklund, Harry C., *Doodle-Art.* (1952) Author, Minneapolis. Saddle-stitch. Orange. 28 pp. 5.5 x 8.5 in. (Measurements and other information have been recorded as accurately as possible.) Chalk talk, Cartoons, Art.

Bjorklund, Harry C., *Doodle-Art.* (1974) Magic Inc., Chicago. Saddle-stitch. Green. 28 pp. 5.5 x 8.5 in. (Measurements and other information have been recorded as accurately as possible.) Chalk talk, Cartoons, Art.

Bjorklund, Harry C., *Fun for All!* (c. 1973) Magic Inc., Chicago. Saddle-stitch. Pink. 32 pp. 5.25 x 8.5 in. Chalk talk, Stunts, Beginner.

Bjorklund, Harry C., *Peppy Picture Stunts for the Chalk Talker.* (1924) Author, Minneapolis. Saddle-stitch. Black. Cover text: Silver; 20 pp. 5.5 x 8.5 in. Chalk talk, Smoke pictures, Rag painting.

Bjorklund, Harry C., *Spell Down Cards.* (1937) Author, Minneapolis. Stapled. White. 2 pp. 8.5 x 14 in. Mimeographed. With author's illustrations. Cards.

Bjorklund, Harry C., *Trickartoons: Book 3.* (1946) Author, Minneapolis. Saddle-stitch. Green. 32 pp. 5.5 x 8.5 in. Chalk talk, Cartoons, Art.

Bjorklund, Harry C., *Trickartoons: Book 3.* (1973) Magic Inc., Chicago. Saddle-stitch. Green. 32 pp. 5.5 x 8.5 in. Chalk talk, Cartoons, Art.

Black Herman, *Secrets of Magic, Mystery, and Legerdemain.* Fifteenth edition. (1938) Dorene Publishing, Dallas, TX. Saddle-stitch. Tan. 128 pp. 5.25 x 7.25 in. Biography, Dreams, Spells, Black magicians.

Black, Ishii, *Magic of Ishii Black, The.* (1992) Robinson Wizard, New York. Comb. Orange. 22 pp. 8.5 x 11 in. Asian magic, History.

Blacke, Thomas, *Little Blacke Book of Magic and Escapes, The.* (2003) Author, UK. Saddle-stitch. Black. 19 pp. 4.25 x 5.5 in. (Information not verified by physical copy.) Close-Up, Stage, Escapes.

Blacke, Thomas, *More Masonic Magic.* (2006) Author, UK. Saddle-stitch. 15 pp. 5.5 x 8.5 in. (Information not verified by physical copy.) Masonry, Bizarre magick.

Blackman, James R., *Big Book of Tricks and Magic, The.* (1962) Random House, New York. Casebound. Yellow. 55 pp. 8.25 x 11.25 in. Retitled edition of "The Jerry Lewis Book of Magic." Beginner, Children's book.

Blackman, James R., *Big Book of Tricks and Magic, The.* (1962) Random House, New York. Perfect. Yellow. 55 pp. 7.75 x 11 in. Retitled edition of "The Jerry Lewis Book of Magic." Beginner, Children's book.

Blackmore, Kent, *Alfred Silvester: The Fakir of Oolu and His Family of Magic.* (2024) Author, Sydney. Casebound. Dark blue. 299 pp. 8.5 x 12 in. Biography, History.

Blackmore, Kent, *Levante: His Life, No Illusion.* (1997) Mike Caveney's Magic Words, Pasadena, CA. Cloth. Green. 239 pp. 7 x 10.5 in. Dust jacket. #724 of 1000. Biography, History.

Blackmore, Kent, *Mentalism.* (1991) Author, Sydney. Stapled. 3 pp. 8.25 x 11.75 in. (Information not verified by physical copy.) See McCullagh, "Under the Southern Cross." Lecture notes. Mentalism.

Blackmore, Kent, *Mentalism.* (1992) Author, Sydney. Stapled. 4 pp. 8.25 x 11.75 in. (Information not verified by physical copy.) See McCullagh, "Under the Southern Cross." Lecture notes. Mentalism.

Blackmore, Kent, *Oscar Eliason: The Original Dante the Great.* (1984) Author, Sydney. Saddle-stitch. Beige. 30 pp. 5.75 x 8.25 in. #99 of 150. Biography, History.

Blackmore, Kent, *Oscar Eliason: The Original Dante the Great.* Revised edition. (1987) Author, Sydney. Saddle-stitch. Beige. 32 pp. 5.75 x 8.25 in. (Information not verified by physical copy.) Biography, History.

Blackstone, Gay, *Around the House Magic.* (1987) Ideals Children's Books, Nashville, TN. Perfect. Black. 48 pp. 6.5 x 9.5 in. Beginner.

Blackstone, Gay, *Blackstone: A Magical Family 1885-2001.* (2001) Author, Redlands, CA. Comb. Blue. 68 pp. 8.5 x 11 in. History, Biography.

Blackstone, Gay, *Magical Century, A.* (2000) Author, Redlands, CA. Strip binding. Orange. 54 pp. 8.5 x 11 in. History, Biography.

Blackstone, Harry, Jr., with Reynolds, Charles and Regina, *Blackstone Book of Magic and Illusion, The.* (1985) Newmarket Press, New York. Cloth. Black. 230 pp. 8.5 x 11 in. Dust jacket. Signed by Charles Reynolds, Regina Reynolds. Biography, History.

Blackstone, Harry, Jr., with Reynolds, Charles and Regina, *Blackstone Book of Magic and Illusion, The.* (1985) Newmarket Press, New York. Cloth. Black. 230 pp. 8.5 x 11 in. Dust jacket. Signed by Harry Blackstone, Jr. and Gay Blackstone. Biography, History.

Blackstone, Harry, Jr., with Reynolds, Charles and Regina, *Blackstone Book of Magic and Illusion, The.* (1985) Newmarket Press, New York. Perfect. Black. 230 pp. 8.5 x 11 in. Biography, History.

Blackstone, Harry, Jr., with Kaufman, Richard, *Blackstone Traveling Magic Show Instructions.* (1988) Pressman Corp., New Brunswick, NJ. Saddle-stitch. White. 28 pp. 7 x 8.5 in. From "Blackstone Traveling Magic Show" set. Magic set manual, Beginner.

Blackstone, Harry, Jr., with Dennison, Milo, *Blackstone's Magic Adventures 1: The Case of the Mummy's Tomb.* (1985) TOR, New York. Perfect. Blue. 125 pp. 4.25 x 6.75 in. Fiction, Beginner.

Blackstone, Harry, Jr., with Dennison, Milo, *Blackstone's Magic Adventures 2: The Case of the Gentleman Ghost.* (1985) T.O.R., New York. Perfect. Purple. 123 pp. 4.25 x 6.75 in. Fiction, Beginner.

Blackstone, Harry, Jr., with Dennison, Milo, *Blackstone's Magic Adventures 3: The Case of the Phantom Treasure.* (1985) T.O.R., New York. Perfect. Green. 126 pp. 4.25 x 6.75 in. Fiction, Beginner.

Blackstone, Harry, Jr., with Dennison, Milo and Cantwell, Lois, *Blackstone's Magical Adventure no. 1: America's Secret King.* (1986) T.O.R., New York. Perfect. Yellow. 64 pp. 5.25 x 7.5 in. Fiction, Beginner.

Blackstone, Harry, Jr., with Dennison, Milo and Cantwell, Lois, *Blackstone's Magical Adventure no. 2: The Secrets of Stonehenge.* (1986) T.O.R., New York. Perfect. Orange. 64 pp. 5.25 x 7.5 in. Fiction, Beginner.

Blackstone, Harry, Jr., *Instructions for Blackstone Instant Magic!* (1981) Magic Magic Magic Unlimited, Mamaroneck, NY. Saddle-stitch. White. 18 pp. 5.5 x 8.5 in. Magic set manual.

Blackstone, Harry, Jr., *Magic World of Blackstone Secret Instruction Book, The.* (1983) Pressman Corp., New York. Saddle-stitch. White. 31 pp. 5.25 x 8.25 in. Magic set manual.

Blackstone, Harry, Jr., with Reynolds, Charles and Regina, *My Life as a Magician.* (1992) Pocket Books, New York. Perfect. Red. 124 pp. 5 x 7.5 in. Biography, Children's book.

Blackstone, Harry, Jr., with Behnke, Leo, *There's One Born Every Minute.* First printing. (February 1978) Jove, New York. Perfect. Beige. 159 pp. 4.25 x 7 in. Stunts, Bets.

Blackstone, Harry, Jr., with Behnke, Leo, *There's One Born Every Minute.* Second printing. (March 1978) Jove, New York. Perfect. Beige. 159 pp. 4.25 x 7 in. Stunts, Bets.

Blackstone, Harry, Jr., with Behnke, Leo, *There's One Born Every Minute.* Third printing. (1978) Jeremy B. Tarcher Inc., Los Angeles. Perfect. Yellow. 149 pp. 7.25 x 7 in. Bound oblong. Signed by Harry Blackstone, Jr. Stunts, Bets.

Blackstone, Harry, Sr., *200 Magic Tricks Anyone Can Do.* (1995) Wings Books, New York. Cloth. Yellow, blue. 212 pp. 5.75 x 8.5 in. Dust jacket. Beginner.

Blackstone, Harry, Sr., *Blackstone Dream Book.* (c. 1925) Author, Chicago. Saddle-stitch. White. 32 pp. 6 x 8.25 in. Dream guide, Souvenir book.

Blackstone, Harry, Sr., *Blackstone the Magic Detective Reveals Magic Tricks Everyone Can Do!* (1946) Blackstone Magic Enterprises, New York. Saddle-stitch. Red. 6 pp. 6 x 9 in. Beginner, Premium, Radio.

Blackstone, Harry, Sr., *Blackstone's Annual of 1929.* (1929) Cooper Printing Co., Philadelphia. Saddle-stitch. Yellow. 48 pp. 7 x 10 in. Two signatures by ghostwriter Walter B. Gibson, one to James C. Wobensmith, one decades later to Todd Karr. Signed by Walter B. Gibson. Beginner, Cards, Close-Up, Stage.

Blackstone, Harry, Sr., *Blackstone's Famous Rope Trick.* (1965) Hollywood Magic Shop, Hollywood, CA. Stapled. White. 7 pp. 8.5 x 11 in. Transcribed by Blackstone assistant Bill Chaudet. Rope, Escapes, Comedy, Stage.

Blackstone, Harry, Sr., *Blackstone's Magic: Every Trick Illustrated.* (1929) Jacobsen Publishing, New York. Perfect. Orange. 98 pp. 5.25 x 8 in. Beginner.

Blackstone, Harry, Sr., *Blackstone's Magic.* (1930) Shade Publishing Co., Philadelphia. Saddle-stitch. Color. 60 pp. 7.5 x 10.75 in. Signed by Harry Blackstone, Sr., Walter B. Gibson. Beginner.

Blackstone, Harry, Sr., *Blackstone's Modern Card Tricks.* (1932) George Sully and Co., New York. Cloth. Red. 204 pp. 5 x 7.5 in. Dust jacket. Cards, Beginner.

Blackstone, Harry, Sr., *Blackstone's Modern Card Tricks.* (1932) A. L. Burt and Co., New York. Cloth. Red. 204 pp. 5.25 x 8.25 in. Dust jacket. Signed by Harry Blackstone, Sr. Cards, Beginner.

Blackstone, Harry, Sr., *Blackstone's Modern Card Tricks.* (1958) Garden City Books, Garden City, NY. Cloth. Black. Cover text: Yellow; 164 pp. 5.5 x 8.5 in. Dust jacket. Listed price: $2.50. Cards, Beginner.

Blackstone, Harry, Sr., *Blackstone's Modern Card Tricks.* (1958) Doubleday, Garden City, NY. Cloth. Black. Cover text: Yellow; 164 pp. 5.5 x 8.5 in. Dust jacket. Listed price: $3.95. Cards, Beginner.

Blackstone, Harry, Sr., *Blackstone's Modern Card Tricks.* (n.d.) Doubleday, Garden City, NY. Cloth. Black. 164 pp. 5.75 x 8.5 in. Dust jacket. Photo of a ribbon around a deck on front cover of jacket. Listed price: $5.95. Cards, Beginner.

Blackstone, Harry, Sr., *Blackstone's Modern Card Tricks.* (1979) Wilshire Book Co., North Hollywood, CA. Perfect. Orange. 164 pp. 5.5 x 8.5 in. Listed price: $3. Cards, Beginner.

Blackstone, Harry, Sr., *Blackstone's Modern Card Tricks and Secrets of Magic.* (1941) Garden City Publishing Co., Garden City, NY. Cloth. Red. Cover text: Black; 263 pp. 5.5 x 8 in. Dust jacket. Beginner, Cards.

Blackstone, Harry, Sr., *Blackstone's Modern Card Tricks and Secrets of Magic.* (1941) Garden City Publishing Co., Garden City, NY. Cloth. Maroon. Cover text: Gold; 263 pp. 5.5 x 8 in. Beginner, Cards.

Blackstone, Harry, Sr., *Blackstone's Modern Card Tricks and Secrets of Magic.* (1941) Garden City Publishing Co., Garden City, NY. Cloth. Black. Cover text: Red; 263 pp. 5.5 x 8 in. Beginner, Cards.

Blackstone, Harry, Sr., *Blackstone's Modern Card Tricks and Secrets of Magic.* (1941) Garden City Publishing Co., Garden City, NY. Cloth. Salmon. Cover text: Black; 263 pp. 5.5 x 8 in. Dust jacket. Beginner, Cards.

Blackstone, Harry, Sr., *Blackstone's Modern Card Tricks and Secrets of Magic.* (1941) Garden City Publishing Co., Garden City, NY. Cloth. Brown. Cover text: Black; 301 pp. 5.25 x 8 in. Thin version. Beginner, Cards.

Blackstone, Harry, Sr., *Blackstone's Modern Card Tricks and Secrets of Magic.* (1941) Garden City Publishing Co., Garden City, NY. Cloth. Gray. Cover text: Black; 301 pp. 5.25 x 8 in. Pulp pages. Beginner, Cards.

Blackstone, Harry, Sr., *Blackstone's Modern Card Tricks and Secrets of Magic.* (1941) Garden City Publishing Co., Garden City, NY. Cloth. Maroon. Cover text: Gold; 301 pp. 5.25 x 8 in. Dust jacket. Beginner, Cards.

Blackstone, Harry, Sr., *Blackstone's Modern Card Tricks and Secrets of Magic.* (1941) Garden City Publishing Co., Garden City, NY. Cloth. Tan. Cover text: Black; 301 pp. 5.25 x 8 in. Dust jacket. Beginner, Cards.

Blackstone, Harry, Sr., *Blackstone's Secrets of Magic.* (1929) George Sully and Co., New York. Cloth. Brown. 265 pp. 5.5 x 8.25 in. Dust jacket. With check endorsed by Blackstone. Signed by Harry Blackstone, Sr. Beginner.

Blackstone, Harry, Sr., *Blackstone's Secrets of Magic.* Second printing. (1930) George Sully and Co., New York. Cloth. Brown. 265 pp. 5.5 x 8.25 in. Dust jacket. Signed by Harry Blackstone, Sr. Beginner.

Blackstone, Harry, Sr., *Blackstone's Secrets of Magic.* Third printing. (1932) George Sully and Co., New York. Cloth. Red. 265 pp. 5.25 x 7.5 in. Dust jacket. Beginner.

Blackstone, Harry, Sr., *Blackstone's Secrets of Magic.* Second edition. (n.d.) A. L. Burt, New York and Chicago. Cloth. Blue. 265 pp. 5.5 x 8 in. Dust jacket. Beginner.

Blackstone, Harry, Sr., *Blackstone's Secrets of Magic.* (1958) Doubleday, Garden City, NY. Cloth. Black. Cover text: Blue; 164 pp. 5.5 x 8.5 in. Dust jacket. Listed price: $2.50. Signed by Harry Blackstone, Sr. Beginner.

Blackstone, Harry, Sr., *Blackstone's Secrets of Magic.* (n.d.) Doubleday, Garden City, NY. Cloth. Black. Cover text: Blue; 164 pp. 5.5 x 8.5 in. Dust jacket. Listed price: $3.95. Beginner.

Blackstone, Harry, Sr., *Blackstone's Secrets of Magic.* (n.d.) Doubleday, Garden City, NY. Cloth. Black. Cover text: Blue; 164 pp. 5.5 x 8.5 in. Dust jacket. Listed price: $4.95. Beginner.

Blackstone, Harry, Sr., *Blackstone's Secrets of Magic.* New revised edition. (n.d.) Doubleday, Garden City, NY. Cloth. Black. 164 pp. 5.75 x 8.5 in. Dust jacket. Photo of a scarf in an egg on front cover of jacket. Listed price: $4.95. Beginner.

Blackstone, Harry, Sr., *Blackstone's Secrets of Magic.* (1974) Wilshire Book Co., North Hollywood, CA. Perfect. Black. 164 pp. 5.25 x 8.25 in. Listed price: $2. Beginner.

Blackstone, Harry, Sr., *Blackstone's Secrets of Magic.* (1975) Wilshire Book Co., North Hollywood, CA. Perfect. Black. 164 pp. 5.25 x 8.25 in. Listed price: $2. Beginner.

Blackstone, Harry, Sr., *Blackstone's Secrets of Magic.* (1977) Wilshire Book Co., North Hollywood, CA. Perfect. Black. 164 pp. 5.25 x 8.25 in. Listed price: $2. Beginner.

Blackstone, Harry, Sr., *Blackstone's Secrets of Magic.* (n.d.) Wilshire Book Co., North Hollywood, CA. Perfect. Black. 164 pp. 5.25 x 8.25 in. Listed price: $3. Beginner.

Blackstone, Harry, Sr., *Blackstone's Tricks Anyone Can Do.* (1948) PermaBooks, New York. Casebound. Black. 233 pp. 4.25 x 6.5 in. Beginner.

Blackstone, Harry, Sr., *Complete Magic Show.* (c. 1920) Author, Chicago. Saddle-stitch. White. 16 pp. 3.25 x 6.5 in. With rules of the Blackstone Junior Magicians (BJM). Beginner.

Blackstone, Harry, Sr., *Easy Magic for Everyone.* (c. 1920) Author, Chicago. Saddle-stitch. Blue, red, black. 16 pp. 5.5 x 8.5 in. Cover says "Blackstone's Secrets." Beginner, Impromptu, Close-Up.

Blackstone, Harry, Sr., *Easy Magic for Everyone.* (1920) Arthur P. Felsman, Chicago. Stapled. Blue. 16 pp. 5.75 x 8.75 in. Bound at top. Beginner, Impromptu, Close-Up.

Blackstone, Harry, Sr., *My Secrets of Magic.* (1947) Blackstone Magic Enterprises, New York. Saddle-stitch. Black. 32 pp. 4.5 x 6 in. Same as Blackstone's "Mysteries of Magic." Beginner, Souvenir book.

Blackstone, Harry, Sr., *Mysteries of Magic.* (c. 1947) Author, New York. Saddle-stitch. Black. 32 pp. 4.5 x 6 in. Address box has printed note from Blackstone. Beginner, Souvenir book.

Blackstone, Harry, Sr., *Mysteries of Magic.* (1947) Blackstone Magic Enterprises, New York. Saddle-stitch. Black. 32 pp. 4.5 x 6 in. Address says "Magic for Advertisers, Proskauer and Gibson." Beginner, Souvenir book.

Blackstone, Harry, Sr., *Mysteries of Magic.* (1947) Blackstone Magic Enterprises, New York. Saddle-stitch. Black. 32 pp. 4.5 x 6 in. Beginner, Souvenir book.

Blackwood, Dan, *Psychic Entertainer's Handbook of Professional Presentations, The.* (1984) Author, South Plainfield, NJ. Comb. Black. 62 pp. 8.5 x 11 in. Mentalism.

Blade, Alex, *Utopian Prediction and Other Mysteries.* (2008) Who's Magic Media. Saddle-stitch. Black. 28 pp. 5.5 x 8.5 in. (Information not verified by physical copy.) Mentalism.

Blaine, David, *Mysterious Stranger.* (2002) Villard, New York. Casebound. Black. 214 pp. 7.25 x 9.25 in. Inscribed "To Michele with peace." Signed by David Blaine. Biography, History.

Blaine, David, *Mysterious Stranger.* (2002) Channel 4, London. Cloth. Black. 214 pp. 7.75 x 9.5 in. Dust jacket. Biography, History.

Blaine, David, *Mysterious Stranger.* (2006) Villard, New York. Perfect. White. 212 pp. 7.25 x 9 in. Inscribed "To Brian the Great Inquisitor. Peace." Signed by David Blaine. Biography, History.

Blaisdell, Frank, *8-King Setup for the Mentalist.* (1982) Magic Limited, Oakland, CA. Saddle-stitch. Blue. 24 pp. 5.5 x 8.5 in. Mentalism, Prearranged deck.

Blaisdell, Frank, *Just Ropes: Rings and Ropes, Rope Escapes.* (1981) Magic Limited, Oakland, CA. Perfect. Red. Cover text: Silver; 95 pp. 6 x 9 in. Rope, Ring and rope, Escapes.

Blaisdell, Frank, *Magical Fun with Magic Squares.* (1978) Author, Watsonville, CA. Perfect. Beige. 85 pp. 8.5 x 10.75 in. Magic squares, Mathematical magic.

Blaisdell, Frank, *More of Magic.* (1980) Magic Limited, Oakland, CA. Cloth. Gray. 97 pp. 8.25 x 9.25 in. Stage, Close-Up, Cards, Mentalism.

Blaisdell, Frank, *Naughty Not Knots.* Revised edition. (1959) Author, Watsonville, CA. Stapled with tape. Beige. 22 pp. 8.75 x 11.25 in. Purple ditto ink, file folder-like cover. Hand-colored cover art. String, Rings, Close-Up, Bibliography.

Blake, Anthony, *Lecture: Meeting of the Minds.* (2013) Author, Madrid. Stapled. Black. 8.5 x 11 in. (Information not verified by physical copy.) Lecture notes. Mentalism.

Blake, George, *Comedy Magic.* (1966) Author, Leeds, UK. Stapled with tape. Orange. 54 pp. 8.5 x 11 in. Mimeographed. Comedy, Stage, Cards.

Blake, George, *Comedy Magic.* (1974) Micky Hades, Calgary, Canada. Stapled with tape. Blue. 56 pp. 8.5 x 11 in. Mimeographed. Comedy, Stage, Cards.

Blake, George, *Commercial Card Magic.* (1972) Micky Hades, Calgary, Canada. Comb. Blue. 47 pp. 8.5 x 11 in. Cards.

Blake, George, *Devil Divination.* (1959) Supreme Magic, Bideford, UK. Saddle-stitch. White, black. 6 pp. 7.75 x 9.75 in. Mimeographed. Cards.

Blake, George, *Dream Poker.* (2007) Colombini Magic, Tampa, FL. Saddle-stitch. Blue. 12 pp. 5.5 x 8.5 in. (Information not verified by physical copy.) Cards, Poker.

Blake, George, *Fairy-Light (The Tantalising Tapers).* (1955) Author, Leeds, UK. Single page. White. 8 x 10 in. Mimeographed. Candles, Stage, Instruction sheet.

Blake, George, *Forgotten Magic.* Second edition. (1972) Micky Hades, Calgary, Canada. Stapled with tape. Green. 56 pp. 8.5 x 11 in. Mimeographed. Stage, Close-Up, Comedy, Stunts.

Blake, George, *Loopy Loop.* (1972) Micky Hades, Calgary, Canada. Stapled with tape. Yellow. 23 pp. 8.5 x 11 in. Mimeographed. Con games, Endless chain.

Blake, George, *Major Magic.* (1968) Author, Leeds, UK. Stapled with tape. Orange. 55 pp. 8.5 x 11 in. Mimeographed. Comedy, Stage, Cards.

Blake, George, *Master Magic.* (1961) Author, Leeds, UK. Stapled with tape. Green. 30 pp. 8 x 10 in. Mimeographed. Stage.

Blake, George, *Master Magic.* (1961) Author, Leeds, UK. Stapled with tape. Orange. 32 pp. 8 x 10 in. Mimeographed. Stage.

Blake, George, *Master Magic.* Second edition. (1975) Micky Hades, Calgary, Canada. Stapled with tape. Yellow. 41 pp. 8.5 x 11 in. Stage.

Blake, George, *More Master Magic.* Second edition. (1975) Micky Hades, Calgary, Canada. Stapled with tape. Yellow. 77 pp. 8.5 x 11 in. Stage.

Blake, George, *Perfected Five Card Trick, The.* (1980) Supreme Magic, Bideford, UK. Saddle-stitch. White. 12 pp. 7.5 x 9.75 in. Cards.

Blake, George, *Set-Up Reset, A.* (1980) Supreme Magic, Bideford, UK. Saddle-stitch. White, blue. 12 pp. 7.25 x 9.75 in. Cards, Eight Kings, Prearranged deck.

Blake, George, *Take a Note.* (1975) Micky Hades, Calgary, Canada. Stapled with tape. Blue. 53 pp. 8.5 x 11 in. (Measurements and other information have been recorded as accurately as possible.) Bills.

Blake, George, *Wun-Dek.* (2007) Author, Leeds, UK. 5 pp. Mimeographed. (Information not verified by physical copy.) Cards.

Blake, John, *3 Ring Routine, A.* (1997) Louis Tannen, New York. Saddle-stitch. Blue. 32 pp. 4.25 x 7.5 in. Linking Rings.

Blanche, Abel, *Tireurs de Music-Hall, Les.* (1927) H. Billy, Paris. Saddle-stitch. Light blue. 32 pp. 4.5 x 7 in. Bullet Catch, Stage. French.

Blanco, Allec, *Glimpse into My Mind: Discoveries and Thoughts.* (2015) Author, Cairo, NY. Stapled. White. 14 pp. 8.5 x 11 in. (Information not verified by physical copy.) Cards.

Bland, Joseph, *Illustrated Catalog of Extraordinary and Superior Conjuring Tricks.* (1982) Volker Huber, Offenbach, Germany. Boards. Blue. 144 pp. 6 x 9.75 in. No. 3 of Huber reprint series. Limited to 250 copies. Catalog reprint.

Blankenship, Bryan D., *Van Doren's Guide to Successful Magic Camps.* (2006) Author, Summerville, SC. Coil. Yellow. 72 pp. 5.5 x 8.5 in. (Information not verified by physical copy.) Business, Children's magic, Camp shows.

Blantz, Father James, *Lecture Notes.* (1967) Author, South Bend, IN. Stapled. White. 6 pp. 8.5 x 11 in. Mimeographed. Lecture notes. Cards, Close-Up, Stage.

Blass-Tchang, Primo, *De Si-phering Mysteries.* Second edition. (1998) Author, Cuernavaca, Mexico. Comb. Black. Cover text: Gold; 26 pp. 8.75 x 11.5 in. Plastic cover. Lecture notes. Cards, Mentalism.

Blau, Ben, *Asymptotes.* (2015) AMS Books, Nanaimo, Canada. Cloth. Black. 339 pp. 6.5 x 9.5 in. Dust jacket. Mentalism, Cards.

Blau, Ben, *Good Heads.* (2004) Author, Royal Oak, MI. Stapled. (Information not verified by physical copy. Bibliographical details are as accurate as possible.) Mentalism.

Blau, Ben, *Ten-Card Poker Deal.* (2005) Author, Royal Oak, MI. Stapled. Dust jacket. (Information not verified by physical copy. Bibliographical details are as accurate as possible.) Mentalism, Cards.

Blau, Ben, *Truth Fables.* (2018) AMS Books, Nanaimo, Canada. Cloth. Black. 498 pp. 6 x 9 in. Dust jacket. (Information not verified by physical copy. Bibliographical details are as accurate as possible.) Mentalism.

Blau, Bob, *Bob Blau's World of Magic and the Secret of the Spirit Cabinet.* (1985) Author, Houston, TX. Comb. Red, black, white. 53 pp. 8.5 x 11 in. (Information not verified by physical copy.) Close-Up, Stage, Spirit Cabinet.

Blau, Bob, *Spirits on the Stage.* (1994) Author, Houston, TX. Coil. 30 pp. (Information not verified by physical copy.) Bizarre magick, Spirit effects.

Blei, Felix, *Hindu Rope Trick, The.* (n.d.) Author, Cincinnati, OH. Stapled. White. 3 pp. 8.5 x 11 in. (Information not verified by physical copy.) History, Indian magic, Indian Rope Trick.

Blevins, David, *Invisible Thread Reel: A How-To Guide 4 Everyone.* (2000) Magic City, Paramount, CA. Saddle-stitch. Yellow. 24 pp. 5.5 x 8.5 in. Gimmicks, Thread, Reels.

Blind, Adolphe (See also Clarke, Sidney W.), *Automates Truqués, Les.* (1927) Eggiman and Bossard, Geneva and Paris. Perfect. Beige. 80 pp. 7 x 10 in. With sheet for Le Monde des Automates. History, Automata. French.

Blismon, Ana-Gramme (Simon Blocquel), *Mille et Un Amusements de Société.* (1850) Delarue, Paris. Leather. Red. 397 pp. 3.75 x 5.75 in. Beginner, Cards. French.

Blismon, Ana-Gramme (Simon Blocquel), *Mille et Un Amusements de Société.* (1850) Delarue, Paris. Perfect. Beige. 397 pp. 4 x 6 in. Beginner, Cards. French.

Blismon, Ana-Gramme (Simon Blocquel), *Mille et Un Tours.* (c. 1856) Delarue, Paris. Perfect. Green. 349 pp. 4 x 6 in. Beginner, Cards. French.

Blitz, François R., *Blitz's Book of Magic.* (1870) Hurst and Co., New York. 30 pp. 4.75 x 7.5 in. (Information not verified by physical copy.) Toole Stott no. 943. Beginner, Fire-eating.

Blitz, François R., *Blitz's Book of Magic and Songs.* (c. 1880) New York Popular Publishing, New York. Saddle-stitch. Color. 16 pp. 4.75 x 7.5 in. Cover says "Blitz's Magic Song Book." Toole Stott no. 944. In Copperfield collection. Beginner, Fire-eating.

Blitz, Signor Antonio (Professor Blitz), *Boy's Own Book of Indoor and Outdoor Sports, The.* (c. 1874) Hurst and Co., New York. Cloth. Red. Multiple sections. 5.25 x 7.5 in. Beginner, Stunts.

Blitz, Signor Antonio (Professor Blitz), *Boys' Own Book of Indoor Sports and Choice Parlor Games, The.* Arlington Edition. (c. 1874) Hurst and Co., New York. Cloth. Brown. Multiple sections. 5 x 7.5 in. Spine says "Boys' Own Book of Indoor Sports." Square floral design on cover. Includes four books. Toole Stott 942. Beginner, Stunts.

Blitz, Signor Antonio (Professor Blitz), *Boys' Own Book of Indoor Sports and Choice Parlor Games, The.* Arlington Edition. (c. 1874) Hurst and Co., New York. Cloth. Brown. Multiple sections. 5 x 7.5 in. Spine says "Indoor Sports." Square floral design on cover. Includes four books. Toole Stott 942. Beginner, Stunts.

Blitz, Signor Antonio (Professor Blitz), *Boys' Own Book of Indoor Sports and Choice Parlor Games, The.* Arlington Edition. (c. 1874) Hurst and Co., New York. Cloth. Gray. Multiple sections. 5 x 7.5 in. Spine says "Indoor Sports." Square floral design on cover. Includes four books. Toole Stott 942. Beginner, Cards, Coins, Stage.

Blitz, Signor Antonio (Professor Blitz), *Boys' Own Book of Indoor Sports and Choice Parlor Games, The.* Arlington Edition. (c. 1874) Hurst and Co., New York. Cloth. Red. Multiple sections. 5 x 7.5 in. Spine says "Indoor Sports." Square floral design on cover. Includes four books. Toole Stott 942. Beginner, Ventriloquism.

Blitz, Signor Antonio (Professor Blitz), *Boys' Own Book of Indoor Sports and Choice Parlor Games, The.* Arlington Edition. (c. 1874) Hurst and Co., New York. Cloth. Blue. Multiple sections. 5 x 7.5 in. Spine says "Indoor Sports." Angled torch on cover. Includes four books. Toole Stott 942. Beginner, Ventriloquism.

Blitz, Signor Antonio (Professor Blitz), *Boys' Own Book of Indoor Sports and Choice Parlor Games, The.* Arlington Edition. (c. 1874) Hurst and Co., New York. Cloth. Dark green. Multiple sections. 5 x 7.5 in. Spine says "Indoor Sports." Angled torch on cover. Includes four books. Toole Stott 942. Beginner, Ventriloquism.

Blitz, Signor Antonio (Professor Blitz), *Boys' Own Book of Indoor Sports and Choice Parlor Games, The.* Arlington Edition. (c. 1874) Hurst and Co., New York. Cloth. Maroon. Multiple sections. 5 x 7.5 in. Spine says "Indoor Sports." Angled torch on cover. Includes four books. Toole Stott 942. Beginner, Ventriloquism.

Blitz, Signor Antonio (Professor Blitz), *Boys' Own Book of Indoor Sports and Choice Parlor Games, The.* Arlington Edition. (c. 1874) Hurst and Co., New York. Cloth. Green. Multiple sections. 5 x 7.25 in. Spine says "Boys Indoor Sports." Winged horse head on cover. Includes three books. Toole Stott 942. Beginner, Ventriloquism.

Blitz, Signor Antonio (Professor Blitz), *Boys' Own Book of Indoor Sports and Choice Parlor Games, The.* Arlington Edition. (c. 1874) Hurst and Co., New York. Cloth. Gray. Multiple sections. 5 x 7.5 in. Later edition of Toole Stott 942. Square floral design on cover. Includes four books. Beginner, Ventriloquism.

Blitz, Signor Antonio (Professor Blitz), *Every Body a Ventriloquist.* (1854) Herald Book and Job Printing Establishments, New York. 32 pp. 4.75 x 7.25 in. (Information not verified by physical copy.) Toole Stott no. 97. Ventriloquism.

Blitz, Signor Antonio (Professor Blitz), *Every Body a Ventriloquist.* (1856) Brown's Steam-Power and Job Printing Establishment, Philadelphia. 32 pp. 5 x 7.75 in. (Information not verified by physical copy.) Toole Stott nos. 98, 1044. Ventriloquism.

Blitz, Signor Antonio (Professor Blitz), *Fifty Years in the Magic Circle.* (1871) Belknap and Bliss, Hartford, CN. Cloth. Green. Cover text: Gold; 432 pp. 5.25 x 8.25 in. Toole Stott no. 100. Biography.

Blitz, Signor Antonio (Professor Blitz), *Fifty Years in the Magic Circle.* (1871) Belknap and Bliss, Hartford, CN. Cloth. Brown. Cover text: Gold; 432 pp. 5.25 x 8.25 in. Toole Stott no. 100. Biography.

Blitz, Signor Antonio (Professor Blitz), *Fifty Years in the Magic Circle.* (1872) Belknap and Bliss, Hartford, CN. Cloth. Green. Cover text: Gold; 432 pp. 5.5 x 8.25 in. Toole Stott no. 100. Biography.

Blitz, Signor Antonio (Professor Blitz), *Fifty Years in the Magic Circle.* (1871) A. L. Bancroft, San Francisco. Cloth. Brown. Cover text: Gold; 432 pp. 5.25 x 8.25 in. Toole Stott no. 99. Biography.

Blitz, Signor Antonio (Professor Blitz), *Fifty Years in the Magic Circle.* (1871) A. L. Bancroft, San Francisco. Cloth. Green. Cover text: Gold; 432 pp. 5.5 x 8.25 in. Toole Stott no. 99. Biography.

Blitz, Signor Antonio (Professor Blitz), *Indoor Sports and Choice Parlor Games.* (c. 1870) Hurst and Co., New York. Multiple sections. 4.75 x 7.5 in. (Information not verified by physical copy.) Toole Stott no. 941. Beginner, Ventriloquism, Cards.

Blitz, Signor Antonio (Professor Blitz), *Parlor Book of Magic, The.* (1889) Hurst and Co., New York. Cloth. Blue. Multiple sections. 5 x 7.5 in. George Washington on cover. With three books: Prof. Raymond, "Parlor Pastimes," 96 pp.; Gilbert's Book of Pantomimes (1878), 120 pp.; Lorento's Wizard's Guide, 30 pp. Beginner.

Blitz, Signor Antonio (Professor Blitz), *Parlor Book of Magic, The.* (1889) Hurst and Co., New York. Cloth. Green. Multiple sections. 5 x 7.5 in. George Washington on cover. With three books: Prof. Raymond, "Parlor Pastimes," 96 pp.; Gilbert's Book of Pantomimes (1878), 120 pp.; Lorento's Wizard's Guide, 30 pp. Beginner.

Blitz, Signor Antonio (Professor Blitz), *Parlor Book of Magic, The.* Arlington Edition. (1889) Hurst and Co., New York. Cloth. Red. Multiple sections. 5 x 7.5 in. George Washington on cover. With three books: Prof. Raymond, "Parlor Pastimes," 96 pp.; Gilbert's Book of Pantomimes (1878), 120 pp.; Lorento's Wizard's Guide, 30 pp. Beginner.

Blitz, Signor Antonio (Professor Blitz), *Parlor Book of Magic, The.* Arlington Edition. (1889) Hurst and Co., New York. Cloth. Light blue. Multiple sections. 5 x 7.5 in. Torch on cover. Includes two books: "Snip, Snap, Snorum," 117 pp.; Prof. Raymond, "Parlor Pastimes" (1875, Toole Stott 593) 96 pp. Beginner.

Blitz, Signor Antonio (Professor Blitz), *Parlor Book of Magic, The.* Arlington Edition. (1889) Hurst and Co., New York. Cloth. Gray. Multiple sections. 5 x 7.5 in. Winged horse head on cover. With two books: "Snip, Snap, Snorum," 117 pp.; Prof. Raymond, "Parlor Pastimes" (1875) 96 pp. Beginner.

Blitz, Signor Antonio (Professor Blitz), *Parlor Book of Magic, The.* Arlington Edition. (1889) Hurst and Co., New York. Cloth. Red. Multiple sections. 5 x 7.25 in. Winged horse head on cover. With two books: "Snip, Snap, Snorum," 117 pp.; Prof. Raymond, "Parlor Pastimes" (1875, Toole Stott 593) 96 pp. Beginner.

Blitz, Signor Antonio (Professor Blitz), *Parlor Book of Magic, The.* Arlington Edition. (1889) Hurst and Co., New York. Cloth. Tan. Multiple sections. 5 x 7.5 in. Winged horse head on cover. With two books: "Snip, Snap, Snorum," 117 pp.; Prof. Raymond, "Parlor Pastimes" (1875) 96 pp. Beginner.

Blitz, Signor Antonio (Professor Blitz), *Vagaries of a Ventriloquist, The.* (1851) United States Steam Power Book and Job Printing Office, Philadelphia. 24 pp. 4.5 x 7.25 in. (Information not verified by physical copy.) Toole Stott no. 96. Ventriloquism.

Bloch, Rich, *I Hate Rope Tricks.* (2008) Author, Washington D.C. Perfect. Black. 113 pp. 8.5 x 11 in. Signed by Rich Bloch. Emcee, Comedy, Showmanship, Stage.

Bloch, Rich, *Some Thoughts on Magic.* (c. 1996) Author, Washington D.C. Saddle-stitch. Black. 48 pp. 8.5 x 11 in. Close-Up, Cards, Mentalism.

Bloch, Rich, *These Are a Few of My Favorite Things.* (1985) Collectors Workshop, Washington D.C. Saddle-stitch. White, blue. 29 pp. 5.5 x 8.25 in. Close-Up, Stage, Mentalism, Cards.

Block, Dan, *Blockbusters: The Magic of Dan Block.* (1996) Kee-West Productions, Key West, FL. Comb. Gray. 52 pp. 5.5 x 8.5 in. (Information not verified by physical copy.) Cards, Close-Up.

Blocquel, Simon-François, *Manuel de l'Amateur des Tours de Cartes.* (1866) Hachette, Paris. Perfect. Brown. 82 pp. 6 x 9.25 in. Reprint of 1864 edition. Cards. French.

Bloom, Gaëtan, *Bloom.* (n.d.) Author, St. Ouen, France. Saddle-stitch. White. 16 pp. 6 x 8.25 in. Lecture notes. Stage, Close-Up, Comedy, Inventions. French.

Bloom, Gaëtan, *Bloomeries.* (1999) Mayette, Paris. Perfect. Black. 152 pp. 6.25 x 9.5 in. Stage, Close-Up, Comedy, Inventions. French.

Bloom, Gaëtan, *Boite à Idées.* (1999) Author, St. Ouen, France. Comb. Orange. 24 pp. 8.25 x 11.75 in. Lecture notes. Stage, Close-Up, Comedy, Inventions. French.

Bloom, Gaëtan, *Bonneteau Escorial.* (1987) Author, St. Ouen, France. Stapled. White. 9 pp. 8.5 x 11 in. Cards, Three-Card Monte. French.

Bloom, Gaëtan, *F.I.S.M. 2006.* (2006) Author, St. Ouen, France. Comb. Orange. 23 pp. 8.25 x 11.75 in. Lecture notes. Stage, Close-Up, Comedy, Inventions. French.

Bloom, Gaëtan, *Full Bloom vol. 1.* (2013) The Miracle Factory, Los Angeles. Cloth. Black. 400 pp. 8.25 x 11.25 in. Dust jacket. Biography, Stage, Close-Up, Inventions.

Bloom, Gaëtan, *Full Bloom vol. 2.* (2013) The Miracle Factory, Los Angeles. Cloth. Black. 336 pp. 8.25 x 11.25 in. Dust jacket. Biography, Stage, Close-Up, Inventions.

Bloom, Gaëtan, *Gaëtan Bloom.* (1987) Académie de Magie Georges Proust, Paris. Stapled. Pink. 30 pp. 8.25 x 11.75 in. Lecture notes. Stage, Close-Up, Comedy, Inventions. French.

Bloom, Gaëtan, *Gaëtan Bloom.* (n.d.) Author, St. Ouen, France. Comb. Orange. 18 pp. 8.25 x 11.75 in. Lecture notes. Stage, Close-Up, Comedy, Inventions. French.

Bloom, Gaëtan, *Gaëtan Bloom.* (2004) Author, St. Ouen, France. Comb. Yellow. 34 pp. 8.25 x 11.75 in. Lecture notes. Stage, Close-Up, Comedy, Inventions. French.

Bloom, Gaëtan, *Gaëtan Bloom 86.* (1986) Jeff Busby Magic, Oakland, CA. Comb. Blue. 36 pp. 8.5 x 11 in. Lecture notes. Stage, Close-Up, Comedy, Inventions.

Bloom, Gaëtan, *Gaëtan Bloom 1999.* (1999) Author, St. Ouen, France. Comb. Yellow. 18 pp. 8.25 x 11.75 in. Lecture notes. Stage, Close-Up, Comedy, Inventions. French.

Bloom, Gaëtan, *Gaëtan Bloom Lecture Notes: Las Vegas – March 1981.* (1981) Ace Place Publications, London. Stapled. White. 10 pp. 8.25 x 11.75 in. Lecture notes. Stage, Close-Up, Comedy, Inventions.

Bloom, Gaëtan, *Gaëtan Bloom Lecture Notes: New Orleans July 1982.* (1982) Ace Place Publications, London. Saddle-stitch. White. 14 pp. 8.25 x 11.75 in. Signed by Gaëtan Bloom. Lecture notes. Stage, Close-Up, Comedy, Inventions.

Bloom, Gaëtan, *Gaëtan Bloom Series no. 1.* (1982) Ace Place Publications, London. Saddle-stitch. Yellow. 12 pp. 8.25 x 11.75 in. Signed by Gaëtan Bloom. Stage, Close-Up, Comedy, Inventions.

Bloom, Gaëtan, *Gaëtan Bloom Series no. 2.* (1982) Ace Place Publications, London. Saddle-stitch. Beige. 14 pp. 8.25 x 10.75 in. Signed by Gaëtan Bloom. Stage, Close-Up, Comedy, Inventions.

Bloom, Gaëtan, *Gaëtan Bloom Series no. 3: Potty Bicycle Pumps.* (1982) Ace Place Publications, London. Saddle-stitch. Light blue. 10 pp. 8.25 x 10.75 in. Stage, Chinese Sticks, Comedy, Inventions.

Bloom, Gaëtan, *Gaëtan Bloom's Potty Bicycle Pumps.* (1982) Ace Place Publications, London. Stapled. Pink. 10 pp. 8.25 x 11.75 in. Signed by Gaëtan Bloom. Stage, Chinese Sticks, Comedy, Inventions.

Bloom, Gaëtan, *Gaëtan Bloom's Visible Monte.* (1986) Jeff Busby Magic, Oakland, CA. Saddle-stitch. Gray. 30 pp. 5.5 x 8.5 in. Includes cards. Cards, Gimmicks, Three-Card Monte.

Bloom, Gaëtan, *Gaëtan Bloom's Zig-Zag Card Trick.* (c. 1981) Ace Place Publications, London. Stapled. Beige. 2 pp. 8.25 x 11.25 in. Includes cards. Cards, Gimmicks, Inventions.

Bloom, Gaëtan, *Geschichten vom Planeten Bloom.* (2002) Author, Paris. Saddle-stitch. Gray. 24 pp. 8.25 x 11.75 in. German. Lecture notes. Stage, Close-Up, Inventions. German.

Bloom, Gaëtan, *Ideas.* (2002) Author, St. Ouen, France. Comb. Color. 23 pp. 8.5 x 11 in. Lecture notes. Stage, Close-Up, Comedy, Inventions.

Bloom, Gaëtan, *Intercessor, The.* (1999) Imagination Unlimited, Las Vegas. Saddle-stitch. Blue. 24 pp. 5.25 x 8.25 in. Gimmicks, Cards, Inventions.

Bloom, Gaëtan, *Methods, Effects, Ideas with the Ultimate Transparent Change Bag.* (1995) Jeff Busby Magic, Oakland, CA. Stapled. White. 4 pp. 8.5 x 11 in. Change Bag, Gimmicks, Inventions.

Blum, Raymond, *Mathemagic.* (1992) Sterling Publishing, New York. Perfect. Purple. 128 pp. 5.25 x 8.25 in. Mathematical, Children's book.

Blunt, John, *Transcornered.* (1974) Supreme Magic, Bideford, UK. Saddle-stitch. Black, white. 8 pp. 7.75 x 9.75 in. Cards.

Blyth, Will, *Effective Conjuring.* (1928) Methuen and Co., London. Cloth. Blue. 224 pp. 5 x 7.5 in. (Measurements and other information have been recorded as accurately as possible.) Beginner.

Blyth, Will, *Effective Conjuring.* Third edition. (1934) Methuen and Co., London. Cloth. Dark gray. 224 pp. 5 x 7.5 in. Beginner.

Blyth, Will, *Effective Conjuring.* Third edition. (1934) Methuen and Co., London. Cloth. Gray. 224 pp. 5 x 7.5 in. Dust jacket. Beginner.

Blyth, Will, *Handkerchief Magic.* (1922) C. Arthur Pearson Ltd., London. Boards. Yellow. 123 pp. 5 x 7.25 in. Introduction by Clive Maskelyne. Handkerchiefs, Silks.

Blyth, Will, *How to Become a Conjuror.* (1934) Methuen and Co., London. Cloth. Gray. 183 pp. 5 x 7.5 in. Dust jacket. Beginner.

Blyth, Will, *How to Become a Conjuror.* (1934) Methuen and Co., London. Cloth. Orange. 183 pp. 5 x 7.5 in. Dust jacket. Beginner.

Blyth, Will, *Impromptu Conjuring.* (1924) C. Arthur Pearson Ltd., London. Boards. Yellow. 122 pp. 5 x 7.25 in. Stunts, Impromptu.

Blyth, Will, *Match-Stick Magic.* (1921) C. Arthur Pearson Ltd., London. Boards. Yellow. 124 pp. 5 x 7.25 in. Introduction by David Devant (Information not verified by physical copy.) Matches, Stunts.

Blyth, Will, *Match-Stick Magic.* Second printing. (1923) C. Arthur Pearson Ltd., London. Boards. Yellow. 124 pp. 5 x 7.25 in. Matches, Stunts.

Blyth, Will, *Match-Stick Magic.* (1939) C. Arthur Pearson Ltd., London. Perfect. White, red, black. 124 pp. 5 x 7.25 in. Matches, Stunts.

Blyth, Will, *Misdirection.* (1936) Author, London. Stapled. White. 12 pp. 8.5 x 11 in. (Information not verified by physical copy.) Lecture notes. Theory, Misdirection.

Blyth, Will, *Money Magic.* (1926) C. Arthur Pearson Ltd., London. Boards. Yellow. 122 pp. 5 x 7.25 in. Introduction by Percy Naldrett. Coins.

Blyth, Will, *Money Magic.* (1926) C. Arthur Pearson Ltd., London. Perfect. White, blue, red. 120 pp. 5 x 7.25 in. Introduction by Percy Naldrett. Coins.

Blyth, Will, *More Paper Magic.* (1923) C. Arthur Pearson Ltd., London. Boards. Yellow. 124 pp. 5 x 7.25 in. Introduction by Nevil Maskelyne. Paper.

Blyth, Will, *Paper Magic.* (1920) C. Arthur Pearson Ltd., London. Boards. Yellow. 99 pp. 5 x 7.25 in. Introduction by Nevil Maskelyne. Paper.

Boardé, C. L., *Borrowed Brain, The.* (1946) Author, New York. Saddle-stitch. White. 12 pp. 5.5 x 8.5 in. In printed envelope. Mentalism.

Boardé, C. L., *Mainly Mental vol. 1: Billet Reading.* (1947) Author, New York. Comb. Black. 98 pp. 7.25 x 9.5 in. Mentalism, Billets.

Boardé, C. L., *Mainly Mental vol. 2: Book Tests.* (1950) Author, New York. Coil. Yellow. 135 pp. 6.25 x 9 in. Mentalism, Book tests.

Boardé, C. L., *Mainly Mental vol. 2: Book Tests.* Reprint. (n.d.) Magico, New York. Cloth. Blue. 135 pp. 6.25 x 9.25 in. Mentalism, Book tests.

Boardé, C. L., *Mainly Mental vol. 3: One-Man Routines.* (1999) Barry H. Wiley, Tacoma, WA. Comb. Yellow. 145 pp. 8.5 x 11 in. Revised version of "The Borrowed Brain." Mentalism.

Boardé, C. L., *One-on-One Mentalism.* (1997) Jack Dean's Stagecraft, Memphis, TN. Comb. Blue. 106 pp. 8.5 x 11 in. Mentalism.

Boaz, Sieur H., *Juggler's Oracle, or The Whole Art of Legerdemain Laid Open.* (1826) William Cole, London. 84 pp. 3.25 x 5.25 in. (Information not verified by physical copy.) Toole Stott no. 101. Beginner, Early magic.

Bobo, J. B., *Bobo Lecture, The.* (c. 1955) Author, Texarkana, TX. Stapled. White. 11 pp. 8.5 x 11 in. Signed by J. B. Bobo. Lecture notes. Cards, Coins, Stage.

Bobo, J. B., *Bobo Lecture, The.* (1964) Ireland Magic Co., Chicago. Stapled. White. 9 pp. 8.5 x 11 in. Folded. Lecture notes. Children's magic, Coins, Close-Up, Stage.

Bobo, J. B., *Bobo Lecture no. Two.* (1984) Author, Texarkana, TX. Stapled. Tan. 10 pp. 8.5 x 11 in. Mimeographed. Lecture notes. Stage, Coins, Close-Up, Children's magic.

Bobo, J. B., *Bobo Magic Show, The.* (1984) Magic Inc., Chicago. Cloth. Black. 189 pp. 8.5 x 11 in. Dust jacket. Children's magic.

Bobo, J. B., *Bobo Magic Show, The.* (1984) Magic Inc., Chicago. Comb. Beige. 189 pp. 8.5 x 11 in. (Measurements and other information have been recorded as accurately as possible.) Children's magic.

Bobo, J. B., *Magia con Monedas.* Second edition. (2008) Páginas Libros de Magia, Madrid. Casebound. Green, white. 574 pp. 7 x 9.75 in. Coins. Spanish.

Bobo, J. B., *Make Believe.* (1952) Author, Texarkana, TX. Single page. White. 5.5 x 8.5 in. Cards, Brainwave deck, Miniature cards. Spanish.

Bobo, J. B., *Modern Coin Magic.* (1952) Carl W. Jones, Minneapolis. Cloth. Beige. 358 pp. 7.25 x 9.75 in. Dust jacket. With original printed mailing box. Coins.

Bobo, J. B., *Modern Coin Magic.* (1952) Carl W. Jones, Minneapolis. Cloth. Beige. 358 pp. 7.25 x 9.75 in. Dust jacket. Signed by J. B. Bobo. Coins.

Bobo, J. B., *Modern Coin Magic.* Second impression. (1952) Carl W. Jones, Minneapolis. Cloth. Beige. 358 pp. 7.25 x 9.75 in. Dust jacket. Coins.

Bobo, J. B., *Modern Coin Magic.* (1982) Dover, New York. Perfect. Green. 358 pp. 5.5 x 8.25 in. (Measurements and other information have been recorded as accurately as possible.) Coins.

Bobo, J. B., *Modern Coin Magic.* (2004) New Dawn Press, UK. Perfect. Purple. 358 pp. 5.5 x 8.5 in. (Measurements and other information have been recorded as accurately as possible.) Coins.

Bobo, J. B., *Modern Coin Magic.* (2007) Houdini Magic, Las Vegas. Perfect. Red. 358 pp. 5.5 x 8.5 in. (Measurements and other information have been recorded as accurately as possible.) Coins.

Bobo, J. B., *Modern Coin Magic.* (2008) D. Robbins, Cranbury, NJ. Perfect. Black. 358 pp. 5.5 x 8.25 in. (Measurements and other information have been recorded as accurately as possible.) Coins.

Bobo, J. B., *Modern Miracles of Magic.* (1965) Author, Texarkana, TX. Stapled. White. 11 pp. 8.5 x 11 in. (Information not verified by physical copy.) Lecture notes.

Bobo, J. B., *New Modern Coin Magic, The.* Revised edition. (1966) Magic Inc., Chicago. Cloth. Blue. 519 pp. 7 x 9.75 in. Dust jacket. Signed by J. B. Bobo. Coins.

Bobo, J. B., *New Modern Coin Magic, The.* Second printing. (1972) Magic Inc., Chicago. Cloth. Blue. 519 pp. 7 x 9.75 in. Dust jacket. Coins.

Bobo, J. B., *Traité de Prestidigitation des Pièces de Monnaie.* (1956) Payot, Paris. Perfect. Beige. 514 pp. 5.5 x 9 in. Coins. French.

Bobo, J. B., *Watch This One!* (1947) Lloyd Jones, Oakland, CA. Cloth. Blue. 124 pp. 5.25 x 8 in. Coins, Cards, Close-Up.

Bodie, Dr. Walford, *Bodie Book, The.* (1905) Caxton Press, London. Cloth. Gray. 193 pp. 5 x 7.25 in. (Information not verified by physical copy.) Hypnotism.

Bodie, Dr. Walford, *Bodie Book, The.* (1907) Caxton Press, London. Perfect. Orange. 193 pp. 4.75 x 7 in. (Measurements and other information have been recorded as accurately as possible.) Hypnotism.

Bodley, Rev. Donald E., *Lessons in Scripture.* (1951) Abbott Magic Co., Colon, MI. Stapled. Beige. 24 pp. 8.5 x 11 in. Mimeographed. Gospel magic.

Bodley, Rev. Donald E., *More Lessons in Scripture.* (1954) Abbott Magic Co., Colon, MI. Stapled with tape. Olive. 28 pp. 8.5 x 11 in. Mimeographed. Gospel magic.

Bohlen, Henry, *Bohleno's Floating Handkerchief.* (1940) Author, London. Stapled. White. 3 pp. 8.5 x 11 in. Mimeographed. (Information not verified by physical copy.) Handkerchiefs, Levitations.

Bohlen, Henry, *Bohleno's Mysteries.* (1947) George Armstrong, London. Saddle-stitch. Red. 26 pp. 5.5 x 8.5 in. Silks, Ring and rope.

Bohlen, Henry, *Bohleno's Mysteries.* (1948) Montandon Magic, Tulsa, OK. Saddle-stitch. Green. 14 pp. 5.5 x 8.5 in. Silks, Ring and rope.

Bokor, Robert, *48 Great Magic Tricks.* (1973) Abracadabra Magic Shop, Colonia, NJ. Saddle-stitch. White. 48 pp. 5.25 x 8.25 in. U. F. Grant effects. Cards, Close-Up, Stage.

Boles, Don, *Compleat Pitchman, The.* (2010) 1878 Press Company, Oxford, CT. Coil. Brown. 101 pp. 8.5 x 11 in. (Measurements and other information have been recorded as accurately as possible.) Pitchman act.

Boles, Don, *Midway Magic.* (1963) Pinchpenny Press, Atlanta. Saddle-stitch. Yellow. 49 pp. 5.5 x 8.5 in. Sideshows, Illusions.

Boles, Don, *Midway Magic.* Reprint. (1963) Pinchpenny Press, Atlanta. Saddle-stitch. Brown. 48 pp. 5.5 x 8.5 in. Sideshows, Illusions.

Boles, Don, *Midway Showman, The.* Reprint. (1967) Pinchpenny Press, Atlanta. Saddle-stitch. Beige. 61 pp. 5.5 x 8.5 in. Introduction by Robert Lund. Sideshows, Illusions.

Boles, Don, *Modern Wizard's Manual, The.* (1970) Pinchpenny Press, Atlanta. Perfect. Gray. 68 pp. 8.5 x 11 in. Stage, Mentalism, Showmanship.

Boley, Col. Bill, *How to Book Shows.* (c. 1979) Author, Hopkinsville, KY. Stapled. Light green. Cover text: Red; 8 pp. 8.5 x 11.25 in. Mimeographed. Business, Promotion.

Boley, Col. Bill, *Performing on Cruise Ships.* (1996) Morris Costumes, Charlotte, NC. Saddle-stitch. White, green. 32 pp. 5.5 x 8.5 in. Cruise ships, Business, Showmanship.

Boley, Col. Bill, *Ventrilo-Magic.* (1977) Maher Ventriloquist Studios, Littleton, CO. Saddle-stitch. Yellow. 44 pp. 5.5 x 8.5 in. Ventriloquism.

Boleware, Tom, *Daycare Magician, The.* (2007) Author, Hattiesburg, MS. Comb. Yellow. 79 pp. 8.5 x 11 in. (Information not verified by physical copy.) Children's magic, School shows, Business.

Bolter, Christopher M., *Memorized–and the Not So Memorized Deck, The.* (2013) Author, Boston. Saddle-stitch. White. 21 pp. 8.5 x 11 in. (Information not verified by physical copy.) Cards, Prearranged deck.

Bolter, Christopher M., *Variations of the Mind.* (2008) Author, Boston. Stapled. White. 27 pp. 8.5 x 11 in. (Information not verified by physical copy.) Lecture notes. Cards, Mentalism.

Bombassei, Roberto, *S. W. Erdnase: Il Misterioso Baro.* (2023) Author, Italy. Perfect. White. 92 pp. 5.75 x 8.25 in. Biography, History, Erdnase. Italian.

Bond, Trixie, *You Entertain Children?* (2002) Author, Houston, TX. Coil. Color. 62 pp. 8.5 x 11 in. (Information not verified by physical copy.) Children's magic.

Bone, Howard, with Waldron, Dan, *SideShow.* (2001) Sun Dog Press, Northville, MI. Perfect. Black. 137 pp. 6 x 9 in. Fakir stunts, Sideshow, History.

Bonerjee, Arun, *Ek Khel Dikhao (Show Us a Trick!). Indian Showcase Series Book no. 3.* (1993) Electro Fun, Calcutta. Comb. Yellow. Cover text: Red; 24 pp. 8 x 11.75 in. Banner flap title over cover. Cards, Indian magic.

Bonfeld, Murray, *Faro Concepts.* (1977) Karl Fulves, Teaneck, NJ. Comb. Light green. 56 pp. 8.5 x 11 in. Cards, Faro, Mathematical.

Bongo, Ali, *Ali Bongo.* (1991) Magic Hands, Germany. 33 pp. (Information not verified by physical copy.) Lecture notes. Stage, Close-Up, Comedy, Inventions. German.

Bongo, Ali, *Ali Bongo's Book of Magic.* (1981) Macdonald, London. Casebound. Orange. 92 pp. 7.75 x 10.5 in. Beginner, Children's book.

Bongo, Ali, *Ali Bongo's Book of Magic.* (1987) Macdonald, London. Perfect. Red. 92 pp. 7.5 x 10.25 in. Beginner, Children's book.

Bongo, Ali, *Be a Magician.* Second edition. (1980) Macdonald, London. Casebound. Yellow. 64 pp. 5.25 x 8 in. Beginner, Comedy, Children's book.

Bongo, Ali, *Big Book of Magic, The.* (1997) Grandreams Ltd., London. Casebound. Blue. 93 pp. 8.75 x 11.5 in. Beginner, Children's book.

Bongo, Ali, *Bongo Book, The.* (1966) Magic Inc., Chicago. Saddle-stitch. White. 64 pp. 5.5 x 8.5 in. Signed by Ali Bongo. Stage, Close-Up, Comedy, Inventions.

Bongo, Ali, *Bongo Book, The.* Second printing. (1972) Magic Inc., Chicago. Saddle-stitch. Pink. 64 pp. 5.5 x 8.5 in. Stage, Close-Up, Comedy, Inventions.

Bongo, Ali, *Bongo Strikes Again.* (1974) Author, London. Saddle-stitch. White. 8 pp. 5 x 6.25 in. Signed by Ali Bongo. Lecture notes. Stage, Close-Up, Comedy, Inventions.

Bongo, Ali, *Bongo's Bazaar.* (c. 1975) Magic Inc., Chicago. Saddle-stitch. White. 12 pp. 5.5 x 8.5 in. Signed by Ali Bongo. Lecture notes. Stage, Close-Up, Comedy, Inventions.

Bongo, Ali (Credited simply to "Ali"), *Gagsterisms.* (1953) Harry Stanley, London. Perfect. Red, black. 67 pp. 5 x 7.25 in. Stage, Close-Up, Comedy, Inventions.

Bongo, Ali, with Francome, Colin and Holland, Charlie, *Juggling for All.* (1991) Carla Publications, Enfield, UK. Perfect. Yellow. 94 pp. 6.5 x 9.75 in. Ali Bongo illustrations. Juggling.

Bongo, Ali, *Lecture Notes by Ali Bongo '94.* (1994) Author, London. Saddle-stitch. Orange. 8 pp. 5.75 x 8.25 in. With folded sheet with effects. Lecture notes. Stage, Close-Up, Comedy, Inventions.

Bongo, Ali, *Lecture Notes by Ali Bongo 1983.* (1983) Author, London. Saddle-stitch. Blue. 12 pp. 3 x 5.75 in. Yellow text pages. Lecture notes. Stage, Close-Up, Comedy, Inventions.

Bongo, Ali, *Lecture Notes by Ali Bongo Geneva 2002.* (2002) Author, London. 16 pp. (Information not verified by physical copy.) Lecture notes. Stage, Close-Up, Comedy, Inventions.

Bongo, Ali, *Lecture Notes by Ali Bongo Las Vegas 2006.* (2006) Author, London. Folded. Yellow. 12 pp. 5.5 x 8.5 in. Yellow text pages. Lecture notes. Stage, Close-Up, Comedy, Inventions.

Bongo, Ali, *Lecture Notes by Ali Bongo Morges 2003.* (2003) Author, London. 12 pp. (Information not verified by physical copy.) Lecture notes. Stage, Close-Up, Comedy, Inventions.

Bongo, Ali, *Lecture Notes for Ali Bongo's Pongolian Delights.* (1978) Author, London. Saddle-stitch. Yellow. 8 pp. 5 x 6.25 in. Signed by Ali Bongo. Lecture notes. Stage, Close-Up, Comedy, Inventions.

Bongo, Ali, *New Penny Express, The.* (1969) Ken Brooke, London. Stapled. Orange. 6 pp. 8.5 x 11 in. (Information not verified by physical copy.) Coins, Handkerchiefs, Children's magic.

Bonnefont, Gaston, *Prestidigitation en Famille, La.* (1913) Chavaray, Mantour, Martin, Paris. Cloth. Red. 220 pp. 5.25 x 8.75 in. Gilt edges. Cover matches De l'Escap and Bellet. Stunts, Science magic. French.

Bonnell, Jack, *Bonnell's Simplified Card Routine.* (1943) The Fun Shop, Memphis, TN. Folded. Beige. 5 pp. 4.5 x 9 in. Cards, Prearranged deck, Eight Kings.

Bonneveine, *Almanach-Manuel de l'Amateur de Tours de Cartes.* (1877) Delarue, Paris. Perfect. Beige. 122 pp. 3.75 x 5.75 in. Cards. French.

Bontjes, J. Gary, *Checklist of Magic Lecture Notes, A.* (1968) F. William Kuethe, Jr., Glen Burnie, MD. Folded. White. 4 pp. 7 x 8.5 in. Supplement to "The Magic Cauldron," no. 27 (March 1968). Bibliography.

Bontjes, J. Gary, *Second Checklist of Magic Lecture Notes, A.* (1969) F. William Kuethe, Jr., Glen Burnie, MD. Folded. White. 4 pp. 7 x 8.5 in. Supplement to "The Magic Cauldron," no. 32 (June 1969). Bibliography.

Bontjes, J. Gary, *Third Checklist of Magic Lecture Notes, A.* (1971) F. William Kuethe, Jr., Glen Burnie, MD. Folded. White. 7 pp. 7 x 8.5 in. Supplement to "The Magic Cauldron," no. 41 (October 1971). Bibliography.

Bontjes, J. Gary, *Fourth Checklist of Magic Lecture Notes, A.* (1974) F. William Kuethe, Jr., Glen Burnie, MD. Folded. White. 13 pp. 7 x 8.5 in. Supplement to "The Magic Cauldron," no. 54 (December 1974). Bibliography.

Bonville, Frank, *Little Secrets, The.* (1904) Author, Chicago. Cloth. Red. Cover text: Gold; 152 pp. 4.75 x 6.5 in. In Byron Walker collection. Cards, Gambling.

Bonville, Frank, *Little Secrets, The.* (1977) Gamblers Book Club, Las Vegas. Saddle-stitch. Tan. 48 pp. 5.5 x 8.5 in. Reprint of 1904 edition. Cards, Gambling.

Bookout, John, with De Nevi, Donald P., Friend, Helen M., *Tricks and Puzzles.* (1973) Silver Dog Press, Oakland, CA. Perfect. Yellow. 215 pp. 7 x 10 in. Reprints of magazine articles from "The Strand," etc. History, Articles.

Booth, John, *Conjurians' Discoveries.* (1992) Ridgeway Press, Los Alamitos, CA. Cloth. Black. 273 pp. 6.25 x 9.25 in. Dust jacket. Signed by John Booth. Biography, History.

Booth, John, *Creative World of Conjuring.* (1990) Ridgeway Press, Los Alamitos, CA. Cloth. Gray. 262 pp. 6.25 x 9.25 in. Dust jacket. Signed by John Booth. Biography, History.

Booth, John, *Dramatic Magic.* (1988) Ridgeway Press, Los Alamitos, CA. Cloth. Black. 240 pp. 6.25 x 9.25 in. Dust jacket. Biography, History.

Booth, John, *Extending Magic Beyond Credibility.* (2001) L & L Publishing, Tahoma, CA. Cloth. Black. 257 pp. 6 x 9.25 in. Dust jacket. Signed by John Booth. Biography, History.

Booth, John, *Fabulous Destinations.* Third edition. (1998) Fairway Press, Lima, OH. Perfect. Blue. 239 pp. 5.5 x 8.25 in. Biography, Essays.

Booth, John, *Fine Art of Hocus Pocus, The.* (1996) Magic Art Book Co., Watertown, MA. Cloth. Black. 287 pp. 6.25 x 9.25 in. Dust jacket. Signed by Ray Goulet. Biography, History.

Booth, John, *Forging Ahead in Magic.* (1939) Kanter's Magic Shop, Philadelphia. Cloth. Maroon. 134 pp. 6 x 9 in. Showmanship, Publicity.

Booth, John, *Forging Ahead in Magic.* Second printing. (October 1944) Kanter's Magic Shop, Philadelphia. Cloth. Maroon. 154 pp. 6 x 9 in. Showmanship, Publicity.

Booth, John, *John Booth Classics.* (1975) Supreme Magic, Bideford, UK. Cloth. Black. 146 pp. 6 x 9 in. Dust jacket. Signed by John Booth. Showmanship, Stage, Biography.

Booth, John, *Keys to Magic's Inner World.* (1999) Magic Art Book Co., Watertown, MA. Cloth. Gray. 171 pp. 6.25 x 9.25 in. Dust jacket. Signed by John Booth. Collecting, History.

Booth, John, *Keys to Magic's Inner World.* Revised edition. (2025) Meir Yedid Magic, Fair Lawn, NJ. Perfect. Olive. 201 pp. 6 x 9 in. Collecting, History.

Booth, John, *Magical Mentalism.* (1931) Seagers Press, Hamilton, Canada. Saddle-stitch. Gray. 32 pp. 5 x 8 in. Signed by John Booth. Mentalism.

Booth, John, *Marvels of Mystery.* (1941) Kanter's Magic Shop, Philadelphia. Cloth. Light blue. 155 pp. 6 x 9.25 in. Signed by John Booth. Stage.

Booth, John, *Marvels of Mystery.* Fourth printing. (1953) Kanter's Magic Shop, Philadelphia. Cloth. Blue. 146 pp. 6 x 9 in. Signed by John Booth. Stage.

Booth, John, *Psychic Paradoxes.* (1984) Ridgeway Press, Los Alamitos, CA. Cloth. Blue. 240 pp. 6 x 9 in. Dust jacket. Signed by John Booth. Biography, History, Psychic.

Booth, John, *Super Magical Miracles.* (1930) Edward Bagshawe, London. Boards. Gray. 63 pp. 5 x 7.5 in. Stage, Mentalism.

Booth, John, *Super Magical Miracles.* (c. 1946) L. Davenport and Co., London. Saddle-stitch. Blue, orange. 46 pp. 5.5 x 8.25 in. Stage, Mentalism.

Booth, John, *Wonders of Magic.* (1986) Ridgeway Press, Los Alamitos, CA. Cloth. Maroon. 285 pp. 6 x 9 in. Signed by John Booth.

Bordo, Vincent, *Magic: Revealing the Mystery.* (1994) Author, Marlton, NJ. Stapled. White. 18 pp. 8.5 x 11 in. Lecture notes. History.

Borer, Christoph, *Forged by Fire.* (2024) Vanishing Inc., Rancho Cordova, CA. Cloth. Red. 268 pp. 6.25 x 9.25 in. Cards, Close-Up, Stage.

Borgh, Alan, *Magicianship.* (1964) Stephen Kelley's Magic Shop, Mishawaka, IN. Stapled with tape. Beige. 34 pp. 8.5 x 11 in. Showmanship, Theory, Stage, Close-Up.

Borland, Kathryn Kilby, with Speicher, Helen Ross, *Harry Houdini: Young Magician.* (1969) Bobbs-Merrill, Indianapolis, IN. Cloth. Orange, blue, white. 200 pp. 5.75 x 7.75 in. Two vignettes and portrait on cover. Cover says "Harry Houdini: Boy Magician." Biography, Houdini, Children's book.

Borland, Kathryn Kilby, with Speicher, Helen Ross, *Harry Houdini: Young Magician.* (1969) Bobbs-Merrill, Indianapolis, IN. Cloth. Red. 200 pp. 5.75 x 7.75 in. Two vignettes and portrait on cover. Biography, Houdini, Children's book.

Borland, Kathryn Kilby, with Speicher, Helen Ross, *Harry Houdini: Young Magician.* (1969) Bobbs-Merrill, Indianapolis, IN. Cloth. Orange, blue, white. 200 pp. 5.75 x 7.75 in. Three vignettes on cover. Cover says "Harry Houdini: Boy Magician." Biography, Houdini, Children's book.

Borland, Kathryn Kilby, with Speicher, Helen Ross, *Harry Houdini: Young Magician.* (1969) Bobbs-Merrill, Indianapolis, IN. Cloth. Yellow, green. 200 pp. 5.75 x 7.75 in. Three vignettes on cover. Cover says "Harry Houdini: Boy Magician." Biography, Houdini, Children's book.

Borland, Kathryn Kilby, with Speicher, Helen Ross, *Harry Houdini: Young Magician.* (1969) Bobbs-Merrill, Indianapolis, IN. Perfect. Tan. 200 pp. 5.75 x 7.75 in. Three vignettes on cover. Cover says "Harry Houdini: Boy Magician." Biography, Houdini, Children's book.

Borland, Kathryn Kilby, with Speicher, Helen Ross, *Harry Houdini: Young Magician.* (1969) Bobbs-Merrill, Indianapolis, IN. Cloth. Orange. 200 pp. 5.75 x 7.75 in. Dust jacket. Text-only cover. Cover says "Harry Houdini: Boy Magician." Biography, Houdini, Children's book.

Born, John B., *Cheating at Texas Hold 'Em.* (2010) Author, Ft. Lauderdale, FL. Cloth. Green. 558 pp. 6.25 x 9.25 in. (Measurements and other information have been recorded as accurately as possible.) Cards, Cheating, Poker.

Born, John B., *Flip Shift, The.* (2010) Author, Ft. Lauderdale, FL. Saddle-stitch. Maroon. 37 pp. 5.5 x 7.5 in. (Measurements and other information have been recorded as accurately as possible.) Cards.

Born, John B., *Matrix God's Way.* First printing. (2003) Author, Ft. Lauderdale, FL. Coil. Blue. 99 pp. 8.5 x 11 in. (Measurements and other information have been recorded as accurately as possible.) Coins, Matrix.

Born, John B., *Meant to Be.* Third printing. (2013) Author, Ft. Lauderdale, FL. Cloth. Red, black. 328 pp. 5.5 x 7.75 in. (Measurements and other information have been recorded as accurately as possible.) Theory, Cards.

Born, John B., *Natural Born Killa's.* (2005) Author, Ft. Lauderdale, FL. Stapled. White. 58 pp. 8.5 x 11 in. Signed by John B. Born. Lecture notes. Close-Up, Cards.

Born, John B., *Seeking the Bridge.* (2012) Author, Ft. Lauderdale, FL. Cloth. Blue, black. 192 pp. 5.75 x 8 in. (Information not verified by physical copy.) Cards, Cheating.

Bornson, Prof. Orestes A., *Rappers, or the Mysteries, Fallacies, and Absurdities of Spirit Rapping, Table-Tipping, and Entrancement.* (1854) H. Long and Another, New York. 282 pp. 4.75 x 7.5 in. (Information not verified by physical copy.) Toole Stott no. 953. Spiritualism, Exposés, Mediums.

Bornstein, Mike, *Eye Popper Money Magic Book no. 5.* (1994) Author, New York. Saddle-stitch. White. 71 pp. 5.5 x 8.5 in. Bills.

Bornstein, Mike, *Latest Money Magic of Mike Bornstein no. III.* (1988) Author, New York. Stapled. Tan. 40 pp. 8.5 x 11 in. (Measurements and other information have been recorded as accurately as possible.) Bills.

Bornstein, Mike, *Lecture no. 2.* (c. 1988) Author, New York. 68 pp. (Information not verified by physical copy.) Lecture notes. Cards, Close-Up.

Bornstein, Mike, *Magic of Mike Bornstein, The.* (1980) Author, New York. Stapled. Tan. 44 pp. 8.5 x 11 in. Includes version of Japanese paper square chain tear. Close-Up, Cards, Bills, Stage.

Bornstein, Mike, *Mike Bornstein's New Commercial Money Magic no. 4.* (1990) Author, New York. Saddle-stitch. Green. 49 pp. 5.5 x 8.5 in. Bills.

Bornstein, Mike, with Weigle, Oscar and Dell, Alan, *Money Magic of Mike Bornstein.* (1980) Magico, New York. Saddle-stitch. Blue. 24 pp. 5.5 x 8.5 in. Close-Up, Bills.

Bornstein, Mike, with Lees, Walt, *More Money Magic of Mike Bornstein.* (1984) Magico Magazine, New York. Saddle-stitch. Yellow. 35 pp. 5.5 x 8.5 in. Bills.

Bornstein, Mike, *Original Commercial Routines with Okito and Boston Boxes.* (1989) Author, New York. Saddle-stitch. Orange. 44 pp. 5.5 x 8.5 in. Coins, Okito Coin Box.

Bornstein, Mike, *Rainbow Matrix.* (1990) Author, New York. Saddle-stitch. Red. 83 pp. 5.5 x 8.5 in. (Measurements and other information have been recorded as accurately as possible.) Coins, Matrix.

Bornstein, Mike, with Lees, Walt, *Triple Threat Reverse (Copper/Silver Matrix).* (1984) Magico, New York. Saddle-stitch. Red. 21 pp. 5.25 x 8.5 in. Coins, Matrix.

Bornstein, Mike, with Lees, Walt, *Triumph Outdone.* (1982) Magico, New York. Saddle-stitch. Green. 56 pp. 5.5 x 8.5 in. Cards, Triumph.

Borodin (trans. by Bill Palmer), *Final Curtain.* (2005) Adesso, Germany. Cloth. Black. 338 pp. 8.75 x 11.25 in. Dust jacket. Mentalism, Bizarre magick.

Borodin (trans. by Bill Palmer), *Sheherezade: Magical Tales, Midnight Stories, Mental Mysteries.* (2003) Adesso, Germany. Cloth. Black. 312 pp. 8.75 x 11.25 in. Dust jacket. German first edition was published in 1999. Mentalism, Bizarre magick.

Bortz, Gerald John, *Reaching and Teaching Kids: Using Magic in the Classroom and Counseling Settings.* (2005) Author, The Woodlands, TX. Perfect. Blue. 170 pp. 7 x 10 in. (Information not verified by physical copy.) Educational, Children's magic, Theory.

Boscar, Professeur, *Dix Séances d'Illusionnisme.* (1928) F. Lanore, Paris. Perfect. White. 323 pp. 5.5 x 7.5 in. Beginner. French.

Bosco, *Moderne Salon-Zaubereien.* (1900) S. Mode's Berlag, Berlin, Germany. Perfect. Olive. 118 pp. 5.75 x 8.25 in. Includes Erdnase Three Ace Trick. Beginner, Cards. German.

Bosco, Carlo, *Zauber-Kabinet oder das Ganze der Taschenspielerkunst.* (1863) Ernst'sche Buchhandlung, Quedlinburg and Leipzig, Germany. Boards. Tan. 196 pp. 4.5 x 7 in. Beginner. German.

Bosco, Carlo, *Zauber-Kabinet oder das Ganze der Taschenspielerkunst.* (1885) Ernst'sche Buchandlung, Quedlinburg and Leipzig, Germany. Boards. Tan. 196 pp. 4.75 x 7.25 in. Beginner.

Bosco, D., *Nuovo Bosco, ossia Il Diavolo Color di Rosa, Il.* (1932) Casa Editrice Bietti, Milan. Perfect. Beige. 232 pp. 4.74 x 7.25 in. Beginner, Cards. Italian.

Bossi, Vanni, with Minch, Stephen, *Aretology of Vanni Bossi, The.* (2016) Hermetic Press, Seattle. Leatherette. Maroon. 192 pp. 8 x 10.25 in. Cards, Close-Up.

Bossi, Vanni, *Escorial '91: The Erdnase Year.* (1991) Author, Castellanza, Italy. 26 pp. (Information not verified by physical copy.) Cards, Erdnase. Italian.

Bossi, Vanni, *Escorial '92: The Marlo Year.* (1992) Author, Castellanza, Italy. Clip. Yellow. 32 pp. 8.25 x 11.75 in. Orange translucent overlay. Inscribed to Jay Marshall. Signed by Vanni Bossi. Cards. Italian.

Bossi, Vanni, *Escorial '93: The Hofzinser Year.* (1993) Author, Castellanza, Italy. 17 pp. (Information not verified by physical copy.) Cards. Italian.

Bossi, Vanni, *New Lecture Notes.* (1992) Author, Castellanza, Italy. Saddle-stitch. Beige. 22 pp. 5.75 x 8.25 in. Signed by Vanni Bossi. Lecture notes. Cards, Coins, Close-Up. Italian.

Bossi, Vanni, *Vanni Bossi Las Vegas Lecture.* (2005) Author, Castellanza, Italy. 31 pp. (Information not verified by physical copy.) Lecture notes. Cards, Close-Up. Italian.

Bossi, Vanni, *Vanni Bossi Las Vegas Lecture.* (2007) Author, Castellanza, Italy. 32 pp. (Information not verified by physical copy.) Lecture notes. Cards, Close-Up. Italian.

Bossi, Vanni, *Vanni Bossi Lecture Notes.* (1995) Author, Castellanza, Italy. 31 pp. (Information not verified by physical copy.) Lecture notes. Cards, Coins, Close-Up. Italian.

Boston, George, *Color I-Do-As-U.* (1979) Supreme Magic, Bideford, UK. Saddle-stitch. White. 5 pp. 7.25 x 9.75 in. Cards.

Boston, George, with Parrish, Robert, *Inside Magic.* (1947) Beechhurst Press, New York. Cloth. Black. 222 pp. 5.5 x 8.5 in. Dust jacket. Signed by Robert Parrish. Biography, History.

Botwinick, Bernie, *Macabre Chemical Magic.* Second printing. (June 1978) B & N Publishing, Clawson, MI. Saddle-stitch. Pink. 27 pp. 5.5 x 8.5 in. Chemical.

Boudreau, Leo, *Psimatrika: New Concepts for the Psychic Entertainer.* (1986) Rustic Press, Arlington, VA. Comb. Red. 121 pp. (Information not verified by physical copy.) Mentalism.

Boudreau, Leo, *Skullduggery: A Hornbook of Binary Magic.* (1989) Rustic Press, Arlington, VA. Comb. Red. 127 pp. (Information not verified by physical copy.) Mentalism.

Boudreau, Leo, *Spirited Pasteboards: Mental Gems for Ordinary Cards.* (1987) Rustic Press, Arlington, VA. Comb. Red. 233 pp. (Information not verified by physical copy.) Mentalism, Cards.

Bouffard, James Charles, *Magician's Fight, The.* (2008) Author. Casebound. Black. 145 pp. 6 x 9 in. (Information not verified by physical copy.) History.

Bowell, Ken, *Magi-Go-Round.* (1958) Supreme Magic, Bideford, UK. Stapled with tape. Red. 22 pp. 8 x 10 in. Mimeographed. Silkscreened cover. Stage, Mentalism.

Bowen, A. F., *Cagliostro and Cornelius: A Magical Minstrel Sketch in One Act.* (c. 1925) Author, Raleigh, NC. Stapled with paper cover. Red. 6 pp. 5.5 x 8.5 in. Mimeographed. Play.

Bowen, A. F., *Lesson in Magic: My Coin Combination, A.* (c. 1925) Thayer Magical Mfg. Co., Los Angeles. Saddle-stitch. Blue. 12 pp. 4 x 6.5 in. Coins.

Bowen, A. F., *Performing Under Difficulties.* (c. 1925) Author, Raleigh, NC. Stapled with paper cover. Olive. 6 pp. 5.5 x 8.5 in. Mimeographed. Showmanship.

Bowen, G. C., *Eyes of Buddha.* (c. 1922) Thayer Magical Mfg. Co., Los Angeles. Stapled. (Information not verified by physical copy. Bibliographical details are as accurate as possible.) Mentalism.

Bowen, O. H., *Retrospect and Prospect.* (1946) Magic Circle, London. Folded. White. 4 pp. 5.5 x 8.5 in. (Information not verified by physical copy.) Supplement to "The Magic Circular," August 1946. Lecture notes.

Bowman, Robert P., *50 Magic Tricks Using Common Objects That Teach Children Strategies for Success.* (2002) YouthLight Inc., Chapin, SC. Perfect. White. 172 pp. 8.5 x 8.75 in. (Information not verified by physical copy.) Educational.

Bowman, Robert P., *Magic Counselor, The.* (2004) YouthLight Inc., Chapin, SC. Perfect. Gray. 91 pp. 8.5 x 11 in. Educational.

Bowman, Stan, *Magical Directory 1962.* (1962) Author, Ipswich, UK. Saddle-stitch. Beige. 10 pp. 5 x 8 in. Directory, Reference.

Bowman, Wallace B., with Bard, William H., *Mental Magic.* (1929) Authors, Mount Vernon, NY. Stapled. Gray. 33 pp. 8 x 10 in. Mimeographed. (Information not verified by physical copy.) Memory, Showmanship.

Boyce, Alexander, *Short Booklet, A.* (2021) Author, New York. Saddle-stitch. Black. 23 pp. 5.5 x 8.5 in. (Information not verified by physical copy.) Cards, Coins, Close-Up, Animals.

Boyce, Wally, with Owen, Anthony, *Bits of Business and More.* (1994) Author, Gravesend, UK. Comb. Yellow. 47 pp. 8.25 x 11.75 in. (Information not verified by physical copy.) Comedy, Stage.

Boyd, David, with Boyd, Mary, *Easy Gospel Magic You Can Do.* (1995) Author, Bega, Australia. Comb. Blue. 14 pp. 8.5 x 11 in. (Information not verified by physical copy.) Lecture notes. Business, Promotion.

Boyd, David, *Making Money Out of Magic.* (1988) Author, Bega, Australia. 14 pp. 8.5 x 11 in. (Information not verified by physical copy.) Lecture notes. Business, Promotion.

Boyd, David, *Magic, Message, and Humor for the Gospel Clown.* (1984) Author, Bega, Australia. Stapled. Blue. 8.5 x 11 in. (Information not verified by physical copy.) Gospel magic, Clowning.

Boyer, Vin (Vynn Boyar), *Blindfold Miracle Stab.* (1951) Author, Forestville, CN. Folded. White. 3 pp. 8.5 x 11 in. (Information not verified by physical copy.) Cards, Card stab, Blindfolds.

Boyer, Vin (Vynn Boyar), *En-E-Dek Rising Card, The.* (1952) Author, Forestville, CN. Loose pages. White. 3 pp. 8.5 x 11 in. Mimeographed. Includes envelope and gimmicked card. Cards, Rising Cards, Instructions.

Boyer, Vin (Vynn Boyar), *Ghostly Seconds.* (1949) Author, Forestville, CN. Folded. White. 4 pp. 8.5 x 11 in. Folded with seal on side. Cards, Second deal.

Boyer, Vin (Vynn Boyar), *Sleights, Secrets, and Suggestions.* (1953) Magicians' Guild of America, New York. Stapled. Orange. 12 pp. 8.5 x 11 in. Mimeographed. Lecture notes. Cards.

Boz, Tom, *K.I.S.S.* (1991) Author, Chicago. Comb. Light blue. 11 pp. 8.5 x 11 in. (Information not verified by physical copy. Bibliographical details are as accurate as possible.) Cards, Close-Up.

Braceland, Prof. Monsieur, *Parlor Amusements, or the Whole Art of Natural Magic.* (1889) Crawford and Co., Philadelphia. Perfect. Orange. 95 pp. 4.75 x 7.25 in. Contains material from Dean. Beginner, Early magic.

Brachetti, Arthur, *Ombre Cinesi, Le.* (2007) Priuli & Verlucca, Scarmagno, Italy. Cloth. Gray. 94 pp. 8 x 8 in. Dust jacket. Shadowgraphy. Italian.

Braddon, Russell, *Piddingtons, The.* Second impression. (1950) Werner Laurie, London. Cloth. Green. 238 pp. 5.25 x 8.25 in. Dust jacket. Biography, Mentalism, Second Sight.

Bradford, William, *Protean Master: LaFollette – Quick Change Artist, A.* (1999) Alex Hargrave Productions, Concord, CA. Comb. Beige. 20 pp. 8.5 x 11 in. Biography, Quick change.

Brady, Ernest W., *Pinnacle Portfolio of Poetry, The.* (1967) Author, Chicago. Vinyl cover. Maroon. 40 pp. 5.5 x 8.5 in. 2 pp. instructions, loose poetry pages in pocket of cover, glassine envelope of numbers. Force book, Book tests, Mentalism.

Brahams, Anthony (See Leech, Al; Norman, Karl), *Rara Avis.* (2006) Cairn Press, Norwich, UK. Cloth. Black. 220 pp. 8.5 x 12 in. Dust jacket. Cards.

Brahma, Pierre, *Histoire d'une F.I.S.M.* (1991) Author, Paris. Perfect. White. 155 pp. 5.25 x 8 in. History, Conventions. French.

Brahma, Pierre, *Jonglerie des Pièces de la Monnaie, La.* (1991) Author, Paris. Perfect. Black. 46 pp. 6 x 9 in. Coins, Manipulation, Juggling. French.

Brahma, Pierre (trans. by Todd Karr), *Magician On Stage: Lecture Notes no. 2.* (1994) Author, Paris. Clip. White. 28 pp. 8.5 x 11 in. Lecture notes. Showmanship, Theory.

Brahma, Pierre, *Magicien en Scène: Notes de Conférence no. 2, Le.* (1990) Author, Paris. Clip. White. 33 pp. 8.5 x 11 in. Inscribed to Todd Karr. Signed by Pierre Brahma. Lecture notes. Showmanship, Theory. French.

Brahma, Pierre, *Magicien en Scène: Notes de Conférence no. 2, Le.* (1991) Author, Paris. Perfect. Red. 42 pp. 6 x 9 in. Inscribed to Todd Karr. Signed by Pierre Brahma. Lecture notes. Showmanship, Theory. French.

Brahma, Pierre, *Malle des Indes, La.* (1979) Juiliiard, Paris. Perfect. Blue. 407 pp. 5.5 x 9 in. Inscribed to Todd Karr. Signed by Pierre Brahma. Biography. French.

Brahma, Pierre, *Malle des Indes, La.* (1979) France Loisirs, Paris. Cloth. Black. 407 pp. 5.5 x 9 in. Dust jacket. (Measurements and other information have been recorded as accurately as possible.) Biography. French.

Braine, Sheila E., *Turkish Automaton, The.* (1899) Blackie and Son, London. Cloth. Black. 288 pp. 5.5 x 7.5 in. In Copperfield collection. Automaton chess player, Fiction.

Branch, Justin, *Cards in Confidence vol. 1.* (1979) Author, Plymouth, UK. Clip. Black. 150 pp. 8.5 x 11.75 in. Mimeographed. Circular silver foil label on cover with title and author. Cards, Manipulation.

Branch, Justin, *Cards in Confidence vol. 2.* (1979) Author, Plymouth, UK. Clip. Black. 154 pp. 8.5 x 11.75 in. Mimeographed. Circular silver foil label on cover with title and author. Includes set of author's "Fan Units" manipulation cards. Cards, Manipulation.

Branch, Justin, *Manipulative Production and Card Routining: Section 1: Exclusive Card Productions.* (1977) Author, Plymouth, UK. Clip. Red. 30 pp. 8.5 x 11.75 in. Mimeographed. Circular gold foil label on cover with title and author and rectangular red label with contents. Cards, Manipulation.

Branch, Justin, *Manipulative Production and Card Routining: Section 1: Exclusive Card Productions.* (1977) Author, Plymouth, UK. Clip. Black. 30 pp. 8.5 x 11.75 in. Mimeographed. Circular gold foil label on cover with title and author and rectangular label with contents. Cards, Manipulation.

Branch, Justin, *Manipulative Production and Card Routining: Sections 2, 3, 4: Ball and Coin Productions, Card Routining, Advanced Coin Productions.* (1977) Author, Plymouth, UK. Clip. Black. 75 pp. 8.5 x 11.75 in. Mimeographed. Circular gold label, rectangular yellow label. Cards, Manipulation, Balls, Coins.

Branch, Justin, *Manipulative Production and Card Routining: Section 3: Practice Summary.* (1977) Author, Plymouth, UK. Saddle-stitch. Orange. 22 pp. 5.75 x 8.25 in. Mimeographed. Cards, Manipulation.

Branch, Justin, *Manipulative Production and Card Routining: Sections 5, 6, 7: Packet Magic, Card Handling, Diversities, plus The Green Star Manuscript.* (1977) Author, Plymouth, UK. Clip. Orange. 40 pp. 8.5 x 11.75 in. Mimeographed. Circular gold label, rectangular orange label. Cards, Manipulation.

Branch, Justin, *Manipulative Production and Card Routining: Photographic Index.* (1977) Author, Plymouth, UK. Clip. Black. 6 pp. 8.5 x 11.75 in. Mimeographed. Circular gold foil label on cover with title and author and rectangular blue label with contents. Cards, Manipulation.

Branch, Justin, *Multiple Assemblies.* (1983) Author, Plymouth, UK. Comb. Yellow. 65 pp. 8.25 x 11.75 in. Includes errata sheet. Cards.

Branch, Justin, *Poker Prediction.* (n.d.) Author, Plymouth, UK. Clip. White. 6 pp. 8.5 x 11.75 in. Mimeographed. Cards.

Branch, Justin, *Progressive Card Magic.* (1985) Author, Plymouth, UK. Comb. Yellow. 101 pp. 8.25 x 11.75 in. (Measurements and other information have been recorded as accurately as possible.) Cards.

Brandeth, Gyles, *Shazzam! Magic Show.* (1978) Nutmeg Press, UK. Perfect. Yellow. 64 pp. 5 x 7.75 in. Children's book, Beginner.

Brando (Harry Bernstein), *Lecture Notes.* (c. 1970) Author, New York. Stapled. 16 pp. 8.5 x 11 in. (Information not verified by physical copy.) Stage.

Brandon, Arthur, *Milo and Roger: A Magical Life.* (1999) Hermetic Press, Seattle. Cloth. Maroon. 418 pp. 6 x 9 in. Dust jacket. Biography.

Brandon, Don and Joyce, *Memoirs and Confessions of a Stage Magician.* (1995) TAG Publications, San Antonio, TX. Cloth. Black. 306 pp. 6.25 x 9.25 in. Biography.

Brandon, James, *Second Step.* (1993) Author, New York. Clip. Black. 57 pp. 8.5 x 11 in. (Information not verified by physical copy.) Stage, Creativity, Doves.

Brandon, Joan, *Art of Hypnotism, The.* (1956) Fawcett Publications, New York. Perfect. Blue. 96 pp. 6.75 x 9.25 in. Hypnotism.

Branson, Maj. Lionel H., *Indian Conjuring.* (1922) Routledge and Dutton, London and New York. Boards. Beige, orange. 103 pp. 5 x 7.5 in. Indian magic.

Branson, Maj. Lionel H., *Lifetime of Deception, A.* (1953) Robert Hale, London. Cloth. Red. 209 pp. 5.5 x 8.25 in. Dust jacket. Signed by Maj. L. H. Branson. Biography, Indian magic.

Branson, Maj. Lionel H., *Magic of India, The.* (1973) Pinchpenny Press, Atlanta. Saddle-stitch. Beige, red. 103 pp. 4.25 x 6.5 in. Retitled reprint of "Indian Conjuring." Indian magic.

Brant, Bob, *As I See It.* (n.d.) Author, Attleboro, MA. Comb. Beige. 18 pp. 8.5 x 11 in. (Information not verified by physical copy. Bibliographical details are as accurate as possible.) Close-Up, Stage.

Braude, Ben B., *Tricks and Treats.* (1972) Haines House of Cards, Norwood, OH. Saddle-stitch. White, orange. 37 pp. 6 x 9 in. Cards, Stage.

Braue, Frederick, *Fred Braue Notebooks vols. 1-8, The.* (1985) Jeff Busby Magic, Oakland, CA. Wire binding. Beige. 30 pp. 8.5 x 11 in. First eight of fifteen planned volumes, each 30 pp. Rounded corners. Cards, History.

Braue, Frederick, *Fred Braue Notebooks Prospectus, The.* (1985) Jeff Busby Magic, Oakland, CA. Saddle-stitch. Beige. 8 pp. 8.5 x 10.75 in. With order form and envelope. Rounded corners. Cards, History.

Braue, Frederick, with Busby, Jeff, *Fred Braue on False Deals.* (1978) Jeff Busby Magic, Oakland, CA. Comb. Beige, red, blue. 44 pp. 8.5 x 11 in. Cards, Second deal.

Braun, Brent, *Plots, Ploys, and Other Cons.* (2019) The Magic Firm, Louisville, KY. Perfect. Red. 132 pp. 6 x 9 in. (Measurements and other information have been recorded as accurately as possible.) Cards, Close-Up.

Braun, John (See also Judah, Stewart), with Bryson, Rhett; Dunn, Bruce, *A. C. Gilbert / Mysto Company Story, The.* Miniature book. (2000) Bruce Dunn, Kalamazoo, MI. Saddle-stitch. Pink. 7 pp. 3 x 4.25 in. Wee Books by Dunn. From "The Linking Ring," 1957. History, Biography, Magic sets.

Braun, John, *Of Legierdemaine and Diverse Juggling Knacks: Columns from "The Linking Ring," 1949-1966.* (1999) Ken Klosterman, Loveland, OH. Cloth. Maroon. Cover text: Gold; 553 pp. 8.75 x 11.25 in. History, Biography, Magazine columns.

Braun, John, *Stewart Judah's Three Card Monte.* (1964) Ireland Magic Co., Chicago. Saddle-stitch. Blue. 12 pp. 5.5 x 8.5 in. Cards, Three-Card Monte.

Braun, John, *T. Nelson Downs and Edward "Tex" McGuire: Letters (1922-1933).* (1981) Karl Fulves, Teaneck, NJ. Saddle-stitch. Blue. 75 pp. 6 x 9 in. Reprints from "The Linking Ring." Biography, History.

Brearley, John, *ConJunioring.* (1948) Academy of Recorded Arts, Crafts, and Sciences, Croydon, UK. Cloth. Orange. 92 pp. 5.5 x 8.5 in. Children's magic.

Breedon, James, *Rub the Lamp.* (1986) Repro Magic, London. Stapled with tape. White. 125 pp. 8.25 x 11.75 in. (Information not verified by physical copy.) Children's magic.

Breeds, John, *Funny Tricks with Clever Bits.* (2020) Author, UK. Perfect. White. 36 pp. 8.75 x 11.25 in. (Information not verified by physical copy. Bibliographical details are as accurate as possible.) Children's magic.

Breeds, John, *How to Create Kids' Magic and Triple Your Income.* (2008) Author, UK. Perfect. White. 188 pp. (Information not verified by physical copy.) Children's magic.

Breeds, John, *Lots of Magic for Kidz.* (n.d.) UK. Perfect. White. (Information not verified by physical copy. Bibliographical details are as accurate as possible.) Children's magic.

Breene, Katlyn, *Faery Call.* (1997) Mermade Magickal Arts, Las Vegas. Perfect. Green. 152 pp. 5.5 x 8.5 in. Inscribed to Todd Karr. Signed by Katlyn Breene. Spirituality, Art.

Breese, Martin (See also Harbin, Robert; Koran, Al; Wichmann, Ralf), *Basil Horwitz Miracle Wallet, The.* (1982) Martin Breese, London. Folded. Yellow. 24 pp. 6 x 8.25 in. Wallets, Cards.

Breese, Martin, *Bendix Bombshell.* (1983) R.A.R. Magic, London. Saddle-stitch. Yellow. 52 pp. 5.5 x 8.5 in. Wallets, Cards.

Breese, Martin, *Best of Pentagram Card Magic, The.* Second edition. (2003) Martin Breese, London. Perfect. White. 228 pp. 5.75 x 8.25 in. Cards, Magazines.

Breese, Martin, *Chan Canasta: Afterthoughts.* (2001) Martin Breese, London. Saddle-stitch. Black. 13 pp. 6 x 9 in. (Information not verified by physical copy.) Mentalism, Biography, History.

Breese, Martin, *Marked! A Manual of Marked Card Magic.* (1982) Martin Breese, London. Folded. Beige. 7 pp. 5.5 x 8.5 in. Cards, Marked cards.

Breggar, "Jerseyana" Michael, *Raiders of the Lost Card.* (2024) Author, Cherry Hill, NJ. Perfect. Brown. 224 pp. 8.5 x 11 in. (Measurements and other information have been recorded as accurately as possible.) Cards.

Breitenmoser, Retonio, *Quick Change Secrets.* (2016) Dreamfactory, Degersheim, Switzerland. Casebound. Color. 182 pp. 6.75 x 9.75 in. Flipbook pages. Signed by Natalie Breitenmoser. Quick change, Stage.

Brejtfus, Caj, *CAJ: The Clowns and Jesters Deck of Magic Gaff Cards.* (2005) Caj Magic, La Puente, CA. Saddle-stitch. Yellow. 16 pp. 5.5 x 8.5 in. Cards, Gimmicked decks.

Brennan, Father Dermont, *If You Can't Invent, Adapt! A Lesson in Creative Magic.* (1983) Author, Yorktown, NY. Stapled. White. 20 pp. 8.5 x 11 in. (Information not verified by physical copy.) Lecture notes. Creativity.

Brent, Christopher, *Flying Silk, The.* (2002) Magic That Works, Fort Worth, TX. Clip. White. 14 pp. 8.5 x 11 in. (Information not verified by physical copy.) Silks, Thread.

Breslaw, Philip, *Breslaw's Last Legacy, or The Magical Companion.* (1784) T. Moore, London. 120 pp. 4.25 x 6 in. (Information not verified by physical copy.) Toole Stott no. 120. Early magic.

Breslaw, Philip, *Breslaw's Last Legacy, or The Magical Companion.* Second edition. (1784) T. Moore, London. 132 pp. 4.25 x 6.75 in. (Information not verified by physical copy.) Toole Stott no. 121. Early magic.

Breslaw, Philip, *Breslaw's Last Legacy, or The Magical Companion.* Fourth edition. (1784) T. Moore, London. 132 pp. 3.75 x 6.5 in. (Information not verified by physical copy.) Toole Stott no. 966. Early magic.

Breslaw, Philip, *Breslaw's Last Legacy, or The Magical Companion.* Fifth edition. (1791) W. Lane, London. 132 pp. 4.25 x 6.75 in. (Information not verified by physical copy.) Toole Stott no. 122. Early magic.

Breslaw, Philip, *Breslaw's Last Legacy, or The Magical Companion.* (1792) J. Barker, London. 112 pp. 4.25 x 6.75 in. (Information not verified by physical copy.) Toole Stott no. 131. Early magic.

Breslaw, Philip, *Breslaw's Last Legacy, or The Magical Companion.* Sixth edition. (1792) W. Lane, London. 144 pp. 4 x 7 in. (Information not verified by physical copy.) Toole Stott no. 967. Early magic.

Breslaw, Philip, *Breslaw's Last Legacy, or The Magical Companion.* Sixth edition. (1793) J. Rice, Dublin. 132 pp. 3.75 x 6.75 in. (Information not verified by physical copy.) Toole Stott no. 123. Early magic.

Breslaw, Philip, *Breslaw's Last Legacy, or The Magical Companion.* Twelfth edition. (1794) J. Barker, London. 88 pp. 4.25 x 7 in. (Information not verified by physical copy.) Toole Stott no. 132. Early magic.

Breslaw, Philip, *Breslaw's Last Legacy, or The Magical Companion.* (1794) P. Byrne, Dublin. 144 pp. 3.75 x 6.75 in. (Information not verified by physical copy.) Toole Stott no. 124. Early magic.

Breslaw, Philip, *Breslaw's Last Legacy, or The Magical Companion.* (1795) W. Lane, London. 144 pp. 4.25 x 6.75 in. (Information not verified by physical copy.) Toole Stott no. 125. Early magic.

Breslaw, Philip, *Breslaw's Last Legacy, or The Magical Companion.* (1803) T. Plummer, London. 40 pp. 4.25 x 6.75 in. (Information not verified by physical copy.) Toole Stott no. 968. Early magic.

Breslaw, Philip, *Breslaw's Last Legacy, or The Magical Companion.* (1806) T. and R. Hughes, London. 38 pp. 4.5 x 7.5 in. (Information not verified by physical copy.) Toole Stott no. 126. Early magic.

Breslaw, Philip, *Breslaw's Last Legacy, or The Magical Companion.* (c. 1807) T. Hughes, London. 40 pp. 4 x 6.75 in. (Information not verified by physical copy.) Toole Stott no. 135. Early magic.

Breslaw, Philip, *Breslaw's Last Legacy, or The Magical Companion.* (c. 1809) J. D. Dewick, London. 38 pp. 3 x 6.75 in. (Information not verified by physical copy.) Toole Stott no. 127. Early magic.

Breslaw, Philip, *Breslaw's Last Legacy, or The Magical Companion.* (c. 1810) J. Martin, Dublin. 38 pp. 4.5 x 7.5 in. (Information not verified by physical copy.) Toole Stott no. 128. Early magic.

Breslaw, Philip, *Breslaw's Last Legacy, or The Magical Companion.* (c. 1810) Thomas Tegg, London. 40 pp. 4 x 6.75 in. (Information not verified by physical copy.) Toole Stott no. 134. Early magic.

Breslaw, Philip, *Breslaw's Last Legacy, or The Magical Companion.* (1811) Philadelphia. 48 pp. 4.25 x 6.75 in. (Information not verified by physical copy.) Toole Stott no. 129. Early magic.

Breslaw, Philip, *Breslaw's Last Legacy, or The Magical Companion.* (1812) Thomas Tegg, London. 36 pp. 4.25 x 7.5 in. (Information not verified by physical copy.) Toole Stott no. 133. Early magic.

Breslaw, Philip, *Breslaw's Last Legacy, or The Magical Companion.* (1824) C. Crookes, Dublin. 40 pp. 4.5 x 7.5 in. (Information not verified by physical copy.) Toole Stott no. 130. Early magic.

Breslaw, Philip, *Breslaw's Last Legacy, or The Magical Companion.* (1997) Stevens Magic, Wichita, KS. Casebound. Brown. 144 pp. 4.75 x 6.25 in. Reprint of 1795 edition. #511 of 560. History, Early magic.

Bresler, Elliott J., *Billet Machine, The.* (2007) Author. eBook. White. Multiple sections. 8.5 x 11 in. Printed copy of ebook. Mentalism, Billets.

Bresler, Elliott J., *Switchcraft: The Billet Work of Elliott J. Bresler.* (2006) Author. eBook. White. 206 pp. 8.5 x 11 in. Printed copy of ebook. Mentalism, Billets.

Brewe, William H., *Silks.* (1984) Author, Cincinnati, OH. Stapled. White. 20 pp. 8.5 x 11 in. (Measurements and other information have been recorded as accurately as possible.) Lecture notes. Silks, Stage.

Brewer, Doug, *Coin Box Killers.* (2009) Author, San Diego. Coil. Black. 60 pp. 8.5 x 11 in. (Information not verified by physical copy.) Coins, Okito Coin Box.

Brewer, Doug, *High Impact Card Magic.* (1999) Ohmigosh Productions, San Diego. Saddle-stitch. Yellow. 41 pp. 8.5 x 11 in. Cards.

Brewer, Doug, *High Impact Coin Magic.* (1999) Ohmigosh Productions, San Diego. Saddle-stitch. White. 21 pp. 8.5 x 11 in. (Information not verified by physical copy.) Coins.

Brewer, Doug, *It's in the Other Hand!* (1997) Author, San Diego. Comb. White. 30 pp. 8.5 x 11 in. (Information not verified by physical copy.) Lecture notes. Cards, Coins, Close-Up.

Brewer, Doug, *Magic Castle Lecture.* (2002) Author, San Diego. Saddle-stitch. White. 21 pp. 8.5 x 11 in. (Information not verified by physical copy.) Lecture notes. Cards, Close-Up.

Brewer, Doug, *Modern Coin Cup.* (2003) Author, San Diego. Saddle-stitch. White. 63 pp. 5.5 x 8.5 in. (Information not verified by physical copy.) Coins, Cups, Close-Up.

Brewer, Doug, *Three Miracle Routines with the Miracle Coin Cup.* (1997) Author, San Diego. Saddle-stitch. White. 14 pp. 8.5 x 11 in. (Information not verified by physical copy.) Coins, Cups, Close-Up.

Brewer, Doug, *Unexpected Visitor, The.* (2001) MagicSmith, Laguna Niguel, CA. Perfect. Gray. 86 pp. 7 x 9 in. (Information not verified by physical copy.) Coins, Close-Up.

Brewster, Sir David, *Letters on Natural Magic.* (1832) John Murray, New York. 351 pp. 3 x 6 in. (Information not verified by physical copy.) Toole Stott no. 136. History, Automata.

Brewster, Sir David, *Letters on Natural Magic.* (1832) J. and J. Harper, New York. Cloth. Gray. 314 pp. 4 x 6.25 in. Toole Stott no. 137. History, Automata.

Brewster, Sir David, *Letters on Natural Magic.* (1833) J. Murray, London. 351 pp. 4 x 6 in. Toole Stott no. 969. History, Automata.

Brewster, Sir David, *Letters on Natural Magic.* (1838) J. and J. Harper, New York. Boards. Tan. 314 pp. 4 x 6.25 in. History, Automata.

Brewster, Sir David, *Letters on Natural Magic.* (1839) Harper and Brothers, New York. 314 pp. 3.5 x 6 in. Toole Stott no. 970. History, Automata.

Brewster, Sir David, *Letters on Natural Magic.* (1842) Harper and Brothers, New York. 314 pp. 3.5 x 6 in. Toole Stott no. 971. History, Automata.

Brewster, Sir David, *Letters on Natural Magic.* (1870) Harper and Brothers, New York. 314 pp. 3.5 x 6 in. Toole Stott no. 972. History, Automata.

Bridwell, Jack, *B-Witcheries.* (1978) Supreme Magic, Bideford, UK. Saddle-stitch. Yellow. 31 pp. 7.25 x 9.75 in. Spirit effects, Stage.

Bridwell, Jack, *Golden Galaxy of Mentalism.* (1988) Micky Hades, Calgary, Canada. Comb. Yellow. 25 pp. 8.5 x 11 in. Mentalism.

Bridwell, Jack, *Just for Laughs.* (1966) Abbott Magic Co., Colon, MI. Stapled. White. 19 pp. 8.5 x 11 in. Mimeographed inside printed cover. Clowning, Comedy.

Bridwell, Jack, *Mental Flashes from Jack Bridwell.* (1979) Micky Hades, Calgary, Canada. Saddle-stitch. Olive. 28 pp. 5.25 x 8.25 in. Mentalism.

Bridwell, Jack, *Pull-ing Ahead with Your Magic.* (1982) Micky Hades, Calgary, Canada. Stapled with tape. Yellow. 20 pp. 8.5 x 11 in. Pulls, Gimmicks.

Briggs, J. Albert, *Book of Magic, The.* (c. 1922) Author, Sydney. 6.25 x 8.75 in. (Information not verified by physical copy.) Bound collections of Briggs magazines. See McCullagh, "Under the Southern Cross." Magazines.

Briggs, J. Albert (as "Merbak"), *Clever Card Tricks.* (c. 1933) Conjurer Publishing Co., Sydney. 16 pp. (Information not verified by physical copy.) See McCullagh, "Under the Southern Cross." Cards.

Briggs, J. Albert, *Dinkum Magic.* (1928) Austral Magic Co., Alexandria, Australia. Stapled with paper cover. Orange. 38 pp. 5.75 x 8.75 in. Stage.

Briggs, J. Albert (as "Merbak"), *Magical Revelations.* (1935) Briton Publications, Sydney. 71 pp. (Information not verified by physical copy.) See McCullagh, "Under the Southern Cross." Close-Up, Stage, Illusions.

Briggs, J. Albert, *Paper Tearing Made Easy.* (n.d.) Author, Sydney. Stapled. 7 pp. Bound at top. (Information not verified by physical copy.) See McCullagh, "Under the Southern Cross." Paper, Paper tearing.

Briggs, J. Albert, *Patter Book no. 1 Miscellaneous.* (n.d.) Author, Sydney. Folded. 7 pp. (Information not verified by physical copy.) See McCullagh, "Under the Southern Cross." Patter.

Briggs, J. Albert, *Patter Book no. 2 Handkerchief and Card Tricks.* (n.d.) Author, Sydney. Stapled. 5 pp. Bound at top. (Information not verified by physical copy.) See McCullagh, "Under the Southern Cross." Handkerchiefs, Cards.

Briggs, J. Albert (as "Merbak"), *Practical Magic.* (1946) Author, Sydney. 28 pp. (Information not verified by physical copy.) See McCullagh, "Under the Southern Cross." Beginner.

Briggs, J. Albert, *Six Easy to Build Illusionettes.* (n.d.) Author, Sydney. Stapled with tape. Green. 7 pp. Bound at top. (Information not verified by physical copy.) See McCullagh, "Under the Southern Cross." Illusions.

Briggs, J. Albert, *Stage Magic no. 1.* (n.d.) Author, Sydney. Stapled. 9 pp. Bound at top. (Information not verified by physical copy.) See McCullagh, "Under the Southern Cross." Stage.

Brill, A. K., *Bible of Building Plans.* Second edition. (c. 1959) A. B. Enterprises, Peoria, IL. Perfect. Brown. 319 pp. 4.25 x 5.5 in. Catalog 15 of illusion, sideshow, and game plans. Illusions, Sideshow, Catalog.

Brill, A. K., *Fifteen Smaller Illusions: Smaller Magic Tricks.* (c. 1959) Author, Peoria, IL. 16 pp. (Information not verified by physical copy.) Illusions, Plans.

Brill, A. K., *First Supplement to A. Brill's Bible of Building Plans.* Second edition. (c. 1959) A. B. Enterprises, Peoria, IL. Stapled. Black. 71 pp. 4 x 5.75 in. Illusions, Sideshow, Catalog.

Brill, A. K., *Strait Jacket, Dungeon Chains, and Anchor Rods Escape.* (c. 1959) A. B. Enterprises, Peoria, IL. 8 pp. (Information not verified by physical copy.) Escapes, Plans, Chains.

Brinegar, Ron, *Desperado Deals.* (1976) Micky Hades, Calgary, Canada. Comb. Red. 32 pp. 8.5 x 11 in. (Measurements and other information have been recorded as accurately as possible.) Cards.

Brinson, Christopher, *Owen Clark: A Genius Forgotten.* (2011) Author, UK. Perfect. 250 pp. 7.25 x 8.5 in. (Information not verified by physical copy.) Biography, History.

Britland, David (See also Berglas, David; Rogers, Terri), *Angel Card Rise and Spooky.* (1979) Author, London. Saddle-stitch. Pink. 16 pp. 6 x 8.25 in. Cards, Rising Cards.

Britland, David, *Angel Card Rise Plus.* (1985) Martin Breese, London. Saddle-stitch. Silver. 28 pp. 5.75 x 8.25 in. Cards.

Britland, David, *Apple Turnover.* (1984) Martin Breese, London. Strip binding. Green. 4 pp. 8.25 x 11.75 in. Includes envelope with cards. Cards.

Britland, David, *Card Kinetics.* Second edition. (1988) Martin Breese, London. Saddle-stitch. Beige. 42 pp. 5.75 x 8.25 in. Signed by David Britland. Cards.

Britland, David, *Chan Canasta: A Remarkable Man.* (2000) Martin Breese, London. Casebound. Gray. 111 pp. 6 x 9.5 in. Signed by David Britland. Biography, Mentalism, Cards.

Britland, David, *Chan Canasta: A Remarkable Man vol. 2.* (2001) Martin Breese, London. Perfect. Black. 45 pp. 6 x 9 in. Signed by David Britland. Biography, Mentalism, Cards.

Britland, David, *Cutting Remarks.* (1990) Martin Breese, London. Saddle-stitch. Red. 20 pp. 5.75 x 8.25 in. (Measurements and other information have been recorded as accurately as possible.) Cards.

Britland, David, *Deckade.* (1982) Martin Breese, London. Stapled with tape. Brown. 20 pp. 8.25 x 11.5 in. (Measurements and other information have been recorded as accurately as possible.) Cards.

Britland, David, *Equinox.* (1984) Martin Breese, London. Cloth. Red. 56 pp. 6 x 8.5 in. Dust jacket. (Measurements and other information have been recorded as accurately as possible.) Cards.

Britland, David, *Lady Through and Through, A.* (1984) Martin Breese, London. Comb. Black. 10 pp. 8.25 x 11.75 in. Cards.

Britland, David, *Magnificent Seven of the Talon, The.* (1984) Micky Hades, Calgary, Canada. Boards. Blue. 109 pp. 6 x 8.25 in. Bound set of "Talon" magazines. Magazine, Cards, Close-Up.

Britland, David, *Master of the Game.* (1988) Martin Breese, London. Saddle-stitch. Green. 16 pp. 5.75 x 8.25 in. With cards in envelope. Cards.

Britland, David, *Mind and Magic of David Berglas, The.* (2002) Hahne, Burbank, CA. Cloth. Maroon. 566 pp. 8.75 x 10.25 in. Signed by David Britland. Mentalism.

Britland, David, *Parallax.* (1986) Martin Breese, London. Saddle-stitch. White, red. 21 pp. 5.75 x 8 in. (Measurements and other information have been recorded as accurately as possible.) Cards.

Britland, David, *Phantoms of the Card Table.* (2003) High Stakes, London. Cloth. Black. 256 pp. 6 x 9 in. Dust jacket. Signed by David Britland. Biography, Cards.

Britland, David, *Psychomancy.* (1986) Martin Breese, London. Saddle-stitch. White, blue. 56 pp. 5.75 x 8 in. Blue pages. Hull Magicians' Circle bookplate. Mentalism, Cards.

Britland, David, *Tearing a Lady in Two.* (1989) Martin Breese, London. Saddle-stitch. Yellow. 15 pp. 5.75 x 8.25 in. Cards.

Britland, David, *Trick Card Trickery.* (1978) Supreme Magic, London. Saddle-stitch. White. 16 pp. 7.5 x 9.5 in. Cards, Gimmicks.

Britland, David, *Zennerism.* (1980) Author, London. Comb. White, black. 7 pp. 8.75 x 11 in. (Measurements and other information have been recorded as accurately as possible.) Cards, Mentalism.

Brock, Tudor, *Great Wong's Routine for the Chinese Rings, The.* (1964) Author, Cadoxton, UK. Saddle-stitch. Red. 16 pp. 7.25 x 9.75 in. Linking Rings.

Brock, Tudor, *Great Wong's Routine for the Chinese Rings, The.* Revised edition. (1989) L. Davenport and Co., London. Comb. Black. 65 pp. 8.25 x 11.75 in. Linking Rings.

Brodien, Marshall, *25 Amazing Magic Tricks.* (1996) Harmony Toy, Elmsford, NY. Saddle-stitch. Black. 23 pp. 5.5 x 8.5 in. From 1996 "Marshall Brodien's Magic Show" set. Magic set manual, Beginner.

Brodien, Marshall, *50 Magic Tricks.* (1992) Harmony Toy, Elmsford, NY. Saddle-stitch. White. 40 pp. 5.5 x 8.5 in. Magic set manual, Beginner.

Brodien, Marshall, *50 Magic Tricks You Can Do!* (2008) Nowstalgia Toys, Columbus, OH. Saddle-stitch. Black. 16 pp. 5.5 x 8.5 in. From 2008 "TV Magic Show" set. Magic set manual, Beginner.

Brodien, Marshall, *100 Magic Tricks.* (1992) Harmony Toy, Elmsford, NY. Folded. White. 24 pp. 5.5 x 8.25 in. Magic set manual, Beginner.

Brodien, Marshall, *100 Magic Trick Instruction Book.* (2002) Cadaco, Chicago. Saddle-stitch. Black. 55 pp. 5.5 x 8.25 in. From 2002 Cadaco "Marshall Brodien's Magic Show" set. Magic set manual, Beginner.

Brodien, Marshall, *101 Card Tricks.* (n.d.) TV Magic Ltd., Schaumberg, IL. Saddle-stitch. White. 36 pp. 5.5 x 8.5 in. Magic set manual, Beginner, Cards.

Brodien, Marshall, *102 Magic Tricks.* (1972) TV Magic Ltd., Schaumberg, IL. Saddle-stitch. White. 24 pp. 5.5 x 8.5 in. Magic set manual, Beginner.

Brodien, Marshall, *Amazing Magic Tricks.* (2004) Cadaco, Chicago. Saddle-stitch. Black. 7 pp. 5.5 x 8.5 in. In "Marshall Brodien Magic Show" set. Magic set manual, Beginner.

Brodien, Marshall, *Bill Bixby The Magician: 50 Magic Tricks.* (1974) TV Magic Ltd., Palatine, IL. Saddle-stitch. White. 28 pp. 5.5 x 8.5 in. In "Bill Bixby TV Magic Set." Magic set manual, Beginner.

Brodien, Marshall, *Bill Bixby The Magician Magic Set Secret Instructions.* (1974) TV Magic Ltd., Palatine, IL. Saddle-stitch. White. 28 pp. 5.5 x 8.5 in. In "Bill Bixby TV Magic Set." Magic set manual, Beginner.

Brodien, Marshall, *Columbia House of Magic Course.* (1977) Columbia House, New York. Box. Black. Unpaginated. 4.5 x 8.5 in. Set of about 300 cards plus dividers in custom box. Course, Beginner.

Brodien, Marshall, *Fifty TV Magic Tricks.* (n.d.) TV Magic Ltd., Schaumberg, IL. Saddle-stitch. White. 24 pp. 5.5 x 8.5 in. Magic set manual, Beginner.

Brodien, Marshall, *Magic Tricks: 239 Magic Tricks You Can Do Yourself.* (1980) Marshall Brodein Magic, Schaumberg, IL. Saddle-stitch. White. 61 pp. 5.5 x 8.5 in. Promotional booklet from Marion Laboratories with ad on back. Beginner, Premium.

Brodien, Marshall, *Magician's Great Escapes.* (2000) Cadaco, Chicago. Saddle-stitch. Black. 11 pp. 5.5 x 8.5 in. In "Magician's Great Escapes" set. Magic set manual, Beginner.

Brodien, Marshall, *Marshall Brodien Magic Show Secret Instruction Book.* (1992) Harmony Toy, Elmsford, NY. Saddle-stitch. Black. 22 pp. 5.5 x 8.5 in. From "Marshall Brodien Magic Show" set. Magic set manual, Beginner.

Brodien, Marshall, *Marshall Brodien's Magic and Illusion Show: 100 Magic Tricks Instruction Book.* (2001) Cadaco, Chicago. Saddle-stitch. Black. 47 pp. 5.5 x 8.5 in. From Cadaco 2001 "Marshall Brodien's Magic and Illusion Show" set. Magic set manual, Beginner.

Brodien, Marshall, *Marshall Brodien's Magic Hat: Secrets of 75 Amazing Magic Tricks.* (2004) Cadaco, Chicago. Saddle-stitch. Black. 38 pp. 5.5 x 8.5 in. From Cadaco 2004 "Marshall Brodien's Magic Hat" set. Magic set manual, Beginner.

Brodien, Marshall, *Marshall Brodien's Magic Show: 100 Magic Tricks Instruction Book.* (2002) Cadaco, Chicago. Saddle-stitch. Black. 55 pp. 5.5 x 8.5 in. From Cadaco 2002 "Marshall Brodien's Magic Show" set. Magic set manual, Beginner.

Brodien, Marshall, *Marshall Brodien's Magic Show Secret Instruction Book.* (1994) Harmony Toy, Elmsford, NY. Saddle-stitch. Black. 40 pp. 5.5 x 8.5 in. In "Video Magic" set. Magic set manual, Beginner.

Brodien, Marshall, *Money Magic Show Secret Instructions.* (1976) TV Mystery Products, Schaumberg, IL. Saddle-stitch. Black, white. 19 pp. 5.25 x 8.25 in. From "Money Magic" 15 tricks set. Magic set manual, Beginner.

Brodien, Marshall, *Money Magic Show Secret Instructions.* (1976) TV Mystery Products, Schaumberg, IL. Saddle-stitch. Black, white. 31 pp. 5.25 x 8.25 in. From "Money Magic" 25 tricks set. Magic set manual, Beginner.

Brodien, Marshall, *My First Magic Set Secret Instruction Booklet.* (1999) Cadaco, Chicago. Saddle-stitch. Black. 15 pp. 5.5 x 8.5 in. From 1999 Cadaco "My First Magic Set." Magic set manual, Beginner.

Brodien, Marshall, *Secrets of 100 Magic Tricks.* (1992) Cadaco, Chicago. Folded. Black. 17 pp. 5.5 x 8 in. From 1992 Harmony Toy "Marshall Brodien Magic Show" set. Magic set manual, Beginner.

Brodien, Marshall, *Secrets of 100 Magic Tricks.* (2005) Cadaco, Chicago. Saddle-stitch. Black. 45 pp. 5.5 x 8.5 in. In "Video Magic" set. Magic set manual, Beginner.

Brodien, Marshall, *Siegfried and Roy Spectacular Magic Secret Instruction Book.* (1980) Marshall Brodein Magic, Schaumberg, IL. Saddle-stitch. Black, white. 54 pp. 5.5 x 8.5 in. In "Siegfried and Roy Spectacular Magic" set. Magic set manual, Beginner.

Brodien, Marshall, *TV Magic Set Secret Instructions.* (n.d.) TV Magic Ltd., Schaumberg, IL. Saddle-stitch. White. 7 pp. 5.5 x 8.5 in. From "12 TV Magic Tricks Set." Magic set manual, Beginner.

Brodien, Marshall, *TV Magic Set Secret Instructions.* (1974) TV Magic Ltd., Schaumberg, IL. Saddle-stitch. White. 20 pp. 5.5 x 8.5 in. From TV Magic "15 Magic Tricks Set." Magic set manual, Beginner.

Brodien, Marshall, *TV Magic Show Instruction Book.* (2008) Nowstalgia Toys, Columbus, OH. Saddle-stitch. Black. 15 pp. 5.5 x 8.5 in. From 2008 "TV Magic Show" set. Magic set manual, Beginner.

Broekel, Ray, with White, Laurence B., Jr., *Now You See It: Easy Magic for Beginners.* (1979) Little, Brown, Boston. Cloth. Red. 57 pp. 6.5 x 8.5 in. Dust jacket. Library copy. Beginner, Children's book.

Brolaski, Harry, *Easy Money, or Fishing for Suckers.* (1911) Searchlight Press, Cleveland, OH. Cloth. Yellow. 328 pp. 5.5 x 8 in. Gambling, Cheating, Cards.

Bronson, Rick, with Acer, David, *7 by Rick Bronson.* (2005) David Acer, Montreal. Saddle-stitch. White. 39 pp. 5.5 x 8.5 in. Cards, Stage.

Bronstrup, Dr. Charles L., II, *Showlines and Snappy Bits.* (2000) H. Marshall and Co., Mogadore, OH. Saddle-stitch. Green. 20 pp. 5.5 x 8.5 in. (Information not verified by physical copy.) Comedy, Hecklers.

Brook, Charles, *Magic in the Real World.* (2001) Author, Portugal. Comb. Yellow. 29 pp. 8.25 x 11.75 in. Lecture notes. Cards.

Brook, Paul, *Book of Lies, The.* (2010) Author, UK. Perfect. White, black. 229 pp. 5.5 x 8.5 in. (Information not verified by physical copy.) Close-Up, Impromptu, Stage.

Brook, Paul, *Brook Test, The.* (2007) Author, UK. Perfect. White, black. 91 pp. 5.5 x 8.5 in. (Information not verified by physical copy.) Mentalism, Book tests.

Brook, Paul, *NIX4.* (2013) Author, UK. Cloth. Black. 226 pp. (Information not verified by physical copy. Bibliographical details are as accurate as possible.) Mentalism, Cards.

Brook, Paul, with McLeod, Colin, *This Way Up.* (2011) Authors, UK. Cloth. 253 pp. 6 x 9 in. Dust jacket. (Information not verified by physical copy.) Mentalism.

Brook, Tony, *Hidden in Plain Sight.* (2001) Author, UK. Comb. White. 21 pp. 8.25 x 11.75 in. (Information not verified by physical copy.) Theory, Misdirection, Showmanship.

Brooke, Ken (See also Koornwinder, Dick), *Beam Shot Book, The.* (c. 1972) Ken Brooke, London. Stapled. Orange. 14 pp. 8 x 10 in. Electronics, Gimmicks, Mentalism, Cards.

Brooke, Ken, *It's Better Than Digging Roads.* (1987) Martin Breese, London. Comb. Yellow. 27 pp. 8.25 x 11.75 in. Includes two cassettes. Biography, Stage, Egg Bag, Mentalism.

Brooke, Ken, *K.B. Coins Thru Table.* (1962) Unique Magic Studios, London. Saddle-stitch. Yellow. 9 pp. 6 x 9 in. Coins, Coins Through Table.

Brooke, Ken, *Ken Brooke and Friends and the Malini Egg Bag.* (1974) Magic Inc., Chicago. Stapled. Blue. 21 pp. 8.5 x 11 in. Collected from various sources. Egg Bag.

Brooke, Ken, *Ken Brooke Cup and Ball Routine, The.* Third printing. (c. 1948) Ken Brooke, London. Loose pages. White. 5 pp. 8.25 x 11.75 in. Mimeographed. Blue text color. Cups and Balls, Close-Up.

Brooke, Ken, *Ken Brooke Routine with Trilby, The.* Fourth printing. (1950) Ken Brooke, London. Loose pages. White. 8 pp. 8.25 x 11.75 in. Mimeographed. Cards.

Brooke, Ken, *Ken Brooke Series no. 1: The Magic Box.* (1981) Paul Stone, London. Comb. Gray. 11 pp. 8.5 x 12 in. Coins, Close-Up, Stage.

Brooke, Ken, *Ken Brooke Series no. 2: The Chop Cup.* (1981) Paul Stone, London. Comb. Brown. 10 pp. 8.5 x 12 in. Chop Cup, Close-Up, Stage.

Brooke, Ken, *Ken Brooke Series no. 3: The Nap Hand and the Multiplying Martini Bottles.* (1981) Paul Stone, London. Comb. Blue. 11 pp. 8.5 x 12 in. Cards, Multiplying Bottles, Stage.

Brooke, Ken, *Ken Brooke Series no. 4: The Sidewalk Shuffle.* (1981) Paul Stone, London. Comb. Red. 14 pp. 8.5 x 12 in. Cards.

Brooke, Ken, *Ken Brooke Series no. 5: The Dancing and Floating Cork.* (1981) Paul Stone, London. Comb. Green. 12 pp. 8.5 x 12 in. Includes card with thread. Thread, Floating effects.

Brooke, Ken, *Ken Brooke Series no. 6: Al Koran's Three Silver Rings.* Second edition. (2009) Stevens Magic, Wichita, KS. Saddle-stitch. Orange. 16 pp. 8.5 x 11 in. Linking Rings.

Brooke, Ken, *Ken Brooke Series no. 7: The Finn Jon Zombie Routine, Roy Johnson's Cent, The Malcolm Davison Book Test.* (1981) Paul Stone, London. Comb. Yellow. 16 pp. 8.5 x 12 in. Zombie, Coins, Book tests.

Brooke, Ken, *Ken Brooke Series no. 8: Roy Johnson's Flawless, Ken Brooke on The Hamman Count.* (1984) Paul Stone, London. Comb. Blue. 21 pp. 8.5 x 12 in. Mentalism, Cards.

Brooke, Ken, *Ken Brooke Series no. 9: Ken Brooke's Ring and Stick Routine, The Backward Card Trick.* (1984) Paul Stone, London. Comb. Brown. 9 pp. 8.5 x 12 in. Rings, Wands, Cards.

Brooke, Ken, *Ken Brooke Series no. 10: Beam Shot, The Koornwinder Kar, Edelweiss.* (1984) Paul Stone, London. Comb. Green. 14 pp. 8.5 x 12 in. Cards, Stage, Close-Up.

Brooke, Ken, *Ken Brooke Treatise on "Dirty Deal," The.* (1970) Ken Brooke, London. Stapled. Pink. 6 pp. 8.25 x 11.75 in. Mimeographed. Techniques for Bruce Cervon's effect. Cards, Packet tricks, Counts.

Brooke, Ken, *Ken Brooke's Cups and Balls Routine.* (1981) Supreme Magic, Bideford, UK. Saddle-stitch. White. 5 pp. 7.5 x 10 in. Cups and Balls.

Brooke, Ken, *Ken Brooke's Magic: The Unique Years.* (1982) Supreme Magic, Bideford, UK. Cloth. Maroon. 222 pp. 8 x 10 in. Dust jacket. Beginner, Stage, Close-Up.

Brooke, Ken, *Ken Brooke's Magic Place.* (1994) L & L Publishing, Tahoma, CA. Cloth. Black. 320 pp. 8.5 x 11 in. Beginner, Stage, Close-Up.

Brooke, Ken, *Letter for the Conjurer, A.* (1951) Ken Brooke, London. Stapled. White. 3 pp. 8 x 10 in. Mimeographed. (Information not verified by physical copy.) Children's magic, Comedy.

Brooke, Ken, with Cook, Steve (ed.), *Legend: An Anecdotal Tribute to Ken Brooke.* (2008) Steve Cook, London. 220 pp. (Information not verified by physical copy.) Biography, History.

Brooke, Ken, *Lifetime of Joy, A.* (1982) Jeff Busby Magic, Oakland, CA. Comb. White. 16 pp. 8.5 x 11 in. (Measurements and other information have been recorded as accurately as possible.) Comedy.

Brooke, Ken, with Kaps, Fred, *Sidewalk Shuffle, The.* (1974) Ken Brooke, London. Stapled. White. 9 pp. 8.25 x 11.75 in. Cards, Monte, Jumbo cards, Stage.

Brooke, Ken, *Something from Nothing.* (1953) Author, Bradford, UK. Stapled. White. 3 pp. 7.75 x 12.25 in. Close-Up, Matrix.

Brookings, Atlas, with Brown, Andrew, *Crusade, The.* (2013) Author, UK. Perfect. Color. 109 pp. (Information not verified by physical copy.) Mentalism.

Brookings, Atlas, *Prodigal, The.* (2013) Author, UK. Perfect. Blue. 155 pp. (Information not verified by physical copy.) Mentalism.

Brookings, Atlas, *Real Thing, The.* (c. 2013) Author, UK. Perfect. Blue. 84 pp. (Information not verified by physical copy.) Mentalism.

Brookings, Atlas, *Intrepid Rogue's Manual of Deception, The.* (c. 2013) Author, UK. Casebound. Green. 224 pp. (Information not verified by physical copy.) Mentalism, Close-Up, Essays.

Brookings, Atlas, *Intrepid Rogue's Manual of Deception, The.* (c. 2013) Author, UK. Perfect. White. 224 pp. (Information not verified by physical copy.) Mentalism, Close-Up, Essays.

Brookings, Atlas, with Fletcher, Joshua, *Underhanded: The Gimmickless Business Card Peek Perfected.* (2018) Authors, UK. Perfect. Blue. 84 pp. 5.5 x 8.5 in. Mentalism, Business cards.

Brooks, Arthur C., *Penny Book of Puzzles and Tricks, The.* (1902) Author, UK. Saddle-stitch. Light blue. 16 pp. 6.25 x 10 in. In Copperfield collection. Beginner, Stunts.

Brooks, Lewis R., *Stack Attack, The.* (1997) Author, Las Vegas. Comb. Yellow. 35 pp. 8.5 x 11 in. Cards, Prearranged deck.

Brooks, Lewis R., *Stack Attack.* Second edition. (1998) Magic Fun Factory, Las Vegas. Comb. Blue. 43 pp. 8.5 x 11 in. Iridescent blue cover. The second edition omitted "The" from the title. Cards, Prearranged deck.

Broughton, Christopher, *Creating Your Own Character.* (c. 1989) Author, Los Angeles. Strip binding. Yellow. 16 pp. 8.5 x 11 in. Translucent yellow cover. Lecture notes. Showmanship, Stage, Theory.

Brown, Bob, *Entertainmentalist, The.* (1980) Author, Davenport, IA. Stapled. Beige. 22 pp. 8.5 x 11 in. Lecture notes. Mentalism, Stage, Escapes.

Brown, Bob, *Extra Act, The.* (n.d.) Author, Davenport, IA. Stapled. Yellow. 11 pp. 8.5 x 11 in. Lecture notes. Memory, Stage.

Brown, Bob, *Magical Miscellany II: Jottings of a Generalist.* (c. 1985) Author, Davenport, IA. Comb. Blue. 36 pp. 8.5 x 11 in. Stage, Close-Up.

Brown, Derren, *Absolute Magic.* (2001) Author, London. Cloth. Brown. Cover text: Gold; 224 pp. 6 x 8.5 in. Close-Up, Theory.

Brown, Derren, *Absolute Magic.* Second edition. (2003) H & R Magic Books, Humble, TX. Cloth. Green. 251 pp. 6 x 9 in. Close-Up, Theory.

Brown, Derren, *Book of Secrets, A.* (2021) Bantam, London. Cloth. Black. 293 pp. 6.25 x 9.5 in. Dust jacket. Essays, Self-help.

Brown, Derren, *Book of Secrets, A.* (2021) Penguin Books, London. Perfect. Blue. 292 pp. 5 x 7.5 in. (Measurements and other information have been recorded as accurately as possible.) Essays, Self-help.

Brown, Derren, *Happy.* (2016) Bantam, London. Cloth. Blue. 442 pp. 6 x 9.5 in. Dust jacket. (Measurements and other information have been recorded as accurately as possible.) Biography.

Brown, Derren, *Little Happier, A.* (2020) Bantam, London. Cloth. Maroon. 115 pp. 5.25 x 8 in. Dust jacket. Biography, Essays.

Brown, Derren, *Magie Absolue.* (2004) CC Editions, Chasseneuil, France. Cloth. Black. 244 pp. 6.5 x 9.5 in. Dust jacket. Translation of "Absolute Magic." Close-Up, Theory. French.

Brown, Derren, *Meet the People with Love.* (2018) Bantam, London. Casebound. Black. 103 pp. 11.75 x 9.25 in. Photography.

Brown, Derren, *Notes from a Fellow Traveler.* (2023) Neat Books, London. Cloth. Beige. Cover text: Red; 519 pp. 5.75 x 8.25 in. Biography, Mentalism, Theory.

Brown, Derren, *Pure Effect.* (1999) Author, Clifton Village, UK. Wire binding. 182 pp. 6 x 9 in. (Information not verified by physical copy.) Mentalism, Cards.

Brown, Derren, *Pure Effect.* Third printing. (2000) H & R Magic Books, Humble, TX. Cloth. Brown. 164 pp. 6 x 9 in. Dust jacket. Mentalism, Cards.

Brown, Derren, *Tricks of the Mind.* (2007) Channel 4, London. Perfect. Color. 392 pp. 5 x 7.75 in. Mentalism, Hypnosis, Stunts.

Brown, Derren, *Tricks of the Mind.* Sixth printing. (2007) Channel 4, London. Perfect. Color. 390 pp. 6 x 9 in. Mentalism, Hypnosis, Stunts.

Brown, Dota "Mysterious," *Neil Foster.* Second printing. (1988) Author, Palm Desert, CA. Saddle-stitch. Yellow. 48 pp. 5.5 x 8.5 in. Biography.

Brown, Edward G., *Sleights and Subtleties.* (1947) Magic Circle, London. Saddle-stitch. White. 12 pp. 5.5 x 8.5 in. (Information not verified by physical copy.) Supplement to "The Magic Circular," May 1947. Lecture notes. Cards, Close-Up.

Brown, Floyd D., *25 Methods for Switching Decks.* (1943) U. F. Grant, Columbus, OH. Saddle-stitch. Yellow. 17 pp. 3.5 x 6 in. Cards, Deck switches.

Brown, Floyd D., *25 Methods for Switching Decks.* (n.d.) U. F. Grant, Columbus, OH. Stapled. White. 6 pp. 8.5 x 11 in. Mimeographed. Cards, Deck switches.

Brown, Floyd D., *25 Methods for Switching Decks.* (n.d.) U. F. Grant, Columbus, OH. Comb. White, red. 11 pp. 3.5 x 6 in. Later edition. Cards, Deck switches.

Brown, Floyd D., *25 Methods for Switching Decks.* (n.d.) O'Neal Magic, Rockbridge, OH. Stapled. Light green. 9 pp. 8.5 x 11 in. Cards, Deck switches.

Brown, Gary R., *Coney Island Fakir: The Magical Life of Al Flosso.* Deluxe edition. (1997) L & L Publishing, Tahoma, CA. Leather. Black. 229 pp. 6 x 9 in. (Information not verified by physical copy.) Signed by Jackie Flosso, Gary Brown. Biography.

Brown, Gary R., *Coney Island Fakir: The Magical Life of Al Flosso.* (1997) L & L Publishing, Tahoma, CA. Cloth. Black. 229 pp. 6 x 9 in. Dust jacket. Includes Annemann's "Buried Treasures." Biography.

Brown, Gary R., *Wandcraft.* (2020) Theory of Art and Magic Press, Las Vegas. Casebound. Red. 94 pp. 6.5 x 9.25 in. Dust jacket. Wands, Building.

Brown, James Chandler, *Cleanmagic II: The Lecture.* (1995) Author, Los Angeles. Stapled. 14 pp. 8.5 x 11 in. (Information not verified by physical copy.) Lecture notes. Stage, Topit.

Brown, Jeff, *Crayon Magic.* (2000) SPS Publications, Tavares, FL. Saddle-stitch. White, red, blue. 60 pp. 5.5 x 8.5 in. (Information not verified by physical copy.) Children's magic, Crayons.

Brown, Jeff, *Sherlock Holmes Book of Magic, The.* (2000) Piccadilly Books, Colorado Springs, CO. Perfect. Black. 96 pp. 5.5 x 8.5 in. Effects themed to Holmes stories. Fiction, Close-Up, Stage.

Brown, Jim and Daisy, with Miller, J. K., *Care and Feeding of Feather Flowers, The.* (n.d.) Author, Miami, FL. Stapled. Green. 8.5 x 11 in. (Information not verified by physical copy.) Flowers, Feather flowers.

Brown, Jim, *Magic.* (c. 1988) Author, Miami, FL. Stapled. White. 15 pp. 8.5 x 11 in. (Information not verified by physical copy.) Close-Up, Stage, Showmanship.

Brown, Jimmy, *Magic of Jimmy Brown, The.* (1991) Author, Union, NJ. Comb. Yellow. 40 pp. 8.5 x 11 in. (Information not verified by physical copy.) Lecture notes. Close-Up, Stage, Showmanship.

Brown, John, *Snow White Dove Production.* (n.d.) The Elders, Dallas, TX. Stapled. White. 8 pp. 8.5 x 11 in. Doves, Stage, Gimmicks.

Brown, Judge Gary, *Inventive Magician's Handbook, The.* (2024) Theory of Art and Magic Press, Washington D.C. Casebound. Red. 208 pp. 7.25 x 10.25 in. Includes props. Creativity, Inventions.

Brown, Professor, *Handbook of Magic.* (1892) Author, St. Thomas, Canada. Saddle-stitch. Beige. 16 pp. 4 x 5.75 in. In Copperfield collection. Beginner.

Browning, Craig, *Thoth's Wisdom.* (2014) Pro Shop, Colchester, VT. Casebound. 78 pp. (Information not verified by physical copy.) Mentalism, Tarot.

Brownstein, Gabriel, *Man from Beyond, The.* (2005) W. W. Norton and Co., New York. Cloth. Green. 298 pp. 5.75 x 8.5 in. Dust jacket. Houdini, Fiction.

Bruecker, Steve, with Rogers, Mike, *Three Shell Game Routine.* (1985) Jeff Busby Magic, Oakland, CA. Saddle-stitch. Beige. 15 pp. 4.25 x 5 in. Three Shell Game.

Brumfield, A. W. C., *Perfection One Man Mind Reading Act.* (1926) Welworth Company, Indianapolis, IN. Stapled with paper cover. Blue. 7 pp. 5.5 x 8.5 in. Mimeographed. Mentalism.

Brumfield, A. W. C., *Perfection Slate Miracle, The.* (1927) Welworth Company, Indianapolis, IN. Brads. White. 2 pp. 8.5 x 11 in. Bound at top. Mimeographed. Actual hand-penned portions of illustrations. Mentalism.

Brummett, Joey, *Making the Impossible Funny.* (2008) Author. Blue. 15 pp. (Information not verified by physical copy.) Comedy.

Brunel, George, *Fun with Magic.* (1901) H. M. Caldwell Co., New York and Boston. Cloth. Brown. 175 pp. 5.5 x 7.75 in. All-over Japanese children design on cover. Beginner, Science magic, Stunts, Shadowgraphy.

Brunel, George, *Fun with Magic.* (1901) H. M. Caldwell Co., New York and Boston. Cloth. Brown. 175 pp. 5.25 x 7.5 in. Japanese children in robes on cover. Beginner, Science magic, Stunts, Shadowgraphy.

Brunel, George, *Fun with Magic.* (1901) H. M. Caldwell Co., New York and Boston. Cloth. Maroon. 175 pp. 5.25 x 7.5 in. Japanese costumed children on cover. Beginner, Science magic, Stunts, Shadowgraphy.

Brunel, George, *Fun with Magic.* (1901) Hurst and Co., New York. Cloth. Beige. 175 pp. 4 x 6 in. Boys in canoe on cover. Beginner, Science magic, Stunts, Shadowgraphy.

Brunel, George, *Fun with Magic.* (1901) Hurst and Co., New York. Cloth. Brown. 175 pp. 4 x 6 in. Boy reading by fire on cover. Beginner, Science magic, Stunts, Shadowgraphy.

Brunel, George, *Fun with Magic.* (1901) Hurst and Co., New York. Cloth. Green. 175 pp. 4 x 6 in. Boys fishing on cover. Beginner, Science magic, Stunts, Shadowgraphy.

Brunelle, Jon, *Mixed Bag.* (1979) Author, Chicago. Stapled. White. 16 pp. 8.5 x 11 in. (Information not verified by physical copy.) Lecture notes. Cards, Close-Up, Stage.

Brunelle, Jon, *Strange Science.* (1998) Author, Chicago. Stapled. White. 20 pp. 8.5 x 11 in. (Information not verified by physical copy.) Close-Up, Stage.

Brunelle, Jon, *Tips and Quick Effects.* (1990) Author, Chicago. Stapled. Blue. 4 pp. 8.5 x 11 in. (Information not verified by physical copy.) Cards, Close-Up, Tips.

Brunelle, Jon, *Ways to Improve Your Coin Magic.* (1988) Author, Chicago. Saddle-stitch. Yellow. 8 pp. 8.5 x 11 in. (Information not verified by physical copy.) Coins, Theory, Misdirection, Showmanship.

Bruno, *25 Card Tricks.* Miniature book. (n.d.) Russell Manufacturing Co., Leicester, MA. Saddle-stitch. Yellow. 25 pp. 3.25 x 4 in. In "Beginner Edition" deck-book set. Cards, Beginner.

Bruno, *25 Card Tricks.* Miniature book. (n.d.) Russell Manufacturing Co., Leicester, MA. Saddle-stitch. Red. 25 pp. 3.25 x 4 in. In "Intermediate Edition" deck-book set. Cards, Beginner.

Bruno, *25 Card Tricks.* Second edition. (n.d.) Author, Des Moines, IA. Saddle-stitch. Brown, orange, white. 25 pp. 3.25 x 4 in. Cards, Beginner.

Bruno, *25 Famous Card Tricks.* Miniature book. (n.d.) Author, Des Moines, IA. Saddle-stitch. Brown, red. 25 pp. 3.5 x 4 in. (Measurements and other information have been recorded as accurately as possible.) Cards.

Bruno, *25 Famous Card Tricks.* Miniature book. (n.d.) Author, Des Moines, IA. Saddle-stitch. Yellow, red. 25 pp. 3.25 x 4 in. (Measurements and other information have been recorded as accurately as possible.) Cards.

Bruno, *Magic from Holland.* (1964) Author, Des Moines, IA. Saddle-stitch. Yellow. 28 pp. 5.5 x 8.5 in. Signed by Bruno. Close-Up, Stage.

Bruno, Joe, *12 Steps to Creative Magic.* (2013) Author, Randallstown, MD. Perfect. Blue. 64 pp. 5.5 x 8.5 in. (Information not verified by physical copy.) Theory, Creativity.

Bruno, Joe, *Anatomy of Misdirection, The.* (c. 1979) Author, Randallstown, MD. 68 pp. (Information not verified by physical copy.) Theory, Misdirection, Psychology, Essays.

Bruno, Joe, *Anatomy of Misdirection, The.* (2013) Author, Randallstown, MD. Perfect. Blue. 84 pp. 5.5 x 8.5 in. Theory, Misdirection, Psychology, Essays.

Bruno, Joe, *Beth Tfiloh Magic Class 1.* (1997) Author, Randallstown, MD. Saddle-stitch. Gray. 34 pp. 5.5 x 8.5 in. Signed by Joe Bruno. Beginner, Course.

Bruno, Joe, *Beth Tfiloh Magic Class 2.* (1997) Author, Randallstown, MD. Saddle-stitch. Gray. 30 pp. 5.5 x 8.5 in. Signed by Joe Bruno. Beginner, Course.

Bruno, Joe, *Beth Tfiloh Magic Class 3.* (1998) Author, Randallstown, MD. Saddle-stitch. Gray. 34 pp. 5.5 x 8.5 in. Signed by Joe Bruno. Beginner, Course.

Bruno, Joe, *Beth Tfiloh Magic Class 4.* (1998) Author, Randallstown, MD. Saddle-stitch. Gray. 30 pp. 5.5 x 8.5 in. Signed by Joe Bruno. Beginner, Course.

Bruno, Joe, *Beth Tfiloh Magic Class 5.* (2000) Author, Randallstown, MD. Saddle-stitch. Gray. 32 pp. 5.5 x 8.5 in. Signed by Joe Bruno. Beginner, Course.

Bruno, Joe, *Beth Tfiloh Magic Class 6.* (2001) Author, Randallstown, MD. Saddle-stitch. Gray. 32 pp. 5.5 x 8.5 in. Signed by Joe Bruno. Beginner, Course.

Brush, Charles "Baffles," *Flower Magic.* (1933) Author, Randallstown, MD. Stapled. Olive. 18 pp. 8.5 x 11 in. Mimeographed. (Measurements and other information have been recorded as accurately as possible.) Flowers.

Brushwood, Brian, *Scam School.* (2013) Skyhorse Publishing, New York. Perfect. Black. 240 pp. 5 x 7 in. Bets, Stunts, Impromptu.

Brushwood, Brian, *Scam School Academy.* (2016) Skyhorse Publishing, New York. Perfect. Blue. 304 pp. 5 x 7 in. Bets, Stunts, Impromptu.

Brusselback, Bryan, *Right Way to Buy Magic, The.* (2000) Author, Pasadena, TX. Clip. White. 7 pp. 8.5 x 11 in. (Information not verified by physical copy.) Business.

Bruton, Paul, *Amusing Yourself with Paper and String.* (1949) Universal Publications, London. Saddle-stitch. Red, blue. 66 pp. 4 x 6.5 in. Paper, Stunts.

Bruton, Paul, *Modern Conjuring: 50 Novel Illusions.* (1940) Universal Publications, London. Saddle-stitch. Red, blue. 90 pp. 4 x 6.5 in. Beginner, Stage.

Bryant, Steve, *Bryant on Cards.* (1977) Author, Bloomington, IN. Comb. Beige. 81 pp. 6.5 x 9 in. (Information not verified by physical copy. Bibliographical details are as accurate as possible.) Cards.

Bryant, Steve, *Little Egypt Book of Ghosts, The.* (2008) H & R Magic Books, Humble, TX. Cloth. Black. 230 pp. 8.5 x 11 in. Dust jacket. Spirit effects, Séances, Close-Up, Stage.

Bryant, Steve, *Little Egypt Book of Numbers, The.* (2004) H & R Magic Books, Humble, TX. Cloth. Blue. 128 pp. 8.5 x 11 in. Dust jacket. Cards, Close-Up.

Bryant, Steve, *Little Egypt Card Tricks.* (1991) Author, Bloomington, IN. Coil. Beige. 122 pp. 8.5 x 11 in. (Information not verified by physical copy.) Cards.

Bryden, Dean, *Fun with Cards.* (1927) George Sully and Co., New York. Cloth. Red. 165 pp. 5 x 7.5 in. Dust jacket. Card games, Cards, History.

Bryson, Rhett (See also Dunn, Bruce; Goldin, Horace; Massey, Edward), with Andrews, Charlton, *Ballade of the Would Be Mage, The.* Miniature book. (1999) Author, Greenville, SC. Saddle-stitch. Beige. 9 pp. 2 x 2.5 in. From "The Jinx," March 1938, p. 290. Fiction.

Bryson, Rhett, *Devil's Prayerbook, The.* Miniature book. (1999) Author, Greenville, SC. Saddle-stitch. Beige. 33 pp. 3.25 x 4.5 in. (Information not verified by physical copy.) Cards, Storytelling magic.

Bryson, Rhett, *Enigmatic India.* Miniature book. (2000) Bruce Dunn, Kalamazoo, MI. Saddle-stitch. Orange. 19 pp. 3 x 4 in. Wee Books by Dunn. From "The Wizard," 1906. History, Indian magic.

Bryson, Rhett, *Magic Collection Miscellanea, A.* Miniature book. (2005) Author, Greenville, SC. Folded. White. Multiple sections. 2.75 x 4.25 in. Fifteen miniature books in outer bands. History.

Bryson, Rhett, *Magic Tricks: vols. 1-6.* Miniature book. (1999) Author, Greenville, SC. Saddle-stitch. Blue. Multiple sections. 2.75 x 4 in. Set of six reprints of Whitman booklets. (Information not verified by physical copy.) History.

Bryson, Rhett, *Most Dramatic Trick in the History of Magic, The.* Miniature book. (2000) Bruce Dunn, Kalamazoo, MI. Saddle-stitch. Yellow. 12 pp. 3 x 4.25 in. Wee Books by Dunn. From "The Mentor," 1927. History, Biography.

Bryson, Rhett, *Small Magical Ideas.* Miniature book. (1989) Jester's Press, Greenville, SC. Comb. Blue gray. 62 pp. 5 x 2.5 in. Material by Daryl, Gardner, and others. #140 of 300. Close-Up, Stage, Mentalism.

Buchanan, Lovell, *Magic Lamp.* (1977) Author, Lancaster, PA. Stapled. Pink. 30 pp. 8 x 10 in. (Information not verified by physical copy.) Close-Up, Stage, Doves.

Buck, Dan and Dave, *Artifice, Ruse, and Subterfuge in the Hands.* Second edition. (2001) DMB Publications, Sonora, CA. Clip. Green. 60 pp. 8.5 x 11 in. Cards, Flourishes.

Buck, Dan and Dave, *Artifice, Ruse, and Subterfuge in the Hands.* Second edition. (2001) DMB Publications, Sonora, CA. Loose pages. White. 60 pp. 8.5 x 11 in. Cards, Flourishes.

Buck, Dan and Dave, *Card Men.* (2014) Authors, Los Angeles. Perfect. Black, white. 61 pp. 6.75 x 10.25 in. Cards, Flourishes.

Buck, Dan and Dave, *Five.* (2003) Authors, Los Angeles. Saddle-stitch. White. 24 pp. 8.5 x 11 in. Signed by Dan and Dave Buck. Cards, Flourishes.

Buck, Dan and Dave, *If an Octopus Could Palm.* (2011) Authors, Los Angeles. Cloth. Yellow. 89 pp. 9.5 x 12 in. Dust jacket. Signed by Dan and Dave Buck. Cards, Flourishes.

Buck, Dan and Dave, *If an Octopus Could Palm.* Second edition. (2021) Authors, Los Angeles. Perfect. Olive. 80 pp. 9.5 x 12 in. Cards, Flourishes.

Buck, Dan and Dave, *Nursery Rhymes vol. 1.* (2001) Authors, Los Angeles. Coil. White. 27 pp. 8.5 x 11 in. Signed by Dan and Dave Buck. Cards, Flourishes.

Buck, Dan and Dave, *Nursery Rhymes vol. 2.* (2002) Authors, Los Angeles. Coil. White. 48 pp. 8.5 x 11 in. Signed by Dan and Dave Buck. Cards, Flourishes.

Buck, Dan and Dave, *Nursery Rhymes vol. 3.* (2003) Authors, Los Angeles. Coil. White. 39 pp. 8.5 x 11 in. Signed by Dan and Dave Buck. Cards, Flourishes.

Buck, Dan and Dave, *Organic.* (2008) Authors, Los Angeles. 28 pp. (Information not verified by physical copy.) Theory, Improv magic, Cards.

Buck, Dan and Dave, *Sleightly Magical.* (2006) Authors, Los Angeles. Saddle-stitch. Green, orange. 33 pp. 8.5 x 11 in. (Information not verified by physical copy.) Cards, Flourishes.

Buck, Dan and Dave, *Splay.* Standard edition. (2022) The Neat Review, UK. Cloth. Black. 229 pp. 9.75 x 11.75 in. Cards, Flourishes.

Buck, Dan and Dave, with Hansford, Alexander, *Tangram vol. 1: Going into Wonder.* (2021) Art of Play, UK. Sewn covers. White, black. 127 pp. 9 x 11.5 in. Magazine, Essays, Art.

Buckingham, Geoffrey, *50 Years of Magic.* (1976) Author, UK. Stapled. White. 22 pp. 8.5 x 11 in. Lecture notes. Cards, Manipulation, Stage, Hindu Thread.

Buckingham, Geoffrey, *Flying Sorcerers, The.* (1950) Magic Circle, London. Stapled. White. 46 pp. 5.5 x 8.5 in. Supplement to "The Magic Circular," January 1951. Lecture notes.

Buckingham, Geoffrey, *It's Easier Than You Think.* (1952) H. Clarke and Co., London. Cloth. Black. 191 pp. 6.25 x 9.25 in. Dust jacket. Billiard balls, Manipulation, Coins.

Buckingham, Geoffrey, *It's Easier Than You Think vol. 1.* Lecture Tour Edition. (1970) Magic Inc., Chicago. Saddle-stitch. Green. 76 pp. 5.5 x 8.5 in. Billiard balls, Manipulation, Coins.

Buckingham, Geoffrey, *It's Easier Than You Think vol. 2.* Lecture Tour Edition. (1970) Magic Inc., Chicago. Saddle-stitch. Red. 72 pp. 5.5 x 8.5 in. Billiard balls, Manipulation, Coins.

Buckingham, Geoffrey, *It's Easier Than You Think vol. 3.* Second printing. (1982) Magic Inc., Chicago. Comb. Green. 104 pp. 5.5 x 8.5 in. Billiard balls, Manipulation, Coins.

Buckingham, Geoffrey, *Magic Moments.* (c. 1976) Author, London. Stapled. White. 15 pp. 8.5 x 11 in. Signed by Geoffrey Buckingham. Lecture notes. Cards, Close-Up, Stage.

Buckingham, Geoffrey, *Manipulation with the Accent on Thimbles: A Report of a Lecture.* (1947) Magic Circle, London. Saddle-stitch. White. 12 pp. 5 x 8 in. Supplement to "The Magic Circular," April 1947. Thimbles, Manipulation.

Buckingham, Geoffrey, *Suggestions for the Manipulator.* (1949) Magic Circle, London. Saddle-stitch. White. 8 pp. 5.5 x 8.5 in. (Information not verified by physical copy.) Supplement to "The Magic Circular," March 1949. Lecture notes. Manipulation.

Buckley, Arthur, *Astrological Forecasts.* (c. 1928) Author, Adelaide, Australia. Saddle-stitch. 32 pp. 4.75 x 7.25 in. (Information not verified by physical copy.) See McCullagh, "Under the Southern Cross." Astrology, Pitch book.

Buckley, Arthur, *Astrology.* (1928) Author, Sydney. Saddle-stitch. 48 pp. 4.75 x 7.25 in. (Information not verified by physical copy.) See McCullagh, "Under the Southern Cross." Astrology, Pitch book.

Buckley, Arthur, *Buckley's New and Improved Effects with Cards no. 1: The Triple Climax.* (August 1921) Magic Products Co., Chicago. Saddle-stitch. Gray. 10 pp. 6 x 9 in. Cards.

Buckley, Arthur, *Buckley's New and Improved Effects with Cards no. 2: The Burglar.* (September 1921) Magic Products Co., Chicago. Saddle-stitch. Gray. 10 pp. 6 x 9 in. Cards.

Buckley, Arthur, *Buckley's New and Improved Effects with Cards no. 3: With a Pack of Cards and Four Pockets.* (October 1912) Magic Products Co., Chicago. Saddle-stitch. Gray. 10 pp. 6 x 9 in. Cards.

Buckley, Arthur, *Buckleys' Articles: Mind Reading, The.* (n.d.) Author, Chicago. Stapled. White. 22 pp. 8.5 x 11 in. Mimeographed. Mentalism, Second Sight.

Buckley, Arthur, *Card Control.* First edition. (1946) Author, Springfield, IL. Cloth. Black. 219 pp. 6.25 x 9.25 in. Signed by Arthur Buckley. Cards.

Buckley, Arthur, *Card Control.* Second edition. (1946) Author, Springfield, IL. Cloth. Black. 222 pp. 6 x 9 in. (Measurements and other information have been recorded as accurately as possible.) Cards.

Buckley, Arthur, *Card Control.* (1973) Gamblers Book Club, Las Vegas. Perfect. Light blue. 220 pp. 5.25 x 8.25 in. $4 price on cover. Cards.

Buckley, Arthur, *Card Control.* (1973) Gamblers Book Club, Las Vegas. Perfect. Blue. 220 pp. 5.25 x 8.25 in. (Measurements and other information have been recorded as accurately as possible.) Cards.

Buckley, Arthur, *Card Control.* (1993) Dover, New York. Perfect. Gray. 219 pp. 5.25 x 8.5 in. (Measurements and other information have been recorded as accurately as possible.) Cards.

Buckley, Arthur, *Card Control.* (2013) Houdini Publishing, Las Vegas. Perfect. Black, red. 219 pp. 6 x 9 in. (Measurements and other information have been recorded as accurately as possible.) Cards.

Buckley, Arthur, *Card Problems.* (1930) American Studios, San Francisco. Stapled with paper cover. Beige. 57 pp. 8.5 x 11 in. Mimeographed. Cards.

Buckley, Arthur, with Dunn, Bruce, *Easy Thimble Production.* Miniature book. (1996) Bruce Dunn, Kalamazoo, MI. Saddle-stitch. Pink. 7 pp. 2 x 3 in. Wee Books by Dunn. From "Dunn's Thimble Series" set. Author misspelled as "Buckle." History, Thimbles.

Buckley, Arthur, with Cook, John Brown, *Gems of Mental Magic.* (1947) Author, Springfield, IL. Cloth. Black. 132 pp. 6 x 9 in. Mentalism.

Buckley, Arthur, with Cook, John Brown, *Gems of Mental Magic.* (1973) Gamblers Book Club, Las Vegas. Perfect. Light blue. 132 pp. 5.25 x 8.25 in. $4 price on cover. Mentalism.

Buckley, Arthur, with Cook, John Brown, *Gems of Mental Magic.* (1973) Gamblers Book Club, Las Vegas. Perfect. Color. 132 pp. 5.25 x 8.25 in. Mentalism.

Buckley, Arthur, *Improved and Original Card Problems: Series 2.* (1924) Z. Goldenberg, San Francisco. Saddle-stitch. White. 11 pp. 3.75 x 6.75 in. Cards.

Buckley, Arthur, *More Power.* (1928) Author, Sydney. 48 pp. 5 x 7.25 in. (Information not verified by physical copy.) See McCullagh, "Under the Southern Cross." Astrology, Self-help, Pitch book.

Buckley, Arthur, *Principles and Deceptions.* (1948) Author, Springfield, IL. Cloth. Black. 224 pp. 6 x 9 in. Coins, Balls, Theory, Close-Up.

Buckley, Arthur, *Principles and Deceptions.* (1973) Gamblers Book Club, Las Vegas. Perfect. Light blue. 222 pp. 5.25 x 8.25 in. $4 price on cover. Coins, Balls, Theory, Close-Up.

Buckley, Arthur, *Principles and Deceptions.* (1973) Gamblers Book Club, Las Vegas. Perfect. Blue. 222 pp. 5.25 x 8.25 in. Coins, Balls, Theory, Close-Up.

Buckner, Charles A., *Charlie's Brain Twisters.* (1997) Author, Birmingham, AL. Comb. Green. 34 pp. 8.5 x 11 in. (Measurements and other information have been recorded as accurately as possible.) Mentalism.

Buckner, Charles A., *Charlie's Brain Twisters II.* (1997) Author, Birmingham, AL. Binder spine. Light green. 19 pp. 8.5 x 11 in. Mentalism.

Buckner, Charles A., *Charliex.* (2000) Author, Birmingham, AL. Clip. White. 13 pp. 8.5 x 11 in. (Information not verified by physical copy. Bibliographical details are as accurate as possible.) Lecture notes. Stage.

Buckner, Charles A., *Dunninger.* (1996) Author, Birmingham, AL. Strip binding. Gray. 135 pp. 8.5 x 11 in. Biography, History, Mentalism.

Budd, David, *Milton Woodward: The Magician That Changed Magic.* (2021) Author, Bidford-on-Avon, UK. Perfect. Red. 119 pp. 8.25 x 10 in. (Information not verified by physical copy.) Biography, History.

Buescher, John Benedict, *Radio Psychics.* (2021) McFarland and Co., Jefferson, NC. Perfect. Maroon. 422 pp. 7 x 10 in. History, Radio, Biography.

Buff, R. C. (See also Dayton, Ronald J.), with Schmidt, Joseph K., *Best of Buff, The.* (1987) Jeff Busby Magic, Oakland, CA. Comb. White. 30 pp. 8.5 x 11 in. Rope.

Buff, R. C., *Floating Cane, The.* (1956) Author, Knoxville, TN. Stapled. White. 8 pp. 8.5 x 11 in. Mimeographed. (Information not verified by physical copy.) Canes, Dancing Cane.

Buff, R. C., *Ghost of the Past.* (1978) Author, Knoxville, TN. 15 pp. (Information not verified by physical copy. Bibliographical details are as accurate as possible.) Biography.

Buff, R. C., with Schmidt, Joseph K., *Knot on the Square.* (1987) Jeff Busby Magic, Oakland, CA. Comb. White. 21 pp. 8.5 x 11 in. Rope.

Buff, R. C., *Square and Circle Magic.* (1946) Author, Knoxville, TN. Boards. Red. 14 pp. 8.5 x 11 in. Mimeographed. (Measurements and other information have been recorded as accurately as possible.) Stage.

Buff, R. C., *Wizard of Knotsville, The.* (1985) Micky Hades, Calgary, Canada. Comb. Beige. 42 pp. 8.5 x 11 in. (Measurements and other information have been recorded as accurately as possible.) Rope.

Buffaloe, Jim, *Buffaloe'd.* (1998) Dan Garrett, Lithonia, GA. Cloth. Black. 222 pp. 8.75 x 11.25 in. (Measurements and other information have been recorded as accurately as possible.) Close-Up, Stage.

Buffaloe, Jim, *Buffaloe'd.* (2024) Meir Yedid Magic, Fair Lawn, NJ. Perfect. Black. 236 pp. 8.5 x 11 in. (Acquired from the reprint's publisher.) Close-Up, Stage.

Buffum, Richard, *Brema Brasses, The.* (1981) Abracadabra Press, Balboa Island, CA. Cloth. Blue. 149 pp. 5.25 x 8.5 in. Dust jacket. Signed by Richard Buffum. #250 of 350. History, Biography, Collecting.

Buffum, Richard, *Cone and Balls, The.* (1961) Sorcerer's Press, Goleta, CA. Saddle-stitch. Yellow. 10 pp. 4.75 x 7 in. Balls, Cone and Ball, Stage.

Bull, Jane, *Magic Book, The.* (2002) Dorling Kindersley Books, London. Casebound. Purple. 48 pp. 8.75 x 11 in. Children's book, Beginner.

Bull, Webster, *Marco the Magi's Production of Le Grand David and His Own Spectacular Magic Company: The Early Years in Photographs.* (2008) White Horse Productions, Beverly, MA. 91 pp. (Information not verified by physical copy.) History, Photography.

Bullivant, C. H., *Drawing Room Entertainer, The.* Fourth edition. (1922) C. Arthur Pearson Ltd., London. Boards. Yellow. 122 pp. 4.75 x 7.25 in. Beginner, Stunts.

Bundy, John, *Tricks 'n' Treats: The Book of Halloween Magic.* (2016) 1878 Press Company, Oxford, CT. Perfect. Black. 210 pp. 8.5 x 11 in. (Information not verified by physical copy.) Illusions, Halloween.

Buonocore, Bud, *How? Being a Treatise on My Own Methods of Sleeving Small Objects.* (c. 1972) Author, Washington D.C. Stapled. Tan. 10 pp. 8.5 x 11 in. (Information not verified by physical copy.) Sleeving, Cards, Coins, Close-Up.

Burden, Rev. Lawrence, *Latest Magical Gospel Lessons no. 4.* (1974) Abbott Magic Co., Colon, MI. Stapled. Yellow. Cover text: Blue; 36 pp. 8.5 x 11 in. Mimeographed. (Information not verified by physical copy.) Gospel magic, Stage.

Burden, Rev. Lawrence, *Magical Gospel Lessons.* (1955) Abbott Magic Co., Colon, MI. Stapled with tape. Beige. 30 pp. 8.5 x 11 in. Mimeographed. Gospel magic.

Burden, Rev. Lawrence, *Magical Gospel Lessons.* (1955) Abbott Magic Co., Colon, MI. Saddle-stitch. Tan. 28 pp. 8.25 x 10.25 in. Gospel magic.

Burger, Eugene (See also Hass, Lawrence; Solomon, David), *Audience Involvement: A Lecture.* Second edition. (1983) Philip R. Willmarth, Arlington Heights, IL. Saddle-stitch. Yellow. 27 pp. 5.5 x 8.5 in. Inscribed to Todd Karr. Signed by Eugene Burger. Lecture notes. Theory, Close-Up, Cards.

Burger, Eugene, *Catching a Spook.* (1985) Author, Chicago. Stapled. White. 8 pp. 8.5 x 11 in. (Information not verified by physical copy.) Lecture notes. Bizarre magick, Séances, Spirit effects.

Burger, Eugene, *Chicago Visions.* (2004) The Miracle Factory, Los Angeles. Perfect. Black. 64 pp. 5.25 x 7.5 in. Included with "The Chicago Tapes" DVD set. Theory, Close-Up, Cards.

Burger, Eugene, *Craft of Magic, The.* (1984) Philip R. Willmarth, Arlington Heights, IL. Saddle-stitch. Red. 64 pp. 5.5 x 8.5 in. Inscribed to Todd Karr. Signed by Eugene Burger. Theory, Close-Up, Cards.

Burger, Eugene, with Morey, David and McLaughlin, John E., *Creating Business Magic.* (2018) Mango Publishing Group, Coral Gables, FL. Cloth. Black. 293 pp. 5.75 x 8.75 in. Dust jacket. Business.

Burger, Eugene, *Deception and Self-Deception.* (c. 1990) Author, Chicago. Stapled. White. 4 pp. 8.5 x 11 in. Theory, Essays.

Burger, Eugene, *Devil's Deck.* (1989) Author, Chicago. Saddle-stitch. White. 8 pp. 5.5 x 8.5 in. Includes deck. Cards, Manual.

Burger, Eugene, with Hass, Lawrence, *Eugene Burger: From Beyond.* (2019) Theory of Art and Magic Press, Memphis, TN. Cloth. Black. 204 pp. 8.5 x 11 in. Dust jacket. Theory, Close-Up.

Burger, Eugene, *Eugene Burger on Matt Schulien's Fabulous Card Discoveries.* (1983) Philip R. Willmarth, Arlington Heights, IL. Saddle-stitch. Beige. 44 pp. 5.5 x 8.5 in. Inscribed to Todd Karr. Signed by Eugene Burger. Cards.

Burger, Eugene, *Eugene Burger on Matt Schulien's Fabulous Card Discoveries.* Third printing. (2022) Magic Methods, Greenville, SC. Saddle-stitch. White. 44 pp. 5.5 x 8.5 in. Cards.

Burger, Eugene, with Hass, Lawrence, *Eugene Burger: The Workshop Transcripts.* (2023) Theory of Art and Magic Press, Las Vegas. Cloth. Gray. 160 pp. 8.5 x 11 in. Dust jacket. Signed by Lawrence Hass. #700 of 850. Theory, Essays, Close-Up, Stage.

Burger, Eugene, *Eugene Burger's Unpublished Secrets: The Spot Card.* (2012) Theory of Art and Magic Press, Las Vegas. Stapled. White. 10 pp. 5.5 x 8.5 in. Folded. Includes prop. Stage, Comedy.

Burger, Eugene, *Experience of Magic, The.* (1989) Kaufman and Greenberg, New York. Cloth. Black, white, red. 140 pp. 8.5 x 11 in. Dust jacket. Inscribed to Todd Karr. Signed by Eugene Burger. Theory, Close-Up, Cards, Mentalism.

Burger, Eugene, *Experience of Magic, The.* (n.d.) Kaufman and Greenberg, New York. Casebound. Black, white, yellow. 140 pp. 8.5 x 11 in. Later reprint. Signed by Eugene Burger. Theory, Close-Up, Cards, Mentalism.

Burger, Eugene, *Ghostly Visitors: An Essay on Nineteenth Century Spiritualism.* (1977) Spirit Theatre Company, Evanston, IL. Stapled with tape. Beige. 50 pp. 8.5 x 11 in. Spiritualism, History.

Burger, Eugene, *Growing in the Art of Magic.* Second edition. (1996) Author, Chicago. Saddle-stitch. Beige. 45 pp. 5.5 x 8.5 in. The "first edition" apparently refers to the earlier audio cassette set transcribed for this book. Inscribed to Todd Karr. Signed by Eugene Burger. Theory, Close-Up, Cards.

Burger, Eugene, with Neale, Robert E., *Magic and Meaning.* First edition. (1995) Hermetic Press, Seattle. Cloth. Black. 189 pp. 6 x 9 in. Dust jacket. Inscribed to Todd Karr. Signed by Eugene Burger. Theory, Close-Up, Cards.

Burger, Eugene, with Neale, Robert E., *Magic and Meaning (Expanded).* Second edition. (2009) Hermetic Press, Seattle. Cloth. Black. 224 pp. 6 x 9 in. Dust jacket. Theory, Close-Up, Cards.

Burger, Eugene, *Mastering the Art of Magic.* (2000) Kaufman and Co., Washington D.C. Cloth. Black. 228 pp. 8.5 x 11 in. Dust jacket. Inscribed to Todd Karr. Signed by Eugene Burger. Theory, Close-Up, Cards, Mentalism.

Burger, Eugene, with McBride, Jeff, *Mystery School.* Limited deluxe edition. (2003) The Miracle Factory, Seattle. Cloth. Black. 448 pp. 8.25 x 10.25 in. Dust jacket. In box with CD and antique-style lock and key. Signed by Eugene Burger, Todd Karr, Max Maven, Jeff McBride. #1 of 125. Theory, Close-Up, Stage, Bizarre magick.

Burger, Eugene, with McBride, Jeff, *Mystery School.* (2003) The Miracle Factory, Seattle. Cloth. Black. 448 pp. 8.25 x 10.25 in. Dust jacket. Theory, Close-Up, Stage, Bizarre magick.

Burger, Eugene, *Performance of Close-Up Magic, The.* (1987) Kaufman and Greenberg, New York. Cloth. Black. 134 pp. 8.5 x 11 in. Dust jacket. Inscribed to Todd Karr. Signed by Eugene Burger. Theory, Close-Up, Cards, Mentalism.

Burger, Eugene, *Performance of Close-Up Magic, The.* (n.d.) Kaufman and Company, Washington D.C. Casebound. Black, white, red. 134 pp. 8.5 x 11.25 in. Theory, Close-Up, Cards, Showmanship.

Burger, Eugene, with Sanvert, Jean-Jacques (trans.), *Redécouvertes.* (1997) Author, France. Saddle-stitch. White. 23 pp. 8.25 x 11.75 in. Translation of "Rediscoveries." Lecture notes. Close-Up, Cards, Theory. French.

Burger, Eugene, *Rediscoveries.* Second edition. (1996) Author, Chicago. Saddle-stitch. Beige. 27 pp. 5.5 x 8.5 in. Inscribed to Todd Karr. Signed by Eugene Burger. Close-Up, Cards.

Burger, Eugene, *Secret of Restaurant Magic, The.* (1983) Author, Chicago. Saddle-stitch. White. 28 pp. 5.5 x 8.5 in. Inscribed to Todd Karr. Signed by Eugene Burger. Lecture notes. Theory, Close-Up, Cards, Automaton chess player.

Burger, Eugene, *Secrets and Mysteries for the Close-Up Performer.* (1982) Philip R. Willmarth, Chicago. Saddle-stitch. Black. 98 pp. 5.5 x 8.5 in. Inscribed to Todd Karr. Signed by Eugene Burger. Theory, Close-Up, Cards.

Burger, Eugene, *Spirit Scarf, The.* (1998) Author, Chicago. Stapled. White. 4 pp. 8.5 x 11 in. Silks, Spirit effects, Close-Up.

Burger, Eugene, *Spirit Theater.* (1986) Kaufman and Greenberg, New York. Cloth. Black. 192 pp. 8.5 x 11 in. Dust jacket. Includes audio flexi-disc. Inscribed to Todd Karr. Signed by Eugene Burger. Séances, Spirit effects, Mentalism.

Burger, Eugene, *Spirit Theater.* Third printing. (1986) Kaufman and Greenberg, New York. Casebound. Black. 192 pp. 8.5 x 11 in. Inscribed to Todd Karr. Signed by Eugene Burger. Séances, Spirit effects, Mentalism.

Burger, Eugene, *Strange Ceremonies.* (1991) Kaufman and Greenberg, New York. Cloth. Black. 104 pp. 8.5 x 11 in. Dust jacket. Inscribed to Todd Karr. Signed by Eugene Burger, Jeff McBride. Bizarre magick, Close-Up, Cards, Mentalism.

Burger, Eugene, *Théâtre Spirite.* (2019) Marchand de Trucs, Lorient, France. Casebound. Black. 251 pp. 8.5 x 12 in. Translation of "Spirit Theater." Séances, Spirit effects, Mentalism. French.

Burger, Eugene, *Van Warren's Four Magical Elements.* (1990) Van Warren, Santa Fe, NM. Saddle-stitch. Gray. 32 pp. 8.5 x 11 in. With Van Warren's miniature props. (Information not verified by physical copy.) Bizarre magick, Manual.

Burger, Eugene, *Wachsen in der Kunst der Magie.* (1997) Wonder Workshop, Berlin, Germany. Saddle-stitch. Yellow. 71 pp. 5.75 x 8.25 in. Translation of "Growing in the Art of Magic." Theory, Close-Up, Cards. German.

Burger, Eugene, *Wiederentdeckungen.* (1997) Wonder Workshop, Berlin, Germany. Saddle-stitch. Green. 28 pp. 5.75 x 8.25 in. Translation of "Rediscoveries." Theory, Close-Up, Cards. German.

Burghardo, Dondo, *Jeu Avec le Subconscient.* (1984) Éditions de Spectacle, Strasbourg. Saddle-stitch. White. 23 pp. 6 x 8.75 in. Mentalism, Contact mind-reading.

Burgoon, Tom, *Breaking Bones for Fun and Profit.* (2004) Author, Kansas City, MO. Saddle-stitch. Blue. 20 pp. 5.5 x 8.5 in. (Information not verified by physical copy.) Comedy, Gimmicks.

Burgoon, Tom, *Tom Burgoon's Magic Lecture Notes.* (2004) Author, Kansas City, MO. Saddle-stitch. White. 20 pp. 5.5 x 8.5 in. (Information not verified by physical copy.) Lecture notes. Comedy, Close-Up, Stage.

Burgoon, Tom, *Tom Burgoon's Magic Lecture Notes no. 2.* (2005) Author, Kansas City, MO. Saddle-stitch. White. 5.5 x 8.5 in. (Information not verified by physical copy.) Lecture notes. Comedy, Close-Up, Stage.

Burgoon, Tom, *Ultra Magic: The Secret Lecture Notes of Tom Burgoon.* (1995) Author, Kansas City, MO. Saddle-stitch. White. 5.5 x 8.5 in. (Information not verified by physical copy.) Lecture notes. Comedy, Showmanship, Routining.

Burke, Corey, *Kardmasutra.* (2002) Author, Vancouver, WA. Saddle-stitch. White. 18 pp. 5.5 x 8.5 in. (Measurements and other information have been recorded as accurately as possible.) Cards, Card Case.

Burke, Corey, *Sense.* (2002) Author, Vancouver, WA. Saddle-stitch. Gray. 20 pp. 5.5 x 8.5 in. (Measurements and other information have been recorded as accurately as possible.) Coins.

Burke, Eddie, *Club and Cabaret Mentalism.* (1970) MagicTrix Publications, Stoke-on-Trent, UK. Stapled with tape. Yellow. 27 pp. 8 x 10 in. Mimeographed. Mentalism, Showmanship.

Burke, Eddie, *Design in Mind.* (2000) Author, UK. Saddle-stitch. White. 9 pp. (Information not verified by physical copy. Bibliographical details are as accurate as possible.) Mentalism.

Burke, Eddie, *Hunting the Headlines.* (2000) Author, UK. Comb. Orange. 18 pp. (Information not verified by physical copy.) Mentalism, Newspaper.

Burke, Eddie, *Man Who Knows Mind Reading Act, The.* (n.d.) Author, UK. 17 pp. (Information not verified by physical copy.) Mentalism.

Burke, Eddie, *Marvillo's and Burke's Card to Almost Anywhere.* (2000) Author, UK. 12 pp. (Information not verified by physical copy.) Cards.

Burke, Eddie, *Mind Reach.* (2000) Author, UK. 13 pp. (Information not verified by physical copy. Bibliographical details are as accurate as possible.) Mentalism.

Burke, Eddie, *More Professional Mental Secrets.* (n.d.) Author, UK. Comb. White. (Information not verified by physical copy. Bibliographical details are as accurate as possible.) Mentalism.

Burke, Eddie, *Pro-Menta Card Prediction.* (n.d.) Author, UK. 5 pp. (Information not verified by physical copy.) Mentalism, Cards.

Burke, Eddie, *Psychic Divination.* (2003) Author, UK. 15 pp. (Information not verified by physical copy.) Mentalism.

Burke, Eddie, *Question and Answer Act, The.* (n.d.) Author, UK. 18 pp. (Information not verified by physical copy.) Mentalism, Question and answer.

Burke, Eddie, *Thru Other Eyes.* (2001) Author, UK. 19 pp. (Information not verified by physical copy. Bibliographical details are as accurate as possible.) Mentalism.

Burke, Eddie, *Ultimate Tele-Phoney.* (n.d.) Author, UK. 14 pp. (Information not verified by physical copy.) Telephone effects, Mentalism.

Burkhart, G., *G. Burkhart: King of Coins.* (c. 1900) Author, Brooklyn, NY. Saddle-stitch. Beige. 12 pp. 5 x 6.75 in. Combination of book and catalog. Close-Up, Stage, Catalog. Pulp.

Burley, Ross A., *Are You Seein' Things?* (1939) Nelmar, Chicago. Stapled. Tan. 45 pp. 8.5 x 11 in. Mimeographed. Optical illusions, Stage.

Burley, Ross A., with Nelmar, *Burley's Baffling Black Boards.* (1945) Nelmar, Chicago. Stapled. White. 40 pp. 8.5 x 11 in. Mimeographed. With prospectus and original mailing envelope. Slates, Mentalism, Spirit effects.

Burley, Ross A., *Burley's Bridge Demonstration no. 1.* (1945) Author, Pontiac, MI. Loose pages. 2 pp. Handwritten. Address is G.M. Truck Co. (Information not verified by physical copy.) Cards.

Burley, Ross A., *Burley's Bridge Demonstration no. 2.* (1945) Author, Pontiac, MI. Loose pages. 2 pp. Handwritten. Address is G.M. Truck Co. (Information not verified by physical copy.) Cards.

Burley, Ross A., *Complete Routine for Art with the Shears.* (1933) Elmer Eckam, Rochester, NY. Stapled. White. 15 pp. 8.5 x 11 in. Mimeographed. (Information not verified by physical copy.) Paper, Cutting effects.

Burley, Ross A., *Figure Fiend, The.* (1941) Nelmar, Chicago. Cloth. Maroon. 69 pp. 8.5 x 11 in. Mimeographed. Sid Lorraine bookplate. Mathematical, Lightning calculation, Magic squares.

Burley, Ross A., with Nelmar, *Laughing at Language.* (1945) Nelmar, Chicago. Stapled. 20 pp. 8.5 x 11 in. Mimeographed. (Information not verified by physical copy.) Mentalism.

Burley, Ross A., *Musical Mindreading Supreme.* (1942) Author, Norfolk, VA. Stapled inside paper cover. 5 pp. Mimeographed. Nelmar advertised this title as "Telepathy in Melody" in "The Sphinx," Oct. 1942. Mentalism.

Burley, Ross A., with Nelmar, *Nelmar's Nite-Club Version of Burley's Baffling Black Boards.* (1945) Nelmar, Chicago. Stapled. White. 6 pp. 8.5 x 11 in. Mimeographed. With prospectus and original mailing envelope. Included as bonus with original Burley routine. Slates, Mentalism, Spirit effects.

Burlingame, H. J., *Around the World with a Magician and a Juggler.* (1891) Clyde Publishing, Chicago. Cloth. Red. 172 pp. 5.25 x 7.75 in. Inscribed New Year's 1908. Signed by H. J. Burlingame. History, Biography.

Burlingame, H. J., *Around the World with a Magician and a Juggler.* (2009) Magico, New York. Cloth. Red. 132 pp. 5.5 x 8.5 in. History, Biography.

Burlingame, H. J., *Herrmann the Magician.* (1897) Laird and Lee, Chicago. Cloth. Yellow, red. 298 pp. 5.5 x 8 in. Biography, History.

Burlingame, H. J., *Herrmann the Magician.* (1897) Laird and Lee, Chicago. Cloth. Blue. 298 pp. 5 x 7.5 in. Biography, History.

Burlingame, H. J., *Herrmann the Great.* (1897) Laird and Lee, Chicago. Perfect. Color. 298 pp. 5.25 x 7.25 in. Color portrait cover. Biography, History.

Burlingame, H. J., *Herrmann the Magician.* (1897) Laird and Lee, Chicago. Perfect. White, red. 298 pp. 5 x 7 in. Biography, History.

Burlingame, H. J., *Herrmann the Magician.* (1897) Whitman, Chicago. Perfect. White. 298 pp. 5.25 x 7.5 in. Biography, History.

Burlingame, H. J., *Herrmann the Magician.* (2007) Magico, New York. Cloth. Beige. 295 pp. 5.5 x 8.5 in. Biography, History.

Burlingame, H. J., *Herrmann the Magician.* (1942) Wilcox and Follett, Chicago. Perfect. Black. 298 pp. 5.25 x 7.5 in. Title on cover: "Magician's Handbook." Biography, History.

Burlingame, H. J., *History of Magic and Magicians.* (1895) Chas. L. Burlingame Inc., Chicago. Perfect. Gray. 50 pp. 6 x 7.5 in. History, Biography.

Burlingame, H. J., *History of Magic and Magicians.* (1974) Magic Inc., Chicago. Saddle-stitch. Orange. 50 pp. 5.5 x 8.5 in. History, Biography.

Burlingame, H. J., *How to Read People's Minds.* (1904) Author, Chicago. Perfect. Beige, blue. 53 pp. 5 x 7 in. Mentalism, History. Pulp.

Burlingame, H. J., *How to Read People's Minds.* (1905) Clyde Publishing, Chicago. Saddle-stitch. Tan. 48 pp. 5.75 x 8.75 in. Mentalism, History. Pulp.

Burlingame, H. J., *How to Read People's Minds.* (n.d.) Author, Chicago. Perfect. Light blue. 53 pp. 5.25 x 7.75 in. Mentalism, History. Pulp.

Burlingame, H. J., *How to Read People's Minds.* (n.d.) Author, Chicago. Saddle-stitch. Yellow. 53 pp. 5.25 x 7.75 in. Mentalism, History. Pulp.

Burlingame, H. J., *How to Read People's Minds.* (n.d.) Author, Chicago. Perfect. White, blue. 53 pp. 5 x 7.25 in. Mentalism, History. Pulp.

Burlingame, H. J., *How to Read People's Minds.* (n.d.) Stein Publishing House, Chicago. Perfect. Yellow, blue. 53 pp. 5.25 x 8 in. Mentalism, History. Pulp.

Burlingame, H. J., *How to Read People's Minds.* (n.d.) Stein Publishing House, Chicago. Perfect. Yellow, red. 53 pp. 5.25 x 7.5 in. Mentalism, History. Pulp.

Burlingame, H. J., *Leaves from Conjurers' Scrap Books.* (1891) Donohue, Henneberrry, and Co., Chicago. Cloth. Green. 274 pp. 5.5 x 8.75 in. Ad in back for planned Willmann translation, "Modern Wonders." History, Biography.

Burlingame, H. J., *Leaves from Conjurers' Scrap Books.* (1891) Donohue, Henneberrry, and Co., Chicago. Cloth. Red. 274 pp. 5.5 x 8.75 in. Ad in back for planned Willmann translation, "Modern Wonders." History, Biography.

Burlingame, H. J., *Leaves from Conjurers' Scrap Books.* (1891) Donohue, Henneberrry, and Co., Chicago. Cloth. Gray. 274 pp. 5.5 x 8.75 in. Ad in back for planned Willmann translation, "Modern Wonders." History, Biography.

Burlingame, H. J., *Leaves from Conjurers' Scrap Books.* (1891) Donohue, Henneberrry, and Co., Chicago. Cloth. Green. 274 pp. 5.5 x 8.75 in. Inscribed "With compliments of the author" by Burlingame. Signed by H. J. Burlingame. History, Biography.

Burlingame, H. J., *Leaves from Conjurers' Scrap Books.* (1891) Donohue, Henneberrry, and Co., Chicago. Cloth. Tan. 274 pp. 5.5 x 8.75 in. No ads. History, Biography.

Burlingame, H. J., *Leaves from Conjurers' Scrap Books.* (1891) Donohue, Henneberrry, and Co., Chicago. Cloth. Dark red. 274 pp. 5.5 x 8.75 in. No ads. Plain text on spine. No gilt on front cover. History, Biography.

Burlingame, H. J., *Leaves from Conjurers' Scrap Books.* (1891) Donohue, Henneberrry, and Co., Chicago. Cloth. Light red. 274 pp. 5.5 x 8.75 in. No ads. Plain text on spine. No gilt on front cover. History, Biography.

Burlingame, H. J., *Leaves from Conjurers' Scrap Books.* (1971) Singing Tree Press, Detroit. Cloth. Maroon. 274 pp. 5.5 x 8.75 in. History, Biography.

Burlingame, H. J., *Magician's Handbook. Herrmann the Magician.* (1967) Universal Book and Stationery Co., Delhi, India. Perfect. Blue, yellow. 202 pp. 4.75 x 7 in. Biography, History.

Burlingame, H. J., *Tricks in Magic vol. 1.* (1895) Chas. L. Burlingame Inc., Chicago. Perfect. Blue. 95 pp. 5.25 x 7.5 in. Stage, Close-Up, Mentalism.

Burlingame, H. J., *Tricks in Magic vol. 1.* (1895) Chas. L. Burlingame Inc., Chicago. Perfect. Blue. 95 pp. 5.25 x 7.5 in. Stage, Close-Up, Mentalism.

Burlingame, H. J., *Tricks in Magic vol. 1.* (1895) Chas. L. Burlingame Inc., Chicago. Perfect. Blue. 95 pp. 5.25 x 7.5 in. Stage, Close-Up, Mentalism.

Burlingame, H. J., *Tricks in Magic vol. 2.* (1896) Chas. L. Burlingame Inc., Chicago. Perfect. Gray. 63 pp. 5.25 x 7.5 in. Includes "Bibliotecha Magica" section, an early conjuring bibliography. Stage, Close-Up, Mentalism, Bibliography.

Burlingame, H. J., *Tricks in Magic vol. 3.* (1898) Chas. L. Burlingame Inc., Chicago. Perfect. Orange. 57 pp. 5.25 x 7.5 in. Stage, Close-Up, Mentalism.

Burlingame, H. J., *Tricks in Magic vols. 1-3.* (1895-8) Chas. L. Burlingame Inc., Chicago. Cloth. Maroon. Multiple sections. 5.25 x 7.5 in. Milton A. Bridges bookplate. Three volumes bound. Stage, Close-Up, Mentalism.

Burlingame, Price, *Three Ring Routine: A Presentation of Jerry Salazar.* (1980) Colin M. Cochrane, San Francisco. Saddle-stitch. Red. 32 pp. 5.5 x 8.5 in. Linking Rings, Street magic.

Burns, Stanley, *Other Voices.* (2000) Author, New York. Cloth. Black. 380 pp. 9.25 x 10.5 in. Dust jacket. (Measurements and other information have been recorded as accurately as possible.) Ventriloquism.

Burrows, J. F., *Lightning Artist, The.* (1904) Hamley Brothers, London. Stapled with paper cover. Green. 82 pp. 5.5 x 8.5 in. Chalk talk, Rag painting, Smoke Painting, Paper.

Burrows, J. F., *Programmes of Magicians.* Second edition. (n.d.) Author, London. Saddle-stitch. Red. 36 pp. 5.5 x 8.5 in. History, Programs.

Burrows, J. F., *Programmes of Famous Magicians.* (c. 1945) L. Davenport and Co., London. Saddle-stitch. Yellow. 40 pp. 5.5 x 8.5 in. History, Programs.

Burrows, J. F., *Some New Magic.* (1904) Hamley Brothers, London. Saddle-stitch. Green. 37 pp. 5.5 x 8.5 in. (Measurements and other information have been recorded as accurately as possible.) Stage.

Burrows, J. F. (Karlyn), *Secrets of Stage Hypnotism, Stage Electricity, and Bloodless Surgery.* (1912) George Routledge and Sons, London. Boards. Red. 71 pp. 5 x 7 in. Hypnotism, Fakir stunts.

Bursill, Henry, *Hand Shadows to Be Thrown Upon the Wall.* (1859) Griffith and Farran, London. 16 pp. (Information not verified by physical copy.) Toole Stott no. 778. Shadowgraphy.

Bursill, Henry, *Hand Shadows to Be Thrown Upon the Wall.* Second edition. (1859) Griffith and Farran, London. 17 pp. (Information not verified by physical copy.) Toole Stott no. 1241. Shadowgraphy.

Bursill, Henry, *Hand Shadows to Be Thrown Upon the Wall.* Third edition. (1859) Griffith and Farran, London. 17 pp. (Information not verified by physical copy.) Toole Stott no. 1242. Shadowgraphy.

Bursill, Henry, *Hand Shadows to Be Thrown Upon the Wall.* Fourth edition. (1860) Griffith and Farran, London. Boards. Salmon. 17 pp. 7.5 x 10 in. Shadowgraphy.

Bursill, Henry, *Hand Shadows to Be Thrown Upon the Wall.* (1967) Dover, New York. Saddle-stitch. Blue. 17 pp. 6.5 x 9.25 in. Shadowgraphy.

Bursill, Henry, *Second Series of Hand Shadows to Be Thrown Upon the Wall, A.* (1860) Griffith and Farran, London. 16 pp. (Information not verified by physical copy.) Toole Stott no. 779. Shadowgraphy.

Bursill, Henry, *Second Series of Hand Shadows to Be Thrown Upon the Wall, A.* (1879) Griffith and Farran, London. 16 pp. (Information not verified by physical copy.) Later edition of Toole Stott no. 779. Shadowgraphy.

Bursill, Henry, *More Hand Shadows to Be Thrown Upon the Wall.* (1971) Dover, New York. Saddle-stitch. Maroon. 30 pp. 6.5 x 9.25 in. Reprint of "A Second Series of Hand Shadows to Be Thrown Upon the Wall." Shadowgraphy.

Bursky, Alan, *Honest Cheat Comedy Poker Routine.* (2008) Divine Goddess 23 Productions, Los Angeles. Saddle-stitch. Black. 7 pp. 5.5 x 8.5 in. Cards, Comedy.

Bursky, Alan, *Poker Sam.* (2009) Divine Goddess 23 Productions, Los Angeles. Saddle-stitch. Black. 7 pp. 5.5 x 8.5 in. Cards.

Burtis, Randy, *Gospel Illusions.* (2019) Rose Publishing, Peabody, MA. Perfect. Green. 111 pp. 8.5 x 11 in. Gospel magic.

Burton, Lance, *12 Magic Tricks Instruction Book.* (n.d.) Harmony Toy, Elmsford, NY. Folded. Black. 7 pp. 5.5 x 8.5 in. In "Lance Burton Magic Set." Magic set manual, Beginner.

Burton, Lance, *12 Tricks Magic Set Secret Instruction Book.* (2000) Cadaco, Chicago. Saddle-stitch. Black. 9 pp. 5.5 x 8.5 in. In "12 Amazing Tricks set." Magic set manual, Beginner.

Burton, Lance, *50 Magic Tricks.* (n.d.) Harmony Toy, Elmsford, NY. Folded. Black. 9 pp. 5.5 x 8.5 in. In "Lance Burton Magic Set." Magic set manual, Beginner.

Burton, Lance, *Advice.* (2001) Author, Las Vegas. Saddle-stitch. Maroon. 33 pp. 5.5 x 8.5 in. Showmanship, Theory, Business.

Burton, Lance, *Magic Blank Deck.* (1995) Harmony Toy, Elmsford, NY. Folded. White. 5 pp. 3.75 x 6 in. In "Magic Deck Set." Magic set manual, Beginner, Cards, Mental Photography deck.

Burton, Lance, *Magic Card Box and Deck.* (1995) Harmony Toy, Elmsford, NY. Folded. White. 8 pp. 3.5 x 11.25 in. In "Magic Deck Set." Magic set manual, Beginner, Cards, Card Case.

Burton, Lance, *Magic Magician's Deck.* (1995) Harmony Toy, Elmsford, NY. Folded. White. 6 pp. 3.75 x 9 in. In "Magic Deck Set." Magic set manual, Beginner, Cards, Svengali deck.

Burton, Lance, *Magic Mystery Deck.* (1995) Harmony Toy, Elmsford, NY. Folded. White. 8 pp. 3.75 x 9 in. In "Magic Deck Set." Magic set manual, Beginner, Cards, Stripper deck.

Burton, Lance, *Secrets of 100 Magic Tricks.* (2000) Cadaco, Chicago. Folded. Black. 17 pp. 5.5 x 8 in. In "12 Amazing Tricks" set. With Robbins material from booklet. Magic set manual, Beginner.

Burton, Lance, *Video Magic.* (1999) Cadaco, Chicago. Saddle-stitch. Black. 24 pp. 5.5 x 8.5 in. In "Video Magic" set. Magic set manual, Beginner.

Burton, Steve (See also Tarbell, Harlan), *Tarbell Companion, The.* (1994) Steve Burton Magic, Cypress, TX. Perfect. Blue, white. 148 pp. 6 x 8.75 in. Anthology of Tarbell and other material of interest. Course, Essays, History.

Burton, Steve, *Tarbell Volume Eight Notebook.* (1993) Steve Burton Magic, Cypress, TX. Comb. Gray. 80 pp. 5.5 x 8.5 in. Course, Close-Up, Stage, Index.

Busby, Jeff (See also Braue, Frederick; Müller, Reinhard; Nielsen, Gene; Takagi, Shigeo), *Back to Back.* (1977) Hank Lee's Magic Factory, Boston. Saddle-stitch. Beige. 24 pp. 5.5 x 8.5 in. Cards.

Busby, Jeff, *Dominique Duvivier's Chameleon Card.* (1995) Jeff Busby Magic, Wallace, ID. Comb. White. 45 pp. 5.5 x 8.5 in. With deck and original label. Cards.

Busby, Jeff, *Epoptica Yearbook All-Trick Special.* (1984) Jeff Busby Magic, Oakland, CA. Comb. Beige. 42 pp. 8.5 x 11 in. Cards.

Busby, Jeff, *Into the 4th Dimension – and Beyond.* Second printing. (1980) Magic Inc., Chicago. Comb. Yellow. 17 pp. 8.5 x 11 in. Cards.

Busby, Jeff, with Matsuura, Gene, *Notes on the Magic of Frank Shields.* (1975) Author, Oakland, CA. Stapled. White. 8 pp. 8.5 x 11 in. Mimeographed. Cards, Coins, Close-Up.

Busby, Jeff, *Paul Fox's Miracle Gimmick.* (1983) Jeff Busby Magic, Oakland, CA. Saddle-stitch. White. 30 pp. 5.5 x 8.5 in. With gimmick and promotional flyers. Cards, Mentalism.

Busby, Jeff, *Routines and Handlings for the Sterling Egg Bag.* (1982) Jeff Busby Magic, Oakland, CA. Comb. White. 27 pp. 8.5 x 11 in. With Chuck Smith routine. Egg Bag.

Busby, Jeff, *Royal Runaway.* (1973) Magic Limited, Oakland, CA. Saddle-stitch. Tan. 4 pp. 8.5 x 11 in. Includes cards in envelope. Cards.

Busby, Jeff, *Secret of the Palmettos, The.* (1998) Jeff Busby Magic, Wallace, ID. Comb. White, red, black. 124 pp. 5.5 x 8.5 in. With deck. Cards, Cheating.

Busch, Richard, *Destiny Response, The.* (2004) Author, Pittsburgh, PA. Saddle-stitch. White. 52 pp. 5.5 x 8.5 in. (Information not verified by physical copy.) Mentalism.

Busch, Richard, *Mind Over Number.* (2002) Author, Pittsburgh, PA. Saddle-stitch. Green. 32 pp. 5.5 x 8.5 in. (Information not verified by physical copy.) Mentalism.

Busch, Richard, *Mother's Home Companion.* (1996) Author, Pittsburgh, PA. Clip. White. 20 pp. 8.5 x 11 in. Signed by Richard Busch. Mentalism, Book tests.

Busch, Richard, *Number–Please?* (2002) Author, Pittsburgh, PA. Saddle-stitch. Yellow. 44 pp. 5.5 x 8.5 in. (Information not verified by physical copy.) Mathematical.

Busch, Richard, *Peek Performances.* (2007) Magic Inspirations, Houston, TX. Cloth. Blue. 209 pp. 7.25 x 10.25 in. Dust jacket. Mentalism, Cards.

Butler, Paul, *Jim Ravel's Theatrical Pickpocketing.* Second printing. (1991) Magic Words, Pasadena, CA. Cloth. Maroon. 137 pp. 7.25 x 10.25 in. Dust jacket. Pickpocket, History.

Butterworth, Philip, *Magic on the Early English Stage.* (2005) Cambridge University Press, Cambridge, UK. Cloth. Black. 295 pp. 6 x 9 in. Dust jacket. History.

Cabral, Tony (as Antonio M. Cabral), *Faces of Magic-Con, The.* (2010) Blurb Inc., Watertown, MA. Saddle-stitch. Black. 22 pp. 7.75 x 9.75 in. #24 of 100. Caricatures.

Cabral, Tony, *Brown Shoe Lecture Notes (or How I Learned to Stop Worrying and Teach Some Card Tricks), The.* (2012) Author, Boston. Saddle-stitch. Black. 35 pp. 8.5 x 11 in. (Information not verified by physical copy.) Lecture notes. Cards.

Cabral, Tony, *Card Tricks for the Untrustworthy: The Usual Suspect Lecture Notes.* (2011) Author, Boston. Saddle-stitch. Green, black. 53 pp. 8.5 x 11 in. (Information not verified by physical copy.) Lecture notes. Cards.

Cabral, Tony, *Notes from a Mechanic: The Motor City Lecture Notes.* (2014) Author, Boston. Saddle-stitch. White. 35 pp. 5.5 x 8.5 in. (Information not verified by physical copy.) Lecture notes. Cards.

Cabral, Tony, *Things to Do in Denver When You're Dead: The Rocky Mountain Session Lecture Notes.* (2019) Author, Boston. Saddle-stitch. Black. 29 pp. 5.5 x 8.5 in. (Information not verified by physical copy.) Lecture notes. Cards.

Cacciato, Carmelo, *Magie Originale, Une.* (2004) Académie de Magie Georges Proust, Paris. Perfect. White. 124 pp. 7.5 x 10.5 in. Inscribed to Todd Karr. Signed by Carmelo Cacciato. Stage. French.

Cachadiña, Tony, *Lecture Notes.* (1991) Author, Spain. Stapled. White. 21 pp. 8.5 x 11 in. (Information not verified by physical copy.) Lecture notes. Cards, Coins, Close-Up.

Caesar, The Great, *Trouble-Wit or Magic Fan.* (n.d.) Ellis Stanyon, London. Stapled. White. 4 pp. 5.5 x 8.5 in. Bound at top. With additional one-page "Trouble-Wit: Hints on the Manipulation" printed instruction sheet by Ellis Stanyon and small mimeographed slip with more suggestions. Troublewit, Paper.

Caffrey, Lance, *Asian Hustle: Secrets of the Hindu Shuffle, The.* (2013) Author, Singapore. Cloth. Black. 108 pp. 5.75 x 8.25 in. Dust jacket. Limited to 250 copies. (Information not verified by physical copy.) Cards, Hindu shuffle.

Cagle, Charles W., *Mental Effects for the Gospel Worker.* (c. 1980) Author, South Pittsburg, TN. Saddle-stitch. Yellow. 24 pp. 5.25 x 8 in. Gospel magic, Mentalism.

Cain, Dan, *Conceptual Misdirections.* (2012) Author, Centreville, MD. Perfect. White. 36 pp. 8.5 x 11 in. Signed by Dan Cain, Charlie Joseph. Theory.

Cain, Ron, *Secret to Reading Cards and Clients, The.* (1991) Flora and Company, Albuquerque, NM. Comb. Beige. 37 pp. 8.5 x 11 in. (Information not verified by physical copy.) Cold reading, Divination, Mentalism.

Calhoun, Phil, *Publicity Digest.* Second printing. (1978) Author, Pasadena, CA. Saddle-stitch. Yellow. 46 pp. 5.5 x 8.5 in. Business, Promotion, Publicity.

Callahan, George W., *Art of Ventriloquism, The.* (c. 1915) Johnson Smith and Co., Racine, WI. Saddle-stitch. Green. 26 pp. 5.25 x 7.5 in. Large ad section. Ventriloquism.

Callahan, George W., *Art of Ventriloquism, The.* (c. 1915) Johnson Smith and Co., Detroit. Saddle-stitch. Olive. 32 pp. 5.25 x 8 in. Ventriloquism.

Calvert, John, *Five Magic Keys, The.* (c. 2004) Author, Meritt Island, FL. Envelope. White. Multiple sections. 12.75 x 9.75 in. Large signed outer envelope with five booklets. Signed by John Calvert. Showmanship, Stage, Promotion, Hypnotism.

Calvert, John, *Five Magic Keys: Blindfold Ballyhoo, The.* (c. 2004) Author, Meritt Island, FL. Saddle-stitch. White. 8 pp. 8.5 x 11 in. From set of five booklets. Publicity, Blindfolds, Promotion.

Calvert, John, *Five Magic Keys: Easy to Learn Stage Hypnosis, The.* (c. 2004) Author, Meritt Island, FL. Saddle-stitch. White. 8 pp. 8.5 x 11 in. From set of five booklets. Hypnotism, Stage.

Calvert, John, *Five Magic Keys: Memoronics, The.* (c. 2004) Author, Meritt Island, FL. Saddle-stitch. White. 8 pp. 8.5 x 11 in. From set of five booklets. Memory.

Calvert, John, *Five Magic Keys: The Magic Key to Fame and Fortune, The.* (c. 2004) Author, Meritt Island, FL. Saddle-stitch. White. 40 pp. 8.5 x 11 in. From set of five booklets. Showmanship, Stage, Promotion.

Calvert, John, *Five Magic Keys: The Television Eye Mystery, The.* (c. 2004) Author, Meritt Island, FL. Saddle-stitch. White. 8 pp. 8.5 x 11 in. From set of five booklets. Mentalism, Blindfolds.

Calvert, John, *How to Live to Be a Hundred.* (2011) Epic Productions, Bowling Green, KY. Casebound. Black. 67 pp. 6.25 x 9.25 in. Signed by John Calvert. Biography, Self-help.

Calvert, John, *John Calvert's Book of Instructions.* (n.d.) Magic City Toy Co., Birmingham, AL. Saddle-stitch. Beige. 14 pp. 4.25 x 5.25 in. Magic set manual, Beginner.

Calvert, John, *John Calvert's Lecture and Program.* (n.d.) Author, Meritt Island, FL. Comb. White, black. 20 pp. 8.5 x 11 in. Signed by John Calvert. Lecture notes. Stage, Biography, Programs.

Calvert, John, *John Calvert's Lecture Notes.* (n.d.) Author, Meritt Island, FL. Comb. White, black. 20 pp. 8.5 x 11 in. Envelope and souvenir bill. Lecture notes. Stage, Biography.

Calvert, John, *John Calvert's Torn and Restored Magazine.* (1980) Martin Breese, London. Saddle-stitch. White. 8 pp. 8.25 x 11.75 in. Newspaper, Stage.

Calvert, John, *Solving the Amazing Facets of Magic for Performing Magicians.* (n.d.) Author, Meritt Island, FL. Saddle-stitch. White. 14 pp. 8.5 x 11 in. With Calvert business card. Signed by John Calvert. Lecture notes. Showmanship, Biography.

Camardo, David, *Minimalist Magic.* (c. 1990) Author, Jackson, CA. Saddle-stitch. Blue. 36 pp. 5.5 x 8.5 in. Close-Up, Stage.

Camaro, Jerry, *Behind the Bar with Jerry Camaro.* (c. 1990) Author, Santa Rosa, CA. Comb. Blue. 10 pp. 8.5 x 11 in. Cards, Bar magic.

Camaro, Jerry, *Behind the Bar with Jerry Camaro 2.* (c. 1995) Author, Santa Rosa, CA. Saddle-stitch. Gray. 16 pp. 5.5 x 8.5 in. Cards, Bar magic.

Camaro, Jerry, *Big Cents.* (c. 1995) Author, Santa Rosa, CA. 8 pp. (Information not verified by physical copy.) Coins, Close-Up.

Camaro, Jerry, *Magic of Jerry Camaro, The.* (c. 1995) Author, Santa Rosa, CA. Comb. White. 24 pp. 5.5 x 8.5 in. (Information not verified by physical copy.) Cards, Close-Up.

Cameron, Charles W., *Castle Dracula Mentalism.* (1997) Breese Books, London. Cloth. Black. Cover text: Red; 87 pp. 6.25 x 9.5 in. Bizarre magick, Mentalism.

Cameron, Charles W., *Devil's Diary.* (1976) Supreme Magic, Bideford, UK. Saddle-stitch. Pink, black. 52 pp. 7.25 x 9.75 in. Bizarre magick.

Cameron, Charles W., *Handbook of Horror.* Second impression. (1977) Supreme Magic, Bideford, UK. Saddle-stitch. Yellow. 43 pp. 5.25 x 8.25 in. Bizarre magick.

Cameron, Charles W., *Macabre and Mental Mysteries.* (1981) Supreme Magic, Bideford, UK. Saddle-stitch. Green. 63 pp. 5.5 x 8.5 in. Bizarre magick.

Cameron, Charles W., *"Mind" Your Magic.* (1973) Supreme Magic, Bideford, UK. Saddle-stitch. White, black. 63 pp. 5.75 x 8.5 in. Signed by Charles W. Cameron. Mentalism.

Cameron, Charles W., *Witches' Brew.* (1968) Supreme Magic, Bideford, UK. Saddle-stitch. Light green. 35 pp. 6.5 x 8 in. Mentalism, Bizarre magick.

Cameron, Douglas, *Steve Lindsay: More Than a Magician: The Magic of Steve Hamilton.* (2013) International Magic, London. Cloth. Red. 174 pp. 6.75 x 9.5 in. Dust jacket. Cards, Close-Up.

Cameron, Judson J., *Cheating at Bridge.* (1933) Dorrance and Co., Philadelphia. Cloth. Red. 188 pp. 5 x 7.25 in. John Northern Hilliard's copy with his signature and annotations. Cards, Cheating.

Cameron, Judson J., *Cheating at Bridge.* (1933) Dorrance and Co., Philadelphia. Cloth. Blue. 188 pp. 5 x 7.25 in. Cards, Cheating.

Cameron, Judson J., *Cheating at Bridge.* (1933) Dorrance and Co., Philadelphia. Cloth. Maroon. 188 pp. 5 x 7.25 in. Pebbled cloth. Cards, Cheating.

Cameron, Judson J., *Cheating at Bridge.* (1973) Gamblers Book Club, Las Vegas. Perfect. Pink. 188 pp. 4.75 x 7.25 in. Cards, Cheating.

Cameron, Judson J., *Cheating at Bridge.* (1973) Gamblers Book Club, Las Vegas. Perfect. Red. 188 pp. 5.25 x 8.25 in. Cards, Cheating.

Cameron, Nell, *Manual for Magicians and Their Assistants.* (1949) Hal Cameron, Boston. Stapled. Blue. 20 pp. 6 x 9.5 in. Mimeographed. Folded. Textured plastic cover. Theory, Assistants, Stagecraft.

Camí, Jordi, with Martinez, Luis M., *Illusionist Brain: The Neuroscience of Magic, The.* (2022) Princeton University Press, Princeton, NJ. Cloth. Purple. 234 pp. 6.25 x 9.5 in. Dust jacket. Theory, Psychology.

Camp, Len, *Magic You'll Like.* (c. 1978) Author, Ottumwa, IA. (Information not verified by physical copy.) Gospel magic, Close-Up, Stage.

Campana, Benoit, *N.L.P. and Magic.* (2010) Mathieu Bich, Paris. Perfect. White. 95 pp. 5.25 x 8.25 in. Theory, Psychological, Mentalism.

Campbell, C. Samuel, *Exposure of Mediums' Tricks and Rackets, An.* (c. 1930) Haldeman-Julius Co., Girard, KS. Saddle-stitch. Green. 32 pp. 3.25 x 5 in. Little Blue Book. Spirit effects, Exposés, Mediums.

Campbell, Dave, *Duplicity.* (1988) Martin Breese, London. Saddle-stitch. Green. 16 pp. 5.75 x 8.25 in. (Measurements and other information have been recorded as accurately as possible.) Cards.

Campbell, Dave, *You Won't Believe Your Eyes.* (1988) Martin Breese, London. Saddle-stitch. Red. 16 pp. 5.75 x 8.25 in. Cards.

Campbell, Jeffrey, *Trick-tion-ary.* (1988) Author, Waukesha, WI. 26 pp. (Information not verified by physical copy.) Humor, Cartoons.

Campbell, Loring, *Magic That is Magic.* (1946) Abbott Magic Co., Colon, MI. Saddle-stitch. Beige. 76 pp. 6 x 9 in. Stage, Children's magic.

Campbell, Loring, *This is Magic!* (1945) Abbott Magic Co., Colon, MI. Stapled. Red. 64 pp. 8.5 x 11 in. Later reprint. Stage, Close-Up.

Campbell, Loring, *This is Magic!* (1945) Abbott Magic Co., Colon, MI. Perfect. Red. 64 pp. 6 x 9 in. Inscribed to Bill Taylor at PCAM, 1946. Signed by Loring Campbell. Stage, Close-Up.

Campbell, Loring, *This is Magic!* (1945) Abbott Magic Co., Colon, MI. Cloth. Black. Cover text: Silver; 64 pp. 6 x 9 in. Limited hardbound edition. (Information not verified by physical copy.) Stage, Close-Up.

Canaldi, Bruno, *Bella-Magia Impossible!* (1997) Martini's Magic Company, Delta, PA. Saddle-stitch. Green. 2 pp. 5.5 x 8.5 in. (Information not verified by physical copy.) Cards.

Canar, Harry A., *Poker Deal.* (1958) Magic Limited, Oakland, CA. Saddle-stitch. Gray. 13 pp. 6 x 9 in. Cards, Poker deal.

Canasta, Chan, *Book of Oopses.* (1966) Harrap, London. Saddle-stitch. Black. 48 pp. 5.5 x 7.25 in. Mentalism, Self-working.

Canasta, Chan, *Miracle Discovery, A.* (1960) Harry Stanley, London. Stapled. Green. 4 pp. 8 x 10 in. Bound at top. Green text pages with no cover page. In Byron Walker collection. Cards, Mentalism.

Canasta, Chan, *Miracle Discovery, A.* (1960) Harry Stanley, London. Stapled. Blue. 4 pp. 8 x 10 in. Bound at top. White text pages with blue cover page. In Byron Walker collection. Cards, Mentalism.

Canasta, Chan, *Miracle Discovery, A.* (1975) Supreme Magic, Bideford, UK. Saddle-stitch. Black. 4 pp. 5.25 x 8.25 in. (Information not verified by physical copy.) Cards, Mentalism.

Canfield, Kid, *Card Sharpers Tricks Exposed!* (c. 1950) Stein Publishing House, Chicago. Perfect. White. Multiple sections. 5.5 x 7.75 in. With six pages on Canfield plus Hoffmann "Modern Magic" material. Cards, Gambling, Cheating. Pulp.

Canfield, Kid, *Confidence-Gambling and Card Sharpers' Tricks Exposed.* (c. 1920) Author, Chicago. Perfect. Yellow. Cover text: Black; 48 pp. 5.25 x 7.5 in. Hand with fan in circle of cards on cover. States "By a Reformed Confidence Man and Gambler." Cards, Gambling. Pulp.

Canfield, Kid, *Confidence-Gambling and Card Sharpers' Tricks Exposed.* (c. 1920) Author, Chicago. Perfect. Yellow. Cover text: Black; 48 pp. 5.25 x 7.5 in. Hand with fan in circle of cards on cover. States "By Famous Reformed Confidence Man and Gambler." Cards, Gambling. Pulp.

Canfield, Kid, *Confidence-Gambling and Card Sharpers' Tricks Exposed.* (c. 1920) Author, Chicago. Perfect. Beige. Cover text: Black; 48 pp. 5.25 x 7.5 in. Hand with fan in circle of cards on cover. States "By Famous Reformed Confidence Man and Gambler." Cards, Gambling. Pulp.

Canfield, Kid, *Confidence-Gambling and Card Sharpers' Tricks Exposed.* (c. 1930) Stein Publishing House, Chicago. Perfect. Yellow. Cover text: Blue; 48 pp. 5.25 x 7.5 in. Hand with fan in circle of cards on cover. States "By Famous Reformed Confidence Man and Gambler." Cards, Gambling. Pulp.

Canfield, Kid, *Confidence-Gambling and Card Sharpers' Tricks Exposed.* (c. 1930) Stein Publishing House, Chicago. Perfect. White. Cover text: Blue; 106 pp. 5.25 x 7.75 in. With six pages on Canfield plus Hoffmann "Modern Magic" material. Cards, Gambling. Pulp.

Canfield, Kid, *Confidence-Gambling and Card Sharpers' Tricks Exposed.* (c. 1930) Stein Publishing House, Chicago. Perfect. Beige. Cover text: Blue; 100 pp. 5.25 x 7.5 in. With six pages on Canfield plus Hoffmann "Modern Magic" material. Cards, Gambling. Pulp.

Canfield, Kid, *Confidence-Gambling and Card Sharpers' Tricks Exposed.* (c. 1930) Stein Publishing House, Chicago. Perfect. Beige. Cover text: Brown; 106 pp. 5.25 x 7.75 in. With six pages on Canfield plus Hoffmann "Modern Magic" material. Cards, Gambling. Pulp.

Canfield, Kid, *Confidence-Gambling and Card Sharpers' Tricks Exposed.* (c. 1930) H. C. Evans and Co., Chicago. Perfect. Beige. Cover text: Brown; 106 pp. 5.25 x 7.75 in. Cover says "Hoffman's Tricks with Cards" and spine says "Be a Card Expert." With six pages on Canfield plus Hoffmann "Modern Magic" material. Cards, Gambling. Pulp.

Canfield, Kid, *Kid Canfield: The Reformed Confidence Man and Gambler.* (1911) Author, New York. Perfect. Yellow. Cover text: Black; 48 pp. 5.25 x 7.5 in. Gold Rush prospector on cover. Cards, Gambling. Pulp.

Canfield, Kid, *Kid Canfield: The Reformed Confidence Man and Gambler.* (1911) Author, New York. Perfect. Yellow. Cover text: Black; 48 pp. 5.25 x 7.5 in. Photo portrait of Kid Canfield on cover. Cards, Gambling. Pulp.

Canfield, Kid, *Kid Canfield: The Reformed Confidence Man and Gambler.* (c. 1928) Stein Publishing House, Chicago. Perfect. White. Cover text: Blue; 48 pp. 5.25 x 8 in. Photo portrait of Kid Canfield on cover. Ad on back for "Gems of Inspiration." Cards, Gambling. Pulp.

Canfield, Kid, *Kid Canfield: The Reformed Confidence Man and Gambler.* (n.d.) Stein Publishing House, Chicago. Perfect. Beige. Cover text: Blue; 48 pp. 5.25 x 8 in. Photo portrait of Kid Canfield on cover. Ad on back includes ad for Thurston's "Tricks with Cards" with image of magician holding fan of cards. Cards, Gambling. Pulp.

Canick, Michael, *Clayton Rawson: Magic and Mystery.* (1999) Volcanick Press, New York. Stapled. Pink. 32 pp. 8.5 x 11 in. With prospectus, letter from author. Bibliography, Collecting, Fiction, History.

Canick, Michael, *Magic in Fiction: A Short-Title Checklist.* (1998) Volcanick Press, New York. Saddle-stitch. Blue. 40 pp. 8.5 x 11 in. Bibliography, Collecting, Fiction, History.

Canick, Michael, *Price Guide to Magic Books 1639-1990, A.* Second printing. (1997) Volcanick Press, New York. Comb. Beige. 192 pp. 8.5 x 11 in. With three bookmarks with abbreviation guide. Price Guide, Bibliography, Collecting, Reference.

Cannell, J. C., *100 Best Tricks, The.* (c. 1933) Hutchinson, London. Perfect. Red. 230 pp. 5.25 x 7 in. (Information not verified by physical copy.) Beginner, General.

Cannell, J. C., *Hundred Best Tricks, The.* (1932) Hutchinson, London. Cloth. Orange. 250 pp. 5 x 7.5 in. Beginner, General.

Cannell, J. C., *Hundred Best Tricks, The.* (c. 1933) Hutchinson, London. Cloth. Beige. 250 pp. 5.25 x 7.5 in. Dust jacket. With 40 pp. publisher's catalog at back. Beginner, General.

Cannell, J. C., *Hundred Best Tricks, The.* (c. 1934) Hutchinson, London. Boards. Red, orange. 250 pp. 5 x 7.5 in. Beginner, General.

Cannell, J. C., *Master Book of Magic.* Third edition. (1935) Quaker Oats Limited, London. Perfect. Blue. 64 pp. 4.25 x 6.5 in. Beginner, Premium.

Cannell, J. C., *Modern Conjuring.* (1940) E. G. Ellisdon Ltd., London. Perfect. Color. 96 pp. 5.25 x 8 in. (Measurements and other information have been recorded as accurately as possible.) Beginner.

Cannell, J. C., *Modern Conjuring for Amateurs.* (1938) E. G. Ellisdon Ltd., London. Cloth. Yellow. 333 pp. 5.25 x 8 in. Dust jacket. Beginner, General.

Cannell, J. C., *Modern Conjuring for Amateurs.* (1950) C. Arthur Pearson Ltd., London. Cloth. Red. 333 pp. 5.5 x 8.25 in. Dust jacket. Beginner, General.

Cannell, J. C., *Secrets of Houdini.* First edition. (1931) Hutchinson, London. Cloth. Maroon. 279 pp. 5.25 x 8.5 in. Biography, Escapes, Houdini.

Cannell, J. C., *Secrets of Houdini.* Second impression. (1931) Hutchinson, London. Cloth. Brown. 279 pp. 5.25 x 8.5 in. Biography, Escapes, Houdini.

Cannell, J. C., *Secrets of Houdini.* Eighth Thousand. (1932) Hutchinson, London. Cloth. Beige. 279 pp. 5.5 x 8.5 in. Biography, Escapes, Houdini.

Cannell, J. C., *Secrets of Houdini.* 38th Thousand. (1938) Hutchinson, London. Perfect. Red. 252 pp. 4.25 x 7 in. Biography, Escapes, Houdini.

Cannell, J. C., *Secrets of Houdini.* (1973) Dover, New York. Perfect. Blue. 279 pp. 5.25 x 8.5 in. Biography, Escapes, Houdini.

Cannell, J. C., *Secrets of Houdini.* (1989) Bell, New York. Cloth. Black. 279 pp. 6 x 9 in. Dust jacket. Biography, Escapes, Houdini.

Canning, Doug, *Canning's Card Capers.* (1992) Author, Dallas, TX. Saddle-stitch. Green. 43 pp. 5.5 x 8.5 in. (Measurements and other information have been recorded as accurately as possible.) Cards.

Cannon, Mark (See also McColl, Ian), *21st Century Escape Lecture, The.* (2002) Author, Yucaipa, CA. Saddle-stitch. Color. 23 pp. 8.5 x 11 in. (Information not verified by physical copy.) Lecture notes. Escapes.

Cantor, Eddie, *Eddie Cantor's Book of Magic.* (1935) Lehn and Fink, New York. Saddle-stitch. Red, blue. 22 pp. 4.75 x 6.75 in. With original mailing envelope. Beginner, Premium, Stunts.

Cantor, Michael, *Herrmann the Great: A Journey Through Media.* (2015) Author, Baltimore, MD. Perfect. Black. 379 pp. 8.5 x 11 in. Signed by Michael Cantor. Biography, History.

Cantor, Michael, *Magician's New Hat: On Art and Illusion, The.* (2015) Author, Baltimore, MD. Perfect. Black. 90 pp. 5 x 8 in. Signed by Michael Cantor. Theory, Showmanship.

Capehart, Chris, with Fulves, Karl, *Chris Capehart's 3-Ring Routine.* New Stars of Magic vol. 1, no. 13. (1981) Louis Tannen, New York. Saddle-stitch. White. 15 pp. 8.5 x 11 in. Linking Rings.

Capehart, Chris, *Chris Capehart's Favorite Card Tricks.* (2020) Author, New York. Saddle-stitch. Orange. 24 pp. 8.5 x 11 in. (Information not verified by physical copy. Bibliographical details are as accurate as possible.) Cards.

Capehart, Chris, *Magic: Make $1500 a Week Doing It on the Streets.* (1998) Author, New York. Clip. Yellow. 26 pp. 8.5 x 11 in. Business, Promotion.

Capps, H. Wayne, *Magicians at War.* (2020) Author, Mt. Pleasant, SC. Perfect. Beige. 83 pp. 5.5 x 8.5 in. (Measurements and other information have been recorded as accurately as possible.) History, War magicians.

Caputo, Chuck, *Pittsburgh Magic: A Magician's Story.* (2013) Author, Pittsburgh, PA. Perfect. Black. 75 pp. 6 x 9 in. Biography, Close-Up.

Caputo, Chuck, with Guevara, Eddie, *Skull Magic Unleashed.* (2023) Author, Pittsburgh, PA. Perfect. Black. 80 pp. 8 x 10 in. Bizarre magick.

Carbone, Angelo (See also Owen, Anthony), *Humbug: A Visual Vanishing Deck.* (1994) Author, Surrey, UK. Saddle-stitch. Black. 21 pp. 5.75 x 8.25 in. (Information not verified by physical copy.) Cards, Manual.

Carbone, Angelo, *Original Out of Order, The.* (1995) Author, Surrey, UK. Saddle-stitch. Orange. 15 pp. 5.75 x 8.25 in. (Information not verified by physical copy.) Cards, Self-working.

Carbonnier, Yves, *Grand Livre de Cartomagie.* (2019) Marchand de Trucs, Lorient, France. Casebound. Black. 289 pp. 8.5 x 12 in. Cards. French.

Cardex, Prof. Leon, *Easy Card Tricks.* (n.d.) Play Shop, Melbourne. 23 pp. 4.25 x 7 in. (Information not verified by physical copy.) Same contents as Levante's Easy Card Tricks. See McCullagh, "Under the Southern Cross."

Cards, Jimmy (Jim Molinari), *Reversed Prediction, A.* (1980) Author, Oak Park, IL. Stapled. White. 25 pp. 8.5 x 11 in. Photocopied card effects. Cards.

Carey, Chris, *Do the Stuff That's You!* (1989) Author, Atlanta. Cloth. Blue. 271 pp. 5.5 x 8.5 in. Dust jacket. Signed by Chris Carey. Showmanship, Children's magic, Stage.

Carey, Elwyn L., *Messages in Magic.* (1968) Jim Club of America, Bemus Point, NY. Comb. Blue. 62 pp. 8.5 x 11 in. Mimeographed. Gospel magic.

Carey, John, *Carey Files vol. 1, The.* (2016) Haresign Press, UK. Perfect. Green. 128 pp. 6 x 9 in. (Information not verified by physical copy.) Cards, Mentalism.

Carey, John, *Carey's Way.* (2018) Author, UK. Casebound. Blue. 184 pp. 6 x 9 in. (Information not verified by physical copy. Bibliographical details are as accurate as possible.) Cards.

Carey, John, *Crafted with Carey.* (2024) MagicSeen, Norton, UK. Perfect. Green. 200 pp. 6 x 9 in. (Measurements and other information have been recorded as accurately as possible.) Cards.

Carey, John, *Dublin City Session, The.* (2014) Author, UK. Saddle-stitch. White, purple. 28 pp. 8.25 x 11.75 in. (Information not verified by physical copy.) Cards.

Carey, John, *John Carey and Friends.* (n.d.) Author, UK. Casebound. Colors. 270 pp. 6 x 8.5 in. (Information not verified by physical copy.) Cards, Mentalism.

Carey, John, *John Carey and Friends II.* (n.d.) Author, UK. Casebound. Black. 500 pp. 6 x 8.5 in. (Information not verified by physical copy.) Cards, Mentalism.

Carey, John, *John Carey and Friends III.* (n.d.) Author, UK. Casebound. Black. 350 pp. 6 x 8.5 in. (Information not verified by physical copy.) Cards, Mentalism.

Carey, John, *Me, My Cards, and I.* (2017) Haresign Press, UK. Casebound. White. 149 pp. 6 x 9 in. (Information not verified by physical copy.) Cards, Mentalism.

Carey, John, *Minimalistica.* (2015) Author, UK. Casebound. Red, black. 275 pp. 6 x 9 in. (Information not verified by physical copy. Bibliographical details are as accurate as possible.) Cards, Mentalism.

Carey, John, *Myriad.* (n.d.) Author, UK. Casebound. Black. 6 x 9 in. (Information not verified by physical copy. Bibliographical details are as accurate as possible.) Cards, Mentalism.

Carey, John, *Reflections.* (n.d.) Author, UK. Casebound. Blue. 196 pp. 6 x 9 in. (Information not verified by physical copy. Bibliographical details are as accurate as possible.) Cards, Mentalism.

Carey, John, *Streamlined: The Commercial Magic of John Carey.* (2014) Author, UK. Stapled. White. 28 pp. 8.25 x 11.75 in. (Information not verified by physical copy.) Lecture notes. Cards.

Carey, John, *Very Best of John Carey, The.* (2021) Author, UK. Casebound. Brown. 356 pp. 6 x 9 in. (Information not verified by physical copy.) Cards, Mentalism.

Carey, Vin (as Vin Cary), *Jap Mirako Act.* (1941) Abbott Magic Co., Colon, MI. Stapled. Yellow. 7 pp. 8.5 x 11 in. Variety, Writing act.

Carey, Vin, *Sleeving: How to Do It, What to Do With It.* (1942) American Magic Co., Baltimore, MD. Stapled. Olive. 8 pp. 8.5 x 11 in. Mimeographed. Sleeving.

Carey, Vin, *Simple Sleeving: How to Do It, What to Do With It.* (c. 1940) Author, Pittsfield, MA. Stapled. White. 8 pp. 8.5 x 11 in. Reprint of original with new title page. Sleeving.

Carl, James, *Practical Conjuring.* (1911) Author, Derby, UK. Boards. White. 27 pp. 5.5 x 8.5 in. Signed by Jack Gwynne. Beginner, Stage.

Carlini (Carl A. Blessing), *Carlini Lecture Notes.* (1980) Author, N. Tonawanda, NY. Stapled. Yellow. 13 pp. 8.5 x 11 in. (Information not verified by physical copy. Bibliographical details are as accurate as possible.) Lecture notes. Stage, Manipulation, Deaf magicians.

Carlisle, Stanton, *Dynamic Mentalism.* (1979) Supreme Magic, Bideford, UK. Comb. White, blue. 84 pp. 7.5 x 9.75 in. Mentalism.

Carlisle, Stanton, *E.S.P.-ecially Yours.* (1980) Supreme Magic, Bideford, UK. Saddle-stitch. Yellow. 36 pp. 7.25 x 9.5 in. Mentalism, Book tests, Billets.

Carlisle, Stanton, *Magic of E.S.P., The.* (1978) Supreme Magic, Bideford, UK. Saddle-stitch. Red. 29 pp. 7 x 9.75 in. Mentalism, E.S.P. cards.

Carlisle, Stanton, *Master-Mentality*. (1976) Supreme Magic, Bideford, UK. Cloth. Black. 87 pp. 7.25 x 10 in. Dust jacket. Mentalism.

Carlisle, Stanton, *Mentalism: Inner Secrets I*. (1990) Exclusive Magical Publications, Mexico City. Perfect. Blue. 87 pp. 5.5 x 8.5 in. Mentalism.

Carlo, *Carlo's Great Card Mysteries*. (c. 1945) Carlo Magic Company, Toledo, OH. Folded. Tan. 4 pp. 6 x 8 in. Unfolded. Cards, Si Stebbins.

Carlo, *Three for One*. (1944) Carlo's Magic Shop, Toledo, OH. Loose pages. Tan. 2 pp. 8.5 x 11 in. Mimeographed. Close-Up, Liquids, Cigarettes, Coins.

Carlo, Jimmy, *Kid-ability*. (c. 1990) Author, UK. Comb. White. 8.5 x 11 in. (Information not verified by physical copy.) Lecture notes. Children's magic.

Carlsen, Rune, *My 10 Go-To Card FX*. (2024) Murphy's Magic Supplies, Rancho Cordova, CA. Casebound. Black. 250 pp. 6.25 x 9.25 in. Cards.

Carlson, George, *Fun-Time Stunts*. (1937) Platt and Munk, New York. Saddle-stitch. Color. 13 pp. 7.5 x 8.5 in. Includes some color pages. Beginner, Stunts.

Carlson, Laurie, *Harry Houdini for Kids*. (2009) Chicago Review Press, Chicago. Perfect. Yellow. 136 pp. 11 x 8.5 in. Bound oblong. Houdini, Biography, History, Children's book.

Carlton, *Twenty Years of Spoof and Bluff*. (1920) Herbert Jenkins, London. Cloth. Maroon. 299 pp. 5.25 x 8 in. Biography, History.

Carlton, Paul, *Magician's Handy Book of Cigarette Tricks*. (1933) R. J. Reynolds, Winston-Salem, NC. Saddle-stitch. Yellow. 36 pp. 4.5 x 6.5 in. Beginner, Premium.

Carlyle, E. Raymond, *Lecture Notes*. (1998) Author, Virginia Beach, VA. Coil. Yellow. 24 pp. 8.5 x 11 in. (Information not verified by physical copy.) Lecture notes. Mentalism.

Carlyle, E. Raymond, *Medium's Grip*. (1988) Scott Davis and Assoc., Ellicott City, MD. Saddle-stitch. Gray. 8 pp. 5.5 x 8.5 in. Spirit effects, Mediums, Séances.

Carlyle, E. Raymond, *Medium's Grip*. (1999) Author, Virginia Beach, VA. 6 pp. (Information not verified by physical copy.) Spirit effects, Mediums, Séances.

Carlyle, Francis, *Botany Book of Magic.* (1940) Botany Worsted Mill, Pasaic, NJ. Saddle-stitch. Red, white. 12 pp. 3 x 6 in. Beginner, Premium.

Carlyle, Francis, *Decapitation.* Stars of Magic series 4, no. 1. (1947) Stars of Magic, Inc., New York. Folded. White. 4 pp. 8.5 x 11 in. Matches, Close-Up.

Carlyle, Francis, *Francis Carlyle Lecture Notes.* (c. 1985) Jeff Busby Magic, Oakland, CA. Comb. White. 8 pp. 8.5 x 11 in. Cards.

Carlyle, Francis, *Homing Card.* Stars of Magic series 4, no. 2. (1947) Stars of Magic, Inc., New York. Folded. White. 4 pp. 8.5 x 11 in. Cards.

Carlyle, Francis, *Wrist Watch Steal.* Stars of Magic series 4, no. 3. (1947) Stars of Magic, Inc., New York. Folded. White. 4 pp. 8.5 x 11 in. Pickpocket, Watch steal, Close-Up, Coins.

Carmel, Simon J., *Invisible Magic.* (2013) Author, West Palm Beach, FL. Perfect. Black. 404 pp. 6 x 9 in. Biography, History, Deaf magicians.

Carmel, Simon J., *Karmel's Kwik-Kuts.* (2003) Author, West Palm Beach, FL. 13 pp. (Information not verified by physical copy.) Paper, Cards.

Carmel, Simon J., *Out of the Magic Cloak.* (2020) Author, West Palm Beach, FL. Perfect. White. 187 pp. 6 x 9 in. (Information not verified by physical copy.) Biography, History, Deaf magicians.

Carmel, Simon J., *Silent Magic: Biographies of Deaf Magicians in the United States from the 19th to 21st Centuries.* (2008) Author, Eustis, FL. Perfect. Beige. 158 pp. 8.5 x 10.75 in. Signed by Simon J. Carmel. Biography, History, Deaf magicians.

Carmel, Simon J., *Three Selected Cards Simply Revealed.* (2003) Author, West Palm Beach, FL. Stapled. White. 3 pp. 8.5 x 11 in. (Information not verified by physical copy.) Cards.

Carmichael, Carrie, *Secrets of the Great Magicians.* (1977) Raintree Children's Books, Milwaukee, WI. Casebound. Brown. 48 pp. 6.25 x 9.25 in. Children's book, Beginner.

Carnazzo, Paul, *Altriotto.* (2012) Author, Boston. Saddle-stitch. White. 62 pp. 6 x 9 in. (Information not verified by physical copy.) Mentalism, Stage.

Carnegie, Dean, *Robert Heller: The Versatile Artist, Pianist, Conjurer, Comedian, and Wit.* (2024) Author, Nashville, TN. Saddle-stitch. White. 30 pp. 8.5 x 11 in. Biography, History.

Carney, John, *Book of Secrets, The.* Limited deluxe edition. (2002) Author, Los Angeles. Leather. Black. 309 pp. 6 x 9 in. (Information not verified by physical copy.) Mentalism.

Carney, John, *Book of Secrets, The.* First edition. (2002) Author, Los Angeles. Cloth. Red. 309 pp. 6 x 9 in. Close-Up, Stage, Theory.

Carney, John, *Book of Secrets, The.* Second edition. (2004) Author, Los Angeles. Cloth. Orange. 309 pp. 6 x 9 in. Close-Up, Stage, Theory.

Carney, John, *Carney Knowledge.* (1983) Magical Publications, Sierra Madre, CA. Saddle-stitch. Maroon. 57 pp. 5.25 x 8.25 in. Signed by John Carney. Close-Up, Cards.

Carney, John, *Carney Uncovered.* (1987) Catman Publications, Los Angeles. Comb. Yellow. 32 pp. 5.5 x 8.5 in. (Measurements and other information have been recorded as accurately as possible.) Cards, Close-Up.

Carney, John, *Carney Uncovered.* (1987) Catman Publications, Los Angeles. Saddle-stitch. White. 32 pp. 5.5 x 8.5 in. Cards, Close-Up.

Carney, John, *Carney Up Close.* (1987) Catman Publications, Los Angeles. Saddle-stitch. White. 28 pp. 5.5 x 8.5 in. Cards, Close-Up.

Carney, John, with Minch, Stephen, *Carneycopia.* (1991) L & L Publishing, Tahoma, CA. Cloth. Black. 266 pp. 5.5 x 9 in. Dust jacket. Signed by John Carney. Close-Up, Stage.

Carney, John, *Conjurers Journal.* (1979) Author, Des Moines, IA. Stapled. Yellow. 16 pp. 8.5 x 11 in. Signed by John Carney. Close-Up, Cards.

Carney, John, *Conjuring Con Carney.* (1987) Catman Publications, Los Angeles. Saddle-stitch. White. 24 pp. 5.5 x 8.5 in. Cards, Close-Up, Coins.

Carney, John, *Enigma.* (1976) Author, Des Moines, IA. Stapled. Yellow. 16 pp. 8.5 x 11 in. Signed by John Carney. Lecture notes. Close-Up, Coins, Cards.

Carney, John, *Legerdemain One: Suite for Coins and Handkerchief.* (2021) Author, Studio City, CA. Saddle-stitch. Blue. 29 pp. 8.5 x 11 in. Close-Up, Coins, Handkerchiefs, Magazines.

Carney, John, with Baker, Al, *Lightning Pull.* (1997) Catman Press, Studio City, CA. Stapled. White. 15 pp. 8.5 x 11 in. Silks.

Carney, John, *Logic of Deception: An Introduction to Magic Theory, The.* (c. 1977) Author, Des Moines, IA. Saddle-stitch. Yellow. 18 pp. 5.5 x 8.5 in. (Measurements and other information have been recorded as accurately as possible.) Signed by John Carney. Theory.

Carney, John, *Notebook.* (c. 1984) Author, Des Moines, IA. Folded. White. 8 pp. 5.5 x 8.5 in. (Measurements and other information have been recorded as accurately as possible.) Signed by John Carney. Close-Up, Cards.

Carney, John, *Sleights and Insights.* Limited deluxe edition. (2020) Author, Los Angeles. Leather. Black. 315 pp. 8.75 x 11.25 in. Slipcase. Signed by John Carney. #115 of 150. Close-Up, Stage, Theory.

Carney, John, *Sleights and Insights.* (2020) Author, Los Angeles. Cloth. Blue. 315 pp. 8.75 x 11.25 in. Close-Up, Stage, Theory.

Carney, John, *Torn and Restored.* (1995) Catman Press, San Francisco. Stapled. Beige. 12 pp. 8.5 x 11 in. Signed by John Carney. Cards.

Carney, John, *Torn and Restored Card.* (2022) Vanishing Inc., Rancho Cordova, CA. Perfect. White. 24 pp. 6 x 6 in. From publisher's "Western Adventure Retreat Gift Pack." (Information not verified by physical copy.) Cards, Torn and Restored Card.

Carney, John, *Using Your Head.* (1999) Author, Studio City, CA. Stapled. 33 pp. 8.5 x 11 in. (Information not verified by physical copy.) Theory, Showmanship, Coins.

Carney, John, *Wizard Academy.* (2011) Author, Studio City, CA. Perfect. Color. 79 pp. 7 x 10 in. Signed by John Carney. Beginner.

Caroly, *Étude Sur les Nouveaux Escamotages de Pièces et Sur le Numéro du "Roi des Dollars."* (1902) Author, Paris. Saddle-stitch. Beige. 32 pp. 5.5 x 8.5 in. Analyzes the successful act of T. Nelson Downs, billed as the "King of Koins" ("le Roi du Dollar"). Coins, Manipulation, Miser's Dream. French.

Caroly, *Illusionniste 1902-1906, L'.* (c. 1906) Author, Paris. Boards. Green. Multiple sections. 8 x 11.25 in. Magazine. French.

Caroly, *Illusionniste 1907-1910, L'.* (c. 1910) Author, Paris. Boards. Green. Multiple sections. 8 x 11.25 in. Magazine. French.

Caroly, *Illusionniste 1911-1914, L'.* (c. 1916) Author, Paris. Boards. Green. Multiple sections. 8 x 11.25 in. Magazine. French.

Caroly, *Tours de Cartes Faciles Pour Jeunes Gens.* (1911) A. Eichler, Paris. Perfect. Color. 188 pp. 4.5 x 6.5 in. Cards. French.

Caroly, *Tours Faciles d'Escamotage.* (1901) A. L. Guyot, Paris. Perfect. Beige, color. 188 pp. 4.25 x 6.25 in. Beginner. French.

Caroly, *Tours Faciles d'Escamotage.* (1921) A. L. Guyot, Paris. Perfect. Beige, black. 191 pp. 4.25 x 6.25 in. Beginner. French.

Carpenter, Jack, *3 Card Monte Routine.* (n.d.) Author, Seattle. Stapled. White. 6 pp. 8.5 x 11 in. (Measurements and other information have been recorded as accurately as possible.) Cards, Three-Card Monte.

Carpenter, Jack, with Mayhew, Steve, *Angels May Shuffle But the Devil Still Deals.* (1999) Author, Seattle. Coil. White, gray. 25 pp. 8.5 x 11 in. Includes 2 pp. "Freedom aka The Mayhew Poker Deal" insert and 1 p. author note. Cards.

Carpenter, Jack, with Masterson, Jamie, *Carpenter's Conceptions.* (2024) Author, Seattle. Cloth. Black. 150 pp. 8.75 x 11.25 in. Dust jacket. Cards.

Carpenter, Jack, *Castle Collection.* (1994) Author, Seattle. Stapled. White. 21 pp. 8.5 x 11 in. (Measurements and other information have been recorded as accurately as possible.) Cards.

Carpenter, Jack, *Expert's Portfolio no. 1.* (1997) Author, Seattle. Coil. White. 102 pp. 8.5 x 11 in. (Measurements and other information have been recorded as accurately as possible.) Cards.

Carpenter, Jack, *Expert's Portfolio no. 2.* (2017) Out-in-the-Bathroom Productions, Seattle. Coil. White. 91 pp. 8.5 x 11 in. Cards.

Carpenter, Jack, with Hobbs, Stephen, *Modus Operandi: The Card Magic of Jack Carpenter.* Second printing. (1992) Hermetic Press, Seattle. Cloth. Black. 163 pp. 6 x 9 in. Dust jacket. Cards.

Carpenter, Jack, *Pasteboard Palette.* (2006) Author, Seattle. Coil. White. 51 pp. 8.5 x 11 in. (Information not verified by physical copy. Bibliographical details are as accurate as possible.) Cards.

Carpenter, Jack, *Pocket Interchange.* (c. 1997) Author, Seattle. Stapled. White. 4 pp. 8.5 x 11 in. (Measurements and other information have been recorded as accurately as possible.) Cards.

Carpenter, Jack, with Masterson, Jamie, *Shadow and Shake.* (2020) Author, Seattle. Coil. Gray. 35 pp. 8.5 x 11 in. (Measurements and other information have been recorded as accurately as possible.) Cards.

Carpenter, Jack, *Ultimate False Dealing Demonstration.* (2006) Author, Seattle. Coil. White. 18 pp. 8.5 x 11 in. (Information not verified by physical copy.) Cards.

Carpenter, Woodrow, *Instructions for Carpenter's Junior Magic Show.* (1947) Author, Frankfort, IN. Saddle-stitch. Yellow. 13 pp. 5.25 x 7.5 in. In "Carpenter's Junior Magic Show" set. Magic set manual, Beginner.

Carreon, Luis, *Poquito Lecture Notes, Un.* (2022) Author, Chicago. Stapled. White. 39 pp. 8.5 x 11 in. (Information not verified by physical copy.) Lecture notes. Cards, Close-Up.

Carrington, Hereward, *Boy's Book of Magic, The.* (1920) Dodd, Mead, New York. Cloth. Blue. 284 pp. 5 x 7.5 in. Carrington's copy with his bookplate and clippings. Beginner.

Carrington, Hereward, *Boy's Book of Magic, The.* (1920) Dodd, Mead, New York. Cloth. Red. 284 pp. 5 x 7.25 in. Beginner.

Carrington, Hereward, *Boy's Book of Magic, The.* (1925) Dodd, Mead, New York. Cloth. Red. 284 pp. 5 x 7.25 in. Beginner.

Carrington, Hereward, *Boy's Book of Magic, The.* (1925) Dodd, Mead, New York. Cloth. Tan. 284 pp. 5 x 7.25 in. Beginner.

Carrington, Hereward, *Boy's Book of Magic, The.* (c. 1920) George Routledge and Sons, London. Cloth. Brown. 284 pp. 5.25 x 7.75 in. Dust jacket. Beginner.

Carrington, Hereward, *Boy's Book of Magic, The.* (c. 1920) George Routledge and Sons, London. Cloth. Green. 284 pp. 5.25 x 7.75 in. Dust jacket. Beginner.

Carrington, Hereward, *Case for Psychic Survival, The.* (1957) Citadel Press, New York. Cloth. Black. 157 pp. 5.5 x 8.25 in. Dust jacket. Psychic, Spiritualism, Occult.

Carrington, Hereward, *Coming Science, The.* Second edition. (1920) American Universities Publishing Co., New York. Cloth. Green. 393 pp. 5.25 x 8.25 in. Carrington's copy with his bookplate. Psychic, Spiritualism.

Carrington, Hereward, *Essays in the Occult.* Second edition. (1958) Thomas Yoseloff, New York. Cloth. Blue. 326 pp. 5.75 x 8.75 in. Dust jacket. Psychic, Spiritualism, Occult.

Carrington, Hereward, *Eusapia Palladino and Her Phenomena.* (1909) B. W. Dodge and Co., New York. Cloth. Green. Cover text: Gold; 353 pp. 5.5 x 8.25 in. Spiritualism, Mediums.

Carrington, Hereward, *Gamblers' Crooked Tricks.* Miniature book. (1928) Haldeman-Julius Co., Girard, KS. Saddle-stitch. Beige. 32 pp. 3.5 x 5 in. Little Blue Book; Gambling, Cheating, Cards.

Carrington, Hereward, *Gamblers' Crooked Tricks.* Miniature book. (1928) Haldeman-Julius Co., Girard, KS. Saddle-stitch. Green. 32 pp. 3.5 x 5 in. Little Blue Book; Gambling, Cheating, Cards.

Carrington, Hereward, *Gamblers' Crooked Tricks.* Miniature book. (1928) Haldeman-Julius Co., Girard, KS. Saddle-stitch. Orange. 32 pp. 3.5 x 5 in. Little Blue Book; Gambling, Cheating, Cards.

Carrington, Hereward, *Gamblers' Crooked Tricks.* Miniature book. (1928) Haldeman-Julius Co., Girard, KS. Saddle-stitch. Tan. 32 pp. 3.5 x 5 in. Little Blue Book; Gambling, Cheating, Cards.

Carrington, Hereward, *Handcuff Tricks.* (1913) A. M. Wilson, Kansas City, MO. Stapled with paper cover. Blue. 61 pp. 5 x 7 in. Escapes, Handcuffs.

Carrington, Hereward, with Fodor, Nandor, *Haunted People.* (1951) E. P. Dutton and Co., New York. Cloth. Beige. 225 pp. 5.5 x 8.25 in. Dust jacket. Inscribed by author to "A ghost if there ever was one!" Signed by Hereward Carrington. Occult.

Carrington, Hereward, *Higher Psychical Development (Yoga Philosophy).* (1920) Dodd, Mead, New York. Cloth. Black. 296 pp. 5.5 x 8.25 in. Psychic, Yoga.

Carrington, Hereward, *Hindu Magic.* (1909) Annals of Psychical Science, London. Boards. Olive. 52 pp. 4.75 x 7.25 in. Indian magic, Close-Up.

Carrington, Hereward, *Hindu Magic.* (1913) A. M. Wilson, Kansas City, MO. Perfect. Blue. 51 pp. 4.75 x 7.25 in. Indian magic, Close-Up.

Carrington, Hereward, *Hindu Magic Self Taught.* Miniature book. (1928) Haldeman-Julius Co., Girard, KS. Saddle-stitch. Beige. 32 pp. 3.5 x 5 in. Indian magic, Close-Up.

Carrington, Hereward, *Hindu Magic Self Taught.* Miniature book. (1928) Little Blue Books, Girard, KS. Saddle-stitch. Yellow. 32 pp. 3.5 x 5 in. Indian magic, Close-Up.

Carrington, Hereward, *Hindu Magic Self Taught.* Miniature book. (1928) Little Blue Books, Girard, KS. Saddle-stitch. Gray. 32 pp. 3.25 x 5 in. Indian magic, Close-Up.

Carrington, Hereward, *Invisible World, The.* (1946) Beechhurst Press, New York. Cloth. Beige. 190 pp. 5.75 x 8.25 in. Dust jacket. Occult.

Carrington, Hereward, *Letters to Hereward Carrington.* (1964) Fieldcrest Publishing, New York. Comb. Yellow. 91 pp. 8.5 x 11 in. History, Spiritualism.

Carrington, Hereward, *Letters to Hereward Carrington.* (1998) Health Research Books, Pomeroy Washington. Comb. Beige. 92 pp. 8.5 x 11 in. Reprint. History, Spiritualism.

Carrington, Hereward, *Magic and Escapology.* (1977) Drake Publishing, New York. Perfect. Blue. 151 pp. 5 x 7.5 in. Excerpts from Carrington's "Boy's Book of Magic." Beginner, Escapes.

Carrington, Hereward, *Magic for Every One.* (1927) Dodd, Mead, New York. Cloth. Red. 138 pp. 5.25 x 7.5 in. Beginner.

Carrington, Hereward, *Magic for Every One.* (1942) World Publishing Co., Cleveland and New York. Cloth. Light green. 138 pp. 5.5 x 8.25 in. Dust jacket. Title on dust jacket: "Magic for Everyone." Tower Books edition. Beginner.

Carrington, Hereward, *Magic for Every One.* Second printing. (1942) World Publishing Co., Cleveland and New York. Cloth. Green. 138 pp. 5.25 x 8 in. Dust jacket. Beginner.

Carrington, Hereward, *Magic for Every One.* Third printing. (1943) World Publishing Co., Cleveland and New York. Cloth. Green. 138 pp. 5.5 x 8.25 in. Dust jacket. Beginner.

Carrington, Hereward, *Magic is Fun.* (1920) New Power Publications, New York. Perfect. Red. 138 pp. 5.25 x 7.5 in. Beginner.

Carrington, Hereward, *Modern Psychical Phenomena.* (1919) Dodd, Mead, New York. Cloth. Black. 331 pp. 5.5 x 8.25 in. Psychic.

Carrington, Hereward, *Personal Experiences in Spiritualism.* (1913) T. Werner Laurie, London. Cloth. Green. 274 pp. 5.5 x 8.5 in. With Carrington's stories of medium Palladino. (Information not verified by physical copy.) Biography, Spiritualism.

Carrington, Hereward, *Phantasms of the Dead or True Ghost Stories.* (1920) American Universities Publishing Co., New York. Cloth. Green. 246 pp. 5.25 x 8.25 in. Psychic, Ghosts.

Carrington, Hereward, *Physical Phenomena of Spiritualism, The.* Third edition. (1920) American Universities Publishing Co., New York. Cloth. Green. 426 pp. 5.25 x 8.25 in. Spiritualism, Mediums.

Carrington, Hereward, *Psychic Oddities.* (1952) Ryder and Company, London. Cloth. Blue. 183 pp. 5.5 x 8.5 in. Dust jacket. Psychic, Spiritualism, Occult.

Carrington, Hereward, *Psychic Series 1-6.* (1920) Psychical Publishing Co., New York. Cloth. Black. 96 pp. 5 x 7 in. Six booklets with orange covers bound into one volume. Psychic, Dreams, Crystal gazing.

Carrington, Hereward, *Psychical Phenomena and the War.* (1919) Dodd, Mead, New York. Cloth. Green. 363 pp. 5.5 x 8.25 in. Spiritualism, Psychics.

Carrington, Hereward, *"Psycho" Mind Reading Act, The.* (1945) Thayer's Studio of Magic, Los Angeles. Saddle-stitch. Beige. 16 pp. 5.5 x 8.5 in. Mentalism.

Carrington, Hereward, *Side-Show and Animal Tricks.* (1913) A. M. Wilson, Kansas City, MO. Perfect. Blue. 66 pp. 5 x 7.5 in. Sideshows, Performing animals.

Carrington, Hereward, *Side-Show and Animal Tricks.* (1973) Pinchpenny Press, Atlanta. Saddle-stitch. Blue. 66 pp. 5.5 x 8.5 in. Reprint. (Information not verified by physical copy.) Sideshows, Performing animals.

Carrington, Hereward, *Side-Show Tricks Explained.* Miniature book. (1928) Haldeman-Julius Co., Girard, KS. Saddle-stitch. Gray. 32 pp. 3.5 x 5 in. Little Blue Book. Sideshows.

Carrington, Hereward, *Side-Show Tricks Explained.* Miniature book. (1928) Haldeman-Julius Co., Girard, KS. Saddle-stitch. Yellow. 32 pp. 3.5 x 5 in. Little Blue Book. Sideshows.

Carrington, Hereward, with Walsh, James J., *Spiritualism: A Fact / Spiritualism: A Fake.* (1925) Stratford Company, Boston. Cloth. Maroon. 150 pp. 5.25 x 7.5 in. Double-sided book with "Spiritualism: A Fake." Spiritualism.

Carrington, Hereward, *Story of Psychic Science, The.* (1931) Ives Washburn, New York. Cloth. Maroon. 400 pp. 6 x 9 in. Spiritualism, Mediums.

Carrington, Hereward, *Ventriloquism Self-Taught.* Miniature book. (1928) Haldeman-Julius Co., Girard, KS. Saddle-stitch. Beige. 32 pp. 3.5 x 5 in. Illustration of ventriloquist on cover. Ventriloquism.

Carrington, Hereward, *Ventriloquism Self-Taught.* Miniature book. (1928) Haldeman-Julius Co., Girard, KS. Saddle-stitch. Yellow. 32 pp. 3.5 x 5 in. Illustration of ventriloquist on cover. Razor blades ad on back. Ventriloquism.

Carrington, Hereward, *Ventriloquism Self-Taught.* Miniature book. (1928) Little Blue Books, Girard, KS. Saddle-stitch. Beige. 32 pp. 3.5 x 5 in. Little Blue Book. Ventriloquism.

Carrington, Hereward, *Ventriloquism Self-Taught.* Miniature book. (1928) Haldeman-Julius Co., Girard, KS. Saddle-stitch. Tan. Cover text: Brown; 32 pp. 3.5 x 5 in. Little Blue Book. Ventriloquism.

Carrington, Hereward, *Walter-Kerwin Thumb Prints, The.* (1934) Boston Society for Psychic Research, Boston. Perfect. Maroon. 85 pp. 6 x 8.75 in. Research on Margery case. Spiritualism.

Carrington, Hereward, *Your Psychic Powers and How to Develop Them.* (1920) Dodd, Mead, New York. Cloth. Dark blue. 358 pp. 5.5 x 8.25 in. Carrington's copy with his bookplate. Psychic.

Carroll, Charles Michael, *Great Chess Automaton, The.* (1975) Dover, New York. Perfect. Brown. 114 pp. 5.25 x 8.5 in. History, Automata, Automaton chess player.

Carroll, Don, *Feats of Memory.* (1983) Supreme Magic, Bideford, UK. Saddle-stitch. Gray. 16 pp. 7.75 x 9.75 in. Memory, Mathematical magic.

Carroll, Harrison, *Shell Game, The.* (1994) Author, Clarence, NY. Comb. Gray. 25 pp. 8.75 x 11.25 in. (Information not verified by physical copy.) Three Shell Game.

Carroll, Jene, *Magic Routines You'd Love to Steal.* (1982) Author, Fort Myers, FL. Comb. Yellow. 72 pp. 8.25 x 11.75 in. (Information not verified by physical copy.) Cards, Close-Up.

Carroll, José, *52 Amantes vol. 1.* (1988) Editorial Frakson, Madrid. Perfect. Pink. 129 pp. 7 x 9.25 in. Dust jacket. (Information not verified by physical copy.) Cards. Spanish.

Carroll, José, *52 Amantes vol. 2.* (1991) Editorial Frakson, Madrid. Perfect. Pink. 129 pp. 7 x 9.25 in. (Information not verified by physical copy.) Cards. Spanish.

Carroll, José, *52 Lovers vol. 1.* (1988) Editorial Frakson, Madrid. Cloth. Red. 163 pp. 7 x 9.25 in. Dust jacket. Cards.

Carroll, José, *52 Lovers vol. 2.* (1991) Editorial Frakson, Madrid. Perfect. Pink. 123 pp. 7 x 9.25 in. (Measurements and other information have been recorded as accurately as possible.) Cards.

Carroll, José, *52 Lovers: Through the Looking Glass.* (2019) Páginas Libros de Magia, Madrid. Casebound. Green. 287 pp. 8.75 x 12.25 in. Cards.

Carroll, José, *Effects and Presentations.* (1983) Author, Madrid. Comb. Orange. 28 pp. 8.5 x 11 in. (Information not verified by physical copy. Bibliographical details are as accurate as possible.) Cards.

Carroll, Neil, *Barry Govan Lecture.* (1986) Author, Melbourne. Stapled. 17 pp. 8.25 x 11.75 in. (Information not verified by physical copy.) See McCullagh, "Under the Southern Cross." Lecture notes. Close-Up.

Carrothers, Ted, *Magic Toothpaste.* (1984) Ted Carrothers Magic Studio, Toledo, OH. Saddle-stitch. Yellow. 28 pp. 5.5 x 8.5 in. Comedy, Stage.

Carter, Charles J., *Carter's Magic and Magicians.* (1903) J. S. Ogilvie Publishing Co., New York. Perfect. Green, red, black. 152 pp. 5.25 x 7.75 in. Blank back cover. Cards, Coins, Handkerchiefs.

Carter, Charles J., *Carter's Magic and Magicians.* (1903) J. S. Ogilvie Publishing Co., New York. Perfect. Green, red, black. 152 pp. 5.25 x 7.75 in. Bottom white margin of front cover says "Sleight-of-Hand, Etc., Etc." Cards, Coins, Handkerchiefs.

Carter, Charles J., *Carter's Magic and Magicians.* (1903) J. S. Ogilvie Publishing Co., New York. Perfect. Dark green, red, black. 152 pp. 4.75 x 7.25 in. No bottom border on front cover. Cards, Coins, Handkerchiefs.

Carter, Charles J., *Carter's Magic and Magicians.* (1903) J. S. Ogilvie Publishing Co., New York. Perfect. Blue, red, black. 152 pp. 4.75 x 7.25 in. No top border on front cover; bottom says "Sleight-of-Hand, Etc., Etc." Cards, Coins, Handkerchiefs.

Carter, Charles J., *Carter's Magic and Magicians.* (1903) J. S. Ogilvie Publishing Co., New York. Perfect. Green, red, black. 152 pp. 4.75 x 7.25 in. No bottom border on front cover. Cards, Coins, Handkerchiefs.

Carter, Charles J., *Carter's Magic and Magicians.* (1903) J. S. Ogilvie Publishing Co., New York. Perfect. Dark green, red, black. 152 pp. 4.75 x 7.25 in. No bottom border on front cover. Cards, Coins, Handkerchiefs.

Carter, Charles J., *Carter's Magic and Magicians.* (1903) J. S. Ogilvie Publishing Co., New York. Perfect. Dark blue, red, black. 152 pp. 4.75 x 7.25 in. No bottom border on front cover; top border cut off. Cards, Coins, Handkerchiefs.

Carter, Charles J., *Personal Magnetism.* (1930) Author, San Francisco. Cloth. Blue. Cover text: Silver; 62 pp. 4.75 x 6.25 in. (Measurements and other information have been recorded as accurately as possible.) Self-help.

Carter, Charles J., *Personal Magnetism.* (1930) Author, San Francisco. Perfect. Brown. Cover text: Black; 62 pp. 4.75 x 6.25 in. Self-help.

Carter, Christopher, *Jack Spade and Other Strange Stories.* (1990) Author, Springfield, IL. Saddle-stitch. Beige. 27 pp. 8.5 x 11 in. (Information not verified by physical copy.) Cards, Storytelling magic.

Carter, Christopher, *Lecture Notes.* (1990) Author, Springfield, IL. Saddle-stitch. Blue. 20 pp. 8.5 x 11 in. (Measurements and other information have been recorded as accurately as possible.) Cards, Close-Up, Stage.

Carter, Christopher, *Reading Minds with Paper.* (2023) Author, Springfield, IL. Comb. 18 pp. 8.5 x 11 in. (Information not verified by physical copy. Bibliographical details are as accurate as possible.) Mentalism.

Cartier, René, *Prestidigitateur Moderne, Le.* (n.d.) Librairie Hayard, Paris. Folded. Tan. 8 pp. 5.25 x 8.75 in. (Measurements and other information have been recorded as accurately as possible.) Beginner. French.

Cartlidge, Ron, *Blue Book of Magic 2004: An Internet Price Guide to Magic.* (2004) Author, Austin, TX. Coil. White. 114 pp. 8.5 x 11 in. (Information not verified by physical copy.) Price guide, Bibliography, Collecting, Reference.

Cartlidge, Ron, *Blue Book of Magic 2005.* (2005) Author, Austin, TX. Coil. White. 122 pp. 8.5 x 11 in. (Information not verified by physical copy.) Price guide, Bibliography, Collecting, Reference.

Cartlidge, Ron, *Blue Book of Magic 2006.* (2006) Author, Austin, TX. Coil. Yellow. 94 pp. 8.5 x 11 in. (Information not verified by physical copy.) Price guide, Bibliography, Collecting, Reference.

Cartlidge, Ron, *Blue Book of Magic 2007-2008.* (2007) Author, Austin, TX. Coil. Yellow. 103 pp. 8.5 x 11 in. (Information not verified by physical copy.) Price guide, Bibliography, Collecting, Reference.

Cartlidge, Ron, *Houdini's Texas Tours 1916 and 1923.* (2002) Author, Austin, TX. Cloth. Red. 119 pp. 6 x 9 in. Dust jacket. Houdini, History.

Carton, Bernard, *Conjuring for Connoisseurs.* Magic Wand Shilling Series no. 1. (1921) George Johnson, London. Saddle-stitch. Tan. 32 pp. 4 x 5.75 in. Close-Up, Stage, Illusions.

Carver, Dr., *Dr. Carver's Tricks and Diversions with Cards.* (n.d.) Modern Publishing Co., Sydney. Perfect. 134 pp. 4.75 x 7.25 in. (Information not verified by physical copy.) See McCullagh, "Under the Southern Cross." Cards.

Casart, René, *Tours de Cartes.* (c. 1870) Bernardin-Bechet, Paris. Saddle-stitch. Tan. 23 pp. 3.75 x 5.5 in. (Measurements and other information have been recorded as accurately as possible.) Cards. French.

Casaubon, Dr. George E. (Msr. VIncent Foy), *Deceptions with a Short Card.* (1946) Abbott Magic Co., Colon, MI. Saddle-stitch. Yellow. 56 pp. 5.5 x 8.25 in. Cards, Gimmicks.

Casaubon, Dr. George E., *Deceptions with a Short Card.* (c. 1960) Supreme Magic, Bideford, UK. Stapled with tape. Tan. 29 pp. 8 x 10 in. Mimeographed. Cards, Gimmicks.

Casaubon, Dr. George E., *Salt Sorcery.* (1978) Magic Limited, Oakland, CA. Perfect. White. 95 pp. 8.5 x 11 in. (Measurements and other information have been recorded as accurately as possible.) Cards.

Cashion, Cathy, *Card and Coin Tricks.* (1977) Tree Communications, New York. Perfect. Blue. 48 pp. 8.75 x 10 in. Beginner, Children's book, Cards, Coins.

Cashion, Cathy, *Magic.* (1977) Tree Communications, New York. Perfect. Purple. 48 pp. 8.75 x 10 in. Beginner, Children's book.

BIBLIOGRAPHY OF MAGIC

Cassette, Miss, *Mysteries of Omaha: 3316 Center Street – David P. Abbott's House of Mystery.* (2024) Omaha Magical Society, Omaha, NE. Perfect. Black. 321 pp. 8.25 x 11 in. History, Biography.

Cassidy, John, *Klutz Book of Magic, The.* (1990) Klutz Press, Palo Alto, CA. Coil. White. 88 pp. 6 x 9 in. (Measurements and other information have been recorded as accurately as possible.) Beginner.

Cassidy, Robert E., *3 Miracles.* (2003) Author, Seattle. eBook. 24 pp. 8.5 x 11 in. Printed from PDF. (Information not verified by physical copy.) Mentalism.

Cassidy, Robert E. (See also Mann, Al), *2009 Lecture Notes.* (2009) Author, Seattle. Stapled. Yellow. 30 pp. 8.5 x 11 in. Lecture notes. Mentalism.

Cassidy, Robert E., *2010 MindVention Lecture Notes.* (2010) Author, Seattle. 22 pp. (Information not verified by physical copy.) Lecture notes. Mentalism.

Cassidy, Robert E., *21st Century Q & A.* (2008) Author, Seattle. eBook. 25 pp. 8.5 x 11 in. Printed from PDF. Mentalism, Question and answer.

Cassidy, Robert E., *Art du Mentalisme 2, L'.* (2009) CC Editions, Paris. 297 pp. (Information not verified by physical copy.) Mentalism. French.

Cassidy, Robert E., *Art of Mentalism, The.* (1983) Author, Morristown, NJ. Comb. Green. 126 pp. 8.5 x 11 in. With errata sheet. Signed by Bob Cassidy. Mentalism.

Cassidy, Robert E., *Art of Mentalism, The.* Second edition. (1984) Collectors Workshop, Washington D.C. Cloth. Black. 96 pp. 6.25 x 9.25 in. Dust jacket. Mentalism.

Cassidy, Robert E., *Art of Mentalism, The.* Third edition. (1984) Collectors Workshop, Washington D.C. Cloth. Blue. 92 pp. 8.5 x 11 in. Mentalism.

Cassidy, Robert E., *Art of Mentalism 2, The.* (1995) Dream Crow Press, Seattle. Comb. Beige. 40 pp. 8.5 x 11 in. Mentalism.

Cassidy, Robert E., with Filippini, Matteo, *Arte del Mentalismo.* (2018) Author, Seattle. Perfect. Black. 142 pp. 6 x 9 in. Translation of "The Art of Mentalism." Mentalism. Italian.

Cassidy, Robert E., *Artful Mentalism of Bob Cassidy, The.* (2004) H & R Magic Books, Humble, TX. Cloth. Black. 290 pp. 6 x 9 in. Dust jacket. Anthology. Signed by Bob Cassidy. Mentalism.

Cassidy, Robert E., *Artful Mentalism of Bob Cassidy vol. 2: Fundamentals, The.* (2013) H & R Magic Books, Humble, TX. Cloth. Black. 413 pp. 6.25 x 9.25 in. Dust jacket. Anthology. Mentalism.

Cassidy, Robert E., *Bent on Strange.* (2002) Author, Seattle. eBook. 18 pp. 8.5 x 11 in. Printed from PDF. (Information not verified by physical copy.) Mentalism, Key bending.

Cassidy, Robert E., *Black Book of Mentalism, The.* (2003) Author, Seattle. eBook. 29 pp. 8.5 x 11 in. Printed from PDF. (Information not verified by physical copy.) Mentalism.

Cassidy, Robert E., *Book of the Golden Tortoise, The.* (2004) Author, Seattle. eBook. 21 pp. 8.5 x 11 in. Printed from PDF. (Information not verified by physical copy.) Mentalism, Divination.

Cassidy, Robert E., *Bottle of Truth, The.* (2002) Author, Seattle. eBook. 4 pp. 8.5 x 11 in. Printed from PDF. (Information not verified by physical copy.) Mentalism, Forcing, Bottles.

Cassidy, Robert E., *But Stranger Still.* (2002) Author, Seattle. eBook. Printed from PDF. (Information not verified by physical copy.) Mentalism.

Cassidy, Robert E., *Confessions of Dr. Crow.* (2002) Author, Seattle. eBook. 17 pp. 8.5 x 11 in. Printed from PDF. (Information not verified by physical copy.) Mentalism.

Cassidy, Robert E., *Crossroads Crosswords.* (2003) Author, Seattle. eBook. 17 pp. 8.5 x 11 in. Printed from PDF. (Information not verified by physical copy.) Mentalism.

Cassidy, Robert E., *Dart Shoot, The.* (2006) Author, Seattle. eBook. 15 pp. 8.5 x 11 in. Printed from PDF. (Information not verified by physical copy.) Mentalism.

Cassidy, Robert E., *Doctor Crow's Magazine Test.* (2016) Author, Seattle. eBook. Printed from PDF. Mentalism, Magazine tests.

Cassidy, Robert E., *Dreams and Devices.* (2003) Author, Seattle. eBook. 19 pp. 8.5 x 11 in. Printed from PDF. (Information not verified by physical copy.) Mentalism.

Cassidy, Robert E., *Exclusive Routines.* (2003) Author, Seattle. eBook. 15 pp. 8.5 x 11 in. Printed from PDF. (Information not verified by physical copy.) Mentalism.

Cassidy, Robert E., *Extremely Remote.* (2003) Author, Seattle. eBook. 26 pp. 8.5 x 11 in. Printed from PDF. (Information not verified by physical copy.) Mentalism.

Cassidy, Robert E., *Fundamentals.* (2002) Author, Seattle. eBook. 89 pp. 8.5 x 11 in. Printed from PDF. (Information not verified by physical copy.) Revised edition: 2005. Mentalism.

Cassidy, Robert E., *Glance.* (1980) Author, Seattle. Strip binding. Gray. 8 pp. 8.5 x 11 in. (Measurements and other information have been recorded as accurately as possible.) Mentalism.

Cassidy, Robert E., *Guide to the Jinx.* (2012) Author, Seattle. Saddle-stitch. White. 16 pp. 5.5 x 8.5 in. Includes reprints of "The Jinx" nos. 1 and 2. Mentalism.

Cassidy, Robert E., *Hanussen Proof, The.* (2003) Author, Seattle. eBook. 28 pp. 8.5 x 11 in. Printed from PDF. (Information not verified by physical copy.) Revised edition: 2005. Mentalism.

Cassidy, Robert E., *Heathen Devices, The.* (2006) Author, Seattle. eBook. 24 pp. 8.5 x 11 in. Printed from PDF. Mentalism.

Cassidy, Robert E., *Heresies, The.* (2003) Author, Seattle. eBook. 25 pp. 8.5 x 11 in. Printed from PDF. (Information not verified by physical copy.) Mentalism.

Cassidy, Robert E., *Hidden Mysteries of Dr. Crow, The.* (2004) Author, Seattle. eBook. 27 pp. 8.5 x 11 in. Printed from PDF. (Information not verified by physical copy.) Mentalism.

Cassidy, Robert E., *Hoodoo Brew.* (2003) Author, Seattle. eBook. 35 pp. 8.5 x 11 in. Printed from PDF. (Information not verified by physical copy.) Mentalism.

Cassidy, Robert E., *Impromptu Psychic, The.* (2006) Author, Seattle. eBook. 24 pp. 8.5 x 11 in. Printed from PDF. (Information not verified by physical copy.) Mentalism, Impromptu.

Cassidy, Robert E., *Intuitively Yours.* (2005) Author, Seattle. eBook. 21 pp. 8.5 x 11 in. Printed from PDF. (Information not verified by physical copy.) Mentalism.

Cassidy, Robert E., *Invisible Billet, The.* (2009) Author, Seattle. eBook. 26 pp. 8.5 x 11 in. Printed from PDF. Mentalism.

Cassidy, Robert E., *Invisible Mirror, The.* (2003) Author, Seattle. eBook. 14 pp. 8.5 x 11 in. Printed from PDF. (Information not verified by physical copy.) Mentalism.

Cassidy, Robert E., *Journey Through the Fourth Dimension, A.* (2007) Author, Seattle. eBook. 34 pp. 8.5 x 11 in. Printed from PDF. Mentalism.

Cassidy, Robert E., *Laboratory Conditions.* (2003) Author, Seattle. eBook. 9 pp. 8.5 x 11 in. Printed from PDF. (Information not verified by physical copy.) Mentalism.

Cassidy, Robert E., *Mag-Eye Move Revisited, The.* (2008) Author, Seattle. eBook. 9 pp. 8.5 x 11 in. Printed from PDF. (Information not verified by physical copy.) Mentalism, Billets.

Cassidy, Robert E., *Mastermind Papers, The.* (2003) Author, Seattle. eBook. 25 pp. 8.5 x 11 in. Printed from PDF. (Information not verified by physical copy.) Mentalism.

Cassidy, Robert E., *Mentalism and Magick.* (2002) Author, Seattle. eBook. 24 pp. 8.5 x 11 in. Printed from PDF. (Information not verified by physical copy.) Mentalism.

Cassidy, Robert E., *Messenger Disks, The.* (2003) Author, Seattle. eBook. 9 pp. 8.5 x 11 in. Printed from PDF. (Information not verified by physical copy.) Mentalism.

Cassidy, Robert E., *Messing Effect, The.* (2004) Author, Seattle. eBook. 44 pp. 8.5 x 11 in. Printed from PDF. (Information not verified by physical copy.) Mentalism.

Cassidy, Robert E., *Millennial Medium, The.* (2005) Author, Seattle. eBook. 11 pp. 8.5 x 11 in. Printed from PDF. (Information not verified by physical copy.) Mentalism, Spirit effects.

Cassidy, Robert E., *Mind Burners.* (2003) Author, Seattle. eBook. 24 pp. 8.5 x 11 in. Printed from PDF. (Information not verified by physical copy.) Mentalism.

Cassidy, Robert E., *Mind Explosions.* (2003) Author, Seattle. eBook. 25 pp. 8.5 x 11 in. Printed from PDF. (Information not verified by physical copy.) Mentalism.

Cassidy, Robert E., *Mind Games.* (2000) Author, Seattle. Stapled. 12 pp. 8.5 x 11 in. Printed from PDF. (Information not verified by physical copy.) Mentalism.

Cassidy, Robert E., *Mind Razor.* (2003) Author, Seattle. eBook. 12 pp. 8.5 x 11 in. Printed from PDF. (Information not verified by physical copy.) Mentalism.

Cassidy, Robert E., *Modern Mentalism.* (1982) Author, Seattle. Stapled. White. 12 pp. 8.5 x 11 in. Signed by Bob Cassidy. Lecture notes. Mentalism.

Cassidy, Robert E., *Modern Mentalism II.* (1982) Author, Seattle. Stapled. White. 9 pp. 8.5 x 11 in. Lecture notes. Mentalism.

Cassidy, Robert E., *Moldavian Switch, The.* (2003) Author, Seattle. eBook. 16 pp. 8.5 x 11 in. Printed from PDF. (Information not verified by physical copy.) Mentalism.

Cassidy, Robert E., *Nameless Secret, The.* (2015) Author, Seattle. eBook. 13 pp. 8.5 x 11 in. Printed from PDF. Mentalism, Séances, Spirit effects, Mediums.

Cassidy, Robert E., *One-Man Billet Routines.* (2006) Author, Seattle. eBook. 21 pp. 8.5 x 11 in. Printed from PDF. (Information not verified by physical copy.) Mentalism, Billets.

Cassidy, Robert E., *Pendulum of Fate, The.* (2004) Author, Seattle. eBook. 20 pp. 8.5 x 11 in. Printed from PDF. (Information not verified by physical copy.) Mentalism, Pendulums.

Cassidy, Robert E., *Principia Mentalia: Fire.* Elements of Mentalism vol. 1. (1995) Author, Seattle. Saddle-stitch. Beige. 72 pp. 5.5 x 8.5 in. Mentalism.

Cassidy, Robert E., *Principia Mentalia: Earth.* Elements of Mentalism vol. 2. (1996) Author, Seattle. Saddle-stitch. Green. 56 pp. 5.5 x 8.5 in. Mentalism.

Cassidy, Robert E., *Principia Mentalia: Air.* Elements of Mentalism vol. 3. (1996) Author, Federal Way, WA. Saddle-stitch. Blue. 56 pp. 5.5 x 8.5 in. Mentalism.

Cassidy, Robert E., *Principia Mentalia: Water.* Elements of Mentalism vol. 4. (1996) Author, Seattle. Saddle-stitch. Light blue. 52 pp. 5.5 x 8.5 in. Mentalism.

Cassidy, Robert E., *Protean Eye, The.* (2010) Author, Seattle. eBook. 9 pp. 8.5 x 11 in. Printed from PDF. Mentalism.

Cassidy, Robert E., *Pseudo-Mentally Yours.* Second revised edition. (1977) Bob Lynn, Warwick, NJ. Saddle-stitch. Gray. 32 pp. 5.5 x 8.5 in. Supplement to Invocation. Mentalism.

Cassidy, Robert E., *Psi Apps.* (2004) Author, Seattle. eBook. 29 pp. 8.5 x 11 in. Printed from PDF. (Information not verified by physical copy.) Mentalism.

Cassidy, Robert E., *Psychic of the Deep.* (2012) Author, Seattle. eBook. 26 pp. 8.5 x 11 in. Printed from PDF. Mentalism.

Cassidy, Robert E., *Psychic Secrets.* (2002) Author, Seattle. eBook. 34 pp. 8.5 x 11 in. Printed from PDF. (Information not verified by physical copy.) Mentalism.

Cassidy, Robert E., *Psychic Tarot, The.* (2006) Author, Seattle. eBook. 27 pp. 8.5 x 11 in. Printed from PDF. (Information not verified by physical copy.) Mentalism, Tarot.

Cassidy, Robert E., *Psychopath: Further Secrets of Doctor Crow.* (2015) Author, Seattle. eBook. 27 pp. 8.5 x 11 in. Printed from PDF. Mentalism.

Cassidy, Robert E., *Puzzled.* (2005) Author, Seattle. eBook. 15 pp. 8.5 x 11 in. Printed from PDF. Mentalism, Stage.

Cassidy, Robert E., *Real Work of Cold Reading, The.* (2004) Author, Seattle. eBook. 58 pp. 8.5 x 11 in. Printed from PDF. (Information not verified by physical copy.) Mentalism, Cold reading.

Cassidy, Robert E., *Real Work of Stage Hypnotism, The.* (2005) Author, Seattle. eBook. 48 pp. 8.5 x 11 in. Printed from PDF. (Information not verified by physical copy.) Mentalism, Hypnosis.

Cassidy, Robert E., *Remote Viewing Tester, The.* (2003) Author, Seattle. eBook. 18 pp. 8.5 x 11 in. Printed from PDF. (Information not verified by physical copy.) Mentalism.

Cassidy, Robert E., *Resurrection of Doctor Crow, The.* (2012) Author, Seattle. eBook. 24 pp. 8.5 x 11 in. Printed from PDF. Mentalism.

Cassidy, Robert E., *Return of the White Dwarf, The.* (2011) Author, Seattle. eBook. 24 pp. 8.5 x 11 in. Printed from PDF. Mentalism.

Cassidy, Robert E., *Return to the Crossroads.* (2003) Author, Seattle. eBook. 20 pp. 8.5 x 11 in. Printed from PDF. (Information not verified by physical copy.) Mentalism.

Cassidy, Robert E., *Schattenjaeger: Shadow Hunter.* (2003) Author, Seattle. eBook. 16 pp. 8.5 x 11 in. Printed from PDF. (Information not verified by physical copy.) Mentalism.

Cassidy, Robert E., *Screen Test.* (1981) Author, Seattle. 6 pp. (Information not verified by physical copy. Bibliographical details are as accurate as possible.) Mentalism.

Cassidy, Robert E., *Side Effects.* (2003) Author, Seattle. eBook. 17 pp. 8.5 x 11 in. Printed from PDF. (Information not verified by physical copy.) Mentalism.

Cassidy, Robert E., *Sleightly Mental.* (2003) Author, Seattle. eBook. 21 pp. 8.5 x 11 in. Printed from PDF. (Information not verified by physical copy.) Mentalism.

Cassidy, Robert E., *Staging It.* (2004) Author, Seattle. eBook. 23 pp. 8.5 x 11 in. Printed from PDF. (Information not verified by physical copy.) Mentalism.

Cassidy, Robert E., *Strange Impressions.* (2002) Author, Seattle. Stapled. 20 pp. 8.5 x 11 in. Printed from PDF. (Information not verified by physical copy.) Mentalism.

Cassidy, Robert E., *Swami Tech.* (2005) Author, Seattle. eBook. 25 pp. 8.5 x 11 in. Printed from PDF. (Information not verified by physical copy.) Mentalism.

Cassidy, Robert E., *Techniques of Mentalism.* (2002) Author, Seattle. Stapled. 16 pp. 8.5 x 11 in. (Information not verified by physical copy.) Lecture notes. Mentalism.

Cassidy, Robert E., *Test Conditions Mentalism.* (1979) Bob Lynn, Warwick, NJ. Saddle-stitch. Beige. 15 pp. 4.75 x 7.75 in. Supplement to "Invocation." Mentalism.

Cassidy, Robert E., *Theories and Methods for the Practical Psychic.* (2002) Sacred Chao Productions, Federal Way, WA. Comb. Red. 68 pp. 8.5 x 11 in. Signed by Bob Cassidy. Mentalism.

Cassidy, Robert E., *Triple Edge.* (2003) Author, Seattle. eBook. 46 pp. 8.5 x 11 in. Printed from PDF. (Information not verified by physical copy.) Mentalism.

Cassidy, Robert E., *Unified Remote Viewing: A Fly on the Wall.* (2008) Author, Seattle. eBook. 25 pp. 8.5 x 11 in. Printed from PDF. (Information not verified by physical copy.) Mentalism.

Cassidy, Robert E., *Universe, The.* (2005) Author, Seattle. eBook. 27 pp. 8.5 x 11 in. Printed from PDF. (Information not verified by physical copy.) Mentalism.

Cassidy, Robert E., *Wadcutter Effect, The.* (2005) Author, Seattle. eBook. 31 pp. 8.5 x 11 in. Printed from PDF. (Information not verified by physical copy.) Bullet Catch, Fakir stunts.

Cassidy, Robert E., *Working It.* (2004) Author, Seattle. eBook. 25 pp. 8.5 x 11 in. Printed from PDF. (Information not verified by physical copy.) Mentalism.

Cassill, George N., *Acme of Perfection in Card Work, The.* (n.d.) Broadway Magic Mfg. Co., New York. Saddle-stitch. Dark green. 8 pp. 6 x 8.25 in. Cards.

Castelli, Antoine, *Amusemens Physiques.* (1810) Author, Paris. Wraps. Beige. 12 pp. 3.5 x 6 in. (Information not verified by physical copy.) Early magic. French.

Castle, Fred, *Magic with Giant Cards.* (1981) Emerson and West, Washington D.C. Saddle-stitch. White. 16 pp. 5.5 x 8.5 in. (Information not verified by physical copy.) Cards, Jumbo cards.

Castro, Rick, *Cardfather, The.* (2001) Author, Los Angeles. Saddle-stitch. Red. 5.5 x 8.5 in. (Information not verified by physical copy. Bibliographical details are as accurate as possible.) Cards.

Caswells, Brian, *Trilogy Streamline.* (2007) Alakazam Magic, Ashford, UK. Saddle-stitch. White. 4 pp. 5.75 x 8.25 in. Revised method for card effect. Cards.

Cattarius, Manfred, *Exzellente Seilroutinen.* (1995) Magic Hands Editions, Herrenburg, Germany. Stapled. White. 54 pp. 8.5 x 11 in. Rope.

Cavaillé, A., *Filouteries du Jeu, Les.* (1870) A. Ghio, Paris. Cloth. Green. 353 pp. 4.75 x 7.25 in. Rebound with original cover inside. Marbled endpapers. Gambling, Cards, Cheating. French.

Cavalli, Paolo, *Cavalli Files part 1: Upsilon, The.* (2013) Author. Perfect. Blue. 108 pp. 6 x 9 in. (Information not verified by physical copy.) Mentalism.

Cavalli, Paolo, *Cavalli Files part 2: Omicron, The.* (2013) Author. Perfect. Green. 116 pp. 6 x 9 in. (Information not verified by physical copy.) Mentalism.

Cavalli, Paolo, *Cavalli Files part 3: Sigma, The.* (2013) Author. Perfect. Black. 114 pp. 6 x 9 in. (Information not verified by physical copy.) Mentalism.

Cavalli, Paolo, *Cavalli Files part 4: The Flytrap Experience, The.* (2013) Author. Perfect. Black. 140 pp. 6 x 9 in. (Information not verified by physical copy.) Mentalism.

Cavalli, Paolo, *Cavalli Files part 5: Notes from the Lord's Diary 1, The.* (2013) Author. Perfect. Black. 112 pp. 6 x 9 in. (Information not verified by physical copy.) Mentalism.

Cavalli, Paolo, *Cavalli Files part 6: Notes from the Lord's Diary 2, The.* (2013) Author. Perfect. Black. 112 pp. 6 x 9 in. (Information not verified by physical copy.) Mentalism.

Caveney, Mike (See also Anderson, Harry), *Carter the Great.* Limited deluxe edition. (1995) Mike Caveney's Magic Words, Pasadena, CA. Cloth. Green. 375 pp. 8.75 x 11.75 in. Slipcase. Dust jacket. (Information not verified by physical copy.) With Carter memorabilia. Limited to fifty copies. Biography, History.

Caveney, Mike, *Carter the Great.* (1995) Mike Caveney's Magic Words, Pasadena, CA. Cloth. Green. 375 pp. 8.5 x 11.5 in. Dust jacket. Signed by Mike Caveney. Biography, History.

Caveney, Mike, *Classic Correspondence from Egyptian Hall Museum vol. 1.* Limited deluxe edition. (2010) Mike Caveney's Magic Words, Pasadena, CA. Cloth and leather. Green, maroon. 288 pp. 6.25 x 9.25 in. Slipcase. Limited to 50 copies. (Information not verified by physical copy.) Signed by Mike Caveney. History, Correspondence.

Caveney, Mike, *Classic Correspondence from Egyptian Hall Museum vol. 2.* Limited deluxe edition. (2014) Mike Caveney's Magic Words, Pasadena, CA. Cloth and leather. Blue, maroon. 378 pp. 6.25 x 9.25 in. Slipcase. Signed by Mike Caveney. #34 of 50. History, Correspondence.

Caveney, Mike, *Classic Correspondence from Egyptian Hall Museum vol. 3.* Limited deluxe edition. (2016) Mike Caveney's Magic Words, Pasadena, CA. Cloth and leather. Blue, maroon. 411 pp. 6.25 x 9.25 in. Slipcase. Signed by Mike Caveney. #32 of 50. History, Correspondence.

Caveney, Mike, *Classic Correspondence from Egyptian Hall Museum vol. 4.* Limited deluxe edition. (2021) Mike Caveney's Magic Words, Pasadena, CA. Cloth and leather. Purple, maroon. 394 pp. 6.25 x 9.25 in. Slipcase. Signed by Mike Caveney. #8 of 50. History, Correspondence.

Caveney, Mike, *Classic Correspondence from Egyptian Hall Museum vols. 1-4.* (2010-21) Mike Caveney's Magic Words, Pasadena, CA. Cloth and leather. Multiple sections. 6 x 9 in. Regular editions of series. History, Correspondence.

Caveney, Mike, *Final Conference Illusions, The.* (2023) Mike Caveney's Magic Words, Pasadena, CA. Leather. Green, maroon. 155 pp. 8.5 x 11.5 in. Includes "It's Magic" program and John Daniels brochure. Signed by Mike Caveney. History, Illusions.

Caveney, Mike, *Great Leon, The.* (1987) Magical Publications, Pasadena, CA. Cloth. Green. 133 pp. 7 x 10 in. Signed by Mike Caveney. Biography, History.

Caveney, Mike, *Harry Anderson: Wise Guy.* Limited deluxe edition. (1993) Mike Caveney's Magic Words, Pasadena, CA. 187 pp. 8.75 x 9.5 in. Slipcase. Dust jacket. Limited to 100 signed and numbered copies. With photo of author. Signed by Harry Anderson. Biography, Stage, Cards.

Caveney, Mike, *Harry Anderson: Wise Guy.* (1993) Mike Caveney's Magic Words, Pasadena, CA. Cloth. Green. 187 pp. 8.75 x 9.5 in. Dust jacket. Signed by Harry Anderson. Biography, Stage, Cards.

Caveney, Mike, *Ideas.* (1982) Magical Publications, Sierra Madre, CA. Saddle-stitch. White, orange. 28 pp. 5.5 x 8.5 in. Signed by Mike Caveney. Lecture notes. Stage, Close-Up.

Caveney, Mike, *Ideas.* Second edition. (1982) Magical Publications, Sierra Madre, CA. Saddle-stitch. Green. 28 pp. 5.5 x 8.5 in. Signed by Mike Caveney. Lecture notes. Stage, Close-Up.

Caveney, Mike, *Impromptu Linking Coat Hangers.* (n.d.) Mike Caveney's Magic Words, Pasadena, CA. Folded. Yellow. 2 pp. 5.5 x 8.5 in. With wire gimmick. Stage, Comedy, Impromptu.

Caveney, Mike, with Miesel, William P., *Kellar's Wonders.* Deluxe edition. (2003) Mike Caveney's Magic Words, Pasadena, CA. Leather. Maroon. 584 pp. 9.75 x 12 in. Slipcase. Dust jacket. Limited to 50 numbered copies. With bonus Kellar portrait. Signed by Mike Caveney. #28 of 1000. Biography, History.

Caveney, Mike, with Miesel, William P., *Kellar's Wonders.* (2003) Mike Caveney's Magic Words, Pasadena, CA. Cloth. Maroon. 584 pp. 9.5 x 11.75 in. Dust jacket. Signed by Mike Caveney. #28 of 1000. Biography, History.

Caveney, Mike, *Linking Coat Hangers.* Third edition. (1985) Magical Publications, Pasadena, CA. Saddle-stitch. White. 32 pp. 5.5 x 8.5 in. Signed by Mike Caveney. Stage.

Caveney, Mike, *MagiComedy.* (1981) Magical Publications, Sierra Madre, CA. Leather. Brown. 171 pp. 5.5 x 8.5 in. Dust jacket. Signed by Mike Caveney. Stage, Comedy, Close-Up.

Caveney, Mike, *One Hundred Years of Sawing.* Limited deluxe edition. (2021) Mike Caveney's Magic Words, Pasadena, CA. Cloth. Green. 457 pp. 9.25 x 11.75 in. Slipcase. Dust jacket. Includes John Daniels brochure and CD. Signed by Mike Caveney. #17 of 100. History, Illusions, Sawing.

Caveney, Mike, *Servais Le Roy: Monarch of Mystery.* (1999) Mike Caveney's Magic Words, Pasadena, CA. Cloth. Gray. 320 pp. 8.5 x 11.5 in. Dust jacket. Signed by Mike Caveney. #965 of 1000.

Caveney, Mike with the Left-Handed League, *Wenii.* (1982) Magical Publications, Sierra Madre, CA. Saddle-stitch. Red, white. 44 pp. 8.5 x 11 in. Satire of "Genii" magazine written by Caveney, Harry Anderson, Martin Lewis, and others. Satire, Magazine.

Caveney, Mike, *Wonders and the Conference Illusions: The Conference Illusions.* (2015) Mike Caveney's Magic Words, Pasadena, CA. Leather. Green, maroon. 255 pp. 8.5 x 11.5 in. Slipcase. From two-volume set. With poster. History, Illusions, Stage.

Caveney, Mike, *Wonders and the Conference Illusions: Wonders.* (2015) Mike Caveney's Magic Words, Pasadena, CA. Leather. Green, maroon. 455 pp. 8.5 x 11.5 in. Slipcase. From two-volume set. History, Illusions, Stage.

Cazeneuve, Marius, *À la Cour de Madagascar.* (1896) Delagrave, Paris. Perfect. Yellow. 342 pp. 4.75 x 7.25 in. Biography, History. French.

Cecil, Harry, *Magic That Perks.* (1937) Author, Detroit. Saddle-stitch. Beige. 72 pp. 6.5 x 9.75 in. (Measurements and other information have been recorded as accurately as possible.) Cards, Stage.

Cecil, Harry, *You Won't Believe Your Own Eyes.* (1952) Author, Detroit. Stapled. White. 72 pp. 6.5 x 9.75 in. (Measurements and other information have been recorded as accurately as possible.) Cards, Stage.

Ceillier, Rémi, *Manuel Pratique d'Illusionnisme et de Prestidigitation vol. 1.* (1935) Payot, Paris. Perfect. Gray. 310 pp. 5.75 x 9 in. Introduction by Auguste Lumière. Beginner. French.

Ceillier, Rémi, *Manuel Pratique d'Illusionnisme et de Prestidigitation vol. 2.* (1935) Payot, Paris. Perfect. Gray. 310 pp. 5.75 x 9 in. Introduction by Auguste Lumière. Beginner. French.

Ceillier, Rémi, *Manuel Pratique d'Illusionnisme et de Prestidigitation vol. 1.* (1936) Payot, Paris. Perfect. Beige. 310 pp. 5.75 x 9 in. Introduction by Auguste Lumière. Beginner. French.

Ceillier, Rémi, *Manuel Pratique d'Illusionnisme et de Prestidigitation vol. 2.* (1953) Payot, Paris. Perfect. Beige. Cover text: Orange; 383 pp. 5.75 x 9 in. Beginner. French.

Cellini, Jim, with McFalls, Eileen M., *Cellini: The Royal Touch: A Guide to the Art of Street Magic.* (1997) Magical Classics, Zurich. Casebound. Gray. 187 pp. 9.5 x 12.5 in. Street magic, Close-Up, Stage.

Cellini, Jim, with McFalls, Eileen M., *Cellini's Lord of the Rings.* (c. 2004) Magical Classics, Zurich. Saddle-stitch. White. 15 pp. 5.5 x 8.5 in. (Information not verified by physical copy.) Linking Rings.

Cellini, Jim, *Lecture Notes.* (2006) Author, Zurich. Stapled. White. 31 pp. 8.5 x 11 in. (Information not verified by physical copy.) Lecture notes. Close-Up, Stage.

Cépak, Abel, *Ce Qu'On Peut Faire Avec des Oeufs.* (1889) J. Michelet, Paris. Leather. Black. 165 pp. 4.75 x 7.25 in. Scarce. Excellent overview of early magic books. Eggs, Bibliography.

Cerceda, Adolfo, with King, William, *Folding Money Book, The.* Fourth printing. (1973) Magic Inc., Chicago. Comb. Orange. 46 pp. 8.5 x 11 in. Combined with "Make Money Selling Money" by William King. Bills, Origami, Publicity, Promotion.

Cerruti, V. A., *Three Master Card Mysteries.* (1939) Author, Nashville, TN. Folded. White. 4 pp. 6 x 9 in. With hand-typed additional effect. Signed by V. A. Cerruti. Cards.

Cervon, Bruce, *Black and White Trick and Other Assorted Mysteries, The.* (1989) L & L Publishing, Tahoma, CA. Cloth. Black. 151 pp. 5.5 x 8.5 in. Dust jacket. With black and white cards in envelope. Signed by Bruce Cervon. Cards, Oil and Water.

Cervon, Bruce, *Bruce Cervon's Castle Notebooks vol. 1.* (2007) L & L Publishing, Tahoma, CA. Leather. Black. 409 pp. 7 x 10 in. Limited to 500 copies. Letter T. Cards.

Cervon, Bruce, *Bruce Cervon's Castle Notebooks vol. 2.* (2007) L & L Publishing, Tahoma, CA. Leather. Black. 263 pp. 7 x 10 in. Limited to 500 copies. Letter T. Cards.

Cervon, Bruce, *Bruce Cervon's Castle Notebooks vol. 3.* (2007) L & L Publishing, Tahoma, CA. Leather. Black. 341 pp. 7 x 10 in. Limited to 500 copies. Letter T. Cards.

Cervon, Bruce, *Bruce Cervon's Castle Notebooks vol. 4.* (2007) L & L Publishing, Tahoma, CA. Leather. Black. 372 pp. 7 x 10 in. Limited to 500 copies. Letter T. Cards.

Cervon, Bruce, *Bruce Cervon's Castle Notebooks vol. 5.* (2007) L & L Publishing, Tahoma, CA. Leather. Black. 333 pp. 7 x 10 in. Limited to 500 copies. Letter T. Cards.

Cervon, Bruce, *Bruce Cervon's Dirty Deal.* (1970) Ken Brooke, London. Folded. White. 4 pp. 8 x 10 in. See also the publisher's "Ken Brooke Treatise on 'Dirty Deal.'." Cards, Packet tricks.

Cervon, Bruce, *Card Secrets of Bruce Cervon.* (1976) Author, Los Angeles. Saddle-stitch. Black. 64 pp. 5.5 x 8.5 in. Signed by Bruce Cervon. Cards.

Cervon, Bruce, *Cervon File, The.* (1988) Magical Publications, Pasadena, CA. Cloth. Blue. 254 pp. 7 x 10 in. Dust jacket. Cards.

Cervon, Bruce, *Cervon Monte, The.* (1984) Author, Los Angeles. Saddle-stitch. Beige. 35 pp. 5.5 x 8.5 in. With cards in envelope. Cards, Three-Card Monte.

Cervon, Bruce, with Minch, Stephen, *Hard-Boiled Mysteries.* (1998) L & L Publishing, Tahoma, CA. Cloth. Black. 178 pp. 8.5 x 11 in. Dust jacket. Cards.

Cervon, Bruce, *Perpetual Motion Card Routine.* (1967) Author, Hollywood, CA. Stapled. White. 5 pp. 8.5 x 11 in. Includes cue sheet in envelope. Cards, Prearranged deck.

Cervon, Bruce, *Tricks of Conjuring.* (c. 1970) Author, Hollywood, CA. Clip. Yellow. 17 pp. 8.5 x 11 in. Gold seal label on cover. Signed by Bruce Cervon. Lecture notes. Close-Up, Cards.

Cervon, Bruce, with Minch, Stephen, *Ultra Cervon.* Deluxe edition. (1990) L & L Publishing, Tahoma, CA. Leather. Red. Cover text: Gold; 176 pp. 8.5 x 11 in. Slipcase. Limited to 50 signed, numbered copies. Signed by Bruce Cervon. Cards.

Cervon, Bruce, with Minch, Stephen, *Ultra Cervon.* (1990) L & L Publishing, Tahoma, CA. Cloth. Black. 176 pp. 8.5 x 11 in. Dust jacket. Cards.

Cestkowski, Gerald P., *Encyclopedia of Playing Card Flourishes.* (2002) Author, Denver, CO. Cloth. Black. 545 pp. 8.5 x 11 in. Cards, Flourishes.

Chadvalli, Professor, *Conjuring Tricks and How to Perform Them.* (c. 1920) Chad Valley Co., Harborne, UK. Folded. White. 8 pp. 5 x 8 in. In Chad Valley Co. "Conjuring Up to Date" magic set. Magic set manual, Beginner.

Chadwick, Bruce, *Illusion Builder Does Stand-Up, An.* (1995) Author, Fort Worth, TX. Comb. Beige. 30 pp. 8.5 x 11 in. (Information not verified by physical copy.) Illusions, Stage.

Chadwick, Bruce, *Illusion Ministry.* (2002) Author, Fort Worth, TX. Comb. White. 52 pp. 8.5 x 11 in. (Information not verified by physical copy.) Gospel magic, Stage.

Chadwick, Hector, *Complete Mental Mysteries of Hector Chadwick, The.* (2021) Vanishing Inc., Rancho Cordova, CA. Cloth. Black. 258 pp. 6.25 x 9.25 in. Derren Brown introduction. Mentalism.

Chadwick, Hector, *Florin Spun, A.* (2023) Author, London. Cloth. Yellow. 151 pp. 5.25 x 8 in. Mentalism, Coins, Bets.

Chadwick, Hector, *Miscellanea.* (2017) Author, London. Perfect. Gray. 68 pp. 5.75 x 8.25 in. (Information not verified by physical copy.) Theory, Essays, Mentalism, Cards.

Chadwick, Hector, *Thirteen Things to Think About Pertaining to the Creation of Original Content Within the World of Magic.* (2017) Author, London. Saddle-stitch. White. 22 pp. 5.75 x 8.25 in. (Information not verified by physical copy.) Theory, Essays.

Chadwick, Hector, *Vok Voak Vokay: A Set of Miscellaneous Thoughts, Notes, and Doodles Relating to the Performance of Equivoque.* (2014) Author, London. Saddle-stitch. Blue. 20 pp. 5.75 x 8.25 in. (Information not verified by physical copy.) Equivoque, Mentalism.

Chadwick, Robert, *Complete Course in Christian Magic.* (n.d.) Author, Birmingham, AL. Comb. Tan. Unpaginated. 8.25 x 11 in. Blank pages. Signed by Robert Chadwick. Gospel magic, Blank book.

Chaikin, Josh, *X-Rated Card and Other Mysteries, The.* (2010) Author, Lenexa, KS. Saddle-stitch. Color. 16 pp. 5.5 x 8.5 in. (Information not verified by physical copy.) Cards.

Chambers, Lloyd W., *Original Ideas in Magic.* (1941) Chambers Magic Co., Topeka, KS. Saddle-stitch. Red. 26 pp. 6 x 9 in. Velour cover. Stage, Close-Up.

Chandaue, Mark, *Harpacrown.* (2016) Author, UK. Casebound. Green. 264 pp. 6 x 9 in. (Information not verified by physical copy.) Mentalism.

Chandaue, Mark, *Harpacrown Too.* (2021) Haresign Press, UK. Cloth. Black. 446 pp. 6.5 x 9.25 in. (Information not verified by physical copy.) Mentalism.

Chandaue, Mark, *Totally Free Will.* (2019) Author, UK. Perfect. Black. 176 pp. 6 x 9 in. (Information not verified by physical copy.) Mentalism.

Chandler, Harold, *Chandu's Magical Varieties.* (1970) Micky Hades, Calgary, Canada. Stapled with tape. Yellow. 34 pp. 8.5 x 11 in. Mimeographed. Stage.

Chandler, Harold, *Let's Make Magic.* (1968) Author, Martinborough. Stapled. Pink. 35 pp. 8.5 x 10.25 in. (Measurements and other information have been recorded as accurately as possible.) Stage.

Chandler, Ryan, *Magic Book.* (2019) Author, Omaha, NE. Perfect. Black. 98 pp. 8.5 x 11 in. (Information not verified by physical copy.) The book also serves as a prop in the routines explained. Cards, Close-Up, Invisible Deck.

Chang, Dr., with Glover, Russel J., *KneeSlappers and Gaggers.* (1981) Author, Silver Spring, MD. Saddle-stitch. Yellow. 16 pp. 5.5 x 8.5 in. Signed by Dr. Chang. Comedy.

Chang, Tony, with Wilson, Tyler, *I Was Kidnapped Left in Taiwan and All I Got Were These Notes.* (2013) Cherry Villain, London. Saddle-stitch. White. 41 pp. 6 x 9 in. (Information not verified by physical copy.) Cards.

Chanin, Jack, *3-to-1 Rope Trick.* (1937) Author, Philadelphia. Single page. White. 8.5 x 11 in. Mimeographed inside printed cover. (Information not verified by physical copy.) Rope.

Chanin, Jack, *Ball-o-Tube Mystery.* (1939) Author, Philadelphia. Saddle-stitch. Yellow. 4 pp. 5.5 x 8.5 in. Four pages folded into cover. Signed by Jack Chanin. Ball and Tube, Close-Up.

Chanin, Jack, *Famous 3 Shell Game from the Private Files of Chanin, The.* (c. 2004) School for Scoundrels, Los Angeles. Stapled. Pink. 2 pp. 8.5 x 11 in. Cover and one page. Three Shell Game.

Chanin, Jack, *Further Adventures of the Seven in One.* (1938) Author, Philadelphia. Saddle-stitch. Red. 15 pp. 5.5 x 8.5 in. Introduction by Al Baker. Cards.

Chanin, Jack, *Handle with Gloves: J.C. Coin Routines.* (1941) Author, Philadelphia. Saddle-stitch. Orange. 31 pp. 5.5 x 8.5 in. Signed by Jack Chanin. Coins, Close-Up.

Chanin, Jack, *Hello, Sucker! The 3 Shell Game.* (1934) Author, Philadelphia. Stapled. Salmon. 6 pp. 5.5 x 8.5 in. Three Shell Game, Close-Up.

Chanin, Jack, *Human Volcano.* (1965) Author, Philadelphia. Stapled. White. 4 pp. 8.5 x 11 in. Mimeographed. (Information not verified by physical copy.) Fire, Fakir stunts.

Chanin, Jack, *I Don't Believe It Rope Trick.* (1952) Author, Philadelphia. Stapled. White. 2 pp. 8.5 x 11 in. Mimeographed. (Information not verified by physical copy.) Rope.

Chanin, Jack, *Illustrated Lecture Based on the Chanin System, An.* (c. 1963) Author, Philadelphia. Stapled. White. 13 pp. 8.5 x 11 in. (Information not verified by physical copy.) Lecture notes. Close-Up, Stage.

Chanin, Jack, *In the Dark: A Most Fantastic Series of Card Effects.* (1958) Author, Philadelphia. Single page. White. 2 pp. 8.5 x 11 in. Ditto. Cards.

Chanin, Jack, *J.C. Cigar Magic: Cigar Manipulations.* (1937) Author, Philadelphia. Saddle-stitch. Brown. 80 pp. 5.25 x 8.25 in. Cigars, Close-Up, Stage, Manipulation.

Chanin, Jack, *J.C. Cigar Magic: Cigar Manipulations.* Second edition. (1937) Author, Philadelphia. Saddle-stitch. Green. 80 pp. 5.25 x 8.25 in. Cigars, Close-Up, Stage, Manipulation.

Chanin, Jack, *J.C. Climax Envelope Mystery.* (1940) Author, Philadelphia. Stapled. White. 2 pp. 8.5 x 11 in. Mimeographed. (Information not verified by physical copy.) Cards, Envelopes.

Chanin, Jack, *J.C. Grand Finale: Silk at Your Finger Tips.* (1940) Author, Philadelphia. Cloth. Red. 96 pp. 5.5 x 8.75 in. Signed by Jack Chanin. Silks, Stage.

Chanin, Jack, *J.C. Grand Finale: Silk at Your Finger Tips.* (1940) Author, Philadelphia. Stapled. Blue. 13 pp. 5.5 x 8.5 in. Silks, Stage.

Chanin, Jack, *J.C. Grand Finale: Silk at Your Finger Tips.* Revised edition. (1951) Author, Philadelphia. Comb. Beige. 96 pp. 5.5 x 8.5 in. Silks, Stage.

Chanin, Jack, *Jaysee Silk: Color Change Supreme.* (1936) Author, Philadelphia. Stapled. Yellow. 10 pp. 5.5 x 8.5 in. Silks, Stage.

Chanin, Jack, *New Twist to Your Magic, A.* (1952) Author, Philadelphia. Stapled. White. 12 pp. 8.5 x 11 in. Includes loose pages of instructions. Lecture notes. Stage, Close-Up.

Chanin, Jack, *Right and Wrong Way of Doing Your Magic or Mistakes Most Often Made.* (1954) Author, Philadelphia. Stapled. White. 7 pp. 8.5 x 11 in. (Information not verified by physical copy.) Lecture notes. Showmanship, Routining.

Chanin, Jack, *Seven in One Card Routine.* (1931) Author, Philadelphia. Stapled. White. 2 pp. 8.5 x 11 in. Mimeographed. (Information not verified by physical copy.) Cards.

Chanin, Jack, *Sleeve Magic: Encyclopedia of Sleeving.* (1947) Author, Philadelphia. Saddle-stitch. Beige. 58 pp. 5.5 x 8.5 in. Essays by Paul Rosini and Al Baker. Coins, Sleeving, Close-Up.

Chanin, Jack, *U-Can-Do Card Act.* (1950) Author, Philadelphia. Stapled. White. 7 pp. 8.5 x 11 in. Mimeographed. (Information not verified by physical copy.) Cards.

Chapman, Frank, *Barnyard Phantasy.* (1945) Author, Ross, CA. Single page. White. 8.5 x 14 in. Mimeographed. Comedy, Liquids, Apparatus.

Chapman, Frank, *Chap's Scrapbook.* (1978) Magico Magazine, New York. Saddle-stitch. Brown. 96 pp. 7 x 10 in. Anthology. Signed by Rabbi Shmuel Gringras. Magazine.

Chapman, Frank, *Fountain of Silks.* (1942) Author, Burlingame, CA. Saddle-stitch. White. 6 pp. 6 x 9 in. (Measurements and other information have been recorded as accurately as possible.) Silks, Stage.

Chapman, Frank, *Magic Tricks for Every Member of the Family.* (1934) Oakite Products, New York. Saddle-stitch. Red, blue. 16 pp. 5 x 7 in. Uncredited. Beginner, Premium.

Chapman, Frank, *Popsicle Magic Coin Book. 20 Clever Coin Tricks.* (1933) Increased Sales Inc., Baltimore, MD. Saddle-stitch. Red, black, white. 24 pp. 5 x 7 in. Uncredited. Beginner, Premium, Coins.

Chapman, Frank, *Quick Tricks.* (1942) Author, Burlingame, CA. Saddle-stitch. White. 9 pp. 6 x 9 in. (Measurements and other information have been recorded as accurately as possible.) Close-Up.

Chapman, Frank, *Six Bits More.* (1947) Author, Burlingame, CA. Saddle-stitch. Green. 8 pp. 6 x 9 in. (Measurements and other information have been recorded as accurately as possible.) Close-Up.

Chapman, Frank, *Ten Stunners with a Nail Writer.* (1941) Author, Burlingame, CA. Saddle-stitch. White. 8 pp. 6 x 9 in. Mentalism, Nail writer.

Chapman, Frank, *Three Six Bits.* (1947) Lloyd Jones, Oakland, CA. Cloth. Gray. Cover text: Gold; 21 pp. 6 x 9.25 in. Scarce clothbound edition. Close-Up.

Chapman, Frank, *Three Six Bits.* (1947) Lloyd Jones, Oakland, CA. Saddle-stitch. Yellow. 21 pp. 6 x 9 in. (Measurements and other information have been recorded as accurately as possible.) Close-Up.

Chapman, Frank, *Twenty Stunners with a Nail Writer.* Second enlarged edition. (1944) Kanter's Magic Shop, Philadelphia. Saddle-stitch. Beige. 25 pp. 6 x 9 in. The first edition was "Ten Stunners with a Nail Writer." Circled K on back cover. Close-Up, Nail writer.

Chapman, Frank, *Twenty Stunners with a Nail Writer.* Second enlarged edition. (1944) Kanter's Magic Shop, Philadelphia. Saddle-stitch. Green. 25 pp. 6 x 9 in. Circled K on back cover. Close-Up, Nail writer.

Chapman, Frank, *Twenty Stunners with a Nail Writer.* Second enlarged edition. (1944) Kanter's Magic Shop, Philadelphia. Saddle-stitch. Beige. 25 pp. 6 x 9 in. No circled K on back cover. Close-Up, Nail writer.

Chapman, Frank, *Wand of Laughter, The.* (c. 1944) Thayer Magical Mfg. Co., Los Angeles. Single page. White. 8.5 x 11 in. Mimeographed. Wands, Comedy.

Chapman, Greg, *Architettura I.* (2021) Author, Isle of Wight, UK. Perfect. Green. 70 pp. 6 x 9 in. (Measurements and other information have been recorded as accurately as possible.) Cards, Prearranged deck, Run-up systems.

Chapman, Greg, *Architettura II.* (2021) Author, Isle of Wight, UK. Perfect. Green. 67 pp. 6 x 9 in. (Measurements and other information have been recorded as accurately as possible.) Cards, Prearranged deck, Run-up systems.

Chapman, Greg, *Details of Deception.* (2017) Author, Isle of Wight, UK. Cloth. Black. 223 pp. 6.25 x 9.25 in. Dust jacket. Cards, Run-up systems, Prearranged deck.

Chapman, Greg, *Devil's Staircase, The.* (2014) Author, Isle of Wight, UK. Cloth. Black. 223 pp. 6.25 x 9.25 in. Dust jacket. Cards, Run-up systems, Prearranged deck.

Chapman, Greg, *Faro Fundamentals.* (2020) Author, Isle of Wight, UK. Perfect. Light blue. 54 pp. 6 x 9 in. (Measurements and other information have been recorded as accurately as possible.) Cards, Faro, Prearranged deck.

Chapman, Greg, *Greg and Felicity's History of Magic.* (2023) Author, Isle of Wight, UK. Perfect. Black. 191 pp. 6 x 9 in. (Information not verified by physical copy.) History.

Chapman, Greg, *Overhand Run-Up Shuffles.* (2021) Author, Isle of Wight, UK. Perfect. Gray. 51 pp. 6 x 9 in. Cards, Run-up systems, Cheating.

Charles III (Charles McPherson), with Barron, Bob and Corbitt, Steve, *Miracle Book, The.* (1990) Charles III, Burlington, CO. Coil. Dark blue. 33 pp. 8.5 x 11 in. Title handwritten on cover with silver marker. Close-Up, Cards, Coins.

Charles III (Charles McPherson), *Personalized Magical Entertainment.* (1997) Charles III, Burlington, CO. Coil. Yellow. 33 pp. 8.5 x 11 in. Close-Up, Cards, Coins.

Charles, Christopher, *Chris Charles Record Vanish.* (n.d.) Author. Stapled with paper cover. Dark pink. 2 pp. 6 x 9 in. Mimeographed. Stage.

Charles, Christopher, *Without Mirrors.* (1947) Lloyd Jones, Oakland, CA. Boards. Black. 20 pp. 6 x 9 in. Patter, Comedy.

Charles, Christopher, *Without Mirrors.* (1947) Lloyd Jones, Oakland, CA. Saddle-stitch. Tan. 20 pp. 6 x 9 in. Patter, Comedy.

Charles, John, *Lecture Notes.* (1973) Author, Arlington, VA. Stapled. White. 4 pp. 8.5 x 11 in. (Information not verified by physical copy.) Lecture notes. Close-Up, Stage.

Charles, John, *They Don't Make Them Like That Anymore.* (1999) Author, Arlington, VA. Stapled. White. 4 pp. 8.5 x 11 in. (Information not verified by physical copy.) Rope.

Charles, John, *World's Most Abused Rope Trick, The.* (1992) Author, Arlington, VA. Stapled. White. 6 pp. 8.5 x 11 in. (Information not verified by physical copy.) Rope.

Charles, Kirk, *Complete Guide to Restaurant and Walk-Around Magic, The.* (1998) Hermetic Press, Seattle. Cloth. Blue. 240 pp. 6 x 9 in. Dust jacket. Signed by Kirk Charles. Close-Up, Showmanship, Marketing.

Charles, Kirk, *Going Mental for Kids.* (1999) Author, Seattle. Stapled with tape. Green. 7 pp. 8.5 x 11 in. Mentalism, Children's magic.

Charles, Kirk, with Wild, Boris, *Hidden in Plain Sight.* (2005) Fun Inc., Seattle. Perfect. Blue. 137 pp. 5.5 x 8.5 in. Cards, Marked deck.

Charles, Kirk, *Marked for Life.* (2002) Hermetic Press, Seattle. Perfect. Blue. 96 pp. 5.5 x 8.5 in. Signed by Kirk Charles. Cards, Marked deck.

Charles, Kirk, *Mixed Bag of Tricks Lecture.* (2002) Author, Seattle. Stapled. Blue. 10 pp. 8.5 x 11 in. (Measurements and other information have been recorded as accurately as possible.) Cards.

Charles, Kirk, *Read 'Em and Reap: Tips, Tricks, and Tactics with a Marked Deck.* (1998) Author, Seattle. Clip. Yellow. 27 pp. 8.5 x 11 in. Signed by Kirk Charles. Cards, Marked deck.

Charles, Kirk, *Standing Up Surrounded.* (1989) Hermetic Press, Seattle. Perfect. White, red, black. 94 pp. 5.5 x 8.5 in. Signed by Kirk Charles. Close-Up, Showmanship, Marketing.

Charles, Kirk, *Standing Up Surrounded.* (1989) Hermetic Press, Seattle. Perfect. Yellow. 94 pp. 5.5 x 8.5 in. Signed by Kirk Charles. Close-Up, Showmanship, Marketing.

Charles, Kirk, *Tips on Table-Hopping.* (1981) Author, Seattle. Stapled. Blue. 33 pp. 8.5 x 11 in. (Information not verified by physical copy.) Close-Up, Strolling magic.

Charles, Kirk, *Tricked and Tricked Again.* (1991) Author, Seattle. Comb. White. 17 pp. 8.5 x 11 in. (Measurements and other information have been recorded as accurately as possible.) Cards, Close-Up.

Charles, Kirk, *Tricked, Too.* (1991) Author, Seattle. Stapled. White. 22 pp. 8.5 x 11 in. (Information not verified by physical copy.) Cards, Close-Up, Stage, Mentalism.

Charles, Kirk, *Walk Talk: Essays on Magic in the Real World.* (1998) Author, Seattle. Clip. Yellow. 31 pp. 8.5 x 11 in. Signed by Kirk Charles. Theory, Showmanship.

Charles, Kirk, *"What Can You Do with This?" or Improv Magic.* (1977) Author, Seattle. Stapled. Blue. 16 pp. 8.5 x 11 in. Signed by Kirk Charles. Close-Up, Improv magic, Impromptu.

Charles, Lance, *Magic for the Few.* (1933) Charles Lantz, Walnut Grove, MN. Boards. Gray, tan. Cover text: Gold; 29 pp. 6 x 9 in. Inscribed by author with his real name. Signed by Charles Lantz (Lance Charles). Cards, Balls, Stage.

Charles, Lance, *Magic for the Few.* (1935) Charles Lantz, Walnut Grove, MN. Saddle-stitch. Green. 29 pp. 6 x 9 in. Cards, Balls, Stage.

Charles, Martin S., with Underwood, Ralph E., *Spook Crooks!* (n.d.) Author, Los Angeles. Saddle-stitch. Orange. 32 pp. 5.5 x 8.5 in. Spiritualism.

Charleson, Prof., *Magic: Some of Its Wonders and Mysteries.* (c. 1880) C. Clark, Manchester. Saddle-stitch. Gray. 16 pp. 5 x 7.5 in. In Copperfield collection. Title on cover: "Modern Magic." Beginner.

Charney, David H., *Magic: The Great Illusions Revealed and Explained.* (1976) New American Library, New York. Perfect. Black. 247 pp. 5.25 x 8 in. Material from Albert A. Hopkins' "Magic." History, Illusions, Close-Up, Stage.

Charvet, David, *Alexander: Before He Knew – The Lost Alaska Gold Rush Diary of Claude Alexander Conlin 1898-1900.* (2021) Charvet Studios, Lake Oswego, OR. Cloth. Black. Cover text: Gold; 87 pp. 8.75 x 8.75 in. Biography, History, Diary.

Charvet, David, with Pomeroy, John, *Alexander: The Man Who Knows.* (2004) Mike Caveney's Magic Words, Pasadena, CA. Cloth. Black. Cover text: Red; 218 pp. 8 x 10.25 in. Dust jacket. #298 of 1000. Biography, History, Mentalism.

Charvet, David, with Pomeroy, John, *Alexander: The Man Who Knows.* Expanded edition. (2007) Mike Caveney's Magic Words, Pasadena, CA. Cloth. Red. Cover text: Gold; 267 pp. 8 x 10.25 in. Dust jacket. Biography, History, Mentalism.

Charvet, David, *Banquet Magician's Handbook, The.* Second edition. (1997) Charvet Studios, Tigard, OR. Perfect. White, yellow. 107 pp. 5.25 x 8.25 in. Showmanship, Business, Stage.

Charvet, David, *Behind Their Curtain.* (2014) Charvet Studios, Lake Oswego, OR. Saddle-stitch. Red. 24 pp. 8.5 x 11 in. Signed by David Charvet. History, Biography.

Charvet, David, *Bill in Lemon Book: Featuring the Life and Times of Emil Jarrow, The.* (1990) Charvet Studios, Tigard, OR. Perfect. White, yellow. 70 pp. 8.5 x 11 in. Stage, Bills, Bill in Lemon.

Charvet, David, *Conjurors and Their Cars.* (2023) Charvet Studios, Lake Oswego, OR. Saddle-stitch. Brown. 16 pp. 8.5 x 11 in. Signed by David Charvet. History.

Charvet, David, *Golden Age of Magic in Southern California 1893-1963, The.* (2024) Charvet Studios, Lake Oswego, OR. Saddle-stitch. White. 12 pp. 8.5 x 11 in. Signed by David Charvet. History, Biography.

Charvet, David, *Great Jester: Magician, Hypnotist, Vaudevillian, The.* (2022) Charvet Studios, Lake Oswego, OR. Saddle-stitch. Black. 20 pp. 8.5 x 11 in. Includes two Jester tickets. Signed by David Charvet. #7 of 100. Biography, History.

Charvet, David, *Great Nicola: Globetrotting Magician, The.* (2019) Charvet Studios, Lake Oswego, OR. Saddle-stitch. Maroon. 32 pp. 8.5 x 11 in. Signed by David Charvet. Biography, History.

Charvet, David, *Great Virgil, The.* (1991) Charvet Studios, Vancouver, WA. Leather. Brown. 232 pp. 8.5 x 11 in. Signed by David Charvet. Biography, Illusions, History.

Charvet, David, *Great Virgil Scrapbook, The.* (1998) Charvet Studios, Tigard, OR. Comb. White, color. 20 pp. 8.5 x 11 in. History, Posters, Biography, Illusions.

Charvet, David, *Jack Gwynne.* (1988) Charvet Studios, Brush Prairie, WA. Perfect. Black. 296 pp. 8.5 x 11 in. Biography, Illusions.

Charvet, David, *Jarrow: The Humorist Trickster.* (2013) Charvet Studios, Lake Oswego, OR. Casebound. Brown. 168 pp. 6.25 x 9.25 in. Signed by David Charvet. Biography, Stage.

Charvet, David, *Rise and Fall of Rag Pictures, The.* (2011) Charvet Studios, Lake Oswego, OR. Saddle-stitch. Color. 16 pp. 8.5 x 11 in. Signed by David Charvet. #57 of 100. Rag paintings.

Charvet, David, *Willard: A Life Under Canvas.* (2008) Mike Caveney's Magic Words, Pasadena, CA. Cloth. Beige. 370 pp. 8.75 x 11.25 in. Slipcase. With photo, prospectus. Signed by David Charvet, Frances Willard. #110 of 150. Biography, Traveling shows, Spirit Cabinet, Séances.

Chaudhuri, Tony, *Bedazzled!* (1977) Author, Ann Arbor, MI. Saddle-stitch. Green. 68 pp. 5.25 x 8.5 in. #412 of 500. Cards, Coins, Close-Up.

Chaudhuri, Tony, *MagiBank.* (1979) Author, Ann Arbor, MI. Saddle-stitch. Tan. 18 pp. 5.25 x 8.25 in. Coins, Gimmicks.

Chavel, *Reelistic Magic.* (1950) Harry Stanley, London. Stapled. Beige. 29 pp. Mimeographed. (Information not verified by physical copy.) Reels.

Chavez, Marian, *Chavez Course in Magic, The.* (1946) Chavez College of Magic, La Verne, CA. Looseleaf binder. Black. Multiple sections. 8.5 x 11 in. Original course with photographic illustrations. Course, Manipulation, Stage, Showmanship.

Chavez, Marian, *Chavez Course in Magic, The.* (c. 1975) Chavez College of Magic, La Verne, CA. Looseleaf binder. Black. Multiple sections. 8.5 x 11 in. Looseleaf binder with photocopied pages as issued later for students. Course, Manipulation, Stage, Showmanship.

Chavez, Marian, *Encyclopedia of Dove Magic.* (1979) Louis Tannen, New York. Perfect. Black. 152 pp. 8.5 x 11 in. Stage, Doves.

Chavigny, Jean, *Roman d'un Artiste: Robert-Houdin – Rénovateur de la Magie Blanche, Le.* (1970) Author, Blois, France. Perfect. Tan. 231 pp. 5.5 x 9 in. With folding plates and business card. #329 of 450. Biography, Robert-Houdin, History. French.

Chelman, Christian, *Capricornian Tales.* (1993) L & L Publishing, Tahoma, CA. Boards. Black. 105 pp. 8.25 x 11.25 in. Bizarre magick.

Chelman, Christian, *Hauntiques: The Magic of Christian Chelman.* (2006) MP Magic, Brussels, Belgium. Cloth. Black. 173 pp. 8.5 x 12 in. Dust jacket. Bizarre magick.

Chelman, Christian, *Paradise Lost.* (2009) MP Magic, Brussels, Belgium. Saddle-stitch. Green. 20 pp. (Information not verified by physical copy. Bibliographical details are as accurate as possible.) Mentalism, Bizarre magick.

Chen-Kai, *Chen Kai's Lecture no. 1.* (1978) Author, Mexico City. Saddle-stitch. White, black. 16 pp. 5.5 x 8.5 in. Owner address label. Signed by Chen-Kai. Lecture notes. Doves, Stage, Candles.

Chen, Anson, *Reality is Magic.* (2023) Neat Review, London. Cloth. Black. 221 pp. 5.5 x 8.5 in. Finely printed and bound. Cards.

Cheng, Danny, *Coin Monster.* (2020) Author, Chicago. 43 pp. (Information not verified by physical copy.) Coins, Okito Coin Box.

Chesbro, Bob, *Tipnician, The.* (1982) Author, Williamstown, MA. Cloth. Black. Cover text: Silver; 64 pp. 5.5 x 8.5 in. (Measurements and other information have been recorded as accurately as possible.) Thumb tip.

Chesbro, Verne, with West, Larry, *Tricks You Can Count On.* Second printing. (1984) Kee-West Productions, Key West, FL. Saddle-stitch. Yellow. 31 pp. 5.5 x 8.5 in. Cards, Bills.

Chesbro, Verne, *Ultimate Color Separation no. 1.* (1963) Author, Loudonville, NY. Saddle-stitch. Light blue. 40 pp. 5.5 x 8.25 in. (Measurements and other information have been recorded as accurately as possible.) Cards.

Chesbro, Verne, *Ultimate Color Separation no. 2.* (1969) Author, Loudonville, NY. Saddle-stitch. Green. 37 pp. 5.5 x 8.5 in. Includes cards. Cards.

Chester, *Chester's Book of Magic.* (1919) Stein Publishing House, Chicago. Saddle-stitch. Brown. Multiple sections. 5 x 7.5 in. Cover has "Magic: A Treatise of Modern Magical Mysteries." Ad on back for Chester's Magic Shop. Beginner. Pulp.

Cheung, Bill, *Lecture Note 2018.* (2018) Author, Austria. Stapled. 22 pp. 8.5 x 11 in. (Information not verified by physical copy. Bibliographical details are as accurate as possible.) Cards, Coins.

Chevrie, Lonnie, *Magic of the Maestro.* (2005) Author, Abilene, TX. Saddle-stitch. Purple. 26 pp. 5.5 x 8.5 in. (Information not verified by physical copy.) Close-Up, Hindu Thread, Silks, Storytelling magic.

Ching, Mike, *New Animations: The Dancing Handkerchief Book.* Second edition. (1996) Magical Entertainments, Honolulu, HI. Perfect. Black. Cover text: Silver; 140 pp. 8.5 x 11 in. Levitations, Handkerchiefs, Thread, Stage.

Chislett, T. H., *Spirits in the House.* (1949) Goodliffe Publications, Birmingham, UK. Cloth. Blue. 118 pp. 5 x 7.25 in. Dust jacket. Spiritualism, Mentalism, Stage, Electrical.

Chock, Yona, *Magic of Clippo, The.* (2002) Author, Hawaii. Stapled. White. 14 pp. 8.5 x 11 in. (Information not verified by physical copy. Bibliographical details are as accurate as possible.) Paper, Clippo.

Chosse, Paul, *Thoughts on Jack McMillan.* (c. 2014) Author, San Francisco. Stapled. White. 21 pp. 8.5 x 11 in. (Information not verified by physical copy.) Biography, Cards.

Choquette, Alain, *Tribute to Gary Ouellet 1945-2002, A.* (2007) Author, Sainte-Adèle, Canada. Coil. Black. 38 pp. 8.5 x 11 in. (Information not verified by physical copy.) Cards, Close-Up.

Choudhury, Deepak Roy, *Jadoo Aur Kahani (Magic and Story). Indian Showcase Series Book no. 4.* (1993) Electro Fun, Calcutta. Comb. Yellow, red. 21 pp. 8 x 11.75 in. Banner flap title over cover. Cards, Indian magic, Stage.

Chrighton, Knox, *Magi Magoria.* (1978) Supreme Magic, Bideford, UK. Cloth. Dark blue. 167 pp. 7.5 x 9.75 in. Dust jacket. Stage, Close-Up, Cards.

Christenberry, Earle J., Jr., *Do a Trick.* (1966) Author, New Orleans. Stapled. White. 3 pp. 8.5 x 11 in. (Information not verified by physical copy.) Lecture notes.

Christensen, Theron, *Plotting Astonishment.* (2020) Author, Omaha, NE. Perfect. 137 pp. 6 x 9 in. Theory, Close-Up, Stage, Routining.

Christian, Brad, *Official Ellusionist Color Book, The.* (2020) Ellusionist, Tiburon, CA. Perfect. White. 102 pp. 8.25 x 11.75 in. For 20th year of company. Coloring book.

Christian, Brad, *Kard Klub: Heat of the Battle.* (2003) Ellusionist, Tiburon, CA. Saddle-stitch. Orange. 28 pp. 5.5 x 8.5 in. no. 4757. Cards.

Christian, Brad, *Kard Klub: Underground Training Manual.* (2005) Ellusionist, Tiburon, CA. Saddle-stitch. Orange. 28 pp. 5.5 x 8.5 in. (Information not verified by physical copy.) Cards.

Christian, Dick, *Working Mentalist's Guide to Forcing Books and Book Tests, The.* (2010) Author, Alexandria, VA. 40 pp. (Information not verified by physical copy.) Lecture notes. Mentalism, Book tests.

Christianer, Louis, *Cigarette Manipulation.* (1923) Thayer Magical Mfg. Co., Los Angeles. Stapled with paper cover. Gray. 4 pp. 8.5 x 11 in. Mimeographed. Cigarettes, Manipulation.

Christianer, Louis, *Cigarette Tricks.* (1916) Eagle Magician, Minneapolis. Saddle-stitch. Brown. 18 pp. 3 x 5.25 in. Mimeographed. Vest Pocket Series of Magic no. 2. Cigarettes, Manipulation.

Christianer, Louis, *Effective Card Tricks.* Second edition. (1916) Thayer Magical Mfg. Co., Los Angeles. Saddle-stitch. Brown. 16 pp. 4.75 x 6.75 in. Cards.

Christianer, Louis, *Effective Coin Act, An.* (1916) Thayer Magical Mfg. Co., Los Angeles. Saddle-stitch. Yellow. 16 pp. 4.75 x 6.75 in. Coins.

Christianer, Louis, *Effective Tricks.* (1916) Thayer Magical Mfg. Co., Los Angeles. Saddle-stitch. Gray. 16 pp. 4.75 x 6.75 in. (Measurements and other information have been recorded as accurately as possible.) Stage.

Christianer, Louis, *Magical Notions.* (1917) Thayer Magical Mfg. Co., Los Angeles. Saddle-stitch. Brown. 24 pp. 4.75 x 6.75 in. (Measurements and other information have been recorded as accurately as possible.) Stage.

Christianer, Louis, *Modern Magical Effects.* (1917) Thayer Magical Mfg. Co., Los Angeles. Saddle-stitch. Olive. 20 pp. 4.75 x 6.75 in. Stage.

Christianer, Louis, *Modern Ventriloquism.* (1918) Thayer Magical Mfg. Co., Los Angeles. Stapled with paper cover. Red. 3 pp. 9 x 11.5 in. Bound at top. Mimeographed. Folded. Green printed label stating "Thayer's Eureka Magical Series: Art of Ventriloquism." Ventriloquism.

Christianer, Louis, *More Effective Card Tricks.* (1919) E. F. Rybolt, Los Angeles. Saddle-stitch. Orange. 24 pp. 4.75 x 6.75 in. Cards.

Christianer, Louis, *More Effective Tricks.* (1916) A. M. Wilson, Kansas City, MO. Saddle-stitch. Beige. 40 pp. 5.25 x 7.75 in. Stage.

Christianer, Louis, *New Magical Conceptions.* (1919) Thayer Magical Mfg. Co., Los Angeles. Saddle-stitch. Tan. 15 pp. 5 x 7 in. Close-Up, Cards, Stage.

Christianer, Louis, *Original Deceptions.* (1919) E. F. Rybolt, Los Angeles. Saddle-stitch. Red. 24 pp. 4.75 x 6.75 in. Stage.

Christianer, Louis, *Selected Tricks.* (1923) Thayer Magical Mfg. Co., Los Angeles. Saddle-stitch. Olive. 24 pp. 4.75 x 6.75 in. (Measurements and other information have been recorded as accurately as possible.) Stage.

Christianer, Louis, *Shell Coin Revised, The.* (1923) Thayer Magical Mfg. Co., Los Angeles. Stapled with paper cover. Red. 4 pp. 5.5 x 8.75 in. Mimeographed. Coins, Gimmicks.

Christianer, Louis, *Sleight of Hand with Coins.* (c. 1923) Thayer Magical Mfg. Co., Los Angeles. Stapled. White. 7 pp. 8.5 x 11 in. Mimeographed. (Information not verified by physical copy.) Coins.

Christianer, Louis, *String Tricks.* Miniature book. (1932) Eagle Magician, Minneapolis. Saddle-stitch. Olive. 12 pp. 3.25 x 4.5 in. Vest Pocket Series of Magic no. 4. String.

Christianer, Louis, *Tissue Paper Mystery, A.* (1918) Thayer Magical Mfg. Co., Los Angeles. Stapled. White. 8.5 x 11 in. Mimeographed. (Information not verified by physical copy.) Paper.

Christianer, Louis, *Thimble Manipulation.* (1923) Thayer Magical Mfg. Co., Los Angeles. Stapled with paper cover. Light blue. 6 pp. 8.5 x 11 in. Mimeographed. Blueprint illustration sheet. Thimbles, Manipulation.

Christianer, Louis, *What You Can Do with a Paper Napkin.* (1923) Thayer Magical Mfg. Co., Los Angeles. Stapled. White. 8.5 x 11 in. Mimeographed. (Information not verified by physical copy.) Napkins, Paper, Impromptu.

Christianer, Louis, *What You Can Do with a Stripper Deck.* (1923) Thayer Magical Mfg. Co., Los Angeles. Stapled. White. 8.5 x 11 in. Mimeographed. (Information not verified by physical copy.) Cards, Stripper deck, Gimmicked decks.

Christiansen, Mortenn, *Mortenn's Notes.* (2023) Author, Horsens, Denmark. Saddle-stitch. Beige. 59 pp. 5.75 x 8.25 in. (Information not verified by physical copy.) Lecture notes. Cards, Coins, Close-Up.

Christopher, Dee, *Black Heart and Bourbon.* (2014) Author, UK. Perfect. Black. 80 pp. 6 x 9 in. (Information not verified by physical copy.) Mentalism.

Christopher, Dee, *Deep Shadows.* (2014) Author, UK. Perfect. Black. 275 pp. 6 x 9 in. (Information not verified by physical copy.) Mentalism.

Christopher, Dee, *Proximity Effects.* (2011) Merchant of Magic, UK. Saddle-stitch. Black. 36 pp. 6 x 9 in. (Information not verified by physical copy.) Cards, Close-Up, Stage, Mentalism.

Christopher, Dee, *Weapons of Mass Deception.* (c. 2011) Author, UK. Saddle-stitch. Black. 18 pp. 6 x 9 in. (Information not verified by physical copy.) Fakir stunts, Mentalism.

Christopher, Maurine, with Hansen, George P., *Milbourne Christopher Library 1589-1900, The.* (1994) Mike Caveney's Magic Words, Pasadena, CA. Cloth. Red. 160 pp. 8.25 x 11.25 in. Dust jacket. Bibliography.

Christopher, Maurine, with Hansen, George P., *Milbourne Christopher Library II 1901-1996, The.* (1998) Mike Caveney's Magic Words, Pasadena, CA. Cloth. Blue. 339 pp. 8.25 x 11.25 in. Dust jacket. Bibliography.

Christopher, Milbourne, *100 Latest Tips on Tricks.* (1953) Louis Tannen, New York. Saddle-stitch. Green. 41 pp. 6 x 9 in. Stage, Close-Up.

Christopher, Milbourne, *50 Tricks with a Thumb Tip.* (1948) D. Robbins, New York. Saddle-stitch. Beige. 24 pp. 6 x 9 in. Brown rectangle extends to bottom of cover. Close-Up, Stage, Thumb tip.

Christopher, Milbourne, *50 Tricks with a Thumb Tip.* Second edition. (1948) D. Robbins, New York. Saddle-stitch. Beige. 24 pp. 5.5 x 8.5 in. Different listings of books in ad. Close-Up, Stage, Thumb tip.

Christopher, Milbourne, *50 Tricks with a Thumb Tip.* Third edition. (n.d.) D. Robbins, New York. Saddle-stitch. Beige. 24 pp. 5.5 x 8.5 in. Brown rectangle extends to bottom of cover. Close-Up, Stage, Thumb tip.

Christopher, Milbourne, *50 Tricks with a Thumb Tip.* Third edition. (1976) D. Robbins, New York. Saddle-stitch. White, orange, purple. 24 pp. 5.5 x 8.5 in. Close-Up, Stage, Thumb tip.

Christopher, Milbourne (ed.), *Baking's Believing.* (1963) General Mills Inc., Minneapolis. Saddle-stitch. Purple. 24 pp. 8 x 4.5 in. Bound oblong. Promotional booklet for cake mix. Psychedelic artwork. Beginner, Stunts, Premium, Recipes.

Christopher, Milbourne, *Christopher's Favorite Routines.* (2000) Collectors Workshop, Washington D.C. Casebound. Red. 186 pp. 8.5 x 11 in. Stage, Close-Up.

Christopher, Milbourne, *Cig-Card Case Tricks.* (1949) Ralston Inc., Bordentown, NJ. Saddle-stitch. Yellow. 8 pp. Cards, Card Case, Cigarettes, Close-Up.

Christopher, Milbourne, *Conjuring with Christopher.* (1949) Max Holden, New York. Perfect. Beige. 71 pp. 6 x 9 in. Stage, Close-Up.

Christopher, Milbourne, *E.S.P., Seers, and Psychics.* (1979) Thomas Y. Crowell, New York. Cloth. Black. 268 pp. 5.5 x 8.5 in. Dust jacket. Spiritualism, Psychics, Occult.

Christopher, Milbourne, *Flash Rope Penetration.* (1942) Author, Baltimore, MD. Stapled. White. 3 pp. 8.5 x 11 in. Mimeographed. (Information not verified by physical copy.) Illustrated by author. Rope, Stage.

Christopher, Milbourne, *Houdini: A Pictorial Biography.* (1976) Gramercy Books, New York. Cloth. Blue. 218 pp. 8.5 x 11 in. Dust jacket. Biography, History, Houdini.

Christopher, Milbourne, *Houdini: A Pictorial Life.* (1976) Thomas Y. Crowell, New York. Cloth. Red. 214 pp. 8.5 x 11 in. Dust jacket. Signed by Milbourne Christopher. Biography, History, Houdini.

Christopher, Milbourne, *Houdini: A Pictorial Life.* Collector's Edition. (2010) 1878 Press Company, Oxford, CT. Casebound. Gray. 242 pp. 8.5 x 11 in. With envelope with Houdini memorabilia reproductions. Biography, History, Houdini.

Christopher, Milbourne, *Houdini: The Untold Story.* First edition. (1969) Thomas Y. Crowell, New York. Cloth. Red. 281 pp. 5.5 x 8.5 in. Dust jacket. Signed by Milbourne Christopher. Biography, History, Houdini.

Christopher, Milbourne, *Houdini: The Untold Story.* (1969) Cassell and Co, London. Cloth. Red. 281 pp. 5.5 x 8.5 in. Dust jacket. Biography, History, Houdini.

Christopher, Milbourne, *Houdini: The Untold Story.* (1970) Pocket Books, New York. Perfect. White. 298 pp. 4.25 x 7 in. Inscribed to Todd Karr. Signed by Milbourne Christopher. Biography, History, Houdini.

Christopher, Milbourne, *Houdini: The Untold Story.* Third printing. (1975) Pocket Books, New York. Perfect. Blue. 298 pp. 4.25 x 7 in. Inscribed to Todd Karr. Signed by Milbourne Christopher. Biography, History, Houdini.

Christopher, Milbourne, *Houdini: The Untold Story.* Deluxe edition. (2013) 1878 Press Company, Oxford, CT. Cloth. Blue. Cover text: Gold; 281 pp. 5.75 x 8.75 in. #216 of 300. Biography, History, Houdini.

Christopher, Milbourne, *Howard Thurston's Illusion Show Work Book.* (1991) Magical Publications, Pasadena, CA. Cloth. Tan. 228 pp. 8 x 10.25 in. Slipcase. #308 of 500. History, Illusions.

Christopher, Milbourne, *Howard Thurston's Illusion Show Work Book II.* (1992) Magical Publications, Pasadena, CA. Cloth. Blue. 254 pp. 8 x 10.25 in. Slipcase. #192 of 500. History, Illusions.

Christopher, Milbourne, *Howard Thurston's Illusion Show Work Book Prosepectus.* (1991) Magical Publications, Pasadena, CA. Saddle-stitch. Red. 8 pp. 5.5 x 8.5 in. Tissue overlay. Prospectus.

Christopher, Milbourne, *Illustrated History of Magic, The.* (1973) Thomas Y. Crowell, New York. Cloth. Black. 452 pp. 7.5 x 10 in. Dust jacket. Warmly inscribed to New York magic collector José Famadas. Signed by Milbourne Christopher. History.

Christopher, Milbourne, *Illustrated History of Magic, The.* Expanded edition. (1996) Heinemann, Portsmouth, NH. Casebound. Gray. 484 pp. 7.5 x 10 in. Dust jacket. History.

Christopher, Milbourne, *Illustrated History of Magic, The.* Updated edition. (2006) Carrol and Graf, New York. Perfect. Yellow. 514 pp. 7.5 x 10 in. Dust jacket. History.

Christopher, Milbourne, *Impromptu Effect with a Cigarette.* (c. 1940) Author, Baltimore, MD. Single page. Brown. 8.5 x 11 in. Cigarettes, Rising effects.

Christopher, Milbourne, with Fetsch, "Hen," *Magic at Your Finger Tips.* (1947) Maryland Magic Studios, Baltimore, MD. Saddle-stitch. Orange. 46 pp. 6 x 9 in. Illustrated by Sid Lorraine. Stage, Close-Up.

Christopher, Milbourne, *Magic from M-U-M.* (1954) Society of American Magicians, Forestville, CN. Saddle-stitch. Yellow. 44 pp. 6 x 9 in. Beginner.

Christopher, Milbourne, *Magic: A Picture History.* (1991) Dover, New York. Perfect. White. 216 pp. 8.25 x 11.25 in. Same as "Panorama of Magic." History.

Christopher, Milbourne, *Mediums, Mystics, and the Occult.* (1975) Thomas Y. Crowell, New York. Cloth. Black. 275 pp. 5.75 x 9 in. Dust jacket. Signed by Milbourne Christopher. Spiritualism, Psychics, Occult.

Christopher, Milbourne, *Milbourne Christopher Lecture Resume.* (1969) Author, New York. Single page. White. 8.5 x 11 in. Lecture notes. Stage, Close-Up.

Christopher, Milbourne, *Milbourne Christopher's Magazine Test.* (1949) Author, New York. Stapled. White. 8.5 x 11 in. (Information not verified by physical copy.) Mentalism, Magazine, Book tests.

Christopher, Milbourne, *Milbourne Christopher's Magic Book.* (1977) Thomas Y. Crowell, New York. Cloth. Black. 240 pp. 7 x 9 in. Dust jacket. Signed by Milbourne Christopher. Beginner, General.

Christopher, Milbourne, *Milbourne Christopher's Magic Book.* (1979) New American Library, New York. Perfect. Orange. 216 pp. 4.25 x 7 in. Beginner, General.

Christopher, Milbourne, *Milbourne Christopher's Magic Book.* (1985) Barnes and Noble, New York. Perfect. Blue. 209 pp. 5.25 x 8.25 in. Beginner, General.

Christopher, Milbourne, *More One-Man Mental Magic.* (1954) Louis Tannen, New York. Saddle-stitch. Olive. 15 pp. 6 x 9 in. Mentalism.

Christopher, Milbourne, *More Tips on Tricks.* (1945) Prestidigitators Press, Baltimore, MD. Saddle-stitch. Beige. 20 pp. 6.25 x 9 in. Beginner, Stage, Close-Up.

Christopher, Milbourne, *One-Man Mental Magic.* (1952) Louis Tannen, New York. Saddle-stitch. Beige. 11 pp. 6 x 9 in. Mentalism.

Christopher, Milbourne, *One-Man Mental Magic and More One-Man Mental Magic.* Second edition. (1952) Louis Tannen, New York. Saddle-stitch. Beige. 15 pp. 6 x 9 in. Combined edition of two books. Mentalism.

Christopher, Milbourne, *Panorama of Magic.* (1962) Dover, New York. Perfect. Orange. 216 pp. 8.25 x 11.25 in. Inscribed to Todd Karr. Signed by Milbourne Christopher. History.

Christopher, Milbourne, *Panorama of Magic.* (1962) Dover, New York. Perfect. Blue. 216 pp. 8.25 x 11.25 in. Signed by Milbourne Christopher. History.

Christopher, Milbourne, *Panorama of Magic.* (1962) Dover, New York. Perfect. Light blue. 216 pp. 8.25 x 11.25 in. History.

Christopher, Milbourne, *Panorama of Magic.* (1962) Dover, New York. Perfect. White. 216 pp. 8.25 x 11.25 in. History.

Christopher, Milbourne, *Panorama of Prestidigitators.* (1956) Author, New York. Saddle-stitch. Beige. 44 pp. 6 x 9 in. Signed by Milbourne Christopher. History.

Christopher, Milbourne, *Search for the Soul.* (1979) Thomas Y. Crowell, New York. Cloth. Blue. 206 pp. 6 x 9.5 in. Dust jacket. Spiritualism, Psychics, Occult.

Christopher, Milbourne, *Seers, Psychics, and E.S.P.* (1970) Cassell and Co, London. Cloth. Yellow. 268 pp. 5.5 x 8.5 in. Dust jacket. Same as "E.S.P., Seers, and Psychics." Psychic, Mentalism.

Christopher, Milbourne, *Stretching a Rope.* Second printing. (1946) Kanter's Magic Shop, Philadelphia. Saddle-stitch. Beige. 13 pp. 5.5 x 8.5 in. Signed by Milbourne Christopher. Rope.

Christopher, Milbourne, *Surprise Element, The.* (1951) Author, New York. Stapled. White. 10 pp. 8.5 x 11 in. Mimeographed. From Magicians Guild talk. Lecture notes. Stage, Close-Up.

Christopher, Milbourne, *Tips on Tricks.* (1942) Berland Magical Creations, Chicago. Saddle-stitch. Yellow. 26 pp. 6 x 9 in. Stage, Close-Up.

Christopher, Milbourne, *Triple Thimble Tricks.* (1949) Author, Baltimore. Stapled. White. 4 pp. 8.5 x 11 in. Mimeographed. (Information not verified by physical copy.) Thimbles, Manipulation.

Christopher, Milbourne, *Varied Deceptions.* (1953) Harry Stanley, London. Cloth. Red. 152 pp. 5.5 x 8.5 in. Dust jacket. Stage, Close-Up.

Christopher, Milbourne, *Varied Deceptions.* (1980) Supreme Magic, Bideford, UK. Cloth. Red. 152 pp. 6 x 9 in. Dust jacket. Stage, Close-Up.

Chun, Kelvin Y. S., *21st Century Guide to Asian Magic.* (2008) Author, Honolulu, HI. 11 pp. (Information not verified by physical copy.) Lecture notes. Asian magic, Stage, Parasols, Rope.

Chung, Derrick, *Nacho Card Notes, The.* (2022) Author, New York. 50 pp. (Information not verified by physical copy.) Lecture notes. Cards.

Cimò, Salvatore, *Cartomagia.* (1973) Ceschina, Milan. Perfect. Orange. 308 pp. 5.25 x 7.75 in. (Measurements and other information have been recorded as accurately as possible.) Cards. Italian.

Cimò, Salvatore, *Divinazioni Mentali.* (1973) Ceschina, Milan. Perfect. Orange. 258 pp. 5.25 x 7.75 in. Mentalism. Italian.

Cimò, Salvatore, *Prestidigitazione con Ditali e Sigarette.* (1973) Ceschina, Milan. Perfect. Orange. 178 pp. 5.25 x 7.75 in. Thimbles, Cigarettes. Italian.

Cimò, Salvatore, *Prestidigitazione con le Corde.* (1973) Ceschina, Milan. Perfect. Orange. 317 pp. 5.25 x 7.75 in. Rope. Italian.

Cimò, Salvatore, *Prestidigitazione con Monete ed Anelli.* (1973) Ceschina, Milan. Perfect. Orange. 338 pp. 5.25 x 7.75 in. Coins, Rings. Italian.

Cimò, Salvatore, *Prestidigitazione con Palline ed Uova.* (1973) Ceschina, Milan. Perfect. Orange. 232 pp. 5.25 x 7.75 in. Balls, Eggs. Italian.

Cinémathèque Française, *Dada no. 248: Méliès.* (2020) Éditions Arola, Paris. Perfect. Black, red. 49 pp. 8.25 x 9.5 in. Magicians in cinema, History, Magazine, Biography.

Cinémathèque Française, *Méliès: La Magie du Cinéma.* (2020) Flammarion, Paris. Casebound. Black. 381 pp. 9 x 12 in. Magicians in cinema, History, Biography.

Cinémathèque Française, *Musée Méliès: La Magie du Cinéma.* (2021) Flammarion, Paris. Perfect. Purple, green. 96 pp. 6 x 8.75 in. Magicians in cinema, History.

Circolo Amici della Magia di Torino, *Figures de Magie Blanche Dévoilée.* (1979) Circolo Amici della Magia di Torino, Turin, Italy. Saddle-stitch. Beige. 14 pp. 5.75 x 8.25 in. History, Early magic. Italian.

Cirs and Nops, *Productions de Cartes Pour la Scène, Les.* (1980) Éditions de Spectacle, Strasbourg. Saddle-stitch. Blue. 60 pp. 7.75 x 9 in. Manipulation, Cards. French.

Citino, Bill, *Coinsomnia: The Random Conjurings of a Sleep Deprived Mind.* (2008) Author, Philadelphia. Perfect. Blue. 83 pp. 6 x 9 in. (Information not verified by physical copy.) Coins, Close-Up.

Citino, Bill, *T3: Tested, Tweaked, True.* (2008) Author, Philadelphia. Comb. Tan. 35 pp. 6 x 9 in. (Information not verified by physical copy.) Cards, Coins, Close-Up.

Citino, Bill, *You Do Cards?! Selected Card Tricks from a Coin Guy (and Some of His Friends!).* (2025) Author, Philadelphia. Casebound. White. 86 pp. 7.25 x 10.25 in. Cards.

Citron, Gabriel, *Houdini-Price Correspondence, The.* (1998) Legerdemain, London. Perfect. Black. 192 pp. 5.25 x 8.5 in. Foreword by David Berglas. #209 of 350. Houdini, History, Spiritualism.

Ciuró, P. Wenceslao, *Cartomagia volumen 1.* (1970) Mens et Manus, Madrid. Perfect. Red. 688 pp. 5.25 x 7.75 in. Cards. Spanish.

Ciuró, P. Wenceslao, *Cartomagia volumen 1.* (2009) Páginas Libros de Magia, Madrid. Perfect. Red. 688 pp. 5.25 x 7.75 in. Cards. Spanish.

Ciuró, P. Wenceslao, *Cartomagia volumen 2.* (1972) Mens et Manus, Madrid. Perfect. Green. 583 pp. 5.25 x 7.75 in. Cards. Spanish.

Ciuró, P. Wenceslao, *Ilusionismo de Salon.* (1967) Paraninfo, Madrid. Perfect. Blue. 248 pp. 4.75 x 6.75 in. Beginner, Stage. Spanish.

Ciuró, P. Wenceslao, *Ilusionismo Elemental.* (1965) Mens et Manus, Madrid. Perfect. Red. 293 pp. 5.25 x 7.5 in. Beginner. Spanish.

Ciuró, P. Wenceslao, *Juegos de Magia: Ilusionismo Elemental. Juegos de Salon vol. 8.* (2007) Páginas Libros de Magia, Madrid. Casebound. Orange. 208 pp. 8.5 x 12 in. Beginner. Spanish.

Ciuró, P. Wenceslao, *Juegos de Magia: Juegos de Sobremesa. Juegos de Salon vol. 5.* (2010) Páginas Libros de Magia, Madrid. Casebound. Green, yellow, red. 139 pp. 8.5 x 12 in. Beginner, Close-Up. Spanish.

Ciuró, P. Wenceslao, *Juegos de Manos de Bolsillo Tomo 1. Trucos de Micromagia.* (1961) Mens et Manus, Madrid. Perfect. Green. 166 pp. 4.75 x 6.75 in. Close-Up. Spanish.

Ciuró, P. Wenceslao, *Juegos de Manos de Bolsillo Tomo 2. Trucos de Micromagia.* (1961) Author, Madrid. Perfect. Red. 234 pp. 4.75 x 6.75 in. Close-Up. Spanish.

Ciuró, P. Wenceslao, *Juegos de Manos de Bolsillo Tomo 3. Trucos de Micromagia.* (1962) Author, Madrid. Perfect. Orange. 236 pp. 4.75 x 6.75 in. Close-Up. Spanish.

Ciuró, P. Wenceslao, *Juegos de Manos de Bolsillo Tomo 4. Trucos de Micromagia.* (1968) Author, Madrid. Perfect. Blue. 264 pp. 4.75 x 6.75 in. Close-Up. Spanish.

Ciuró, P. Wenceslao, *Juegos de Manos Sobremesa.* (1956) Mens et Manus, Madrid. Perfect. Blue. 174 pp. 4.75 x 6.75 in. Close-Up. Spanish.

Ciuró, P. Wenceslao, with Verdejo, C., *Juegos para Todos.* (1972) Editorial Ramon Sopena, Barcelona. Cloth. Green. 682 pp. 6 x 8.25 in. Beginner, Stunts. Spanish.

Ciuró, P. Wenceslao, with Verdejo, C., *Juegos para Todos.* (1978) Editorial Ramon Sopena, Barcelona. Cloth. Green. 682 pp. 6 x 8.25 in. Beginner, Stunts. Spanish.

Ciuró, P. Wenceslao, *Magia con Pañuelos vol. II.* (1977) Editorial Cymus, Madrid. Cloth. Blue. 327 pp. 6.25 x 8.75 in. Dust jacket. Silks, Stage. Spanish.

Ciuró, P. Wenceslao, *Mnemotecnia Teatral.* (1959) Editorial Paraninfo, Madrid. Perfect. Blue. 259 pp. 5.25 x 7.75 in. Memory, Mentalism. Spanish.

Ciuró, P. Wenceslao, *Mnemotecnia Teatral.* (2008) Páginas Libros de Magia, Madrid. Perfect. Blue. 207 pp. 6.75 x 9.5 in. Memory, Mentalism. Spanish.

Ciuró, P. Wenceslao, *Prestidigitación al Alcance de Todos, La.* (1948) Instituto Editorial Reus, Madrid. Perfect. Blue. 532 pp. 5.25 x 7.75 in. Beginner, General. Spanish.

Ciuró, P. Wenceslao, *Prestidigitación al Alcance de Todos, La.* (2005) Páginas Libros de Magia, Madrid. Casebound. Brown. 280 pp. 8.5 x 12 in. In box with booklet. Beginner, General. Spanish.

Ciuró, P. Wenceslao, *Trucos de Magia.* (1957) Mens et Manus, Madrid. Perfect. Beige. 189 pp. 4.75 x 6.5 in. Beginner. Spanish.

Claflin, Edward, with Sheridan, Jeff, *Street Magic.* (1977) Dolphin Books, New York. Perfect. Blue. 136 pp. 8.25 x 11 in. Signed by Jeff Sheridan. History, Street magic.

Claflin, Edward, with Sheridan, Jeff, *Street Magic.* Second edition. (1998) Kaufman and Co., Washington D.C. Perfect. Black. 156 pp. 8.5 x 11 in. Limited to 1000 copies. History, Street magic.

Clapham, Harry L., *Melody Magic.* (1932) Author, Washington D.C. Cloth. Red. 72 pp. 9 x 12.25 in. Signed by Henry Ridgely Evans. #271 of 1000. Biography.

Clark, Bobby, *Magic is an Art.* (c. 1973) Jean Clark, Robbins, CA. Saddle-stitch. Orange. 21 pp. 5.5 x 8.5 in. Stage, Close-Up.

Clark, Hyla M., *World's Greatest Magic, The.* (1976) Bonanza-Crown, New York. Cloth. Black. 298 pp. 8.5 x 11 in. Slipcase. Dust jacket. Special edition signed by subjects, limited to 30 copies. (Information not verified by physical copy.) Biography, History, Photography.

Clark, Hyla M., *World's Greatest Magic, The.* (1976) Bonanza-Crown, New York. Cloth. Black. 382 pp. 8.5 x 11 in. Dust jacket. Signed by Hyla M. Clark. Biography, History, Photography.

Clark, James L., *Easy-to-Master Mental Magic.* (2010) Dover, New York. Perfect. Black, blue. 109 pp. 5.25 x 8.5 in. (Information not verified by physical copy.) Beginner, Mentalism.

Clark, James L., *Mind Magic and Mentalism for Dummies.* (2012) John Wiley and Sons, West Sussex, UK. Perfect. Yellow. 370 pp. 7.5 x 9.25 in. (Information not verified by physical copy.) Beginner, Mentalism.

Clark, Keith, *Celebrated Cigarettes.* (1943) Silk King Studios, Cincinnati, OH. Saddle-stitch. Orange. 24 pp. 5.5 x 8.5 in. Cigarettes, Manipulation.

Clark, Keith, *Celebrated Cigarettes.* (1943) Silk King Studios, Cincinnati, OH. Saddle-stitch. Light blue. 24 pp. 5.5 x 8.5 in. Cigarettes, Manipulation.

Clark, Keith, *Encyclopedia of Cigarette Magic.* First edition. (1937) Author, New York and Paris. Cloth. Black. 307 pp. 6 x 9 in. Signed by Keith Clark. Cigarettes, Manipulation.

Clark, Keith, *Encyclopedia of Cigarette Tricks.* Second edition. (1952) Louis Tannen, New York. Cloth. Gray. 304 pp. 6 x 9.25 in. Cigarettes, Manipulation.

Clark, Keith, *Encyclopedia of Cigarette Magic.* (1953) Louis Tannen, New York. Cloth. Gray. 304 pp. 6 x 9 in. Dust jacket. Cigarettes, Manipulation.

Clark, Keith (trans. by Maurice Sardina), *Encyclopédie des Tours de Cigarettes.* (1958) Payot, Paris. Perfect. Beige, red, brown. 331 pp. 5.5 x 9 in. Cover states Clark's real name as "Pier Cartier" rather than the familiar spelling "Pierre Cartier." Cigarettes, Manipulation. French.

Clark, Keith, *Nite Club Act.* (1944) Silk King Studios, Cincinnati, OH. Cloth. Blue. 50 pp. 5.5 x 8.5 in. (Measurements and other information have been recorded as accurately as possible.) Silks.

Clark, Keith, *Rope Royale.* (1942) Silk King Studios, Cincinnati, OH. Saddle-stitch. Dark blue. 16 pp. 5.5 x 8.5 in. Rope.

Clark, Keith, *Silks Supreme.* (1942) Silk King Studios, Cincinnati, OH. Saddle-stitch. Maroon. 18 pp. 5.5 x 8.5 in. Silks.

Clark, Robert, *Magic: Sleightly Done.* (1954) R. C. Buff, Knoxville, TN. Stapled with paper cover. Green. 14 pp. 6 x 9 in. Mimeographed. Sid Lorraine bookplate. Inscribed by publisher Buff. Signed by R. C. Buff. Comedy, Stage.

Clark, Tony, *Art of Magic 2.0, The.* (c. 2013) Author, Los Angeles. Saddle-stitch. Black. 16 pp. 5.5 x 8.5 in. (Information not verified by physical copy.) Lecture notes. Cards, Close-Up.

Clark, Tony, *Tony Clark Unmasks: Award-Winning Dove Techniques.* First edition. (1992) Author, Los Angeles. Comb. Black. 20 pp. 8.5 x 11 in. Clear overlay with white title and mask seem to unmask the photo below. Doves.

Clark, Tony, *Tony Clark Unmasks: Award-Winning Dove Techniques.* Second edition. (1997) Tony Clark Productions, Los Angeles. Perfect. Black. 74 pp. 7 x 10 in. Doves.

Clarke, Graham S., *Book That Never Was, The.* (1990) Author, Colchester, UK. Saddle-stitch. Blue. 37 pp. 5.5 x 8.5 in. (Information not verified by physical copy.) Cards, Close-Up, Stage.

Clarke, Graham S., *Oliver's More.* (1997) Author, Colchester, UK. Saddle-stitch. Blue. 34 pp. 5.5 x 8.5 in. (Information not verified by physical copy.) Cards, Close-Up, Stage.

Clarke, Harry, *Magic: Burke's Pastime Series for Boys.* (1962) Burke Publishing, London. Cloth. Blue. 127 pp. 7.5 x 10 in. Dust jacket. Johnny Hart color photo on cover. Beginner.

Clarke, K. T., *Zera's Art of Magic.* (1876) Merrihew and Son, Philadelphia. 48 pp. 4 x 6 in. (Information not verified by physical copy.) Toole Stott no. 150. Early magic.

Clarke, Sidney W., *Annals of Conjuring, The.* (1983) Magico, New York. Cloth. Maroon. 291 pp. 5.5 x 8.75 in. Essay and index by Robert Lund. History.

Clarke, Sidney W. (ed. by Todd Karr and Edwin A. Dawes with Bob Read), *Annals of Conjuring, The.* Limited deluxe edition. (2001) The Miracle Factory, Seattle. Cloth. Black. 619 pp. 8.25 x 10.25 in. Dust jacket. In box with ribbon tie. Signed by Edwin A. Dawes, Bob Read, Todd Karr. Letter T of 25 presentation copies. History.

Clarke, Sidney W. (ed. by Todd Karr and Edwin A. Dawes with Bob Read), *Annals of Conjuring, The.* (2001) The Miracle Factory, Seattle. Cloth. Black. 619 pp. 8.25 x 10.25 in. Dust jacket. History.

Clarke, Sidney W., *Annals of Conjuring, The.* (n.d.) Cloth. Black. 185 pp. 6 x 9.25 in. Dust jacket. Publisher not noted. Later reprint of "The Magic Wand" series. History.

Clarke, Sidney W., with Blind, Adolphe, *Bibliography of Conjuring and Kindred Deceptions, The.* (1920) George Johnson, London. Boards. Blue. 84 pp. 5.5 x 8.5 in. Bibliography, History, Collecting, Reference.

Clarke, Sidney W., with Blind, Adolphe, *Bibliography of Conjuring and Kindred Deceptions, The.* (1999) Martino Books, Mansfield Centre, CT. Cloth. Green. 84 pp. 6.25 x 9 in. Reprint of 1920 edition. Bibliography, History, Collecting, Reference.

Clarke, Sidney W., *Miracle Play in England, The.* (1897) William Andrews and Co., London. Cloth. Blue. 94 pp. 5.25 x 7.75 in. History.

Clarke, William C., *Boy's Own Book, The.* (1828) Viztelly, Branston, and Co., London. 447 pp. 4 x 5.25 in. (Information not verified by physical copy.) Toole Stott no. 151. Early magic, Beginner.

Clarke, William C., *Boy's Own Book, The.* (1829) Monroe and Francis, Boston. 316 pp. 4.5 x 5.25 in. (Information not verified by physical copy.) Toole Stott no. 152. Early magic, Beginner.

Clarke, William C., *Boy's Own Book, The.* (1996) Applewood Books, Bedford, MA. Perfect. Light blue. 316 pp. 4.5 x 5.5 in. Reprint of 1829 edition. History, Early magic, Beginner.

Clary, Bill, *Bill Clary Lecture.* (1990) Author, Rochester, NY. Stapled. White. 10 pp. 8.5 x 11 in. (Information not verified by physical copy. Bibliographical details are as accurate as possible.) Lecture notes. Close-Up, Stage, Cups and Balls.

Claxton, Michael, *Don't Fool Yourself: The Magical Life of Dell O'Dell.* (2014) Squash Publishing, Chicago. Cloth. White, red. 332 pp. 6.25 x 9.25 in. Dust jacket. Biography, History.

Clayton, *Ultimate Linking Rings, The.* (c. 1985) Author, Baltimore. Folder. Orange. 26 pp. 8.5 x 11 in. (Information not verified by physical copy.) Linking Rings.

Clayton, Mihlon F., *One on a Match.* Trick of the Month Club series 2, no. 7. (January 1933) Thayer Magical Mfg. Co., Los Angeles. Folded. Yellow. 6 pp. 3.75 x 6.75 in. Cards, Mentalism.

Clayton, Mihlon F., *Rope Trick You Can Do, A.* (1924) Author, Asbury Park, NJ. Folded single page. Gray. 6 x 9 in. Hand-tinted photo strip and text page inside folded cover with title. Rope.

Cleveland, H. G., *New Ring and Rope Release, A.* Trick of the Month Club series 3, no. 1. (July 1933) Thayer's Studio of Magic, Los Angeles. Folded. Beige. 4 pp. 3.75 x 6.75 in. Ring and rope, Stage.

Clever, Eddie, *Backs Up.* Trick of the Month Club series 3, no. 10. (April 1934) Thayer's Studio of Magic, Los Angeles. Folded. Green. 5 pp. 3.75 x 6.75 in. Cards.

Clever, Eddie, with Cleveland, H. G., *Celebro and Magic Squares.* Trick of the Month Club series 3, no. 12. (June 1934) Thayer's Studio of Magic, Los Angeles. Folded. Yellow. 12 pp. 3.75 x 6.75 in. (Information not verified by physical copy.) Mentalism, Magic squares.

Clever, Eddie, *Effects with Alphabet Cards.* (1943) Midwest Magic Service, Portsmouth, OH. Saddle-stitch. Beige. (Information not verified by physical copy.) Cards, Alphabet cards, Close-Up, Stage.

Clever, Eddie, *Entertaining Children with Magic.* (1939) Evangel Press, Portsmouth, OH. Stapled with tape. Beige. 78 pp. 6 x 8.75 in. Children's magic.

Clever, Eddie, *Thought Wings Onward.* (1939) Abbott Magic Co., Colon, MI. Stapled with tape. Beige, red. 121 pp. 5.75 x 8.75 in. Mentalism.

Clever, Eddie, *Thought Wings Onward.* (1939) Abbott Magic Co., Colon, MI. Stapled with paper cover. Beige. 121 pp. 5.75 x 8.75 in. Mentalism.

Clever, Eddie, *Thought Wings Onward.* Second edition. (1945) Abbott Magic Co., Colon, MI. Stapled with paper cover. Olive. 121 pp. 5.75 x 8.75 in. Mentalism.

Cliffe, Norman, with Bee, Percy, *Great "Socko" Comedy Watch Routine, The.* (c. 1947) Author, Bournemouth, UK. Stapled with tape. Green. 8 pp. 8.25 x 10.25 in. Mimeographed. Comedy, Watches.

Clive, Paul, *Card Tricks Without Skill.* (1946) Paul Clive and Co., London. Cloth. Orange. 190 pp. 5 x 7.5 in. Dust jacket. Cards.

Clive, Paul, *Card Tricks Without Skill.* Third edition. (1959) Faber and Faber, London. Cloth. Tan. 264 pp. 4.75 x 7.25 in. Dust jacket. Cards.

Clive, Paul, *Card Tricks Without Skill.* Third edition. (1959) Faber and Faber, London. Perfect. White, blue, red. 264 pp. 4.75 x 7.25 in. Cards, Beginner.

Clivette, *Entertaining Recreation of Parlor Magic, The.* (1897) Author, Atlantic City, NJ. Saddle-stitch. Gray. 18 pp. 4.75 x 7.25 in. In Copperfield collection. Close-Up, Stage.

Close, Michael, *Complete Workers Series vols. 1-5, The.* (2024) Author, Las Vegas. Casebound. White. 491 pp. 8.5 x 11 in. Cards, Close-Up, Routining.

Close, Michael, *Complete Workers Series vols. 1-5, The.* (2004) Author, Las Vegas. Perfect. Blue. 653 pp. 8.5 x 11 in. Cards, Close-Up, Routining.

Close, Michael, *Forget-Me-Notes.* (2007) Author, Las Vegas. Saddle-stitch. White. 13 pp. 5.5 x 8.5 in. (Information not verified by physical copy.) Lecture notes. Cards, Prearranged deck.

Close, Michael, *Hemi-Demi-Semi-Quavers: Lecture no. 1.* (1992) Author, Las Vegas. Saddle-stitch. Light blue. 12 pp. 5.5 x 8.5 in. Lecture notes. Cards, Close-Up.

Close, Michael, *On the Road Again.* (2005) Author, Las Vegas. Coil. White. 165 pp. 8.5 x 11 in. (Information not verified by physical copy.) Lecture notes. Cards, Close-Up.

Close, Michael, *On the Road Again UK Tour.* (2006) Author, Las Vegas. Coil. White. 119 pp. 8.5 x 11 in. (Information not verified by physical copy.) Lecture notes. Cards, Close-Up, Theory.

Close, Michael, *That Reminds Me: Finding the Funny in a Serious World.* (2007) Author, Las Vegas. Perfect. White. 211 pp. 6 x 9 in. (Information not verified by physical copy.) Comedy.

Close, Michael, *While I'm Gone.* (c. 1998) Author, Las Vegas. Comb. Beige. 18 pp. 8.5 x 11 in. Lecture notes. Cards, Close-Up, Theory.

Close, Michael, *Workers Series Sampler, A.* (1994) Author, Carmel, IN. Comb. White. 21 pp. 8.5 x 11 in. Lecture notes. Cards, Close-Up, Routining.

Close, Michael, *Workers vol. 1.* (1990) Author, Carmel, IN. Comb. Gray. 36 pp. 8.5 x 11 in. Cards, Close-Up, Routining.

Close, Michael, *Workers vol. 2.* (1991) Author, Carmel, IN. Comb. Gray. 64 pp. 8.5 x 11 in. Cards, Close-Up, Routining.

Close, Michael, *Workers vol. 3.* (1993) Author, Carmel, IN. Comb. Gray. 138 pp. 8.5 x 11 in. Cards, Close-Up, Routining.

Close, Michael, *Workers vol. 4.* (1994) Author, Carmel, IN. Comb. Gray. 64 pp. 8.5 x 11 in. Cards, Close-Up, Routining.

Close, Michael, *Workers vol. 5.* (1996) Author, Carmel, IN. Comb. Gray. 167 pp. 8.5 x 11 in. Signed by Michael Close. Cards, Close-Up, Routining.

Closson, George E., *Original Secrets of Magic.* (1909) Author, Troy, NY. Cloth. Dark brown. Unpaginated. 6 x 9.25 in. Combined reprint of "Brotherhood Secrets" magazine vols. 1 and 2. Photos of contributors. Magazine, Close-Up, Stage, Illusions.

Clothier, Tim, *Advanced Illusion Projects.* (2005) Author, Las Vegas. Perfect. White. 156 pp. 8.5 x 11 in. (Information not verified by physical copy. Bibliographical details are as accurate as possible.) Illusions.

Cloutier, Carl, *Lecture Notes.* (1993) Author, Canada. Saddle-stitch. Black, white. 25 pp. 8.25 x 11.75 in. (Information not verified by physical copy.) Lecture notes. Cards, Coins, Close-Up.

Clower, R. L., *Book of Shadows, The.* (1983) Author, Duncanville, TX. Saddle-stitch. Tan. 24 pp. 8.5 x 11 in. (Information not verified by physical copy.) Bizarre magick.

Clute, Cedric, Jr., with Lewin, Nick, *Sleight of Crime.* (1977) Henry Regnery, Chicago. Perfect. White. 301 pp. 5.5 x 8.25 in. Anthology. Fiction.

Cobalt, Shane, *50 Faces North.* (2012) Author, Toronto. Saddle-stitch. White. 9 pp. 8.5 x 11 in. (Information not verified by physical copy. Bibliographical details are as accurate as possible.) Cards.

Cobalt, Shane, *Acorn Notes: An Unofficial Guide to The Expert at the Card Table, The.* (2019) Author, Toronto. Saddle-stitch. White. 48 pp. 8.5 x 11 in. (Information not verified by physical copy.) Cards, Erdnase, History.

Cobalt, Shane, *Chasing Dovetails.* (2012) Author, Toronto. Saddle-stitch. White. 33 pp. 8.5 x 11 in. (Information not verified by physical copy.) Cards, Close-Up.

Cobalt, Shane, *CTRL: A Collection of Controls for the Modern Card Conjuror.* (2012) Author, Toronto. Saddle-stitch. White. 17 pp. 8.5 x 11 in. (Information not verified by physical copy.) Cards.

Cobalt, Shane, *Trick for Chuck, A.* (2012) Author, Toronto. Saddle-stitch. White. 10 pp. 8.5 x 11 in. (Information not verified by physical copy. Bibliographical details are as accurate as possible.) Cards.

Cobalt, Shane, *Visible Deck.* (2012) Author, Toronto. Saddle-stitch. White. 9 pp. 8.5 x 11 in. (Information not verified by physical copy. Bibliographical details are as accurate as possible.) Cards.

Cobb, Vicki, *Magic – Naturally!* (1976) J. P. Lippincott, Philadelphia. Perfect. Yellow. 159 pp. 5.25 x 8 in. Beginner, Science magic.

Coby, Rudy, *How to Become a World Famous Magician.* (1997) Author, Los Angeles. Stapled. Yellow. 24 pp. 8.5 x 11 in. Signed by Rudy Coby. Lecture notes. Showmanship, Stage.

Coby, Rudy, *How to Become the Coolest Magician on Earth.* (c. 2011) Author, Los Angeles. Stapled. Beige. 8.5 x 11 in. Lecture notes. Showmanship, Stage.

Coby, Rudy, *Labman Sourcebook.* (1996) Image Comics, Fullerton, CA. Saddle-stitch. White, black. 14 pp. 5.5 x 8.5 in. Comic book.

Coghlan, Arthur, *Original Escapes of Arthur Coghlan, The.* (2024) Author, Brisbane, Australia. Perfect. 108 pp. (Information not verified by physical copy.) Escapes.

Cohen, Al, *Magical Mish-Mosh (and Other Tricky Trivia).* (1985) Author, Washington D.C. Saddle-stitch. Beige. 16 pp. 5.5 x 8.5 in. Signed by Al Cohen. Stage, Close-Up, Tips.

Cohen, Andy, *Follow the Other Hand.* (2009) iUniverse, New York. Perfect. White, red. 172 pp. 5.5 x 8.5 in. Biography, Beginner.

Cohen, Bill, *Money in Kid Shows.* (1988) Martini's Magic, Delta, PA. Comb. 11 pp. 8.5 x 11 in. (Information not verified by physical copy.) Children's magic, Business.

Cohen, Steve, *Confronting Magic.* Limited deluxe edition. (2021) Assouline, New York. Cloth. Color. 207 pp. 7.75 x 11 in. Inscribed to Todd Karr. Includes printed scarf. Signed by Steve Cohen. #4 of 300. Biography, History.

Cohen, Steve, *Evergreen.* (2018) Vanishing Inc., Rancho Cordova, CA. Perfect. Black. 57 pp. 6 x 6 in. Astonishing Essays no. 1. Essays.

Cohen, Steve, *Ink Matrix.* (c. 1990) Author, New York. Stapled. Blue. 6 pp. 8.5 x 11 in. Folded. (Information not verified by physical copy.) Cards, Matrix, Close-Up.

Cohen, Steve, with Kaufman, Richard, *Japan Ingenious.* (2013) Kaufman and Co., Washington D.C. Casebound. Yellow. 251 pp. 7.25 x 10.25 in. Dust jacket. Two-thirds-length dust jacket. Close-Up, Stage, Cards, Inventions. Japanese.

Cohen, Steve, *Max Malini: King of Magicians, Magician of Kings.* (2021) Squash Publishing, Chicago. Cloth. Blue. 521 pp. 8.25 x 10.25 in. Biography, History, Cards.

Cohen, Steve, *Max Malini: King of Magicians, Magician of Kings.* Second edition. (2024) Squash Publishing, Chicago. Cloth. Red. 521 pp. 8.25 x 10.25 in. Biography, History, Cards.

Cohen, Steve, *Millionaire's Magician, The.* (2018) Brick Hat, New York. Perfect. Color. 113 pp. 8.75 x 10.25 in. Signed by Steve Cohen. Graphic novel.

Cohen, Steve, *Redhead from New York, A.* (1987) Author, New York. Stapled. White. 25 pp. 8.5 x 11 in. (Information not verified by physical copy.) Lecture notes. Close-Up, Stage.

Cohen, Steve, *Win the Crowd.* (2005) Harper Collins, New York. Cloth. Beige. 182 pp. 6.25 x 9.25 in. Dust jacket. Showmanship, Stagecraft.

Cohn, Richard Steven, *Brooklyn Magicians.* (2007) Author, New York. Saddle-stitch. Beige. 22 pp. 5.5 x 8.5 in. History.

Cole, Bryan, *Lecture Notes no. 2: Bits and Pieces.* (c. 1950) Author, Allentown, PA. Saddle-stitch. Beige. 8 pp. 5.5 x 8.5 in. (Information not verified by physical copy.) Lecture notes. Coins, Close-Up, Stage.

Cole, Joe, *MicroEconomics.* (2006) Author, Omaha, NE. Comb. White. 67 pp. 8.5 x 11 in. (Information not verified by physical copy.) Coins, Cigars, Apparatus.

Cole, Joe, *Table Hopping Tonics.* (2006) Author, Omaha, NE. Coil. White. 36 pp. 8.5 x 11 in. (Information not verified by physical copy. Bibliographical details are as accurate as possible.) Close-Up, Stage.

Coleman, David B., *Original Doc Hokum Medicine Pitch, The.* (1959) Ireland Magic Co., Chicago. Saddle-stitch. Red. 8 pp. 5.5 x 8.5 in. Pitchman act, Comedy.

Coleman, Earle J., *Magic: A Reference Guide.* (1987) Greenwood Press, New York. Cloth. Black. 198 pp. 6.25 x 9.5 in. History.

Coleman, Glenn, *Magician's Guide to Making and Using Lockpicks.* (1988) Abbott Magic Co., Colon, MI. Saddle-stitch. Beige. 44 pp. 5.5 x 8.5 in. Escapes, Lockpicking.

Collen, Jay, *Magic Unconcealed.* (2021) Author, Chicago. Casebound. Black. 210 pp. 7.25 x 10.25 in. (Information not verified by physical copy.) Showmanship, Close-Up, Stage.

Collier, L. C., *Big Ring on String.* (2003) Author, Kansas City, MO. Saddle-stitch. White. 12 pp. 5.5 x 8.5 in. (Information not verified by physical copy.) Rings, Ring and rope, String, Close-Up.

Collier, L. C., *Complete Two Ball Sponge Ball Routine.* (2003) Author, Kansas City, MO. Saddle-stitch. White. 9 pp. 5.5 x 8.5 in. (Information not verified by physical copy.) Sponge balls, Close-Up.

Collier, L. C., *Full Circle Rope Routine.* (2003) Author, Kansas City, MO. Saddle-stitch. White. 16 pp. 5.5 x 8.5 in. (Information not verified by physical copy. Bibliographical details are as accurate as possible.) Rope.

Collier, L. C., *How to Perform for Kids and Stay Out of Trouble.* (2003) Author, Kansas City, MO. Saddle-stitch. Yellow. 24 pp. 5.5 x 8.5 in. (Information not verified by physical copy.) Children's magic.

Collier, L. C., *Three Ring Routine, A.* (2003) Author, Kansas City, MO. Saddle-stitch. Red. 12 pp. 5.5 x 8.5 in. (Information not verified by physical copy.) Linking Rings.

Collier, L. C., *Three Way Coloring Book Routine.* (2003) Author, Kansas City, MO. Saddle-stitch. Light green. 10 pp. 5.5 x 8.5 in. (Information not verified by physical copy.) Children's magic, Blow books.

Colino, Joe, *Pensando en Mnemonica Mayor.* (2020) Author, Spain. Perfect. Gray. 90 pp. 6 x 9 in. Cards, Prearranged deck. Spanish.

Colley, C. Michael, *Young Magicians, The.* (2011) Echo Library, London. Perfect. Blue. 245 pp. 8.5 x 11 in. History of Young Magicians Competition. History, Contests, Biography.

Collins, A. Frederick, *Amateur Entertainer, The.* (1926) D. Appleton and Co., New York. Cloth. Orange. 201 pp. 5.25 x 7.5 in. Extensive magic content. Different material than Collins' "Book of Magic." Beginner, General, Cards.

Collins, A. Frederick, *Book of Magic, The.* (1915) D. Appleton and Co., New York. Cloth. Tan. 177 pp. 4.75 x 7.5 in. Beginner, General, Cards, Coins.

Collins, A. Frederick, *Book of Magic, The.* (1916) D. Appleton and Co., New York. Cloth. Tan. 177 pp. 4.75 x 7.5 in. Beginner, General, Cards, Coins.

Collins, A. Frederick, *Book of Magic, The.* (1918) D. Appleton and Co., New York. Cloth. Tan. 177 pp. 4.75 x 7.5 in. Beginner, General, Cards, Coins.

Collins, A. Frederick, *Book of Magic, The.* (1919) D. Appleton and Co., New York. Cloth. Tan. 177 pp. 4.75 x 7.5 in. Dust jacket. Inscribed by author to C. R. Tracy in NYC 1932. Beginner, General, Cards, Coins.

Collins, A. Frederick, *Book of Puzzles, The.* (1927) D. Appleton and Co., New York. Cloth. Orange. 190 pp. 5.25 x 7.5 in. Puzzles, Magic squares.

Collins, A. Frederick, *Book of Magic, The.* (1936) D. Appleton and Co., New York. Cloth. Tan. 177 pp. 4.75 x 7.5 in. Dust jacket. Orange dust jacket. Beginner, General, Cards, Coins.

Collins, A. Frederick, *Book of Magic, The.* (1939) D. Appleton and Co., New York. Cloth. Tan. 177 pp. 4.75 x 7.5 in. Beginner, General, Cards, Coins.

Collins, A. Frederick, *Boys' Book of Amusements, The.* (1939) D. Appleton and Co., New York. Cloth. Olive. 197 pp. 5 x 7.5 in. Magic and stunts from earlier Collins books. Beginner, Stunts, Puzzles.

Collins, A. Frederick, *Fun with Figures.* (1928) D. Appleton and Co., New York. Cloth. Yellow. 253 pp. 5.25 x 7.5 in. Mathematical, Magic squares.

Collins, A. Frederick, *Magia de Salón.* First edition. (1946) José Monteso, Barcelona. Cloth. Gray. 208 pp. 5.25 x 7.25 in. Translation of "The Book of Magic." Beginner, General, Cards, Coins. Spanish.

Collins, A. Frederick, *Magia de Salón.* Second edition. (1950) José Monteso, Barcelona. Casebound. Orange, blue, black. 208 pp. 5.25 x 7.25 in. Translation of "The Book of Magic." Beginner, General, Cards, Coins. Spanish.

Collins, A. Frederick, *Magic of Science, The.* (1917) Fleming H. Revel Co., New York. Cloth. Tan. 215 pp. 5 x 7.75 in. Stunts, Chemical magic, Science magic, Pepper's Ghost.

Collins, A. Frederick, *Mirth and Mystery.* (1931) Coward-McCann, New York. Cloth. Red. 312 pp. 5 x 7.5 in. Beginner.

Collins, A. Frederick, *Money-Making Hobbies.* (1942) World Publishing Co., Cleveland and New York. Cloth. Gray. 322 pp. 5.5 x 8.25 in. Section details Collins' "Book of Magic" and recommends Brooklyn magician Prince Mendes as the world's greatest card manipulator. Beginner.

Collins, Doug, *Doves.* (1981) Author, Marshall, MI. Saddle-stitch. Blue. 11 pp. 5.5 x 8.5 in. Layout by Jack Barrows. Doves, Stage.

Collins, Harry, *Helpful Hints on Magic.* (c. 1960) Author, Louisville, KY. Stapled. White, color. 20 pp. 8.5 x 11 in. (Information not verified by physical copy.) Lecture notes. Showmanship, Business, Stagecraft.

Collins, Jack, *Clowning Around for Children.* (1979) Supreme Magic, Bideford, UK. Saddle-stitch. Red. 71 pp. 7.25 x 9.5 in. Clowning.

Collins, Stanley, *Collins' Card Conceits.* (1925) Author, London. Saddle-stitch. Olive. 48 pp. 5.5 x 8.5 in. (Measurements and other information have been recorded as accurately as possible.) Cards.

Collins, Stanley, with Gordon, Paul (ed.), *Collins' Card Conceits.* (2007) Natzler Enterprises, London. Saddle-stitch. Green. 51 pp. 5.75 x 8.25 in. Cards.

Collins, Stanley, *Conjuring Mélange, A.* (1947) Fleming Book Co., Berkeley Heights, NJ. Cloth. Blue. 244 pp. 5.5 x 8 in. Dust jacket. Stage.

Collins, Stanley, with Findlay, James B., *Conjuring on Cigarette and Trade Cards.* (1979) PFCC Press, Southfield, MI. Saddle-stitch. White. 15 pp. 2.75 x 4.25 in. With 1935 Lloyd's card set reprint in envelope. Supplement to "Periodical for Collecting Conjurers." Collecting, History, Trade cards.

Collins, Stanley, *Deceptive Conceptions in Magic.* (1920) London Magical Co., London. Boards. Green. 112 pp. 4.75 x 7.25 in. Signed with the notation "Author's copy" and Collins' bookplate. Signed by Stanley Collins. Cards, Stage.

Collins, Stanley, *Original Magical Creations.* (1915) Will Goldston Ltd., London. Boards. White. 111 pp. 4.75 x 7.25 in. Signed by Thomas Chislett. Cards, Stage.

Collins, Stanley, *Transcendental Book Mystery.* (1929) Author, Peckham, UK. Single page. 8.5 x 11 in. Carbon copy. (Information not verified by physical copy.) Mentalism, Book tests.

Collins, Stanley, *Whisper-Word.* (1931) Author, Peckham, UK. Stapled. 2 pp. 8.5 x 11 in. (Information not verified by physical copy.) Mentalism.

Collins, Ted, *Original Panama Rope Mystery, The.* (1949) Mecca Magic, Bloomfield, NJ. Folded. White. 4 pp. 5.5 x 8.5 in. Inside printed envelope. With one-page "Startling Improvements for the Panama Rope Mystery." Rope.

Collis, Len, *Magic Tricks.* (1989) Barrons Educational Service, New York. Perfect. White. 95 pp. 5.75 x 8.25 in. Beginner.

Collosini, *Mental Meanderings.* (c. 1950) Supreme Magic, Bideford, UK. Stapled with tape. Blue, red. 13 pp. 8 x 10 in. Mimeographed. Mentalism.

Colman, Matt, *Those Damn American Coins.* (c. 2008) Author, Liverpool, UK. Comb. White. 7 pp. 8.5 x 11 in. (Information not verified by physical copy.) Coins.

Colombini, Aldo, *11 Great Tricks.* (c. 2008) Colombini Magic, Tampa, FL. Saddle-stitch. Green. 32 pp. 5.5 x 8.5 in. (Information not verified by physical copy.) Rubber bands.

Colombini, Aldo (See also Duffie, Peter; Fabian; Ganson, Lewis; Yedid, Meir), *Anytime, Anyplace, Anywhere with a Deck of Cards.* (2007) Colombini Magic, Tampa, FL. Comb. Beige. 24 pp. 8.5 x 11 in. (Information not verified by physical copy.) Cards.

Colombini, Aldo, *Band, The.* (1993) Mamma Mia Magic, Modena, Italy. Comb. Green. 19 pp. 8.5 x 11 in. (Information not verified by physical copy.) Rubber bands.

Colombini, Aldo, *Baroque Cards.* (2008) Mamma Mia Magic, Granada Hills, CA. Saddle-stitch. White. 40 pp. 8.5 x 11 in. (Information not verified by physical copy.) Cards.

Colombini, Aldo (as Fabian), *Burtini's Cups and Balls Routine.* (1946) Author, Smethwick, UK. Saddle-stitch. White. 8 pp. 5.5 x 8.75 in. (Information not verified by physical copy.) Cups and Balls.

Colombini, Aldo (as Fabian), *Burtini's Linking Rings Routine.* (1947) Author, Smethwick, UK. Saddle-stitch. Light green. 16 pp. 4.75 x 7.25 in. Linking Rings.

Colombini, Aldo, *Card Journal: Card Routines for Everyone.* (2008) Colombini Magic, Tampa, FL. Saddle-stitch. Yellow. 31 pp. 5.5 x 8.5 in. (Information not verified by physical copy.) Magnets.

Colombini, Aldo, *Card Shadows.* (2004) Colombini Magic, Tampa, FL. Comb. White. 20 pp. 8.5 x 11 in. (Information not verified by physical copy.) Cards.

Colombini, Aldo, *Card Trips.* (2004) Mamma Mia Magic, Newbury Park, CA. Coil. White. 48 pp. 8.5 x 11 in. (Information not verified by physical copy.) Cards.

Colombini, Aldo, *Cards in Action.* (2008) Colombini Magic, Tampa, FL. Comb. White, green. 24 pp. 8.5 x 11 in. (Information not verified by physical copy.) Cards.

Colombini, Aldo, *Cardsdotcom.* (2004) Mamma Mia Magic, Barcelona. Coil. White. 44 pp. 8.5 x 11 in. Cards. Spanish.

Colombini, Aldo, *Cartas Barrocas.* (2006) Ediciones Marré, Barcelona. Perfect. Color. 111 pp. 8.25 x 6.75 in. Cards. Spanish.

Colombini, Aldo, *Chinese Purse, The.* (2000) Mamma Mia Magic, Thousand Oaks, CA. Folded. White. 2 pp. 8.5 x 11 in. (Information not verified by physical copy.) Coins, Chinese coins, Close-Up. Spanish.

Colombini, Aldo, *Close-Up Magic of Aldo Colombini, The.* (1994) L & L Publishing, Tahoma, CA. Cloth. Black. 172 pp. 8.5 x 11 in. Dust jacket. Signed by Aldo Colombini. Close-Up, Cards.

Colombini, Aldo, with Colombini, Rachel, *Colombini Farewell Tour, The.* (2011) Colombini Magic, Tampa, FL. Saddle-stitch. Color. 8.5 x 11 in. (Information not verified by physical copy.) Lecture notes. Close-Up, Stage.

Colombini, Aldo, with Colombini, Rachel, *Comedy Mind-Reading Act (for Two Performers).* (2009) Colombini Magic, Tampa, FL. Comb. White. 10 pp. 8.5 x 11 in. (Information not verified by physical copy.) Comedy, Mentalism, Stage.

Colombini, Aldo, *Cone-Tact.* (1998) Mamma Mia Magic, Thousand Oaks, CA. Saddle-stitch. White. 20 pp. 5.5 x 8.5 in. (Information not verified by physical copy.) Stage, Ball and Cone.

Colombini, Aldo, *Crisis of Identity.* (1993) Author, Modena, Italy. Saddle-stitch. Yellow. 10 pp. 5.5 x 8.5 in. (Information not verified by physical copy.) Cards.

Colombini, Aldo, *Cut Above the Rest: New Impromptu Card Routines, A.* (2007) Colombini Magic, Tampa, FL. Saddle-stitch. Blue. 36 pp. 5.5 x 8.5 in. (Information not verified by physical copy.) Cards, Impromptu.

Colombini, Aldo, *Cut Deeper: Incredible Impromptu Routines Performed with Just a Regular Deck of Cards, A.* (2007) Colombini Magic, Tampa, FL. Saddle-stitch. Yellow. 32 pp. 5.5 x 8.5 in. (Information not verified by physical copy.) Cards, Impromptu.

Colombini, Aldo, *Direct Hits: Imaginative Card Magic.* (1996) Mamma Mia Magic, Granada Hills, CA. Saddle-stitch. White, red. 48 pp. 8.5 x 11 in. Cards.

Colombini, Aldo, *Easy Coins: Seven Easy Coin Routines.* (2008) Colombini Magic, Tampa, FL. Saddle-stitch. White. 12 pp. 5.5 x 8.5 in. (Information not verified by physical copy.) Coins.

Colombini, Aldo, *Ensemble: Four Dazzling Card Routines.* (1999) Mamma Mia Magic, Thousand Oaks, CA. Saddle-stitch. White. 8.5 x 11 in. (Information not verified by physical copy.) Cards.

Colombini, Aldo (as Fabian), *Fabian's Magic Notes.* (1986) Supreme Magic, Bideford, UK. Saddle-stitch. White. 52 pp. 8 x 10 in. Cards, Rope.

Colombini, Aldo, *Final Cut: 25 Incredible Impromptu Routines Performed with Just a Regular Deck of Cards.* (2008) Colombini Magic, Tampa, FL. Saddle-stitch. White. 32 pp. 5.5 x 8.5 in. (Information not verified by physical copy.) Cards, Impromptu.

Colombini, Aldo, *Fireworks: An Amazing Twelve-Card Revelation Routine.* (2004) Mamma Mia Magic, Newbury Park, CA. Saddle-stitch. White. 20 pp. 8.5 x 11 in. (Information not verified by physical copy.) Cards, Multiple revelations.

Colombini, Aldo, *First Aid Lines.* (2005) Colombini Magic, Tampa, FL. Comb. White. 16 pp. 8.5 x 11 in. (Information not verified by physical copy.) Comedy, Jokes.

Colombini, Aldo, *First Impressions.* (1999) Mamma Mia Magic, Granada Hills, CA. Saddle-stitch. White, red. 28 pp. 8.5 x 11 in. (Information not verified by physical copy.) Lecture notes. Cards, Close-Up, Stage.

Colombini, Aldo, *F.I.S.M. Lecture Notes.* (1991) Author, Modena, Italy. Stapled. Yellow. 16 pp. 5.75 x 8.25 in. (Information not verified by physical copy.) Lecture notes. Cards, Close-Up, Stage.

Colombini, Aldo, *Fun with Matches.* (2007) Colombini Magic, Tampa, FL. Saddle-stitch. White. 28 pp. 8.5 x 11 in. (Information not verified by physical copy.) Matches, Stunts, Bets, Puzzles.

Colombini, Aldo, *Funny Stuff.* (2003) Mamma Mia Magic, Newbury Park, CA. Saddle-stitch. Yellow. 28 pp. 8.5 x 11 in. (Information not verified by physical copy.) Comedy, Jokes.

Colombini, Aldo, *Get the Ball Rolling.* (1999) Mamma Mia Magic, Thousand Oaks, CA. Saddle-stitch. White, red, black. 16 pp. 5.5 x 8.5 in. (Information not verified by physical copy.) Balls, Close-Up.

Colombini, Aldo, *Impact: Coins, Cards, Ropes, and Rings.* (1991) Micky Hades, Calgary, Canada. Coil. White, pink. 145 pp. 6 x 9 in. Cards, Coins, Rope, Rings.

Colombini, Aldo, *Impromptu Card Magic.* (2003) Mamma Mia Magic, Granada Hills, CA. Perfect. White. 126 pp. 8.5 x 11 in. Cards, Impromptu.

Colombini, Aldo, *Keep 'Em Laughing!* (2009) Colombini Magic, Tampa, FL. Comb. White. 20 pp. 8.5 x 11 in. (Information not verified by physical copy.) Comedy, Jokes.

Colombini, Aldo, *Laser Cup.* (2003) Loomis Magic, Camino, CA. Saddle-stitch. Beige. 11 pp. 5.5 x 8.5 in. Chop Cup, Close-Up.

Colombini, Aldo, *Life-Saver Lines.* (c. 1990) Colombini Magic, Granada Hills, CA. Saddle-stitch. Yellow. 22 pp. 8.5 x 11 in. (Information not verified by physical copy.) Comedy, Jokes.

Colombini, Aldo, *LOL (Laughing Out Loud).* (2004) Mamma Mia Magic, Newbury Park, CA. Saddle-stitch. White. 40 pp. 5.5 x 8.5 in. (Information not verified by physical copy.) Comedy, Jokes.

Colombini, Aldo, *Magic Cartoons.* (1994) Mamma Mia Magic, Granada Hills, CA. Saddle-stitch. Blue. 16 pp. 5.5 x 8.25 in. Children's magic.

Colombini, Aldo, with Colombini, Rachel, *Magic of Rachel Colombini, The.* (2011) Colombini Magic, Tampa, FL. Comb. White. 24 pp. 8.5 x 11 in. (Information not verified by physical copy.) Close-Up, Stage.

Colombini, Aldo, *Magic You Can Use.* (2011) Colombini Magic, Tampa, FL. Comb. White. 38 pp. 8.5 x 11 in. (Information not verified by physical copy.) Close-Up, Stage.

Colombini, Aldo, *Make 'Em Laugh.* (2003) Colombini Magic, Granada Hills, CA. Saddle-stitch. White. 12 pp. 8.5 x 11 in. (Information not verified by physical copy.) Comedy, Jokes.

Colombini, Aldo, *Mamma Mia Magic.* (c. 1980) Author, Modena, Italy. Saddle-stitch. Green. 14 pp. 8.25 x 11.75 in. (Information not verified by physical copy.) Rope, Cards, Rubber bands, Cups.

Colombini, Aldo, *Mamma Mia Magic Lecture Notes.* (1995) Mamma Mia Magic, Granada Hills, CA. Saddle-stitch. Orange. 28 pp. 5.5 x 8.5 in. (Information not verified by physical copy.) Lecture notes. Cards, Close-Up, Stage.

Colombini, Aldo, *Mamma Mia Rope Routine.* (c. 1980) Author, Modena, Italy. Saddle-stitch. White, green. 12 pp. 8.25 x 11.75 in. (Information not verified by physical copy.) Rope.

Colombini, Aldo, *Mamma Mia Rope Routine.* Second edition. (1994) Author, Modena, Italy. Saddle-stitch. Yellow. 16 pp. 5.5 x 8.5 in. (Information not verified by physical copy.) Rope.

Colombini, Aldo, *My Favorite Linking Ring Columns.* (2011) Colombini Magic, Tampa, FL. Comb. White. 80 pp. 8.5 x 11 in. (Information not verified by physical copy.) Magazine columns, Close-Up, Stage.

Colombini, Aldo, *Nailed Down Lecture Notes.* (2005) Mamma Mia Magic, Thousand Oaks, CA. Saddle-stitch. White, red, black. 24 pp. 5.5 x 8.5 in. (Information not verified by physical copy.) Lecture notes. Cards, Close-Up, Stage, Rope.

Colombini, Aldo, *On the Ropes: A Collection of Rope Routines.* (1996) Mamma Mia Magic, Granada Hills, CA. Saddle-stitch. White, blue. 18 pp. 8.5 x 11 in. Lecture notes. Rope.

Colombini, Aldo, *Pot of Gold: Four Stunning Routines with the Rainbow Deck, A.* (1994) Author, Modena, Italy. Saddle-stitch. Yellow. 10 pp. 5.5 x 8.5 in. (Information not verified by physical copy.) Cards.

Colombini, Aldo, *Pre-Deck-Ability.* (1996) Mamma Mia Magic, Granada Hills, CA. Saddle-stitch. Orange. 8 pp. 5.5 x 8.5 in. (Information not verified by physical copy.) Cards.

Colombini, Aldo, *Professor's Math.* (2004) Mamma Mia Magic, Thousand Oaks, CA. Saddle-stitch. White, red, black. 12 pp. 8.5 x 11 in. (Information not verified by physical copy.) Rope.

Colombini, Aldo, *Put Comedy in Your Magic!* (2009) Colombini Magic, Tampa, FL. Comb. White. 20 pp. 8.5 x 11 in. (Information not verified by physical copy.) Comedy, Patter.

Colombini, Aldo, *React.* (1994) Micky Hades, Calgary, Canada. Coil. White, blue. 103 pp. 6 x 9 in. Cards, Coins, Rope, Stage.

Colombini, Aldo, *Ringing Around Too.* (1998) Mamma Mia Magic, Thousand Oaks, CA. Saddle-stitch. White, red, black. 16 pp. 5.5 x 8.5 in. (Information not verified by physical copy.) Lecture notes. Cards, Close-Up, Stage.

Colombini, Aldo, *Rubber Illusion, The.* (c. 1996) Mamma Mia Magic, Granada Hills, CA. Saddle-stitch. Purple. 7 pp. 5.5 x 8.5 in. (Information not verified by physical copy.)

Colombini, Aldo, *Set-Up with Aldo: Five Incredible Routines with a Deck of Cards, A.* (2007) Colombini Magic, Tampa, FL. Saddle-stitch. Blue. 12 pp. 5.5 x 8.5 in. (Information not verified by physical copy.) Cards.

Colombini, Aldo, *Side Splitters.* (2010) Colombini Magic, Tampa, FL. Comb. White. 14 pp. 8.5 x 11 in. (Information not verified by physical copy.) Comedy, Jokes.

Colombini, Aldo, *Snake Eyes.* (2006) Mamma Mia Magic, Newbury Park, CA. Saddle-stitch. White, blue. 52 pp. 5.5 x 8.5 in. (Information not verified by physical copy.) Cards, Dice.

Colombini, Aldo, *Solutions.* (2002) Mamma Mia Magic, Thousand Oaks, CA. Saddle-stitch. White. 20 pp. 5.5 x 8.5 in. (Information not verified by physical copy.) Cards.

Colombini, Aldo, *Spaghetti Magic.* (1991) Mamma Mia Magic, Modena, Italy. Saddle-stitch. Green. 16 pp. 5.75 x 8.25 in. (Information not verified by physical copy.) Close-Up, Stage, Cups and Balls.

Colombini, Aldo, *Special Effects.* (2004) Mamma Mia Magic, Thousand Oaks, CA. Saddle-stitch. Yellow. 16 pp. 5.5 x 8.5 in. (Information not verified by physical copy.) Close-Up, Stage.

Colombini, Aldo, *Standing Room Only.* (2003) Mamma Mia Magic, Thousand Oaks, CA. Saddle-stitch. Green. 16 pp. 8.5 x 11 in. (Information not verified by physical copy.) Lecture notes. Cards, Close-Up, Stage, Rope.

Colombini, Aldo, *Still Ringing.* (2004) Mamma Mia Magic, Thousand Oaks, CA. Saddle-stitch. White. 12 pp. 8.5 x 11 in. (Information not verified by physical copy.) Ring and rope.

Colombini, Aldo, *That'll Be the Day.* (c. 2009) Mamma Mia Magic, Thousand Oaks, CA. Comb. White. 20 pp. 8.5 x 11 in. (Information not verified by physical copy.) Cards, Packet tricks.

Colombini, Aldo, *Throw in the Sponge.* (1996) Mamma Mia Magic, Granada Hills, CA. Saddle-stitch. Yellow. 11 pp. 5.5 x 8.5 in. (Information not verified by physical copy.) Sponge balls.

Colombini, Aldo, *Tight Rope.* (1997) Mamma Mia Magic, Granada Hills, CA. Saddle-stitch. White, red, black. 16 pp. 8.5 x 11 in. (Information not verified by physical copy.) Rope.

Colombini, Aldo, *To Die For: An Outstanding Collection of Tricks and Routines with Dice and Cards.* (2009) Colombini Magic, Tampa, FL. Comb. White. 24 pp. 8.5 x 11 in. (Information not verified by physical copy.) Cards, Dice.

Colombini, Aldo, *Top Ten.* (n.d.) Author, Modena, Italy. Comb. Yellow. 14 pp. 8.25 x 11.75 in. (Information not verified by physical copy. Bibliographical details are as accurate as possible.) Cards.

Colombini, Aldo, with Colombini, Rachel, *Two's Company.* (2009) Colombini Magic, Tampa, FL. Saddle-stitch. White. 28 pp. 8.5 x 11 in. (Information not verified by physical copy.) Close-Up, Stage.

Colombini, Aldo, *What's Up Deck?* (1995) Mamma Mia Magic, Granada Hills, CA. Cloth. Black. 147 pp. 8.5 x 11 in. Dust jacket. (Information not verified by physical copy.) Cards.

Colombini, Aldo, *Yo Quiero Vivir Para Siempre y Por Ahora la Cosa Va Bien.* (2005) Páginas Libros de Magia, Madrid. Perfect. Orange. 47 pp. 8.75 x 8.75 in. Comedy, Gags. Spanish.

Colombini, Aldo, *Your Host for Tonight: The Professional Emcee's Handbook.* (2010) Colombini Magic, Tampa, FL. Comb. Peach. 20 pp. 8.5 x 11 in. Emcee.

Colombini, Rachel, *Book of Book Tests, The.* (2010) Colombini Magic, Tampa, FL. Comb. White. 28 pp. 8.5 x 11 in. (Information not verified by physical copy.) Mentalism, Book tests.

Colombini, Rachel (as Rachel Wild), with Jones, Tom, *Magnets for Magic.* (2002) Wild Magic, San Antonio, FL. Saddle-stitch. White, blue, red. 20 pp. 5.5 x 8.5 in. Magnets, Close-Up, Stage, Gimmicks.

Colombini, Rachel, *Magnets for Magic.* (2002) Colombini Magic, Granada Hills, CA. Saddle-stitch. White. 12 pp. 5.5 x 8.5 in. (Information not verified by physical copy.) Magnets.

Colombini, Rachel (as Rachel Wild), with Jones, Tom, *Wild About Harry: Unique Routines for Magic Shows That Include a Young Wizard Theme.* (2002) Wild Magic, San Antonio, FL. Saddle-stitch. Purple. 20 pp. 5.5 x 8.5 in. (Information not verified by physical copy.) Children's magic.

Colombini, Rachel, *Wild About Harry: Unique Routines for Magic Shows That Include a Young Wizard Theme.* (2007) Colombini Magic, Tampa, FL. Saddle-stitch. Red. 20 pp. 5.5 x 8.5 in. (Information not verified by physical copy.) Children's magic.

Colucci, Donato, *Encyclopedia of Egg Magic, The.* (2002) Hermetic Press, Seattle. Cloth. Beige. 305 pp. 11.25 x 8.75 in. Bound oblong. Dust jacket. Eggs.

Colwell, Nathan, *Lorem Ipsum: Style Over Substance.* (2021) Author, Chicago. Saddle-stitch. White. 41 pp. 5.5 x 8.5 in. Cards.

Colwell, Nathan, *Theseus.* (2021) Magic Inc., Chicago. Cloth. Brown. 108 pp. 6.25 x 9.25 in. (Measurements and other information have been recorded as accurately as possible.) Cards.

Comte, M., *Nouveau Manuel Complet des Sorciers, ou La Magie Blanche Dévoilée.* Reprint. (1970) Éditions Charles Moreau, Paris. Perfect. Green. 426 pp. 4.5 x 6.75 in. Fold-out plates. Beginner. French.

Commons, Terry, with Docherty, Doc; Hartman, M. K., *Forged Mettle from Dreams and Nightmares.* (2023) Mystique, Provo, UT. Casebound. Black. 183 pp. 8.75 x 10.5 in. History, Close-Up, Restaurant magic, Stage.

Conde Ramsés, *Magirama vol. 4.* (1981) Author, Belém-Pará, Brazil. Cloth. Black. 333 pp. 8.75 x 12.75 in. Mimeographed. One of 200 copies. Course, Close-Up, Stage, Cards. Portuguese.

Congreave, Chris, *Commercial Killers.* (2023) Author, UK. Cloth. Black. Cover text: Gold; 112 pp. 6 x 8.5 in. (Information not verified by physical copy.) Cards, Close-Up.

Congreave, Chris, *Congreave's Curiosities.* (2017) MagicSeen, Norton, UK. Perfect. Black. 116 pp. 6 x 9 in. (Information not verified by physical copy.) Cards, Coins, Close-Up.

Congreave, Chris, *Curiouser and Curiouser.* (2021) Author, UK. Cloth. Black. Cover text: Gold; 104 pp. 6 x 8.5 in. (Information not verified by physical copy.) Cards, Coins, Close-Up.

Congreave, Chris, *Curiously Enough.* (2023) Author, UK. Cloth. Black. Cover text: Gold; 128 pp. 6 x 8.5 in. (Information not verified by physical copy.) Cards, Close-Up.

Congreave, Chris, *More Commercial Killers.* (2024) Author, UK. Cloth. Red. Cover text: Gold; 112 pp. 6 x 8.5 in. (Information not verified by physical copy.) Cards, Close-Up.

Conley, Craig, with Meyer, Gordon; Turner, Fredrick, *Jinx Companion.* (2011) Author, Raleigh, NC. Perfect. Black, white, yellow. 150 pp. 7 x 10 in. Mentalism, History, Cards.

Conley, Craig, *Magic Archetypes.* (2005) Author, Raleigh, NC. Perfect. Beige. 109 pp. 6.5 x 10.25 in. Signed by Craig Conley, Jeff McBride. Theory.

Conley, Craig, with Meyer, Gordon; Turner, Fredrick, *One Jinxed Year.* (2010) Authors, Raleigh, NC. Clip. Beige. 224 pp. 8.5 x 11 in. Anthology. (Information not verified by physical copy.) Mentalism, Cards, Magazine.

Conley, Craig (as Prof. Oddfellow), *Revealed at Last: Why Magicians Pull Coins from Ears (and What It Means for Your Weekend).* (2018) Author, Raleigh, NC. Perfect. Pink, blue. 36 pp. 6 x 9 in. Humor, Essays.

Conley, Ron, *Chicken Soup for Magicians.* (2007) Author, Salem, OR. Coil. White. 19 pp. 8.5 x 11 in. (Information not verified by physical copy.) Showmanship, Business.

Conley, Ron, *Drugs, Strangers, and Other Dangers.* (1997) SPS Publications, Eustis, FL. Saddle-stitch. Yellow, black. 96 pp. 8.5 x 11 in. (Information not verified by physical copy.) Children's magic, School shows.

Conn, Doug, with Racherbaumer, Jon, *Conn-Fidential.* (1997) Author, Charlotte, NC. Comb. Yellow. 31 pp. 8.5 x 11 in. (Information not verified by physical copy.) Cards, Coins, Close-Up.

Conn, Doug, *Connjuring.* (2004) Author, Charlotte, NC. Clip. White. 41 pp. 8.5 x 11 in. (Information not verified by physical copy. Bibliographical details are as accurate as possible.) Cards, Coins, Close-Up.

Conn, Doug, *Connjuring 2.* (2003) Author, Charlotte, NC. Saddle-stitch. Blue. 32 pp. 5.5 x 8.5 in. (Information not verified by physical copy. Bibliographical details are as accurate as possible.) Close-Up.

Conn, Doug, *Purse'n'l Coin Routine.* (c. 1997) Author, Charlotte, NC. Saddle-stitch. White. 26 pp. 5.5 x 8.5 in. (Information not verified by physical copy.) Coins, Purse frame.

Conn, Doug, with Cummins, Paul W., *Tricks of My Trade: The Magic of Doug Conn.* (1999) FASDIU Press, Jacksonville, FL. Casebound. Green. 190 pp. 8.5 x 11 in. Signed by Paul W. Cummins. Cards, Coins, Close-Up.

Connolly, Kevin, *Story Behind the Houdini Keys, The.* (1995) Author, New Milford, NJ. Folded. Tan. 4 pp. 5.5 x 8.5 in. Includes color photo and price list. Houdini, History, Collecting, Escapes.

Connor, R. Brooks, Jr., *McAbee Rings, The.* (2001) Magikraft Studios, Moreno Valley, CA. Saddle-stitch. Beige. 12 pp. 5.5 x 8.5 in. (Information not verified by physical copy.) Rings, Close-Up.

Conover, Tim, with York, Scotty, *Revolutionary Routines with Aces.* (1993) FYEO Creations, Alexandria, VA. Coil. White. 33 pp. 5.5 x 8.5 in. Cards.

Conradi, Friedrich W. (See also Robinson, Richard), *Book of Exquisite Conjuring, The. Magic Library no. 1.* (1928) Horsterscher Verlag, Berlin, Germany. Stapled. Tan. 46 pp. 8.75 x 10.75 in. Some pictures hand-colored. Stage, Rag painting.

Conradi, Friedrich W., *Démonstrations mystérieuses.* (1904) Horsterscher Verlag, Berlin, Germany. Leather. Brown. 188 pp. 6 x 9 in. Cards, Stage. German.

Conradi, Friedrich W., *Explanations to Conradi's "Box-Tricks."* (n.d.) Conradi-Horster, Berlin, Germany. Stapled. Beige. 12 pp. 8.75 x 11.5 in. Magic set manual.

Conradi, Friedrich W., *Feuerzauber.* (1922) Horsterscher Verlag, Berlin, Germany. Saddle-stitch. Maroon. 16 pp. 6 x 9 in. Fire, Stage. German.

Conradi, Friedrich W., *Ich Kann Zaubern.* (1950) Bergwald, Köln, Germany. Perfect. Beige, red, black. 80 pp. 5 x 7.25 in. Beginner. German.

Conradi, Friedrich W., *Im Reiche der Wunder. Der Tausenkünstler.* (1905) Peter J. Oeitergaard, Berlin, Germany. Cloth. Olive. 391 pp. 6.25 x 9.5 in. Cards, Close-Up, Stage. German.

Conradi, Friedrich W., *Im Reich der Wunder.* (1985) Edition Olms, Zurich. Cloth. Black. 391 pp. 5.5 x 9 in. Dust jacket. Reprint of 1905 edition. Stage, History. German.

Conradi, Friedrich W., *Letzen Schlager der Magie, Die.* (1928) Horsterscher Verlag, Berlin, Germany. Stapled. Purple. 45 pp. 8.75 x 11 in. Stage, Cards. German.

Conradi, Friedrich W., *Magische Juwelen.* (1912) Horsterscher Verlag, Berlin, Germany. Cloth. Purple. 252 pp. 6.25 x 9.25 in. Signed by F. W. Conradi. Cards, Stage, Close-Up. German.

Conradi, Friedrich W., *Moderne Kartenkünstler, Der.* (1896) Borwig and Horster, Dresden, Germany. Cloth. Tan. 232 pp. 6.25 x 9 in. Cards. German.

Conradi, Friedrich W., *Moderne Kartenkünstler, Der.* (1896) Borwig and Horster, Dresden, Germany. Cloth. Black. 232 pp. 6 x 9 in. Cards. German.

Conradi, Friedrich W., *Moderne Kartenkünstler, Der.* (1980) Edition Olms, Zurich. Cloth. Black. 232 pp. 5 x 7.5 in. Dust jacket. Reprint of 1896 edition. Cards. German.

Conradi, Friedrich W., *Neue Humorostische Zauberkünstler, Der.* (1958) Joe Wildon, Bielefeld, Germany. Perfect. Yellow, white. 55 pp. 5.75 x 8.25 in. Cards. German.

Conradi, Friedrich W., *Universum der Magie, Das.* (1912) Horsterscher Verlag, Berlin, Germany. Cloth. Dark blue. 200 pp. 6.25 x 9 in. Cards, Coins, Balls. German.

Conradi, Friedrich W., *Vollendete Karten-Künstler, Der.* (1920) Eysler, Berlin, Germany. Perfect. Red. 159 pp. 5.75 x 8.75 in. Cards. German.

Conradi, Friedrich W., *What You Can Do with a Pack of Giant Cards.* (c. 1925) Author, Berlin, Germany. Saddle-stitch. Beige, blue. 12 pp. 7.25 x 10.5 in. Cards, Jumbo cards. German.

Conradi, Friedrich W., *Wunder der Kartenkünst.* (1920) Horsterscher Verlag, Berlin, Germany. Cloth. Black. 47 pp. 6 x 9 in. Cards. German.

Conradi, Friedrich W., *Zauberkataloge.* (1984) Volker Huber, Offenbach, Germany. Cloth. Red. 32 pp. 6.25 x 9.5 in. No. 9 in Huber catalog series. #155 of 250. Catalog reprint. German.

Conran, Edward P., *Choice Selections of Conran's Subtle Secrets.* (c. 1920) Author, Philadelphia. Stapled. Green. 8.5 x 11 in. Mimeographed. (Information not verified by physical copy.) Mentalism, Close-Up, Stage.

Constant, P., *Petit Manuel de Tours de Physique.* (1925) Librairie Bernardin-Béchet, Paris. Perfect. Black, red, yellow. 106 pp. 3.75 x 6 in. Beginner, Stunts. French.

Contento, Marcelo, *Medal-lions.* (1994) Author, Boston. Saddle-stitch. White. 5 pp. 5.5 x 8.5 in. (Information not verified by physical copy. Bibliographical details are as accurate as possible.) Close-Up.

Contento, Marcelo, *Notes.* (1998) Author, Watertown, MA. Coil. White. 15 pp. 8.5 x 11 in. (Information not verified by physical copy.) Cards, Close-Up.

Converse, Tim "Santiago," *Scrolls: A Book of Storytelling Magic Theatre.* (2007) Leaping Lizards Magic, Orlando, FL. Perfect. Brown. 125 pp. 8.5 x 11 in. (Information not verified by physical copy.) Storytelling magic.

Conway, Pat, with Lees, Walt, *Pat Way to Con, The.* (1988) Magico, New York. Cloth. Brown. 157 pp. 6.25 x 9.25 in. Close-Up, Cards, Stage.

Cook, Cecil, *Fifty-One Impromptu Conjuring Tricks.* (1946) Author, Sydney. Saddle-stitch. Orange. 48 pp. 4.75 x 7 in. Impromptu, Close-Up.

Cook, Irv, *G Powder Slush: My Favorite Effects.* (1989) Author, Daytona Beach, FL. Comb. Blue. 12 pp. 5.5 x 8.5 in. (Information not verified by physical copy.) Slush powder.

Cook, James W., *Arts of Deception, The.* (2001) Harvard University Press, Cambridge, MA. Perfect. Beige. 314 pp. 6 x 9 in. History.

Cook, Steve, *24 Ct. Gold.* (2025) Haresign Press, UK. Casebound. Maroon. Cover text: Gold; pp. (Information not verified by physical copy.) Mentalism, Stage.

Cook, Steve, *Cool: Based on a Basil Horwitz Routine.* (2006) Author, UK. Comb. White, blue. 11 pp. 6 x 9 in. (Information not verified by physical copy.) Mentalism.

Cook, Steve, *Fake Genius.* (2018) Haresign Press, UK. Cloth. Black. 176 pp. 6 x 9 in. Dust jacket. (Information not verified by physical copy.) Mentalism.

Cook, Steve, *Fake Genius 2.* (2021) Haresign Press, UK. Cloth. Black. 192 pp. 6 x 9 in. Dust jacket. (Information not verified by physical copy.) Mentalism.

Cook, Steve, *Point Blank.* (1992) Haresign Press, UK. 176 pp. Dust jacket. (Information not verified by physical copy.) Mentalism.

Cook, Steve, *Psychological Subtlety and Devious Ruse.* (2010) Author, UK. Stapled. 43 pp. Limited to 15 copies. (Information not verified by physical copy.) Lecture notes. Mentalism.

Cooke, Conrad William, *Automata Old and New.* (2000) A Real Miracle, Malibu, CA. Perfect. Beige. 117 pp. 4.5 x 5.5 in. Reprint of 1893 edition. Signed by Burton Sperber. #19 of 25 copies. History, Automata.

Cooke, Palmer, *Spiritualistic Secrets. Cover says "Secrets."* (n.d.) Attica, IN. Saddle-stitch. Blue. 36 pp. 4.5 x 5.75 in. Spiritualism.

Coomer, Bill, *Magic of Bill Coomer, The.* (c. 1990) Author, Cape Girardeau, MO. Comb. Beige. 20 pp. 5.5 x 8.5 in. (Information not verified by physical copy.) Cards, Ambitious Card, Close-Up.

Cooper, John, *How to Increase Your Birthday Party Business!* (1990) Smilemakers Entertainment, Forest Park, GA. Saddle-stitch. Blue. 11 pp. 5.25 x 8.5 in. Children's magic, Business, Promotion.

Cooper, Johnny, *Polished Presentations.* (1980) Supreme Magic, Bideford, UK. Saddle-stitch. Purple. 59 pp. 7.25 x 9.75 in. Stage, Children's magic, Comedy, Close-Up.

Cooper, Tommy, *Just Like That! Jokes and Tricks.* (1975) Jupiter Books, London. Cloth. Blue. 176 pp. 6.25 x 9.5 in. Dust jacket. Beginner, Stunts, Comedy.

Cooper, Tommy, *Just Like That! Jokes and Tricks.* (1976) Wyndham Books, London. Perfect. White. 175 pp. 5 x 7.5 in. Beginner, Stunts, Comedy.

Copper, Ger, *Magic from Holland.* (1970) Author, Amsterdam. Stapled. Blue. 9 pp. 8.5 x 11 in. Lecture notes. Stage, Close-Up.

Copper, Ger, *Magic from Holland.* (1970) Author, Amsterdam. Saddle-stitch. White. 8 pp. 6 x 8.25 in. Signed by Ger Copper. Lecture notes. Stage, Close-Up.

Copperfield, David, *David Copperfield's Beyond Imagination.* (1996) HarperPrism, New York. Cloth. Black. 353 pp. 6.25 x 9.25 in. Dust jacket. Signed by David Copperfield. Fiction.

Copperfield, David, *David Copperfield's History of Magic.* (2021) Simon and Schuster, New York. Cloth. Black. 256 pp. 8.5 x 11 in. Dust jacket. Barnes and Noble signed edition with second inscription to Todd Karr signed in person. Signed by David Copperfield. History.

Copperfield, David, *David Copperfield's History of Magic audiobook.* (2021) Audioworks, New York. CD. Brown. Audiobook pp. 5 x 6 in. CD in box. History, Audiobook.

Copperfield, David, *David Copperfield's Tales of the Impossible.* (1995) HarperPrism, New York. Cloth. Black. 385 pp. 6.5 x 9.5 in. Dust jacket. Fiction.

Copperfield, David, *David Copperfield's Project Magic.* (c. 1984) Author, Las Vegas. Comb. White, purple, black. 74 pp. 8.5 x 11 in. From the magician's physical therapy foundation. Beginner.

Copperfield, David, *David Copperfield's Project Magic Handbook.* (2002) Author, Las Vegas. Cloth. White. 291 pp. 9.5 x 9.25 in. Dust jacket. Beginner.

Coram, *How to Become a Ventriloquist.* (c. 1919) London Magical Co., London. Saddle-stitch. Tan. 16 pp. 5.5 x 8.5 in. Ventriloquism.

Corbier, Gaston, *Méthode Tours de Cartes.* (c. 1925) Author, Paris. Saddle-stitch. Orange. 8 pp. 5.5 x 8.5 in. Cards, Beginner. French.

Corbitt, Steve, *Everybody's Favorite Uncle.* (2001) Author, St. Louis, MO. Comb. Blue. 19 pp. 8.5 x 11 in. (Information not verified by physical copy.) Comedy, Close-Up.

Corbitt, Steve, *Lighten Up!* (c. 2000) Author, St. Louis, MO. Saddle-stitch. White. 52 pp. 5.5 x 8.5 in. (Information not verified by physical copy.) Close-Up, Stage, Storytelling magic.

Corcos, Christine A., *Law and Magic: A Collection of Essays.* (2010) Carolina Academic Press, Durham, NC. Perfect. Black. 429 pp. 7 x 10 in. Essays, Legal, Reference.

Corinda, Tony (See also Mason, Eric), *13 Escalones del Mentalismo.* (2016) Páginas Libros de Magia, Madrid. Perfect. Black, gold. 397 pp. 6.75 x 9.5 in. Mentalism. Spanish.

Corinda, Tony, *13 Steps to Mentalism.* (1964) Accuba, London. Cloth. Black. 424 pp. 5.5 x 8.25 in. (Measurements and other information have been recorded as accurately as possible.) Mentalism.

Corinda, Tony, *13 Steps to Mentalism.* Second printing. (1968) Louis Tannen, New York. Cloth. Green. 424 pp. 5.5 x 8.5 in. Smooth pages. Photos opening chapters and not skulls. New illustrations and typesetting. Mentalism.

Corinda, Tony, *13 Steps to Mentalism, nos. 1-13.* Second printing. (1964) Accuba Ltd., London. Saddle-stitch. Black, white. Multiple sections. 5.5 x 8.5 in. Covers feature large skull. Mentalism.

Corinda, Tony, *Amazing Memory Systems.* (1960) Author, London. Saddle-stitch. Beige, red. 20 pp. 5.5 x 8.25 in. Reprint of Step Three of "Thirteen Steps to Mentalism." Memory, Mentalism.

Corinda, Tony, with Read, Ralph W., *Complete Guide to Billet-Switching, The.* (1976) Louis Tannen, New York. Saddle-stitch. Blue. 46 pp. 5.5 x 8.5 in. Mentalism, Billets.

Corinda, Tony, *Corinda's Selected Effects no. 1.* (1959) Corinda's Magic Studio, London. Saddle-stitch. Yellow. 8 pp. 5.5 x 8.5 in. Includes phone dial paper square for center tear. Mentalism, Center Tear.

Corinda, Tony, *Corinda's Step One of Thirteen Steps to Mentalism: The Swami Gimmick.* (1958) Corinda's Magic Studio, London. Saddle-stitch. Yellow. 24 pp. 5.5 x 8.5 in. Mentalism, Nail writer.

Corinda, Tony, *Corinda's Step Two of Thirteen Steps to Mentalism: Pencil, Lip, Sound, Touch, and Muscle Reading.* (1958) Corinda's Magic Studio, London. Saddle-stitch. Blue. 24 pp. 5.5 x 8.5 in. Mentalism, Muscle reading.

Corinda, Tony, *Corinda's Step Three of Thirteen Steps to Mentalism: Mnemonics and Mental Systems.* (1958) Corinda's Magic Studio, London. Saddle-stitch. Red. 22 pp. 5.5 x 8.5 in. Memory, Mnemonics.

Corinda, Tony, *Corinda's Step Four of Thirteen Steps to Mentalism: Predictions.* (1958) Corinda's Magic Studio, London. Saddle-stitch. Yellow. 38 pp. 5.5 x 8.5 in. Mentalism.

Corinda, Tony, *Corinda's Step Five of Thirteen Steps to Mentalism: Blindfolds and X-Ray Eyes.* (1958) Corinda's Magic Studio, London. Saddle-stitch. Gray. 30 pp. 5.5 x 8.5 in. Mentalism, Blindfolds.

Corinda, Tony, *Corinda's Step Six of Thirteen Steps to Mentalism: Billets.* (1959) Corinda's Magic Studio, London. Saddle-stitch. Yellow. 30 pp. 5.5 x 8.5 in. Mentalism, Billets.

Corinda, Tony, *Corinda's Step Seven of Thirteen Steps to Mentalism: Book Tests and Supplement.* (1959) Corinda's Magic Studio, London. Saddle-stitch. Blue. 31 pp. 5.5 x 8.5 in. Mentalism, Book tests.

Corinda, Tony, *Corinda's Step Eight of Thirteen Steps to Mentalism: Two-Person Telepathy.* (1959) Corinda's Magic Studio, London. Saddle-stitch. Purple. 33 pp. 5.5 x 8.5 in. Mentalism, Code acts.

Corinda, Tony, *Corinda's Step Nine of Thirteen Steps to Mentalism: Mediumistic Stunts.* (1959) Corinda's Magic Studio, London. Saddle-stitch. Green. 26 pp. 5.5 x 8.5 in. Mentalism, Spirit effects, Séances.

Corinda, Tony, *Corinda's Step Ten of Thirteen Steps to Mentalism: Card Tricks.* (1959) Corinda's Magic Studio, London. Saddle-stitch. Beige. 25 pp. 5.5 x 8.5 in. Mentalism, Cards.

Corinda, Tony, *Corinda's Step Eleven of Thirteen Steps to Mentalism: Question and Answer (Readings).* (1959) Corinda's Magic Studio, London. Saddle-stitch. Green. 20 pp. 5.5 x 8.5 in. Mentalism, Question and answer.

Corinda, Tony, *Corinda's Step Twelve of Thirteen Steps to Mentalism: Publicity Stunts.* (1960) Corinda's Magic Studio, London. Saddle-stitch. Beige. 20 pp. 5.5 x 8.5 in. Mentalism, Publicity stunts, Promotion.

Corinda, Tony, *Corinda's Step Thirteen of Thirteen Steps to Mentalism: Patter and Presentation.* (1960) Corinda's Magic Studio, London. Saddle-stitch. Light green. 30 pp. 5.5 x 8.5 in. Mentalism, Patter, Routining, Showmanship.

Corinda, Tony, *Mini-Slate Magic.* (1958) Corinda's Magic Studio, London. Stapled with tape. White. 20 pp. 8.25 x 6.5 in. Bound oblong. Mimeographed inside printed cover. Slates, Mentalism, Close-Up.

Corinda, Tony, *Nail Writer: "Swami Gimmic," The.* (c. 1971) Louis Tannen, New York. Saddle-stitch. Blue. 24 pp. 5.5 x 8.5 in. Mentalism, Gimmicks, Nail writer.

Corinda, Tony, *Powers of Darkness, The.* (1958) Corinda's Magic Studio, London. Saddle-stitch. 5.5 x 8.5 in. (Information not verified by physical copy.) Stage, Psychological.

Corinda, Tony, *Powers of Darkness, The.* (1958) Ireland Magic Co., Chicago. Saddle-stitch. White. 11 pp. 5.5 x 8.5 in. Stage, Psychological.

Corinda, Tony, *Tele-Trickery.* (1961) Corinda's Magic Studio, London. Stapled with tape. Pink. 13 pp. 8 x 10 in. Mentalism.

Cornelius, John, with Pierce, Lance, *Award-Winning Magic of John Cornelius, The.* (2001) L & L Publishing, Tahoma, CA. Cloth. Black. 181 pp. 8.5 x 11 in. Dust jacket. Close-Up, Creativity, Cards, Inventions.

Cornelius, John, *Borrowed Bill Routine.* (1984) Author, San Antonio, TX. Stapled. Black, white. 7 pp. 5.5 x 8.5 in. Bills.

Cornelius, John, *Cornelius Card System, The.* (1979) Author, San Antonio, TX. Stapled with paper cover. Yellow. 6 pp. 5.5 x 8.5 in. Cards, Prearranged deck.

Cornelius, John, *Creative Secrets no. 1.* (1988) Author, San Antonio, TX. Saddle-stitch. White. 34 pp. 5.5 x 8.5 in. Close-Up, Stage, Creativity, Inventions.

Cornelius, John, *Fickle Nickle.* (1974) Author, San Antonio, TX. Stapled. White. 6 pp. 8.5 x 11 in. Photo illustrations. Folded in printed envelope with title "The Vanishing Nickle." Coins, Gimmicks.

Cornelius, John, *Fickle Nickle.* (1974) Author, San Antonio, TX. Stapled. White. 6 pp. 8.5 x 11 in. Version with drawings as illustrations. Coins, Gimmicks.

Cornelius, John, *Magic of John Cornelius, no. 1, The.* (1980) Author, San Antonio, TX. Saddle-stitch. Blue. 12 pp. 5.5 x 8.5 in. Lecture notes. Close-Up, Stage, Creativity, Inventions.

Cornelius, John, *Pen Through Everything.* Second edition. (1994) Author, San Antonio, TX. Saddle-stitch. Gray. 24 pp. 5.5 x 8.5 in. Material by Michael Close, Jim Krenz. Pens, Bills, Gimmicks, Close-Up.

Cornelius, John, *Perfect Pen.* (1996) Author, San Antonio, TX. Loose pages. White. 6 pp. 8.5 x 11 in. Pens, Bills, Gimmicks, Close-Up.

Cornelius, John, *Shrinking Card Case.* (1978) Author, San Antonio, TX. Stapled. White. 2 pp. 8.5 x 11 in. Cards, Card cases, Close-Up.

Cosmo (Gabriel Trelawney), *Ten Exclusive Magic Secrets.* (c. 1920) Author, UK. Saddle-stitch. Beige. 8 pp. 4.75 x 6 in. In Copperfield collection. Cards, Close-Up.

Cosmo (Gabriel Trelawney), *Ten Exclusive Magic Secrets.* (c. 1920) Author, UK. Saddle-stitch. Beige. 8 pp. 5.25 x 7.25 in. Different layout. In Copperfield collection. Cards, Close-Up.

Costello, Matthew J., *Magic Everywhere!* (1999) Three Rivers Press, New York. Perfect. White. 144 pp. 5.5 x 8 in. (Information not verified by physical copy.) Beginner.

Costi, Davide, *Close-Up Elegance.* (2004) Cairn Press, Norwich, UK. Cloth. White. 144 pp. 7.25 x 10 in. Close-Up, Cards, Coins.

Costi, Davide, *For Friends Only.* (1987) Author, Milan. Comb. Gold. 79 pp. 8.25 x 11.75 in. (Measurements and other information have been recorded as accurately as possible.) Close-Up, Cards, Coins.

Cotgrave, John (J. C.), *Wits Interpreter.* (1655) N. Brook, London. Multiple sections. 4 x 6.75 in. (Information not verified by physical copy.) Toole Stott no. 185. Early magic.

Cotgrave, John (J. C.), *Wits Interpreter.* (1662) N. Brook, London. 496 pp. 4.75 x 6.5 in. (Information not verified by physical copy.) Toole Stott no. 186. Early magic.

Cotgrave, John (J. C.), *Wits Interpreter.* Third edition. (1671) N. Brook, London. 520 pp. 4.75 x 6.5 in. (Information not verified by physical copy.) Toole Stott no. 187. Early magic.

Cotler, Jordan, *Impromptu Svengali Deck Principle, The.* Second edition. (2009) Author, Chicago. Wire binding. Black, red, blue. 30 pp. 8.5 x 11 in. (Information not verified by physical copy.) Cards, Svengali deck, Impromptu.

Cotler, Jordan, *Impromptu Svengali Deck Routine vol. 1, The.* (2007) Author, Chicago. Stapled. White. 29 pp. 8.5 x 11 in. (Information not verified by physical copy.) Cards, Svengali deck, Impromptu.

Cotton, Charles, *Compleat Gamester, The.* (1725) J. Wilford, London. 224 pp. 3.75 x 6.5 in. (Information not verified by physical copy.) Toole Stott no. 188. Gambling, Cards, Early magic.

Cotton, Charles, *Compleat Gamester, The.* (1726) J. Wilford, London. 224 pp. 3.75 x 6.25 in. (Information not verified by physical copy.) Toole Stott no. 189. Gambling, Cards, Early magic.

Cotton, Charles, *Compleat Gamester, The.* (1970) Imprint Society, Barre, MA. Cloth. Brown. 176 pp. 5.25 x 8.5 in. Slipcase. Artist signature. Signed by Joseph Low. #257 of 1950. Gambling, Cards, Early magic.

Cotton, Charles, *Compleat Gamester, The.* (1972) Cornmarket, Cambridge, UK. Cloth. Red. 230 pp. 4 x 6.25 in. Reprint of 1674 edition. Gambling, Cards, Early magic.

Cotton, Charles, *Games and Gamesters of the Restoration: The Compleat Gamester and Lives of the Gamesters.* (1971) Kennikat Press, Port Washington, NY. Cloth. Gray. 282 pp. 5.75 x 8.75 in. Gambling, Cards, Early magic.

Cottone, Joseph, *Joseph Cottone's Continuous Card Production.* (1946) Carlo's Magic Shop, Toledo, OH. Stapled with paper cover. Beige. 3 pp. 5.5 x 8.25 in. Cards, Manipulation, Interlocked card production.

Couden, Doug, *Playing and Booking School Assemblies.* (1947) Roger Montandon, Tulsa, OK. Saddle-stitch. Yellow. 12 pp. 5.5 x 8.5 in. Children's magic, School shows, Business, Promotion.

Count, The, *Inquisition of Shuffling and Dealing.* (2006) Author, Tulsa, OK. Coil. White. Unpaginated. 8.5 x 11 in. Cards.

Courville, Paul, *Magic Tokens.* (2018) Magic Token, Greenwood, IN. Perfect. White. 136 pp. 8.5 x 11 in. (Measurements and other information have been recorded as accurately as possible.) Collecting, Tokens.

Couture, Sylvian A., *Magic Tricks You Can Do.* (c. 1915) Sylvian's Magic Shop, Providence, RI. Saddle-stitch. Yellow. 16 pp. 5.25 x 7.25 in. Beginner.

Covey, Lynn, *Novel Concepts in Magic vol. 1.* (1979) Author, Pittsburgh, PA. Stapled. Yellow. 15 pp. 8.5 x 11 in. Cards, Close-Up, Stage.

Cowan, Geoffrey, *Fun with Magic.* (1973) Grosset and Dunlap, New York. Casebound. Orange. 45 pp. 9.25 x 12.5 in. Beginner, Children's book.

Cowolsky Richard, *Straw Struck.* (1978) Author, Morris Plains, NJ. Saddle-stitch. Gray, red, blue. 40 pp. 5.5 x 8.5 in. (Information not verified by physical copy.) Straws, Close-Up.

Cox, Chris, *Cannibal Rap.* (1988) Author, Sweden. Saddle-stitch. Pink. 15 pp. 5.75 x 8.25 in. Cards, Cannibal Cards.

Cox, Clinton, *Houdini: Master of Illusion.* (2001) Scholastic Press, New York. Cloth. Black. 194 pp. 5.75 x 8.5 in. Dust jacket. Biography, Houdini, History.

Cox, J. Randolph, *Man of Magic and Mystery: A Guide to the Work of Walter B. Gibson.* (1988) Scarecrow Press, Metuchen, NJ. Cloth. Black. 382 pp. 5.5 x 8.5 in. (Information not verified by physical copy.) Bibliography, History.

Cox, L. Raymond, *Tips and Tricks.* (1934) Author, Denver, CO. Stapled. Blue. 19 pp. 8.5 x 11 in. Mimeographed. (Information not verified by physical copy.) Cards, Close-Up, Stage.

Cox, Robert, *Cox at the Castle.* (1996) Author, UK. Saddle-stitch. White, green. 28 pp. 5.5 x 8.5 in. (Information not verified by physical copy.) Lecture notes. Cards, Close-Up, Magnets.

Cox, Robert, *Magic from the Front Line.* (1994) Author, UK. Clip. White. 50 pp. 8.5 x 11 in. (Information not verified by physical copy.) Close-Up, Children's magic.

Cox, Robert, *Trouble with Magic Is, The.* (2003) Author, UK. Comb. Gray, red, black. 36 pp. 8.5 x 11 in. (Information not verified by physical copy.) Close-Up, Strolling magic.

Cox, William Edward, *Mentalism and Magicians: Some Conclusive Arguments About a Modern Problem.* (1972) Stamford College Press, Singapore. Saddle-stitch. White. 20 pp. 5.5 x 8.25 in. Theory, Mentalism.

Crabb, Charles G., *Spirit Spots a Prevaricator, A.* Trick of the Month Club series 2, no. 1. (July 1932) Thayer Magical Mfg. Co., Los Angeles. Folded. Yellow. 6 pp. 3.75 x 6.75 in. Spirit effects, Slates, Cards.

Crabb, Tabby, *Tabman Magic.* (2009) Ancient Spring Publishing, Houston, TX. Perfect. Black. 240 pp. 8 x 10 in. (Information not verified by physical copy.) Stage, Building.

Craddock, Justin, with Linian, Alex, *19/20.* (2020) Authors, Buffalo, NY. Perfect. Black. 194 pp. 6 x 9 in. (Information not verified by physical copy.) Cards, Coins, Close-Up, Theory.

Craggs, Douglas, *A.B.C. of Ventriloquism.* (1944) Academy of Recorded Crafts, Arts, and Sciences, Croydon, UK. Stapled with tape. Brown. 52 pp. 8.5 x 13.5 in. Ventriloquism.

Craggs, Douglas, *Masterpieces of Magic vol. 1.* (1946) Academy of Recorded Arts, Crafts, and Sciences, Croydon, UK. Cloth. Red. 77 pp. 6.75 x 8.5 in. Close-Up, Cards, Stage.

Craggs, Douglas, *Ventriloquism from A to Z.* (1969) Faber and Faber, London. Cloth. Orange. 104 pp. 5.5 x 8.25 in. Dust jacket. Ventriloquism.

Craig, Mystic, *Elusive Canary, The.* (1936) Mystic Craig. Saddle-stitch. Brown. 33 pp. 5.75 x 8.75 in. Velour fabric cover. Inscribed 1937. Signed by Mystic Craig. Stage, Vanishing Birdcage.

Crambrook, W. H. M., *Crambrook's Catalogue of Mathematical and Mechanical Puzzles, Deceptions, and Magical Curiosities.* (1843) W. H. M. Crambrook, London. 48 pp. 4.5 x 7.5 in. (Information not verified by physical copy.) Toole Stott no. 190. Catalog.

Crambrook, W. H. M., *Crambrook's Catalogue of Magical Curiosities and Deceptions.* (1991) Collectors Workshop, Washington D.C. Folder. Gray. 48 pp. 8.75 x 11.25 in. Saddle-stitch beige-cover reprint of 1843 catalog inside outer cover. #1 of 300. Catalog reprint, History.

Cramer, Stuart, *Germain the Wizard.* Deluxe edition. (2002) The Miracle Factory, Seattle. Leather. Black. 624 pp. 8.25 x 10.25 in. Dust jacket. In box with ribbon tie, hand-painted signature sheet, poem with rose petals, CD. Signed by Katlyn Breene, Stuart Cramer, Todd Karr, Teller,. #1 of 100. History, Biography, Stage, Close-Up.

Cramer, Stuart, *Germain the Wizard.* (2002) The Miracle Factory, Seattle. Cloth. Black. 624 pp. 8.25 x 10.25 in. Dust jacket. History, Biography, Stage, Close-Up.

Cramer, Stuart, *Germain the Wizard and His Legerdemain.* (1966) Buffum Publishing Co., Goleta, CA. Cloth. Dark blue. 152 pp. 5.5 x 8.5 in. Signed by Stuart Cramer. History, Biography, Stage, Close-Up.

Cramer, Stuart, *Germain the Wizard and His Legerdemain.* (1966) Buffum Publishing Co., Goleta, CA. Casebound. Blue. 152 pp. 5.5 x 8.5 in. History, Biography, Stage, Close-Up.

Cramer, Stuart, *Germain the Wizard and His Legerdemain.* (1966) Buffum Publishing Co., Goleta, CA. Perfect. Blue. 152 pp. 5.5 x 8.5 in. Signed by Stuart Cramer. History, Biography, Stage, Close-Up.

Cramer, Stuart (as S. Phones Cramer), *Golden Stream, The.* (1978) Mr. Meriweather and Co., Vermilion, OH. Saddle-stitch. Yellow. 32 pp. 5.5 x 8.5 in. Humor, Scatological.

Cramer, Stuart, *Mr. Meriweather's Book of Magic Tricks You Can Do.* (1963) Author, Cleveland Hts., OH. Saddle-stitch. White. 16 pp. 3.5 x 9 in. Beginner, Premium.

Cramer, Stuart, *Secrets of Karl Germain, The.* (1962) Mr. Meriweather and Co., Cleveland Hts., OH. Perfect. Red. 70 pp. 5.5 x 8.5 in. Signed by Stuart Cramer. History, Biography, Stage.

Crandall, Clarke "The Senator" (See also Marshall, Jay), *Bartender Dice Routine.* (1959) Edward O. Drane, Chicago. Saddle-stitch. Blue. 4 pp. 8.5 x 11 in. Dice stacking.

Crandall, Clarke "The Senator," *Best of "Senator" Crandall.* (1969) Abbott Magic Co., Colon, MI. Saddle-stitch. White. 108 pp. 8.5 x 11 in. Foreword by Robert Lund. Humor, Biography, Columns.

Crandall, Clarke "The Senator," *Entertaining with Magic: A Lecture.* (1952) Author, Chicago. Stapled. White. 14 pp. 8.5 x 11 in. (Information not verified by physical copy.) Lecture notes. Close-Up.

Crandall, Clarke "The Senator," *How to Stack Dice for Fun and No $!* (1973) Author, Hollywood, CA. Saddle-stitch. White. 16 pp. 5.5 x 8.5 in. Dice stacking.

Crandall, Clarke "The Senator," *It's Not Magic.* (1948) Author, Chicago. Stapled. White. 5 pp. 8.5 x 11 in. Mimeographed. (Information not verified by physical copy.) Cards.

Crandall, Clarke "The Senator," *Meet the Senator.* (c. 1980) Magic Inc., Chicago. Saddle-stitch. Orange. 15 pp. 5.5 x 8.5 in. Comedy, Stage.

Crandall, Clarke "The Senator," *Ment-a-Maze.* (1957) Author, Chicago. Stapled. White. 6 pp. 8.5 x 11 in. Mimeographed. Includes cards. Cards, Mentalism.

Crandall, Clarke "The Senator," *One Hundred Percent All American Ball Assembly.* (c. 1959) Author, Chicago. Stapled. White. 2 pp. 8.5 x 11 in. Mimeographed. (Information not verified by physical copy.) Balls, Comedy.

Crandall, Clarke "The Senator," *Senator Crandall's Duck Deck Routine.* (1962) Magic Inc., Chicago. Saddle-stitch. White, blue. 9 pp. 5.5 x 8.5 in. Essay by Frances Marshall: "Anatomy of a Trick." Comedy, Stage.

Crandall, Clarke "The Senator," *Senator Returns, The.* (1959) Author, Chicago. Stapled. Yellow. 16 pp. 8.5 x 11 in. Comedy.

Crandall, Clarke "The Senator," *"X" Salted Shaker, The.* (1957) Author, Chicago. Single page. Yellow. 2 pp. 8.5 x 11 in. Mimeographed. Routine for Robert Haskell's effect. Stage, Salt effects.

Crasson, Sara J., *Own Your Magic.* (2019) Author, Studio City, CA. Perfect. Black. 132 pp. 6.75 x 9.5 in. (Measurements and other information have been recorded as accurately as possible.) Business, Legal.

Craven, Tom (See also Gordon, Paul; Quine, John), *20th Annual Battle of the Magicians Lecture.* (2011) Author, Kent, OH. Comb. 18 pp. 8.5 x 11 in. (Information not verified by physical copy.) Lecture notes. Cards, Close-Up, Stage.

Craven, Tom, *24th Annual Hall of Fame of Famous Unknown Magicians and Clowns Convention Lecture Notes.* (n.d.) Author, Kent, OH. Comb. 15 pp. 8.5 x 11 in. (Information not verified by physical copy.) Lecture notes. Cards, Close-Up, Stage.

Craven, Tom, *2010 SCAM Lecture Notes, The.* (2010) Author, Kent, OH. Comb. 13 pp. 8.5 x 11 in. (Information not verified by physical copy.) Lecture notes. Cards, Close-Up, Stage.

Craven, Tom, *Another Special Lecture of Ring no. 2.* (n.d.) Author, Kent, OH. Comb. 44 pp. 8.5 x 11 in. (Information not verified by physical copy.) Lecture notes. Cards, Close-Up, Stage.

Craven, Tom, *Atlanta Lecture, The.* (n.d.) Author, Kent, OH. Comb. 14 pp. 8.5 x 11 in. (Information not verified by physical copy.) Lecture notes. Cards, Close-Up, Stage.

Craven, Tom, *Bag o' Tricks Lecture, A.* (n.d.) Author, Kent, OH. Comb. 15 pp. 8.5 x 11 in. (Information not verified by physical copy.) Lecture notes. Cards, Close-Up, Stage.

Craven, Tom, *Close-Up Stand-Up Mental Lecture, A.* (2008) Author, Kent, OH. Comb. 14 pp. 8.5 x 11 in. (Information not verified by physical copy.) Lecture notes. Cards, Close-Up, Stage, Mentalism.

Craven, Tom, *FABulous Lecture for the FAB Convention, A.* (2012) Author, Kent, OH. Comb. White. 10 pp. 8.5 x 11 in. (Information not verified by physical copy.) Cards, Close-Up.

Craven, Tom, *Farewell Lecture Tour, The.* (2017) Author, Kent, OH. Comb. Orange. 8.5 x 11 in. (Information not verified by physical copy.) Lecture notes. Cards, Close-Up, Stage.

Craven, Tom, *Fort Walton Beach Lecture, The.* (2013) Author, Kent, OH. Comb. 12 pp. 8.5 x 11 in. (Information not verified by physical copy.) Lecture notes. Cards, Close-Up, Stage.

Craven, Tom, *Fun Things to Do in Lakeland.* (n.d.) Author, Kent, OH. Comb. 14 pp. 8.5 x 11 in. (Information not verified by physical copy.) Lecture notes. Cards, Close-Up, Stage.

Craven, Tom, *H. H. Lecture (Hilton Head Low Country Magicians), The.* (n.d.) Author, Kent, OH. Comb. 13 pp. 8.5 x 11 in. (Information not verified by physical copy.) Lecture notes. Cards, Close-Up, Stage.

Craven, Tom, *Hat Full of Stuff, A.* (1998) Author, Kent, OH. Comb. Green. 20 pp. 8.5 x 11 in. Lecture notes. Cards, Mentalism, Stage.

Craven, Tom, *Instruction Cards, The.* (1992) Author, Kent, OH. Saddle-stitch. Yellow. 4 pp. 5.5 x 8.5 in. (Information not verified by physical copy. Bibliographical details are as accurate as possible.) Cards.

Craven, Tom, *Lecture for a Special Club: Ring 2.* (1981) Author, Kent, OH. Stapled. White. 8 pp. 8.5 x 11 in. (Information not verified by physical copy.) Lecture notes. Cards, Close-Up, Stage.

Craven, Tom, *Lecture Series no. 9.* (n.d.) Author, Kent, OH. Comb. 20 pp. 8.5 x 11 in. (Information not verified by physical copy.) Lecture notes. Cards, Close-Up, Stage.

Craven, Tom, *Magic You Can Do.* (1992) Author, Kent, OH. Comb. Blue. 24 pp. 8.5 x 11 in. Lecture notes. Cards, Mentalism, Stage.

Craven, Tom, *Marietta Lecture, The.* (2010) Author, Kent, OH. Comb. 16 pp. 8.5 x 11 in. (Information not verified by physical copy.) Lecture notes. Cards, Close-Up, Stage.

Craven, Tom, *Michigan Magic Day Lecture, The.* (2015) Author, Kent, OH. Comb. 10 pp. 8.5 x 11 in. (Information not verified by physical copy.) Lecture notes. Cards, Close-Up, Stage.

Craven, Tom, *My (Almost) 50 Years in Magic.* (2011) Author, Kent, OH. Casebound. Gray. 190 pp. 8.5 x 11 in. Cards, Biography.

Craven, Tom, *My First.* (1978) Author, Kent, OH. Stapled. White. 16 pp. 8.5 x 11 in. (Information not verified by physical copy.) Lecture notes. Cards, Close-Up, Stage.

Craven, Tom, *NEMCON Lecture, The.* (2008) Author, Kent, OH. Comb. 11 pp. 8.5 x 11 in. (Information not verified by physical copy.) Lecture notes. Cards, Close-Up, Stage.

Craven, Tom, *New Lecture for All Skill Levels of Magicians, A.* (n.d.) Author, Kent, OH. Comb. 10 pp. 8.5 x 11 in. (Information not verified by physical copy.) Lecture notes. Cards, Close-Up, Stage.

Craven, Tom, *New Twists on Old Tricks.* (2005) Author, Kent, OH. Comb. Beige. 18 pp. 8.5 x 11 in. Lecture notes. Cards, Mentalism, Stage.

Craven, Tom, *Pallbearers Review Lecture.* (1981) Author, Auburndale, FL. Comb. Black, white. 22 pp. 8.5 x 11 in. Lecture notes. Cards, Close-Up, Stage.

Craven, Tom, with Gordon, Paul, *Something Old, Something New, Something Borrowed, Something for You.* (2007) Author, Kent, OH. Perfect. White. 114 pp. 6 x 9 in. Lecture notes. Cards, Mentalism, Stage.

Craven, Tom, *T.I.P.S.: Tom in Print Somewhere.* (c. 1990) Author, Kent, OH. Comb. Gray. 42 pp. 5.5 x 8.5 in. (Measurements and other information have been recorded as accurately as possible.) Cards.

Craven, Tom, *Tom Craven's 16th Card Book.* (1982) Author, Kent, OH. Comb. White. 25 pp. 8.5 x 11 in. (Information not verified by physical copy.) Cards.

Craven, Tom, *Tom Craven's Mini Lecture.* (n.d.) Author, Kent, OH. Comb. 8 pp. 8.5 x 11 in. (Information not verified by physical copy.) Lecture notes. Cards, Close-Up, Stage.

Craven, Tom, *Trade Show Lecture, A.* (1984) Author, Kent, OH. Comb. White. 13 pp. 8.5 x 11 in. Lecture notes. Trade shows.

Craven, Tom, *Untitled Lecture Notes.* (n.d.) Author, Kent, OH. Comb. 7 pp. 8.5 x 11 in. (Information not verified by physical copy.) Lecture notes. Cards, Close-Up, Stage.

Cravens, M. N., *Lecture on Close-Up Magic.* (1967) Author, Albuquerque, NM. Stapled. White. 6 pp. 8.5 x 11 in. (Information not verified by physical copy.) Lecture notes. Close-Up.

Craver, Nowlin (See also Evans, Eric), *Nowlin Craver Sells Out: A Conventional Dove Lecture.* (2002) Author, Austin, TX. Stapled. Pink. 25 pp. 8.5 x 11 in. (Information not verified by physical copy.) Lecture notes. Doves, Stage.

Crayford, Charles (See also Roberts, Charles), *50 Best Conjuring Tricks, The.* (1924) Foulsham, London. Perfect. Yellow. 63 pp. 4.75 x 7.25 in. Yellow. Dust jacket. Beginner.

Crayford, Charles, *50 Best Conjuring Tricks, The.* (1924) Foulsham, London. Perfect. Beige. 63 pp. 4.75 x 7.25 in. Vignettes. Beginner.

Crayford, Charles, *A.B.C. of Conjuring.* (c. 1925) Drane's, London. Cloth. Red. 72 pp. 4.25 x 5.5 in. In Copperfield collection. Close-Up, Stage.

Crayford, Charles, *Magical Deceptions.* (1946) Mitre Publishing Co., London. Saddle-stitch. Red. 40 pp. 5 x 7.25 in. Beginner.

Crayford, Charles, *New and Original Conjuring Tricks.* (1926) Austin Rogers and Co., London. Perfect. Beige. 64 pp. 4.75 x 7 in. Beginner, General.

Crayford, Charles, *New and Original Conjuring Tricks.* (1926) Austin Rogers and Co., London. Perfect. Yellow. 64 pp. 4.75 x 7 in. Beginner, General.

Creasey, Scott, *Escape: An In-Depth Look at the Underwater Handcuff Escape.* (2014) Author, UK. Stapled. White. 50 pp. 8.5 x 11 in. (Information not verified by physical copy.) Escapes, Handcuffs.

Creasey, Scott, *Escaping the Restraints of Reality.* (2004) Author, UK. Saddle-stitch. White. 50 pp. 8.5 x 11 in. (Information not verified by physical copy.) Lecture notes. Close-Up, Stage, Mentalism.

Creasey, Scott, *Mental(Magic)ism.* (2008) Author, UK. Clip. White. 48 pp. 8.25 x 11.75 in. (Information not verified by physical copy.) Mentalism.

Cremer, W. H., Jr. (ed.), *Hanky Panky.* (1872) John Camden Hotten, London. Cloth. Green. 328 pp. 4.75 x 7.5 in. Color Robert-Houdin frontispiece. Tissue over frontispiece. Toole Stott 193. Beginner.

Cremer, W. H., Jr. (ed.), *Hanky Panky.* (1874) John Grant, Edinburgh. Cloth. Yellow. 328 pp. 5.25 x 7.5 in. Robert-Houdin frontispiece. Tissue over frontispiece. Toole Stott no. 1016. Beginner, Stunts, Cards, Close-Up.

Cremer, W. H., Jr. (ed.), *Hanky Panky.* (1902) Chatto and Windus, London. Cloth. Red. 328 pp. 5.25 x 7.75 in. Robert-Houdin frontispiece. Beginner, Stunts, Cards, Close-Up.

Cremer, W. H., Jr. (ed.), *Magic No Mystery.* (1875) Chatto and Windus, London. Cloth. 328 pp. 5.25 x 7.75 in. Toole Stott no. 1017. (Information not verified by physical copy.) Beginner.

Cremer, W. H., Jr. (ed.), *Magic No Mystery.* (1876) Chatto and Windus, London. Cloth. Tan. 333 pp. 5 x 7.25 in. Toole Stott no. 195. Beginner.

Cremer, W. H., Jr. (ed.), *Magic No Mystery.* (c. 1900) John Grant, Edinburgh. Cloth. Red. 333 pp. 5 x 7.5 in. Beginner.

Cristall, Leslie, *My 25 Years in Magic.* (1966) Author, Eastbourne, UK. Saddle-stitch. Blue. 26 pp. 7.5 x 9.75 in. Signed by Leslie Cristal. #251. Stage.

Crockett, Jeremy, *Crockett Calling.* (c. 1977) Supreme Magic, Bideford, UK. Saddle-stitch. White, green. 17 pp. 8 x 10 in. (Information not verified by physical copy.) Close-Up, Stage.

Crockwell, Colin, *Business of Children's Entertainment, The.* (1990) Author, Exeter, UK. Comb. Red. 50 pp. 8.25 x 11.75 in. (Information not verified by physical copy.) Children's magic, Business.

Crone, Tom, *Misdirection for Close-Up Magicians.* (1999) Author, Minneapolis. Stapled with tape. Yellow. 67 pp. 8.5 x 11 in. Theory, Misdirection, Close-Up.

Cros, Daniel, *Close-Up Magic of Daniel Cros, The.* (1983) Author, Las Vegas. Saddle-stitch. White. 16 pp. 5.5 x 8.5 in. Effect with Paul Harris. Signed by Daniel Cros. Close-Up, Coins, Three Shell Game.

Cros, Daniel, *Daniel's Seahorse.* (1983) Author, Las Vegas. Saddle-stitch. White. 8 pp. 5.5 x 8.5 in. (Measurements and other information have been recorded as accurately as possible.) Thread, Close-Up.

Cros, Daniel, *Magic by Request.* (1980) Author, Las Vegas. Stapled. 13 pp. 8.5 x 11 in. (Information not verified by physical copy.) Coins, Close-Up, Three Shell Game.

Cros, Daniel, *Super Twilight.* (1983) Author, Las Vegas. Saddle-stitch. White. 8 pp. 5.5 x 8.5 in. Signed by Daniel Cros. Coins.

Crosbie, Tom, *Just Be Croz.* (2013) Author, UK. Perfect. Black. 200 pp. 6 x 9 in. (Information not verified by physical copy.) Cards, Coins, Close-Up.

Croskery, Bob Forsythe, *Magic Profit Primer, The.* (1987) Author, Toledo, OH. Clip. White. 141 pp. 5.5 x 8.5 in. (Information not verified by physical copy.) Business, Promotion.

Cross, Pat, *Magic Circus Party.* (1992) Author, UK. Comb. White. 30 pp. 8.5 x 11 in. (Information not verified by physical copy.) Children's magic, Games.

Crosthwaite, Roger (See Marlo, Edward; Vincent, Michael), *Arcadia.* (1999) Cairn Press, Norwich, UK. Cloth. Black. 198 pp. 6.25 x 9.25 in. Dust jacket. Cards.

Crosthwaite, Roger, with Higham, Justin, *Card Notes: Lecture Notes 1.* (1982) Martin Breese, London. Saddle-stitch. Yellow. 50 pp. 8.25 x 12 in. Cards.

Crosthwaite, Roger, with Lees, Walt, *Commercial Card Magic of Roger Crosthwaite, The.* (1981) Walt Lees, London. Saddle-stitch. White. 47 pp. 8 x 10 in. Cards.

Crosthwaite, Roger, *Foundations 1.* (c. 1980) Martin Breese, London. Stapled. White. 13 pp. 8.25 x 11.75 in. (Information not verified by physical copy. Bibliographical details are as accurate as possible.) Cards, False shuffles, Counts.

Crosthwaite, Roger, *Goodliffe Memorial Lecture, The.* (1998) Natzler Enterprises, Worthing, UK. Saddle-stitch. White. 30 pp. 5.5 x 8.5 in. (Information not verified by physical copy.) Lecture notes. Cards.

Crosthwaite, Roger, *Lecture Notes 2.* (1982) Author, UK. Comb. White. 49 pp. 8.25 x 11.75 in. (Information not verified by physical copy.) Lecture notes. Cards.

Crosthwaite, Roger, *Mindboggler.* (1982) Eaton Magic Graphics, Derby, UK. Folded. White. 5 pp. 8.25 x 11.75 in. Signed by Roger Crosthwaite. Cards.

Crosthwaite, Roger, *Nine by Northwest.* (2000) Natzler Enterprises, London. 13 pp. (Information not verified by physical copy.) Cards.

Crosthwaite, Roger, *Roger's Real Gone Aces.* (2000) Chazpro, Eugene, OR. Saddle-stitch. Gray. 36 pp. 5.25 x 8.5 in. Cards.

Crosthwaite, Roger, with Higham, Justin, *Roger's Thesaurus.* (1994) L & L Publishing, Tahoma, CA. Cloth. Maroon. 234 pp. 8.5 x 11 in. Dust jacket. Cards.

Crosthwaite, Roger, *Saga of the 21 Card Trick, The.* (2001) Author, UK. Stapled. 16 pp. (Information not verified by physical copy.) Cards.

Crosthwaite, Roger, *Six Tricks.* (2003) Magick Enterprises, Sheffield, UK. Saddle-stitch. Red. 19 pp. 5.75 x 8.25 in. Cards.

Crosthwaite, Roger, *Tribute to Farelli.* (c. 2005) Natzler Enterprises, London. Saddle-stitch. White. 34 pp. 5.75 x 8.25 in. (Information not verified by physical copy.) Cards, Close-Up, Biography, History.

Croucher, Donald, *Magic by Miller.* (2015) Author, London, KY. Casebound. Blue. 266 pp. 8.75 x 11.25 in. Dust jacket. With Miller business card. Signed by Douglas Crowther, Clarence S. Miller. #159 of 195. History, Apparatus, Building.

Crouter, Fred, *Advanced Psychic Readings: Monograph no. 3.* (2002) Author, Omaha. Stapled. White. 33 pp. 8.5 x 11 in. (Information not verified by physical copy.) Mentalism.

Crouter, Fred, *Inner Secrets of Cold Reading: Monograph no. 2, The.* (2002) Author, Omaha. Stapled. White. 23 pp. 8.5 x 11 in. (Information not verified by physical copy.) Mentalism, Cold reading.

Crow, Bran, *Seeing Thread.* (2022) Orion Magic Productions, Athens, Greece. Saddle-stitch. Black. 52 pp. 5.5 x 8.5 in. (Information not verified by physical copy.) Mentalism.

Crow, Raymonde, *As the Crow Flies.* (2003) Author, Nampa, ID. Comb. White. 99 pp. 8.5 x 11 in. (Information not verified by physical copy.) Close-Up, Stage.

Crow, Raymonde, *Bird's Eye, The.* (2007) Author, Nampa, ID. Comb. White. 68 pp. 8.5 x 11 in. (Information not verified by physical copy.) Cards, Close-Up.

Crow, Raymonde, *Powerful Magic.* (c. 2007) Author, Nampa, ID. Coil. White. 68 pp. 8.5 x 11 in. (Information not verified by physical copy.) Cards, Close-Up.

Crowe, Jay, *Game: The Most Perfect Mind Readings in History, The.* (2008) Author, Los Angeles. Saddle-stitch. Black. 24 pp. 5.5 x 8.5 in. (Information not verified by physical copy.) Mentalism.

Crowe, Jay, *Ultimate Secrets Revealed.* (2021) Enigmagia, Los Angeles. Saddle-stitch. Black. 37 pp. 5.5 x 8.5 in. Close-Up, Stage.

Crowe, Raymond, *Crowe Feats: Foot Notes.* (2000) Author, South Australia. Stapled. 10 pp. 8.25 x 11.75 in. (Information not verified by physical copy.) Lecture notes. Billiard balls, Dancing Cane, Zombie.

Crowe, Raymond, *Crowe Feats no. 2.* (1995) Author, South Australia. Stapled. 8 pp. 8.25 x 11.75 in. (Information not verified by physical copy.) Lecture notes. Stage.

Crowe, Raymond, *Crowe's Feats: A Lecture of Tricky Stuff.* (1991) Author, South Australia. Stapled. 9 pp. 8.25 x 11.75 in. (Information not verified by physical copy.) Lecture notes. Stage.

Crowe, Raymond, *Hand Shadows.* (2000) Author, South Australia. Saddle-stitch. Black. 16 pp. 5.75 x 8.25 in. Signed by Raymond Crowe. Shadowgraphy.

Crowe, Raymond, *Wonderful World of Hand Shadows, A.* (2007) The Miracle Factory, Los Angeles. Saddle-stitch. Black. 24 pp. 5.5 x 7 in. Shadowgraphy.

Crowl, Tom, *Magic of the Renaissance.* (1996) Author, Westminster, MD. Comb. 23 pp. 8.5 x 11 in. (Information not verified by physical copy.) Stage, Fairs.

Cruikshank, George, *Discovery Concerning Ghosts: With a Rap at the "Spirit-Rappers."* (1894) Routledge, London. Saddle-stitch. Beige. 60 pp. 6.25 x 9.75 in. In Copperfield collection. Spiritualism, Exposés, Davenport Brothers.

Crush, Peter, *Folding Coin Secrets.* (1981) Author, Ilford, UK. Saddle-stitch. Beige. 32 pp. 5.75 x 8.25 in. (Measurements and other information have been recorded as accurately as possible.) Coins, Folding coins.

Cuesta, Manolo, *Dai Vernon: Análisis Estadístico de Sus Libros, Juegos, Efectos y Técnicas.* (1997) Author, Madrid. Stapled. 9 pp. Spanish Escorial event publication. (Information not verified by physical copy.) Cards.

Culliton, Patrick, *Houdini Unlocked Book One: The Tao of Houdini.* (1997) Kieran Press, Los Angeles. Cloth. Orange. 399 pp. 8.5 x 11 in. Limited to 250 copies. (Information not verified by physical copy.) Houdini, Biography, History.

Culliton, Patrick, *Houdini Unlocked Book Two: The Tao of Houdini.* (1997) Kieran Press, Los Angeles. Cloth. Orange. 397 pp. 8.5 x 11 in. Limited to 250 copies. (Information not verified by physical copy.) Houdini, Biography, History.

Culliton, Patrick, with Williams, T. L., *Houdini's Strange Tales.* (1992) Kieran Press, Los Angeles. Perfect. Black. 96 pp. 8.5 x 11 in. Houdini, Fiction.

Culpitt, Frederic, *Laughter and Legerdemain.* (1928) George Johnson, London. Perfect. Beige. 72 pp. 4.25 x 6.5 in. Stage, Comedy.

Cumberland, Stuart, *People I Have Read.* (1905) C. Arthur Pearson Ltd., London. Cloth. Green. Cover text: Gold; 192 pp. 5 x 7.25 in. (Information not verified by physical copy.) Biography, Mentalism, Psychic.

Cumberland, Stuart, *People I Have Read.* (1905) C. Arthur Pearson Ltd., London. Boards. Yellow. 192 pp. 4.75 x 7.25 in. (Information not verified by physical copy.) Biography, Mentalism, Psychic.

Cumberland, Stuart, *Spiritualism: The Inside Truth.* (1919) Odhams Ltd., London. Cloth. Red. 157 pp. 4.5 x 6.75 in. Spiritualism, History.

Cumberland, Stuart, *That Other World.* (1918) Grant Richards, London. Cloth. 253 pp. 6 x 9 in. Occult, Mediums.

Cumberland, Stuart, *Thought Reader's Thoughts, A.* (1888) Sampson, Low, Marston, Searle, and Rivington, London. Cloth. Blue. 325 pp. 5.75 x 8 in. (Information not verified by physical copy.) Biography, Mentalism.

Cummings, Walter E., *Billiard Balls: Manipulation, Routine, and Sleights.* (1980) Author, Utica, NY. Saddle-stitch. Yellow, green. 25 pp. 8.5 x 11 in. Text in blue. (Information not verified by physical copy.) Billiard balls, Manipulation.

Cummings, Walter E., *Cummings' Crash Lecture Notes.* (n.d.) Author, Utica, NY. Saddle-stitch. White. 9 pp. 8.5 x 11 in. Foreword by Laurant. Lecture notes. Manipulation, Cards, Stage.

Cummins, Kent, *Comedy Magic.* (1985) Author, Austin, TX. Stapled. Yellow. 6 pp. 8.5 x 11 in. (Information not verified by physical copy.) Lecture notes. Comedy, Jokes.

Cummins, Kent, *Ethics in Magic.* (1997) Author, Austin, TX. Comb. Gray. 53 pp. 8.5 x 11 in. Gray section dividers. Legal, Ethics.

Cummins, Kent, *Marketing for Magicians.* (1993) Author, Austin, TX. Coil. 30 pp. 8.5 x 11 in. (Information not verified by physical copy.) Lecture notes. Business, Marketing, Promotion.

Cummins, Kent, *Marketing Magic.* (2017) Author, Austin, TX. Perfect. Red. 120 pp. 6 x 9 in. (Information not verified by physical copy.) Business, Marketing, Promotion.

Cummins, Kent, *Pricing for Magicians.* (1993) Author, Austin, TX. Coil. 30 pp. 8.5 x 11 in. (Information not verified by physical copy.) Lecture notes. Business, Marketing, Promotion.

Cummins, Kent, *Publicity for Magicians.* (1993) Author, Austin, TX. Coil. 30 pp. 8.5 x 11 in. (Information not verified by physical copy.) Lecture notes. Business, Marketing, Promotion.

Cummins, Kent, *Self-Eating Watermelon, The.* (1996) Author, Austin, TX. Comb. Red. 34 pp. 8.5 x 11 in. (Information not verified by physical copy.) Lecture notes. Business, Marketing, Promotion.

Cummins, Kent, *Tricks of the Trade: 50 Years of Magic.* (2003) Author, Austin, TX. Comb. White. 132 pp. 8.5 x 11 in. Includes DVD. (Information not verified by physical copy.) Biography, Close-Up, Stage.

Cummins, Paul W. (See also Conn, Doug), *Acme Card Magic Workshop.* (2004) FASDIU Enterprises, Jacksonville, FL. Comb. White. 39 pp. 8.5 x 11 in. Lecture notes. Cards.

Cummins, Paul W., *FASDIU: From a Shuffled Deck in Use part 1.* (1996) Author, Jacksonville, FL. Comb. Maroon. 42 pp. 8.5 x 11 in. Dated July 1996. Signed by Paul W. Cummins. Cards.

Cummins, Paul W., *FASDIU: From a Shuffled Deck in Use part 2.* (1996) Author, Jacksonville, FL. Comb. Dark blue. 36 pp. 8.5 x 11 in. Dated July 1996. Cards.

Cummins, Paul W., *FASDIU: From a Shuffled Deck in Use parts 1 and 2.* Fourth revision. (1999) Author, Jacksonville, FL. Comb. Red. 72 pp. 8.5 x 11 in. Two parts comb-bound in red cover. Cards.

Cummins, Paul W., with Eason, Doc, *Fusillade: A Treatise on the Multiple Selection Routine.* (2000) FASDIU Press, Jacksonville, FL. Saddle-stitch. White. 75 pp. 8.5 x 11 in. Cards, Bar magic.

Cummins, Paul W., *Souvenir.* (2000) FASDIU Press, Jacksonville, FL. Stapled. 24 pp. 8.5 x 11 in. (Information not verified by physical copy.) Cards.

Curry, Paul, *Color Changing Deck, The.* (1978) Author, Phoenicia, NY. Stapled with paper cover. Yellow. 3 pp. 6 x 9 in. Includes cards in triangular pocket. Cards.

Curry, Paul, *Dirty Tricks.* (1976) Author, Phoenicia, NY. Loose pages. White. 5 pp. 8.5 x 11 in. (Measurements and other information have been recorded as accurately as possible.) Cards.

Curry, Paul, *Magician's Magic.* (1965) Franklin Watts Inc., New York. Cloth. Black. 269 pp. 6 x 9.25 in. Dust jacket. Lecture notes. Beginner, Cards, History.

Curry, Paul, *Multiple Thought Power.* (1976) Author, Phoenicia, NY. Loose pages. White. 3 pp. 8.5 x 11 in. (Measurements and other information have been recorded as accurately as possible.) Cards.

Curry, Paul, *Never in a Lifetime.* (1975) Author, Phoenicia, NY. Stapled with paper cover. White. 4 pp. 5.5 x 8.5 in. Red seal on side. Cards, Out of This World.

Curry, Paul, *Out of This World.* (1942) Author, Phoenicia, NY. Loose pages. White. 2 pp. 8.5 x 14 in. With Ed Mishell-art envelope. (Measurements and other information have been recorded as accurately as possible.) Cards.

Curry, Paul, *Out of This World – and Beyond.* (1975) Author, Phoenicia, NY. Saddle-stitch. Yellow. 20 pp. 8.5 x 11 in. Cards.

Curry, Paul, *Paul Curry Presents.* (1974) Author, Phoenicia, NY. Perfect. Red. 108 pp. 8.5 x 11 in. (Measurements and other information have been recorded as accurately as possible.) Cards.

Curry, Paul, *Power of Concentration.* (c. 1995) Louis Tannen, New York. Stapled. White. 8 pp. 5.25 x 8.25 in. (Measurements and other information have been recorded as accurately as possible.) Cards.

Curry, Paul, *Power of Thought, The.* (1947) Author, Phoenicia, NY. Stapled with paper cover. Beige. 5 pp. 5.5 x 8.5 in. Cards.

Curry, Paul, *Probability Zero.* (1944) Author, Phoenicia, NY. Stapled. Blue. 5 pp. 5.5 x 8.5 in. Mimeographed. (Measurements and other information have been recorded as accurately as possible.) Cards.

Curry, Paul, *Simply Miraculous.* (1977) Author, Phoenicia, NY. Stapled with paper cover. Green. 2 pp. 5.5 x 9 in. Includes cards in triangular pocket. Cards.

Curry, Paul, *Sliding Knot and Restoration Supreme, The.* Second printing. (1979) Author, Phoenicia, NY. Saddle-stitch. White. 6 pp. 8.5 x 11 in. With original mailing envelope. Rope.

Curry, Paul, *Something Borrowed, Something New.* (1941) Author, Phoenicia, NY. Stapled with tape. Yellow. 35 pp. 6.5 x 8.5 in. Introduction by Oscar Weigle. Cards.

Curry, Paul, *Spaced Out.* (1978) Author, Phoenicia, NY. Stapled with paper cover. Blue. 2 pp. 8.5 x 11 in. (Measurements and other information have been recorded as accurately as possible.) Cards.

Curry, Paul, *Special Effects.* (1977) Author, Phoenicia, NY. Perfect. Yellow. 92 pp. 8.5 x 11 in. (Measurements and other information have been recorded as accurately as possible.) Cards.

Curry, Paul, *Stamp-It.* (1939) Holden's Magic Studio, New York. Single page. White. 8.5 x 11 in. (Measurements and other information have been recorded as accurately as possible.) Cards.

Curry, Paul, *Worlds Beyond.* Second printing. (2009) Hermetic Press, Seattle. Cloth. Green. 382 pp. 7.25 x 10.25 in. Dust jacket. Cards.

Curtin, Kevin E., *Lecture Notes for I.B.M. Lecture 11/9/92.* (1992) Author, Las Vegas. Comb. Yellow. 15 pp. 8.5 x 11 in. Lecture notes. Coins, Close-Up.

Curzon, Paul, with McOwan, Peter W., *Conjuring with Computation.* (2023) World Scientific, Hackensack, N.J. Perfect. Black. 386 pp. 6 x 9 in. Computing, Mathematical.

Curzon, Roger, *Blood on the Tricks.* (1995) Author, UK. Coil. Red. 58 pp. 8.25 x 11.75 in. (Information not verified by physical copy. Bibliographical details are as accurate as possible.) Cards.

Curzon, Roger, *Dark Matters: The Arcane Thaumaturgy of Doctor Jacob Tordoff.* (2017) Author, UK. Cloth. Black. 138 pp. 6 x 9 in. Dust jacket. (Information not verified by physical copy. Bibliographical details are as accurate as possible.) Mentalism, Bizarre magick.

Curzon, Roger, *Roger Curzon's Lecture Notes.* (1980) Author, UK. Saddle-stitch. Blue. 16 pp. 8.25 x 11.75 in. (Information not verified by physical copy.) Lecture notes. Cards.

Curzon, Roger, *Roger Curzon's Lecture Notes.* (1980) Author, UK. Saddle-stitch. Yellow. 16 pp. 8.25 x 11.75 in. (Information not verified by physical copy.) Lecture notes. Cards.

Curzon, Roger, *Roger Curzon's Lecture Notes: Guild of Magicians Nottingham.* (1989) Author, UK. Wire binding. Beige. 17 pp. 8.25 x 11.75 in. (Information not verified by physical copy.) Lecture notes. Cards.

Curzon, Roger, *Sublimations.* (2006) Magick Enterprises, Sheffield, UK. Casebound. Beige. 149 pp. 8.25 x 11.75 in. (Information not verified by physical copy.) With DVD. Mentalism, Bizarre magick.

Curzon, Roger, *Theomancy.* (2008) Magick Enterprises, Sheffield, UK. Perfect. Blue. 8.25 x 11.75 in. (Information not verified by physical copy.) With DVD. Mentalism, Bizarre magick.

Cuthbert, Jim, *What Has Scotland Ever Done for Magic?* (2009) Author, Scotland. Wire binding. White. 112 pp. 8.5 x 11 in. Scottish magic bibliography. (Information not verified by physical copy.) Bibliography, History.

Cuthbertson, Rod, *How to Make a Magician of Yourself.* (1970) Australian Society of Magicians, Melbourne. Perfect. Yellow. 202 pp. 5.5 x 8.5 in. (Information not verified by physical copy.) Showmanship, History, Magic clubs.

Cyprian, Father, *10: You Are Magic no. 10.* (1983) Author, Garrison, NY. Stapled. Orange. 29 pp. 8.5 x 11 in. Lecture notes. Cards, Close-Up.

Cyprian, Father, *Adventure in E.S.D.: Extra-Sensory Deception, An.* (1967) Author, Garrison, NY. Stapled. 14 pp. 8.5 x 11 in. (Information not verified by physical copy.) Cards.

Cyprian, Father, *Bottom Collectors, The.* (1975) Louis Tannen, New York. Saddle-stitch. White. 52 pp. 8.5 x 11 in. Cards.

Cyprian, Father, with Garcia, Frank, *Bullseye.* New Stars of Magic vol. 1, no. 11. (1978) Louis Tannen, New York. Saddle-stitch. White. 16 pp. 8.5 x 11 in. Cards, Portable hole effects.

Cyprian, Father, *Charisma-Elan-Panache: You are Magic no. 10-1/2.* (1986) Author, Garrison, NY. Stapled. Tan. 26 pp. 8.5 x 11 in. Lecture notes. Cards.

Cyprian, Father, *Door to Door Card Sharp: You are Magic no. 7.* (1979) Author, Garrison, NY. Stapled. Blue. 10 pp. 8.5 x 11 in. Cards.

Cyprian, Father, with Garcia, Frank, *Elegant Card Magic of Father Cyprian, The.* (1980) Author, New York. Saddle-stitch. Red. 80 pp. 5.5 x 8.5 in. Cards.

Cyprian, Father, *Evening of Extra-Sensory Deception, An.* (c. 1986) Author, Garrison, NY. Stapled. Tan. 8.5 x 11 in. (Information not verified by physical copy.) Lecture notes. Cards, Close-Up.

Cyprian, Father, with Fulves, Karl, *Fr. Cyprian on the Hofzinser Card Problem.* (1978) Author, Teaneck, NJ. Saddle-stitch. Tan. 24 pp. 6.75 x 8.5 in. Cards.

Cyprian, Father, with Fulves, Karl, *Fr. Cyprian's T.V. Card Rise.* (1982) Author, Teaneck, NJ. Saddle-stitch. Yellow. 40 pp. 6.75 x 8.5 in. Effects by Fr. Cyprian, Rick Johnsson, Gene Maze, Tom Gagnon. Cards, Rising Cards.

Cyprian, Father, *Illusions of Power: Magic in the Movies.* (1986) Author, Garrison, NY. Comb. Beige. 46 pp. 8.5 x 11 in. History, Cinema.

Cyprian, Father, *Lecture Notes no. 11.* (1989) Author, Garrison, NY. Stapled. White. 35 pp. 8.5 x 11 in. (Information not verified by physical copy.) Lecture notes. Cards, Close-Up.

Cyprian, Father, *Lecture Without a Name, The.* (n.d.) Author, Garrison, NY. Stapled. Brown. 16 pp. 8.5 x 11 in. Brown pages. Lecture notes. Cards.

Cyprian, Father, *Let 'Er Rip, Father Cyp: Close-Up Lecture Notes.* (1980) Author, Garrison, NY. Stapled. White. 6 pp. 8.5 x 11 in. (Information not verified by physical copy.) Lecture notes. Cards, Close-Up.

Cyprian, Father, *Light Touch: Lecture no. 12, The.* (1990) Author, Garrison, NY. Stapled. Tan. 16 pp. 8.5 x 11 in. (Information not verified by physical copy.) Lecture notes. Cards, Close-Up.

Cyprian, Father, *Nostalgia Torn and Restored Card.* (1983) Author, Garrison, NY. Saddle-stitch. Blue. 8 pp. 5.5 x 8.5 in. (Information not verified by physical copy.) Cards, Torn and Restored Card.

Cyprian, Father, *R & R: Rings and Routining Lecture.* (c. 1980) Author, Garrison, NY. Stapled. White. 2 pp. 8.5 x 11 in. Lecture notes. Linking Rings, Showmanship.

Cyprian, Father, *Stand Up Close: You are Magic no. 8.* (1980) Author. Saddle-stitch. Beige. 29 pp. 5.5 x 8.5 in. Cards, Close-Up.

Cyprian, Father, *You Are Magic: Close-Up Lecture Notes.* (c. 1980) Author, Garrison, NY. Stapled. White. 16 pp. 8.5 x 11 in. Signed by Fr. Cyprian. Lecture notes. Cards, Close-Up.

Cyprian, Father, *You Are Magic: Lecture Notes.* (1978) Author, Garrison, NY. Stapled. White. 20 pp. 8.5 x 11 in. Lecture notes. Cards, Dice.

Cyprian, Father, *You Are Magic no. 6: Featuring "A Holey Trick."* (1977) Author, Garrison, NY. Stapled. White. 14 pp. 8.5 x 11 in. (Information not verified by physical copy.) Lecture notes. Cards, Close-Up.

Cyprian, Father, *You Are Magic: Stand Up Close: You are Magic no. 8.* (1980) Author, Garrison, NY. Saddle-stitch. White. 29 pp. 5.5 x 8.5 in. Lecture notes. Cards, Close-Up.

Dacri, Steve, *Commercial Close-Up: Lecture no. 1.* (1973) Imperial Products, Worcester, MA. Stapled. White. 23 pp. 8.5 x 11 in. (Information not verified by physical copy.) Cards, Close-Up.

Dacri, Steve, *Commercial Close-Up: Lecture no. 1.* Second edition. (1979) Author, N. Hollywood, CA. Saddle-stitch. Beige. 18 pp. 8.5 x 11 in. Cards, Close-Up.

Dacri, Steve, *Fooling People.* (1984) Author, N. Hollywood, CA. Comb. Blue. 142 pp. 8.5 x 11 in. (Information not verified by physical copy.) Beginner.

Dacri, Steve, *Magic Secrets: The Magic Circle Lecture.* (2001) Author, Los Angeles. Stapled. White, blue, red, yellow. 32 pp. 8.5 x 11 in. (Information not verified by physical copy.) Lecture notes. Close-Up, Stage.

Dacri, Steve, *Master Routines, The.* (2002) Imperial Products, Worcester, MA. Comb. White. 26 pp. 8.5 x 11 in. (Information not verified by physical copy.) Cards, Close-Up, Stage.

Dacri, Steve, with Lorraine, Sid, *Penny Fantasy.* (1975) Imperial Products, Worcester, MA. Stapled. Blue. 8 pp. 8.5 x 11 in. Folded. Includes "Tricks with Micro-Penny" by Lorraine. Cards, Comedy.

Dacri, Steve, *Tricks with Gag Card.* Second printing. (1974) Imperial Products, Worcester, MA. Saddle-stitch. Blue. 7 pp. 5.5 x 8.5 in. Cards, Comedy.

Daggers, Ben, with Katsuragawa, Shimpei, *Campanella: Etudes and Sonatas with Playing Cards, La.* (2022) Impossible Co., Osaka, Japan. Cloth. Red. Cover text: Gold; 158 pp. (Information not verified by physical copy.) Cards.

Daggers, Ben, *Elusive Illusive, The.* (2022) Vanishing Inc., Rancho Cordova, CA. Cloth. Blue. 218 pp. 6.25 x 8.25 in. Cards, Close-Up.

Daily, George L., Jr., *Periodicals of U. F. Grant, The.* (1976) Cauldron Press, Glen Burnie, MD. Folded. White. 4 pp. 7 x 8.5 in. Supplement to "The Magic Cauldron," no. 59, December 1975. Bibliography, Magazines.

Dakota, Andrew, *S.F.B. 2000: The Ultimate Animated Bill Trick.* (1999) Proof Positive Magic, South Lyon, MI. Saddle-stitch. Purple. 24 pp. 8.5 x 11 in. With gimmicked bill in envelope. Bills, Thread, Close-Up.

Dalal, Sam (See also Morris, Bud), *42 Amazing Tricks and Stunts with Rope.* (2002) Electro Fun, Calcutta. Saddle-stitch. Green. 47 pp. 5.5 x 8.5 in. Rope, Stunts.

Dalal, Sam, *All You Wanted to Know About Change Bags and 101 Tricks You Can Do with Them.* (2002) Electro Fun, Calcutta. Saddle-stitch. Color. 48 pp. 5.5 x 8.25 in. Change Bag, Stage.

Dalal, Sam, *Cabaret Capers vol. 1.* (c. 1972) Ramdev and Sons, Calcutta. Saddle-stitch. White. 19 pp. 4.75 x 7.25 in. Mentalism, Stage.

Dalal, Sam, *Chinese Linking Rings.* (2002) Funtime Innovations, Calcutta. Saddle-stitch. Pink. 32 pp. 5.5 x 4 in. Bound oblong. Linking Rings, Manual.

Dalal, Sam, *Chinese Linking Rings.* (2002) Funtime Innovations, Calcutta. Saddle-stitch. Red. 32 pp. 4 x 5.25 in. Linking Rings, Manual.

Dalal, Sam, *Chop Cup and Chop Cup Combo Tutor.* (1993) Electro Fun, Calcutta. Clip. Gray. 20 pp. 5.5 x 8 in. (Information not verified by physical copy.) Chop Cup, Cups and Balls, Close-Up, Beginner.

Dalal, Sam, *Chop Cup and Chop Cup Combo Tutor.* (2006) Funtime Innovations, Calcutta. Saddle-stitch. Purple. 24 pp. 4 x 5.25 in. Chop Cup, Cups and Balls, Close-Up, Beginner.

Dalal, Sam, *Getting the Best of Your Himber Wallet.* (2003) Author, Calcutta. Saddle-stitch. Yellow. 16 pp. 5.75 x 8 in. Wallets, Close-Up.

Dalal, Sam, *Indian Cups and Balls Primer.* (c. 1972) Ramdev and Sons, Calcutta. Saddle-stitch. White. 15 pp. 9.75 x 7.25 in. Bound oblong. Cups and Balls, Indian magic.

Dalal, Sam, *Incredible Instant Insanity Prediction.* (1992) Electro Fun, Calcutta. Saddle-stitch. Beige. 18 pp. 5.5 x 8.5 in. Mentalism.

Dalal, Sam, *Magic with a Marked Deck.* (1972) Author, Calcutta. Stapled with tape. Tan. 13 pp. 8.5 x 11 in. Cards, Marked deck.

Dalal, Sam, *Magic with a Marked Deck.* Second edition. (1976) Micky Hades, Calgary, Canada. Comb. Yellow. 14 pp. 8.5 x 11 in. Cards, Marked deck.

Dalal, Sam, *Magic with a Marked Deck.* Third edition. (1992) Author, Calcutta. Stapled with tape. Beige. 15 pp. 8.5 x 11 in. (Information not verified by physical copy.) Cards, Marked deck.

Dalal, Sam, *Magic with an E.S.P. Deck.* (1977) Accent Products, Calcutta. Saddle-stitch. Brown. 32 pp. 5.5 x 8.5 in. Includes envelope with E.S.P. cards. Mentalism, E.S.P. cards.

Dalal, Sam, *Magic with an E.S.P. Deck.* (1992) Author, Calcutta. Stapled with tape. Red. 15 pp. 8.25 x 11.75 in. Mentalism, E.S.P. cards.

Dalal, Sam, *Magic with an E.S.P. Deck.* (1995) Author, Calcutta. Saddle-stitch. White. 22 pp. 8.5 x 11 in. Mentalism, E.S.P. cards.

Dalal, Sam, *Magic by Apparatus.* (1996) Learner's Press, New Delhi, India. Perfect. Red, green. 96 pp. 5 x 7.75 in. (Information not verified by physical copy.) Beginner.

Dalal, Sam, *Magic by Misdirection.* (1996) Learner's Press, New Delhi, India. Perfect. Red, blue. 96 pp. 5 x 7.75 in. (Information not verified by physical copy.) Beginner.

Dalal, Sam, *Magic with Ease.* (1996) Learner's Press, New Delhi, India. Perfect. Red, yellow. 95 pp. 5 x 7.75 in. Beginner.

Dalal, Sam, *Magic with Thimbles.* (2004) Funtime Innovations, Calcutta. Saddle-stitch. Purple. 16 pp. 5.5 x 4 in. Bound oblong. Thimbles.

Dalal, Sam, *Menta Color.* (1974) Author, Calcutta. Stapled. White. 5 pp. 8.25 x 11.75 in. (Information not verified by physical copy.) Mentalism.

Dalal, Sam, *Patterns of Perfection.* (1993) Author, Calcutta. Comb. Beige. 28 pp. 8.25 x 11.75 in. (Measurements and other information have been recorded as accurately as possible.) Magic squares.

Dalal, Sam, *Psychic Dominoes.* (2004) Funtime Innovations, Calcutta. Saddle-stitch. Olive. 16 pp. 5.75 x 8.25 in. Dominoes, Mentalism.

Dalal, Sam, *Rabbit Production Puppet.* (2003) Electro Fun, Calcutta. Saddle-stitch. Blue. 14 pp. 5.75 x 8.25 in. No author noted. Children's magic, Puppetry, Manual.

Dalal, Sam, *Secrets of Magic, The.* (2001) New Dawn, New Delhi, India. Perfect. Blue. 184 pp. 4.5 x 6 in. (Measurements and other information have been recorded as accurately as possible.) Beginner.

Dalal, Sam, *Sound Mentalism.* (1971) Supreme Magic, Bideford, UK. Comb. Black. 16 pp. 7.75 x 9.75 in. Rounded corners. Mentalism, Sounds.

Dalal, Sam, *Subtle Ways of Using the Swami Gimmick.* (1990) Supreme Magic, Bideford, UK. Saddle-stitch. Yellow. 24 pp. 5.75 x 8.25 in. Mentalism, Nail writer.

Dalal, Sam, *Swami Gimmick, The.* (1990) Sam Dalal, Calcutta. Saddle-stitch. Green. 32 pp. 5.5 x 8.5 in. Mentalism, Nail writer.

Dalal, Sam, *Swami Mantra.* (1997) Kaufman and Company, Washington D.C. Casebound. Brown. Multiple sections. 8.5 x 11 in. Magazine, Mentalism.

Dalal, Sam, *Swami vol. 1.* (1971) Ramdev and Sons, Calcutta. Cloth. Blue. 48 pp. 8.75 x 11.5 in. Magazine, Mentalism.

Dalal, Sam, *Swami vol. 2.* (1973) Ramdev and Sons, Calcutta. Cloth. Black. 48 pp. 8.5 x 10.75 in. Magazine, Mentalism.

Dalal, Sam, *Uses for the Giant E.S.P. Deck.* (1988) Author, Calcutta. Saddle-stitch. White, red. 15 pp. 5.75 x 8.25 in. Mentalism, E.S.P. cards.

Dalal, Sam, *X-Ray Eyes.* (1985) Author, Calcutta. Stapled with paper cover. Beige. 11 pp. 8.25 x 10.75 in. Mentalism, Blindfolds.

Dale, Will, *General Magic.* (1937) Author, Glasgow. Stapled with paper cover. Orange. 13 pp. 8.5 x 11 in. Mimeographed. Cards, Stage.

Daley, Dr. Jacob (See also Scarne, John), *Cards Up the Sleeve.* Stars of Magic series 7, no. 1. (1950) Stars of Magic, Inc., New York. Saddle-stitch. White. 8 pp. 8.5 x 11 in. Cards.

Daley, Dr. Jacob, *Cavorting Aces, The.* Stars of Magic series 7, no. 3. (1950) Stars of Magic, Inc., New York. Folded. White. 4 pp. 8.5 x 11 in. Cards.

Daley, Dr. Jacob, *Itinerant Pasteboards, The.* Stars of Magic series 7, no. 2. (1950) Stars of Magic, Inc., New York. Folded. White. 4 pp. 8.5 x 11 in. Cards.

Daley, Dr. Jacob, with Csuri, Frank F. (ed.), *Jacob Daley's Notebooks.* (1975) Karl Fulves, Teaneck, NJ. Comb. Yellow. 194 pp. 8.5 x 11 in. (Information not verified by physical copy.) Cards.

Daly, Steve, *Daycare Dollars.* (2011) Author. Folder. White. 8.5 x 11 in. (Information not verified by physical copy.) Children's magic, Promotion.

Dameon (Hal Meyers), *Back 2 Back.* (1993) Magic Source, Glen Ridge, NJ. Saddle-stitch. Purple. 19 pp. 5.5 x 8.5 in. (Information not verified by physical copy.) Showmanship, Doves, Manipulation.

Dameon (Hal Meyers), *Dameon.* (c. 1993) Author, Glen Ridge, NJ. Clip. Green. 14 pp. 8.5 x 11 in. (Information not verified by physical copy.) Lecture notes. Doves, Stage, Showmanship.

Damon, Dwight, *Balloonatrix.* (1962) La Wain's House of Magic, Monmouth, IL. Saddle-stitch. White. 48 pp. 5.5 x 8.5 in. Balloons, Stage.

Damon, Dwight, *Balloonatrix.* Second edition. (1980) La Wain's House of Magic, Monmouth, IL. Saddle-stitch. Blue. 48 pp. 5.5 x 8.5 in. Balloons, Stage.

Damon, Dwight, *How to Make Money with Magic.* Third edition. (1977) Author, Merrimack, NJ. Saddle-stitch. Yellow. 20 pp. 5.5 x 8.5 in. Business, Promotion.

Damon, Dwight, *Lecture Notes of Dwight Damon.* (1975) Author, Merrimack, NJ. Saddle-stitch. Beige. 20 pp. 5.5 x 8.5 in. Signed by Dwight Damon. Lecture notes. Business, Promotion.

Damon, Dwight, *TV's Original Balloonatic.* (1958) La Wain's House of Magic, Monmouth, IL. Saddle-stitch. White, black. 21 pp. 6 x 7.5 in. Illustration sheet in back cover. Balloons.

Danata, Mike, *Floating Golden Stick.* (1985) Martin Breese, London. Comb. White, purple. 17 pp. 8.25 x 11.75 in. Thread, Floating effects, Stage.

Dancey, Charlie, *Every Trick in the Book.* (2023) Overlook Duckworth, New York. Casebound. White. 702 pp. 5.25 x 8 in. Beginner, Cards, Mentalism, Children's book.

Dancy, Luke, *On the Floor.* (2005) Author, Charlotte, NC. Saddle-stitch. Beige. 20 pp. 8.5 x 11 in. (Information not verified by physical copy. Bibliographical details are as accurate as possible.) Cards, Close-Up.

Daniel, Noel (ed.), *Livre de la Magie, La.* (2018) Taschen, Köln, Germany. Cloth. Beige. 527 pp. 7 x 9.75 in. Translation of "Magic: 1400s to 1950s." Color half-sleeve. History. French.

Daniel, Noel (ed.), *Magic: 1400s to 1950s.* (2009) Taschen, Köln, Germany. Cloth. Black. 637 pp. 11.5 x 17.5 in. Dust jacket. Oversized first edition with ribbon bookmark. Introduction by Ricky Jay. Text by Mike Caveney and Jim Steinmeyer. History.

Daniel, Noel (ed.), *Magic: 1400s to 1950s.* (2013) Taschen, Köln, Germany. Cloth. Black. 535 pp. 10 x 13 in. Slipcase. Dust jacket. History.

Daniel, Noel (ed.), *Magic: 1400s to 1950s.* (2013) Taschen, Köln, Germany. Cloth. Black. 535 pp. 10 x 13 in. Slipcase. Dust jacket. Spanish, Italian, Portuguese edition. History. Spanish, Italian, Portuguese.

Daniel, Noel (ed.), *Magic: 1400s to 1950s.* (2015) Taschen, Köln, Germany. Casebound. Color. 373 pp. 8.75 x 13.5 in. History.

Daniel, Noel (ed.), *Magic Book, The.* (2018) Taschen, Köln, Germany. Cloth. Beige. 527 pp. 7 x 9.75 in. Retitled edition of "Magic: 1400s to 1950s." Color half-sleeve. History.

Daniel, Noel (ed.), *Magic Book, The.* Deluxe edition. (2018) Taschen, Köln, Germany. Leather. Black, red, gold. 527 pp. 7 x 9.75 in. Translation of "Magic: 1400s to 1950s." Ribbon bookmark, gilt edges. History.

Daniels, Joseph, *Conjurations.* (2015) Author, Lincolnton, NC. Perfect. Black. 44 pp. 5.5 x 8.5 in. (Information not verified by physical copy. Bibliographical details are as accurate as possible.) Close-Up, Stage.

Daniels, Paul, *50 Easy Card Tricks.* (1993) Author, Middlesex. Perfect. Color. 57 pp. 6 x 8.25 in. (Measurements and other information have been recorded as accurately as possible.) Beginner, Cards.

Daniels, Paul, *77 Popular Card Games and Tricks.* (1985) Fanfare Books, London. Perfect. Color. 128 pp. 5.25 x 7.75 in. Beginner, Cards.

Daniels, Paul, *Adult Magic.* (1989) Michael O'Mara Books, London. Cloth. Black. 160 pp. 7.75 x 10.75 in. Dust jacket. Beginner.

Daniels, Paul, *Everybody's Magic.* (2004) Magic Tricks UK, London. Perfect. Color. 120 pp. 6 x 8.25 in. Charity book with Wayne Dobson and others. Beginner.

Daniels, Paul, *How to Make Money by Magic.* (2019) Meir Yedid Magic, Rego Park, NY. Perfect. Gray. 351 pp. 8.5 x 11 in. Business, Promotion.

Daniels, Paul, *More Magic.* (1981) Piccolo Books, London. Perfect. Color. 75 pp. 4.25 x 7 in. (Measurements and other information have been recorded as accurately as possible.) Beginner.

Daniels, Paul, *My Magic Life: The Autobiography.* (2016) John Blake, London. Perfect. Color. 423 pp. 5 x 7.75 in. Retitled from Under No Illusion. Biography.

Daniels, Paul, *Paul Daniels Magic Annual, The.* (1978) World International, Manchester, UK. Boards. Color. 61 pp. 7.75 x 10.5 in. Beginner.

Daniels, Paul, *Paul Daniels Magic Annual, The.* (1982) World International, Manchester, UK. Boards. Color. 61 pp. 7.75 x 10.5 in. Beginner.

Daniels, Paul, *Paul Daniels' Magic Book.* (1980) Piccolo Books, London. Perfect. Orange. 125 pp. 4.25 x 7 in. Beginner.

Daniels, Paul, *Paul Daniels' Magic Journey.* (1983) Piccolo Books and British Airways, London. Perfect. Blue. 48 pp. 7 x 9.75 in. History.

Daniels, Paul, *Under No Illusion: My Autobiography.* (2000) Blake Publishing, London. Cloth. Black. 313 pp. 6.25 x 9.5 in. Dust jacket. Biography.

Daniels, Paul, with Murray, Barry, *You Don't Have to Be a Kid to Pull a Rabbit Out of a Hat.* (1997) Barricade Books, New York. Perfect. Orange. 159 pp. 7.5 x 10.25 in. Beginner.

Dante, *50 Mysteries.* (1936) Author, Copenhagen. Saddle-stitch. Color. 32 pp. 9 x 12.25 in. (Measurements and other information have been recorded as accurately as possible.) Beginner, Souvenir book.

Dante, *50 Mysteries.* Catellan edition. (1936) Author, Copenhagen. Saddle-stitch. Color. 24 pp. 9 x 12.25 in. Beginner, Souvenir book. Catellan.

Dante, *50 Mysteries.* Chinese edition. (1936) Author, Copenhagen. Saddle-stitch. Color. 24 pp. 9 x 12.25 in. Bound on right; Chinese characters. Beginner, Souvenir book. Chinese.

Dante, *50 Tricks for Everybody.* (1936) Author, Copenhagen. Saddle-stitch. Red, black, white. 24 pp. 9 x 12 in. Beginner, Souvenir book.

Dante, *Dante 35th Year Trunk Book.* (1941) Author, Prague. Saddle-stitch. Green. 62 pp. 12.5 x 19 in. Promotional book printed in Czechoslovakia when Dante could not bring his show's earnings out of the country. Biography, Souvenir book, Promotion.

Dante, *Libro Magico di Dante.* Catellan edition. (n.d.) Author, Copenhagen. Saddle-stitch. Color. 10 pp. 9.25 x 12.25 in. Beginner, Souvenir book. Catellan.

Dante, *Tricks for Everybody.* New edition. (1938) Author, Copenhagen. Saddle-stitch. Color. 24 pp. 9.25 x 12.25 in. Beginner, Souvenir book.

DaOrtiz, Dani, *Card in Bottle.* (2018) Grupokaps, Spain. Saddle-stitch. Black. 36 pp. 5.75 x 8.25 in. (Information not verified by physical copy. Bibliographical details are as accurate as possible.) Cards, Bottles.

DaOrtiz, Dani, *Five.* (2022) Grupokaps, Spain. Cloth. Brown. 66 pp. 6.5 x 6.5 in. With card with Internet information. Cards.

DaOrtiz, Dani, *Freedom of Expression.* (2021) Grupokaps, Spain. Casebound. Black. 152 pp. 7 x 8.75 in. Cards, Forcing, Psychological.

DaOrtiz, Dani, with Engblom, Christian, *Lecture Notes.* (2007) Authors, Spain. Coil. White. 37 pp. 8.5 x 11 in. (Information not verified by physical copy.) Lecture notes. Cards.

DaOrtiz, Dani, *Playing.* (2005) Author, Spain. 30 pp. (Information not verified by physical copy. Bibliographical details are as accurate as possible.) Cards, Close-Up.

DaOrtiz, Dani, *Semi Automatic.* (2019) Vanishing Inc., Rancho Cordova, CA. Saddle-stitch. White. 19 pp. 8.25 x 8.25 in. From publisher's "Costa Rica Retreat Gift Pack." (Information not verified by physical copy.) Cards.

DaOrtiz, Dani, *Semi Automatic 2.* (2013) Author, Spain. 36 pp. (Information not verified by physical copy. Bibliographical details are as accurate as possible.) Cards.

D'Arcy, Peter, *Children's Parties a Specialty.* (1972) Goodliffe Publications, Alcester, UK. Cloth. Blue. 96 pp. 5.75 x 9 in. Dust jacket. Children's magic.

Dardant, Michael, *Bitten by a Wizard.* (2013) Author, New Orleans. Stapled. White. 61 pp. 8.5 x 11 in. (Information not verified by physical copy. Bibliographical details are as accurate as possible.) Lecture notes. Cards, Close-Up, Stage.

Dare, Sterling, *Money Menagerie.* (2004) H & R Magic Books, Humble, TX. Saddle-stitch. Beige. 48 pp. 8.5 x 11 in. Origami, Bills.

Darling, Aage, *I'll Read Your Mind.* (1953) George Armstrong, London. Cloth. Black. 56 pp. 5.5 x 8.75 in. (Measurements and other information have been recorded as accurately as possible.) Mentalism.

Darling, Aage, *Mentale Mysterier.* (1948) C. Steffensen, Copenhagen. Saddle-stitch. 42 pp. (Information not verified by physical copy.) Mentalism. Danish.

Darugh, Fred, *Magic as a Hobby.* (1974) Author, Albuquerque, NM. Saddle-stitch. Olive. 107 pp. 8.5 x 11 in. (Measurements and other information have been recorded as accurately as possible.) Stage.

Darwin, Gary, *101 Fillers.* (2009) Darwin Publications, Las Vegas. Saddle-stitch. Pink. 16 pp. 4.25 x 5.5 in. Foreword by Fielding West. Comedy, Patter.

Darwin, Gary, *101 Thumb Tip Tricks.* (1994) Geno Munari, Las Vegas. Saddle-stitch. Yellow. 24 pp. 5.5 x 8.5 in. Foreword by Blackstone. Effects by Lance Burton and others. Thumb tip, Close-Up.

Darwin, Gary, *101 Thumb Tip Tricks.* Second printing. (1995) Geno Munari, Las Vegas. Saddle-stitch. Red. 23 pp. 5.5 x 8.5 in. Foreword by Blackstone. Effects by Lance Burton and others. Thumb tip, Close-Up.

Darwin, Gary, with Munari, Geno, *101 Thumb Tip Tricks.* (2000) Houdini Magic, Las Vegas. Saddle-stitch. Black. 24 pp. 5.5 x 8.5 in. Revised edition omitting the words "Thumb Tip" from the title on the cover. Thumb tip, Close-Up.

Darwin, Gary, *201 Jokes for Card Magicians.* (1998) Author, Las Vegas. Saddle-stitch. Gold. 20 pp. 5.5 x 8.5 in. Comedy, Cards.

Darwin, Gary, *Darwin's Close-Up Miracles.* (1982) Author, Las Vegas. Saddle-stitch. Blue. 40 pp. 5.5 x 8.5 in. Signed by Gary Darwin. Close-Up.

Darwin, Gary, *Darwin's Inexpensive Illusions.* (1996) Author, Las Vegas. Saddle-stitch. Silver. 25 pp. 8.5 x 11 in. Illusions, Building.

Darwin, Gary, *Darwin's Thumb Tip Miracles.* (1981) Author, Las Vegas. Perfect. Red. 129 pp. 5.75 x 9 in. Thumb tip, Close-Up.

Darwin, Gary, *Darwin's Thumb Tip Secrets no. 1.* (1984) Author, Las Vegas. Saddle-stitch. Red. 19 pp. 8.5 x 11 in. Foreword by Reveen. Thumb tip, Close-Up.

Darwin, Gary, with Alafrez, Abdul (trans.), *Grandes Illusions Impromptues.* (1999) Académie de Magie Georges Proust, Paris. Saddle-stitch. White, red, black. 25 pp. 8.25 x 11.75 in. Translation of "Darwin's Inexpensive Illusions." Cover by James Hodges. Illusions. French.

Darwin, Gary, *Magic Autograph Poster Gallery.* (1989) Author, Las Vegas. Perfect. White. 267 pp. 8.5 x 11 in. Caricatures, Art.

Darwin, Gary, *Thumb Tip Thinking.* (1986) Author, Las Vegas. Saddle-stitch. Gold. 20 pp. 5.5 x 8.5 in. Foreword by Johnny Paul. Thumb tip, Close-Up.

Darwin, Gary, *Who Invented the Magic?* (1988) Author, Las Vegas. Saddle-stitch. Silver. 28 pp. 8.5 x 11 in. With envelope hand-addressed by Darwin. Signed by Gary Darwin, Geno Munari. #52 of 300. Reference, History.

Daryl (Martinez; See also Fleischer, Adam J.), *3 Fly III.* (1999) Author, Anaheim, CA. Saddle-stitch. Color. 14 pp. 5.5 x 8.5 in. (Information not verified by physical copy.) Coins.

Daryl, *4F XII.* (2012) Author, Auburn, CA. Saddle-stitch. Gray. 60 pp. 5.5 x 8.5 in. Lecture notes. Cards, Rope, Close-Up, Stage.

Daryl, with Minch, Stephen, *Ambitious Card Omnibus.* (1987) Author, Anaheim, CA. Cloth. Red. 140 pp. 9.25 x 7.5 in. Dust jacket. Cards, Ambitious Card.

Daryl, *Balance.* (2014) Author, Auburn, CA. Saddle-stitch. Blue. 23 pp. 8.25 x 11.75 in. (Measurements and other information have been recorded as accurately as possible.) Cards, Close-Up, Coins.

Daryl, *Bounce No-Bounce Ball Booklet, The.* (c. 1985) Author, Anaheim, CA. Saddle-stitch. Red. 12 pp. 5.5 x 8.5 in. Balls, Close-Up.

Daryl, *Bounce No-Bounce Ball Booklet, The.* (c. 1985) Author, Anaheim, CA. Saddle-stitch. Pink. 12 pp. 5.5 x 8.5 in. Balls, Close-Up.

Daryl, *Bounce No-Bounce Ball Booklet, The.* (c. 1985) Author, Anaheim, CA. Saddle-stitch. Red. 12 pp. 5.5 x 8.5 in. Different cover. Balls, Close-Up.

Daryl, *Clea-zean Mea-zagic.* (2009) Author, Auburn, CA. Saddle-stitch. Black. 63 pp. 5.5 x 8.5 in. Signed by Daryl Martinez. Cards, Close-Up, Stage, Rope.

Daryl, *Daryl Does Den Haag.* (1988) Author, Anaheim, CA. Saddle-stitch. Maroon. 28 pp. 5.5 x 8.5 in. Includes sheet of illustrations. Lecture notes. Cards, Close-Up.

Daryl, *Daryl Does Den Haag.* (1988) Author, Anaheim, CA. Saddle-stitch. Red. 28 pp. 5.5 x 8.5 in. Includes sheet of illustrations. Lecture notes. Cards, Close-Up.

Daryl, with Goldstein, Phil, *Daryl's Cardboard Chameleons.* (1981) Author, Anaheim, CA. Saddle-stitch. Beige. 6 pp. 5.5 x 8.5 in. Written and illustrated by Phil Goldstein. Signed by Daryl Martinez. Cards, Packet tricks.

Daryl, *Daryl's Psychological Assembly, or The Jolly Jumping Jokers.* (1985) Author, Anaheim, CA. Saddle-stitch. Red. 12 pp. 8.5 x 11 in. With 4 pp. Daryl catalog. Cards, Packet tricks.

Daryl, *Daryl's Rope Routine.* (1987) Author, Anaheim, CA. Folded single page. White. 40 x 48 in. Single large sheet with step-by-step photos. Rope.

Daryl, with Racherbaumer, Jon, *Double-Dazzling Triumph.* (1979) Author, Anaheim, CA. Stapled. Blue. 3 pp. 8.5 x 11 in. Cards.

Daryl, with Racherbaumer, Jon, *Double-Dazzling Triumph.* Second printing. (1982) Author, Anaheim, CA. Saddle-stitch. Purple. 4 pp. 5.5 x 8.5 in. Cards.

Daryl, with Minch, Stephen, *Elbow, Knee, and Neck.* (1990) L & L Publishing, Tahoma, CA. Folded. White. 4 pp. 5.5 x 8.5 in. Excerpt from "Spectacle" (1990), ed. by Minch. Coins, Close-Up.

Daryl, *F.F.F.F. Session 1992.* (1992) Author, Anaheim, CA. Saddle-stitch. Orange. 16 pp. 5.5 x 8.5 in. Lecture notes. Cards, Close-Up.

Daryl, *Fooler Droolers.* (2003) Author, Anaheim, CA. Saddle-stitch. Yellow. 12 pp. 8.5 x 11 in. Lecture notes. Cards, Rope.

Daryl, with Minch, Stephen, *For Your Entertainment Pleasure.* (1982) Author, Anaheim, CA. Saddle-stitch. Beige. 90 pp. 5.5 x 8.5 in. Cards, Coins.

Daryl, *For Your Entertainment Pleasure and Secrets of a Puerto Rican Gambler.* Limited deluxe edition. (2016) Vanishing Inc., Rancho Cordova, CA. Leather. Black. Multiple sections. 6.25 x 9.25 in. Slipcase. Two-volume set. Signed by Daryl Martinez. #63 of 250. Cards, Close-Up.

Daryl, *Hyper-Bent-Elation.* (2007) Author, Auburn, CA. Comb. White. 4 pp. 8.5 x 11 in. Includes cards. Cards, Topological.

Daryl, *Lecture Notes to Convention Session no. 1.* (1980) Author, Anaheim, CA. Saddle-stitch. Beige. 28 pp. 5.5 x 8.5 in. Signed by Daryl Martinez. Lecture notes. Cards, Theory.

Daryl, *Magic Lecture Notes.* (n.d.) Author, Anaheim, CA. Saddle-stitch. White. 8 pp. 5.5 x 8.5 in. Inscribed April 29, 1981. Signed by Daryl Martinez. Lecture notes. Cards, Close-Up.

Daryl, *Magic Lecture Notes.* Second printing. (1975) Author, Anaheim, CA. Stapled. Red. 8 pp. 8.5 x 11 in. Signed by Daryl Martinez. Lecture notes. Close-Up, Stage.

Daryl, *New Millennium World Tour.* (1999) Author, Anaheim, CA. Saddle-stitch. Red. 24 pp. 8.5 x 11 in. Signed by Daryl Martinez. Lecture notes. Cards, Close-Up.

Daryl, *New Millennium World Tour.* Reprint. (n.d.) Author, Anaheim, CA. Stapled. Yellow. 24 pp. 8.5 x 11 in. Lecture notes. Cards, Close-Up.

Daryl, *Out of This Hemisphere.* (1989) Author, Anaheim, CA. Saddle-stitch. Red. 10 pp. 5.5 x 8.5 in. Cards, Out of This World.

Daryl, *Out of This Hemisphere.* (1989) Author, Anaheim, CA. Saddle-stitch. Orange. 10 pp. 5.5 x 8.5 in. Cards, Out of This World.

Daryl, *Secrets of a Puerto Rican Gambler.* Second printing. (1980) Author, Anaheim, CA. Saddle-stitch. Green. 115 pp. 5.5 x 8.5 in. Cards, Coins.

Daryl, *Something for Everyone: Magic Lecture no. 2.* (1982) Author, Beverly Hills, CA. Saddle-stitch. Light blue. 14 pp. 5.5 x 8.5 in. Includes two envelopes with cards. Lecture notes. Cards.

Daryl, *Tour de France 2007.* (2007) Author, Auburn, CA. Stapled. Yellow. 20 pp. 6 x 8.25 in. With illustration sheet. Signed by Daryl Martinez. Lecture notes. Cards, Close-Up. French.

Das, B. (Bisweshar Das), *Chopper Secrets.* (2001) Electro Fun, Calcutta. Stapled with tape. 15 pp. 8 x 11.5 in. (Information not verified by physical copy.) Illusions, Cutting effects.

Das, B., *Levitation Secrets.* (1999) Electro Fun, Calcutta. Stapled with tape. Red. 18 pp. 8 x 11.5 in. Illusions, Levitations.

Das, B., *Sawing Illusion Secrets.* (2000) Electro Fun, Calcutta. Stapled with tape. Olive. 24 pp. 8 x 11.25 in. Illusions, Sawing.

Daugherty, Tom, *Addition to Nate Leipzig's Poker Deal.* (c. 1990) Secret World, Covington, KY. Comb. White. 10 pp. 8.5 x 11 in. Cards, Poker deal.

Daugherty, Tom, *Another Force.* (c. 1990) Secret World, Covington, KY. Comb. Yellow. 10 pp. (Information not verified by physical copy.) Cards, Forcing.

Daugherty, Tom, *Before the Twists.* (c. 1990) Secret World, Covington, KY. Comb. Blue. 4 pp. (Information not verified by physical copy.) Cards.

Daugherty, Tom, *Beyond Control.* (c. 1990) Secret World, Covington, KY. Comb. Blue. 4 pp. (Information not verified by physical copy.) Cards.

Daugherty, Tom, *Bingo!* (c. 1990) Secret World, Covington, KY. Comb. Yellow. 4 pp. (Information not verified by physical copy.) Cards.

Daugherty, Tom, *But Four Wrongs Do!* (c. 1990) Secret World, Covington, KY. Comb. Blue. 2 pp. (Information not verified by physical copy.) Cards.

Daugherty, Tom, *Count Subtula.* (c. 1990) Secret World, Covington, KY. Comb. Green. 3 pp. (Information not verified by physical copy.) Cards.

Daugherty, Tom, *Date with Destiny, A.* (c. 1990) Secret World, Covington, KY. Comb. Blue. 12 pp. (Information not verified by physical copy.) Mentalism.

Daugherty, Tom, *Daugherty Shuffle, The.* (c. 1990) Secret World, Covington, KY. Comb. Yellow. 9 pp. With Robert Neale's improvement. (Information not verified by physical copy.) Cards.

Daugherty, Tom, *Devastation.* (c. 1990) Secret World, Covington, KY. Comb. Blue. 7 pp. (Information not verified by physical copy.) Cards.

Daugherty, Tom, *Dice-abolical.* (c. 1990) Secret World, Covington, KY. Comb. Pink. 5 pp. (Information not verified by physical copy.) Dice, Cards, Close-Up.

Daugherty, Tom, *Double Double; My Lucky Card; Do You Believe Me?* (c. 1990) Secret World, Covington, KY. Comb. Blue. 8 pp. (Information not verified by physical copy.) Cards.

Daugherty, Tom, *Double Migration.* (c. 1990) Secret World, Covington, KY. Comb. Pink. 8 pp. (Information not verified by physical copy.) Cards.

Daugherty, Tom, *Elevator Card, The.* (c. 1990) Secret World, Covington, KY. Comb. Green. 2 pp. (Information not verified by physical copy.) Cards.

Daugherty, Tom, *F-Cards, The.* (c. 1990) Secret World, Covington, KY. Comb. Yellow. 3 pp. (Information not verified by physical copy.) Cards.

Daugherty, Tom, *Find Your Own.* (c. 1990) Secret World, Covington, KY. Comb. Yellow. 4 pp. (Information not verified by physical copy.) Cards.

Daugherty, Tom, *Folderol.* (c. 1990) Secret World, Covington, KY. Comb. Yellow. 6 pp. (Information not verified by physical copy.) Cards.

Daugherty, Tom, *Fortunate Cookie, The.* (c. 1990) Secret World, Covington, KY. Comb. Blue. 3 pp. (Information not verified by physical copy.) Cards.

Daugherty, Tom, *Future Stack, The.* (c. 1990) Secret World, Covington, KY. Comb. Yellow. 5 pp. (Information not verified by physical copy.) Cards.

Daugherty, Tom, *Gallimaufry Salmagundi.* (c. 1990) Secret World, Covington, KY. Comb. Green. 6 pp. (Information not verified by physical copy.) Cards.

Daugherty, Tom, *Gypsy Shuffle, The.* (c. 1990) Secret World, Covington, KY. Comb. Green. 3 pp. (Information not verified by physical copy.) Cards.

Daugherty, Tom, *Hartman Force, The.* (c. 1990) Secret World, Covington, KY. Comb. Yellow. 2 pp. (Information not verified by physical copy.) Cards.

Daugherty, Tom, *Heavies.* (c. 1990) Secret World, Covington, KY. Comb. Yellow. 3 pp. (Information not verified by physical copy.) Cards.

Daugherty, Tom, *Impossible.* (c. 1990) Secret World, Covington, KY. Comb. Pink. 3 pp. (Information not verified by physical copy.) Cards.

Daugherty, Tom, *Impossible II.* (c. 1990) Secret World, Covington, KY. Comb. Yellow. 2 pp. (Information not verified by physical copy.) Cards.

Daugherty, Tom, *Improbable Impression.* (c. 1990) Secret World, Covington, KY. Comb. Yellow. 3 pp. (Information not verified by physical copy.) Cards.

Daugherty, Tom, *Invisible Dice.* (c. 1990) Secret World, Covington, KY. Comb. Pink. 4 pp. (Information not verified by physical copy.) Cards.

Daugherty, Tom, *It's Lost!* (c. 1990) Secret World, Covington, KY. Comb. Yellow. 3 pp. (Information not verified by physical copy.) Cards.

Daugherty, Tom, *Judah's Wrapped Deck.* (c. 1990) Secret World, Covington, KY. Comb. Yellow. 5 pp. (Information not verified by physical copy.) Cards.

Daugherty, Tom, *Kangaroo Kard, The.* (c. 1990) Secret World, Covington, KY. Comb. Green. 3 pp. (Information not verified by physical copy.) Cards.

Daugherty, Tom, *Kings!* (c. 1990) Secret World, Covington, KY. Comb. Yellow. 3 pp. (Information not verified by physical copy.) Cards.

Daugherty, Tom, *Last Pair, The.* (c. 1990) Secret World, Covington, KY. Comb. Pink. 5 pp. (Information not verified by physical copy.) Cards.

Daugherty, Tom, *Lesson in Telepathy, A.* (c. 1990) Secret World, Covington, KY. Comb. Pink. 7 pp. (Information not verified by physical copy.) Mentalism.

Daugherty, Tom, *Lund Exception, The.* (c. 1990) Secret World, Covington, KY. Stapled. White. 3 pp. (Information not verified by physical copy.) Cards.

Daugherty, Tom, *Magillogical.* (c. 1990) Secret World, Covington, KY. Comb. Blue. 3 pp. (Information not verified by physical copy.) Cards.

Daugherty, Tom, *Martian Mix, The.* (c. 1990) Secret World, Covington, KY. Comb. Pink. 8 pp. (Information not verified by physical copy.) Cards.

Daugherty, Tom, *Matched!* (c. 1990) Secret World, Covington, KY. Comb. Yellow. 4 pp. (Information not verified by physical copy.) Cards.

Daugherty, Tom, *Mathematics Makes Magic.* (c. 1990) Secret World, Covington, KY. Comb. Yellow. 4 pp. (Information not verified by physical copy.) Cards.

Daugherty, Tom, *McDonagh Switch, The.* (c. 1990) Secret World, Covington, KY. Comb. Green. 4 pp. (Information not verified by physical copy.) Cards.

Daugherty, Tom, *Mirage; Sudden Impulse; Choice and Chance.* (c. 1990) Secret World, Covington, KY. Comb. Blue. 10 pp. (Information not verified by physical copy.) Cards.

Daugherty, Tom, *Misdirection Segue.* (c. 1990) Secret World, Covington, KY. Comb. Yellow. 4 pp. (Information not verified by physical copy.) Cards.

Daugherty, Tom, *Monthaumaturgy.* (c. 1990) Secret World, Covington, KY. Comb. Yellow. 4 pp. (Information not verified by physical copy.) Cards.

Daugherty, Tom, *More Magic with the Daugherty Shuffle: Feeling Red, Pyramid Power, That's My Ace!* (c. 1990) Secret World, Covington, KY. Comb. Green. 5 pp. (Information not verified by physical copy.) Cards.

Daugherty, Tom, *Nameless.* (c. 1990) Secret World, Covington, KY. Comb. Pink. 4 pp. (Information not verified by physical copy.) Cards.

Daugherty, Tom, *Nervous Ace, The.* (c. 1990) Secret World, Covington, KY. Comb. Green. 2 pp. (Information not verified by physical copy.) Cards.

Daugherty, Tom, *No Pairs!* (c. 1990) Secret World, Covington, KY. Comb. Pink. 10 pp. (Information not verified by physical copy.) Cards.

Daugherty, Tom, *One-Faced.* (c. 1990) Secret World, Covington, KY. Comb. Green. 3 pp. (Information not verified by physical copy.) Cards.

Daugherty, Tom, *Osmosis; Under Your Spell; The Obvious Choice.* (c. 1990) Secret World, Covington, KY. Comb. Blue. 17 pp. (Information not verified by physical copy.) Cards.

Daugherty, Tom, *Out of This Galaxy.* (c. 1990) Secret World, Covington, KY. Comb. Yellow. 4 pp. (Information not verified by physical copy.) Cards, Out of This World.

Daugherty, Tom, *Outrageous.* (c. 1990) Secret World, Covington, KY. Comb. Green. 2 pp. (Information not verified by physical copy.) Cards.

Daugherty, Tom, *Outside In.* (c. 1990) Secret World, Covington, KY. Comb. Pink. 2 pp. (Information not verified by physical copy.) Cards.

Daugherty, Tom, *Potpourri.* (c. 1990) Secret World, Covington, KY. Comb. Yellow. 8 pp. (Information not verified by physical copy.) Cards, Mentalism.

Daugherty, Tom, *Pseudo Tsunami.* (c. 1990) Secret World, Covington, KY. Comb. Yellow. 3 pp. (Information not verified by physical copy.) Cards.

Daugherty, Tom, *Quetzalcoatl.* (c. 1990) Secret World, Covington, KY. Comb. Yellow. 4 pp. (Information not verified by physical copy.) Cards.

Daugherty, Tom, *Quintimental.* (c. 1990) Secret World, Covington, KY. Comb. White. 14 pp. (Information not verified by physical copy.) Cards.

Daugherty, Tom, *Right? Wrong!* (c. 1990) Secret World, Covington, KY. Comb. Pink. 4 pp. (Information not verified by physical copy.) Cards.

Daugherty, Tom, *Rolling Revelation.* (c. 1990) Secret World, Covington, KY. Comb. Blue. 6 pp. (Information not verified by physical copy.) Cards.

Daugherty, Tom, *Sefaljia Twins, The.* (c. 1990) Secret World, Covington, KY. Comb. Yellow. 3 pp. (Information not verified by physical copy.) Spirit effects, Rope, Rings.

Daugherty, Tom, *Sens-Ace-Tional.* (c. 1990) Secret World, Covington, KY. Comb. Pink. 4 pp. (Information not verified by physical copy.) Cards.

Daugherty, Tom, *Sightless.* (c. 1990) Secret World, Covington, KY. Comb. Yellow. 3 pp. (Information not verified by physical copy.) Cards.

Daugherty, Tom, *Three Applications of the Daugherty Shuffle: Night and Day, Misdirection, Son of Psychedelic.* (c. 1990) Secret World, Covington, KY. Comb. Yellow. 13 pp. (Information not verified by physical copy.) Cards.

Daugherty, Tom, *Three Bears, The.* (c. 1990) Secret World, Covington, KY. Comb. Pink. 28 pp. (Information not verified by physical copy.) Cards.

Daugherty, Tom, *Three Proofs.* (c. 1990) Secret World, Covington, KY. Comb. Pink. 2 pp. (Information not verified by physical copy.) Cards.

Daugherty, Tom, *Topsy-Turvy Twosome.* (c. 1990) Secret World, Covington, KY. Comb. Green. 5 pp. (Information not verified by physical copy.) Cards.

Daugherty, Tom, *Total Confusion.* (c. 1990) Secret World, Covington, KY. Comb. Pink. 10 pp. (Information not verified by physical copy.) Cards.

Daugherty, Tom, *Trick Deck, The.* (c. 1990) Secret World, Covington, KY. Comb. Green. 7 pp. (Information not verified by physical copy.) Cards.

Daugherty, Tom, *Triple Whammy, Triple Migration.* (c. 1990) Secret World, Covington, KY. Comb. Yellow. 7 pp. (Information not verified by physical copy.) Cards.

Daugherty, Tom, *Un-Sandwiched!* (c. 1990) Secret World, Covington, KY. Comb. Yellow. 3 pp. (Information not verified by physical copy.) Cards.

Daugherty, Tom, *Up and Down.* (c. 1990) Secret World, Covington, KY. Comb. Green. 4 pp. (Information not verified by physical copy.) Cards.

Daugherty, Tom, *Utterly Blown Away.* (c. 1990) Secret World, Covington, KY. Comb. Pink. 7 pp. (Information not verified by physical copy.) Cards.

Daugherty, Tom, *Very Best, The.* (c. 1990) Secret World, Covington, KY. Comb. Pink. 3 pp. (Information not verified by physical copy.) Cards.

Daugherty, Tom, *Vice Versa; Switcheroo.* (c. 1990) Secret World, Covington, KY. Comb. Blue. 7 pp. (Information not verified by physical copy.) Cards.

D'Aveno (Harry Cohen), *D'Aveno's Parlour Conjurer.* (c. 1910) Cole's Book Arcade, Melbourne. Saddle-stitch. 32 pp. 5 x 7.25 in. (Information not verified by physical copy.) See McCullagh, "Under the Southern Cross." Beginner.

Davenport, Anne, with Salisse, John, *Candid View of Maskelyne's 1916-17, A.* (1995) John Davenport, Leicester, UK. Perfect. Beige. 72 pp. 8.25 x 11.25 in. History, Illusions.

Davenport, Anne, with Salisse, John, *St. George's Hall: Behind the Scenes at England's Home of Mystery.* (2001) Mike Caveney's Magic Words, Pasadena, CA. Cloth. Purple. 474 pp. 8.25 x 10.25 in. Dust jacket. Maskelyne and Devant. #30 of 1000. History, Stage.

Davenport, L., *Demon Telegraph Vol. 1 1933-1934.* (1934) L. Davenport and Co., London. Cloth. Black. Multiple sections. 5.75 x 8.75 in. Bound issues of vol. 1. Magazine.

Davenport, L., *Wonderful Mysteries of "The Hindoo Yogi" Fully Explained, The.* (c. 1934) L. Davenport and Co., London. Saddle-stitch. White. 10 pp. 5.5 x 8.5 in. Random explanations and material. Indian magic, Stage.

David, Jonathan (Chris Faria), *Now Appearing.* (1985) Author, Denver, CO. Saddle-stitch. Tan. 40 pp. 5.75 x 8.5 in. Signed by Jonathan David. Cards, Close-Up.

D'Avies, Albert M., *Up-to-Date French Card Tricks.* (1904) Mutual Book Co., Boston. Saddle-stitch. White, blue. 24 pp. 3.75 x 6 in. Cards.

D'Avies, Albert M., *Up-to-Date French Card Tricks.* (1904) Mutual Book Co., Boston. Saddle-stitch. White, black. 24 pp. 3.75 x 6 in. Cards.

D'Avies, Albert M., *Up-to-Date French Card Tricks.* (1904) McLeod and Allen, Toronto. Saddle-stitch. White, black. 24 pp. 3.75 x 6 in. Cards.

Davini, Herrmann, *Davini Catalog.* (1983) Volker Huber, Offenbach, Germany. Cloth. Purple. 32 pp. 5.75 x 8.5 in. No. 7 in Huber catalog series. #112 of 250. Catalog reprint. German.

Davis, A. Berkeley, *Miracle of the Eighties (8T's, That Is).* (1989) Author, Jackson, MS. Folder. Orange. 7 pp. 8.5 x 11 in. Pages fastened inside 9 x 11.5 in. folder. Cards, Punch marking.

Davis, A. Berkeley, *Third Sight: Simply a Miracle.* (1989) Author, Jackson, MS. Comb. White. 25 pp. 8.5 x 11 in. (Information not verified by physical copy.) Cards, Punch marking.

Davis, David, *Gambler's Luck.* (c. 1960) Supreme Magic, Bideford, UK. Loose pages. White. 3 pp. 8 x 10 in. Mimeographed. In envelope with label. Cards, Poker deal.

Davis, David, *Super Unnatural.* (1980) Supreme Magic, Bideford, UK. Loose pages. White. 3 pp. 8 x 10 in. Mimeographed. With envelope. Cards.

Davis, Eddie, *Gospel Magic Lecture Notes.* (1977) Author, Little Rock, AR. Stapled with tape. Green. 8.5 x 11 in. (Information not verified by physical copy.) Lecture notes. Gospel magic.

Davis, Hassoldt, *Child's Book of Magic.* Second printing. (1949) Greenberg, New York. Coil. Blue. 32 pp. 4.25 x 6.25 in. Contains envelopes with flat effects and mustache. Beginner, Close-Up, Stunts, Children.

Davis, J. M., *Card "Secrets."* (c. 1927) Modern Magic Publishing Co., New York. Saddle-stitch. Orange. 20 pp. 4.25 x 6 in. Red seal on side. Jack Barren's Trick and Novelty Shop label, San Francisco. Cards, Beginner.

Davis, J. M., *Card "Secrets."* (c. 1927) Modern Magic Publishing Co., New York. Saddle-stitch. Orange. 20 pp. 4.25 x 6 in. No seal. Signed by W. F. Van Zandt. Cards, Beginner.

Davis, Jimmy, *One Balloon Zoo.* (1966) Magic Inc., Chicago. Saddle-stitch. White. 32 pp. 5.5 x 8.5 in. (Measurements and other information have been recorded as accurately as possible.) Balloons.

Davis, Rick, *Totally Useless Skills.* (1991) Perigee, New York. Perfect. Blue. 122 pp. 5.5 x 8.5 in. (Measurements and other information have been recorded as accurately as possible.) Stunts.

Davis, Scott (Scott Moore-Davis), *Medium Rare.* (1992) Jim Magus, Marietta, GA. Comb. 67 pp. 8.5 x 11 in. (Information not verified by physical copy.) Séances, Spirit effects, Bizarre magick.

Davis, Scott, with Piatt, Ray, *Ray Piatt's Caper-Case Book 1.* (1988) Magic Makers, Bath, PA. Comb. Beige. 24 pp. 9 x 11 in. (Information not verified by physical copy.) Close-Up, Gimmicks, Mentalism.

Davis, Scott, with Piatt, Ray, *Ray Piatt's Caper-Case Book 2.* (1988) Magic Makers, Bath, PA. Comb. Beige. 36 pp. 9 x 11 in. (Information not verified by physical copy.) Close-Up, Gimmicks, Mentalism.

Davis, Scott, *Séance.* (1996) Kaufman and Greenberg, New York. Cloth. Black. Multiple sections. 8.5 x 11 in. Magazine, Bizarre magick.

Davis, Scott, *Television for the Mentalist.* (1988) Author, Bath, PA. Saddle-stitch. Gray. 20 pp. 5.5 x 8.5 in. (Information not verified by physical copy.) Television magic, Mentalism.

Davis, Seymour, *Lecture Notes on Apparatus Magic.* (1970) Author, Oklahoma City, OK. Stapled. White. 4 pp. 8.5 x 11 in. (Information not verified by physical copy.) Lecture notes. Stage, Apparatus.

Davis, Stan, *Using Magic to Prevent Drug Abuse.* Revised edition. (2000) SPS Publications, Eustis, FL. Saddle-stitch. White, red, black. 40 pp. 5.25 x 8.5 in. Drug education, Children's magic.

Davis, Stanley, *Tricks Presented.* (1944) George Johnson, London. Saddle-stitch. Blue. 28 pp. 5.5 x 8.5 in. Cards, Stage.

Davison, Donn, *$100 an Hour for Magicians.* First edition. (1978) Author, Atlanta. Comb. Green. 52 pp. 8.5 x 11 in. Business, Publicity, Promotion.

Davison, Donn, *$100 an Hour for Magicians.* Second edition. (1982) Micky Hades, Calgary, Canada. Comb. Yellow. 50 pp. 8.5 x 11 in. Business, Publicity, Promotion.

Davison, Donn, *$800 Magic Day, The.* (1987) Author, Atlanta. Comb. Yellow, red. 17 pp. 8.5 x 11 in. Business, Publicity, Promotion.

Davison, Donn, *Campground Ca$h from Conjuring.* (1982) Author, Atlanta. Stapled with tape. Yellow. 11 pp. 8.5 x 11 in. Business, Publicity, Promotion, Camp shows.

Davison, Donn, *Conjuring for Ca$h.* (1977) Author, Atlanta. Cloth. Black. Cover text: Gold; 248 pp. 8.5 x 11 in. Business, Publicity, Promotion.

Davison, Donn, *Conjuring for Ca$h.* (1977) Micky Hades, Calgary, Canada. Perfect. Beige. 248 pp. 8.5 x 11 in. Includes audiocassette. Business, Publicity, Promotion.

Davison, Donn, *Dynamic Publicity for Magicians.* (1979) Author, Atlanta. Stapled. Yellow. 9 pp. 8.5 x 11 in. Business, Publicity, Promotion.

Davison, Donn, *How I Make $1000 from a School Show!* (1982) Author, Atlanta. Comb. Red. 17 pp. 8.5 x 11 in. Children's magic, School shows, Business, Promotion.

Davison, Donn, *Konjure to Kids for Ka$h.* (1979) Author, Atlanta. Comb. Pink. 20 pp. 8.5 x 11 in. Children's magic, Business, Promotion.

Davison, Donn, *Make $1,000 a Night Entertaining Adults in Movie Theatres.* (1979) Author, Atlanta. Comb. Pink. 24 pp. 8.5 x 11 in. Business, Publicity, Promotion.

Davison, Donn, *Mega Bucks Mental Promotion.* (1983) Author, Atlanta. Stapled. Pink. 24 pp. 8.5 x 11 in. Business, Promotion, Publicity, Mentalism.

Davison, Donn, *Mining Gold Magically.* (1978) Author, Atlanta. Comb. Yellow. 34 pp. 8.5 x 11 in. Business, Promotion, Publicity.

Davison, Donn, *Monster Manual.* (1980) Micky Hades, Calgary, Canada. Comb. 20 pp. 8.5 x 11 in. (Information not verified by physical copy.) Children's magic, Business, Promotion.

Davison, Donn, with Wise, Harry W., *Rip Taylor, Eat Your Heart Out.* (1982) Author, Atlanta. Stapled with tape. Pink. 4 pp. 8.5 x 11 in. Comedy, Gags.

Davison, R. Mark, *Beach House Card Tricks.* (2020) Class LLC, Pawleys Island, SC. Cloth. Maroon. 126 pp. 6.25 x 9.25 in. Cards.

Davison, R. Mark, *Beach House Card Tricks III.* (2022) Class LLC, Pawleys Island, SC. Cloth. Black. 199 pp. 6.25 x 9.25 in. Cards.

Davison, R. Mark, *More Beach House Card Tricks.* (2020) Class LLC, Pawleys Island, SC. Cloth. Blue. 158 pp. 6.25 x 9.25 in. Cards.

Davison, Robert, *Mysteria: A Book of Modern Magical Marvels for Magicians.* (1904) Author, Bolton, UK. Saddle-stitch. Olive. 12 pp. 5 x 7.25 in. Effect by Charles Medrington. Beginner.

Dawes, Edwin A. (See also Berlinski, Allen; Clarke, Sidney W.), *Barrister in the Circle, The.* (1983) Magic Circle, London. Cloth. Beige. 123 pp. 6 x 8.5 in. Signed by Edwin A. Dawes. #131 of 500. History, Biography.

Dawes, Edwin A., *Charles Bertram: The Court Conjurer.* (1997) Kaufman and Co., Washington D.C. Cloth. Black. 360 pp. 8.5 x 11 in. Dust jacket. Signed by Edwin A. Dawes. History, Biography.

Dawes, Edwin A., with Bailey, Michael, *Circle Without End: The Magic Circle 1905-2005.* (2005) Magic Circle, London. Perfect. Blue. 190 pp. 8.25 x 11.75 in. Magic Circle centennial. History, Clubs.

Dawes, Edwin A., with Short, Stephen, *David Nixon: Entertainer with the Magic Touch.* (2009) Northern Arts Publications, Anlaby, UK. Cloth. Blue. 276 pp. 8.5 x 11.25 in. Dust jacket. Inscribed to Charles and Regina Reynolds. Signed by Edwin A. Dawes. Biography, History.

Dawes, Edwin A., *Doctor Ormonde.* (2016) Dawes Partnership, Anlaby, UK. Saddle-stitch. White. 30 pp. 8.25 x 11.75 in. Limited to 100 copies. History, Biography.

Dawes, Edwin A., *Glimpses of Goldston.* (2000) Dane Hill Publications, Anlaby, UK. Saddle-stitch. Yellow. 12 pp. 7 x 8.5 in. Signed by Edwin A. Dawes. #11 of 250. History, Biography.

Dawes, Edwin A., *Great Illusionists, The.* (1979) Chartwell Books, Secaucus, NJ. Cloth. Black. 216 pp. 7.75 x 10 in. Dust jacket. Signed by Edwin A. Dawes. History, Biography.

Dawes, Edwin A., *Great Lyle, The.* (2005) Mike Caveney's Magic Words, Pasadena, CA. Cloth. Blue. 298 pp. 8.25 x 10.5 in. Dust jacket. Signed by Edwin A. Dawes. #23 of 1000. History, Biography.

Dawes, Edwin A., *Harry Leat: Magic Dealer and Crusader.* (2003) Dane Hill Publications, Anlaby, UK. Saddle-stitch. Blue. 28 pp. 5.75 x 8.25 in. Signed by Edwin A. Dawes. History, Biography.

Dawes, Edwin A., *Henry Dean: Eighteenth-Century Best-Selling Magic Author/Compiler.* (2012) Author, Anlaby, UK. Saddle-stitch. Beige. 28 pp. 5.5 x 8.5 in. Signed by Edwin A. Dawes. #44 of 150. History, Biography.

Dawes, Edwin A., *Henry J. Robin: Expositor of Science and Magic.* (1990) Abracadabra Press, Balboa Island, CA. Perfect. White. 57 pp. 6.25 x 8.75 in. With prospectus letter. Signed by Edwin A. Dawes. #173 of 230. History, Biography.

Dawes, Edwin A., *Isaac Fawkes: Fame and Fable.* (1979) Author, Anlaby, UK. Saddle-stitch. Blue. 8 pp. 7.25 x 9.75 in. Signed by Edwin A. Dawes. #103 of 200. History, Biography.

Dawes, Edwin A., with Dawes, Michael E., *John Henry Anderson: The Great Wizard of the North and His Magical Family.* (2014) Conjuring Arts, New York. Cloth. Blue. 303 pp. 6.75 x 10 in. Fold-out family tree. Limited to 400 copies. Biography, History.

Dawes, Edwin A., *Magic of England, The.* (1994) Author, London. Perfect. Olive. 78 pp. 8.5 x 11 in. History, Apparatus, Collecting.

Dawes, Edwin A., with Setterington, Arthur, *Making Magic.* (1986) Multimedia Books, London. Casebound. Black. 190 pp. 9 x 12 in. Dust jacket. Signed by Edwin A. Dawes. History.

Dawes, Edwin A., with Setterington, Arthur, *Making Magic.* (1992) Prion, London. Casebound. Black. 190 pp. 9 x 11.75 in. Dust jacket. History.

Dawes, Edwin A., *Opening the Door of Mystery.* (1979) Author, Anlaby, UK. Saddle-stitch. Beige. 19 pp. 5.75 x 8.25 in. With letter from author. Signed by Edwin A. Dawes. History, Bibliography, Exhibit catalog.

Dawes, Edwin A., *"Out of the Rich Cabinet."* (2004) Dane Hill Publications, Anlaby, UK. Saddle-stitch. Blue. 25 pp. 5.75 x 8.25 in. Signed by Edwin A. Dawes. Lecture notes. History, Biography.

Dawes, Edwin A., *Rich Cabinet Collection vol. I.* (2022) Magicana, Toronto. Casebound. Black. Consecutive pagination between volumes. pp. 9.25 x 11.75 in. Dust jacket. Limited to 250 copies. History, Biography, Collecting.

Dawes, Edwin A., *Rich Cabinet Collection vol. II.* (2022) Magicana, Toronto. Casebound. Black. Consecutive pagination between volumes. pp. 9.25 x 11.75 in. Dust jacket. Limited to 250 copies. History, Biography, Collecting.

Dawes, Edwin A., *Rich Cabinet Collection vol. III.* (2023) Magicana, Toronto. Casebound. Black. Consecutive pagination between volumes. pp. 9.25 x 11.75 in. Dust jacket. Limited to 250 copies. History, Biography, Collecting.

Dawes, Edwin A., *Rich Cabinet Collection vol. IV.* (2023) Magicana, Toronto. Casebound. Black. Consecutive pagination between volumes. pp. 9.25 x 11.75 in. Dust jacket. Limited to 250 copies. History, Biography, Collecting.

Dawes, Edwin A., *Rich Cabinet Collection vol. V.* (2023) Magicana, Toronto. Casebound. Black. Consecutive pagination between volumes. pp. 9.25 x 11.75 in. Dust jacket. Limited to 250 copies. History, Biography, Collecting.

Dawes, Edwin A., *Rich Cabinet Collection vol. VI.* (2023) Magicana, Toronto. Casebound. Black. Consecutive pagination between volumes. pp. 9.25 x 11.75 in. Dust jacket. Limited to 250 copies. History, Biography, Collecting.

Dawes, Edwin A., *Rich Cabinet Collection vol. VII.* (2024) Magicana, Toronto. Casebound. Black. Consecutive pagination between volumes. pp. 9.25 x 11.75 in. Dust jacket. Limited to 250 copies. History, Biography, Collecting.

Dawes, Edwin A., *Rich Cabinet Collection vol. VIII.* (2024) Magicana, Toronto. Casebound. Black. Consecutive pagination between volumes. pp. 9.25 x 11.75 in. Dust jacket. Limited to 250 copies. History, Biography, Collecting.

Dawes, Edwin A., *Rich Cabinet Collection vol. IX.* (2024) Magicana, Toronto. Casebound. Black. Consecutive pagination between volumes. pp. 9.25 x 11.75 in. Dust jacket. Limited to 250 copies. History, Biography, Collecting, Index.

Dawes, Edwin A., *Rich Cabinet of Magical Curiosities: parts 1 and 2, A.* (2010) Peter Scarlett, Surrey, UK. CD. 1990 pp. Collected columns on CD. History, Biography, Collecting, Magazine columns.

Dawes, Edwin A., *Stanley Collins: Conjurer, Collector, and Iconoclast.* (2002) Kaufman and Co., Washington D.C. Cloth. Black. 360 pp. 8.5 x 11 in. Dust jacket. Includes DVD. Signed by Edwin A. Dawes. History, Biography.

Dawes, Edwin A., *Stodare: The Enigma Variations.* (1998) Kaufman and Co., Washington D.C. Cloth. Maroon. 278 pp. 6.25 x 9.25 in. Signed by Edwin A. Dawes. Limited to 500 copies. History, Biography.

Dawes, Edwin A., *Willane: The Story of the Short But Remarkable Career of a Creative Performer.* (2018) Dawes Partnership, Anlaby, UK. Saddle-stitch. White. 22 pp. 8.25 x 11.75 in. Limited to 50 copies. History, Biography.

Daws, Jamie, *Opening Daws.* (2016) Author, UK. Comb. White. 28 pp. 8.25 x 11.75 in. (Information not verified by physical copy.) Lecture notes. Cards, Mentalism, Close-Up.

Dawson, Steve, *Routining and Scripting for Magical Performers.* (1992) The Magic Touch. Comb. Light blue. 60 pp. 8.5 x 11.5 in. Showmanship, Routining, Scripting.

Dawson, Trevor, *Charles Dickens: Conjurer, Mesmerist, and Showman.* (2012) Author, London. Cloth. Green. 231 pp. 6.75 x 10 in. Dust jacket. Biography, History.

Dawson, Trevor, *Signor Arvi: The Forgotten Illusionist.* (2015) Author, London. Cloth. Green. 64 pp. 6.75 x 10 in. Dust jacket. Signed by Trevor Dawson. Biography, History.

Day and Levani, *Conjuring Apparatus Up-to-Date.* (1912) Cassell and Co., London. Perfect. Red, black, white. 152 pp. 4.75 x 7.25 in. Authors are apparently pseudonyms. Stage.

Day, Frederic, *Modern Magic.* (c. 1910) Author, UK. Folded. White. 8 pp. 7.25 x 5 in. Bound oblong. Clever Eight Kings on back page with chart titled "The Mystic Wheel." In Copperfield collection. Beginner.

Day, Jon, *Let's Make Magic.* (1992) Kingfisher, UK. Perfect. White. 96 pp. 7.75 x 10 in. (Information not verified by physical copy.) Beginner.

Day, Professor James, *Secrets of the Handcuff Trick.* (1905) Author, Birmingham, UK. Saddle-stitch. Tan, blue. 8 pp. 5 x 7.25 in. Escapes, Handcuffs.

Dayton, Ronald J., *Brainstorm in My Pajamas.* (2006) Leaping Lizards Magic, Orlando, FL. Perfect. Purple. 177 pp. 8.5 x 11 in. Stage, Close-Up.

Dayton, Ronald J. (as Kotah), *By Darkness Influenced.* (2006) Leaping Lizards Magic, Orlando, FL. Perfect. Brown. 121 pp. 8.5 x 11 in. Bizarre magick.

Dayton, Ronald J., *Conjuror's Collage, A.* (1980) Micky Hades, Calgary, Canada. Comb. Blue. 78 pp. 8.5 x 11 in. Stage, Close-Up, Rope.

Dayton, Ronald J., *Cord-ially Yours.* (1983) Micky Hades, Calgary, Canada. Comb. Beige. 45 pp. 8.5 x 11 in. Rope.

Dayton, Ronald J., with Campbell, Jeffrey L., *Crystal Cups.* (1983) Micky Hades, Calgary, Canada. Comb. Yellow. 15 pp. 8.5 x 11 in. Cups and Balls.

Dayton, Ronald J., *Darker Light, A.* (2005) Leaping Lizards Magic, Orlando, FL. Perfect. Tan, beige. 122 pp. 8.25 x 11 in. Bizarre magick.

Dayton, Ronald J., *Dayton Razor Blade Miracle, The.* (1988) Author, Port Washington, WI. Stapled. Gray. 13 pp. 8.5 x 11 in. Sealed on side with round white label. Clear acetate cover. Stage, Razor blade swallowing.

Dayton, Ronald J., *Dayton Wallet, The.* (2008) Leaping Lizards Magic, Orlando, FL. Saddle-stitch. Black. 10 pp. 5.5 x 8.5 in. (Information not verified by physical copy.) Wallets, Close-Up.

Dayton, Ronald J., *Dayton's Delights.* (1992) Hades Publications, Calgary, Canada. Cloth. Blue. Cover text: Gold; 495 pp. 8.5 x 11 in. Bound collection of several Dayton booklets. Close-Up, Stage.

Dayton, Ronald J., with Campbell, Jeffrey L., *Doing Coin Magic for the Change.* (1986) Hades Publications, Calgary, Canada. Saddle-stitch. White. 15 pp. 6 x 9 in. Coins.

Dayton, Ronald J., *Hung Up on Ropes / Off the Beaten Path.* (1986) Tannen's Magic Manuscript, New York. Perfect. Black. 147 pp. 5.25 x 8.25 in. Double-sided book. Rope, Cards.

Dayton, Ronald J., *Jenny-U-Wan Magic part 1: Silks-n-Ropes-n-Rings.* (1984) Micky Hades, Calgary, Canada. Stapled with tape. Red. 51 pp. 8.5 x 11 in. Silks, Rope, Rings.

Dayton, Ronald J., *Jenny-U-Wan Magic part 2: Tissues-n-Money.* (1984) Micky Hades, Calgary, Canada. Stapled with tape. Blue. 64 pp. 8.5 x 11 in. Paper, Bills, Tissue paper.

Dayton, Ronald J., *Jenny-U-Wan Magic part 3: Magic-n-the Grab Bag.* (1984) Micky Hades, Calgary, Canada. Stapled with tape. Yellow. 60 pp. 8.5 x 11 in. Close-Up, Stage.

Dayton, Ronald J., *Legerdemine.* (1981) Micky Hades, Calgary, Canada. Comb. Blue. 71 pp. 8.5 x 11 in. Stage, Rope.

Dayton, Ronald J., *Magic Playground, The.* (1998) Micky Hades, Calgary, Canada. Comb. White. 55 pp. 6 x 9 in. Stage, Close-Up.

Dayton, Ronald J., *One of a Kind Magic.* (1983) Micky Hades, Calgary, Canada. Comb. Green. 50 pp. 8.5 x 11 in. Cards, Stage, Close-Up.

Dayton, Ronald J., *Press-Tidigitation.* (1981) Micky Hades, Calgary, Canada. Comb. Blue. 73 pp. 8.5 x 11 in. Paper, Newspaper.

Dayton, Ronald J., *Professor's Nightmare: The Awakening.* (2007) Leaping Lizards Magic, Orlando, FL. Perfect. Purple. 40 pp. 6 x 9 in. Rope, Professor's Nightmare.

Dayton, Ronald J., with Buff, R. C., *Rope: Without End.* (1981) Micky Hades, Calgary, Canada. Comb. Yellow. 113 pp. 8.5 x 11 in. Rope.

Dayton, Ronald J., with Schmidt, Joseph K., *Rope Worker: A Tribute to R. C. Buff.* (1993) Micky Hades, Calgary, Canada. Coil. Red, gold. 101 pp. 6 x 9 in. Rope, History.

Dayton, Ronald J., *Ropes with a Different Twist.* (1979) Micky Hades, Calgary, Canada. Comb. Tan. 107 pp. 8.5 x 11 in. Rope, Inventions.

Dayton, Ronald J., *Secret Thoughts.* (1983) Micky Hades, Calgary, Canada. Comb. White. 80 pp. 8.5 x 11 in. Stage, Close-Up.

Dayton, Ronald J., *Simply Amazing.* (1987) Micky Hades, Calgary, Canada. Comb. Black. 42 pp. 8.5 x 11 in. Close-Up, Stage.

Dayton, Ronald J., *Speed Reader Plus.* (1992) Author, Port Washington, WI. Stapled. White. 3 pp. 8.5 x 11 in. Cards, Prearranged deck, Marked cards.

Dayton, Ronald J., *Spoof – It's Magic.* (1993) American Magic Co., Harrisburg, PA. Cloth. Black. 50 pp. 8.5 x 11 in. Effects in parodies of magazines. Close-Up, Stage, Parody.

Dayton, Ronald J., *Strange Reflections.* (1989) Micky Hades, Calgary, Canada. Perfect. White, black. 55 pp. 6 x 9 in. With Diminishing Fan design sheet. Cards, Diminishing Cards.

Dayton, Ronald J., *Three by KOTA.* (2003) Author, Port Washington, WI. Coil. White. 13 pp. 8.5 x 11 in. Printed version of ebook. Cards, Close-Up.

Dayton, Ronald J., *Visual Fantasies.* (1986) Micky Hades, Calgary, Canada. Comb. Beige. 50 pp. 8.5 x 11 in. Stage, Close-Up.

Dayton, Ronald J., *Whole Art of Clippo Revealed – and More!, The.* (1986) Micky Hades, Calgary, Canada. Comb. Yellow. 37 pp. 8.5 x 11 in. Paper, Clippo.

Dé, Té, *Annuaire des Prestidigitateurs.* (1921) Author, Lyons, France. Saddle-stitch. Tan. 27 pp. 5.25 x 8.25 in. Includes a listing for Georges Méliès. Directory, History. French.

Dean, Dicky, *Dean Speaks, The.* (1969) Author, London, Canada. Saddle-stitch. Blue. 54 pp. 5.5 x 8.25 in. With 2 pp. supplement. Showmanship, Theory, Promotion, Essays.

Dean, Dicky, *Magic.* (1975) Author, London, Canada. Stapled with tape. Orange. 83 pp. 8.5 x 11 in. (Measurements and other information have been recorded as accurately as possible.) Beginner.

Dean, Dicky, *Using Magic in Teaching.* (1975) Author, London, Canada. Stapled with tape. Yellow. 206 pp. 5.5 x 7.75 in. Effects matched to various school topics. Educational, Close-Up, Stage.

Dean, Dicky, *Zombie Fire Climax.* (1979) Supreme Magic, Bideford, UK. Saddle-stitch. Black. 8 pp. 7.25 x 9.5 in. Zombie, Stage, Fire.

Dean, George, *Best of George Dean, The.* (1972) Author, Oakland, CA. Stapled. White. 5 pp. 8.5 x 11 in. Lecture notes. Stage, Close-Up, Mentalism.

Dean, George, *Magic Everyone Else Isn't Doing.* (1984) Magic Limited, Oakland, CA. Saddle-stitch. Green. 29 pp. 5.25 x 8.5 in. Cards, Mentalism, Stage, Close-Up.

Dean, Henry, *Hocus Pocus.* (1983) Walter B. Graham, Omaha. Leatherette. Brown. 132 pp. 4.25 x 7.25 in. Reprint of 1763 sixth edition. #148 of 200. History, Early magic.

Dean, Henry, *Whole Art of Legerdemain, or Hocus Pocus in Perfection, The.* (1722) A. Bettesworth, London. 101 pp. 3.25 x 5.75 in. (Information not verified by physical copy.) Toole Stott no. 199. Early magic, Beginner.

Dean, Henry, *Whole Art of Legerdemain, or Hocus Pocus in Perfection, The.* Second edition. (1727) A. Bettesworth, London. 132 pp. 3.25 x 5.25 in. (Information not verified by physical copy.) Toole Stott no. 200. Early magic, Beginner.

Dean, Henry, *Whole Art of Legerdemain, or Hocus Pocus in Perfection, The.* Third edition. (c. 1750) A. Bettesworth, London. 132 pp. 3.5 x 5.5 in. (Information not verified by physical copy.) Toole Stott no. 201. Early magic, Beginner.

Dean, Henry, *Whole Art of Legerdemain, or Hocus Pocus in Perfection, The.* Fourth edition. (c. 1758) J. Hodges, London. 132 pp. 3.25 x 5.75 in. (Information not verified by physical copy.) Toole Stott no. 202. Early magic, Beginner.

Dean, Henry, *Whole Art of Legerdemain, or Hocus Pocus in Perfection, The.* Fifth edition. (c. 1760) J. Hodges, London. 132 pp. 3.5 x 6 in. (Information not verified by physical copy.) Toole Stott no. 203. Early magic, Beginner.

Dean, Henry, *Whole Art of Legerdemain, or Hocus Pocus in Perfection, The.* Fifth edition (Scotland). (c. 1762) Robert Smith, Jr., Glasgow. 119 pp. 3.5 x 5.75 in. (Information not verified by physical copy.) Toole Stott no. 204. Early magic, Beginner.

Dean, Henry, *Whole Art of Legerdemain, or Hocus Pocus in Perfection, The.* Sixth edition. (1763) L. Hawes and Co., London. 132 pp. 3.5 x 5.5 in. (Information not verified by physical copy.) Toole Stott no. 205. Early magic, Beginner.

Dean, Henry, *Whole Art of Legerdemain, or Hocus Pocus in Perfection, The.* Sixth edition (Scotland). (1765) William Duncan, Glasgow. 119 pp. 3.5 x 5.5 in. (Information not verified by physical copy.) Toole Stott no. 206. Early magic, Beginner.

Dean, Henry, *Whole Art of Legerdemain, or Hocus Pocus in Perfection, The.* Seventh edition. (1763) L. Hawes and Co., London. 132 pp. 3.25 x 6 in. (Information not verified by physical copy.) Toole Stott no. 207. Early magic, Beginner.

Dean, Henry, *Whole Art of Legerdemain, or Hocus Pocus in Perfection, The.* Seventh edition. (1772) L. Hawes and Co., London. 132 pp. 3.25 x 6 in. (Information not verified by physical copy.) Toole Stott no. 208. Early magic, Beginner.

Dean, Henry, *Whole Art of Legerdemain, or Hocus Pocus in Perfection, The.* Seventh edition (Scotland). (1769) Robert Duncan, Glasgow. 119 pp. 3.25 x 5.75 in. (Information not verified by physical copy.) Toole Stott no. 209. Early magic, Beginner.

Dean, Henry, *Whole Art of Legerdemain, or Hocus Pocus in Perfection, The.* Eighth edition. (1781) J. Bew, London. 132 pp. 3.5 x 6 in. (Information not verified by physical copy.) Toole Stott no. 210. Early magic, Beginner.

Dean, Henry, *Whole Art of Legerdemain, or Hocus Pocus in Perfection, The.* Eighth edition (Scotland). (1773) R. and T. Duncan, Glasgow. 119 pp. 3.75 x 5.75 in. (Information not verified by physical copy.) Toole Stott no. 211. Early magic, Beginner.

Dean, Henry, *Whole Art of Legerdemain, or Hocus Pocus in Perfection, The.* Eighth edition. (1785) T. Sabine, London. 108 pp. 3.5 x 5 in. (Information not verified by physical copy.) Toole Stott no. 212. Early magic, Beginner.

Dean, Henry, *Whole Art of Legerdemain, or Hocus Pocus in Perfection, The.* Ninth edition. (c. 1789) T. Sabine, London. 95 pp. 4 x 6.5 in. (Information not verified by physical copy.) Toole Stott no. 213. Early magic, Beginner.

Dean, Henry, *Whole Art of Legerdemain, or Hocus Pocus in Perfection, The.* Ninth edition. (1789) J. Bew, London. 132 pp. 3.25 x 6 in. (Information not verified by physical copy.) Toole Stott no. 214. Early magic, Beginner.

Dean, Henry, *Whole Art of Legerdemain, or Hocus Pocus in Perfection, The.* Ninth edition. (1789) T. Sabine, London. 108 pp. 3.5 x 6 in. (Information not verified by physical copy.) Toole Stott no. 215. Early magic, Beginner.

Dean, Henry, *Whole Art of Legerdemain, or Hocus Pocus in Perfection, The.* Tenth edition (Scotland). (1783) J. and M. Robertson, Glasgow. 108 pp. 3.5 x 6 in. (Information not verified by physical copy.) Toole Stott no. 216. Early magic, Beginner.

Dean, Henry, *Whole Art of Legerdemain, or Hocus Pocus in Perfection, The.* Eleventh edition. (c. 1790) Sabine and Son, London. 96 pp. 3.75 x 6 in. (Information not verified by physical copy.) Toole Stott no. 217. Early magic, Beginner.

Dean, Henry, *Whole Art of Legerdemain, or Hocus Pocus in Perfection, The.* Eleventh edition (Scotland). (1791) J. and M. Robertson, Glasgow. 108 pp. 4.25 x 6.75 in. (Information not verified by physical copy.) Toole Stott no. 218. Early magic, Beginner.

Dean, Henry, *Whole Art of Legerdemain, or Hocus Pocus in Perfection, The.* Eleventh edition. (1795) J. Hollis, London. 96 pp. 3.75 x 6.75 in. (Information not verified by physical copy.) Toole Stott no. 219. Early magic, Beginner.

Dean, Henry, *Whole Art of Legerdemain, or Hocus Pocus in Perfection, The.* Eleventh edition (U.S.) (1795) Mathew Carey, Philadelphia. 106 pp. 3.25 x 5.25 in. (Information not verified by physical copy.) Toole Stott no. 220. Early magic, Beginner.

Dean, Henry, *Whole Art of Legerdemain, or Hocus Pocus in Perfection, The.* Twelfth edition (Scotland). (1797) J. and M. Robertson, Glasgow. 108 pp. 3.75 x 6.5 in. (Information not verified by physical copy.) Toole Stott no. 222. Early magic, Beginner.

Dean, Henry, *Whole Art of Legerdemain, or Hocus Pocus in Perfection, The.* Twelfth edition. (c. 1800) J. Hollis, London. 96 pp. 3.75 x 6.5 in. (Information not verified by physical copy.) Toole Stott no. 221. Early magic, Beginner.

Dean, Henry, *Whole Art of Legerdemain, or Hocus Pocus in Perfection, The.* Thirteenth edition (Scotland). (1806) J. and M. Robertson, Glasgow. 108 pp. 3.75 x 6 in. (Information not verified by physical copy.) Toole Stott no. 223. Early magic, Beginner.

Dean, Henry, *Whole Art of Legerdemain, or Hocus Pocus in Perfection, The.* Fourteenth edition (Scotland). (1811) A. Napier, Glasgow. 96 pp. 3.5 x 6 in. (Information not verified by physical copy.) Toole Stott no. 224. Early magic, Beginner.

Dean, Henry, *Whole Art of Legerdemain, or Hocus Pocus in Perfection, The.* Fifteenth edition (U.S.) (c. 1812) Mathew Carey, Philadelphia. 125 pp. 3.5 x 5.75 in. (Information not verified by physical copy.) Toole Stott no. 227. Toole Stott gives the date as 1804. Early magic, Beginner.

Dean, Henry, *Whole Art of Legerdemain, or Hocus Pocus in Perfection, The.* Fifteenth edition (Ireland). (1814) Joseph Smyth, Belfast. 114 pp. 3.5 x 6 in. (Information not verified by physical copy.) Toole Stott no. 225. Early magic, Beginner.

Dean, Henry, *Whole Art of Legerdemain, or Hocus Pocus in Perfection, The.* Fifteenth edition (Scotland). (1817) A. Napier, Glasgow. 95 pp. 3.75 x 6.25 in. (Information not verified by physical copy.) Toole Stott no. 226. Early magic, Beginner.

Dean, Henry, *Whole Art of Legerdemain, or Hocus Pocus in Perfection, The.* Sixteenth edition (U.S.) (c. 1813) Mathew Carey, Philadelphia. 125 pp. 3.5 x 5.75 in. (Information not verified by physical copy.) Toole Stott no. 228. Toole Stott gives the date as 1807. Early magic, Beginner.

Dean, Henry, *Whole Art of Legerdemain, or Hocus Pocus in Perfection, The.* Sixteenth edition. (c. 1825) W. Macnie, Stirling, UK. 24 pp. 3.75 x 6.75 in. (Information not verified by physical copy.) Toole Stott no. 229. Early magic, Beginner.

Dean, Henry, *Whole Art of Legerdemain, or Hocus Pocus in Perfection, The.* Seventeenth edition (U.S.) (1814) E. Duyckinck, New York. 107 pp. 3.5 x 5.5 in. (Information not verified by physical copy.) Toole Stott no. 230. Early magic, Beginner.

Dean, Henry, *Whole Art of Legerdemain, or Hocus Pocus in Perfection, The.* Eighteenth edition (U.S.) (1817) Monroe and Francis, Boston. 107 pp. 3.5 x 5.75 in. (Information not verified by physical copy.) Toole Stott no. 231. Early magic, Beginner.

Dean, Henry, *Whole Art of Legerdemain, or Hocus Pocus in Perfection, The.* Eighteenth edition (Ireland). (c. 1850) James Duffy, Dublin. 144 pp. 3.5 x 5.75 in. (Information not verified by physical copy.) Toole Stott no. 232. Early magic, Beginner.

Dean, Henry, *Whole Art of Legerdemain, or Hocus Pocus in Perfection, The.* Eighteenth edition (Ireland). (1856) C. M. Warren, Dublin. 108 pp. 3.5 x 6 in. (Information not verified by physical copy.) Toole Stott no. 233. Early magic, Beginner.

Dean, Henry, *Wonderful Magical Tricks, or Hocus Pocus.* (1873) Edwin Pearson, London. 8 pp. 6.25 x 9 in. (Information not verified by physical copy.) Toole Stott no. 234. Early magic, Beginner.

Dean, Jack, *Enforcer, The.* (1996) Jack Dean's Stagecraft, Memphis, TN. Comb. Red. 27 pp. 8.5 x 11 in. (Information not verified by physical copy.) Mentalism.

Dean, Jack, *Equivoque Choice, The.* (1994) Jack Dean's Stagecraft, Memphis, TN. Comb. Tan. 35 pp. 8.5 x 11 in. Equivoque, Mentalism.

Dean, Jack, *FouRings.* (1996) Jack Dean's Stagecraft, Memphis, TN. Coil. White. 9 pp. 8.5 x 11 in. (Information not verified by physical copy.) Linking Rings.

Dean, Jack, *Lecture Notes 1.* (c. 1995) Jack Dean's Stagecraft, Memphis, TN. Comb. Red. 13 pp. 8.5 x 11 in. (Information not verified by physical copy.) Lecture notes. Cards, Mentalism, Stage.

Dean, Jack, *Performance Proven Magic.* (1967) Author, Memphis, TN. Stapled. 13 pp. 8.5 x 11 in. (Information not verified by physical copy.) Lecture notes.

Dean, Jack, *Psychic Sight.* (1994) Jack Dean's Stagecraft, Memphis, TN. Comb. Green. 29 pp. 8.5 x 11 in. Mentalism, Blindfolds.

Dean, Jack, *Soothsayer.* (1990) Jack Dean's Stagecraft, Memphis, TN. Comb. Yellow. 47 pp. 8.5 x 11 in. Equivoque, Mentalism.

Dean, Jack, *Voice of the Prophet, The.* (1983) Jack Dean's Stagecraft, Memphis, TN. Saddle-stitch. Green. 20 pp. 5.25 x 7.25 in. Mentalism, Recorded effects.

Dean, Jason, *Pik-a-Nip.* (2003) Author, Kansas City, MO. Saddle-stitch. White. 6 pp. 7 x 8.5 in. (Measurements and other information have been recorded as accurately as possible.) Cards.

Dean, Jason, *Private Parts of Jason Dean, The.* (2006) Author, Kansas City, MO. Saddle-stitch. Black. 5.5 x 8.5 in. (Information not verified by physical copy. Bibliographical details are as accurate as possible.) Cards.

Dean, Jason, *Threesome.* (2012) Vanishing Inc., Rancho Cordova, CA. Saddle-stitch. Gray. 24 pp. 6 x 9 in. Includes cards. Signed by Jason Dean. Coins, Cards, Close-Up.

De Armenteras, Antonio, *Enciclopedia de la Magia, Ilusionismo, y Prestidigitacion.* (1957) De Gasso, Barcelona. Cloth. Black. 331 pp. 5.5 x 7.5 in. Beginner. Spanish.

De Armenteras, Antonio, *Juegos de manos, de ingenio, de prendas y de salon.* (1958) De Gasso, Barcelona. Cloth. Red. 333 pp. 5.5 x 7.75 in. Beginner. Spanish.

Deb, Soumya, *Soumya's Brainstorms.* (1998) Electro Fun, Calcutta. Saddle-stitch. Tan. 26 pp. 5.75 x 8 in. Cards, Close-Up, Stage.

De Barros, Jules, *Baron, The.* (1981) Author, New Orleans. Stapled. White. 15 pp. 8.5 x 11 in. Signed by Jules De Barros. Coins, Close-Up.

De Barros, Jules, *Coins of Ishtar, The.* (1971) Author, New Orleans. Perfect. Pink. 69 pp. 8.5 x 11 in. Signed by Jules De Barros. #492. Coins.

De Barros, Jules, *Techniques and Principles of Sleight-of-Hand vol. 1.* (1982) Author, New Orleans. Saddle-stitch. Blue. 28 pp. 7 x 8.5 in. Coins, Theory, Close-Up.

De Bevere, L., *Alphabetical Mysteries.* (1984) Supreme Magic, Bideford, UK. Saddle-stitch. White. 67 pp. 7.5 x 9.75 in. Mentalism, Key card.

De Bevere, L., *Mnemodexterity.* (1979) Supreme Magic, Bideford, UK. Saddle-stitch. White. 8 pp. 7.5 x 10 in. Cards, Memory.

DeCamps, Eric (See also Ouellet, Gary), *Compositions of Conjuring.* (2001) Author, New York. Saddle-stitch. Black. 51 pp. 8.5 x 11 in. (Information not verified by physical copy.) Cards, Close-Up, Stage.

DeCamps, Eric, *Jokers are Wild.* (1995) Meir Yedid Magic, Fair Lawn, NJ. Saddle-stitch. Light blue. 20 pp. 5.5 x 8.5 in. Cards.

DeCamps, Eric, *Magic of Eric Decamps: Compendium I, The.* (1985) Author, New York. Saddle-stitch. White. 28 pp. 8.5 x 11 in. Cards, Close-Up.

DeCamps, Eric, *Magic of Eric Decamps: Compendium I, The.* (1998) Author, New York. Stapled with tape. White. 28 pp. 8.5 x 11 in. Cards, Close-Up.

DeCamps, Eric, *Stack 'Em If You Got 'Em!* (1997) Author, New York. Stapled. White. 6 pp. 8.5 x 11 in. (Information not verified by physical copy.) Cups and Balls.

De Caston, Alfred, *Marchands de Miracles, Les.* (1864) E. Dentu, Paris. Boards. Green. 338 pp. 4.25 x 7 in. Psychic, History. French.

De Caston, Alfred, *Marchands de Miracles, Les.* (1864) E. Dentu, Paris. Perfect. Beige. 338 pp. 4.25 x 7 in. Psychic, History. French.

De Caston, Alfred, *Tricheurs: Scènes de Jeu, Les.* (1863) E. Dentu, Paris. Perfect. Beige. 347 pp. 4.75 x 7.25 in. Fortune-telling, Cheating, History. French.

De Caston, Alfred, *Vendeurs de Bonne Aventure, Les.* (1866) Librairie Centrale, Paris. Leather. Brown. 347 pp. 4.25 x 7 in. Fortune-telling, History. French.

De Caston, Herbert, *Peerless Prestidigitation.* (1910) Hamley's, London. Boards. White. 30 pp. 5 x 7.5 in. Stage. French.

De Corbecert, Raoul, *Tours d'Escamotage Faciles à Faire!* (c. 1920) Author, Paris. Saddle-stitch. Color. 45 pp. 4 x 6.25 in. Beginner. French.

De Courcy, Ken (See also McComb, Billy; Page, Patrick; Rungay, Herb; Stern, Duke; Yates, Jack), *33 Tricks with the P-A-T-E-O Force.* (1980) Supreme Magic, Bideford, UK. Saddle-stitch. White, purple. 19 pp. 7.25 x 9.5 in. Cards, Forcing.

De Courcy, Ken, *After-Dinner Technique.* (1980) Supreme Magic, Bideford, UK. Saddle-stitch. White, green. 64 pp. 5.25 x 8 in. Impromptu, Close-Up.

De Courcy, Ken, *At the Drop of a Match.* (1972) Supreme Magic, Bideford, UK. Saddle-stitch. Orange. 35 pp. 7.75 x 9.75 in. Matches, Stunts, Impromptu.

De Courcy, Ken, *At the Drop of a Match.* Second edition. (1983) Supreme Magic, Bideford, UK. Saddle-stitch. Purple, green. 34 pp. 7.75 x 9.5 in. Matches, Stunts, Impromptu.

De Courcy, Ken, *Australian Gambling Game of 31, The.* (1974) Supreme Magic, Bideford, UK. Saddle-stitch. Red, white. 8 pp. 7.75 x 9.75 in. Cards, Gambling.

De Courcy, Ken, *Automentalism.* (1953) George Armstrong, London. Saddle-stitch. White. 15 pp. 5.5 x 8.5 in. Mentalism.

De Courcy, Ken, *Blood Feast of the Sun, The.* (1979) Supreme Magic, Bideford, UK. Saddle-stitch. Beige. 7 pp. 8 x 10 in. Bizarre magick.

De Courcy, Ken, *Blue Spotitis.* (1980) Supreme Magic, Bideford, UK. Saddle-stitch. Blue. 20 pp. 7.25 x 9.75 in. Paper, Origami, Close-Up.

De Courcy, Ken, *Calling All Cards.* (1964) Supreme Magic, Bideford, UK. Stapled with tape. Red. 10 pp. 8 x 9.75 in. Mimeographed. Cards.

De Courcy, Ken, *Card in Seven, A.* (1972) Supreme Magic, Bideford, UK. Saddle-stitch. Yellow. 12 pp. 7.5 x 9.25 in. Cards.

De Courcy, Ken, *Cards in Cabaret.* (1980) Supreme Magic, Bideford, UK. Saddle-stitch. Yellow. 67 pp. 7.25 x 9.5 in. Cards.

De Courcy, Ken, *Chinese Ring on Stick.* (1970) Supreme Magic, Bideford, UK. Saddle-stitch. White. 7 pp. 8 x 10 in. Rings, Close-Up, Wands, Ring on stick.

De Courcy, Ken, *Creditable Conjuring.* (1982) Supreme Magic, Bideford, UK. Saddle-stitch. Green. 12 pp. 7.25 x 9.75 in. Credit cards, Close-Up, Stage.

De Courcy, Ken, *Cross-Indexed Comedy Collection.* (1986) Supreme Magic, Bideford, UK. Saddle-stitch. White, red, black. 48 pp. 8 x 10 in. (Information not verified by physical copy.) Comedy, Jokes, Gags.

De Courcy, Ken, *Cross-Indexed Comedy Collection Part Two: Separate Index of Contents.* (1986) Supreme Magic, Bideford, UK. Saddle-stitch. White, red. 8 x 10 in. (Information not verified by physical copy.) Comedy, Jokes, Gags, Index.

De Courcy, Ken, *Danson's Diary Trick.* (1983) Supreme Magic, Bideford, UK. Saddle-stitch. Red, gray. 20 pp. 8 x 10 in. Cards, Mentalism.

De Courcy, Ken, *Deceiver's Discourse.* (1976) Supreme Magic, Bideford, UK. Saddle-stitch. Yellow. 24 pp. 7.75 x 9.75 in. Stage.

De Courcy, Ken, *Diamonds Aren't a Girl's Best Friend.* (1980) Supreme Magic, Bideford, UK. Loose pages. White. 8 x 10 in. Cards, Sam the Bellhop routines, Instructions.

De Courcy, Ken, *Dubbelkross and Simulkross.* (1955) George Armstrong, London. Saddle-stitch. Yellow. 16 pp. 5.5 x 8.25 in. Coins.

De Courcy, Ken, *Easy Everywhere and Nowhere.* (1981) Supreme Magic, Bideford, UK. Saddle-stitch. Yellow. 6 pp. 7.25 x 9.5 in. Cards.

De Courcy, Ken, *Even Stephen.* (1976) Supreme Magic, Bideford, UK. Saddle-stitch. Blue. 10 pp. 7.75 x 9.75 in. Cards.

De Courcy, Ken, *Exclusive Card Magic Series nos. 1-3.* (1986) Author, London. 76 pp. (Information not verified by physical copy.) Cards.

De Courcy, Ken, *Four Aces Intro's.* (1983) Supreme Magic, Bideford, UK. Saddle-stitch. Red, white. 24 pp. 5.75 x 8.25 in. Cards, Four Ace effects.

De Courcy, Ken, *Genial Improbabilities.* (1949) Goodliffe Publications, Birmingham, UK. Saddle-stitch. White, yellow. 62 pp. 5.5 x 8.75 in. Stage, Manipulation, Close-Up.

De Courcy, Ken, *Hot ICE (Imaginative Card Effects) no. 1: A Double Dose.* (1985) Supreme Magic, Bideford, UK. Saddle-stitch. 7 pp. 5.75 x 8.25 in. (Information not verified by physical copy.)

De Courcy, Ken, *Hot ICE (Imaginative Card Effects) no. 2: Hammanesque.* (1985) Supreme Magic, Bideford, UK. Saddle-stitch. Red, white. 7 pp. 5.75 x 8.25 in. Cards.

De Courcy, Ken, *Hot ICE (Imaginative Card Effects) no. 3: The Kosky Cut.* (1985) Supreme Magic, Bideford, UK. Saddle-stitch. 7 pp. 5.75 x 8.25 in. (Information not verified by physical copy.) Cards.

De Courcy, Ken, *Hot ICE (Imaginative Card Effects) no. 4: Straight Prediction.* (1985) Supreme Magic, Bideford, UK. Saddle-stitch. White. 8 pp. 5.75 x 8.25 in. Cards.

De Courcy, Ken, *How to Get More Applause.* (1985) Author, London. Saddle-stitch. Yellow. 24 pp. 7.5 x 10 in. (Information not verified by physical copy.) Showmanship.

De Courcy, Ken, *Ideas Incorporated.* (1985) Author, London. 12 pp. (Information not verified by physical copy.) Lecture notes. Close-Up, Stage.

De Courcy, Ken, *Ideas Incorporated II.* (1989) Author, London. 15 pp. (Information not verified by physical copy.) Lecture notes. Close-Up, Stage.

De Courcy, Ken, *Impromptu Turn-About Card Routine.* (1952) Supreme Magic, Bideford, UK. Stapled with tape. Blue. 7 pp. 8 x 10 in. Mimeographed. Cards, Impromptu.

De Courcy, Ken, *Ken on Kards: Card Magic for Non-Card Men.* (1972) Supreme Magic, Bideford, UK. Saddle-stitch. White. 6 pp. 7.5 x 10 in. (Information not verified by physical copy.) Cards.

De Courcy, Ken, *Koran Newspaper Prediction, The.* (1970) Supreme Magic, Bideford, UK. Saddle-stitch. White, red. 8 pp. 8 x 10 in. (Information not verified by physical copy.) Mentalism, Newspaper, Publicity.

De Courcy, Ken, *Life-Lines.* (1982) Supreme Magic, Bideford, UK. Saddle-stitch. White, purple. 19 pp. 7.25 x 9.75 in. Balloons, Stage.

De Courcy, Ken, *Luck of Lucretia, The.* (2000) PH Marketing, UK. 22 pp. (Information not verified by physical copy.) Cards, Mentalism, Liquids.

De Courcy, Ken, *Magic Balloons.* (1979) Supreme Magic, Bideford, UK. Saddle-stitch. Blue. 20 pp. 7.25 x 9.75 in. Balloons, Stage.

De Courcy, Ken, *Magic Balloons.* (1979) Supreme Magic, Bideford, UK. Saddle-stitch. Green. 20 pp. 7.25 x 9.75 in. Balloons, Stage.

De Courcy, Ken, *Magic in Cabaret Land.* (1966) Supreme Magic, Bideford, UK. Stapled with tape. Yellow, blue. 28 pp. 7.75 x 9.5 in. Silkscreened cover. Stage.

De Courcy, Ken, with Adair, Ian, *Magical Jumbo Chinese Coin, The.* (1983) Supreme Magic, Bideford, UK. Saddle-stitch. Yellow, blue. 19 pp. 8 x 9.75 in. Coins, Chinese coins.

De Courcy, Ken, *Meshed Minds.* (1971) Supreme Magic, Bideford, UK. Comb. Black. 16 pp. 8 x 9.75 in. Rounded corners. Mentalism.

De Courcy, Ken, *Mistress of Pentertain.* (1976) Supreme Magic, Bideford, UK. Saddle-stitch. White, green. 40 pp. 7.25 x 9.75 in. Close-Up, Pens.

De Courcy, Ken, with Hooper, Edwin, *My Card, Sir!* (1968) Supreme Magic, Bideford, UK. Saddle-stitch. Light green, purple. 15 pp. 6.5 x 8 in. Business cards, Close-Up, Promotion.

De Courcy, Ken, *Notes on the Ken De Courcy Lecture.* (n.d.) Author, Herts, UK. Stapled. White. 6 pp. 8.5 x 11 in. Close-Up, Stage.

De Courcy, Ken, *One Dream Bottle.* (1982) Supreme Magic, Bideford, UK. Saddle-stitch. White, red. 5 pp. 6.5 x 8 in. Bottles, Mentalism.

De Courcy, Ken, *Patently Obscure.* (1964) Supreme Magic, Bideford, UK. Stapled. Gray. 9 pp. 8 x 9.75 in. Comedy, Patter.

De Courcy, Ken, *Pentertain.* (1972) Supreme Magic, Bideford, UK. Saddle-stitch. Black, white. 14 pp. 7.25 x 9.75 in. Close-Up, Pens.

De Courcy, Ken, *Pin-Points.* (1980) Supreme Magic, Bideford, UK. Saddle-stitch. Red, white. 16 pp. 7.25 x 9.75 in. Safety pins, Close-Up.

De Courcy, Ken, *Receptive Shroud, The.* (1971) Supreme Magic, Bideford, UK. Folded. White. 3 pp. 8 x 10 in. Mentalism.

De Courcy, Ken, *Ring of EOK, The.* (1977) Supreme Magic, Bideford, UK. Saddle-stitch. White, red. 8 pp. 8 x 9.75 in. Rings, String.

De Courcy, Ken, *Ringmanship.* (1966) Supreme Magic, Bideford, UK. Saddle-stitch. Gray. 23 pp. 8 x 9.75 in. Mimeographed. Rings.

De Courcy, Ken, with Rink, *Rink Goes Loop La-La!* (1980) Supreme Magic, Bideford, UK. Saddle-stitch. White, red. 16 pp. 7.25 x 9.75 in. With inserted mimeographed instructions from Rink effect. Rope, Rings.

De Courcy, Ken, *Round the World with a Pack of Cards.* (1968) Supreme Magic, Bideford, UK. Saddle-stitch. Blue. 16 pp. 6.5 x 8 in. Cards, Stage.

De Courcy, Ken, *Sequacious Aces.* (1974) Supreme Magic, Bideford, UK. Saddle-stitch. White. 14 pp. 7.75 x 9.75 in. Cards.

De Courcy, Ken, *Sequential Comedy.* (1971) Supreme Magic, Bideford, UK. Saddle-stitch. Blue. 28 pp. 6.75 x 8.75 in. Comedy.

De Courcy, Ken, *Slightly Easier.* (1989) Supreme Magic, Bideford, UK. Saddle-stitch. Red, white, black. 36 pp. 5.75 x 8.25 in. Cards.

De Courcy, Ken, *Son of Pentertain.* (1974) Supreme Magic, Bideford, UK. Saddle-stitch. White, green. 16 pp. 8 x 9.75 in. Close-Up, Pens.

De Courcy, Ken, *Stand-Up Sponges.* (1980) Supreme Magic, Bideford, UK. Saddle-stitch. White, green. 12 pp. 7.25 x 9.5 in. Sponge balls.

De Courcy, Ken, *Super Spell.* (1980) Supreme Magic, Bideford, UK. Saddle-stitch. White, red. 8 pp. 7.25 x 9.5 in. Cards.

De Courcy, Ken, *Super Sponges.* (1980) Supreme Magic, Bideford, UK. Saddle-stitch. White, red. 8 pp. 7.25 x 9.75 in. Cards.

De Courcy, Ken, *Systematic Seer, The.* (1976) Supreme Magic, Bideford, UK. Folded. White. 4 pp. 7.25 x 9.75 in. Fortune telling, Mentalism.

De Courcy, Ken, *Tear for Two.* (2007) Colombini Magic, Tampa, FL. Saddle-stitch. White, black. 8 pp. Cards, Torn and Restored Card.

De Courcy, Ken, *Thimbles Three.* (1973) Supreme Magic, Bideford, UK. Saddle-stitch. Green. 16 pp. 7.75 x 9.75 in. Thimbles, Manipulation.

De Courcy, Ken, *Thought Stealer, The.* (1969) Supreme Magic, Bideford, UK. Saddle-stitch. White, blue, gray. 19 pp. 6.5 x 8 in. Mentalism.

De Courcy, Ken, *Tricks for Travelling Tricksters.* (1982) Supreme Magic, Bideford, UK. Saddle-stitch. White, red, black. 56 pp. 8 x 9.5 in. Impromptu, Close-Up, Stage.

De Courcy, Ken, with West, Bill, *Troublewit Routines.* (1971) Supreme Magic, Bideford, UK. Saddle-stitch. White. 16 pp. 8.25 x 10.5 in. Troublewit.

De Courcy, Ken, with McComb, Billy; Adair, Ian, *Wonderful Wine and Water Trick, The.* (1991) Supreme Magic, Bideford, UK. Saddle-stitch. Beige. 5.75 x 8.25 in. (Information not verified by physical copy.) Liquids, Wine and Water, Chemical.

De Courcy, Ken, *World's Fastest Card Trick, The.* (1980) Supreme Magic, Bideford, UK. 20 pp. (Information not verified by physical copy.) Cards.

De Courcy, Ken, *Zodiac Telepathy.* (1951) George Armstrong, London. Saddle-stitch. White. 19 pp. 5.5 x 8.5 in. Mentalism, Astrology.

De Cova, Alexander, *California Lecture 2006, The.* (2006) Author, Asperg, Germany. 47 pp. (Information not verified by physical copy.) Close-Up, Stage, Mentalism.

De Cova, Alexander, *Horizons.* (1990) Author, Asperg, Germany. Comb. Yellow. 40 pp. 8.25 x 11.75 in. (Information not verified by physical copy.) Lecture notes. Close-Up, Stage.

De Cova, Alexander, *Treasures.* (2001) Author, Asperg, Germany. 28 pp. (Information not verified by physical copy. Bibliographical details are as accurate as possible.) Close-Up, Stage.

Decremps, Henri, *Codicile de Jérôme Sharp, La.* (1788) Lesclapart, Paris. Leather. Brown. 286 pp. 5.25 x 8.5 in. Early magic, Beginner. French.

Decremps, Henri, *Codicile de Jérôme Sharp, La.* (1791) F. J. Desoer, Paris. Wraps. Blue. 244 pp. 5.75 x 8.5 in. Frontispiece portrait of Decremps. Early magic, Beginner. French.

Decremps, Henri, *Codicile de Jérôme Sharp, La.* (1793) F. J. Desoer, Paris. 244 pp. (Information not verified by physical copy.) Early magic, Beginner. French.

Decremps, Henri (trans. by Thomas Denton), *Conjuror Unmasked, or La Magie Blanche Dévoilée, The.* (1785) Thomas Denton, London. 89 pp. 5 x 7.5 in. (Information not verified by physical copy.) Toole Stott no. 235. Early magic, Beginner.

Decremps, Henri (trans. by Thomas Denton), *Conjuror Unmasked, or La Magie Blanche Dévoilée, The.* Second edition. (1788) C. Stalker, Thomas Denton, H. Brookes, London. 96 pp. 4.75 x 6.5 in. (Information not verified by physical copy.) Toole Stott no. 236. Early magic, Beginner.

Decremps, Henri (trans. by Thomas Denton), *Conjuror Unmasked, or La Magie Blanche Dévoilée, The.* Third edition. (1790) C. Stalker, London. 128 pp. 4.25 x 6.5 in. (Information not verified by physical copy.) Toole Stott no. 237. Early magic, Beginner.

Decremps, Henri, *Éclaircissements.* (c. 1785) Author, Paris. 32 pp. 5 x 8 in. (Information not verified by physical copy.) Pamphlet with corrections and additions for Decremps' "Supplement à la Magie Blanche Dévoilée." Early magic, Beginner. French.

Decremps, Henri, *Magia Blanca Svelata, La.* (1793) Grande Ospedale, Messina, Italy. 76 pp. (Information not verified by physical copy.) Early magic, Beginner. Italian.

Decremps, Henri, *Magie Blanche Dévoilée, La.* (1784) Langlois Libraire, Paris. 138 pp. 4.75 x 7 in. (Information not verified by physical copy.) Early magic, Beginner. French.

Decremps, Henri, *Magie Blanche Dévoilée, La.* (c. 1784) Cailleau, Paris. 140 pp. 4.75 x 7 in. (Information not verified by physical copy.) Early magic, Beginner. French.

Decremps, Henri, *Magie Blanche Dévoilée, La.* (1788) Chez Lesclapart, Paris. (Information not verified by physical copy.) Early magic, Beginner. French.

Decremps, Henri, *Magie Blanche Dévoilée, La.* (1789) F. J. Desoer, Paris. Wraps. Beige. 118 pp. 5.5 x 8.5 in. Frontispiece of Pinetti. Early magic, Beginner. French.

Decremps, Henri, *Magie Blanche Dévoilée, La.* (1792) J. F. Desoer, Paris. 118 pp. (Information not verified by physical copy.) Early magic, Beginner. French.

Decremps, Henri, *Natuurlyk Toverboek.* (1791) Allart en Van Der Plaats, Amsterdam. Wraps. Tan. 276 pp. 5.25 x 8.75 in. Dutch edition of Decremps without attribution. Early magic, Beginner. Dutch.

Decremps, Henri, *Neuer Beytrag zur Naturlichen Magie.* (1788) Berlin, Germany. Wraps. 159 pp. 4.25 x 6.75 in. No publisher credited. (Information not verified by physical copy.) Early magic, Beginner. German.

Decremps, Henri, *Petites Aventures de Jérôme Sharp, Les.* (1789) Dujardin, Brussels, Belgium. Leather. Brown. 386 pp. 5.25 x 8 in. Early magic, Beginner. French.

Decremps, Henri, *Petites Aventures de Jérôme Sharp, Les.* (1790) F. J. Desoer, Brussels, Belgium. Wraps. Beige. 266 pp. 5.25 x 8.5 in. Early magic, Beginner. French.

Decremps, Henri, *Petites Aventures de Jérôme Sharp, Les.* (1793) F. J. Desoer, Brussels, Belgium. Leather. Brown. 266 pp. 5.25 x 8.25 in. Early magic, Beginner. French.

Decremps, Henri, *Petites Aventures de Jérôme Sharp, Les.* (1989) Champion-Slatkine, Paris. Leather. Blue. 386 pp. 6 x 8.75 in. Early magic, Beginner. French.

Decremps, Henri, *Philosophical Amusements.* (1790) J. Johnson, London. 80 pp. 4.25 x 7 in. (Information not verified by physical copy.) Toole Stott no. 238. Early magic, Beginner.

Decremps, Henri, *Philosophical Amusements.* Second edition. (1797) J. Johnson, London. 72 pp. 4 x 6.25 in. (Information not verified by physical copy.) Toole Stott no. 239. Early magic, Beginner.

Decremps, Henri, *Secreti della Magia Bianca tomo 1.* (1827) Domenico Ercole, Rome. 159 pp. (Information not verified by physical copy.) Early magic, Beginner. Italian.

Decremps, Henri, *Secreti della Magia Bianca tomo 2.* (1827) Domenico Ercole, Rome. 111 pp. (Information not verified by physical copy.) Early magic, Beginner. Italian.

Decremps, Henri, *Spiegazione Fisica di Quaranta Giochi.* (1788) Giulio Trento, Treviso, Italy. 47 pp. (Information not verified by physical copy.) Early magic, Beginner. Italian.

Decremps, Henri, *Spiegazione Fisica di Quaranta Giochi.* (2006) Libreria Antiquaria Mirabilia, Turin, Italy. 47 pp. (Information not verified by physical copy.) Reprint of 1788 edition. Early magic, Beginner. Italian.

Decremps, Henri, *Supplement à La Magie Blanche Dévoilée.* (1785) Langlois Libraire, Paris. 287 pp. (Information not verified by physical copy.) Early magic, Beginner. French.

Decremps, Henri, *Supplement à La Magie Blanche Dévoilée.* (1785) Lesclapart, Paris. Boards. Tan. 287 pp. 5 x 8 in. With 41 pp. "Approbations" section at end. Early magic, Beginner. French.

Decremps, Henri, *Supplement à La Magie Blanche Dévoilée.* (1788) Lesclapart, Paris. Boards. Tan. 287 pp. 5 x 8 in. With 41 pp. "Approbations" section at end. Early magic, Beginner. French.

Decremps, Henri, *Supplement à La Magie Blanche Dévoilée.* (1789) F. J. Desoer, Paris. Wraps. Beige. 270 pp. 5.5 x 8.5 in. Early magic, Beginner. French.

Decremps, Henri, *Supplement à La Magie Blanche Dévoilée.* (1792) F. J. Desoer, Paris. 270 pp. (Information not verified by physical copy.) Early magic, Beginner. French.

Decremps, Henri, *Testament de Jérôme Sharp, Le.* First edition. (1786) Author, Paris. 329 pp. (Information not verified by physical copy.) Early magic, Beginner, Cards. French.

Decremps, Henri, *Testament de Jérôme Sharp, Le.* Second edition. (1786) Author, Paris. Wraps. Marbled. 328 pp. 5.5 x 8.5 in. Marbled wraps. Early magic, Beginner, Cards. French.

Decremps, Henri, *Testament de Jérôme Sharp, Le.* Third edition. (1788) Lesclapart, Paris. Boards. Green, tan. 328 pp. 5 x 8.25 in. Early magic, Beginner, Cards. French.

Decremps, Henri, *Testament de Jérôme Sharp, Le.* (1789) F. J. Desoer, Paris. (Information not verified by physical copy.) Early magic, Beginner, Cards. French.

Decremps, Henri, *Testament de Jérôme Sharp, Le.* (1789) Chez la Veuve Dujardin, Brussels, Belgium. (Information not verified by physical copy.) Early magic, Beginner, Cards. French.

Decremps, Henri, *Testament de Jérôme Sharp, Le.* (1793) F. J. Desoer, Paris. 262 pp. (Information not verified by physical copy.) Early magic, Beginner, Cards. French.

Dedopulos, Tim, *Enigmes d'Houdini, Les.* (2019) Hachette, Paris. Casebound. Blue. 224 pp. 7 x 9.75 in. Houdini, Games, Puzzles, History. French.

Dee, David, *Maximum Profits and Shows with Minimum Time and Effort.* (1999) Author, Alpharetta, GA. Comb. Beige. 92 pp. 8.5 x 11 in. Business, Showmanship, Promotion.

D'Egerdon, Ebert, *Aids to Wizardry.* (1908) Hamley's, London. Perfect. Green. 86 pp. 5.5 x 8.5 in. (Measurements and other information have been recorded as accurately as possible.) Stage, Manipulation.

De Hempsey, Sydney, *How to Do Punch and Judy.* (1955) Abbott Magic Co., Colon, MI. Stapled with paper cover. Yellow. 7 pp. 5.25 x 8.5 in. Folded pages in cover. Puppetry, Punch and Judy.

De Hempsey, Sydney, *How to Do Punch and Judy.* (1976) Magic Inc., Chicago. Comb. White, red, black. 106 pp. 5.75 x 8.5 in. Additional material by Jay Marshall. Puppetry, Punch and Judy, History.

De Hempsey, Sydney, *Mind Reading for Two People.* (1950) Abbott Magic Co., Colon, MI. Stapled. Olive, red. 15 pp. 8 x 10.75 in. Mentalism, Second Sight.

Deighton, Maurice, *Make It Simple – But Make It!* (1981) Author, York, UK. Stapled. White. 6 pp. 8.25 x 11.75 in. (Information not verified by physical copy.) Close-Up, Stage, Children's magic.

Deich, Don, with Hitchcock, Scott; Shaw, John, *Bizarre Magic: An Introduction.* (1993) Authors, Poughkeepsie, NY. Comb. 8.5 x 11 in. (Information not verified by physical copy. Bibliographical details are as accurate as possible.) Bizarre magick.

DeKräm, Dr. A. C., with Fletcher, Ken, *Secrets of the DeKräm Deck.* (1994) Magic Masters, Lithonia, GA. Saddle-stitch. Purple. 28 pp. 5.5 x 8.5 in. Cards, Marked deck.

De La Chapelle, M., *Ventriloque, ou l'Engastrimythe, Première Partie, Le.* (1772) Chez De l'Étanville, London. Leather. Brown. 292 pp. 4.25 x 6.75 in. Two-volume edition ((Information not verified by physical copy.) Ventriloquism. French.

De La Chapelle, M., *Ventriloque, ou l'Engastrimythe, Seconde Partie, Le.* (1772) Chez De l'Étanville, London. Leather. Brown. 280 pp. 4.25 x 6.75 in. Ventriloquism. French.

DeLage, Al, *Lecture Notes no. 3.* (c. 1989) Author, Morristown, TN. Saddle-stitch. Light blue. 16 pp. 5.5 x 8.5 in. (Information not verified by physical copy.) Lecture notes. Close-Up, Stage.

De La Mano, *De la Mano's Great Magic Book: Conjuring, or Magic Made Easy.* (1881) N. Y. Popular Publishing Co., New York. Saddle-stitch. Color. 32 pp. 4 x 6.25 in. Beginner, Stunts.

DeLand, Theodore L., *Did the Devil Invent a Deck of Cards?* (1914) Author, Philadelphia. Saddle-stitch. Red, white. 16 pp. 5 x 8 in. Cards.

De La Torre, Jose (See also Ascanio, Arturo de), *Incredible Linking Pins, The.* (1993) Author, Belleville, NJ. 41 pp. (Information not verified by physical copy.) Safety pins, Close-Up.

De La Torre, Jose, *Knives Routines.* (1976) Author, Belleville, NJ. Stapled with tape. Yellow. 8 pp. 5.5 x 8.5 in. Fred Kaps routine. Knives.

De La Torre, Jose, *Magia con Imperdibles.* (1994) Author, Belleville, NJ. Saddle-stitch. Blue. 16 pp. 5.5 x 8.5 in. Translation of "Magic with Giant Pins." Linking pins, Close-Up. Spanish.

De La Torre, Jose, *Magic with Giant Pins.* (1994) Author, Belleville, NJ. Saddle-stitch. Blue. 16 pp. 5.5 x 8.5 in. Linking pins, Close-Up.

De La Torre, Jose, *Magicana of Havana in New York.* (1975) José's Studio, Belleville, NJ. Perfect. Yellow, red. 80 pp. 8.5 x 10.75 in. Signed by José de la Torre. Cards, Rope.

De La Torre, Jose, *New Jumping Jack.* Second printing. (1978) José's Studio, Belleville, NJ. Saddle-stitch. Blue. 32 pp. 5.5 x 8.5 in. Cards.

De La Torre, Jose, *Real Magic.* (1978) José's Studio, Belleville, NJ. Perfect. Red. 127 pp. 5.5 x 8.5 in. (Measurements and other information have been recorded as accurately as possible.) Cards.

Delaurence, L. W., *Practical Lessons in Hypnotism.* (1902) Frederick J. Drake, Chicago. Cloth. Red. 261 pp. 5.25 x 7.75 in. Hypnotism.

DeLawrence, George, *Another Vaudeville Magic Act.* (1923) Author, Chicago. Saddle-stitch. Tan. 25 pp. 4.75 x 6.75 in. Signed by George DeLawrence. Patter, Stage, Cards.

DeLawrence, George, *Answers for Questions.* (1924) Author, Chicago. Stapled. Blue. 19 pp. 8.5 x 11 in. (Measurements and other information have been recorded as accurately as possible.) Mentalism.

DeLawrence, George, *Answers for Questions.* (c. 1927) Nelson Enterprises, Columbus, OH. Stapled. 14 pp. 8.5 x 13 in. (Information not verified by physical copy.) Mentalism.

DeLawrence, George, *Answers to Questions.* (1924) Author, Chicago. Stapled. Blue. 16 pp. 8.5 x 11 in. (Measurements and other information have been recorded as accurately as possible.) Mentalism.

DeLawrence, George, *How to Answer Questions in Crystal Gazing.* (1922) Author, Chicago. Stapled. 18 pp. 8.5 x 11 in. (Information not verified by physical copy.) Mentalism.

DeLawrence, George, *Impromptu Magic.* (n.d.) T. S. Denison and Co., Chicago. Perfect. Beige, red. 79 pp. 4.75 x 7.25 in. Stunts, Impromptu, Patter, Cards.

DeLawrence, George, *Impromptu Magic with Patter.* (1922) T. S. Denison and Co., Chicago. Cloth. Tan. 80 pp. 4.75 x 7.25 in. Stunts, Impromptu, Patter, Cards.

DeLawrence, George, *Miscellaneous Handkerchief Tricks That You Can Do.* (1921) Heaney Magic Co., Berlin, WI. Saddle-stitch. Beige. 37 pp. 5.25 x 7.75 in. Silks, Handkerchiefs.

DeLawrence, George, with Thompson, James "Kater," *Modern Card Effects and How to Perform Them.* (1920) Arthur P. Felsman, Chicago. Perfect. Blue. 80 pp. 5.5 x 7.75 in. Cards.

DeLawrence, George, with De Jong, Carroll, *Mysteries of Crystal Gazing, The.* (1920) Author, Chicago. Brads. Gray. 22 pp. 8.75 x 11.25 in. Mimeographed. Mentalism.

DeLawrence, George, *Patter for the Sucker Billiard Ball Box.* (1921) Thayer Magical Mfg. Co., Los Angeles. Stapled. White. 2 pp. 8.5 x 11 in. (Information not verified by physical copy.) Patter, Billiard balls, Sucker effects.

DeLawrence, George, *Perfection Crystal Gazing Act, The.* (1923) Author, Chicago. Stapled. White. 20 pp. 8.5 x 11 in. Mimeographed. (Information not verified by physical copy.) Mentalism.

DeLawrence, George, *Pithy Patter for the Parlor and the Professional Prestidigitator.* (1920) Heaney Magic Co., Berlin, WI. Saddle-stitch. Blue. 31 pp. 5 x 7.25 in. Patter.

DeLawrence, George, *Pithy Patter for the Parlor and the Professional Prestidigitator.* (1920) Heaney Magic Co., Berlin, WI. Saddle-stitch. Gray. 31 pp. 5 x 7.25 in. Patter.

DeLawrence, George, *Pithy Patter for the Parlor and the Professional Prestidigitator.* (1920) Heaney Magic Co., Berlin, WI. Saddle-stitch. Purple. 31 pp. 5 x 7.25 in. Patter.

DeLawrence, George, *Pithy Patter for the Parlor and the Professional Prestidigitator.* (1920) Heaney Magic Co., Berlin, WI. Saddle-stitch. Tan. 31 pp. 5 x 7.25 in. Patter.

DeLawrence, George, *Some Card Effects and Magical Talks.* (1919) Thayer Magical Mfg. Co., Los Angeles. Saddle-stitch. Olive, green. 45 pp. 5.25 x 8 in. Cards, Patter, Stage.

DeLawrence, George, *Vaudeville Magic Act, A.* (1919) Author, Chicago. Saddle-stitch. Gray. 27 pp. 4.75 x 6.75 in. Patter, Stage, Cards.

De l'Escap, St.-J., *Secrets de la Prestidigitation, Les.* (1907) Hachette, Paris. Cloth. Red. 230 pp. 6.25 x 10 in. Gilt edges. Beginner. French.

De l'Escap, St.-J., *Secrets de la Prestidigitation, Les.* (1907) Hachette, Paris. Cloth. Red. 230 pp. 6.25 x 10 in. Gilt edges. Different cover and spine. Beginner. French.

De l'Escap, St.-J., *Secrets de la Prestidigitation, Les.* (1923) Hachette, Paris. Cloth. Red. 230 pp. 6.25 x 9.75 in. Plain edges. Beginner. French.

Delgaudio, Derek, *A Coruña.* (2010) Author, Los Angeles. Saddle-stitch. White. 18 pp. 8.5 x 5.5 in. Bound oblong. Photo explanations with no text. (Information not verified by physical copy.) Lecture notes. Cards. Spanish.

Delgaudio, Derek, *Amoralman.* (2021) Alfred A. Knopf, New York. Casebound. Black. 235 pp. 5.75 x 8.5 in. (Measurements and other information have been recorded as accurately as possible.) Essays.

Delgaudio, Derek, *Derek Delgaudio: MagicCon 2010 Lecture Notes.* (2010) Author, Los Angeles. Saddle-stitch. White. 12 pp. 5.5 x 7 in. No title on cover, only author's name. Lecture notes. Cards.

Delgaudio, Derek, *Only Notes.* (2008) Author, Los Angeles. Saddle-stitch. Black. 36 pp. 5.5 x 8.5 in. (Information not verified by physical copy.) Lecture notes. Cards.

Delgaudio, Derek, with Kaino, Glenn, *Secret Has Two Faces, A.* (2017) Delmonico Books, Munich. Cloth. Black. 273 pp. 7.5 x 10.5 in. Theory.

Delgaudio, Derek, *Spain 2011.* (2011) Author, Los Angeles. Stapled. White, black. 26 pp. 5.5 x 8.5 in. (Information not verified by physical copy.) Lecture notes. Cards. Spanish.

Delion, M., *Almanach-Manuel du Magicien des Salons.* (1855) H. Delarue, Paris. Perfect. Yellow. 187 pp. 3.75 x 5.25 in. Beginner. French.

Dell, *Dell's Fabulous Ribbon Fountain.* (1963) Supreme Magic, Bideford, UK. Saddle-stitch. White. 10 pp. 5 x 7.25 in. Stage, Ribbons.

Dell, Ralph, *Magic with a Smile.* (1967) Supreme Magic, Bideford, UK. Comb. Tan, red. 34 pp. 8 x 10 in. Comedy, Stage, Children's magic.

Dellini, The Great (Alan Dell), *Mental Miracles.* (1979) Magico Magazine, New York. Saddle-stitch. Blue. 24 pp. 5.5 x 8.5 in. Mentalism.

Delord, Jacques, *Chroniques de Jacques Delord, Les.* (2024) Magicus Éditions, Paris. Casebound. Red. 158 pp. 8.5 x 12 in. Collected columns from "Magicus" magazine 1987-2006. Theory, Essays, Magazine columns. French.

Delord, Jacques, *Éternel Magicien, L'.* (1973) Éditions G.P., Paris. Casebound. Red. 125 pp. 7.75 x 10.5 in. Third book of trilogy. Beginner, Theory. French.

Delord, Jacques, *Mes Premiers Tours de Magie.* (1978) Solarama, Paris. Perfect. Black. 62 pp. 4.75 x 7 in. Beginner, Theory. French.

Delord, Jacques, *Sois l'Enchanteur.* (1972) Éditions G.P., Paris. Casebound. Red. 126 pp. 7.75 x 10.5 in. Second book of trilogy. Beginner, Theory. French.

Delord, Jacques, *Sois le Magicien.* (1971) Éditions G.P., Paris. Casebound. Blue. 123 pp. 7.75 x 10.5 in. First book of trilogy. Beginner, Theory. French.

Delord, Jacques, *Trilogie, La.* (2013) Marchand de Trucs, Lorient. Cloth. Black. Multiple sections. 7.75 x 11.5 in. Dust jacket. Includes DVD. Reprint of Delord's classic trilogy for beginners. #241 of 500. Beginner, Theory. French.

Delvin, Jack, *Magic in the Family Circle.* (1956) Ellisdons, UK. Perfect. Purple. 100 pp. 4.75 x 7 in. (Measurements and other information have been recorded as accurately as possible.) Beginner.

Delvin, Jack, *Magic of the Masters.* (1977) Arco Publications, London. Cloth. 240 pp. 6.25 x 9.25 in. (Information not verified by physical copy.) Beginner.

Delvin, Jack, *Magic of the Masters.* (1977) Arco Publications, London. Perfect. Black. 240 pp. 4.5 x 7.5 in. Beginner.

Delvin, Jack, *Magic of the Masters.* (1980) Coles, Toronto. Perfect. Black, yellow. 239 pp. 5.25 x 8.25 in. (Measurements and other information have been recorded as accurately as possible.) Beginner.

Delvin, Jack, *Young Ideas in Magic.* (1954) Author, London. Stapled with paper cover. Yellow. 10 pp. 5.25 x 9 in. Mimeographed. Stage.

Demaline, Jesse, *Demagic: The Magic of Jesse Demaline.* (1990) Modern Mystic League, UK. Perfect. Pink. 120 pp. 6 x 9 in. (Information not verified by physical copy.) Mentalism, Close-Up, Children's magic, Stage.

Demanet, Hippolyte, *Nouveau Magicien, Le.* (c. 1865) Le Bailly, Paris. Saddle-stitch. Green. 8 pp. 4.5 x 6.75 in. Collected in wraps with three other booklets as "La Magie Noire et La Magie Blanche." Beginner. French.

Demanet, Hippolyte, *Nouveau Robert-Houdin, Le.* (c. 1865) H. Billy, Paris. Folded. White. 8 pp. 4.5 x 6.75 in. Published at 8, Rue de Carmes, later location of Mayette. Beginner. French.

Demanet, Hippolyte, *Physicien de Société, Le.* (c. 1865) Le Bailly, Paris. Saddle-stitch. Beige. 8 pp. 4.5 x 6.75 in. Collected in wraps with three other booklets as "La Magie Noire et La Magie Blanche." Beginner. French.

Demanet, Hippolyte, *Prestidigitateur Sans Pareil, Le.* (c. 1865) Le Bailly, Paris. Saddle-stitch. White. 8 pp. 4.5 x 6.75 in. Collected in wraps with three other booklets as "La Magie Noire et La Magie Blanche." Beginner. French.

Demanet, Hippolyte, *Sorcier Amusant, Le.* (c. 1865) Le Bailly, Paris. Saddle-stitch. Orange. 8 pp. 4.5 x 6.75 in. Collected in wraps with three other booklets as "La Magie Noire et La Magie Blanche." Beginner. French.

Demanet, Hippolyte, *Surprises Amusantes, Les.* (c. 1865) Maison Aubert, Paris. Folded. White. 8 pp. 4.5 x 6.75 in. Beginner. French.

Demanet, Hippolyte, *Véritable Escamoteur, Le.* (c. 1865) L. Baudot, Paris. Folded. Beige. 8 pp. 4.5 x 6.75 in. 8, Rue de Carmes, later location of Mayette. Beginner. French.

De Meglio, *Magical Programmes and How to Present Them.* (1914) H. Wiles, Manchester, UK. Boards. Black, yellow. 94 pp. 4.75 x 7.25 in. Showmanship, Stage.

De Meglio, *Magical Programmes and How to Present Them.* (1914) H. Wiles, Manchester, UK. Perfect. Green. 94 pp. 4.75 x 7.25 in. Showmanship, Stage.

De Merry, Jean, *Petite Encyclopédie des Tirages.* (1987) Éditions du Spectacle, Strasbourg, France. Perfect. Red. 109 pp. 6 x 8.75 in. Pulls, Gimmicks. French.

De Merry, Jean, *Ventriloquie Pour des Magiciens.* (1980) Éditions du Spectacle, Strasbourg, France. Perfect. 47 pp. (Information not verified by physical copy.) Ventriloquism. French.

DeMilo, Marco, *Bingo Divination.* (1980) Supreme Magic, Bideford, UK. Loose pages. White. 8 x 10 in. Mentalism, Instructions.

De Mirville, J. E., *Question des Ésprits et Leurs Manifestations Diverses.* Second edition. (1854) H. Vrayet de Surcy, Paris. Wraps. Beige. 468 pp. 5.25 x 8 in. Anecdotes about Robert-Houdin. Spiritualism, Robert-Houdin. French.

De Montgon, A., *Robert Houdin.* (1939) Hachette, Paris. Perfect. Beige. 191 pp. 4.75 x 6.5 in. Cursive name on cover. Robert-Houdin misspelled in title without hyphen as "Robert Houdin." Biography, Robert-Houdin. French.

De Montgon, A., *Robert Houdin.* (1939) Hachette, Paris. Perfect. Beige. 191 pp. 4.75 x 6.25 in. Magician on cover. Robert-Houdin misspelled in title without hyphen. Biography, Robert-Houdin. French.

DeMott, George, *Want to Be a Juggler?* (1962) Roger Montandon, Bixby, OK. Cloth. Blue. Cover text: Gold; 81 pp. 6.25 x 9.25 in. Juggling.

DeMott, George, *Want to Be a Juggler?* Second printing. (1973) Roger Montandon, Bixby, OK. Saddle-stitch. Blue. 81 pp. 6 x 9 in. Juggling.

Dempsey, William T. J., *Being a Mentalist.* (1981) Author, Malden, MA. Comb. 42 pp. 8.5 x 11 in. (Information not verified by physical copy.) Lecture notes. Mentalism, Tips, Bibliography.

De Nansouty, Max, *Trucs du Théâtre, du Cirque, et de la Foire.* (1909) Librairie Armand Colin, Paris. Leather. Brown. 159 pp. 5 x 7.75 in. Version of Albert A. Hopkins' "Magic." Illusions, Special effects.

Denemark, Howard A., *Denemark Okito Box Routine, The.* (c. 1980) Devoe Magic Den, St. Louis, MO. Saddle-stitch. Yellow. 6 pp. 5.5 x 8.5 in. Coins, Okito Coin Box.

Denemark, Howard A., *Okito at the Fair.* (1981) Author, St. Louis, MO. Saddle-stitch. 12 pp. 5.5 x 8.5 in. (Information not verified by physical copy.) Coins, Okito Coin Box.

Denhard, Harold, *How to Do Rope Tricks.* (1957) Ireland Magic Co., Chicago. Saddle-stitch. Yellow. 68 pp. 5.5 x 8.5 in. Rope.

Denhard, Harold, *How to Do Rope Tricks.* Fifth printing. (1977) Magic Inc., Chicago. Saddle-stitch. Blue. 68 pp. 5.5 x 8.5 in. Rope.

Denhard, Harold, *How to Do Rope Tricks.* Fifth printing. (1977) Magic Inc., Chicago. Saddle-stitch. Brown. 68 pp. 5.5 x 8.5 in. Rope.

Denhard, Harold, *Magic Lecture.* (1973) Author, Chicago. Stapled. White. 5 pp. 8.5 x 11 in. (Information not verified by physical copy. Bibliographical details are as accurate as possible.) Lecture notes.

Denise, *Puzzledom.* (1903) Denise, Blackpool, UK. Saddle-stitch. Beige. 8 pp. 5 x 7.75 in. (Measurements and other information have been recorded as accurately as possible.) Close-Up, Cards.

Made in the USA
Monee, IL
25 May 2025

7bbafcde-bace-43e0-bf7b-172ab9f793a2R02